Reliable Face Recognition Methods
System Design, Implementation and Evaluation

Reliable Face Recognition Methods
System Design, Implementation and Evaluation

by

Harry Wechsler
George Mason University, USA

 Springer

Harry Wechsler
George Mason University
Dept. of Computer Science
Fairfax, VA 22030
wechsler@gmu.edu

Library of Congress Control Number: 2006932031

Reliable Face Recognition Methods:
System Design, Implementation and Evaluation
by *Harry Wechsler*

ISBN-13: 978-0-387-22372-8
ISBN-10: 0-387-22372-X
e-ISBN-13: 978-0-387-38464-1
e-ISBN-10: 0-387-38464-2

Printed on acid-free paper.

9 8 7 6 5 4 3 2 1

springer.com

With love to my children
Gabriela and Marc

Contents

Preface

Science is a way to teach how something gets to be known, what is known, to what extent things are known (for nothing is known absolutely), how to handle doubt and uncertainty, what the rules of evidence are, how to think about things so that judgments can be made, how to distinguish truth from fraud, and from show (Richard Feynman)

One of the grand challenges for computational intelligence is to understand how people process and recognize each other's face <u>and</u> to develop automated and reliable face recognition systems. This challenge underlies *biometrics*, the science of authenticating people by measuring their physical or external appearance and/or their behavioral or physiological traits. The physical and behavioral traits are not necessarily independent. The face we look at is a mix of both physical characteristics and emotive expressions. Face recognition has become a major biometric technology. Solving the face recognition problem will have a major scientific impact, as recognizing people is a first but critical step towards building intelligent machines that can function in human environments. "The ability to recognize living creatures in photographs or video clips is a critical enabling technology for a wide range of applications including defense, health care, human-computer interaction, image retrieval and data mining, industrial and personal robotics, surveillance and security, and transportation. Despite 40 years of research, however, today's recognition systems are still largely unable to handle the extraordinary wide range of appearances assumed by common objects [including faces] in typical images" (*Designing Tomorrow's Category - Level 3D Object Recognition Systems* [1]).

Biometrics has become the major component in the complex decision-making process associated with security applications. Key concerns related to accuracy and performance, benefits versus costs, information assurance, and security over privacy have surfaced and have yet to be resolved. Skepticism, the heart of scientific method, is needed to ferret out fact from fiction regarding what biometrics can actually do and to what extent. Advancing the field of biometrics for homeland security has taken on a sense of urgency in the post 9/11 world. Even though people can detect and identify faces with little or no effort, building an automated system for such purposes has proven elusive as reliable solutions have yet to be found. The all-encompassing *Face in a Crowd* biometric problem addresses both face detection and face recognition in cluttered environments. Biometric systems have to take into account the dynamic changes that affect the visual stimuli, including variability in the geometry of image formation, such as facial pose and distance from the camera, and illumination. Other factors that affect face recognition include facial expression due to emotion, occlusion and disguise, temporal changes and aging, and last but not least, the lack of adequate training data for learning how to represent and encode human faces.

A few major edited books treat face recognition. Among them are the first and seminal *"Face Recognition: From Theory to Applications"* (Wechsler et al., Springer, 1998), and most recently the *"Handbook of Face Recognition"* (Li and Jain, Springer, 2005). This book is the first to comprehensively address the face recognition problem in its entirety, while drawing inspiration and gaining new insights from complementary fields of endeavor, such as neurosciences, statistics, signal and image processing, computer vision, machine learning and pattern recognition, and statistical learning. The various chapters treat topics related to how people represent, process and/or respond to the human face, modeling and prediction, the face space, identification and verification, face detection, tracking and recognition, 3D, data fusion, denial and de-

---

[1] http://lear.inrialpes.fr/people/schmid/workshop.html

ception using occlusion and disguise, performance evaluation and error analysis, and finally, competing security and privacy considerations.

The underlying theme of the book is that the biometric inputs chart continuous and coherent space and time manifolds, which facilitate their recognition. Face recognition is dynamic rather than static. It continuously iterates, making specific interpretations and assigning confidence to them. Supporting and non-accidental evidence is accrued in an active fashion, leading to lower uncertainty in the recognition decisions made, and resolving ambiguity, if any. Integral to face recognition are advances in pattern recognition. Novel methods are proposed here to handle real life applications where variability, incomplete, noisy, distorted and/or disguised patterns are usually the norm rather than the exception. The overall goal of the book is *applied modern pattern recognition*, with the understanding that the novel methods described here apply to any objects. The face pattern is only one of the object patterns that surround us and need to be recognized. The scope for pattern recognition (Rosenfeld and Wechsler, 2000) is much wider here because among other things both training and testing can take place using incomplete or camouflaged/disguised patterns drawn from single and/or multiple image sets.

The emphasis throughout the book is on proper modeling and prediction. Gregory Chaitin, in the March 2006 issue of the Scientific American, recalls Gottfried Leibniz's 1685 philosophical essay *Discourse de métaphysique* (Discourse on Metaphysics). The essay discusses how one can distinguish between facts that can be described by some law and those that are lawless, irregular facts. Leibniz observed that "a theory has to be simpler than the data it explains, otherwise it does not explain anything. The concept of a law becomes vacuous if arbitrarily high mathematical complexity is permitted, because then one can always construct a law no matter how random and patternless the data really are." The corollary for Chaitin is that "a useful theory is a compression of the data; comprehension is compression." Modeling and prediction, the hallmarks of learning, can be implemented using novel methods driven by semi-supervised learning and transduction, exchangeability and rank order, and martingale. Overall, the book articulates new but promising directions for pattern recognition, while providing the motivation for innovative ways to approach the face recognition challenge.

The title of the book, *Reliable Face Recognition Methods*, refers to the normal expectation one has that face recognition should display robust performance despite suboptimal and/or adverse image acquisition conditions or lack of adequate training data. Even the top-ranked face recognition engines still reject legitimate subjects, while letting impostors pass through. "Reliable," throughout the book, means the ability to deploy consistent, dependable, large-scale and full-fledged operational biometric systems, which is the true hallmark of a mature technology. To that end, a large data base of facial images, such as FERET, is required to test and assess competing technologies. FERET, which was designed and developed at George Mason University under my direction, has become the standard data base used by researchers worldwide for R&D and benchmark studies on face recognition. Science needs to be replicated and tested for validation.

This book can serve both as an interdisciplinary text and as a research reference. Each chapter provides the background and impetus for understanding the problems discussed and the approach taken to solve them. The book can benefit advanced undergraduates ("senior") and graduates taking courses on pattern recognition or biometrics; scientists and practitioners interested in updating their knowledge; and government and industry executives charged with addressing ever-evolving biometric security requirements.

My gratitude goes to many people. Many thanks go to Professor Jack Sklansky, who introduced me to the field of pattern recognition. Much appreciation goes to my former doctoral students Srinivas Gutta, Shen-Shyang Ho, Jeffrey Huang, Fayin Li, and Albert Pujol, with whom I had many productive and rewarding collaborations. I am also grateful for the help and inspiration for this book from Josef Bigun, Vladimir Cherkassky, Clifford Claussen, Victor Chen, Stephen McKenna, Matt Matsuda, and

Barnabas Takacs. My thanks go also to the many people referenced throughout the book from whom I have drawn knowledge and motivation. From my brother Tobi, I learned to appreciate and love the visual arts, which led me to explore the scientific basis for perception-representation and interpretation. Thanks go also to my sister-in-law Nobuko for her friendship and kindness. Last but not least, heartfelt thanks go to my wife Michele for her encouragement and help with completing this book, and to my children Gabriela and Marc for the sparks in their eyes and their smiling faces.

Harry Wechsler
June 2006

1. Introduction

The first rule was never to accept anything as true unless I recognized it to be certainly and evidently such: that is, carefully to avoid all precipitation and prejudgment, and to include nothing in my conclusions unless it presented itself so clearly and distinctly to my mind that there was no reason or occasion to doubt it. The second was to divide each of the difficulties which I encountered into as many parts as possible, and as might be required for an easier solution. The third was to think in an orderly fashion when concerned with the search for truth, beginning with the things which were simplest and easiest to understand, and gradually and by degrees reaching toward more complex knowledge, even treating, as though ordered, materials which were not necessarily so. The last was, both in the process of searching and in reviewing when in difficulty, always to make enumerations so complete and reviews so general, that I would be certain that nothing was omitted.

From Discourse on Method and Meditations by Ren Descartes (1641) (translated by Laurence J. Lafleur and published by Liberal Arts Press, 1960)

Face recognition (Samal and Iyengar, 1992; Chellappa et al., 1995; Daugman, 1997; Jain et al., 1999; Zhao et al., 2003; Bolle et al., 2004; Li and Jain, 2005) has become a major biometric technology. Biometrics involve the automated identification or authentication from personal physical appearance or behavioral traits. Human physical appearance and/or behavioral characteristics are counted as biometrics as long as they satisfy requirements that include universality, distinctiveness or uniqueness, permanence or invariance, collectability, and acceptability (Clarke, 1994). The early belief in the uniqueness aspect of faces (to preempt forgeries) was one of the reasons behind their use, e.g., the face of Queen Victoria on the early stamps (Samal and Iyengar, 1992). Biometric systems, including face recognition systems, can be categorized according to their intended applications. According to Wayman (1999) a suitable self-evident taxonomy will include cooperative vs. non-cooperative, overt vs. covert, habituated vs. non-habituated, attended vs. non-attended, standard vs. non-standard operating environments, and public vs. private.

This book addresses the above taxonomy as it discusses face recognition along the complementary dimensions of science, (information) technology and engineering, culture and society, and visual arts. It is about science because it aims to understand and systematize the fundamental principles behind face processing. Face processing is an all-encompassing term that involves everything that facilitates face recognition, e.g., image capture, enrollment, and face detection and tracking. The scientific dimension is related to the basic research that supports technological progress. The book is about technology and engineering, because it deals with applied science and research aimed at practical ends, e.g., designing and building reliable face recognition systems. It is about culture and society because they affect the role the human face plays in our interactions. The book is also about the visual arts because the human figure has always occupied an important place in personal expression and contemplation. Art connects internal and external realities, provides for new perspectives of the world, and seeks for the ultimate truth and permanent essence embodied by fixed icons such as human faces and ideals. The arts activate abstraction and creativity and can stimulate innovative face recognition research, e.g., using the golden ratio template of human beauty for face recognition-by-parts (See Sect. 6.5 and 9.7). Last but not least, the book is about building completely automatic and full-fledged biometric systems that consider the full range of the face recognition sub-tasks, starting with data acquisition and enrollment and ending with different face authentication scenarios. The ever expanding scope of face recognition includes field operation rather than controlled in vitro lab conditions. This should lead to building search and analysis biometric video engines able to recognize people and/or interpret their activities and intentions from live-fed CCTV.

The book, multidisciplinary and syncretic, frames a modern research agenda for pattern recognition, in general, and face recognition, in particular. The modernity aspect refers to the scope of the enterprise. The book identifies real problems and motivates the need for large scale pattern recognition systems that can handle human diversity, temporal changes, and occlusion and disguise. The book, selective rather than encyclopedic, introduces new topics that require further investigation. It differentiates and motivates among existing problems and their proffered solutions, places emphasis on common threads, and focuses on what is most important. In particular, the book aims to fuse and reconcile the specific disciplines of image and signal processing, computer vision, machine learning and pattern recognition, while charting new but promising research directions.

Computer vision is about "computing properties of the 3D world from one or more digital images. As the name suggests, it involves computers interpreting images. Image analysis and/or understanding are synonyms for computer vision. Image processing and pattern recognition are disciplines related but not identical to computer vision. Image processing concerns image properties and image-to-image transformations, while pattern recognition [involves] recognizing and classifying objects using digital images" (Trucco and Verri, 1998). Learning, which is about generalization and prediction, lies at the interface between computer vision and pattern recognition. It plays a fundamental role in facilitating "the balance between internal representations and external regularities" (Nayar and Poggio, 1996). Face recognition requires new and robust learning paradigms. This includes 'good' classification methods that can work with only limited training data, which was acquired under fairly flexible and general assumptions. "The fewer assumptions a [computer vision] system imposes on its operational conditions, the more robust it is considered to be" (Moeslund and Granum, 2001).

The challenges confronting face recognition are many. First and foremost there is much variability in the image formation process that includes geometry, illumination, occlusion and disguise, and temporal changes (see Fig. 1.1). Even the faces of "identical" twins are different to some extent (see 1.1a). Biometrics in general, and face recognition, in particular, bear directly on the use of forensics in the courts of law. In a provocative *Science* editorial, titled *"Forensic Science: Oxymoron?"* Donald Kennedy, the Editor-in-Chief, makes the obvious point that the reliability of forensics "is unverified either by statistical models of [biometric] variation or by consistent data on error rates. Nor does the problem with forensic methods ends there. Processing and enhancement of such images could mislead jurors who believe they are seeing undoctored originals." Following the 1993 U.S. Supreme Court's Daubert case, the Court "did list several criteria for qualifying expert testimony: peer review, error rate, adequate testing, regular standards and techniques, and general acceptance" (Kennedy, 2003). Similar arguments apply to automatic face recognition and are considered throughout. Other factors adversely affecting face recognition include the lack of enough data to learn reliable and distinguishable face representations, and the large computational resources required to adequately process the biometric data. Comprehensive evaluations of the science underlying forensic techniques in general, and studies on the uniqueness of personal face signatures, in particular, are still lacking. The current Face Recognition Grand Challenge (FRGC) project (Phillips et al., 2005), administered by the US National Institute of Standards and Technology (NIST), aims for

98% average reliability at FAR = 0.1%, "a tough standard, but perhaps not tough enough to handle tens of millions of travelers per year", when one considers the false alarms. The scope for FRGC is relatively narrow compared to the earlier FERET and FRVT evaluations (see Sect. 13.4) because despite the relatively large corpus of data involved, the number of subjects enrolled, 275 and 675 for ver1.0a and ver2.0, respectively, is only in the hundreds and thus much smaller than FRVT2002. FRGC functionality is further limited to verification compared to previous evaluations that also involved identification. Last but not least, the practicality of FRVT during both enrollment and testing is questionable due to its requirement for a large set of face images using different image capture methods.

(a)

(b)

(c)

Fig. 1.1. Human Faces (from FERET). (a) Twins; (b) Temporal Variation; (c) Time Sequence Including Pose Variation.

The book is no panegyrics to some research utopia but rather an attempt to be as informative as possible, avoid heuristics, and last but not least cope with meaningful face recognition tasks (see Descartes' admonishments). The book is inclusive but in a comparative fashion in order to motivate and inspire. Hard or intractable problems, e.g., correspondence, segmentation (Gurari and Wechsler, 1982) and clutter, variability, and/or insufficient and/or missing information, are not avoided or glossed over. Folk wisdom chuckles that the difference between theory and practice finds no difference in theory but only in practice. Vapnik (2000) rightly points out, however, that there is nothing more practical than a good theory. The challenge for reliable face recognition is to show through fair and good experimentation that theory and practice are consistent.

The book is mostly about face recognition but it is quite relevant to categorization and recognition for science and technology in general. The driving and unifying force behind the proposed reconciliation among computer vision, machine learning, and pattern recognition, is the active, progressive and selective accrual of evidence needed to reduce uncertainty. Practical intelligence "modifies the stimulus situation as a part of the process of responding to it" (Vygotsky, 1976). Practical intelligence is actually much more than merely modifying or transforming the input. "For the young child, to think means to recall; but for the adolescent, to recall means to think" (Vygotsky, 1976). Connect "adolescent" to reliable face recognition engines, and connect "think" to reasoning and inference. Faces cannot be reliably located and identified from merely one still image. Rather than static inputs, the language of changes observed, their logical interrelations, and the plausible inferences or transformations over space and time underlie reliable face identification and authentication.

1.1 Tasks and Protocols

The generic (on-line) biometric system used herein for face recognition (see Fig. 1.2) will be referred to throughout the book. The **match** task evaluates to what extent the biometric **signatures** extracted from the unknown face exemplar(s) and the biometric signature(s) stored during the enrollment stage as reference **template(s)** are similar. The match score has to be compared against some a priori defined **threshold** value. Matching takes place against a single template (for **verification**), or against a list of candidate templates (for **identification**). Verification is also referred to as **authentication**. Identification is usually carried out using iterative verification and ranking. The face space, usually the basis needed to generate the templates, is derived using face images acquired ahead of time and independent of those that would be later on enrolled for training or queried on (see top of Fig. 1.2). The biometric templates encode the essential features of the face along the specific dimensions of the face space used. They are stored in some central data base but can be also carried by owners on a smart card.

Face recognition performance is still lacking. According to the December 6, 2003 issue of the Economist "governments are investing a lot of faith in biometric technology as a way to improve security. For the moment, this confidence is misplaced. Body-recognition technology is not the silver bullet many governments imagine it to be. Biometrics [are] too flaky to trust." The experience of the 2001 Super Bowl held in Tampa and the trial held at Boston's Logan International Airport in 2002, which exhibited a failure rate of 38.6% [while the false-positive rate exceeded 50%], are cases in point. Again according to the Economist "given the volume of air traffic, the incidence of false alarms will vastly outnumber the rare occasions when someone tries to subvert the system. The false alarms will either have to be ignored, rendering the system useless, or a time-consuming and expensive secondary-screening system will be needed." This book is about how to improve the state-of-the art for reliable face recognition.

Performance evaluation is an integral part of any serious effort to field reliable face recognition systems. **FERET** (Phillips et al., 1998) and **BANCA** (Bailly-Bailliere et al., 2003), the standard evaluation protocols in use today, are briefly described next. FERET starts by considering target (**gallery**) T and query (**probe**) Q sets. The output for FERET is a full (distance) matrix $S(q,t)$, which measures the **similarity** between each query face, $q \in Q$, and each target face, $t \in T$, pair. The nearest neighbor (NN) classifier authenticates then face images using the similarity scores recorded by S. The availability of the matrix S allows for different "virtual" experiments to be conducted when one selects the specific query P and gallery G as subsets of Q and T. Note that one can expand on the above model using data fusion when sets rather than singletons are matched, and both the query and the gallery sets are acquired using multimodal sensors.

The **closed (universe) set face recognition** model used by FERET for $1:N$ identification, when each probe has always a mate in the gallery, is restrictive and does not reflect the true intricacies of positive and negative biometric enrollment and identification. Under positive enrollment, the client is authenticated to become eligible for "admission" or apprehended if found on some watch list, while under negative identification the biometric system has to determine that the client does not belong to some most-wanted list. Positive identification can be determined using traditional personal tokens, e.g., PIN, but negative identification can only be established using biometrics.

More challenging is the **open (universe) set face recognition** model, which operates under the assumption that not all the probes (unknown test face images) have mates (counterparts) in the gallery (of known subjects) (see Sect. 6.3). Open set face recognition requires the **a priori** availability of a **reject** option to provide for the answer "none of the above" for unknown classes of clients. If the probe is detected rather than rejected, the face recognition engine must then identify/recognize the subject. The operational analogue for open set face recognition is the (usually small) **watch list** or **surveillance** task, which involves (i) negative identification ("rejection") due to the obvious fact that the large majority [almost all] of the people screened at security entry points are law abiding people, and (ii) correct identification for those that make up the watch list. "Performance for the open set problem is quantified over two populations. First the impostors, those persons who are not present in the gallery, i.e., not on the watch list, are used to compute the false match [acceptance] rate, which is needed to quantify rejection capability. Second, for those persons who are "known" (i.e., previously enrolled) to a system, the open set identification rate, is used to quantify user [hit] performance" (Grother, 2004).

The 1 : N open set problem referred to by FRVT2002 (Phillips et al., 2003) as the watch list task, is briefly addressed after two (degenerate) special cases of verification and closed set identification. Verification corresponds to an open set identification for a gallery size of $N = 1$, while closed set identification seeks the match for an image whose mate is known to be in the gallery, i.e., for each image probe $p \in P$ there exists (exactly one) gallery mate $g^* \in G$. The "none of the above" answer is not an option. Cumulative Matching Curves (CMC) and Receiver Operating Characteristics (ROC) are used to display the results for identification and verification, respectively (see Sect. 12.1). FERET results are derived using ground truth for a posteriori setting of optimal thresholds to yield prespecified false alarm rates. Ground truth, however, is not available during real field operation hence the need for a priori setting of decision thresholds.

The BANCA protocol, geared toward the verification task, is designed to work with multi-modal databases. Verification is viewed as hypothesis testing and the (detection) choice is between true clients and impostors. There are two types of errors, false acceptance and false rejection, and their associated costs. Two types of protocols exist, closed and open set, respectively. In closed set verification the population of clients is fixed and anyone not in the training set is considered an impostor. The earlier XM2VTS Lausanne protocol (Bengio et al., 2001) is an example of closed set verification. In open set verification one seeks to add clients without having to redesign the verification system. In particular, BANCA goal is to use the same feature space and the same design parameters including thresholds. In such a scenario, the feature space and the verification system parameters should be trained using calibration data distinct and independent from the data used for specifying the client models (see Fig. 1.2). The BANCA protocol is an example of open set verification protocol.

The use of the open set concept by the BANCA protocol is quite restricted. It only refers to the derivation of the feature (face) space and the parameters needed for verification. This was referred earlier as face space basis derivation (see top of Fig. 1.2 and Sect. 5.1) and should precede enrollment. BANCA protocol, however, does not address the full scope of open set identification, where not all the probes are mated in the gallery. Real world applications are of the open set type. We address this important but usually neglected aspect of face identification using transduction, a local form of estimation and inductive inference (see Sects. 6.3 and 6.4).

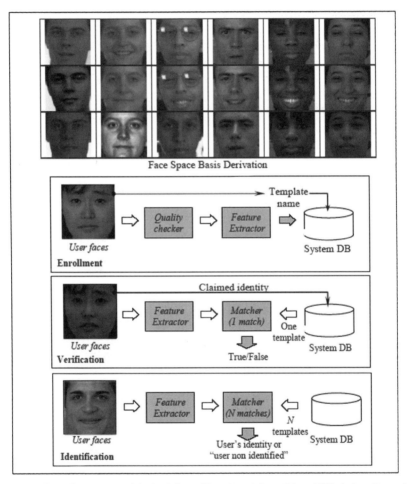

Fig. 1.2. Face Recognition Methodology (Reprinted from Li and Wechsler, Open Set Face Recognition Using Transduction, *IEEE Transactions on Pattern Analysis and Machine Intelligence*, ©2005 IEEE).

1.2 Biometrics System Design

The biometric system is the technological shell needed to realize the face recognition methodology. The focus for biometric technologies is much more than simply "replacing passwords" to being "fundamental components of secure systems, whose use and integration demands very careful planning. This involves the consideration of many issues, such as recognition accuracy, total cost of ownership, acquisition and processing speed, intrinsic and system security, [exception handling], privacy and legal requirements, as well as interface usability and user acceptance" (Bolle et al. 2004).

There are many constraints, both logistical and technical, the biometric system needs to heed. From a logistical view point most important is to become sensitive to the facts that (i) biometrics serve mass screening, e.g., machine readable travel documents (MRTD), and that (ii) the number of wanted and/or impostors is relatively small compared to the large majority of law abiding citizens. The road map for the biometric system is drawn by system engineering (Kotonya and Sommerville, 1998). It involves a complex life cycle process that includes requirements engineering, system prototyping and evaluation, architectural design and specifications, subsystem development (biometrics, communication, storage and retrieval, and security and privacy), system integration, system validation, and system maintenance. The requirements engineering component involves process together with design and techniques, i.e., *what* has to be done and *how*. System engineering addresses the requirements engineering aspect using a *spiral process* that consists of requirement elicitation, analysis and negotiation, requirements documentation and validation, and requirements management (documentation and maintenance). The design criteria used include interoperability and standards, policies, vulnerability and security, privacy, costs/performance/benefits tradeoffs, user acceptance and human factors, documentation and support, software development kit (SDK), and system administration and maintenance.

Biometric systems can be viewed as pattern recognition systems. The specific biometric components include data collection, enrollment and storage, feature extraction and template derivation, matching for different face recognition tasks such as identification and/or verification, and decision-making including post-processing. The matching component is usually referred to as the face recognition engine. Enrollment assumes that the engine has been trained ahead of time and taught how to generate the template signatures needed for enrollment and later on for matching and recognition. The biometric signatures have to be securely stored and transmitted and their vulnerabilities carefully assessed (see Ch. 14).

System validation involves testing and evaluation "to help testers achieve the best possible estimate of field performance while expending the minimum effort in conducting their evaluation, and to improve understanding of the limits of applicability of test results and test methods" (Mansfield and Wayman, 2002) (see Chaps. 12 and 13). Blackburn (2001) provides a structured approach that moves system validation through three major steps: a **technology evaluation**, a **scenario evaluation** and an **operational evaluation**. "Each type of [evaluation] test requires a different protocol and produces different results. [Technology refers to the algorithms used.] The goal for scenario evaluation is to determine the overall system performance in a prototype or simulated application. Testing is carried out [on-line] and using a complete system in an environment that models a real-world target application of interest. In scenario and operational testing any adjustments to the devices and their environment for optimal performance (including image quality and decision thresholds) have to take place **prior** [emphasis added] to data collection [and enrollment]. This should be done in consultation with the vendor" (Mansfield et al., 2001). Alternatively, according to Wayman, technology, scenario, and operational settings correspond to testing the algorithms, testing the human-machine interface, and testing mob behavior, respectively. This requires off-line training while enforcing specific policy management rules for field deployment and operation. Note that FRVT2002 has undertaken only (algorithmic) technology and scenario evaluations.

Deployment of operational biometrics involves an a priori but necessary step of threshold selection. This step is difficult to automate due to the strong dependency of optimal thresholds on image quality and the composition of training data. Much more is also known about the population, [or genuine customers,] of an application than about the enemies, [i.e., the impostors]. Consequently, the probability of a false alarm rate (FAR), [i.e.,] a false match [for screening and positive identification], is hard to estimate. Hence, "the false reject rate (FRR) for a particular decision is easier to estimate than the false alarm rate for that decision, because the biometric samples of the enemy population are not available" (Bolle et al., 2004). Note that FAR and FRR are also referred to as FPR (false positive rate) and FNR (false negative rate), respectively.

The Biometric Evaluation Methodology (BEM) provides "a common criteria scheme for Information Technology Security Evaluation that is mutually recognized by organizations in several countries" [1]. The administrator guidance [AGD] provided by the BEM document specifically refers to the setting of decisions thresholds and notes that "where it is possible to change the matching thresholds used in the comparison [authentication] process, documentation should include the effects of changing these thresholds, the means of changing these thresholds, and the importance of these thresholds in determining security." The decision threshold must be considered to be a security parameter according to BEM (AGD_ADM. 1-5). It must also include, according to BEM - Vulnerability Assessment and Misuse (AVA_MSU2-10) "guidance on how to set matching thresholds, if changing the threshold is permitted." Biometrics systems in general, and face recognition engines, in particular, require significant training for tuning and calibration before "plug and play" becomes feasible, if at all.

1.3 History

An NSF sponsored international workshop, held late in 2003, on *Designing Tomorrow's Category-Level 3D Object Recognition Systems* had a rather grim assessment of the state-of-the art for object recognition. While a distinction was made between identification (recognizing the same object), e.g., personal authentication, and categorization (recognizing a visual object class), e.g., gender and/or ethnicity, no mention is made of personal identification that discriminates between instances from the same category, e.g., human faces that carry different ID tags. The NSF report claims that "for humans, categorization is easier whereas in computer vision individual identification is a much simpler problem. For example, humans can recognize categories such as dogs, cats, horses etc. by the age of three. It appears that in humans categorization precedes [generic rather than personal] identification." The reality for face recognition is quite different. The performance on biometric categorization far exceeds that for personal identification, because there are less biometric categories, and the within class variability, characteristic of human identity, is far greater than that of biometric categories.

With the advent of photography by mid-19th century, police departments started to build local archives of suspected felons. At the beginning, the gallery of sought after criminals included daguerreotypes or mug shots together with associated information, something that today is referred to as soft biometrics. Galleries were compiled by both local police and by private detective services, such as the Pinkerton National Detective Agency. Alphonse Bertillon (1853–1914) is widely acknowledged as the person who started the field of biometrics. A friend of Paul Broca, he held the firm belief that the physical or anthropometrical characteristics of people, e.g., body measurements, are unique and that they are measurable. Specious links between anthropology and criminology, e.g., phrenology [shape of the skull and face reveals mental character and capacity], did emerge too. Bertillon measured various features, including height, arms' length, and the length and breadth of the skull. Beyond obvious bodily measurements,

---

[1] http://www.cesg.gov.uk/site/ast/biometrics/media/BEM_10.pdf

Bertillon's system also included morphological descriptions of body parts including the ear, and marks due to disease, accident, or personally inflicted, e.g., tattoos. "Having made his first 7,336 measurements, Bertillon [handwriting expert at the Dreyfus trial] was able [in 1883] to identify 49 repeat offenders; the following year, 241" (Matsuda, 1996). Bertillon intended to use these biometrics for the Paris prison service, for both physical and "moral" identification, and in 1892 became the first Director of the Paris' *Service d'Identite Judiciare*. Taxonomies across demographics and physical space were also produced. The core of *fiche signaletique* designed by Bertillon, similar to recognition-by-parts today, was to decompose the face first into "its [character] traits" before recomposing it later on for final identification. A culturally bias-based approach is a core weakness of his approach. "Cognition dominated perception, and the eye searched for what it expected to find, that is *resemblance*. Seeing a face was a fine thing, but such memories were easily tricked. According to Bertillon *we only think that which we are able to express in words*" (Matsuda, 1996) (see Sect. 14.6 on photofits).

Long before the Daubert case facing the US Supreme Court, Bertillon was aware of both the difference between early enrollment and delayed identification and authentication, and of the importance that uniqueness plays in biometrics. Towards that end, Bertillon calculated that if 14 different measurements of body parts were taken, the odds of finding two people with identical measurements were 286,435,456 to one. The system proposed by Bertillon did not last for long. In 1898, a Royal Commission sided with Sir Francis Galton - responsible for establishing fingerprints as the method of choice for personal identification and authentication - who argued that the statistical interpretation used by Bertillon is flawed and "the incorrectness lay in treating the measures of different dimensions of the same person as if they were independent variables, which they are not. For example, a tall man is much more likely to have a long arm, foot, or finger, than a short one." In addition to being conceptually flawed, Bertillon's approach failed because it was unreliable and difficult to administer.

As early as 1888, Galton (1888a and 1888b; 1910) proposed a method to classify faces, by indexing different facial (curve) profiles, finding their norms and bounding limits, and classifying new faces from their deviations from the norm. Five cardinal points derived from the face profile were used for matching. The points used included "the notch between the brow and the nose, the tip of the nose, the notch between the nose and the upper lip, parting of the lips and the tip of the chin" (Samal and Iyengar, 1992).

Anthropometry, which includes standardized body measurements, archival and retrieval, came to the United States courtesy of Major McClaughry in 1887. Gates (2004), drawing from Matsuda (1996), further reconstructs some of "the past perfect promise of facial recognition technology." In 1907, medical-legalist Dr. Motet in France transformed "bodies into coded numerical references and circulated those references as a system of signals via telegraph," while in 1912, Dr. Icard, also in France, proposed "bodies as figural landscapes to be plotted cartographically." Soon after Roentgen discovered X-rays, Dr. Foveau de Courmelles suggested the "internal card" as the ultimate identity trace that is least changeable, and established the link between biometrics and personal forensics.

Personal documentation came into vogue around the turn of the 20th century, a time of great mass dislocation when communal identity was shifting fast. The appeal for identity cards and passports, standardization and search efficiency, applied to vagabonds and foreigners alike. Matsuda (1996) recounts Vacher's sensational criminal case, which at the turn of the century ended on the guillotine in 1897. What finally trapped Vacher was "the memory of the state," which Max Weber called "the domination through knowledge, specifically rational" that characterizes modern bureaucratic organizations, i.e., the knowledge of the "file." The "file" includes photographs, measurements, [identity cards] documents, clues and correlations, ultimately "collapsing the distinction between *identity* and *identification*. The memory did more than remember - it was a *memory* which acted." The implications today, for face recognition on one side, and security and privacy, on the other side, are clear. Multi-modal face recognition, soft biometrics, evidence accumulation, and data fusion and integration further the identification and authentication process but at the cost of decreased privacy.

An excellent review for the first 25 years of the modern age, including the contributions made by Galton, comes from Samal and Iyengar (1992). The modern age for face recognition started with Bledsoe (1964). The approach used by Bledsoe was the (local) *feature* or *abstractive approach*. The intuition suggested looking at the major features of the face and comparing them against the same features from the candidate faces available. Fiducial landmarks were located and extracted as major features using manual annotation, e.g., the corners of the eyes, ears, nose, and the mouth. Normalized distances and ratios, computed from these fiducial landmarks to a common reference point, were compared to labeled data for classification. Preston (1965) used the matched filter and correlation (see Sect. 10.6) for identification from a set of six kings. In the late 1960s, Ilya Prokopoff, a Soviet scientist from Moscow University, approached face recognition using hybrid methods that included models of neurons and Rosenblatt's Perceptron. Faces were scanned and matched against a visual database to find local correlations. To address the uniqueness problem Kaya and Kobayashi (1972) used information theory to determine the number of faces that Bledsoe's method could distinguish.

Sakai et al. (1969) were first to program the computer to locate faces in an image. The feature extraction approach continued with Kelly (1970), whose doctoral dissertation was the first to show how to automatically extract outlines for both the head and body, and how to proceed to locate the facial landmarks. Body measurements, e.g., width of shoulders, and close-up head measurements, e.g., head width and the interocular distance, were combined to identify about ten persons. Leon Harmon (1973) asked whether a computer can be programmed to recognize a human face. Faced with the computational limitations of the time, he experimented with "block portraits" and asked what is the minimum resolution required for effective face recognition. He experimented with blurring - progressive defocusing - of photos into coarse 16×16 images using low-pass frequency filters (see Sects. 2.2 and 5.2) and displayed with 8 or 16 gray levels. This process can result in the image shown below (Fig. 1.3) where one can recognize Abraham Lincoln. Another role frequency plays is seen in critical-band masking when adjacent noise lies within two octaves from the signal. Harmon and Julesz (1973) showed that critical-masking is responsible for suppressed recognition (see also Sect. 14.5 on anonymity). The above findings supplemented by additional observations (see Sect. 2.2) suggest that frequency analysis plays a major role in face recognition.

Fig. 1.3. Blurred Image of Abraham Lincoln.

The next question Harmon asked was about what features are most important for face recognition. The sketches drawn by police to identify missing or wanted people start from a catalogue of face portraits drawn from memory and indexed by various head shapes, eye spacing, and lip thickness (see Sect. 14.6 for photofits). The sketching process, which iterates using "pointing to" similar features on other portraits, yields a written description used to create the final sketch. Significant facial details are corrected to enhance discrimination. Enhancing and/or distorting some of the facial features is yet another possibility characteristic of caricatures (see Sect. 5.6). While blurring serves to cancel noise, e.g., sharp edges due to digitization, high-pass filtering sharpens the visual appearance of the features that are deemed most important.

Harmon also built a vocabulary of features and the values they can take for describing and ultimately recognizing faces. The features expanded on the fiducial landmarks used almost one hundred years earlier by Galton and more recently by Bledsoe. They included hair (coverage, length, texture, and shade), forehead, eyebrows (weight and separation), eyes (opening, separation, and shade), ears (length and protrusion), cheeks, nose (length, tip, and profile), mouth, lip (upper - and lower thickness, overlap, and width), and chin (profile). Examples of values the features could take include straight, wavy and curly for hair texture, and sunken, average, and full for the cheeks. Matching between two faces, or equivalently between their feature vectors, was done using the Euclidean distance normalized for the variance observed in the placement of features. The profiles were drawn by artists but the fiducial landmarks were automatically derived (Samal and Iyengar, 1992). Kanade (1973) was the first to program the computer to recognize faces using the feature based approach. He used dedicated subroutines for different parts of the face and was able to automatically identify 15 out of 20 people. Kaufman and Breeding (1976) used profiles for identification. The approach was feature based and the features were extracted from the autocorrelation function expressed in polar form.

The next approaches for face recognition were *holistic* or *template-matching* and *hybrid*, respectively. The holistic approach, *global* in nature, encodes the whole face and achieves identification using template matching or correlation (Baron, 1981). There is unity to the face and the Gestalt or whole is more than the sum of its components. Faces are perceived as a whole rather than disconnected features. The reason for the holistic approach came from the realization that seeking for more and better features is not feasible. More measurements are difficult to come by in an automatic fashion and their quality deteriorates due to noise and occlusion (Brunelli and Poggio, 1993). Eyes were located first using templates via correlation. Standard normalization for faces kept the inter (between the eyes) ocular distance constant for storage and later on for retrieval using correlation. The best candidates were found using template matching. Disadvantages for the global approach include the need for extensive training and the difficulty to interpolate between exemplars and models, e.g., poses. The top ranked faces for global methods can continue to compete using feature matching. The last approach is referred to as *hybrid* due to its use of both template and feature matching.

The field of face recognition was reinvented when Kirby and Sirovich (1990) proposed Principal Component Analysis (PCA) for holistic face recognition. PCA, conceptually similar to Karhunen-Loeve (KL) and factor analysis, is a linear (and unsupervised) model that under Gaussian assumptions derives global and orthogonal "features" that are now routinely referred to as eigenfaces. PCA lacks phase information and its use of global features refers to the fact that the support for each feature comes from the whole face image. Each eigenface represents one of the components or dimensions along which human faces are encoded (see Sect. 5.4). The eigenfaces were one of the first attempts made to define the face space and to compress the facial data into a small and compact biometric signature that can serve as a template for face recognition. A face is then approximated as a weighted combination of some ordered eigenfaces, with the weights found by projecting the face on the face space derived ahead of time using data independent of the faces whose identification or authentication one seeks. The set of weights constitutes the signature or template used later on for personal identification and authentication. Since relatively few eigenfaces are needed to create semblances of most people, this greatly reduces the amount of data that has to be stored in order to compare faces. Kirby and Sirovich were able to encode 115 Caucasian faces using only 40 eigenfaces. Turk and Pentland (1992) refined the techniques that had been pioneered by Kirby and Sirovich. Eigenspaces, were also defined locally as eigen features, to include eigen eyes, eigen mouth and eigen nose (Pentland et al., 1994). The eigenspaces and eigen features capture the global and local appearance of the face.

There are additional ways to define the face space, including Linear Discriminant Analysis (LDA) or (non-orthogonal and supervised) Fisher Linear Discriminant (FLD) (Etemad and Chellappa, 1997), Fisherfaces, which are LDA derived on eigen spaces (Belhumeuer et al., 1997), Independent Component Analysis (ICA) (Bartlett et al., 1998), and Evolutionary Pursuit (EP) (Liu and Wechsler, 2000), a projection pursuit method whose trajectory is traced by Genetic Algorithms (GA). Note that the eigenfaces are expressive rather than discriminative features and their usefulness should apply to face reconstruction rather than face identification and authentication, a role that is more suitable for LDA. Neural networks and Statistical Learning Theory (SLT) are another instantiation of the holistic approach. The WIZARD (Stonham, 1986), self-organizing feature maps (Kohonen, 1989), connectionism (Valentin et al., 1994), and support vector machines (SVM) are major examples for such an approach. There are direct connections between PCA and neural networks. Oja (1982) has shown that the hidden nodes for MLP span the same space as the one spanned by the leading eigen values for PCA. Such connections and their potential use for color compression are discussed later on (see Sect. 5.8). The (compact) hidden unit outputs were used as features by a second MLP (Golomb et al, 1991) for gender categorization.

The feature based approach gave way in the 1990s to a *structural approach*, similar in concept and scope with the earlier hybrid approach. The structural approach is now referred to as the *recognition-by-parts approach*. In addition to features there is a global structure linking the local features or parts. The Dynamic Link Architecture (DLA) (Lades et al., 1993) and its descendant, Elastic Bunch Graph matching (EBGM) (Wiskott, 1997), express the local features in terms of Gabor wavelets using the face as the underlying grid. The local features are linked within a graph with spring-like connections that define the face topography. The role for matching is to align between two (gallery and probe) graphs. EBGM bundles the features into bunches to allow for their variable appearance. Similarity between two faces corresponds to the cost paid for deformation or elastic alignment (Yuille, 1989). Another possible structure linking the 2D features for face recognition is the Hidden Markov Model (Samaria and Young, 1994). Similar to the structural approach in terms of plasticity is the *flexible appearance approach* pioneered by Lanitis et al. (1995). PCA is used to model the principal (inter- and intra- personal) modes of variation for both shape, i.e., face outline, and texture. Some methods can implement both the holistic and structural approach. As an example, Independent Component Analysis (ICA), depending on the architecture used, implements both the global (holistic) model and spatially localized features suitable for recognition-by-parts (Draper et al., 2003). Interestingly enough and what one would expect, the global features are best for face identification, with the local features best at recognizing facial expressions. The Local Features Analysis (LFA) (Penev and Atick, 1996) expands on standard PCA as it tries to fill in for some underlying structure. It does this by extracting sparsely distributed but topographically spaced local features from the global PCA modes. The grid used to index for the LFA kernels is reminiscent of the grid used by DLA and EBGM.

The most recent attempts to address face recognition are characteristic of *recognition-by-parts*. The overall encoding structure is referred to as a constellation (Heisele et al., 2003; Huang et al., 2003) (see Sect.9.7). The current parts or component-based recognition methods, known earlier on as aspect graphs or visual potentials (Koenderink and van Doorn, 1979), are suitable to handle partial occlusion and structural noise. The scope for pattern recognition, in general, and face recognition, in particular, has become much wider because training and/or testing can take place using incomplete or camouflaged/disguised patterns from single or multiple image sets. As we move from 2D stills to time-varying imagery and 3D, video tracking and recognition together with data fusion are the latest approaches for face recognition (see Chaps. 7, 8 and 9).

1.4 Road Map

This book, the first to comprehensively address the face recognition problem in its entirety, draws inspiration and gains new insights from complementary fields of endeavor, such as neurosciences, statistics, signal and image processing, computer vision, machine learning and pattern recognition, and statistical learning. The overall goal of the book is applied modern pattern recognition, with the understanding that the novel methods described are not restricted to faces but rather apply to any objects. The scope for pattern recognition considered is also much wider because both training and testing should take place using incomplete or camouflaged/disguised patterns drawn from single and/or multiple image sets. The various chapters treat topics related to how people represent, process and/or respond to the human face, modeling and prediction, representing the face space, identification and verification, face detection, tracking and recognition, 3D, data fusion, denial and deception under occlusion and disguise, performance evaluation and error analysis, and finally, competing security and privacy considerations.

The specific road map for the book is as follows. Ch. 2 brings forth the complementary dimensions of cognitive neurosciences, psychophysics, social sciences, and aesthetics and arts. They place the endeavor of face recognition in a multidisciplinary context, and provide the motivation and inspiration required to understand and advance the field of reliable face recognition. Perception, in general, and face recognition, in particular, requires training and reasoning or inference. This is discussed in Ch. 3 using the predictive learning framework, starting with the Bayesian approach, and continuing with connectionism or neural networks, statistical learning, and recent approaches such as transduction. The chapter ends with a comparative assessment of generative and discriminative approaches. Biometrics, in general, and face recognition, in particular, start with data capture. Towards that end, Ch. 4 considers sensing and enrollment, the standards required for proper biometric use and evaluation, and the compression means available to facilitate storage and processing. Human faces have to be represented before recognition can take place. Ch. 5 is involved with the means available to represent faces for fidelity purposes and enhanced discrimination. The notions and basics of the face space, scale space and invariance, are motivated and presented first. Specific subspace methods for face representation, e.g., eigenfaces and Fisherfaces, are then described and compared. Feature selection, caricatures, and kernel methods are among the methods proposed for more distinctive face representations that are expected to yield better performance.

Ch. 6 is involved with specific face recognition tasks such as verification and identification, watch list/surveillance, and selection and categorization. The chapter starts with the metrics available for measuring similarity between face representations, and their relative merits. Open set (face) recognition is then introduced and compared with closed set (face) recognition. Methods driven by transduction are described for implementing open set face recognition, and the recognition-by-parts strategy for face recognition is discussed in detail. Ch. 7 addresses the all encompassing problem of face in a crowd. It starts with eye and face detection, and continues with a thoroughly discussion on the related concepts of uncertainty, active learning, and evidence accumulation. Topics such as video break detection and key frame extraction, pose detection and manifolds, joint tracking and recognition, and subspace spatial-temporal analysis are described, and their specific benefits for face recognition using multiple image sets are explained. Ch. 8 considers and evaluates the use of 3D for face recognition. The topics discussed include sensing, the analysis by synthesis strategy of image interpretation, animation, and modeling and recognition in 3D using transformations and morphing to align enrolled and query data and measure their similarity. Ch. 9 is involved with data fusion. The motivation comes from the belief that more but independent sources of data are better at overcoming uncertainty and improving overall performance, or equivalently that the whole is more than the sum of its parts. Data fusion can involve multiple samples, multiple cues, multiple engines, several sensory channels, soft biometrics, or a combination thereof, using a voting scheme such as

AdaBoost. The chapter concludes with a description of how boosting and strangeness implement recognition-by-parts in a fashion characteristic of data fusion.

Biometrics can not assume that the personal signatures they have access to are complete and reliable. Towards that end, Ch. 10 considers means for deception and denial, e.g., occlusion and disguise, and human biases that face recognition algorithms are likely to exhibit. The chapter describes among others a number of counter measures to handle partial faces and camouflage, and determine if the biometric presented is alive. Ch. 10 concludes with a description of how adaptive and robust correlation filters can implement the recognition-by-parts strategy for handling occlusion and disguise. Ch. 11 considers augmented cognition to extend users' and face recognition engines' abilities in order to improve their performance and provide for graceful degradation. The chapter also discusses the important dimension of face expressions for face recognition and social communication. Chaps. 12 and 13 are involved with the important but closely related topics of performance evaluation and error analysis. The topics addressed in Ch. 12 include figures of merit, score normalization to account for different operating conditions, threshold settings and decision-making, choosing among competing face recognition engines, and the data bases available for training and testing face recognition algorithms. Ch. 13 discusses confidence intervals for performance indexes, fallacies that concern the effectiveness of mass screening and intrusion detection,, and anecdotal observations that clients are different with respect to the difficulty they present for being recognized and/or their ability to become imposters, and the means to handle such diversity of clients. The chapter concludes with a critical discussion of large-scale face recognition evaluations.

Ch. 14 expands on reliability to include security and privacy aspects. The chapter addresses the perceived threats and vulnerabilities, and the means to thwart them. The topics covered include aspects related to the diversity and uniqueness of biometrics, cryptographic means, steganography and digital watermarking for and using faces, anonymity and privacy and their preservation, and photofits to recall fleeting observances of biometric data. Ch. 15 is involved with expanding the scope for biometrics and adding to existing knowledge and practice. The rapid increase expected in biometric data volumes is not matched by a commensurate increase in the quantity or quality of data intensive scientific research tools. To meet such biometrics goals, the chapter introduces the idea of agent-based middleware, driven by machine learning, to automate the process of data search, query formulation, workflow configuration and service composition, and collaborative reuse, for enhanced biometric system design and performance. The Epilogue concludes the book with an overall assessment of challenges, and outlines promising R&D directions for their resolution.

2. The Human Face

The Face is the Soul of the Body
(Ludwig Wittgenstein)

Where does the human face come from and how did it evolve? More than 300 million years ago, the features of eyes, nostrils, and a hinged jaw have combined to create a face. Starting with prehistoric tetrapod creatures such as the (late Devonian) fish Panderichthys and the amphibian Acanthostega, the head/face complex has continued to be present and change ever since. "When the human fetus is five and a half weeks old and shaped like a bean, there appear from the underside three outgrowths. These bronchial arches develop, in fish, into gills. In mammals, these buds of tissue merge and mix to form our forehead, face, and throat, with the second arch moving upward to form the face" (Cole, 1998). As recounted by Cole, additional evolutionary changes that are responsible for the human face as we know it today include warm bloodedness that requires insulation and makes the skin softer, and a sense of vision that dominates over smell and touch and makes the eyes the center for the face. The facial hair went away and the jaws can now display face expressions. The new ways the food is ingested further shape and mold the facial bones, muscles, and the skull that harbors the human face.

Mammals are capable of recognizing each other's faces and of picking up important cues from the expressions imprinted on them. Sheep, in particular, excel and can remember other sheep faces after many years of separation (Kendrick et al., 2001). With the dominant sensory centers of hearing, smell, sight, and taste all located within the face framework, and the skull harboring the control center, the face commands much attention. When primates began to walk upright, the sense of sight becomes the most important of the senses. Body posture and vocalization gave way to face language and social intelligence. The face becomes the medium for sharing information and communicating within groups of increasing size. As human language and abstract reasoning have emerged only recently, a tantalizing question concerns the relation between face language and the early manifestations of human language. Face language, to some extent, is universal. Did the universal element of the face language transfer to universal elements for our primeval "mother" language?

The human face today is a collection of two bones (the skull and jaw) and 44 muscles, which are not attached to the bones. This enables a great liberty of movement that allows thousands of different facial expressions. Recognizing faces is absolutely central to our humanity; it is estimated that 50% of our brain function is devoted to vision, and that a lion's share of that goes for facial recognition. It is only natural that we endeavor to endow computers with the same ability. Another practical reason for computerized facial recognition was advanced by Gates (2004). She frames the problem of identification in historical perspective to bear not only on criminology but also on civil identification. In particular, she refers to Arendt (1973), who argued in *Origins of Totalitarianism* that "the claim to authority for determining who belongs and who does not is a central component of sovereignty." This has been "a particular preoccupation of modern states" and is even more so today. The human face also plays an important role in social interaction and communication that is crucial for realistic animation and video games. Last but not least, the face and its apparent beauty has been the focus for aesthetics and arts since the dawn of civilization. The beauty is either inner and hidden and reveals character, or outward and visible, and conveys physical appearance. The face is the messenger in both cases.

The book, mostly about the science and technology of automatic face recognition, brings forth in this chapter the complementary dimensions of cognitive neurosciences, psychophysics, social sciences, and aesthetics and arts. They provide both motivation and inspiration for how to advance the field of reliable face recognition.

2.1 Cognitive Neurosciences

From their early infancy, people have the ability to process faces. Babies have blurry vision at birth, but newborns can still discriminate, using external features, their mother's face from other female faces soon after birth. Infants can also differentiate both facial attractiveness and facial expressions. Is face recognition different from other categorization tasks regarding the processes the brain engages in? Not according to Gauthier and Logothetis (2000). There is neocortical and limbic cell selectivity in response to facial identity in the prefrontal cortex, to gaze direction in the superior temporal sulcus, to face expression in the amygdale, and to overall face configuration for most of the type of cells mentioned. Such selectivity, however, is not unique for face recognition. Gauthier and Logothetis found using neuro imaging on monkeys that preferential cell selectivity applies to "any arbitrary homogeneous class of artificial objects - which the animal has to individually learn, remember, and recognize again and again from a large number of distractors sharing a number of common features with the target. Faces are not "special" but rather the "default special" class in the primate recognition system."

Neurological patients and their syndromes provide a rich trove of information on how the brain is built and how it functions. Ramachandran (1998), like a sleuth always excited to "begin with a set of symptoms that seem bizarre and incomprehensible and then end up - at least in some cases - with an intellectual satisfying account in terms of the neural circuitry in the patient's brain," has worked for many years on the nature of phantom limbs, which are ghosts of arms and legs lost years before but still somehow remembered by the brain. The phantom limbs, according to Oliver Sacks who prefaced the book written by Ramachandran (with Sandra Blakeslee), serve as "experimental epistemology" and are explained by "reorganizations of body image in the sensory cortex." The sensory maps are thus not fixed but malleable. There is "nature" and there is "nurture." Maps can and do change as a result of injury. Neural connections are not fixed but rather plastic. There is a redundancy of connections and new paths can sprout, or even more intriguing paths can exists even for limbs missing since birth or never developed. A hand is lost and it becomes a phantom. Remapping takes place and the face, whose sensory area is right beside the hand, takes over the area previously allotted to the hand. Touching the face generates sensations in the phantom hand. The brain, modular with regard to functionality and localization, "doesn't hold all the answers." Genuine and spontaneous smiles are produced by basal ganglia but smiles on request come courtesy of the cortex.

The body surface is mapped on the surface of the brain behind the central sulcus. The Penfield's "sensory homunculus" is a visual rendering of how different parts of the body are mapped, and to what extent and where. The homunculus distorts the body and the size for different parts corresponding to their relative importance. The face and hand occupy "a disproportionately large share of the map." The explanation given, that "the area involved with lips and fingers takes up as much space as the area involved with the entire trunk of the body. This is presumably because your lips and fingers are highly sensitive to touch and are capable of very fine discrimination," is eminently plausible. The map is not continuous and "the face is not near the neck, where it should be, but is below the hand." The above findings suggest that varying rather than uniform resolution grids are used to represent the face. Self-Organization

Features Maps (SOFM) (see Sect. 5.6) could provide the mechanism used to allocate more grid space to the eyes, nose, and mouth at the expense of the cheeks. This involves competitive learning and Hebbian attractors that trade the real estate for the face representation between the facial areas and its landmarks according to their functional conspicuity and saliency.

While the processes by which the human brain recognizes faces are not fully understood, some clues are available from people affected by *Prosopagnosia*. The name of the disorder combines the Greek words for person and face (prosopon) and impairment (agnosia). More than failing to remember the names associated with the faces seen, individuals affected by prosopagnosia lose the ability to recognize faces [but still display autonomic covert recognition as measured by skin conductance responses], and lack any subjective sense of familiarity, even for their closest family members. Patients experience difficulty in tracking characters from TV shows and rely instead on non-facial information [similar to soft biometrics]. The disorder has to do with recall mechanisms and appears to be caused by an injury in the fusiform gyrus area of the brain, which involves the amygdala. Here, researchers have identified a *Fusiform Face Area* (FFA), an area specialized for face perception (Kanwisher et al., 1997). Yovel and Kanwisher (2004a) have shown, using fMRI studies of FFA, that face perception is domain rather than process specific. Subjects had to discriminate among pairs of upright or inverted faces or houses stimuli that differed in either the spatial distance among parts (configuration) or the shape of the parts. "The FFA showed a much higher response to faces than to houses, but no preference for the configuration task over the part task." Such findings are relevant to recognition-by-parts methods, which are compositional and structural in nature. The above findings appear to suggest that claims made on the existence of a generic dictionary of parts, e.g., geons (Biederman, 1987), are not warranted. The parts are rather different and according to the object they compose. They emerge as a result of competitive pressure encountered during discrimination tasks (see Sect. 9.7).

There are additional areas that appear to be involved in face processing. The result of evolution and functional differentiation, the areas are located in the posterior fusiform (PF), apparently a gateway to higher level processing including emotion, and in the middle temporal gyrus responsible for attention. Interesting also to note is that FFA lies in the "non retinotopic visual association cortex of the ventral visual processing stream" (Halgren et al., 1999). Canonical or configural configurations of face parts were found to trigger greater response vs. randomly rearranged parts within the face outline in the amygdala, superior temporal sulcus (STS), and FFA (Golarai et al., 2004). Deficits in configural processing could account for prosopagnosia (Duchaine et al., 2004). Face processing, however, is more than just configural. Face perception "engages a domain-specific system for processing both configural and part-based information about faces" (Yovel and Kanwisher, 2004b). This is needed to accommodate viewpoint or pose changes, occlusion and/or disguise, and temporal changes. Robust and steady part- or patch- based information can still identify a face despite missing and/or changed patches. Such information is behind the recent upsurge of "constellations" of parts for reliable face recognition (see Sects. 6.5 and 9.7).

It is the sub-ordinate rather than basic-level classification that appears to fire FFA. What about encoding for face recognition? "For stimuli such as faces, which are likely to be encountered by every member of the species, configural representations or [golden ratio] templates may be most effective because the basic stimulus configuration is invariant across the environments in which individuals may live. Thus the predictability of species-specific stimuli may allow for the creation through evolution of complex pattern recognition systems. These systems are tuned at birth but remain plastic through development" (Kanwisher and Moscovitch, 2000). The arguments listed above are relevant to basic-level face detection rather than sub-ordinate face identification. Liu, Harris et al. (2001) have MEG recordings to suggest that "face processing [indeed] proceeds through two stages: an initial stage of [basic] face

categorization [after 100 ms], and a [70 ms] later stage at which the identity of the individual face is extracted."
Dissociations of face and object recognition in developmental prosopagnosia (Duchaine and Nakayama, 2005) support the hypothesis that "face and non-face recognition relies on separate mechanisms." Aware that "the acquisition of mature face perception skills is not complete until late adolescence" and that face recognition is a skill that has to be learned, the developmental aspect of the disorder refers to patients failing to develop the face recognition skills rather than acquiring the deficits as adults due to illness. What is the difference between object and face recognition? As recounted by Duchaine and Nakayama, "object recognition typically involves feature processing, but face recognition also involves holistic and configural processing. Holistic processing is characterized by the integration of facial information into a gestalt, whereas configural processing usually describe sensitivity to the precise spatial layout of the facial features." The development of specific mechanisms starts with external features for newborns, proceeds with internal features around eight weeks, and will continue with holistic and configural processing later on. Aspergers' syndrome is a mild form of autism characterized by an abnormally-sized amygdala. Patients are unable to recognize facial expressions, e.g., fear, and seem to analyze separate elements of a face more than the whole. Brain disorders, in general, and prosopagnosia and Aspergers syndromes, in particular, cannot be explained by any single cause. This makes a strong case for hybrid (local and global) approaches for face recognition that include (internal and external) features together with configural and holistic processing.

Another neurological disorder, reported by Dr. Ramachandran, is the Capgras' syndrome of misidentification, where the patient sees familiar and loved ones as impostors. Again we refer to Oliver Sacks and his explanation that there is "a clear neurological basis for the syndrome - the removal of the usual and crucial affective cues to recognition [leading to] affectless perceptions." Capgras' syndrome is explained by the damaged connections from the face processing areas in the temporal lobe to the limbic system. Patients report something like *she can't be my fiancée because I feel nothing* and record diminished galvanic skin response (GSR). Capgras' delusion suggests that there is more to face recognition than the face itself and that emotions play an important role. Antonio Damasio (1994) argues along similar lines for the role emotions play in rational thinking. Damasio's book *Descartes' Error* is a clever take on the famous *Je Pense donc Je suis* [I think therefore I exist]. Emotions are integral to existence. Some obvious implications for face recognition follow. Face expressions [of inner emotions] rather than being a handicap should help with face recognition as they are unique to each individual, e.g., the mysterious smile of Mona Lisa. Face expressions play also an imported role in interpreting human behaviors and augmented cognition (see Ch. 11). Video sequences rather than single still images for face recognition are thus required to capture the temporal dimension and the unique facial changes experienced. The neurological patient suffering from Capgars' syndrome remembers each face appearance episode but fails to link them into one category. The implications for face recognition are obvious. Multiple image frames are needed to search for the "glue" unique to each individual that makes the temporal sequence coherent.

Capgras' delusion is a mirror image of amnesia. A face is recognized but its authentication fails. Starting from the Capgras' delusion and within the framework of cognitive neuropsychiatry, Ellis and Lewis (2001) raise important epistemological questions on normal face recognition [circuitry] and the corresponding models of modal face recognition. The belief that specific cognitive functions are localized goes back to the anthropologist Paul Broca in the 19th century for whom an area of the frontal lobe is named. Today we witness a revolution in mapping brain functions to understand how the normal mind works. Neuroimaging is a "keystone for the growing field of cognitive neurosciences" (Culham, 2004). The growth of the field is indeed impressive. At the same time, Tulving, in an interview for *Cognitive Neuroscience* (Cooney et al., 2002), remarks that "what is badly needed now, with all these scanners whirring away, is an understanding of exactly what we are observing, and seeing, and measuring, and wondering about." Different but complementary neuroimaging technologies have become available, including electroencephalography (EEG), magnetic electroencephalography (MEG), magnetic resonance imaging (MRI), positron emission tomography (PET) and fMRI. The same technologies are also used to diagnose disorders and to monitor drug treatments. The underlying principle for neuroimaging is that matter, i.e., body or brain tissue, absorb energy at a resonant frequency and reemission or relaxation times that can be differentially measured (Lauterbur, 1973). Originally the devices were called NMR (nuclear magnetic resonance) but for public reassurance the name has changed later on to MRI (magnetic resonance imaging).

f(unctional)MRI, a standard MRI scanner, measures changes in blood-oxygenation-level dependent (BOLD) signals in response to variable magnetic fields. There is functional resolution, which relates neuronal activity and cognitive behavior, and there is also anatomical contrast, which differentiate between different properties of tissue. fMRI provides fine spatial and temporal resolution, 4 mm voxel size, and one second repeatability. This makes fMRI suitable for spatiotemporal event analysis using ICA (see Sect. 7.8). Differences in performance between attending vs. not attending to the stimulus were found higher for faces than for places in FFA, the apparent locus for face processing. This provides strong motivation for using attention mechanisms for face processing. As the temporal (ms) resolution for MEG is much higher than the one for fMRI, integral studies using fMRI and MEG are now being performed. "fMRI adaptation techniques hold excellent potential for evaluating the nature of the mental representations within an area. Both behavioral and fMRI adaptation work on the same principle: with continued stimulation, neurons show reduced responses" (Culham, 2004). The reduced response indicates the dimensions some brain area is sensitive to. As an example, the face selective FFA mentioned earlier yields lower response when subject to extended presentation of the same face compared to versions of different faces.

While suggesting that face recognition is modular [modal], Ellis and Lewis (2001) claim that the etiology behind Capgras' delusion "invokes a second stage at which autonomic [identification] attributions are made." Like Breen et al. (2000), Ellis and Lewis (2001) proposed (see Fig. 2.1) a modified dual-route model of face recognition and misidentification, where recognition takes place along the ventral route, and affective responses are provided by ventral limbic structures, especially the amygdala. In addition, they also proposed a second [integrative] facility that compares the conclusions of the two routes, which must be impaired for the delusion to take place. Abnormalities at locations A and B (see 2.1) are responsible for prosopagnosia and the Capgras' delusion, respectively. An abnormality at location C will not lead to delusions and would imply that damage at A or B could be circumvented. Furthermore, covert face recognition for patients affected by prosopagnosia is fractioned between autonomic and cognitive/behavioral recognition, e.g., face interference in terms of accuracy and latency, as measured by the skin conductance response (SCR) that was referred to earlier as GSR. The conceptual framework provided by the modal architecture has important implications for automatic face recognition. There are person identity nodes but there is also much scope for context and modularity and thus for multimodal and episodic recognition, and data (fusion and) integration.

Another fertile area of research is what information from faces is stored to make them recognizable. It has been noted that we see differences in our own ethnic group with greater ease than we do in other ethnic groups (the other race-effect or "they all look alike to me" syndrome.) Experiments show that we recognize a well done caricature faster than a photographic image, suggesting that the distinctive details of each face and their exaggeration or stereotyping lead to the correct match for identification (see Sect. 5.6).

2.2 Psychophysics

Psychophysics lies between perception and psychology. It is concerned with establishing qualitative and/or quantitative relations between physical stimulation and percep-

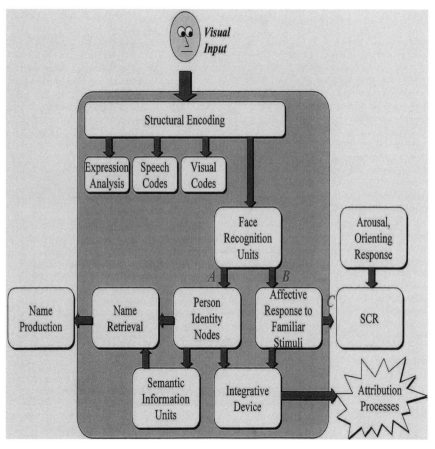

Fig. 2.1. Modal Brain Architecture for Face Recognition and Misidentification (Reprinted from *Trends in Cognitive Sciences*, Vol. 5, Ellis and Lewis, Capgras Delusion: A Window on Face Recognition, ©2001, with permission from Elsevier).

tual events. Psychophysics can provide insights and motivation for a particular line of research, e.g., face recognition. One has to keep in mind that psychophysics is mostly driven by constrained rather than unconstrained environments, and because it is usually done in vitro, it is not situated and thus lacks context. While it should be obvious that mass screening is not something that people routinely engage in, there are other dimensions worth exploring. We start by reporting on preliminary studies that were conducted in our laboratory regarding human sensitivity and bias on face surveillance tasks. Under the face surveillance task, human subjects were asked if a given face image ('probe') belongs to a relatively small set of face images ('gallery'). The performance indexes used for the study, the d' sensitivity and c response bias (Macmillan and Creelman, 1991), are described below together with our psychophysical findings.

d', a function of the hit rate (H) and false alarm rate (F), captures the observer's sensitivity. The miss rate is $M = 1 - H$. A perfectly sensitive subject has a hit rate of 1 and a false alarm rate of zero. A completely insensitive subject, on the other side, is unable to distinguish between two stimuli (old and new) and performs equally well without attending to them. For this subject, the probability of saying 'yes' does not depend on the probe, and $H = F$. d', defined in terms of the inverse of the normal distribution function Z, is defined as $d' = Z(H) - Z(F)$. The transformation Z converts an H or F rate to a Z score using standard deviations units. A rate of 0.5 is converted into a Z-score of 0, larger rates into positive Z-scores, while smaller rates into negative ones. When observers cannot discriminate at all, $H = F$ and $d' = 0$. Perfect accuracy on the other hand implies an infinite d'. Moderate performance implies that d' is near unity (see Sect. 12.1 for related performance indexes).

The response bias index c measures subjects' preference to provide 'yes' responses at the expense of 'no' responses. The bias c is defined as $c = -0.5[Z(H) + Z(F)]$. When the false alarm and miss rates are equal, $Z(F) = Z(1 - H) = -Z(H)$, and the bias is zero. Negative values for the bias arise when the false alarm rate exceeds the miss rate, while positive values for the bias are recorded when $F < M$. Extreme values of c occur when H and F are both large or small. If both H and F equal 0.99 then $c = -2.33$, while when both H and F are equal to 0.01, $c = 2.33$. The range of the bias c is therefore the same as that of d', although 0 is now the center rather than an endpoint. For positive c values, the smaller c is, the more biased the subject is to say 'yes'. Subjects that participated in screening experiments were found to display a significant degree of bias when they have or think they have more evidence about the gallery. Specifically, the bias displayed is reflected in an increased propensity to match a probe against the gallery if (a) the gallery was available for perusal, (b) screeners were trained twice and believed they were better prepared, (c) screeners were tested closer in time to the training session. The same experiments confirmed that fatigue, less training, and/or flashing the gallery on request are likely to decrease the sensitivity of screeners on face surveillance tasks. The explanation for the observed decrease in sensitivity when the gallery is flashed is that the increase in the false alarm rate more than compensates the increase in the probability of detection. Lack of the flash option during testing appears to make the screeners more conservative and thus decreases the false alarm rate.

The fact that frequency analysis plays an important role in face recognition was already known by Harmon (1973) (see Sect. 1.3). Frequency analysis is characteristic of early or low-level vision for both biological and artificial or man-made vision systems. Frequency analysis can be traced back to Fourier. It is based on the simple observation that any (periodic) signal or waveform (of period T) can be composed by adding together an (infinite) series of (sine and cosine) sinusoids waves. The assumptions about periodicity and the use of infinite series are usually relaxed for practical use. The sinusoid frequencies are integer multiples of the basic or fundamental f frequency, $f = 1/T$, and are referred to as harmonics. Frequency, as the name implies, denotes repeatability and is measured in cycles per standard unit of space and/or time. The zero harmonic of the signal, the DC component, has zero frequency and stands for the average of the wave form. The harmonics are further defined in terms of amplitude and phase. The amplitude is about the magnitude of the sinusoid, while the phase or relative position describes how the harmonics are shifted with respect to each other before they are summed up. Both amplitude and phase are important for image reconstruction. The phase is closely related to the image contents and their structure because it carries information about location. The power spectrum, which is the squared amplitude of the Fourier components, is poor in terms of information contents because phase information is absent. The power spectrum is the Fourier transform of the autocorrelation function and provides the link between frequency or Fourier analysis and second order statistics, e.g., principal component analysis (PCA) (see Sect. 5.4). The use of Fourier analysis is quite restrictive. It is relaxed using Gabor or wavelet representations for whom the support is now local (see Sect. 5.2).

Choosing the right harmonics (or equivalently the right PCA components) for signal or face representation (and implicitly for reliable face recognition) is a challenge. The low-frequency harmonics are usually associated with averages and are thus suitable for (face) categorization using demographics. The high frequency harmonics code for details and are relevant for personal identification and verification. The same details, however, can code for noise too and are then a hindrance for face authentication. Bigun et al. (2001) have shown that "the lack of caricature type information (high spatial frequencies) hampers the [face] recognition task significantly more than the lack of silhouette and shading (low spatial frequencies) information. The same test on forensic skills and a following study, using faces that differ significantly in hair style, glasses, expressions, facial hair, and clothing, uncovered that "the female population have better skills in human face recognition tasks than the male population." Men appear to have larger negative bias to hair style and facial expressions than women do. Hair style (including hair cut) change is a great distraction factor for both genders when they recognize faces, but more so for males than females. Males are easier to recognize than females by both genders. (This is a reconfirmation of findings made by other researchers). The test, available on the internet [1], is similar to that shown in Fig. 2.2, where A5 is the right answer! A5 just had a hair cut. 59% of the subjects tested thought that A10, however, is the right answer. The next largest agreement on answers was 9% for A1 and A5 (the correct answer). The rest of the agreements were smaller and indicate random decisions. Note that women were better than males on the test because they are more aware of hair styles. Khurana and Hole (2004) suggest that "women's general predisposition to attend to the internal geometry of the face, familiarity notwithstanding, underlies their efficacy in face processing."

Spectral contents bears on face attractiveness and recognition. Faces appear to be best recognized for a critical band of (middle) spatial frequency (SF) thought to lie between 8 and 16 cycles/face. Liu, Collin et al. (2000) argued earlier that the most important factor for face recognition regarding frequency analysis is the spatial frequency overlap (SFO), which is the range of spatial frequencies shared by the learned and test face images. They showed that "a single octave change in this factor was found to produce differences in accuracy on the order of 20% in some conditions, and manipulations in SFO elicited performance ranging from floor to ceiling" (Collin et al., 2004). SFO is thus more important than the frequency cut-off and this is going to affect human identification from distance (HID) where one expects that SFO drops off significantly. Noise distribution in relation to SFO is yet another factor that affects face recognition.

Frequency analysis is also relevant for assessing beauty, and analyzing face expressions and their contributions to face recognition. Blurred and original face images are found to be similar with respect to attractiveness. This suggests that fine details do not play a significant role on assessing beauty (Sadr et al., 2002). The placement and relative luminance of large regions of dark and light, however, do affect the perceived beauty (Russell et al., 2004). What about face expressions? Goren and Wilson (2004) have shown that there is a differential impact of spatial frequency on facial expression and face recognition. As expected, face expressions rendered using low special frequency (LSF) are harder to recognize than their high spatial frequency equivalents (HSF). "Fear, sadness and happiness show greater detriments than anger when spatial

---

[1] http://www.hh.se/staff/josef/public/sa/face_recog_test/

frequency is lowered. LSF emotion recognition is impaired more than facial identity, suggesting that facial expression recognition is more dependent on an optimal spatial frequency range than facial identity recognition".

What features, if at all, are useful for face recognition, and how should one use them? "The difference in human features must be reckoned great, inasmuch as they enable us to distinguish a single known face among those of thousands of strangers, though they are mostly too minute for measurement. At the same time, they are exceedingly numerous. The general expression of a face is the sum of a multitude of small details, which are viewed in such rapid succession that we seem to perceive them all at a single glance. If any one of them disagrees with the recollected traits of a known face, the eye is quick at observing it, and it dwells upon the difference. One small discordance overweighs a multitude of similarities and suggests a general unlikeness" Galton (1883). The standard features for face recognition are the major facial landmarks, i.e., the eyes, nose, and mouth. Eyebrows, however, appear to be more important than the eyes regarding performance accuracy (Sadr et al., 2003).

Jarudi and Sinha (2003) have considered the relative contributions made by internal and external features in terms of image resolution. External features, e.g., head outline, provide both context and the frame of reference for the internal features, e.g., eyes, mouth, and nose. In addition, the external features are thought more important for recognizing unfamiliar faces, while the internal features hold the advantage for familiar faces. The belief held in the past was that at high resolution, the internal features of familiar faces are more useful for face recognition than the external features. The experiments performed by Jarudi and Sinha (2003) suggest now that "the two feature sets reverse in importance as resolution decreases [due to image degradation] and that the visual system uses a highly non-linear cue-fusion strategy in combining internal and external features along the dimension of image resolution, and that the configural cues that relate the two feature sets play an important role in judgments of facial identity." As an example, when a picture of Vice President Al Gore had its internal features supplanted by those of President Bill Clinton, the judgment on the face perceived was still that of Al Gore despite the fact that the internal features all came from Bill Clinton. Similar findings regarding the role of using external features apply to neonates who are known to lack access to high resolution in their first days of life. A complementary but related finding made by Yip and Sinha (2002) is that "color increasingly contributes to face recognition with decreasing image resolution." When shape (external) cues are degraded, color helps with both face detection and face recognition. The implications are clear. Human identification from distance (HID), under the reasonable assumption of unfamiliarity, should use both color and external cues.

Illumination varies and it affects face recognition. Thoresz and Sinha (2001) suggest the (golden) ratio - template for generating face signatures that are largely invariant to illumination changes and thus suitable for face detection. The templates encode pair-wise ordinal relationships that are invariant. The eye-forehead ratio is more significant than nose-tip-cheek because the last can be affected by hair. A holistic-like approach is required where one has to consider several qualitative relations together for detection and/or categorization. Faces are difficult to identify in contrast negatives. The standard explanation is that lacking shape-from-shading, 3D shape information is absent. An alternative explanation for impaired performance could be, however, that ordinal 2D contrast relationships, e.g., contrast polarity around the eyes, is compromised instead. Towards that end, Sinha and Gilad (2004) created a set of "contrast chimeras," which are photo-negative faces everywhere except in the eye region (thus preserving local contrast polarity in that neighborhood). "Given that such faces have unnatural shading cues over much of their extents, a shape-from-shading based explanation would not predict significant improvements in recognition performance. However, if performance in negatives is compromised, at least in part, due to the destruction of local polarity relations between the eyes and their neighborhood, performance with contrast chimeras is expected to be better than that with contrast negatives." Contrast chimeras were recognized indeed at a significantly higher rate

Count of Q2	Q2										
Gender	A 1	A 2	A 3	A 4	A 5	A 6	A 7	A 8	A 9	A 10	Total
Female	8%	3%	4%	4%	16%	8%	0%	4%	2%	51%	100%
Male	9%	5%	3%	6%	6%	5%	1%	2%	1%	63%	100%
Grand Total	9%	4%	3%	5%	9%	6%	1%	3%	1%	59%	100%

This is a smoothed picture (i.e. no detail information).
Try to find this person among the pictures below.
Choose one of the checkboxes under the pictures

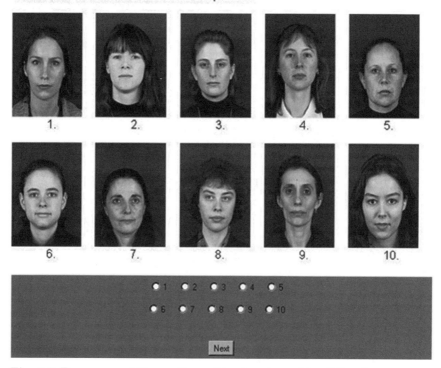

Fig. 2.2. Frequency and Human Recognition (courtesy of Josef Bigun).

than the full negatives. Just a few local patches built around the eyes, for which the ordinal brightness relationships are available, would help with face recognition. Worth also to note is that upside down faces look grotesque and are difficult to recognize. Most likely this occurs because we are not trained to see faces upside down. Pose, one of the factors affecting face recognition, is another dimension that assumes illumination coming from above. Negation disrupts face recognition, however, even more than an upside down condition.

One recent study relevant to the role that the temporal dimension and changes play in face recognition reports that "when people talk, their changing facial expressions and head movements provide dynamic cues for recognition [of both the identity and sex of a person]" (Hill and Johnston, 2001). The results reported further suggest that "whereas recognition of identity seems to be mediated mainly by characteristic [rigid] head movements, recognition of sex seems to be mediated mainly by [non-rigid] changes in facial expression." The rigid and non-rigid motion signals "were then imposed on a computer generated canonical head (a morph-average of 200 actors), so that the motion (but not the facial features) of the original actor was preserved in the reconstituted (silent) video sequence" and "it appears that recognizing a friend may not depend purely on the shape of their face" (Stone, 2001). This finding is not unexpected. We mostly see and interact with people over space and time rather than merely viewing their photographs. Interactions involve both language and paralanguage (see Sect. 11.1) in addition to people moving their heads. The rich changes taking place during such interactions are idiosyncratic, so they should help with face identification and authentication. Another intriguing finding reported was that, "whereas spatial inversion of video sequences - turning them upside down - disrupts the recognition of both sex and identity, temporal reversal - playing them backwards - disrupts the recognition of sex, but not identity" (Hill and Johnston, 2001).

An interesting comment made by Stone (2001) is that "inversion and temporal reversal of video sequences are useful standard tricks for isolating different component processes in recognition, because neither transformation affects the contents of the images presented. So any change in performance induced by these transformations cannot be attributed to changes in the visual cues such as the image gray level or speed, or the perception of structure from motion, shading, or texture, because these cues remain invariant with respect to changes in orientation and temporal direction. The dynamic cues used for identity recognition are [thus] independent of temporal direction, but are not independent of spatial orientation."

The relevance of dynamic cues should come as no surprise. The use of still and impoverished facial imagery has been justified only by the lack of adequate sensory and computational resources. It should by now be clear that advances in face recognition will be driven by using video processing, to allow for flexible matching between multiple image sets. The availability of additional frames facilitates evidence accumulation that overcomes uncertainty or temporary occlusion due to expanded access to face representations.

Human face recognition also has access to 3D information, while the face biometrics are usually rendered in 2D. O'Toole et al. (1999) have shown that "the ability to recognize faces relies both on information that uniquely specifies the 3D shape of the face and on information that uniquely specifies the 2D surface reflectance [albedo] properties of the face." The results reported had access to laser scanners for data acquisition and morphing, and used manual correspondence for modeling purposes. For familiar faces, $\frac{3}{4}$ and full faces are similar in performance but for unfamiliar faces, $\frac{3}{4}$ is better because it offers the advantage of generalization and possibly provides additional information on depth and the nose (Bruce et al., 1987). This facilitates "hallucinating" additional views for matching purposes. Lifeless 3D is, however, insufficient for recognition and "superficial features [shape] and pigmentation are necessary" (Bruce et al., 1991). Shape and color information are also required for ethnicity and gender categorization (Hill and Johnston, 2001).

2.3 The Social Face

The human face has a history of its own that parallels that of human development. Arien Mack (2000) in his editorial introduction to *(Social Research on) Faces*, writes "··· first, the face is that part of us which is usually most visible and recognizable, and so in some cultures it must be masked, veiled, or transformed in a variety of ways. It is the seat of beauty and the mirror of our emotions. It is that part of us which we are most likely to alter, either by cosmetics or cosmetic surgery. Its changing images are seen as the public manifestation of the self, the character, and the soul. Ancient myths and stories portray the dangers of looking at either one's own reflections or into the face of some other (for example, God) and so we endow the face with special power." The face talks with a loud voice about our identity, including age, gender, our feelings and intentions, and it can predict behavior. The social mores in Paris, around the end of the 19th century, show up in the faces that Toulouse-Lautrec painted. Once we stood up, the face language gained primacy over the voice and body language.

"The face flattens, the nose juts out, the chin appears, and the forehead rises to house the ballooning brain" (McNeill, 1998). The furry face gave way to smooth skin and let the face talk. The muzzle we used to have with the teeth thrust outward to maul and attack became obsolete. People became able to make tools and weapons instead. Cole (1998) makes a strong argument that "the development of the face may parallel the evolution of primates and humans, and reveal something about the evolutionary pressures which led to our emergence." The face sends true and/or deceiving signals and it predicts behavior. These characteristics appeared early on during our evolution and are responsible for the development of "social intelligence" (Cole, 1998). The face is also the locus for displaying inner emotions and mental state. It allows for psychoanalysis using the face rather than the voice channel. Last but not least, the face serves as the medium for social communication and interaction. Autism, according to the *American Heritage Dictionary* is "an abnormal introversion and egocentrism; acceptance of fantasy rather than reality." Autism is characterized among others by the inability to "read" the face of others and/or avoiding their face. This breaks down the social link and explains both detachment and the failure to tune to the world around. The face language is predicated on face mobility and its interpretation. Some people affected by the Parkinson disease show difficulty in both expressing emotional faces and in recognizing them and in imaging emotional faces (Jacobs et al., 1995).

The face is the locus where our most direct social interactions take place. Merleau-Ponty, in *The Primacy of Perception*, suggests that "the body [including the face] is more than an instrument or a means, it is our expression in the world." People who lost their sight experience social isolation. The Moebius syndrome, not being able to move the facial muscles and display emotions, is a difficult (congenital) affliction. "Adjusting to acquired blindness may be far more perplexing than to be born blind. In contrast, to have never had a mobile expressive face may be a more profound problem than to have lost facial animation as an adult" (Cole, 2000). The social interactions, the developmental aspect, and the sense for self-confidence suffer as a consequence.

George Orwell said that "After 40, a man is responsible for his face." The way we live imprints itself on our face, which becomes the signature we show to the outside world. In the ancient world, philosophers studied the face as a means to probe and interpret a person's inner qualities, morality, and traits, as well as for clues to a person's likely behavior. One reads from Aristotle's *Physiognomy*, Ch. 2 that "A great and wide mouth shows a man to be bold, warlike, shameless and stout, a great liar and as great a talker, also a great eater, but as to his intellectuals, he is very dull, being for the most part very simple. A little mouth shows the person to be of a quiet and pacific temper, somewhat reticent, but faithful, secret, modest, bountiful, and but a little eater."

In the 18th century, the Swiss thinker Johann Kaspar Lavater (1741-1801) expanded upon the ideas on physiognomy espoused by Aristotle to write *Fragments of Physiognomy for the Increase of Knowledge and Love of Mankind* (1775-1778). Here's an example of Lavater's analysis, for the silhouette "1" shown in Fig. 2.3: "From a section of this forehead, singly considered, without the top and back of the head, something excellent might be expected; so difficult is it to discriminate between this and the best built foreheads. But, as soon as the whole is taken collectively, all expectation of great powers of mind will vanish, and we must content ourselves with discovering, in this head of mediocrity, incapable of profound research, or great productions, a degree of benevolence, not very active, and inoffensive patience." Lavatar's silhouettes anticipate space dimensions for face representation using flexible active models (Lanitis et al., 1997) and chorus of prototypes (Edelman, 1998).

Physiognomy served as semiotics for indexing the "character or as a kind of semaphore signaling inner feelings with the reliable consistency of a code" (Gombrich, 1972). Refuted by Hegel in his *Phenomenology of Mind*, the masks worn, however, are more an act than a sign, performance rather than expression (Trachtenberg, 2000). Physiognomy is a severely flawed pseudo-science, from a time when moral beauty was thought to be impossible without physical beauty. Physiognomy led the way to other attempts to divine character based on facial and cranial measurements. In 1876, the Italian Cesare Lombroso (1836 - 1909) wrote *L'uomo delinquente*, an attempt to categorize faces in order to scientifically determine who was prone to criminal behavior. Lombroso believed that criminals had different and recognizable facial characteristics. The characteristics of people with a propensity for crime would include a small head with a large face, small and sloping forehead, large sinus cavities or bumpy face, large protruding ears, bumps on head, beaked nose or flat nose, strong jaw line, weak chin, etc. Lombroso's work was very influential in his time and Lambroso himself is considered the founder of criminology. Lombroso also claimed as part of his physiognomy studies that facial asymmetry, among others, characterizes the criminal face. Or is it that those different from us are always under suspicion? Franz Joseph Gall (1758 - 1828) is the person one links to the introduction of *phrenology*, which associates bumps and protuberances on the skull rather than face contours with personality and character. Phrenology has been discredited as much as physiognomy has been, if not more. The use of physiognomy and passions as indexes for personality identification have to be traced to the "ideals" proposed by Plato and pursued later on by Kant.

Fig. 2.3. Human Physiognomy (Johann Kaspar Lavater 1775-1778), (Plate 26) (http://www.newcastle.edu.au/discipline/fine-art/pubs/lavater/) (courtesy of Ross Woodrow)

Faces reveal much about people. Like text, faces can be read, interpreted, misunderstood, and deconstructed. Learning using social cues is quite important and is a measure of our (social) intelligence. Human characteristics, e.g., honesty, when deduced from human faces and behavior are not necessarily correlated with ground truth. There seems to be, however, enough agreement among subjects on the traits behind human faces. Stereotypes probably emerged and spread easily due to non conscious inferences. One explanation comes via Richard Dawkins (1976). He has proposed a generalization of evolution that makes it applicable to cultural and thus social constructs. These cultural replicators, under the name of *memes*, are the *genes* for the cultural and social kingdom, stereotypes included. The habitat for the memes is the mind, and they move from mind to mind, subject to the selective pressure of human acceptance. Social experience after all exerts its effect through imitation. The "masks" people wear can be donned at pleasure or can be altered and enhanced using cosmetics and/or surgery. The individual wants to integrate and merge with the society at large. There is the desire to assimilate and blend with the majority to avoid being singled out for some ethnic minority and become subject to real or perceived hardship. Most people want to be inclusive rather than exclusive. The hope is to become almost invisible or hard to recognize and to evade the perceived misfortunes associated with being a minority. An average face or change of identity are sought in order to make authentication by the others more difficult. In addition, cosmetic or aesthetic surgery, for narcissistic reasons and/or or socio-economic gains, aims to undo the ravages of times and to restore a youthful resemblance. Time related changes and cosmetic surgery make face authentication harder (Gates, 2004).

Emotions, or for Descartes, *Les Passions de L'Ame* or *Passions of the Soul*, are one medium to reveal personality. They are immediate but transitory, and depend on context. Both painting and sculpture seek to capture the human's face capacity for expression. The French painter Charles Le Brun (1619-1690) tried to do so in a systematic manner in his *Trait des Passions* series (see Fig. 2.4). Admiration as a passion for Le Brun's is described as "the eyebrows rises, the eye opens a little more than ordinary ··· the mouth half opens" (Trachtenberg, 2000). A succession of calm, silent, restless, deep, and patient grief was illustrated by Lavater (see Fig. 2.4).

Fig. 2.4. Face Expressions (Johann Kaspar Lavater 1775-1778), Physiognomische Fragmente zur Befrderung der Menschenkenntnis und Menschenliebe (plate III) http://www.newcastle.edu.au/discipline/fine-art/pubs/lavater/ (courtesy of Ross Woodrow)

Evolutionary psychology (see Dawkins on memes earlier) is about understanding the design and function of the human mind. It draws its arguments from evolutionary biology, and similar to psychology aims to understand the brain in terms of information processing and observed behavior. According to Cosmides and Tooby [2] for evolutionary psychology "the mind is a set of information processing machines that were designed by natural selection to solve adaptive problems faced by our hunter-gatherer ancestors." The machines or programs are basically instincts or routines that are shared for some common need or purpose. Emotions and face expressions are one example of such instincts or integrative programs. The programs are the result of adaptation and were imprinted through natural selection to handle successful sharing of physical and social space. Adaptation comes in response to both short term and long term changes in our environment. The programs support a modular, specialized and integrated brain architecture (see Ch. 11 on augmented cognition). Evolutionary psychology shares much with sociobiology, which explains social behavior using evolution as the driving force.

Beauty has much to do with the social face. It helps and even "intoxicates" according to Freud. (The discussion on what stands for beauty is deferred to the section on aesthetics and arts.) The looks of Helen of Troy were enough to start a war but also for Homer to give us *The Iliad*, a cultural beacon ever since. Beautiful people are more likely to be successful and in the court of law they appear to draw more sympathy. The looks are often used on the screen to suggest both character and intellect. The cue associates the guilty or mean party with a less than perfect face. Suspense flicks throw the viewer off many times only to reveal later on about the inner beauty or innocence that a plain or ugly face hides, e.g., *Shrek*. Where does the fascination with beauty come from? One explanation comes from evolutionary psychology. Beauty is associated with youth, health and fertility. Beauty is also associated with order whose semiotic reference is the symmetry. Remember that mating and concern about offspring is one of the imprints that drives humanity. Average faces are deemed beautiful for both mating and grouping because they indicate by their wide availability safety, convenience, and familiarity.

Penton-Voak and Perrett (2000) have observed that "Darwinian approaches to the study of facial attractiveness are based on the premise that attractive faces are a biological 'ornament' that signals valuable information, e.g., health and/or reproductive ability, to a potential mate. The rapid learning of attractiveness judgments and impressive cross-cultural consistency indicate that individuals around the world respond fairly similarly to facial attributes." Attractiveness and beauty are interchangeable for most people (on a blind date). An interesting fact is that newborn babies instinctively find some faces more attractive than others, as found by researchers at the University of Exeter in the UK. Babies show positive responses to faces generally considered beautiful and negative responses to people making "ugly" faces. In another experiment, children and adults were asked to rank pictures from most attractive to least attractive, and remarkably the results are almost identical across ages and cultures. While the basic (data-driven) criteria for attractiveness are universally shared, there are individual differences that can be traced to imprinting and learning using evolutionary explanations of behavior (Penton-Voak and Perrett, 2000). The case can be made that both biological "predisposition" and cultural norms influence how attractiveness is defined. Rubenesque faces were thought beautiful in an earlier age and time but not today where food is plentiful. The social face is full of signs. According to Vygotsky (1976) human interactions are mediated using such signs as tools. Furthermore, "like tool systems, sign systems are created by societies over the course of human history and change with the form of society and the level of cultural development." Vygotsky further believed that "the internalization of culturally produced sign systems brings about behavioral transformations and forms the bridge between early and later forms of individual development."

---

[2] www.psych.ucsb.edu/research/cep/primer.html

2.4 Aesthetics and Arts

Aesthetics and arts, according to the American Heritage Dictionary (AHD), "concern the appreciation of beauty," and the "human effort to imitate, supplement or alter the work of nature ⋯ in a manner that affects the sense of beauty," respectively. Both aesthetics and arts have much to do with beauty and by default with the human face. But what is beauty? According to Plato, there are things and there are *forms* or *ideals*. Things are perceived, are not perfect and are continuously changing. They are about appearance and can be deceptive. The forms describe some permanent essence and are only available to reason. The real beauty can be thus reached only by reason, corresponds to character rather than appearance, and it is only an ideal. Indeed, according to *Webster*, beauty is that "which gives the highest degree of pleasure to senses or to the mind and suggests that the object of delight approximates one's conception of an ideal." Sadr et al. (2004) have shown "an intriguing dissociation between the processes subserving face recognition and those which underlie the perception of facial attractiveness. Moreover, that the perception of attractiveness can proceed normally in the absence of the mechanisms necessary for face recognition may well serve to suggest important constraints on theories of facial aesthetics." The dissociation was motivated by prosopagnosia patients "in which the perception of facial attractiveness is severely compromised or, perhaps more remarkably, spared."

Is there a universal ideal for beauty? For McNeill (1998) the average [women] beauties had "higher cheekbones, thinner jaws, and larger eyes relative to face size than the average faces. The distances between chin and mouth, and mouth and nose were also shorter. That is, their lower faces were smaller." An oval or round face and no abnormalities add to beauty. The permanent search for beauty and ideals suggests new features and/or dimensions to represent and process faces. Fox et al. (2004) have recently shown a perceptual basis for the lighting of Caravaggio's faces painted four hundred years ago. "A leader of the Baroque art movement, [Caravaggio] is well known for his departure from the Renaissance ideals of balance and restraint in the portrayal of lighting and facial expression." There is an overwhelming preference to light subjects from the left side relative to the viewer's perspective. This "reveals contrasting regions of harsh light and complete shadow in the faces painted." Subjects tested by Fox et al. (2004) judged the left-lit faces as more emotional than right-lit faces. This fits with cognitive studies that "have shown a left visual field/right hemisphere bias in the perception of both faces and emotions." Similar techniques were used shortly after by George de la Tour for his striking *New Born* painting. Following in the steps of Caravaggio light and shadow were used to much effect later on by Rembrandt. The play or harsh contrast between light and shadows is also characteristic of *chiaroscuro* that heightens the illusion of depth.

Visual rendition of both our environment and our own mental imagery is complementary to visual interpretation. The artist always keeps in mind the inseparability of seeing and interpreting. The mission of art is not merely to copy life but to express and represent it. From the dawn of civilization the human figure had a special place for artists. It is the role of the artist to reflect upon and sometimes advance new ways about how to look around. As ontology recapitulates phylogeny, so too the history of arts follows the evolution of mental development. It traces an evolutionary path starting with figurative and iconic imagery that leads to the nonrepresentational and abstract imagery of today. In particular, the history of arts follows genetic epistemology, a term used by Gablik to denote the genesis and development of systems of knowledge. The episteme is an epistemological space specific to a particular period, or what one would call a *spirit of age*. Development projects itself in different forms that are used to represent "reality." To quote Gablik (1977), "evolution of human cognition has led to changes in the way we experience and represent the world. Art not only relates to the development of knowledge but presupposes it." The artist by the mere act of representation goes beyond mere perception. The artist does not merely copy his subject but uses her knowledge to reconstruct it. Gablik further suggests that "the image is a pictorial anticipation of an action not yet performed, and a reaching forward from what is presently perceived to what may be, but is not yet perceived." Mental imagery, anticipation, and context driven evidence accumulation take place over time. All of them share in enabling the viewer to capture and grasp what the artist has tried to convey, and/or according to Jacques Derrida, to "deconstruct" the image and reconstruct it to personal taste and/or belief. Deconstructing and reconstructing faces from video bears similarities to iterative cycles of image analysis and synthesis.

The figurine shown in Fig. 2.5 is a representative example of the so-called "*canoni-cal*" (that is standard) type of early Cycladic female figurines. Nikolas Papadimitriou, curator at the Museum of Cycladic Art in Athens, Greece, provides an informative summary on such Cycladic figurines. Their characteristics are: standing position, lyre-shaped head tilting backwards, folded arms below the breasts (the right always under the left), straight back, slightly flexed knees, feet standing on the tiptoes. Female figurines were being modelled in marble in the Cyclades (islands) throughout the Early Bronze Age, termed as the "*Early Cycladic period*" (3200-2000 BC). In the earlier part of the period (*Early Cycladic I*, 3200-2800 BC), most figurines were extremely schematic and abstract, although certain anatomical details make it clear that they depicted females. In the mature phase of the period (*Early Cycladic II*, 2800-2300 BC), the representation of females took the standard form described above, hence the term "canonical". More than 90% of excavated Cycladic figurines belong to this type. Male figurines are rare and usually appear as musicians, hunters or drinking figures. In the last phase of the period (*Early Cycladic III*, 2300-2000 BC), canonical figures start to diminish rapidly and cruder, more naturalistic examples make their appearance.

The canonical Cycladic figurines are famous for their simplicity and abstraction. As far as the *face* is concerned, it is interesting that, during the *Early Cycladic II* period, the nose is the only feature that is rendered in plastic form by means of a long triangular protrusion (while both in EC I and III, the mouth, eyes and ears could be incised or modelled in relief). It is only in the larger, life size examples (only two surviving) that ears have also been sculpted. However, modern research has proved, through macroscopic and microscopic examination, that other facial details, such as eyes, eyebrows, ears, mouth and the hair, were rendered *in paint*. Colour was used extensively to decorate Cycladic figurines, not only in the face but also in the body. It seems, thus, quite plausible to assume that originally the Cycladic figurines looked much more "realistic" than they do today. Another interesting aspect of the representation of the face is its shape. Cycladic figurines had round faces with flat top (hence the term "lyre-shaped"), and curving backwards. No convincing explanation has been put forward for this position, but given the probable *ritual* use of these figurines, it is possible that it depicts some accepted symbolic form of veneration. The flat top is another interesting feature, which may have been somehow associated with the representation of hair, which were usually rendered in color. One should stress here that the *thin section* of the head (in fact of the whole of the body) of "canonical" figurines was a limiting factor for the artist, who had practically to work with a two-(instead of three-) dimensional surface. This may explain partly why the face was so wide, as well as why it was preferred to render features other than the nose in paint rather than in relief. Similar rendering of the human face can be found in the modern age, e.g., Brîncusi (see *Ms. Peggy*).

Gablik suggests that development in arts amounts to decentrating and enhancing the objectivity of experiencing reality. Decentration allows for the assimilation of reality, which she calls schemata, and for accommodation, when operational thinking transforms reality. According to her, art history has experienced three major stages of development, which correspond to the enactive, iconic, and symbolic modes. The enactive stage, characteristic of ancient and medieval art, lacks depth representation, and size and/or distances are not preserved. The iconic stage, characteristic of Renaissance, draws on coordinate systems and introduces perspective. It would take another 500 years before Cezanne and Cubism introduced multiple and shifting viewpoints. Face recognition appears to follow a similar developmental path. Technological innovation led to the birth of symbolic movements in the early 1900s. Driven by their interest in motion, the Futurists borrowed from the earlier multiple-exposure pho-

Fig. 2.5. Cycladic Female Figurine (ca. 2800-2300 BC). N. P. Goulandris Foundation - Museum of Cycladic Art, Athens, Greece, Coll. No. NG 207.

tography and/or image sequences created by Muybridge. The parallel today is the growing use of multiple-still images and/or video for face identification and authentication. The descriptive value of lines for defining contours lost its relevance. Even for Goya, "there are no lines in nature, only lighted forms and forms which are in shadow, planes which project and planes which recede." The modern artist thinks about the total volume of a figure and synthesizes the profile and frontal views. Figures drawn by Picasso and Bacon converge and deflect themselves around surrounding space. Multiple appearances not only succeed, but confirm, continue, and complement each other. Time informs spatial-temporal trajectories and makes them coherent. Part based constellation face recognition and video processing approaches have to follow a similar path. Suzi Gablik reminds us that "art is not a recommendation about the way the world is, it is a recommendation that the world ought to be looked at in a given way."

Beauty or attractiveness are thought to reflect average, symmetry, and some golden ratios. An average or composite face is the result of high pass filter and benefits from smoothing over blemishes. The finding about symmetric faces being more beautiful appears to be limited to faces seen frontal rather than in profile. Attractiveness is still probably a combination of the familiar, i.e., the healthy average, and the distinctive, or exotic. Perrett et al. (1994) have shown that the average of highly attractive faces is more attractive than the average of the original set the attractive faces were drawn from. Attractiveness increases further when the differences between the average of most attractive faces and the population average are emphasized. Patnaik et al. (1993) refer to Cunningham (1986) to detail the anatomy of "a beautiful face and smile" in terms of form, size, (smooth) texture, and pigmentation. Cunningham found specific ratios across the face that create harmony and are perceived as beautiful, e.g., wide cheekbones, narrow cheeks, broad smile, wide eyes, and set far apart, large pupils, high eyebrows, small nose, and a long neck. The "average" face is beautiful but "emphasize [caricature] differences and faces become even more alluring" (McNeill, 1998). The exotic simply attracts.

"Divine" proportions or "golden" ratios were criteria used in antiquity for both natural, and man made beauty, e.g., the dimensions of the Parthenon rectangles. Leonardo Da Vinci may have used the *Phi* or "golden ratio" in his paintings. The golden (Fibonacci) ratio of a line AB is obtained by introducing a point C between A and B such that $AB/AC = AC/BC$. Solving $\Phi/1 = (\Phi + 1)/\Phi$ yields $\Phi = (1 + \sqrt{5})/2$ or 1.618 (while its inverse is 0.618). Growth and duplication based on Φ leads to harmony and it appears pleasing to the eye. In addition to lines, the golden ration applies to shapes too, e.g., the golden decagon matrix. Many of Da Vinci's sketches use golden rectangles for features in drawings. Measurements for *Mona Lisa* show that it obeys the proportion 1 : 1.618 in many areas of her face. (Leonardo is known not only for the beauty he depicted but also for his caricature-like grotesque heads. The grotesque reflected for Leonardo the irrational. Caricatures, however, can also express rage and suffering as was the case with Goya.) The width for an ideal face should be about two-thirds of its length. Dr. Stephen Marquardt, a former plastic surgeon, has suggested that "beauty is a mechanism to ensure humans recognize and are attracted to other humans." He has used the golden ratio to prepare an archetype *Phi* mask that he proposes that faces be matched against for beauty assessment and rankings [3]. Anderson and McOwan (2004) have used such masks to develop software for face tracking (see Fig. 6.5).

It is not only harmony but also photometry that affects beauty. Russell (2003) found experimentally that "the luminance difference between the eyes and the mouth and the rest of the face is naturally greater in women than men. In this case increasing or decreasing the luminance difference will make a face more feminine or masculine, respectively, and hence, more or less attractive depending on the sex of the face." The implications for cosmetics are obvious. Beauty is assumed to be in the eye of the beholder but what is made available to the beholder can vary and can deceive (see Umberto Eco's History of Beauty, Rizzoli and Ch. 10 on denial and deception). Photometry affects categorization, e.g., age and gender, and identification. Luminance differences were found in particular helpful with face detection (Thoresz and Sinha, 2001).

Gombrich (1984), the master of psychology and pictorial representation, gives an account of face and head modelling. The Renaissance has brought renewed interest in real life and the human figure. The artists used projective geometry and clarity for their models. Dürer, a major artist, showed keen interest in drawing the human figure and the proportions behind beauty (Dresden Sketchbook and Vier Bucher von Menschlicher Proportionen). Dürer used three orthographic projections on a rectilinear grid to draw the human head. Most fascinating, however, was Dürer's attempt to morph and caricature both faces and human heads using 2D (affine and projective) coordinate transformations. The transformations sought resemblance between different face appearances. The model and schema is subject for revision and refinement or in Gombrich's words, "the starting point which he [artist] will then cloth with flesh and blood." Caricatures (see Fig. 2.6) sparse the face space and facilitate face recognition (see Sect. 5.6).

The standard model - shape and texture - for the human face gave way to pointillism and juxtaposition of complementary colors for Seurat (see *Jeune Femme se Poudrant* and *Le Cirque*) and Signac but one can still recognize human faces. Then there is the *Scream* of Munch and character and personal background in the stylized faces that Modigliani painted. The (futurism, primitivism, and cubism) avant-garde from Picasso through Braque to Diego Rivera teaches a new language for face representation, using multiple perspectives, grid composition, overlapping and flattened planes. Malevitch and Lebedev, famous Russian Suprematists, used flat and bright colors for abstraction that were nevertheless able to suggest human faces. Art and perception have become intimately linked. Helmholtz thought earlier of perception as unconscious inference. For Gombrich (1984), perception "may be regarded as primarily the modification of an anticipation. It is always an active process, conditioned by our expectations and adapted to situations. We notice only when we look for something, and we look when our attention is aroused by some disequilibrium, a difference between our expectations and the incoming message." It is analysis and synthesis all over again and all is subject to predictions and feedback. The world is not accidental. Expectations and purpose drive the way human faces are processed and interpreted.

Early 20th century arts are ripe with bold imagination. Movements include Dadaism, about bizarre and existential disruption, and Surrealism, about mystery

---

[3] http://www.beautyanalysis.com

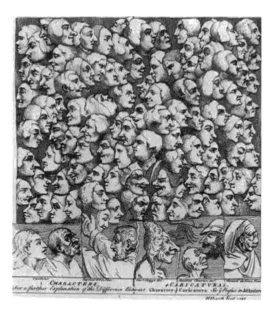

Fig.   2.6.   Characters   and   Caricaturas   (William   Hogarth,   1743)
(http://hograth.althacker.com) (courtesy of Shaun Wourm).

and "fantastic imagery and incongruous juxtaposition of subject matter." Published
in 1928, Andre Breton's *Surrealism and Painting*, is considered the manifesto on Surrealism. It calls for the plastic arts to "refer to a purely internal model." Dali plays
on the irrational with his illusions drawn from eccentric face arrangements, e.g., *Mae
West (Face of Mae West Which Can Be Used as an Apartment)*. This illustrates that
facial landmarks can be substituted but one can still detect the "human face." *Slave
Market with Invisible Bust of Voltaire* painted also by Dali illustrates the same point.
The faces of two figures dressed in black make up the eyes of Voltaire and the sky
stands for his head. The configural plays a major role and multiple interpretations
are feasible. Faces are also detected where one can see only flowers, e.g., *Three Young
Women with Heads of Flowers Finding the Skin of a Grand Piano on the Beach* and
Apparition of Face and Fruit-Dish on a Beach. For Dali, "you have to systematically
create confusion - it sets creativity free. Everything that is contradictory creates life."
Creativity to create and creativity to infer and interpret. Magritte made good company with Dali. In *La Presence d'Esprit* and *Paysage de Baucis* the faces strike you
even that there is no shape or face contour but only big eyes, a huge nose, and the
lips. *Mathematical Logic* is merely a collection of digits but suggestive enough to see
the face as a constellation of landmark parts. *The Lovers* have their faces completely
covered but still so apparent. And then there is the cover for Andre Breton *Qu'est -
ce que Le Surrealisme?* The eyes, nose, and mouth have been replaced with common
objects. One does not lose a beat in seeing the face.

Last but not least among the arts is cinematography. The invention of the Lumière
brothers and known as the 7th art, it had its first screening in 1895. Thought by
August Lumière as "an invention without a future," cinematography has been with
us ever since. Roland Barthes in *Mythologies* reflects on stars like Greta Garbo and
recalls that her face in *Queen Christina* represents "not a painted face, but one set in
plaster" ··· "an archetype of the human face" ··· "the face of Garbo is an Idea" ···
"beautiful certainly, but more importantly revealing an ephemeral essential quality of
a lyricism of Woman."

3. Modeling and Prediction

We know for certain only when we know little.
With knowledge, doubt increases (Goethe).

Perception, in general, and face recognition, in particular, requires training. The accounts provided by Oliver Sacks are illuminating on this point. A blind person, whose vision is suddenly restored, makes sense of the surrounding world only gradually, and as Berkeley has earlier anticipated, partly by connecting visual experiences with tactile ones. Perception for Helmholtz is merely inference. It is through immersion in our surrounding world and through development that people gradually learn to see and recognize objects, and in particular human faces. Nature alone is not enough and rich nurturing, i.e., learning, is paramount.

Learning is mostly about model selection and prediction. Learning denotes "changes in the system that are adaptive in the sense that they enable the system to do the same tasks drawn from the same population more efficiently the next time" (Simon, 1982). In particular, learning models associations that are then used to infer some output given its inputs, i.e., identification from a given face representation. Face appearance varies while its identity remains constant. Eminent for reliable face recognition is the ability to generalize and withstand input variability. As "versatility [generalization] and scalability are desirable attributes in most vision systems," the "only solution is to incorporate learning capabilities within the vision system." Towards that end, learning plays a fundamental role in facilitating "the balance between internal representations and external regularities" (Nayar and Poggio, 1996). The inferences made are merely predictions because learning can only approximate ground truth. The framework for learning and the factors affecting the quality of the predictions made are the topics discussed in this chapter.

In the predictive learning framework, obtaining a good prediction model requires the specification of admissible models (or approximating functions), e.g., the regression estimator, an inductive principle for combining admissible models with available data, and an optimization ("learning") procedure for estimating the parameters of the admissible models (Cherkassky and Mulier, 1998). Note that "the goal for predictive learning is imitation (of the unknown model) rather than its identification." The inductive principle is responsible for the particular model selected and it directly affects the generalization ability in terms of prediction risk, i.e., the performance on unseen/future (test) data. Transduction, one alternative to induction, is discussed in Sect. 3.5. Model selection is geared for optimality only in terms of generalization performance and without regard to what the true underlying model might be. This is one reason to prefer *discriminative* rather than (normative) *generative* (prescriptive) methods (see Sect. 3.6). Conversely, a learning method is a constructive implementation of an inductive principle, i.e., an optimization or (hyper) parameter estimation procedure, for a given set of approximating functions when some specific estimator is sought. The learning method is an algorithm that estimates an unknown mapping (dependency) between the learning system's inputs and outputs using the available data, i.e. known (input, output) samples. Once such a dependency has been estimated, it can be used for predicting/deducing the outputs from the input values. The usual quality assigned to learning is its prediction accuracy or generalization ability. The standard formulation of the learning problem amounts to function estimation, i.e., selecting the 'best' function from a set of admissible functions $f(\mathbf{x}, \mathbf{w})$, $\mathbf{w} \in \Omega$ where Ω is a set of (hyper) parameters of an arbitrary nature. Here the 'best' function (model) is the one minimizing the prediction risk, which is the expected value of the loss incurred when the ground truth and the approximation are different. The choice of the loss function depends, among other things, on the costs incurred when making the wrong choice. The loss function also depends on noise, something that most learning methods usually do not account for. Consider for example regression and an asymptotic setting, i.e., a large number of samples, as robust statistics (Huber, 2004) do. (The term "robust" means that the statistical estimators found are "insensitive to small departures from idealized assumptions for which the estimator was optimized." Small can mean either small deviations for all the data points, or large deviations, e.g., outliers, for a relatively small number of data points.) The optimal loss function for a Gaussian noise density is the quadratic loss function because it provides an asymptotically efficient (best unbiased) estimator (using maximum likelihood) for regression. When the noise density is Laplacian, the best minmax strategy for regression estimation is provided by the least-modulus (or absolute-value) loss. Smola and Scholkopf (1998) have shown that the optimal loss function (in the maximum-likelihood sense) for a known noise density $p(z)$ is

$$L(y, f(\mathbf{x}, \mathbf{w})) = -\log p(y - f(\mathbf{x}, \mathbf{w})) \tag{3.1}$$

The question one still has to address is how to choose the loss function for finite rather than asymptotic settings and unknown noise densities. Towards that end, Cherkassky and Ma (2004) have stated that "with finite-sample estimation problems it may be preferable to use biased estimators" (see Sect. 13.1 for the bias - variance dilemma in statistics). They provide empirical evidence that "Vapnik's ϵ−insensitive loss function $L_\epsilon(y, f(\mathbf{x}, \mathbf{w}))$, equal to 0 if $|y - f(\mathbf{x}, \mathbf{w})| = \epsilon$ and equal to $|y - f(\mathbf{x}, \mathbf{w})| - \epsilon$ otherwise, yields more robust performance and improved prediction accuracy in comparison with quadratic loss and least-modulus loss, especially for noisy high-dimensional data sets." Prediction accuracy is measured as the mean-squared error (MSE) between the (estimated) model and ground truth. Note that support vector machine (SVM) regression minimizes the norm of the linear parameters ($||\mathbf{w}||^2$) and the Vapnik's ϵ−insensitive loss weighted by the term $\frac{C}{n}$, where n is the sample size (see Sects. 3.4). Large values for C reduce SVM linear regression to regularization according to the choice made on the ϵ−value.

Learning is an ill-posed problem since the prediction risk (functional) is unknown (by definition). Neither the loss function nor the distribution the data is drawn from are known. Most model selection methods implement a concept known as 'empirical risk minimization' (ERM), which chooses the model minimizing the empirical risk, or the average loss/empirical error for training data. The key problem for learning, according to Vapnik, is to ensure consistency for the empirical error, i.e., to ensure its convergence to the true error. The ERM approach is only appropriate under parametric settings, i.e. when the parametric form for the unknown dependency is known. Under such a (parametric) approach the unknown dependency is assumed to belong to a narrow class of functions (specified by a given parametric form). In most practical applications parametric assumptions do not hold true, and the unknown dependency is estimated for a wide class of possible models of varying complexity, e.g., degrees of freedom used to describe the model. Since the goal of learning is to obtain a model providing minimal prediction risk, one should choose a model that yields the smallest prediction (generalization) error for future data. Towards that end, the 'simple is beautiful' principle known as Occam's razor considers complexity, and suggests that "no more things should be presumed to exist than are absolutely necessary." Model selection seeks then for "simplicity" while trading off between ERM and complexity; neither overfit nor underfit is acceptable. Existing provisions or inductive principles for model complexity control include Bayesian inference driven by priors, regularization driven by penalties, structural risk minimization (SRM) driven by confidence intervals, and minimum description length (MDL) driven by randomness (Cherkassky and Mulier, 1998).

3.1 Bayesian Inference

The implicit inductive principle behind (asymptotic) statistical or Bayesian inference is minimum classification and/or risk error. Bayes' rule estimates the a posteriori probability $P(C_k|\mathbf{x})$ that an observed pattern $\mathbf{x}$ comes from class C_k as

$$P(C_k|\mathbf{x}) = \frac{P(\mathbf{x}|C_k)P(C_k)}{P(\mathbf{x})} = \frac{P(\mathbf{x}, C_k)}{P(\mathbf{x})} \qquad (3.2)$$

where $P(C_k)$ and $P(\mathbf{x}, C_k)$ stand for the a priori probability for class k and the joint probability for observation $\mathbf{x}$ and class k, respectively. Bayes' decision rule assigns a pattern $\mathbf{x}$ to class C_k using the a posteriori probability and implements the maximum a posteriori probability (MAP) rule.

Once class densities are estimated, decision boundaries, which are the real objective for pattern recognition, in general, and face recognition, in particular, can be determined. The decision boundaries, minimizing the probability for misclassification and induced by MAP, assign $\mathbf{x}$ to C_k if $P(C_k|\mathbf{x}) > P(C_j|\mathbf{x})$ or equivalently if the joint probabilities $P(\mathbf{x}, C_k)$ and $P(\mathbf{x}, C_j)$ satisfy

$$P(\mathbf{x}, C_k) = P(\mathbf{x}|C_k)P(C_k) > P(\mathbf{x}, C_j) = P(\mathbf{x}|C_j)P(C_j) \quad \forall j \neq k \qquad (3.3)$$

Note that the same decision boundaries split the feature space $\mathbf{x}$ into disjoint regions $\mathbf{R_j}$, one for each class. The regions can be further split such that each class is the union of several (disjoint) subclasses. One can easily visualize that MAP is optimal for two classes from the fact that the decision boundary is located where the two joint probability densities intersect (see Fig. 12.1). Note that the nearest neighbor assignment (boundary) rule yields less than twice the Bayes' error for all possible probability distributions (Cover and Hart, 1967; Stone, 1977). The alternative to MAP is to define for each one of the M classes corresponding discriminant function $\{y_1(\mathbf{x}), \cdots, y_M(\mathbf{x})\}$ such that $\mathbf{x}$ is now assigned to C_k if

$$y_k(\mathbf{x}) > y_j(\mathbf{x}) \quad \forall j \neq k \qquad (3.4)$$

The decision boundary between the classes k and j is where $y_k(\mathbf{x}) = y_j(\mathbf{x})$. For two classes the discriminant function is $y(\mathbf{x}) = y_1(\mathbf{x}) - y_2(\mathbf{x})$. One can rewrite the discriminant function for the linear case when $M = 2$ as $y(\mathbf{x}) = \mathbf{w}^T \cdot \mathbf{x} + w_0$, with w_0 referred to as bias or threshold. The multi-class $M > 2$ case is treated similar and yields $y_k(\mathbf{x}) = \sum_{j=0}^{d} w_{kj} x_j$. The last expression for the multi-class linear discriminant makes the link to connectionism (see Sect. 3.2). Bayesian inference derives the discriminants using explicit (parametric) density functions, while (non-parametric) connectionism finds the synaptic weights w_{kj} through (gradient descent) learning, e.g., back propagation (BP). When data for $M = 2$ is generated using multivariate normal PDFs $N(\mu_1, \Sigma_1)$ and $N(\mu_2, \Sigma_2)$, the optimal discriminant $y(\mathbf{x})$ is a (parabolic) quadratic rather than linear (Fukunaga, 1990)

$$y(\mathbf{x}) = \frac{1}{2}(\mathbf{x} - \mu_1)^T \Sigma_1^{-1}(\mathbf{x} - \mu_1) - \frac{1}{2}(\mathbf{x} - \mu_2)^T \Sigma_2^{-1}(\mathbf{x} - \mu_2) \qquad (3.5)$$

The linear discriminant is obtained for $\Sigma_1 = \Sigma_2 = \Sigma$, and the metric induced corresponds to the Mahalanobis rather than Euclidean distance.

Closed solution for linear discriminant functions are found using least-squares techniques. Towards that end one solves $\mathbf{Aw} = \mathbf{c}$ where $\mathbf{w}$ is the weight vector, each row of $\mathbf{A}$ is a data point $\mathbf{x}$, and the column $\mathbf{c}$ consists of corresponding class labels.

The solution found by minimizing $||\mathbf{Aw} - \mathbf{c}||^2$ is $\mathbf{w} = (\mathbf{A}^T\mathbf{A})^{-1}\mathbf{A}^T\mathbf{c} = \mathbf{A}^+\mathbf{c}$ with $\mathbf{A}^+$ the pseudo-inverse of $\mathbf{A}$ (see Sect. 10.7). The singularity condition, due to correlated data, is addressed for m data points through regularization (see Sect. 3.3) using ridge regression with an added penalty on the weight vector (Cherkassky and Mulier, 1998)

$$R_{ridge}(\mathbf{w}) = \frac{1}{m}\sum_{i=1}^{m}(c_i - \mathbf{x_i} \cdot \mathbf{w})^2 + \frac{\lambda}{m}(\mathbf{w} \cdot \mathbf{w}) \tag{3.6}$$

The linear estimator solution for a given λ (found using cross-validation) is

$$\mathbf{w} = (\mathbf{A}^T\mathbf{A} + \lambda\mathbf{I})^{-1}\mathbf{A}^T\mathbf{c} = \mathbf{A}_\lambda\mathbf{c} \tag{3.7}$$

Bayes' decision rule takes into account the relative harm due to different misclassification errors using losses l_{kj} incurred when pattern $\mathbf{x}$ is assigned to class k when in reality it belongs to class j. Bayes' decision rule defines the risk $R_i(\mathbf{x})$ involved in assigning $\mathbf{x}$ to class i

$$R_i(\mathbf{x}) = l_{ii}P(C_i|\mathbf{x}) + l_{ij}P(C_j|\mathbf{x}) \tag{3.8}$$

The risks for two classes C_1 and C_2, e.g., face verification when C_1 corresponds to the correct class while C_2 corresponds to making an incorrect authentication, are

$$R_1(\mathbf{x}) = l_{11}P(C_1|\mathbf{x}) + l_{12}P(C_2|\mathbf{x})$$
$$R_2(\mathbf{x}) = l_{21}P(C_1|\mathbf{x}) + l_{21}P(C_2|\mathbf{x}) \tag{3.9}$$

The decision rule is that $\mathbf{x}$ belongs to C_1 when

$$R_1(\mathbf{x}) < R_2(\mathbf{x}) \tag{3.10}$$

or equivalently

$$\begin{aligned}(l_{12} - l_{22})\,P(C_2|\mathbf{x}) &< (l_{21} - l_{11})P(C_1|\mathbf{x})\\ \frac{P(C_1|\mathbf{x})}{P(C_2|\mathbf{x})} &> \frac{(l_{12} - l_{22})}{(l_{21} - l_{11})}\end{aligned} \tag{3.11}$$

One derives again MAP if no loss is incurred when making the correct assignment, i.e., $l_{11} = l_{22} = 0$, and if incorrect mistakes are deemed equally harmful, i.e., $l_{12} = l_{21}$.

The goal of inference is to approximate functional dependencies that are defined by a small number of parameters and limited by a Gaussian stochastic component (under the Central Limit Theorem) (Vapnik, 1998). The penalty or constraint involves here information from outside of the training data, i.e., priors, an obvious drawback. Straightforward application of the Bayes' rule shows that

$$P(model|data) = \frac{P(data|model)P(model)}{P(data)} \tag{3.12}$$

where $P(model)$, $P(model|data)$, and $P(data|model)$ are $p(\mathbf{w})$, $P(\mathbf{X}|\mathbf{w})$, and $p(\mathbf{w}|\mathbf{X})$, and correspond to the a priori probability of the model (before the data is seen), the a posteriori probability for the specific model (after the data is seen), and the probability that the data are generated by the model specified (and referred to as likelihood), respectively. After observing the data, the wide prior distribution that reflects uncertainty about the "correct" parameter values, i.e., $P(model)$, is converted into $P(model|data)$, a rather narrower posterior distribution (Cherkassky and Mulier, 1998).

$$p(\mathbf{w}|\mathbf{X}) = \frac{P(\mathbf{X}|\mathbf{w})p(\mathbf{w})}{P(\mathbf{X})} \tag{3.13}$$

Model selection or equivalently density estimation amount to estimating the parameters $\mathbf{w}$ that specify the model according to some known probability density function (PDF) and using maximum likelihood (ML) for inductive principle. Training/ learning and classification/interpretation thus use ML and MAP, respectively. Assuming $f(\mathbf{x}, \mathbf{w})$ for model, the maximum likelihood choice for (hyper) parameters $\mathbf{w} \in \Omega$ is the $\mathbf{w}^*$ that maximizes the likelihood for the data points $\mathbf{x_i}$ observed

$$P(\mathbf{X}|\mathbf{w}) = \prod_{i=1}^{m} f(\mathbf{x_i}, \mathbf{w}) \qquad (3.14)$$

or equivalently minimizes the log likelihood risk functional

$$R(\mathbf{w}) = -\sum_{i=1}^{m} \ln f(\mathbf{x_i}, \mathbf{w}). \qquad (3.15)$$

The same maximum likelihood principle is behind the well known *Expectation-Maximization (EM)* algorithm (Dempster et al., 1977). EM is the method of choice used to estimate the parameters for a mixture model, e. g., Gaussian Mixture Model (GMM)

$$P(\mathbf{x}) = \sum_{i=1}^{M} P(\mathbf{x}|i, \theta_i)P(i) \quad \text{and} \quad \sum_{i=1}^{M} P(i) = 1. \qquad (3.16)$$

Each component $P(\mathbf{x}|i, \theta_i)$ is modeled as a Gaussian with parameter θ_i in terms of mean μ_i and covariance $\sum_i = \sigma_i^2 \mathbf{I}$

$$P(\mathbf{x}) \cong \sum_{i=1}^{M} a_i \cdot \frac{1}{(2\pi\sigma_i^2)^{\frac{d}{2}}} \cdot \exp\left\{ \frac{-||\mathbf{x} - \mu_i||^2}{2\sigma_i^2} \right\} \qquad (3.17)$$

where a_i are the mixing weights. Similar to fuzzy clustering, each data sample $\mathbf{x}$ belongs to each component i according to its membership a_i, which is updated on each iteration. The number of components M has to be guessed, possibly using cross-validation. Given data samples $\mathbf{X} = \{\mathbf{x_1}, \cdots, \mathbf{x_m}\}$ whose dimension is d, the log likelihood function is

$$P(\mathbf{X}|\theta) = \sum_{j=1}^{m} \ln \sum_{i=1}^{M} P(\mathbf{x_j}|i, \theta_i)P(i) \qquad (3.18)$$

The *E-step* estimates at each iteration k the probability π_{ji} that data point j was generated by the Gaussian component i

$$\pi_{ji} = \sigma_i^{-d}(k) \cdot \frac{\exp\left\{ \frac{-||\mathbf{x} - \mu_i(k)||^2}{2\sigma_i^2(k)} \right\}}{\sum_{l=1}^{M} \sigma_l^{-d}(k) \cdot \exp\left\{ \frac{-||\mathbf{x} - \mu_l(k)||^2}{2\sigma_l^2(k)} \right\}} \qquad (3.19)$$

The *M-step* finds new values for the mixing weights, mean, and variance to maximize the likelihood for the observations $\mathbf{X}$

$$a_i(k+1) = \frac{1}{m} \sum_{j=1}^{m} \pi_{ji} \qquad (3.20)$$

$$\mu_i(k+1) = \frac{\sum_{j=1}^{m} \pi_{ji}\mathbf{x}_j}{\sum_{j=1}^{m} \pi_{ji}} \qquad (3.21)$$

$$\sigma_i^2(k+1) = \frac{\sum_{j=1}^{m} \pi_{ji}||\mathbf{x} - \mu_i(k+1)||^2}{\sum_{j=1}^{m} \pi_{ji}} \qquad (3.22)$$

EM is relevant when some biometric, in general, or face representation, in particular, is approximated by a mixture of components and the corresponding functional form has to be recovered. The *K-means* clustering algorithm is a special case of soft (fuzzy) EM (Bishop, 1995). Similar to vector quantization (VQ), the goal for K-means is to cluster the given data into K groups C_k. Towards that end one minimizes $\sum_{j=1}^{m} ||\mathbf{x}_j - \mu_j||^2$. Hard ("unique") membership is determined (at the E-step) for each sample such that $\mathbf{x} \in C_k$ if $||\mathbf{x} - \mu_k|| < ||\mathbf{x} - \mu_j|| \ \forall j \neq k$. The M-step updates the centroid that stands for the cluster prototype as

$$\mu_j = \frac{1}{m_j} \sum_{x \in C_k} \mathbf{x} \qquad (3.23)$$

Note that when "using ML it is impossible to estimate a density that is the simplest mixture of two normal densities. Thus, ML can be applied only to a very restrictive set of densities" (Vapnik, 2000). One way for model selection to estimate the unknown density is using *marginalization* that averages over all possible models and finds $\theta(\mathbf{x}|\mathbf{X}) = \int f(\mathbf{x}, \mathbf{w})p(\mathbf{w}|\mathbf{X})d\mathbf{w}$ for solution. "The final model is a weighted sum of all prediction models, with weights given by the evidence (or posterior probability) $p(\mathbf{w}|\mathbf{X})$ that each model is correct. Multidimensional integration, due to the large number of parameters involved, presents, however, a challenging problem. Standard numerical integration is impossible, whereas analytic evaluation may be possible only under restrictive assumptions when the posterior density has the same form as the a priori (typically assumed to be Gaussian) one" (Cherkassky and Mulier, 1998). When Gaussian assumptions do not hold, random sampling, e.g., sequential importance sampling (SIS) is used instead. The other but much simpler alternative is to use that estimate $f(\mathbf{x}, \mathbf{w}^*)$ that maximizes (the) posterior probability (MAP) for complexity control or equivalently model selection. (See Sect. 3.3. for the analogy between MAP and regularization.) Bayesian inference falls short when the class of models chosen is mismatched. In addition, large multivariate problems lead to what Bellman has referred to as the "curse of dimensionality." The increase in the number of (feature) dimensions, performed with the expectation that pattern discrimination and thus class separability will increase, has its own drawbacks. They include exponential growth in the number of hyper-parameters that define the target function sought to approximate the density underlying the sparse multivariate space, the fact that the only multivariate density available, the Gaussian, does not necessarily match the distribution observed, and the computational costs involved. The last concern can be alleviated using the kernel trick (see Sect. 5.7). Another relevant observation is that the (discrimination) performance peaks relatively soon and then degrades as the number of dimensions increases. The opposite to large dimensionality is what is actually sought after and usually done. This is referred to as dimensionality reduction (see Sects. 5.4 and 5.5).

3.2 Connectionism

According to Friedman (1994) "predictive learning is remarkably simple to state, but difficult to solve in general. One has a system under study characterized by several (possibly many) simultaneously measurable (observable) quantities, called variables. The variables are divided into two groups. The variables in one group are referred to as (respectively) as independent variables (applied mathematics), explanatory/predictor variables (statistics), or input variables (neural networks/machine learning). The variables of the other group also have different names depending on the field of study: dependent variables (applied mathematics), responses (statistics), or output variables (neural networks/machine learning). The goal is to develop a computational relationship between the inputs and the outputs (formula/algorithm) for determining/predicting/estimating values for the output variables given only the values of the input variables." Depending on the field of study, different computational approaches have been adopted. As an example, statistical methods use batch processing, while neural networks employ iterative (flow through) methods. Artificial neural networks are generically referred to as connectionism to emphasize, in analogy to biological networks, the (synaptic) connections between the computing units where learning takes place.

The basic but related tasks artificial neural networks have to cope with involve learning adaptive mappings for functional approximation, solving inverse problems within the framework provided by regularization (see next section), and sampling to represent (sensory) inputs using optimal (kernel) bases ('receptive fields'). One expands on the original concept of sampling by moving from mere signal sampling, characteristic of optimal signal representation and restoration, to pattern sampling and active learning, leading to generalization and adaptation, characteristic of pattern classification. Examples of adaptive strategies include optimal sampling using conjoint spatial-(temporal)/frequency wavelet packet representations, and active or progressive sampling driven by selective attention and corrective training.

The renewed interest in neural networks in the 1980s is attributed to several factors. First, the realization that a function of sufficient complexity can approximate any (continuous) target function or PDF with arbitrary accuracy, and second, the ability to train multilayer and non-linear neural networks using back propagation (BP). Approximation theory goes back to Weierstrass' theorem, which states that for any continuous real-valued function f defined on a closed interval $[a, b]$, and for any given positive constant there exists a (real coefficients) polynomial y, such that $\|y(x) - f(x)\| < \epsilon$, for every $x \in [a, b]$. In other words, every continuous function can be uniformly approximated by polynomials, which serve as universal approximators.

Several theoretical results, starting with one from Kolmogorov, have shown that multilayer feed forward networks can serve as universal approximators. Kolmogorov's theorem proves that for any given continuous function $f : [0, 1]^d \to \mathbf{R}^n$, f can be realized by a three-layer feed forward (neural) network having d fan out processing elements in the first $\mathbf{x}$-input layer, $(2d+1)$ processing elements in the middle ('hidden') layer, and n processing elements in the top $\mathbf{y}$-output layer. Theoretical rather than constructive, Kolmogorov's result shows that it is possible to map arbitrary continuous functions from the $d-$dimensional cube $[0, 1]^d$ to the real numbers $\mathbf{R}$, using functions of only one variable. Universal approximation results have also been obtained by Wang and Mendel (1992) using the fuzzy (systems) framework. They consider fuzzy systems represented as series expansions of fuzzy basis functions - algebraic super positions of fuzzy membership functions - and showed that linear combinations of such fuzzy basis functions are capable of uniformly approximating any real continuous function on a compact set to any arbitrary accuracy. Note that universal approximation, however, refers to functional approximation rather than predictive learning from small sample statistics when asymptotic convergence properties do not hold. Approximation and prediction are two different things.

Among connectionist classifiers, back propagation (BP) (Rumelhart et al., 1986) stands out in its use for face recognition (see Ch. 6). BP is characteristic of supervised learning where the difference between the teacher's desired (target) response $\mathbf{t}$ and the network's actual output $\mathbf{o}$ (that results from feed-forward propagation), drives in an iterative fashion the way synaptic weights are set. BP learns across a multi-layer network (MLN) architecture that consists of an input layer, several hidden layers, and an output layer. The units in each layer $l = 1, \cdots, L$, aggregate weighted inputs from the preceding layer $(l-1)$ and subject the result to a sigmoid ('squashing') (unipolar) function f that saturates at 0 and 1

$$y = f(\mathbf{x}) = \frac{1}{1 + \exp\{-(\theta \cdot \mathbf{x})\}} \tag{3.24}$$

where the hyper parameter θ bears on how fast the unit saturates. The weights w_{ji} connect the outputs of unit j from layer $(l-1)$ and unit i from layer l. The input $\mathbf{x}$ for unit i is $\mathbf{w}^T \mathbf{y}$ where $\mathbf{y}$ is the output coming from units in the preceding layer. BP starts by minimizing the total error $E(\mathbf{w})$ for the output layer L

$$E(\mathbf{w}) = \sum_{m=1}^{M} \sum_{q=1}^{Q} [t_q^{(m)} - o_q^{(m)}]^2 \tag{3.25}$$

where M is the number of data points in the training set and Q is the number of nodes for the output layer. Gradient descent and the chain rule iteratively (starting with $n = 1$) update the synaptic weights $\mathbf{w}$ and the hyper parameter θ for each layer l until their settings (almost) stop changing or a fixed number of iterations N has been reached

$$w_{ji}^{(n+1)}(l) = w_{ji}^n(l) + \Delta w_{ji}^n(l) \tag{3.26}$$

with the corresponding change in synaptic weights

$$\Delta w_{ji}^n(l) = -\eta \frac{\partial E}{\partial w_{ji}} \tag{3.27}$$

The unit i at the output layer for data point m yields $o_i^{(m)} = y_i^{(m)}$ using the outputs y_j from the preceding layer $(L - 1)$ so

$$
\begin{aligned}
\frac{\partial E}{\partial w_{ji}} &= \frac{\partial E}{\partial y_j} \cdot \frac{\partial y_j}{\partial x_j} \cdot \frac{\partial x_j}{\partial w_{ij}} \\
&= (t_i^{(m)} - y_i^{(m)}) y_j (1 - y_i) y_i
\end{aligned}
\tag{3.28}
$$

The name for BP comes from the following observation. While it is quite obvious what the error is at the output layer (see above) the error for each hidden layer is not known and has to be back propagated on a node by node basis. The individual errors E_i^l encountered for units i in layer l, weighted by existing weights w_{ji}, are summed up and counted as the errors $E_j^{(i-1)}$ at node j in layer $(l - 1)$

$$E_j^{(l-1)} = \sum_i E_i^l w_{ji} \tag{3.29}$$

The minimization process carried on $E(\mathbf{w})$ is a straightforward realization of the *orthogonality principle* and corresponds to the supervised (2nd) layer of radial basis functions (RBF) (see Sect. 9.2). The network outputs $\mathbf{y}$ live in the space S spanned by kernels serving as basis functions (BF). The least square solution for $\mathbf{y}$, found as the orthogonal projection of $\mathbf{t}$ onto S, minimizes the residual error $\mathbf{e}$ for $(||\mathbf{y} - \mathbf{t}||_2)^2$. Formally $\mathbf{e}$ is the distance from $\mathbf{t}$ to the space S. One finds that $\mathbf{t} = \mathbf{y} + \mathbf{e}$, $\mathbf{e} \perp S$, and $< \mathbf{e}, \mathbf{y} > = 0$. Face representation amounts then to a functional decomposition that consists of the subspace S approximation and the distance of the face from the subspace. This tells how fit the subspace description of the face is.

Fundamental links have been established between statistical pattern recognition and neural networks (see also Sect. 10.6). When back propagation (BP) learning is defined over the error surface $E(\mathbf{w})$ defined as $e(f) = \sum [y_i - f(x_i)]^2$, the regression, among all the functions of $\mathbf{x}$, is the best predictor of y given $\mathbf{x}$ in the mean-square error (MSE) sense (Geman et al., 1992), i.e.,

$$E[(y - f(\mathbf{x}))^2 | \mathbf{x}] \geq E[(y - E(y|\mathbf{x}))^2 | \mathbf{x}] \tag{3.30}$$

Another important result, due to Richard and Lippmann (1991), states that neural network classifiers, e.g., MLN trained using BP or RBF, provide outputs that estimate Bayesian a posteriori probabilities according to the degree to which the training data reflect true likelihood distributions and a priori class probabilities. This allows for the networks outputs to be combined within a probabilistic framework. The results hold only asymptotically - when the number of training samples grows infinitely large

- hence they give little insight regarding learning from small sample statistics. Note that BP is not incremental. This means that retraining should involve both the data BP has already trained on and any new data that has yet to be learned. Last but not least, there is the obvious question on how does connectionism actually learns to generalize. The standard approach for any learning method is to trade off between training or empirical risk, on one side, and some confidence interval, on the other side (see Sects. 3.3 and 3.4). Neural networks learn "by keeping the confidence interval fixed (by choosing an appropriate construction of the [learning MLN] machine) and minimize the empirical risk" (Vapnik, 2000). Structural risk minimization, in general, and support vector machines (SVM) (see Sect. 3.4), in particular, do the opposite. They keep the value for the empirical risk fixed and minimize the confidence interval.

3.3 Regularization

Given a class of mappings $f(\mathbf{x}, \mathbf{w})$, $\mathbf{w} \in \Omega$ where Ω is a set of (hyper) parameters of an arbitrary nature, the search for optimal predictive solutions is narrowed down using penalty (regularization) terms. Similar to the method of Lagrange multipliers, (inductive) inference using regularization consists of the original empirical risk minimization (ERM) for the average loss encountered on training data, i.e., $R_{emp}(\mathbf{w})$, augmented by a penalty term Φ

$$R_{pen}(\mathbf{w}) = R_{emp}(\mathbf{w}) + \lambda \cdot \Phi[f(\mathbf{x}, \mathbf{w})] \qquad (3.31)$$

where the functional Φ measures the extent to which a priori constraints, on the quality of the solution $f(\mathbf{x}, \mathbf{w})$ proposed, are satisfied (Cherkassky and Mulier, 1998). The tradeoff parameter λ controls the relative importance of the a priori constraints. The penalty term can be a stabilizer that measures smoothness or uniqueness, or alternatively, can be a confidence interval for predictions or the complexity of the hypothesis space (see Sect. 3.4). The control parameter λ can be set using resampling methods, e.g., cross-validation. Some architectures for solving regularization keep the confidence interval fixed and minimize the empirical risk, e.g., standard neural networks (see Sect. 3.2), or keep the empirical error fixed and minimize the confidence interval, e.g., support vector machines (see Sect. 3.4). In practice, connectionist networks include the penalty term using early stopping criteria and/or weight decay, similar to ridge regression.

Poggio and Smale (2003) have shown that regularization learns the approximating mapping $f : \mathbf{x} \to Y$ such that

$$f(\mathbf{x}) = \sum_{i=1}^{m} c_i K(\mathbf{x}, \mathbf{x_i}) \qquad (3.32)$$

for $\Phi[f(\mathbf{x}, \mathbf{w})] = \|f\|_k^2 = \mathbf{c}' \mathbf{K} \mathbf{c}$ where K is a symmetric and positive-definite Mercer kernel (see Sect. 5.7), e.g., the Gaussian $K(\mathbf{x}, \mathbf{x}') = \exp\left\{ \frac{-\|\mathbf{x} - \mathbf{x}'\|^2}{2\sigma^2} \right\}$ and σ controls the smoothness of the approximation. When $\sigma \to 0$, the mapping learned implements a table look-up. The linear system of equations $(\mathbf{K} + m \cdot \lambda \cdot \mathbf{I})\mathbf{c} = \mathbf{y}$ is well posed and can be solved for $\mathbf{c}$. The condition number a of the coefficient matrix $(\mathbf{K} + m \cdot \lambda \cdot \mathbf{I})$ of a linear system is a (nonnegative) number that estimates the amount by which small errors in (the right hand side) $\mathbf{y}$, or in $(\mathbf{K} + m \cdot \lambda \cdot \mathbf{I})$ itself, perturb the solution $\mathbf{c}$. Small values of the condition number suggest that the (regularization) algorithm will not be sensitive to errors, while large values for a indicate that small data values or arithmetic errors could lead to large errors in the answer. The condition number is defined in terms of a particular matrix norm, e.g., $a(\mathbf{K} + m \cdot \lambda \cdot \mathbf{I}) = \|(\mathbf{K} + m \cdot \lambda \cdot \mathbf{I})\| \cdot \|(\mathbf{K} + m \cdot \lambda \cdot \mathbf{I})^{-1}\|$. The condition number a is infinite if $(\mathbf{K} + m \cdot \lambda \cdot \mathbf{I})$ is not invertible. The condition number for the mapping f defined above is good if $m \cdot \lambda$ is large (Poggio and Smale, 2003).

The explanation is that a large m amounts to a large data set to learn from and/or a large λ amounts to discounting the training error to avoid overfit. Regularization leads directly to support vector machines (SVM) for whom the coefficients c are found by solving a quadratic optimization problem. The regularization framework discussed above is also behind correlation filters and distributed associative memories (see Sect. 10.6).

The interpretation of the mapping f says that it is synthesized by a weighted superposition of Gaussian blobs, each centered at the location x_i of one of the training exemplars (see analogy to Parzen windows). The weights c found minimize the regularized/penalized empirical error $R_{pen}(w)$. The approach described implements regularized least-square classification (RLSC). The approximation f is equivalent to radial basis functions (see Sect. 9.2) and is also representative of hybrid learning because the number of Gaussian blobs can be narrowed down using (unsupervised) clustering, e.g., K-means or EM, before actual (supervised) regularization takes place. Last but not least the regularization framework can also assume a Bayesian interpretation (Wahba, 1990; Poggio and Smale, 2003). The data term (for fidelity) using a quadratic loss function is optimal in response to additive Gaussian noise, while the penalty term or stabilizer corresponds to priors given on the hypothesis space of admissible models. The mapping f learned by regularization corresponds then to the MAP estimate.

3.4 Structural Risk Minimization

Structural risk minimization (SRM) is the new inductive principle proposed by statistical learning theory (SLT) for model selection. Like regularization, SRM is an example of constraint optimization but with a twist. The tradeoff is now between the empirical risk (ER) encountered during learning the classifier, on one side, and the confidence interval that surrounds ER, on the other side. The confidence interval bounds future performance around the empirical error experienced during training. The smaller the confidence interval is, the higher the generalization ability and the smaller the prediction risk are. The confidence interval actually is an indicator on the uncertainty surrounding the predictions made. It depends on both the sample size of the training set, and the capacity of the classifier, the latter defined using the Vapnik-Chervonenkis (VC) dimension (see below). SRM seeks to minimize the expected or future prediction risk, i.e., the generalization error, while avoiding underfitting and overfitting using model complexity control (Cherkassky and Mulier, 1998) (see Fig. 3.1). Underfitting, when the model selected is too simple to explain the training data, and overfitting when the model selected is too complex and thus undermines generalization. Alternatively, underfitting is characterized by large empirical loss, while overfitting corresponds to a large capacity that explains too much and it is unlikely to generalize well. This draws from the wisdom expressed back in 1685 by Leibniz (see the Preface) that comprehension should entail compression. Complexity and capacity are used interchangeably here. SRM searches for the simplest model that explains the data and this is discussed next.

Complexity or equivalently capacity are measured using the VC-dimension, which is the size of the largest set that can be shattered by the set of functions $f(x, w)$. When the VC-dimension is h there is at least one set of h data points or patterns that can be shattered. The set is shattered if each possible (binary) dichotomy or classification can be modeled by $f(x, w)$ for some $w \in \Omega$. It is easy to see that a linear function in $\mathbf{R}^2$ can shatter three $(n = 3)$ but not four $(n = 4)$ examples, e.g., it cannot shatter XOR. The dichotomies (that can be separated) for two classes (0 and 1) in 2D are $\{000, 001, 010, 011, 100, 101, 110, 111\}$. The VC-dimension for hyperplanes in $\mathbf{R}^d$ is $(d + 1)$. The VC-dimension should not be confused with the number of parameters or degrees of freedom (Vapnik, 2000). One can show that with probability $1 - \eta$,

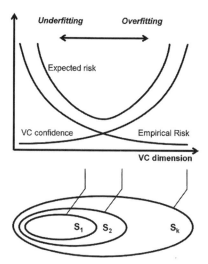

Fig. 3.1. Structural Risk Minimization (Reprinted from *Statistical Learning Theory*, Vapnik, ©2000 Springer).

$$R(\mathbf{w}) = R_{emp}(\mathbf{w}) + \Phi\left(\frac{h}{n}, \frac{\log(\eta)}{n}\right) \tag{3.33}$$

$$R(\mathbf{w}) = R_{emp}(\mathbf{w}) + \sqrt{\frac{h\left(\log\left(\frac{2n}{h}\right) + 1\right) - \log\left(\frac{\eta}{4}\right)}{n}} \tag{3.34}$$

where $n > h$, the constraint Φ refers to model complexity/capacity or alternatively the VC-confidence interval, and $R(\mathbf{w})$ is the penalized risk $R_{pen}(\mathbf{w})$ referred to earlier. The empirical risk decreases as the VC-dimension increases. When the VC-dimension h is low compared to the number of examples n learned from, the confidence interval is narrow. Small capacity/complexity means that there are many samples or facts that cannot be shattered or explained. The model found can fail and is thus falsifiable. This is what makes SRM closely aligned to Kant's demarcation criterion that separates true science from mere beliefs. Popper (2002) goes on to state that "It must be possible for an empirical theory to be refuted by experience. Every good scientific theory is a prohibition; it forbids certain things to happen. The more a theory forbids, the better it is."

SRM seeks the lowest upper bound on the predicted risk or the generalization error. It strikes a balance between the empirical risk and the VC confidence interval while searching for an optimal model with respect to prediction or expected risk (see Fig. 3.1). Towards that end, SRM defines a nested structure of elements S_i

$$S_1 \subset S_2 \subset S_3 \subset \cdots \subset S_i \subset \cdots S_k \tag{3.35}$$

and finds the solutions $f_i(\mathbf{x}, \mathbf{w})$ (of increasing VC-dimension h) that minimize the empirical risk for each element S_i. The model S_i chosen is the one for whom the empirical risk traced to the function $f_i(\mathbf{x}, \mathbf{w})$ together with the corresponding confidence interval achieves minimum for $R(\mathbf{w})$.

Support vector machines (SVM), a realization of SRM for linear models, seek among the learning examples only those examples, called support vectors (SV), which contribute to the derivation of the optimal linear hyper-plane that separates the two classes. It is usually the case that m, the number of SV, is much less that the total number n of learning examples, as most of the training examples are 'far' away from the decision (hyper-planes) boundaries. Vapnik (2000) has shown that for large n the probability of error $P(e)$ on future trials is bounded as

$$P(e) < \frac{m}{n} \qquad (3.36)$$

The optimal hyper-plane $D(\mathbf{x})$ sought by linear SVM

$$D(\mathbf{x}) = D(\mathbf{x}, \mathbf{w}) = <\mathbf{w} \cdot \mathbf{x}> + w_0 \qquad (3.37)$$

is the one that provides for the largest margin that separates between two given classes. The larger the margin (of error) the better the generalization ability is.

Formally, given n training samples $(\mathbf{x_i}, y_i)$, where $y_i \in \{-1, 1\}$ the separating hyper-plane has to satisfy for each i the constraint equation $y_i \cdot D(x_i) \geq 1$. The distance between the separating hyper-plane $D(\mathbf{x})$ and some sample x_i is $\frac{|D(\mathbf{x_i})|}{||\mathbf{w}||}$. The smallest distance between the separating hyper-plane and its closes sample(s), i.e., support vector(s) (SV), is referred to as the margin γ. The separating hyper-plane is optimal if the margin achieves its maximum. The constraint equation, now expressed in terms of margin γ, is

$$\frac{y_i \cdot D(\mathbf{x_i})}{||\mathbf{w}||} \geq \gamma \qquad (3.38)$$

SVM seeks for $\mathbf{w}$ that maximizes the margin γ subject to the normalization constraint $\gamma||\mathbf{w}|| = 1$. A large margin provides more opportunity to avoid misclassification (see Fig. 3.2). The loss outside the margin is zero and no losses are incurred for the separable case. Losses, however, occur for the non separable or soft case as explained later on.

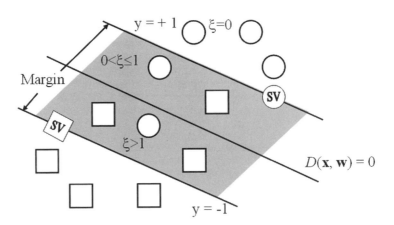

Fig. 3.2. Margin Based Binary Classification.

The search for a large margin involves minimizing the norm $||\mathbf{w}||^2$ subject to the constraint equations given earlier. The SRM nested structure consists of $S_i = \{(\mathbf{w} \cdot \mathbf{x}) + w_0; ||\mathbf{w}||^2 \leq c_i\}$, i.e., hyper-planes $D(\mathbf{x})$ for whom the (coefficients) $\mathbf{w}$ norm is bound by increasing values $c_1 < c_2 < \cdots$. This is consistent with SRM because for hyper-planes $D(\mathbf{x})$ for whom $||\mathbf{w}||^2 \leq c$ the VC-dimension is bound by $h = \min(r^2 c, d) + 1$, where r is the radius of the smallest sphere that contains the training samples, and d is the space dimension. The formal arguments presented above are used to find the minimal structural risk for a (convex) quadratic $J(\mathbf{w})$ (for whom there exists a unique global minimum)

$$\min J(\mathbf{w}) = \frac{1}{2}||\mathbf{w}||^2 \quad \text{subject to} \quad y_i D(\mathbf{x_i}) \geq 1 \tag{3.39}$$

Multi (K)-class problems are solved using K SVM classifiers, each of them tasked to choose between one class $k = 1 \cdots K$ and all the other classes. A winner-take-all (WTA) is declared based on the relative performance of the K classifiers. Tree classifiers can expedite this process.

The SVM solution for the non-separable case has access to slack variables ξ_i that account for data points or patterns that (a) fall within the margin but on the correct side, i.e., $0 \leq \xi_i \leq 1$, or (b) fall on the wrong side of the hyper plane, i.e., $\xi_i > 1$ (see Fig. 3.2). The objective for the non-separable and soft SVM is to find the optimal hyper plane while incurring a minimum of misclassification decisions $\phi(\xi)$. Formally one now solves for

$$\min J(\mathbf{w}, \xi) = \frac{1}{2}||\mathbf{w}||^2 + \frac{C}{n} \sum \xi_i$$
$$\text{subject to} \quad \{y_i D(\mathbf{x_i}) \geq 1 - \xi_i \text{ and } \xi_i \geq 0\} \tag{3.40}$$

where C, in a fashion similar to the penalizers λ (see regularization) trades off between complexity and misclassification, e.g., large values for C lead to fewer misclassification errors. Appropriate values for C can be found using cross-validation. The decision hyper plane (for m support vectors $\mathbf{x_i}$) in the dual space is the same for both the separable and non-separable case

$$D(\mathbf{x}) = \sum_{i=1}^{n} \lambda_i^* y_i <\mathbf{x} \cdot \mathbf{x_i}> +w_0^* \tag{3.41}$$

Non-separable classification problems can become separable when cast in a high dimensional space using non-linear mappings of $\mathbf{x}$ (Cover, 1969). Formally the sequence of mappings, including classification, consists of $\mathbf{x} \rightarrow \varphi(\mathbf{x}) \rightarrow \mathbf{z} \rightarrow \mathbf{w} \cdot \mathbf{z} \rightarrow \mathbf{y}$. As an example, $\varphi : \mathbf{R}^2 \rightarrow \mathbf{R}^3$ where $(\mathbf{x_1}, \mathbf{x_2}) \rightarrow (\mathbf{z_1}, \mathbf{z_2}, \mathbf{z_3}) = (\mathbf{x_1^2}, (\sqrt{2\mathbf{x_1}\mathbf{x_2}}, \mathbf{x_2^2})$. Projections and dot products in the high-dimensional space are implicit using the Mercer condition or the kernel trick (see Sect. 5.7)

$$\langle \varphi(\mathbf{x_i}), \varphi(\mathbf{x_j}) \rangle = K(\mathbf{x_i}, \mathbf{x_j}) \tag{3.42}$$

The complexity of the SVM decision boundary becomes thus independent of the dimensionality of $\mathbf{z}$, which can be very large (or even infinite). Some kernels meeting the Mercer condition and used by non-linear SVM are

The radial basis function (RBF) kernels

$$K(\mathbf{x_i}, \mathbf{x_j}) = \exp\left(-\frac{1}{\sigma^2}||\mathbf{x_i} - \mathbf{x_j}||^2\right) \tag{3.43}$$

Polynomial kernels

$$K(\mathbf{x_i}, \mathbf{x_j}) = (\mathbf{x_i'}\mathbf{x_j} + 1)^p \tag{3.44}$$

and the decision hyper plane (for m support vectors $\mathbf{x_i}$) in the dual (kernel) space is

$$D(\mathbf{x}) = \sum_{i=1}^{n} \lambda_i^* y_i K(\mathbf{x_i}, \mathbf{x}) \tag{3.45}$$

The Lagrange multipliers λ_i are found by maximizing the dual formulation of SVM

$$Q(\lambda) = -\frac{1}{2}\sum_{i=1}^{n}\sum_{j=1}^{n}\lambda_i\lambda_j y_i y_j K(\mathbf{x}_i, \mathbf{x}_j) + \sum_{i=1}^{n}\lambda_i \qquad (3.46)$$

subject to the constraints $\sum_{i=1}^{n}\lambda_i y_i = 0$ and $0 \leq \lambda_i \leq C, i = 1, \cdots, n$, where $K(\mathbf{x}_i, \mathbf{x}_j)$ is a kernel function. For the examples on the margin, the values of the Lagrange multipliers are between 0 and C. The examples outside the margin have zero Lagrange multipliers, while all the examples within the margin share the value of C for their Lagrange multipliers.

We close on SRM by noting that Cherkassky and Ma (2004) have disputed the claim made earlier by Poggio and Smale (2003) that SRM, in general, and SVM, in particular, are merely a special case of regularization. Both the non separable or soft SVM formulation and regularized least squares classification (RLSC) indeed have a single parameter that controls complexity. It is the margin concept that makes SVM unique rather than merely being an instantiation of regularization. The SVM formulation used for regression, according to Cherkassky and Ma, includes two rather than one hyper parameters, i.e., an adaptive $\epsilon-$insensitive loss function and the penalization term $\phi(\xi)$.

3.5 Transduction

Transductive inference is a type of *local* inference that moves from particular to particular (Vapnik, 1998; 2000) (see Fig 3.3). "In contrast to inductive inference where one uses given empirical data to find the approximation of a functional dependency (the inductive step [that moves from particular to general]) and then uses the obtained approximation to evaluate the values of a function at the points of interest (the deductive step [that moves from general to particular]), one estimates [using transduction] the values of a function [only] at the points of interest in one step" (Vapnik, 1998). Transduction incorporates the unlabeled data, like test probes, in the decision-making process responsible for their eventual labeling. This involves some combinatorial optimization process that seeks to maximize the likelihood or fitness for the local model chosen to explain and label the combined training and test data. As an example, the transductive SVM (TSVM) maximizes the margin for both labeled and unlabeled examples (Joachims, 1999), but on a global basis. Transduction "works because the test set can give you a nontrivial factorization of the [discrimination] function class" (Chapelle et al., 2006). One key concept behind transduction is the symmetrization lemma (Vapnik, 1998). The idea is to replace the true risk by an estimate computed on an independent set of data, e.g., unlabeled or test data. The extra data set, referred to as 'virtual' or 'ghost sample', is similar to the hints or constrained used by semi-supervised learning (Chapelle et al., 2006). The simplest mathematical realization for transductive inference is the method of k nearest neighbors. The Cover-Hart (1967) theorem proves that asymptotically the one nearest neighbor algorithm is bounded above by twice the Bayes' minimum probability of error.

Given (labeled) training examples, transduction seeks among the feasible labels available for the (unlabeled probe) test examples the ones that make the error observed during testing consistent with the errors recorded during training. Transduction might be useful, among others, when there are only a few training examples while most of the data available is of the unlabeled type, or when the costs for annotation and/or the efforts involved are prohibitive. Simply put, the test data should affect the very design of the classifier used to label it because more data is now available to learn from. Equivalently, the training classifier should adapt to the distribution of the unlabeled or test data. Training and test data are assumed to come from similar but not identical distributions, are identically independent distributed (i.i.d.), and play symmetric roles. Towards that end, one has to minimize·an *overall risk* functional in order to achieve the most consistent labeling or classification for training and test data as explained next (see also Sects. 6.3 and 6.4). Given a small size training set

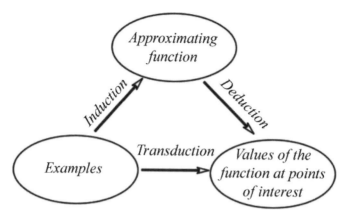

Fig. 3.3. Transductive Inference (Reprinted from *Statistical Learning Theory*, Vapnik, ©2000 Springer).

of examples, T, which consists of l input-output pairs $(\mathbf{x}_i, y_i)$, transduction has to estimate the value of the function $y = \Phi(\mathbf{x})$ at the given [*working* test examples] set W of points $\mathbf{x}_{l+1}, \cdots, \mathbf{x}_{l+m}$. Based on the training set T, the working set W, and a given set of functions $f(\mathbf{x}, \alpha), \alpha \in \Lambda$ where $\Phi(\mathbf{x})$ does not necessarily belong to this set, one has to find $f(\mathbf{x}, \alpha^*)$ that minimizes with a preassigned probability $1 - \eta$ the overall risk of forecasting the values of the function $y_i = \Phi(\mathbf{x}_i)$ on the elements of the working set W – that is, yields with probability $1 - \eta$, a value of the functional

$$R(\alpha) = \sum_{i=1}^{m} \rho(y_{l+i}, f(\mathbf{x}_{l+i}, \alpha)) \tag{3.47}$$

that is close to the minimal one. $\rho(y, f(\mathbf{x}, \alpha))$ measures the discrepancy between y and $f(\mathbf{x}, a)$

$$\rho(y_{l+i}, f(\mathbf{x}_{l+i}, \alpha)) = (y_{l+i} - f(\mathbf{x}_{l+i}, \alpha))^2 \tag{3.48}$$

The above setting #1 minimizes the deviation between the risk on the training and working samples (Vapnik, 1998). The alternative but equivalent setting #2, also due to Vapnik, considers training and working samples [chosen according to a probability distribution function $P(\mathbf{x}, y)$] and seeks algorithm A that will choose a function $f(\mathbf{x}, \alpha_A)$,

$$f(\mathbf{x}, \alpha_A) = f(\mathbf{x}, \alpha_A(\mathbf{x}_1, y_1; \cdots; \mathbf{x}_l, y_l; \mathbf{x}_{l+1}, \cdots, \mathbf{x}_{l+m})) \tag{3.49}$$

that makes the value of the functional

$$R(A) = \int \left(\frac{1}{m} \sum_{i=l+1}^{l+m} \rho(y_i, f(\mathbf{x}_i, \alpha_A)) \right) dP(\mathbf{x}_1, y_1) \cdots dP(\mathbf{x}_l, y_l) dP(\mathbf{x}_{l+m}, y_{l+m}) \tag{3.50}$$

close to the minimal one, when the sum is indexed for (unlabeled) examples i between $l+1$ and $l+m$. Setting #2 labels W, the set of working examples, in a fashion consistent with T, the training set, e.g., but now using minimization over $T \bigcup W$. One possible realization using SVM classifies the joint set of training and working examples over all the possible labels or classifications $\mathbf{L}(W)$ for W, e.g., $\arg\min_{\mathbf{L}(W)} \min_{\mathbf{w}} \frac{1}{2}||\mathbf{w}||^2$ (Saunders et al., 1999). The margin is "a natural way to encode prior knowledge for classifiers and to study the location of exemplars (with respect to the hyper plane), which is not possible for an inductive learner" (Joachims, 1999). A generic transductive scheme is proposed by Weston et al. (2003). It gives the flavor for how binary transduction works and it is described next (see multi-class recognition using transduction for open set face recognition in Sect. 6.3).

Assume an inductive classification algorithm A^I that learns a real valued function $g(\mathbf{x})$ for input-output training pairs $(\mathbf{x_i}, y_i)$, where $\mathbf{x_i} \in \mathbf{R}^d$ and $y_i \in [-1, 1]$. The labels $y = \pm 1$ indicate high confidence in the binary labels assigned, while $y = 0$ indicates lack of knowledge about the label sought after. The (signed) magnitude of $g(\mathbf{x})$ is proportional to the confidence in the label assignments $y = \pm 1$. The other values that can be credited to y signify varying degrees of confidence in the (positive or negative) labels assigned. Given T and W (see above), $D = T \bigcup W, \#T = l, \#W = m$ and $\#D = n$, where $n = l + m$, the update function $u(\mathbf{x})$ takes on each iteration input $g(\mathbf{x})$ and outputs a label $y_i \in [-1, 1]$. The transduction algorithm A^T initializes the labels for W as $y_i = 0$ and iterates over

- Train A^I using D to derive $g(\mathbf{x})$
- Update labels for W such that $y_i = u(g(\mathbf{x}_i))$

until convergence or a preset number of iterations have been performed. The final transductive label assignments for W are $y_i = 1$ if $g(\mathbf{x}_i) > 0$ or $y_i = -1$ otherwise. Note that the labels for T are fixed but this should not always be the case. In particular, for data cleaning purposes or to lower the overall risk, one should update the labels for T as well.

Transduction seeks consistent labels for training and test data. It iterates to relabel the test data using local perturbations on the labels assigned. Poggio et al. (2004) using similar reasoning suggest it is the stability of the learning process that leads to good learning predictivity. In particular, the stability property says that "when the training set is perturbed by deleting one example, the learned hypothesis does not change much. This stability property stipulates conditions on the learning map rather than on the hypothesis space." An open question is the extent to which the concept of stability could be expanded to allow for label changes rather than only training exemplar deletion.

The goal for inductive learning is to generalize for any future test set, while the goal for transductive inference is to make predictions for a specific working set W. Test data is not merely a passive collection of data waiting for authentication but rather an active player ready to make its contribution together with enrollment data. The working or test examples provide additional information about the distribution of face patterns and their explicit inclusion in the problem formulation yields better generalization on problems with insufficient labeled points (Gammerman et al., 1998).

3.6 Generative and Discriminative Methods

The brain is not an organ of thinking but an organ of survival, like claws and fangs. It is made in such a way as to make us accept as truth that which is only advantage. It is an exceptional, almost pathological constitution one has, if one follows thoughts logically through, regardless of consequences. (Albert Szent-Gyorgi)

Modeling and prediction are mostly about decision making. The relative novelty of transduction is that it approaches inference on a local basis. Local estimation still needs access to some classifier and the proper language to express it. To paraphrase Galileo, "in order to understand the Universe you need to know the language was written in and this is the language of mathematics," one still needs to find the proper dialect. The generative, also referred to as informative, and discriminative methods, are two basic approaches that compete today to implement categorization. In a nutshell, the generative methods, normative and prescriptive in nature, synthesize the classifier by learning what appear to be the relevant class distributions and choose their decisions using MAP. The discriminative methods imitate and model only what it takes to make the classification. The discriminative method is in tune with both structural risk minimization and transduction. It is in tune with structural risk minimization because it locks on what is essential for discrimination, and it is in tune with transduction because discrimination is local. Jebara (2002) has actually suggested that imitation should be added to the generative and discriminative methods as another mode of learning. He recalls from Edmund Burke that "it is by imitation, far more than by percept, that we learn everything." Discriminative methods make fewer assumptions and are closer to the dictum enunciated by Leibniz that comprehension entails compression. Fewer assumptions also mean less chance to be mistaken when modeling phenomena of interest.

There are philosophical and linguistic arguments that further support the discriminative approach. Philosophically, it has to do with practical reasoning and epistemology, and according to Hume, to the fact that "all kinds of reasoning consist in nothing but a comparison and a discovery of those relations, either constant or inconstant, which two or more objects bear to each other." The empiricist's stance, that the percept is always a wager, is closely related to likelihood ratios and context. Practical reasoning leads to practical expertise and is reminiscent of linguistics. Language, according to Vygotsky, is closely related to thought and reasoning, and it affects the scope and quality of the inferences made. *Langue* ("language"), according to the official and sanctioned structuralist grammar, is transcendental and beyond experience. *Langue* is different from the *parole* ("word") or the language as it is practiced. This distinction, which goes back to Saussure, focuses on the clash of competence against performance. To paraphrase Szent-Gyorgi, competence is about thinking, while performance is about survival. For Wittgenstein, language functions properly only in context and its expression depends on functionality. Words and sentences have no fixed meanings; the meaning of a word is its use in the sentence. This is why machine translation still lacks and why English-to-from-Russian mechanical translations proffer that "the spirit is willing but the flesh is weak" and "the vodka is good but the meat is rotten" are equivalent. Discriminative modeling for real life situations, both creative and pragmatic, is also what makes us well versed with goal directed speech acts, according to Searle (1969). Idealized human rationality, according to Kahneman and Tversky (2000), is a myth, and so is the rationale behind generative methods.

According to Rubinstein and Hastie (1997), "the goal of pattern classification can be approached from two points of view: informative [generative] - where the classifier learns the class densities, [e.g., HMM] or discriminative - where the focus is on learning the class boundaries without regard to the underlying class densities, [e.g., logistic regression and neural networks]." The informative approach for 0/1 loss classifies some input $\mathbf{x}$ to the class $k \in K$ for whom the class posterior probability $P(y = k|\mathbf{x})$

$$P(y = k|\mathbf{x}) = \frac{P(\mathbf{x}|y = k)P(y = k)}{\sum_i^K P(\mathbf{x}|y = i)P(y = i)} \tag{3.51}$$

yields maximum. The MAP decision requires access to the full log likelihood $P_\theta(\mathbf{x}, y)$. The optimal (hyper) parameters θ are learned using maximum likelihood (ML) and a decision boundary is then induced, which corresponds to a minimum distance classifier. The discriminative approach models directly the conditional log likelihood or posteriors $P_\theta(y|\mathbf{x})$. The optimal parameters are estimated using ML leading to the discriminant function

$$\lambda_k(\mathbf{x}) = \log \left[\frac{P(y = k|\mathbf{x})}{P(y \in K|\mathbf{x})} \right] \tag{3.52}$$

that is very similar to the universal background model (UBM) used for score normalization (see Sect. 12.2). The comparison taking place is between some very specific class membership k and a generic distribution (over K) that describes everything that is known. The discriminative approach was found by Rubinstein and Hastie to be more flexible and robust because fewer assumptions have to be made. The drawback is that it ignores the marginal distribution $P(\mathbf{x})$, which is difficult to estimate anyway. The informative approach is biased when the distribution chosen is incorrect.

The discriminative classifier should be generally preferred to the generative one for the obvious reason that "one should solve the [classification] problem directly and never solve a more general problem as an intermediate step [such as modeling $P(\mathbf{x}|y)$]" (Vapnik, 1998). Jordan (1995) has approached the generative vs. discriminative (referred to as "diagnostic" methods) using the framework of Bayesian belief networks for binary classification. The generative approach has access to the class ω for evidence that influences on the observation vector $\mathbf{x}$ and determines the marginal probability $P(\omega)$ and conditional probability $P(\mathbf{x}|\omega)$. The sought after posterior probability $P(\omega|\mathbf{x})$ can be expressed using the logistic function (eq. 3.26) to model back propagation outputs (see Sect. 3.2) such that for binary classification

$$P(\omega_0|\mathbf{x}) = \frac{1}{\left[1 + \exp\left\{-\log\left[\frac{P(\mathbf{x}|\omega_0)}{P(\mathbf{x}|\omega_1)}\right] - \log\left[\frac{P(\omega_0)}{P(\omega_1)}\right]\right\}\right]} \tag{3.53}$$

Jordan goes on to say that "the statistical advantage of generative network is that if the model specification is nearly correct, then estimation will be more efficient than estimation in diagnostic network (will require fewer data points to obtain a given level of accuracy). The statistical advantage of diagnostic network, on the other hand, is that it is more robust to uncertainty about the data generation process." Ng and Jordan (2001) have shown that when classifiers sharing the same functional form are learned, the asymptotic error for the discriminative classifier is lower or equal to the error that the generative classifier yields. Last but not least, the discriminative and generative methods are complementary to each other when they implement the analysis and synthesis face recognition loop.

4. Data Collection

Permanence is relative, of course; that is, it depends on whether you mean persistence over a day, a year, or a millennium. Almost nothing is forever permanent; nothing is either immutable or mutable. So it is better to speak of persistence under change (James Gibson, The Ecological Approach to Visual Perception).

"Collected biometric samples or features are properly referred to as a "corpus". The information about those images and the clients who produced them is referred to as the "data base". Data collection, which affects both the corpus and the data base, is most relevant for machine readable travel documents (MRTD). Both the corpus and the database can be corrupted by human error [and/or security lapses] during the collection, processing, and storage process (see Ch. 14). "In fact, error rates in the collection process may easily exceed those of the biometric device. Extreme care must thus be taken during data collection to avoid both corpus (images improperly acquired) and data base (mislabeled image) errors" (Mansfield et al., 2001). There are two basic remedies for such errors. The face recognition engine should flush out such errors and/or use manual inspection. There are two types of failures that can be traced to image acquisition errors. The *failure to enroll rate* is the expected proportion of the population for whom the system is unable to generate repeatable [signatures] templates, while the *failure to acquire rate* is defined as the expected proportion of transactions for which the system is unable to capture or locate an image or signal of sufficient quality. The two errors related to image acquisition are handled by repeated attempts until success is observed. *FACE IT* from Visionics (now part of Viisage), during testing and evaluation, collects images over a period of 10 seconds and provides the best (pair wise) match obtained.

In analogy to the way people sense and process images, face recognition is not limited to the use of one still image. Data collection can involve the acquisition of more than just one still image per subject, e.g., *Smart Gate* in Australia and the Face Recognition Grand Challenge (FRGC) (Phillips et al., 2005). Several gallery images, available for each subject, are then matched against one or several probe images. Data fusion and integration methods actually call for the explicit use of multiple images and/or multi modal biometrics from each subject. The full richness of time-varying imagery made available by video processing can and should be harnessed. The temporal dimension facilitates the integration and reconciliation of information over time. As new sensors are introduced, e.g., 3D, additional and valuable facial information becomes available. The next sections address sensors' characteristics, standards for data collection and image compression, and the way data collection affects image quality and the very reliability of face recognition.

4.1 Sensing

Photography, a marvel of technology, appeared in the early 19th century. Photography has made big strides ever since and it is still evolving. Not a substitute for paintings, photography is sometime considered an art. It freezes for posterity the way we look and it provides context that connects image, context and situation, and feelings, e.g., the photos made by Andre Kertesz and Henri-Cartier Bresson. Cameras and the resulting 2D intensity images are the main medium for sensing and processing human faces. 3D sensors and range images are starting to also be considered for their potential contributions to face recognition, e.g., FRGC. Smart dust shaped as "cubes of silicon the size of ants" is no more the subject of science fiction and can provide for each host a sensor, a processor, and wireless-communication hardware. Everything today has become pervasive and transparent. People can now be monitored and recorded, e.g., closed circuit TV (CCTV), with obvious implications for security and privacy.

Trucco and Verri (1998) give a detail account for the 2D and 3D image formation process. Here we address the factors that affect image quality and contents. This is relevant to the interchange standards proposed for MRTD (see Sect. 4.2), and face recognition in general. The most common geometric model for data capture is the perspective or pinhole camera. The fundamental equations are

$$x = f \cdot \frac{X}{Z}, \quad y = f \cdot \frac{Y}{Z} \tag{4.1}$$

where (x, y) and (X, Y) are the image and camera frame coordinates, respectively, Z is the optical axis, and f, the (principal) focal length, is approximately the distance that separates the image (sensor) plane (where all the incoming parallel rays are focused to a point referred to as the principal focal point) and camera frame. The above equations are non-linear. Neither distances between points nor angles between lines are preserved. The focal length corresponds to the magnification factor. Spherical and chromatic aberrations affect the focal length. Preprocessing using image processing and computer vision techniques can make up for most of the technical imperfections induces by the faults introduced during image capture and acquisition. The basic controls using film or digital recording are discussed next.

First and foremost there is the exposure and the amount of light that strikes the "film". The more light strikes the film, the faster the shutter speed and/or the lower ASA film speed or sensitivity should be. Shutter speed can vary from $\frac{1}{2}$ to $\frac{1}{1000}$ sec; night photography requires slow speed, e.g., 4 sec. The aperture is the other factor that affects exposure. Aperture is usually automatically set based on prevalent illumination, film speed and the shutter (release) speed chosen. The scale for aperture, using f-numbers of f/stops, ranges approximately from a maximum size 1.4 to a minimum size of 22. A good choice for fast exposure would use $f/1.8$ lenses. The smaller the aperture, the sharper the image and the larger the depth of field are. A large aperture is useful to isolate the subject from her background. The depth of field d is the range of distances over which faces appear sharp. The capture of mug shots requires that the depth of field should cover the distance from nose to ears. The depth of field is also greater the shorter the focal length of the lens and the greater the distance the subjects is seen from. Focus is related to the sharpness of the image and the amount of detail recorded. Focus, usually an automatic feature for cameras, ranges from 0.8 meter to infinity when using active infrared. A related concept is the circle of confusion C, e.g., the spot size corresponding to the image of a point. It is related to in-focus and diffraction induced blur. Diffraction is caused by spreading of light while passing through some aperture. A large $f/4$ aperture and diffraction yield a 5.4 microns spot size, while a small $f/22$ aperture yields a much larger 30 microns spot size. An increased (f/stop) aperture and diffraction trade off sharpness and focus. The depth of field d is proportional to $\frac{C}{f^2}$. Camera should be held steady for image stabilization to avoid blur and lose of face detail. As an example, the motion of a pedestrian can be frozen at a shutter speed of $\frac{1}{60}$ second. Optical image stabilization, using variable prism is better than electronic image stabilization. Digital image stabilization is yet another alternative.

Unlike standard cameras that use film to capture and store the image, (pocket size, point-and-shoot, and high end) digital cameras known as *digicams* use solid-state devices as array image sensors, e.g., charge-coupled devices (CCD) and complementary metal oxide semiconductors (CMOS). CMOS is newer, cheaper and a faster technology. There is an additional digital-to-analogue converter that records the electrical CCD signals onto digital medium. Digital recordings consist of millions of picture elements referred to as pixels, which capture information about brightness. The image quality depends among other factors on the number of pixels or resolution. The size of the smallest detail that can be captured is a function of resolution. There is absolute or optical resolution, which counts the number of photo sites or equivalently the number of pixels per inch, and there is an interpolated resolution using image processing software. Interpolated resolution is the mode of operation for additive RGB color images when each photo site uses only one of the three filters and neighboring information is used for interpolation. Such chroma sub-sampling, however, can blur color detail.

Point-and-shoot recordings are sampled to produce digital images. Shannon sampling theorem sets the minimum rate for sampling a bandwidth-limited continuous signal so it can be uniquely recovered. The sampling frequency, known as the Nyquist frequency, must be at least twice the largest frequency or the bandwidth of the signal. Otherwise aliasing occurs, e.g., jagged profiles and loss of detail. One possible solution for staying within the Nyquist frequency is to use filters that blur the original signal and thus reduce its effective bandwidth. The size of the digital recording is given by the file size and the total number N of pixels, or by the 2D image array (x, y) where $\#x$ and $\#y$ are the number of rows and columns, respectively, and $N = \#x \times \#y$. The digital image is encoded by an intensity function $I(x, y)$ using gray levels or color. High resolution digital cameras can provide today up to 6-8 million Mega pixels (MP) for an image. A 5 MP camera images a human face across an array that consists of $2,560 \times 1,920$ pixels. Color generates three times as much bytes of information. Some digicams increase the pixel count while shrinking the information contents for each pixel. Scanning, complementary to sampling, affects image quality. Progressive CCD scanning captures full still images while conventional CCD are of the interlace type. Sensitivity typically ranges from 64 to 500 ISO, the latter suitable for indoor photography that requires high sensitivity, and speed for proper exposure.

A zoom lens has a variable focal length. Short focal length or wide-angle lens, e.g., $f/3.1$, are useful for large fields of view (FOV), while a long focal length is needed for distant faces. FOV is the space angle over which faces can be photographed. Most digital cameras have a 3X zoom, with a focal length that ranges from about 35 mm to 105 mm. Digital zoom merely expands the image and yields no information gain compared to optical zoom. Digital sensors automatically provide for white balance, which is a useful feature that adjusts for the light source. It makes white look white, and makes the correction for color temperature, as it would be the case with regular film, unnecessary. There are several memory cards used for storage, e.g., compact flash (CF) cards up to 2 GB, Smart Media ($\sim$ 128 MB), and varying capacity micro drives up to 4 GB. The 2 GB CF allows the 5 MP camera mentioned earlier to store up to 1,120 shots using low JPEG compression. The advantage for CF comes from them being a safe and reliable form of storage that does not require power once the (face) image has been saved. Camera interfaces include USB 1.1, USB 2.0 and FireWire IEEE 1394.

Another factor that affects image quality is the contrast or dynamic range, which is determined by the modulation transfer function (MTF) using the intensity I

$$MTF = \frac{(\max I - \min I)}{(\max I + \min I)} \qquad (4.2)$$

The dynamic range for real scenes is $50,000 : 1$, while for the recording media is bound to around $300 : 1$. Note that contrast also refers to the perceived contrast of a scene, which may be different from the measured dynamic range. Contrast is determined locally, so sharp (incised) edges, e.g., Ming porcelain, would increase the overall contrast but not the dynamic range. A transition is now under way to high(er) dynamic range (HDR) imaging. The quality of the pixels rather than their sheer number will be the hallmark for HDR. More details in the shadows and/or highlights become available so outdoor illumination that adversely affects face recognition is handled better. HDR cameras are expected to accommodate a much wider range of lighting conditions.

Digital and analog camcorders are for video what digital cameras or digicams are for still photography. They are made up of a lightweight, hand-held CCD TV camera, a shrunk VCR for recording, and a viewfinder, possibly LCD, for preview. Better camcorders have lower (illumination) lux ratings for handling low-light environments. Digital camcorders also include an analog-to-digital converter that takes the analog information the camera gathers, and translates it to bytes of digital data rather than analog magnetic patterns. Digital information, stored on a digital medium, e.g., tape, hard disk, DVD, or flash memory cards, doesn't fade with continuous use, and renders itself to copying, editing, and straightforward manipulation. As an example, Digital8 camcorders using standard and thus less expensive Hi-8mm tapes, can hold up to 60 minutes of footage. Digital8 camcorders interface to PCs to transfer the video recorded for editing or Internet use. Similar technologies can be used for wireless and mobile communication. Advanced digital signal processing (DSP) married to digital sensing can enhance image quality preempting the need for further digital processing.

4.2 Standards

The standards refer to the image contents and their quality. They have to be agreed upon and enforced at enrollment or screening time to facilitate face recognition and to improve performance. The standards are more about contents and quality rather than the specific means to achieve them. Sensing is, however, directly involved as it affects both contents and quality. Enrollment is direct, when the subject and the image acquisition operator are physically co-located, or it takes place on line via remote access. Enrollment is deemed successful when the biometric data is complete, e.g., all the major facial landmarks and contours are included, and the image quality is satisfactory. If the data is acquired on line one needs also to thwart deception and check for aliveness (see Sect. 10.3). The standards include framing and photometry, e.g., proper face posture, resolution, contrast and focus, scanning and/or digital conversion, formatting and storage, and interoperability. The challenge for reliable face recognition is to match biometrics that meet the standards with images degraded due to denial and deception (see Ch. 10).

INCITS (The International Committee for Information Technology Standards), which is the ANSI recognized STO (Standards Development Organization) for information technology within USA, and ISO (Int. Standards Organization), through its IEC (Int. Electrotechnical Commission) and the Joint Technical Committee (JTC) subcommittee 37 on Biometrics, have issued drafts for (still evolving) standards that are closely related in design and implementation. ISO/IEC 19794-5-FDIS JTC 1/SC 37 and M1/04-0041 (ANSI) INCITS (385) (Griffin, 2004; 2005) are representative documents that are referred to by the International Civil Aviation Organization (ICAO) regarding the biometric deployment of Machine Readable Travel Documents (MRTD). The scope for ISO is "to develop an image-based interchange for face recognition algorithms and human examination. The header of the format will contain generic attributes of the image, the color characteristics of the image (when available), the eye positions and other significant landmarks of the face required for automatic recognition when available. The data will be gray scale or color face image. Both one-to-one and one-to-many applications will be supported." The purpose and justification for ISO/IEC 19794-5 JTC 1/SC 37 further indicate that the interchange of biometric data should support a large number of user identification and authentication applications. The proposal for the latest standard defines an interchange format for face images suitable to generate face signatures/templates. As there is no standard definition for the face template, the interchange format allows for cross-vendor compatibility and future algorithmic upgrades. The standard on image quality for face recognition will

- Allow interoperability among vendors based on a small data record

- Support the proliferation of large-scale one-to-many face identification
- Allow for human visual identification of subjects

The M1 INCITS [1] standard [2] accepts either a full or a canonical/token image. The full image, e.g., the passport photo, is used for permanent storage, human examination and verification, as well as automatic/computerized face recognition. The face image should include the full head with all hair in most cases, as well as neck and shoulders. The canonical face image extracts and stores face information from the full image at half the resolution of a minimum sized full image. Features points are optional and if available are based on SC29/MPEG4. There are specific requirements that concern the (less than $+/-5$ degrees rotation in every roll, pitch and yaw direction) pose, (neutral) expression, (plain and diffuse) lighting, and no shadows.

The geometry for the full frontal image requires a (image width to head width) ratio between $7:4$ and $2:1$, at least 180 pixels for the width of the head, or roughly 90 pixels from eye center to eye center, which is about 40% the resolution FRGC works with (see Sect. 13.4). The canonical or token image is 240 pixels wide by 320 pixels high. The eye positions in the canonical image are vertically and horizontally centered with an inter-eye distance of 60 pixels. This corresponds to horizontal and vertical displacements of 91 and 145 for the first eye and 150 and 145 for the second eye, if they are raster scanned from the top left corner of the image $(1,1)$ at half the resolution used for the minimum sized full image. The canonical image is obtained via an affine transformation. First rotate to align the eyes, then scale the image to keep a distance of 60 pixels between the eyes, translate and crop the image to properly position the head, and pad the image borders with black pixels if needed. The (tri-stimulus) color space is 24-bit RGB or YUV422. The latter color space takes advantage of the fact that human perception is more sensitive to luminance or brightness (Y) than to the two color channels (U and V). Data compression takes advantage of this and sub-samples the color components by a factor of two, using the ratio $4:2:2$. (PCA analysis also reveals that most of the RGB energy can be represented in a lower two dimensional space.) An alternative standard proposed for color over the internet that is also suitable for digital cameras is sRGB [3], which is derived from the standard 1931 CIE XYZ colometric space with reference to some viewing environment. Last but not least, red eyes are not acceptable.

Some of the attributes specified by the (evolving) M1 INCITS standard include head centering, a frontal face that is full and occupies 70% to 80% of the vertical length of the image, and width to height ratio that ranges between $1:1.25$ and $1:1.33$ (to conform with the $1:1.28$ ratio used in passport photos). The focal length, with a subject 1.5 to 2.5 meter from the camera, should be between 90 mm and 130 mm when using 35 mm photography. The f-stop should be set at two (or more) f-stops below the maximum aperture opening when possible to obtain enough depth of field. The background is expected to be uniform, neither overexposed nor underexposed, and with no shadows behind the face image, while lighting should be equally distributed on each side of the face and from top to bottom. The lighting should produce a natural looking color face image with flesh tones expected for indoor incandescent lighting environments. Note that reflective halogen lighting can maximize ambient light and minimize glare and hot spots. Clear glasses (frames not too heavy and no dark tint) are required so the eye pupils and irises are clearly visible. There should be no lighting artifacts on eyeglasses. The need for high quality photos requires much dedication, effort, and time, from well trained biometrics personnel.

The standards cover also compression and usually include either JPEG or JPEG 2000 (see Sect. 4.3). The best compromise between size and quality is using a Region of Interest (ROI) with a face region compression ratio there of $20:1$ to $24:1$. The standards affect mass screening in terms of efficiency and accuracy. Some of the strict

---

[1] http://www.incits.org/tc_home/m1htm/docs/M1040041.pdf
[2] http://fingerprint.nist.gov/standard/Workshop1/presentations/Griffin-Face-Std-M1.pdf
[3] http://www.w3.org/Graphics/Color/sRGB

standards on data collection can be relaxed if image preprocessing and computer vision techniques, rather than human personnel, are used to enforce them or to adjust the image quality. Digital image file type formats, complementary to the standards used for compression, affect storage, viewing, and subsequent "dark room" like processing. They affect both processing, access and viewing, possibly over the internet. Examples of file types include (unprocessed) RAW, JPG, GIF, and TIFF. The file types can either use lossy or lossless compression. Similar to RAW, Tagged Image File Format (TIFF) is uncompressed and takes about twice as much space as RAW does. It is lossless and provides better image quality but at the price of huge file size. It is useful as a (master) storage medium for editing and reuse. JPG is the format of choice and achieves impressive image quality even at high JPEG compression rates. GIF yields small sized files. It can be the choice made when the number of colors is relatively small and the digital image contains large areas of relatively flat color.

4.3 Data Compression

Image compression affects image quality, matching, and storage. Most important regarding face recognition is (i) to assess the extent to which different compression methods affect performance, and (ii) to determine at what compression rates performance starts to deteriorate in a significant fashion. Compression can be lossless when all the details are retained, or lossy, when some details are discarded. Lossy compression can be a hindrance to both human and computer analysis. Note that some data compression, even when lossy, might actually increase the signal-to-noise (snr) ratio and thus enhance performance (compared against using uncompressed data). Data compression, however, eventually starts to decrease the effective number of degrees of freedom available, and affects the uniqueness of the biometric signature. The compression standards for continuous tone images are JPEG and JPEG2000. Face recognition can use compressed or decompressed faces. The tradeoff is between expediency and fidelity to original detail.

JPEG (Joint Picture Expert Group) decorrelates image contents in order to eliminate redundancy and achieve compression. It is modeled after the DCT (discrete cosine transform) and it samples non-overlapping 8×8 image blocks. The DCT coefficients are quantized and coded using Huffman entropy encoder. Artifacts include blurring and blocking. Compression works hand in hand with feature extraction when the features extracted are the first 15 DCT (frequency) coefficients $(u + v = 4)$ of the face image intensity I, where $I = f(x, y)$ (Eickeler et al., 2000)

$$C(u, v) = \alpha(u)\alpha(v) \sum \sum f(x, y) \cos \left[\frac{(2x + 1)u\pi}{16} \right] \left[\frac{(2y + 1)v\pi}{16} \right] \quad (4.3)$$

The features extracted are then fed to a pseudo 2D HMM (Hidden Markov Model) for face recognition. Lossless JPEG works on $4 - 12$ bit image components and achieves compression rates between $2 : 1$ and $10 : 1$. Similar concepts can be employed for video (and audio) stream compression and analysis using Motion Picture Expert Group (MPEG) standards, e.g., MPEG1, MPEG2, MPEG4, MPEG7, and MPEG21. They span a range of compression, authoring, and delivery methods [4] for multimedia. MPEG2, the common standard for digital video transmission, needs about 6Mbps bandwidth. MPEG4 is the standard used for synchronizing different kind of media objects and supports small devices like cell phones and PDA. MPEG7 is about metadata, indexing and search, rather than a video or audio coding and delivery scheme.

JPEG2000 is a new compression standard that supports both lossy and lossless compression for continuous tone, bi-level, gray-scale, and color digital images. It provides for high flexibility in terms of progressive transmission by resolution, quality,

---

[4] http://stream.uen.org/medsol/digvid/html/2B_mediaarchmpeg1.html

color, and spatial locality or region of interest (ROI) features. The wavelet/trellis coded quantization (WTCQ), the reference used for JPEG2000, is related to the discrete wavelet transform (DWT) (see Sect. 7.2) and is similar to the wavelet scalar quantization (WSQ) used for fingerprint biometrics. Multiple decompositions are available, e.g., dyadic and packet, and difference images, i.e., residuals, support lossless compression. JPEG2000 provides for lossless compression rates up to 200 : 1 and is highly controllable in terms of the compression features used.

JPEG and JPEG2000 provide also lossy compression, which exploits the limitations of human perception. The original and compressed face images are no longer the same but the eye does not perceive the distortions taking place. As the eye perceives small color changes less accurately than small changes in brightness, color is compressed more than brightness so its resolution is lower than that for brightness. Some distortions are, however, perceived as artifacts. Examples of artifacts include blocking, color washout due to chroma sub-sampling, and blurring due to ringing. Lossy compression affects face recognition disregarding if artifacts are present or not. This is discussed next.

A recent analysis on how data compression affects face recognition has been carried out by Terry Hartman from Passports Australia, using 1,000 matching pairs (originals and renewals) of real passports (Griffin, 2004). The passports photos were scanned using 300 dpi resolution according to the ISO standards for image quality. The average size for full images was 71 KB. The normalized (correct match probability rank one statistic) match rate (compared to uncompressed images) starts to deteriorate (by more than 1% − 2%) for JPEG2000 around 20KB (compared to uncompressed data). Performance starts to degrade quickly (compared to uncompressed images) below a compressed file size of 10K.

The same analysis using now cropped (chin-to-crown and ear-to-ear) and canonical images has revealed that performance degrades quickly below a compressed file size of 6KB. Last but not least gray scale compression does not yield a significant improvement when compared with color compression. Maximum compression and file sizes for JPEG/JPEG2000 were also provided. The findings indicate that the compression that yields minimal degradation in performance is:

- For full images, color or grey scale, compression no lower than 11K on average, with JPEG or JPEG2000
- For canonical images, color or grey scale, compression no lower than 6K on average, with JPEG or JPEG2000.
- Canonical images performed relatively better than cropped images, which were extracted as chin-to-crown and ear-to-ear.

Hartman's findings confirmed the expectation that JPEG2000 performs better than JPEG. In addition, JPEG 2000 also offers the richest set of features [against the evaluated standards, namely JPEG, JPEG-LS, MPEG-4 Visual Texture Coding (VTC) and Portable Network Graphics (PNG)]. It is best at lossy compression as it provides superior rate-distortion performance (Santa-Cruz and Ebrahimi, 2000). The canonical face image could be further compressed using the region of interests (ROI) feature of JPEG2000 when the eye alignment is known.

Fractals (Mandelbrot, 1982) are self-similar shapes under magnification and serve for both data compression and feature extraction. The geometry of fractals can be effectively used for both face compression and feature extraction. The Hurst exponent H, related to the space dimension T and the fractal dimension FD, provides a measure of the roughness or irregularities of a surface. (Lacunarity, another useful fractal induced feature, measures how data fills the space compared to the fractal dimension that measures how much space is filled. Lacunarity is small when the texture is fine and large when the texture is coarse.) For 1D signals, when $T = 1$, one obtains H from

$$FD = T + 1 - H = 2 - H \qquad (4.4)$$

The roughness of the surface is connected to the power spectrum and wavelet spectral density. The connection to the power spectrum in 1D is

$$\text{power spectrum} \propto \frac{1}{\omega^\beta} \quad \text{where} \quad \beta = 2H + 1 \qquad (4.5)$$

A precursor to face recognition is the detection and extraction of facial features that are important for face detection, e.g., the eyes and the nose. The eventual extraction of facial features is problematic because it involves image segmentation when human faces are usually mixed and even occluded by clutter or background noise. There are bottom-up and top-down approaches for feature extraction. Bottom-up approaches examine individual pixels and attempt to assemble them into patches from which the features can be then extracted and described. Top-down approaches, on the other hand, examine different windows within an image looking for facial features. While top-down approaches are generally more reliable than bottom-up methods, they are also more expensive computationally. One method for reducing the computational expense of top-down approaches is to look for regions of interest, i.e., areas where useful facial features are most likely to be found. Of course, these regions must be easy to find computationally, otherwise little has been gained. What one needs are a set of attributes that are inexpensive to calculate and the means to determine if a particular set of attribute-value pairs corresponds to a region of interest. The approach that we motivate and describe below for such purposes is called Quad-Q-learning. Characteristic of the control interplay between exploration and exploitation, Quad-Q-learning has been successfully applied to the fractal image compression problem (Clausen and Wechsler, 2000a) and has earned to Clausen and Wechsler in 2004 the US patent 6,775,415 B1. Experimental evidence has shown that at high compression levels, the quality of this fractal image compression approach is superior to JPEG; and that it reduces significantly the compression time compared to other fractal image compression approaches. In addition, Quad-Q-learning provides a novel approach to the problem of reliable face recognition. The compression code produced at enrollment can be compared against the code generated during testing for identification and authentication. The local aspects of the codes produced should be particularly suited to deal with occlusion and disguise, on one side, and pose or temporal change, on the other side.

The purpose of Quad-Q-learning is to divide large intractable problems into smaller, independent problems that can be more readily solved, while minimizing the impact of sub-optimization. Quad-Q-learning, which is an outgrowth of Q-learning (Sutton and Barto, 1998), learns to make a decision to either break-up a large problem into smaller more easily solvable problems, or to solve the larger problem and achieve a better solution. As with all fractal image compression algorithms, this invention compresses images by representing regions of a [face] image (called ranges) as transformed copies of other regions of a [face] image (domains). That is, it exploits the self-similarity of face images. Compression is achieved because the image regions themselves are not actually stored, just the transformations are. As it is advocated throughout this book, it is the change (trajectories) and transformations taking place, rather than merely still images, which characterize faces and are most suitable for reliable face recognition. Quad-Q-learning uses reinforcement learning to reduce computation time by learning to make choices about how to transform one face image sub-region to match another face image sub-region, and how to partition each face image region based upon local characteristics. The particular reinforcement learning algorithm proposed learns to make these choices by generalizing from computationally expensive calculations performed on a small subset of face image regions. Quad-Q-learning finds good domain to range block matches by combining the concept of lean domain pools with the concept of block classification. A lean domain pool is a small subset of all possible domains where each domain is very likely to be transformable so as to match with other regions (ranges) of the image. The use of lean domain pools reduces the search time required to find good domain to range matches. Block classification further reduces search time by classifying range and domain blocks and then only attempting to match domains to ranges that are in the same class. Some of the details involved are described next.

Quad-Q-learning has to identify regions of an image where a facial feature is likely to be found, and by so doing, identifies also regions where that feature is not likely to be found. Towards that end a quad-tree is used to partition an image into regions (see Fig. 4.1). In a quad-tree, an image is partitioned into quadrants. Each quadrant may in turn be further partitioned, thus forming a quad-tree. Each block of a quad-tree can be labeled so as to uniquely identify the block within the image. The Quad-Q-learning method operates in three stages. In the first, it learns to correlate attributes of a region with a decision to 1) mark the region as uninteresting, 2) mark the region as interesting, or 3) further partition the image. This first stage corresponds to exploration. During exploration, Quad-Q-learning learns to generalize from a few faces to any face. During this stage, a feature detector indicates whether or not the feature searched for is in the block, or the likelihood that the feature is found in the block.

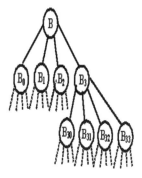
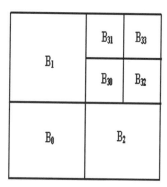

Fig. 4.1. Quad-Tree.

In the second stage the training method partitions the image into a quad-tree, marking the interesting image blocks. The method proceeds by calculating the attributes of a quad-tree block and, using the results of learning, makes one of the decisions described above. Finally, in the third stage, a feature detector looks for a particular facial feature within the blocks marked as interesting. For the third stage, one has to hypothesize a highly reliable algorithm that indicates the existence or absence of a particular facial feature, and if found, to mark its location. This feature detector is usually computationally expensive. However, since the learning method has identified a limited set of blocks in the image, less computation is now required. Note that the feature detector used during stage one is not necessarily the same feature detector used during the third stage. The justification for this is that during learning one has to identify blocks that are likely to have any interesting feature, while during the third stage, one looks for particular features and their locations. The second and third stages are referred together as exploitation.

The overall objective of Quad-Q-learning is to learn an optimal policy function, denoted as π that maps local attributes of an image block to a particular decision from a set $\mathbf{D}$. Once the policy function has been learned, it can make rapid decisions based upon local block attributes on how to partition an image and label each block. Also assumed is the existence of a vector $\mathbf{a} \in \mathbf{A}$ where $\mathbf{A}$ is a finite set that characterizes a block, and a function that maps a region of an image $\mathbf{B}$ into $\mathbf{a} \in \mathbf{A}$. The policy function π maps $\mathbf{a}$ to $d \in \mathbf{D}$. Quad-Q-learning has access to a utility function $Q(\mathbf{a}, d)$,

$\mathbf{a} \in \mathbf{A}$ and $d \in \mathbf{D}$, that returns the utility of decision d, given attribute $\mathbf{a}$. Finally $\pi(\mathbf{a}) = \arg\max Q(\mathbf{a}, d)$ over $d \in \mathbf{D}$.

Before fully characterizing Q, we introduce the reward concept. The reward captures the trade-off between computation time for processing a block and the likelihood of finding a high quality feature within the block. If one excludes a region from being searched for facial features, the computation time is reduced. However, by not processing a block, there is also the chance that a feature of interest will be missed. The larger a block, the larger the computation time required. So, the computational penalty of processing a block is a function of the block size. The likelihood of finding a high quality feature in a block is related to the attribute $\mathbf{a}$ of the block. Let P be a function that maps $S(\mathbf{B})$, the size of block $\mathbf{B}$, into the computational penalty for processing block $\mathbf{B}$. Let G be a random variable that represents the quality (goodness, likelihood) of a feature being found by the stage one feature detector in a block with attribute $\mathbf{a}$. The reward R obtained for labeling block $\mathbf{B}$ as uninteresting is $R = P(S(\mathbf{B})) - \lambda \cdot G(\mathbf{a})$, where λ characterizes the tradeoff between computational cost and the importance of finding a high quality feature. Note that if the reward is negative, then one should prefer labeling the block as interesting. For simplicity of notation, assume that vector $\mathbf{a}$ includes $S(\mathbf{B})$ as one of its features, and write the random variable $R(A(\mathbf{B}), P(S(\mathbf{B})), d)$ as $R(\mathbf{a}, d)$. The reward for a split decision requires that one looks at the expected reward for each of the four blocks that result from splitting block $\mathbf{B}$, assuming that the optimal policy is followed for each of these blocks. Given a policy π, define Q^π as follows:

$$Q^\pi(\mathbf{a}, d) = \begin{cases} E[R(\mathbf{a}, d)] & \text{if } d \text{ is a no split decision} \\ 4\sum_{\mathbf{b} \in A} E[R_\pi(\mathbf{b})]P_{\mathbf{a},\mathbf{b}} & \text{if } d \text{ is a split action} \end{cases} \quad (4.6)$$

In the above summation, $P_{\mathbf{a},\mathbf{b}}$ is the probability that a block with attribute $\mathbf{b}$ results from splitting a block with attribute $\mathbf{a}$. Also, $R_\pi(\mathbf{B})$ is the total sum of rewards for a block $\mathbf{B}$ given that the policy π is pursued. Define now the optimal policy π^* such that for every $\mathbf{a} \in \mathbf{A}$, $d \in \mathbf{D}$, and policy π, $Q \geq Q^\pi$ where Q stands for the function derived from the optimal policy π^*. To calculate Q an iterative procedure that can be proven to converge to the optimal Q is used. That is, calculate a series Q_n that converges to Q as $n \to \infty$. Start with an arbitrary Q_0 and find Q_n after n iterations of

$$Q_{n+1}(\mathbf{a}, d) = \begin{cases} (1 - \alpha_n)Q_n(\mathbf{a}, d) + \alpha_n r_n(\mathbf{a}, d) & \text{if } d \text{ is a no split decision} \\ \\ (1 - \alpha_n)Q_n(\mathbf{a}, d) \\ + \alpha_n(\max_{d_0} Q_n(\mathbf{a_0}, d_0)) \\ + \max_{d_1} Q_n(\mathbf{a_1}, d_1) \\ + \max_{d_2} Q_n(\mathbf{a_2}, d_2) \\ + \max_{d_3} Q_n(\mathbf{a_3}, d_3)) & \text{if } d \text{ is a split action} \end{cases}$$

$$(4.7)$$

In the above equation, α_n is a learning rate such that $\sum \alpha_n^2 < \infty$ and $\sum_{k=0}^n \alpha_k \to \infty$ as $n \to \infty$. The $r_n(\mathbf{a}, d)$ are instances of the random variable $R(\mathbf{a}, d)$ describe above. The indices $\mathbf{a_0}, \mathbf{a_1}, \mathbf{a_2}$, and $\mathbf{a_3}$ are the attribute values of the four blocks that result when the block with attribute value $\mathbf{a}$ is split. Finally, d_i corresponds to a decision about the block with attribute vector $\mathbf{a_i}$ that would result from splitting the block with attribute vector $\mathbf{a}$.

Quad-Q-learning, characteristic of reinforcement learning in general, and Q-learning, in particular, is suitable for solving coordination problems that involve delayed rewards. Here the coordination problem is that of finding the best facial features at minimal cost. Similar to control, exploration and exploitation compete for attention. Quad-Q-learning implements an *off* policy using a quad type of (split) exploration. It indirectly learns an optimal policy π^* by directly learning the value of a state-action pair from exploring and interacting with the environment. The (strategy) control policies π that are found generate then feasible and optimal actions. Fig. 4.2 shows the partitioning for the *Lena* face image that Quad-Q-learning yields. The block attribute vector **a**, consists of variance and block size. The stage one feature detector looks for (fractal) self-similarity. That is, it looks for blocks that can be easily expressed as a multiple of another block. Blocks that are easily represented as multiples of other blocks are considered uninteresting and left un-split. Only the smallest blocks are considered interesting. Note that the feature detector used for learning is not the same feature detector that would ultimately be used to identify facial features. In fact, multiple different feature detectors could be used in the final step, one for each facial feature of interest. Finally, one can observe from Fig. 4.2 that the grid resolution for features varies across the face. As expected more facial real estate is allocated to the eyes than to the cheeks. The same problem is revisited using Hebbian learning and Self-Organization Feature Maps (SOFM) in the context of caricatures (see Sect. 5.6).

Fig. 4.2. Regions of Interest for Lena Found Using Quad-Q-Learning.

5. Face Representation

Imagination abandoned by reason produces impossible monsters; united with her, she is the mother of arts and the source of their wonders (Los Caprichos # 43, Goya)

Human faces have to be represented before recognition can take place. The role played by representation is most important, and it probably exceeds that played by recognition, known also as classification or identification. Kant described the problem of how anything in the mind can be a "representation" of anything outside the mind as the most difficult riddle in philosophy. We can recognize transformed and dimensionally-reduced as well as original human faces in their "raw" form. Gerald Edelman (1987) has described innate neural architectures that generically implement what is referred to as neural Darwinism. The representations, learned through visual experience, are directly related to the context they operate within and the tasks they have to accomplish. The non-accidental properties of human faces are the particular dimensions the human face representations become tuned for. Such properties eventually induce the features extracted to represent human faces. The features correspond to coordinate axes and they define the face space.

The interplay between nature and nurture suggested by Edelman is straightforward. Neural Darwinism is discriminative and selective rather than descriptive and instructive. It corresponds to closed loop systems whose behavior is driven by performance. Features are proposed ("extracted") and kept ("selected") according to their utility in recognition. Similar viewpoints have also been formulated by Barlow (1989a,b), who argued that redundancy minimization and decorrelation, on one side, and adaptation, on the other side, are the basic functionalities for the visual cortex. This led to a growing interest in (a) statistical characterization of natural images (Ruderman, 1994); and (b) relationships between the statistical properties of natural images and the optimization of the visual system. Specific examples of such optimization criteria and their realization for representing human faces include decorrelation and minimization of the reconstruction error leading to principal component analysis (PCA); and maximization of information transmission (infomax) leading to independent component analysis (ICA).

5.1 The Face Space

The basis functions, similar in concept to receptive field (RF) profiles, are the dimensions that define the face space. The raw face data is projected on the basis functions to yield the features needed for initial face representation. Such representations, subject to further transformations, are then used for identification and/or authentication. The face space, learned and fixed ahead of time, encodes human faces during enrollment and testing (see Fig. 1.2). This eliminates the need to recompute the face basis and provides for consistent operation and meaningful evaluations. The face space concept is motivated by the way natural images are represented. In particular, the coding of natural scenes has been shown to take advantage of intrinsic image statistics leading to the derivation of a "universal" basis (Hancock et al., 1992; Olshausen and Field, 1996). The universal basis functions closely approximated the receptive fields of simple cells in the mammalian primary visual cortex. The profiles for the receptive fields found resembled derivative-of-Gaussian (DOG) functions, which are spatially localized, oriented, and band-pass like filters (see Sect. 5.2). Olshausen and Field (1996) derived such receptive fields based on a criterion of sparseness, while Bell and Sejnowski (1995) used an independence criterion to derive qualitatively similar results. Barlow et al. (1989) has earlier argued that such receptive fields might arise from unsupervised learning, subject to redundancy reduction or minimum-entropy encoding.

Sparse codes fit well with psychological and physiological evidence for parts-based representations, and with computational theories of recognition by parts. Lee and Seung (1999) have described a non-negative matrix factorization (NMF) algorithm able to learn the parts of human faces. They have further argued that vector quantization (VQ), similar to self-organization feature maps (SOFM) (see Sect. 5.6), can discover a basis consisting of prototypes, each of which is a whole face, and that eigenfaces, which are the basis images for PCA might resemble distorted versions of the whole face. The NMF basis, however, is radically different: its coordinate images are localized features that correspond better with intuitive notions of facial parts. Li et al. (2001) impose further locality constraints on NMF leading to an improved Local Non-Negative Matrix Factorization (LNMF) method. Locality, while useful for recognition-by-parts, does not necessarily make the features found by LNMF discriminant enough for face recognition.

The search to find an adequate natural basis for faces can draw from several different but related disciplines, all of them attempting to achieve sparse functional approximation. The objectives for a face basis are two fold. The basis should be complete and low-dimensional, and allow the efficient derivation of suitable representations that can adequately express the contents of face images. The emphasis should be on being expressive and discriminative rather than merely generative and reconstructive. Expressiveness depends first and foremost on the availability of a coherent and representative dictionary of receptive fields or alternatively of computable kernels. Coherence means that most of the energy or face contents can be captured by as few elements ("atoms") as possible, leading to representations characterized by low-dimensionality. The face space could require functional composition, e.g., Fisherfaces using PCA and LDA (see Sect. 5.4), when the representational objectives include both low-dimensionality and discrimination ability.

Once the face basis has been derived, the faces subject to enrollment and/or testing are represented as multi-dimensional points using their projections along the axes that define the basis. A "universal" and frozen face basis, however, is lacking. In particular, the basis may be too general to account for the inherent variability found within large and diverse populations. If the patterns under consideration are human faces rather than natural images, several specific face spaces rather than a universal basis might be needed. Categorization indexes the population according to gender, ethnicity and age, and determines the appropriate face space that should be used (see Sect. 6.6). The face representations we hold for other people also appear to be not unique. After getting rid of my beard some 20 years ago, people I knew reacted in several ways when seeing me. Some didn't see any difference, some noted a difference but couldn't tell what it was, and some acquaintances would pass by without even recognizing me. Learning low-dimensional representations of visual patterns using prior knowledge has been discussed by Edelman (1999), who claims that "perceptual tasks such as similarity judgment tend to be performed on a low-dimensional representation of the sensory data. Low dimensionality is especially important for learning, as the number of examples required for attaining a given level of performance grows exponentially with the dimensionality of the underlying representation space." This shows that both adaptive selection and dimensionality reduction are intrinsically connected in deriving the face ("feature") space.

The face space paradigm can be now visualized in terms of a specific basis that consists of images that are learned or evolved, e.g., eigenfaces (see Figs. 5.1 and 5.4).

The dimension of the face space is usually ad-hoc truncated to the extent that the resulting sub-space is still expressive and discriminative enough. The images that define the basis can bear resemblance to human faces or not. Any face to be enrolled is projected on the face space and a signature of the projection coefficients **w** is assembled to serve as a template for future identification and authentication. Face recognition can be then achieved using nearest neighbor classification or more complex methods might be called for (see Sect. 6.2).

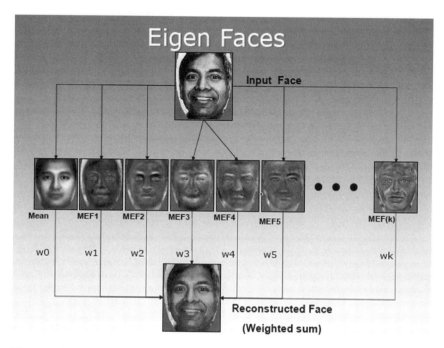

Fig. 5.1. Eigenfaces (courtesy of Anil Jain).

The face space F is a set where a metric or distance/norm function d between elements of the set has been defined. Each face $f \in F$ is represented by its coordinates along the basis functions defining the face space. The metric is non-negative, symmetric and obeys the triangle inequality. Both the geometry and layout for the face space F, on one side, and relative face recognition performance, on the other side, depend on the similarity and metric chosen. Similarity affects the relative density of the face space. Face spaces that are rather dense are more difficult to use for discrimination compared to uniform or sparse face spaces.

The major face space candidates competing for attention in the neuropsychological and computational communities are holistic and parts-based, respectively. The holistic space is global. It extracts and integrates information from the whole (up-right) face. Subsequent to deriving the holistic face space, one wants to reduce its dimensionality. The parts-based space gathers information using local features, which are then combined into (geometric) constellations. The basic difference between the holistic and parts-based face spaces is that the first integrates information implicitly, while the latter integrates information in an explicit fashion. There is evidence that each approach contributes to face recognition and accounts for covert changes in appearance. McKone et al. (2001) note that "anecdotally, it is clear that changes in hairstyle or the shaving off of a beard can lead to initial failures to identify even highly familiar people." Such findings have major implications for face recognition, in general, and coping with occlusion and disguise, in particular. McKone et al. (2001) further argue that overall "local features provide insufficient information to ensure the accurate discrimination of identity and, thus, configural processing of the face is also necessary." Local features and/or parts, however, can accommodate missing or disguised parts because their inputs are narrowly defined and are thus not perturbed by changes taking place elsewhere.

Evidence for the holistic face space comes from "the detrimental effects of manipulations that disrupt the holistic structure of the face but leave individual features intact" (McKone et al., 2001), e.g., scrambling of the face, misaligning the lower and upper halves of the face, and inverted faces. Moscovitch et al. (1997) argue that only a vertical half is necessary to activate configural face processing (see Sect. 10.5 for half face recognition using ensembles of radial basis functions) and that holistic processing has access to enough information to fill in for missing parts (see Sect. 10.6 for occlusion and disguise using adaptive correlation filters). McKone et al. (2001) have shown that holistic processing can operate in isolation from (local) feature-based identification. In particular, they have shown that holistic processing is called for during fine discrimination tasks (on upright but not inverted faces) when the local cues for identity are unreliable, e.g., faces lacking distinguishable features, heavy (structural) noise due to illumination, mismatch of orientation between gallery and probe, expression, and makeup. The holistic and parts-based/constellation face recognition approaches appear thus to be complementary to each other.

5.2 Scale Space

Scale space representation and analysis extend from the apparent but simple idea, which can be easily tested, that different characteristics of an image reveal themselves at different levels of resolution (see Fig. 1.3). Scale space can be traced to the heat equation. Assume the image intensity $f(x, y)$ to be a function of spatial variables x and y. (Scale space can be extended for the multidimensional case as well.) The heat equation seeks a function $u(x, y, t)$ such that after t units of time, the initial function $f(x, y)$ will diffuse to $u(x, y, t)$. Formally, one seeks to solve

$$\frac{\partial u}{\partial t} = \nabla^2 u \tag{5.1}$$

$$u(x, y, 0) = f(x, y) \tag{5.2}$$

where ∇^2 is the Laplacian operator $\nabla^2 f \cong \left(\frac{\partial^2}{\partial x^2}\right) f + \left(\frac{\partial^2}{\partial x^2}\right) f$. The solution to the heat equation is derived by blurring ("filtering") $f(x, y)$ with Gaussians G of increasing widths. Blurring, is equivalent to convolution and yields

$$u(x, y, t) = \int \int G(x', y', t) f(x - x', y - y') dx' dy' = G(x, y, t) \otimes f(x, y) \tag{5.3}$$

The Gaussian itself is a solution for the heat equation

$$\frac{\partial G}{\partial t} = \nabla^2 G = \lim_{\alpha \to 0} \frac{[G(x, y, t + \alpha) - G(x, y, t)]}{\alpha} \tag{5.4}$$

The difference of Gaussians (DOG) approximates the $\nabla^2 G$ operator and can derive a scale space representation. The filtered images making up the scale space representation $\hat{f}(x, y, t)$ are found using several alternative formulations

$$\begin{aligned} \hat{f}(x, y, t) &= \nabla^2 G \otimes f \\ &= G \otimes \nabla^2 f \\ &= \nabla^2 (G \otimes f) \end{aligned} \tag{5.5}$$

The scale space can be thus derived by either (i) filtering the original face image with the Laplacian of a Gaussian (or alternatively with DOG); (ii) convolving the Laplacian of the original face image with Gaussians of increasing widths; or (iii) taking the Laplacian of the face images resulting from convolving the original face image with Gaussians of increasing widths. Recall that the Fourier transform of a Gaussian is a Gaussian too but of different amplitude and width. If a face image is blurred with a Gaussian (like in DOG) then the Gaussian acts like a transfer function and stands for a band-limiting (of some width) operator in the frequency domain. The scale space is thus a multi-channel representation in the frequency domain where a channel corresponds to some specific bandwidth.

Frequency analysis underlies much of the early stages of the human visual system. There is strong evidence that the processes responsible early on are both compact and local in nature. The receptive fields or filter profiles that facilitate such processing can be adequately described using Gabor functions that enjoy optimal conjoint localization in the spatial and spatial frequency domains. Locality means that frequency now depends on location and that events separated in space and/or time can be uniquely characterized and identified from their spectral signatures. This is quite different from the Fourier transform where such events are confounded in the spectral domain. Gabor (1946) has developed a discrete joint time-frequency signal representation. It is referred to as the information diagram and it is derived by computing the coefficients or logons of a signal expansion in terms of time shifted and frequency modulated Gaussian functions. The logons, each of them occupying a rectangular cell in the time frequency plane, provide a discrete quantum of information about the signal. The search is for a compact signal decomposition that is highly concentrated in terms of the number of cells used. The cells provide the equivalent of a coherent and expressive dictionary to rewrite the raw face images using some of the conjoint scale space available.

The Gabor (kernel, filter) wavelets appear to be a good approximation to the filter profiles encountered experimentally in cortical neurons (Daugman, 1980; Pollen and Ronner, 1981; Daugman, 1990) (see also Sect. 7.2 for wavelet packets). They capture the corresponding properties of spatial localization, orientation and spatial frequency selectivity, and quadratic phase relationship. The Gabor filters t are sinusoidal s at some particular frequency modulated by a Gaussian envelope G

$$t(x,y) = s(x,y) \cdot G(x,y) = \exp[-j2\pi(u_0 x + v_0 y)] \cdot \frac{1}{\sqrt{2\pi\sigma^2}} \exp\left[\frac{x^2}{\sigma_x^2} + \frac{y^2}{\sigma_y^2}\right] \quad (5.6)$$

The frequency response or transfer function T for the above Gabor filter is

$$\begin{aligned} T(u,v) &= G(u - u_0, v - v_0) \\ &= 2\pi\sigma_x\sigma_y\{\exp(-2\pi^2[(u - u_0)^2\sigma_x^2 + (v - v_0)^2\sigma_y^2])\} \\ &= \frac{1}{2\pi\sigma_u\sigma_v} \exp\left(-\frac{1}{2}\left[\frac{(u - u_0)^2}{\sigma_u^2} + \frac{(v - v_0)^2}{\sigma_v^2}\right]\right) \end{aligned} \quad (5.7)$$

The Gaussian, translated in frequency by (and centered at) (u_0, v_0), is at distance $(u_0^2 + v_0^2)^{-\frac{1}{2}}$ from the origin of the spectral (frequency) domain and its orientation is given by $\tan^{-1} = \frac{u_0}{v_0}$. Alternatively and in analogy to how the receptive fields of simple cells are modeled (Pollen and Ronner, 1981; Daugman, 1990), the Gabor kernel are defined as

$$\psi_j(\mathbf{z}) = \frac{k_j^2}{\sigma^2} \exp\left(-\frac{k_j^2}{2\sigma^2}z^2\right)\left(\exp(i\mathbf{k}_j\mathbf{z}) - \exp\left(-\frac{\sigma^2}{2}\right)\right) \quad (5.8)$$

where $\mathbf{z} = (x, y)$, $\mathbf{k}_j$ is the central frequency of the (wave vector) filter, $\exp(i\mathbf{k}_j\mathbf{z})$ is the complex-valued sinusoid, the Gaussian envelope is $\exp\left(-\frac{k_j^2}{2\sigma^2}x^2\right)$, $\exp\left(-\frac{\sigma^2}{2}\right)$ removes the DC component, and $\frac{k_j^2}{\sigma^2}$ compensates for the frequency-dependent decrease of the power spectrum in natural images (Field, 1987). The working definition for the Gabor filters $\Theta_{\mu,\nu}(\mathbf{z})$ (see below and Sect. 6.5 for their specific use in face recognition) is

$$\Theta_{\mu,\nu}(\mathbf{z}) = \frac{||k_{\mu,\nu}||^2}{\sigma^2} \exp\left(-\frac{||k_{\mu,\nu}||^2||\mathbf{z}||^2}{2\sigma^2}\right) \left(\exp(jk_{\mu,\nu}\mathbf{z}) - \exp\left(-\frac{\sigma^2}{2}\right)\right) \quad (5.9)$$

where μ and ν define the orientation and scale of the Gabor kernels, $\mathbf{z} = (x,y)$, the wave vector $k_{\mu,\nu}$ is defined as $k_{\mu,\nu} = k_\nu \cdot \exp(j\Phi_\mu)$, $k_\nu = \frac{k_{max}}{f^\nu}$, $\Phi_\mu = \frac{\pi\mu}{8}$, and f is the spacing factor between the kernels in the frequency domain (Lades et al., 1993). The Gabor kernels are self-similar since they can be generated from one filter, the mother wavelet, by scaling and rotation using the wave vector $k_{\mu,\nu}$. Each kernel is a product of a Gaussian envelope and a complex plane wave, with the first term in the last bracketed expression determining the oscillatory part of the kernel and the second term compensating for the DC value. The effect of the DC term is negligible when the parameter σ, which determines the ratio of the Gaussian window width to wavelength, attains a sufficiently high value. In most cases Gabor wavelets at five different scales, $\nu \in \{0, \cdots, 4\}$ and eight orientations $\mu \in \{0, \cdots, 7\}$ are used. Fig. 5.2 shows the real part of the Gabor kernels at five scales and eight orientations (Fig. 5.2a), the corresponding filter magnitudes using the parameters $\sigma = 2\pi$, $k_{max} = \frac{\pi}{2}$, and $f = \sqrt{2}$ are shown in Fig. 5.2b, while the magnitude for face images is shown in Fig. 5.2c. The kernels show strong characteristics of spatial locality and orientation selectivity, making them a suitable choice for feature extraction when the objective is to derive local and discriminative features for face recognition.

The power spectrum for the Fourier transform $F(\mathbf{w})$ consists of the magnitude $P(\mathbf{w})$ and the phase $\Psi(\mathbf{w})$ such that $P(\mathbf{w}) = |F(\mathbf{w})|$ and $\Psi(\mathbf{w}) = \arctan\left\{\frac{Im[F(\mathbf{w})]}{Re[F(\mathbf{w})]}\right\}$. The phase, related to internal structure, plays an important role in reconstruction and image characterization. The same holds true concerning the role of the phase for Gabor kernels. The Gabor real and imaginary parts are

$$Re(\Theta_{\mu,\nu}) = \frac{k_{\mu,\nu}^2}{\sigma^2} \exp\left(-\frac{k_{\mu,\nu}\mathbf{z}^2}{2\sigma^2}\right) \left[\cos(k_{\mu,\nu}\mathbf{z}) - \exp\left(-\frac{\sigma^2}{2}\right)\right] \quad (5.10)$$

$$Im(\Theta_{\mu,\nu}) = \frac{k_{\mu,\nu}^2}{\sigma^2} \exp\left(-\frac{k_{\mu,\nu}\mathbf{z}^2}{2\sigma^2}\right) \sin(k_{\mu,\nu}\mathbf{z}) \quad (5.11)$$

The corresponding magnitude and phase features are found from $\{[Re(\Theta_{\mu,\nu})]^2 + [Im(\Theta_{\mu,\nu})]^2\}^{\frac{1}{2}}$ and $\arctan \frac{Im(\Theta_{\mu,\nu})}{Re(\Theta_{\mu,\nu})}$, respectively.

The convolution of the face image with the Gabor kernels $\Theta_{\mu,\nu}(\mathbf{z})$ defines a set of local features $\mathbf{J}$ called jets, expressed in terms of magnitude $a(\mathbf{z})$ and phase as $J_i = a_i \cdot \exp(j\Phi_i)$. The magnitude varies slowly with position, while the phase $\phi_i(\mathbf{z})$ rotates with a rate set by the spatial frequency or the wave vector $k_{\mu,\nu}$ of the kernels. As a result of phase rotation, jets that are derived from face locations only a few pixels apart and stand for almost similar local features vary and lead to severe mismatch for faces carrying the same ID. The use of phase provides, however, two advantages for face recognition when properly controlled (Wiscott et al., 1997) "Firstly, phase information is required to discriminate between patterns with similar magnitudes, should they occur. Secondly, since phase varies so quickly with location, it provides a means for accurate jet localization in an image." This is particularly important for face registration and normalization, in general, and eye detection, in particular. The phase is also important to choose weak classifiers for face recognition in the later stages of AdaBoost (Zhang et al., 2004) (see Sects. 9.3 and 9.7 for weak classifiers and AdaBoost).

The Gabor filters, while optimal in terms of their conjoint ("simultaneous") localization in the space and frequency domains, have drawbacks. As the maximum bandwidth is limited to about one octave, one needs multiple Gabor filters to cover a wide spectrum. (The bandwidth of a band-pass filter is the ratio of the upper and

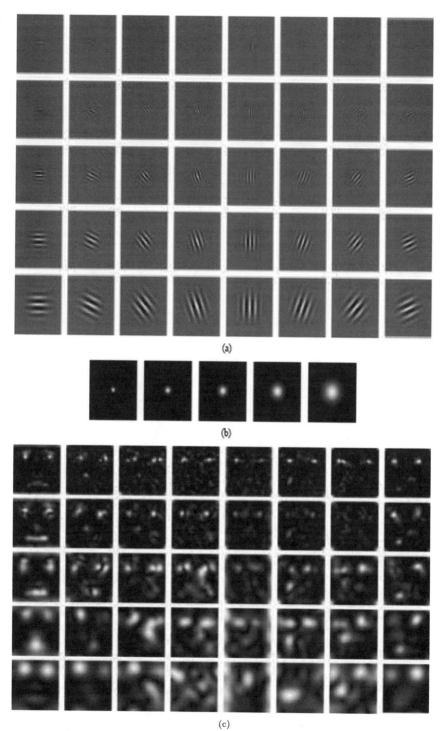

(a)

(b)

(c)

Fig. 5.2. Gabor Wavelets and Their Magnitude for Face Images (Reprinted from Liu and Wechsler, Independent Component Analysis of Gabor Features for Face Recognition, *IEEE Transactions on Neural Networks*, ©2003 IEEE).

lower cut-off frequencies using base 2 logarithms.) Furthermore, the Gabor filters over represent low frequencies at the expense of high frequencies where most of the face details show up. Such limitations can be addressed using the log-Gabor filters (Field, 1987), which can be modeled with arbitrary bandwidth and minimal spatial support. The log transformation, useful on its own and known to be part of cortical processing, expands the range, while for invariance to scale and rotation purposes it conformally maps the image domain (in polar coordinates) (see Sect. 5.3). Replace now the linear with the logarithmic frequency scale (Bigun and du Buf, 1994) and the transfer function (in the frequency domain) for the log-Gabor filters, when $\mathbf{w_0}$ is the filter's centre frequency, becomes Gaussian

$$G(\mathbf{w}) = \exp\left(\frac{-\log\left(\frac{\mathbf{w}}{\mathbf{w_0}}\right)^2}{2\log\left(\frac{k}{\mathbf{w_0}}\right)^2}\right) \tag{5.12}$$

The log-Gabor filters have no DC component and, similar to natural images, their transfer function $G(\mathbf{w})$ displays a long tail at the high frequency end or alternatively their amplitude spectrum falls like $\frac{1}{\mathbf{w}}$. In polar (radial, angular) coordinates (r, θ), the 2D transfer function for the log-Gabor filters (Bigun and du Buf, 1994) is

$$G(r, \theta) = G(r) \cdot G(\theta) = \exp\left(-\frac{\log\left(\frac{r}{r_0}\right)^2}{2\log\left(\frac{k}{r_0}\right)^2}\right) \cdot \exp\left(\frac{(\theta - \theta_0)^2}{2\sigma_\theta^2}\right) \tag{5.13}$$

where k and r_0 are the bandwidth and the center frequency of the filter, respectively, s_θ is a scale factor, and $\sigma_\theta = \frac{\Delta\theta}{s_\theta}$. Face recognition using masked log-polar PCA selection of log-Gabor magnitude features showed very good results on 1196 persons from FERET, 97% - 98% rank one recognition and 0.3% - 0.4% equal error rate (EER) (Perlibakas, 2006). Kovesi provides additional details on the characteristics and construction of log-Gabor filters [1]. Last but not least, the scale space is dense and requires sub-sampling. Dimensionality reduction (see Sect. 5.4) and/or feature selection methods (see Sect. 5.5) are the methods used to make the subsequent computation involved in face identification and authentication effective and efficient.

5.3 Invariance

The high degree of computational complexity in face recognition comes from the inherent variability in the appearance of human faces. The data varies but the human faces seem to preserve their identity. *Plus ça change plus c'est la même chose – The more things change, the more they stay the same.* Reliable biometric identification and authentication ultimately depend on the computational ability to capture invariants and respond to them appropriately. The sources for variability are due to changes in the geometry and illumination of the image formation process and temporal change. The geometric sources that include linear transformations in terms of shift, scale, and rotation are addressed here. Evidence accumulation via spatiotemporal processing to handle temporal variability is discussed in Ch. 7.

The multi scale concept discussed in the preceding section can be expanded to include geometric invariance as well. Towards that end, Lowe (2004) has proposed the Scale Invariant Feature Transform (SIFT) to find stable and oriented local features at different scales. It has been empirically found that SIFT is "invariant to image scale and rotation, and provides robust matching across a substantial range of affine distortion, change in 3D viewpoint, addition of noise, and change in illumination." The local SIFT descriptors, indexed by position and scale at points found interesting,

---

[1] http://www.csse.uwa.edu.au/pk/Research/MatlabFns/PhaseCongruency/ Docs/convexpl.html

e.g., local peaks or corners in the scale space, are filtered to preserve only those key points (of interest) that are invariant. A summary description that is compact and distinctive is subsequently derived. The SIFT derivation involves scale-space peak selection, key point localization, orientation assignment, and key point description. Peak selection takes place in the scale space using the difference of Gaussians (DOG). Stable key points are localized to sub-pixel accuracy and their dominant orientation θ is determined within the local patch centered at the key point. The same local patch, once normalized, i.e., rotated by θ and properly scaled, yields the final description based upon the image gradients surrounding the key point, in terms of magnitude and orientation. SIFT consists of two independent stages, the localization stage and most important, the description stage (Mikolajczyk and Schmid, 2003). Instead of using SIFT smoothed weighted histograms, Ke and Sukthankar (2004) showed that "PCA based descriptors are more distinctive, more robust to image deformations, and more compact than the standard SIFT (histogram) representation."

Formal and systematic invariance to scale and rotation can also be achieved using log-polar mappings that realize the equivalent of a retinotopic sampling grid (Schwartz, 1981; Takacs and Wechsler, 1998a). The grid can be used for both facial landmark localization and person identification and authentication. The local frequency plane must be covered as uniformly as possible. "When only a small number of frequency channels is employed, however, the Gaussian spectrum of filters results in an excessive overlap towards the (densely sampled) origin of the frequency plane, while the high frequencies are poorly covered. This is due to the fact that each Gaussian weights high as well as low frequencies in its support in a symmetric manner, whereas the decomposition itself is coarser at high frequencies" (Smeraldi and Bigun, 2002). To compensate for that, modified Gabor filters $G(\xi, \varphi)$ tuned to orientation φ_0 and angular frequency $\omega_0 = \exp(\xi_0)$ are defined as

$$G(\xi, \varphi) = A \exp\left(-\frac{(\xi - \xi_0)^2}{2\sigma_\xi^2}\right) \cdot \exp\left(-\frac{(\varphi - \varphi_0)^2}{2\sigma_\varphi^2}\right) \tag{5.14}$$

where A is a normalization constant. (ξ, φ) are the log-polar frequency coordinates such that eccentricity and angular orientation are measured along the x- and y-axes, respectively,

$$(\xi, \varphi) = \left(\log(|\mathbf{w}|), \arctan\left(\frac{w_y}{w_x}\right)\right) \tag{5.15}$$

Translations along φ and ξ represent now rotations and scale changes in the face domain. The log-polar (conformal) maps the (x, y) face domain into the (ξ, φ) domain. A complete bank of filters is designed by arranging a set of identical Gaussians in a rectangular lattice in the log-polar frequency plane. The log-polar transformation considers image domain points $\mathbf{z} = (x, y) = x + jy = (Re(\mathbf{z}), Im(\mathbf{z}))$, $z = r \cdot \exp(j\theta)$, $r = |\mathbf{z}| = (x^2 + y^2)^{0.5}$ and $\theta = \arg(\mathbf{z}) = \tan^{-1}\left(\frac{y}{x}\right)$. The conformal map, $\mathbf{w} = \ln(\mathbf{z}) = \ln[r \cdot \exp(j\theta)] = \ln(r) + j\theta$, decouples eccentricity from angular orientation. After the log-polar transformation, rotation and scale about the origin in the Cartesian domain become linear shifts in the $\theta(mod\ 2\pi)$ and $\ln(r)$ directions, respectively. Invariance to linear shifts (and thus implicit invariance to rotation and scale) can be now easily achieved from the shift invariance property for the magnitude of the Fourier transform $F(u, v)$

$$F(u, v) = \int_{-\infty}^{+\infty} \int_{-\infty}^{+\infty} f(x, y) \exp[-2\pi j(ua + vb)] dx dy \tag{5.16}$$

Shift by (a, b) for the face image function $f(x, y)$ yields $f_1 = f(x - a, y - b)$. The related Fourier transforms are $F_1(u, v) = \exp[-2\pi j(ua + vb)]F(u, v)$ such that $|F_1(u, v)| = |F(u, v)|$ and the magnitude thus stays invariant. Scale change by α when $f_1 = f(\alpha x, \alpha y)$ yields $F_1(u, v) = F(\frac{u}{\alpha}, \frac{v}{\alpha})$. Using polar coordinates, when the face is rotated by τ, one finds that $x = r \cdot \cos\theta, y = r \cdot \sin\theta, u = \rho \cdot \cos\varphi, v = \rho \cdot \sin\varphi$, and $F_1(u,v) = F(\rho, \varphi + \tau)$. Combine scale change by α and rotation by τ for the transformed face $f_1 = f(\alpha r, \varphi + \tau)$ and the corresponding Fourier transforms are now related as $F_1(u,v) = \frac{1}{\alpha} F(\frac{\rho}{\alpha}, \varphi + \tau)$. Translation, scale, and rotation invariant features are eventually obtained by eliminating the factor through normalization, letting $\lambda = \ln \rho$ to yield $F(\rho, \varphi)$, $F(e^\lambda, \varphi) = G(\lambda, \varphi)$, $F(\frac{\rho}{\alpha}, \varphi + \tau) = G(\lambda - \ln \alpha, \varphi + \tau)$, and observing that $G(\lambda - \ln \alpha, \varphi + \tau)$ is a translated version of $G(\lambda, \varphi)$ that is made invariant by taking its magnitude (Lai et al., 2001). A spectroface representation is suggested for invariant (to translation, scale, and on-plane rotation) face recognition. The low frequency sub band of the wavelet transform (WT), which is less sensitive to the variability induced by face expressions, is derived first and is subject to the Fast Fourier Transform (FFT), a polar coordinate transformation (with the origin centered at the centroid) is made, and finally $\lambda = \ln \rho$ followed by FFT yield the invariant spectroface.

The circular Fourier and radial Mellin transform (FMT) for $f(r, \theta)$ of order s and circular harmonic expansion order $m = 0, \pm 1, \pm 2, \cdots$, is an equivalent formal route to gain invariance to linear transformations (LT) (Sheng and Lejeune, 1991)

$$FMT_{s,m} = \int_{-\infty}^{\infty} \int_0^{2\pi} r^{s-1} f(r, \theta) \cdot \exp(-jm\theta) r \, dr \, d\theta \qquad (5.17)$$

When s is purely imaginary, i.e., $s = -jw$, FMT reduces to the 2D FT in log-polar coordinates ($\rho = \ln r, \theta$)

$$FMT_{s,m} = \int_{-\infty}^{\infty} \int_0^{2\pi} f(\rho, \theta) \cdot \exp(-jw\rho) \cdot \exp(-jm\theta) d\rho \, d\theta \qquad (5.18)$$

and its magnitude is invariant to linear transformations. When s is an integer, $s = 0, 1, 2$, the FMT is directly related to Hu (1962) invariant moments (Terrillon et al., 2000). Without loss of generality the origin of the polar coordinate system is located at the centroid.

5.4 Subspace Methods

The most popular subspace representation is **Principal Component Analysis (PCA)**, which is similar to the Karhunen-Loeve transform (KLT). The optimization objectives met by PCA are to decorrelate the dimensions of the original face images and to find linear projections that maximize the overall scatter. PCA assumes Gaussian data distributions. In the case of non-Gaussian data, PCA underestimates the likelihood for data distribution in its dense and sparse areas. Given a set of n faces $\mathbf{X}_i \in \mathbf{R}^N$, PCA seeks a linear transformation $\Phi^T : \mathbf{R}^N \to \mathbf{R}^M$, where Φ is an orthonormal matrix and ^{T} stands for the transpose. The total scatter or covariance matrix Σ with μ as the mean face image is

$$\Sigma = \sum_{i=1}^{n} (\mathbf{X_i} - \mu)(\mathbf{X_i} - \mu)^T \qquad (5.19)$$

The scatter for the PCA transformation is $\Phi^T \Sigma \Phi$ using the projection matrix Φ that maximizes the index $\hat{\Phi} = \arg\max_\Phi |\Phi^T \Sigma \Phi| = [\varphi_1, \varphi_2, \cdots, \varphi_M]$, where φ_i are eigenvectors (of the same size as the original faces), which correspond to the M largest eigenvalues λ_i (to capture a large degree of variance) that are derived by solving the eigenvalue problem $\Sigma \Phi = \Phi \Lambda$. The eigenvectors φ_i of Σ are referred to as principal components or eigenfaces (see Fig. 5.3) and the PCA transformed data is $\mathbf{Y} = \Phi^T \cdot \mathbf{X}$. It can be shown that for any choice of M, the PCA subspace spanned by the corresponding M eigenvectors yields the lowest L_2 reconstruction error. Note that the PCA face subspace should be learned ahead of time using faces that are different from those that will be enrolled (see Fig. 1.2). The optimality for PCA is limited to reconstruction rather than enhanced discrimination as it is the case with Linear Discriminant Analysis (LDA), which is discussed later on. The use of PCA for discrimination purposes, while not warranted, is still widespread. PCA is best suited for data compression and dimensionality reduction, i.e., $dim(\mathbf{Y}) = M < dim(\mathbf{X}) = N$. The main disadvantages for PCA include inability to (a) distinguish within and between class scatters; and (b) discriminate distributions separated not by mean-differences but by covariance-differences. The whitening transformation $\mathbf{V} = \Gamma \mathbf{Y}$ where $\Gamma = diag[\lambda_1^{0.5}, \cdots, \lambda_M^{0.5}]$ counteracts the fact that the MSE criterion, which underlies PCA, favors the low-order components. In addition, Γ increases the reachable space of solutions to include non orthogonal bases.

Computational details regarding PCA implementation are important and are discussed next. Prior to PCA, faces are raster scanned as 1D vectors and normalized such that their mean and variance become 0 and 1, respectively. (See J. Yang et al. (2004) for full fledged 2D PCA that preserves topography.) The average face is $\mathbf{X} = \frac{1}{n} \sum_{i=1}^{n} \mathbf{X}_i$ and the normalized faces become $\mathbf{U}_i = \frac{(\mathbf{X}_i - \mathbf{X})}{\sigma^2}$. The search is after orthonormal vectors φ_i to form a basis and span the face space. Towards that end one defines $\Sigma = \frac{1}{n} \sum_{i=1}^{n} \mathbf{U}_i \mathbf{U}_i^T = \mathbf{A}\mathbf{A}^T$ such that $\mathbf{A} = [\mathbf{U}_1, \cdots, \mathbf{U}_n]$. Note that the (raster 1D) vector dimension of Σ is $N^2 \times N^2$ making the problem intractable. When $n < N^2$ there are only $(n-1)$ rather than N^2 meaningful eigenvectors, the remaining ones being associated with zero eigenvalues. Consider solving instead for the eigenvectors of $\mathbf{A}^T\mathbf{A}$ whose dimension is $n \times n$ rather than $N^2 \times N^2$. The transformed eigenvalue problem is $\mathbf{A}^T\mathbf{A}\mathbf{v}_i = \gamma_i \mathbf{v}_i$. $\mathbf{A}\mathbf{A}^T\mathbf{A}\mathbf{v}_i = \gamma_i \mathbf{A}\mathbf{v}_i$, the orthonormal vectors φ_i are $\varphi_i = \mathbf{A}\mathbf{v}_i$ and that the required computation is now feasible. The actual eigen-decomposition is carried out using Singular Value Decomposition (SVD). $\Sigma_{SVD} = \mathbf{U}\mathbf{C}\mathbf{V}^T$ and the columns of $\mathbf{U}$ and $\mathbf{V}$ are the eigenvectors of $\mathbf{A}\mathbf{A}^T$ and $\mathbf{A}^T\mathbf{A}$, respectively. The singular values on the diagonal of $\mathbf{C}$ are the square roots of the eigenvalues for both $\mathbf{A}\mathbf{A}^T$ and $\mathbf{A}^T\mathbf{A}$. We conclude by noting that $\Sigma = \Phi\mathbf{D}\Phi^T$ where $\mathbf{D} = diag(\lambda_1, \cdots, \lambda_n)$ and the trace $\Sigma = \Sigma_{i=1}^{n}\lambda_i$.

A qualitative interpretation has been proposed for the PCA eigenvectors in the context of face recognition. The low-order PCA components are surmised to code for gender and ethnicity (O'Toole et al., 1994). The apparent age of a face can also be related to its proximity to the average of the face space. The first component or DC codes for the average human face.

Penev and Sirovitch (2000) have argued that the generalization ability for PCA "depends strongly on both the ensemble composition and size, with statistics for populations as large as 5500 still not stationary. Further, the assumption of mirror symmetry of the ensemble [if a picture is a face, its mirror is a face too] improves the quality of the results substantially." The number M of eigenface components that have to be kept is the other key issue addressed by Penev and Sirovitch. This number can be adjudicated using the perceptual quality of face reconstruction or the relative entropic cost and signal to noise (SNR) ratio. H, the entropy of the reconstructed image, is computed as the average (over M) of the components' (projected) squared lengths. Using a probabilistic PCA interpretation, the probability P of a particular face image is $P \sim \exp\left(-\frac{1}{2}H\right)$; $-\log P$, which approximates the information content of the signal (Barlow, 1989b), is proportional to the length of the optimal code. One can see that if the entropy H for some reconstructed face image goes down, its likelihood goes up. One draws $S - H$ diagrams to observe how much of the signal-to-noise-ratio can be inexpensively captured; afterwards, even if one were to increase the SNR, i.e., get a better approximation, the face reconstruction obtained is very improbable - not likely. One assumes that $SNR = \log_2\left(\frac{||\Phi||^2}{||\Phi_M^{err}||^2}\right)$, $\Phi_M^{err} = \Phi - \Phi_M^{rec}$ when Φ_M^{err} and Φ_M^{rec} are the approximation error and the reconstructed face using M eigenfaces, respectively. Penev and Sirovitch argue that "even with large statistics, the dimensionality of the PCA subspace necessary for adequate representation of the identity information in relatively tightly cropped faces is in the 400-700 range, and that a dimensionality of 200 is inadequate."

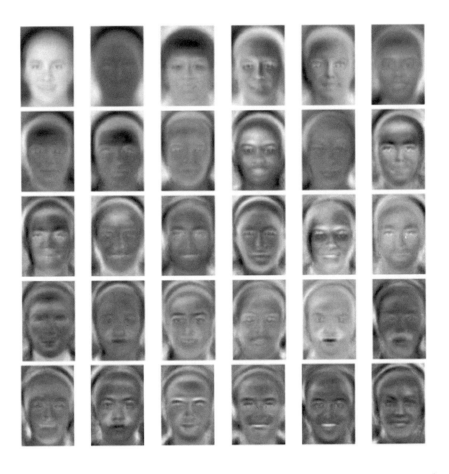

Fig. 5.3. Eigenfaces (Reprinted from Liu and Wechsler, Evolutionary Pursuit and Its Application to Face Recognition, *IEEE Transactions on Pattern Analysis and Machine Intelligence,* ©2000 IEEE).

Penev and Attick (1996) have advanced the concept of local feature analysis (LFA) as a substitute for global ("holistic") PCA for face recognition. In terms of local processing for feature extraction, LFA is conceptually similar to the use of Gabor jets (see Sect. 6.5) or the attempts made to define eigenimages corresponding to specific facial landmarks such as the eyes, nose and mouth. LFA derives local and topographic kernels $\mathbf{K}$ that are spatially indexed and sparsified. Independent Component Analysis (ICA) (see below) provides yet another example of a transformation that connects local information and recognition-by-parts methods. The LFA kernels, the rows of $\mathbf{K}$, are found for the covariance matrix Σ from $\mathbf{K} = \Phi \mathbf{D}^{-\frac{1}{2}} \Phi$ where $\mathbf{D}^{-\frac{1}{2}} = \text{diagonal} \left(\frac{1}{\sqrt{\lambda_i}} \right)$. The effect of sparsification is to reduce the dimensionality of the base representation using the mean reconstruction error to rank and induce relative order among the filters $\mathbf{K}$ derived. Independent Component Analysis (ICA) implemented using architecture I (see below, Sect. 6.5, and Ch. 15) finds basis images, which are localized edge filters (Bell and Sejnowski, 1997) and are suitable for recognition-by-parts methods.

Linear Discriminant Analysis (LDA) (Etemad and Chellappa, 1997), another major subspace method, is different from PCA as it considers class membership to build a transformed face space that is discriminative in nature. LDA performs dimensionality reduction while seeking for the linear transformation $\Phi^T : \mathbf{R}^N \to \mathbf{R}^M$ that maximizes the Fisher criterion, i.e., the ratio of the between-class scatter SB and the within-class scatter S_W for

$$\mathbf{S}_B = \sum_{i=1}^{c} \frac{N_i}{n} (\mu_i - \mu)(\mu_i - \mu)^T = \sum_{i=1}^{c} P(C_i)(\mu_i - \mu)(\mu_i - \mu)^T \quad (5.20)$$

$$\mathbf{S}_W = \sum_{i=1}^{c} \frac{N_i}{n} \sum (\mathbf{X}_k - \mu_i)(\mathbf{X}_k - \mu_i)^T = \sum_{i=1}^{c} P(C_i)\Sigma_i \quad (5.21)$$

when μ_i is the mean for N_i faces $\mathbf{X}_i$ from class C_i and μ is the average for n faces. When $\mathbf{S}_W$ is not singular the optimal projection $\hat{\Phi}$ is $\hat{\Phi} = \arg\max_\Phi \frac{|\Phi^T \mathbf{S}_B \Phi|}{|\Phi^T \mathbf{S}_W \Phi|} = [\varphi_1, \varphi_2, \cdots, \varphi_M]$ where φ_i correspond to the M largest eigenvalues λ_i for the eigenvalue problem $\mathbf{S}_B \Phi = \mathbf{S}_W \Phi$. The optimal projection for two classes ($c = 2$), e.g., face detection, is along the direction of the principal eigenvector for $\hat{\Phi} = \mathbf{S}_W^{-1}(\mu_1 - \mu_2)$. The discrimination power or equivalently separability can be defined as $\text{trace}(\mathbf{S}_W^{-1}\mathbf{S}_B)$. The rank ($\mathbf{S}_B$) is less or equal to ($c - 1$) and therefore there are at most ($c - 1$) non-zero generalized eigenvalues for c classes. This can be a limiting factor leading to a shortage of features for reliable face recognition. The transformed LDA data becomes $\mathbf{Y} = \Phi^T \cdot \mathbf{X}$ along possibly non-orthogonal axes. One can derive LDA using maximum likelihood (ML) for the case of normal class conditional distributions when the covariance matrices are equal. One potential problem with LDA concerns the fact that $\mathbf{S}_W$ is likely to be singular. This can happen since rank ($\mathbf{S}_W$) = ($n - c$) when $n = \sum_{i=1}^{c} N_i$ because n is usually much smaller than the number of pixels in each face image. The concerns regarding the large size of the face image can be alleviated by applying LDA in the PCA subspace spanned by the original faces. This leads to the **Fisherfaces** subspace method (Belhumeur et al., 1997) (see Fig. 5.4). Another alternative used to deal with the singularity aspect of $\mathbf{S}_W$ is to find the optimal projection for $\hat{\Phi} = \arg\max_\Phi \frac{|\Phi^T \mathbf{S}_B \Phi|}{|\Phi^T \mathbf{S}_t \Phi|}$ where $\mathbf{S}_t = \mathbf{S}_B + \mathbf{S}_W$.

LDA is highly sensitive to outliers and occlusion, and requires a large number of face images to derive the between and within scatters needed for proper generalization. When there are not enough face images for such a purpose one should use PCA instead (Martinez and Kak, 2001) or generate additional faces from the original ones using symmetry and/or noisy or slightly distorted (by geometrical transformations) versions of the original face images. This expands on the repertoire of faces available for learning the LDA subspace and leads to better performance.

Fig. 5.4. Fisherfaces.

The next important subspace described is derived using **Independent Component Analysis (ICA)**. We start with some preliminaries on statistical independence. Random (zero-mean) variables $\mathbf{S}_1, \mathbf{S}_2, \cdots, \mathbf{S}_m$ are statistically independent (versus linear independence in algebra) if their joint PDF can be factorized using marginal densities

$$p(\mathbf{S}_1, \mathbf{S}_2, \cdots, \mathbf{S}_m) = p(\mathbf{S}_1)p(\mathbf{S}_2)\cdots p(\mathbf{S}_m) \qquad (5.22)$$

Independence is much stronger than lack of correlatation, which merely implies zero covariance, i.e., $E(\mathbf{S}_i, \mathbf{S}_j) = E(\mathbf{S}_i) \cdot E(\mathbf{S}_j)$ for $i \neq j$. When the joint PDF $p(\mathbf{S}_1, \mathbf{S}_2, \cdots, \mathbf{S}_m)$ is Gaussian, independent and uncorrelated events are equivalent. ICA implements non-Gaussian factor analysis, while PCA implements Gaussian factor analysis. Another immediate distinction between PCA and ICA is that PCA is limited to second order statistics, while ICA usually involves higher order statistics. One important application for ICA is blind source separation known also as the cocktail party problem. People surrounding you at a party are simultaneously talking but you can still tune to independent (voice) conversations from their n "joint" conversations. Mixed faces in a crowd is a particular case of the cocktail party problem. Following Hyvarinen et al. (2001) ICA seeks a linear transformation ϕ for random vectors $\mathbf{X}_i$ such that $\mathbf{S} = \phi\mathbf{X}$ with the (non-Gaussian) components $\mathbf{S}_j$ as independent as possible according to some criterion $f(\mathbf{S}_1\mathbf{S}_2\cdots\mathbf{S}_m)$. $\mathbf{X} = \{\mathbf{X}_i\}$ is under the noise free ICA model by the "mixing" matrix $\mathbf{A}$ as $\mathbf{X} = \mathbf{AS} = \sum_{j=1}^{m} \mathbf{a}_j\mathbf{S}_j$. Similar to projection pursuit, ICA searches for "interesting" projections that are assumed to be independent. The matrix $\mathbf{A}$ is not identifiable for Gaussian independent components, i.e., the scatter is dense everywhere and information about useful directions for projections is lacking. Hence the search for "non-Gaussian" dimensions. The mixing matrix $\mathbf{A}$ is estimated first and then one computes its inverse ϕ to obtain the independent components.

The number of observed linear mixtures n is at least as large as the number of independent components m, i.e., $n = m$; the matrix $\mathbf{A}(n, m)$ must be of full column rank. The columns of $\mathbf{A}$ can be estimated up to a multiplicative constant. Note that in contrast to PCA there is no specific order for the independent components found. Formally, using some permutation matrix $\mathbf{P}$ and its inverse $\mathbf{P}^{-1}$ one can consider a new ICA model $\mathbf{X} = \mathbf{AP}^{-1}\mathbf{PS}$ where $\mathbf{PS}$ reorders the original independent variables. There are two options available to order the independent components. One option is to use the norms of the columns of the mixing matrix $\mathbf{A}$, which indicate the contributions of the independent components to the variance of the mixed observations $\mathbf{X}_i$. The other option, similar to projection pursuit indexes, is to use the non-Gaussian property of the independent components $\mathbf{S}_j$. One way to probe for non-Gaussian characterization for (zero-mean) random variables $\mathbf{X}_i$ is to use the kurtosis k, which measures their fourth moment with respect to the variance (2nd moment), i.e., $k = \frac{E(X^4)}{E(X^2)^2} - 3$, or alternatively $k = \sum \frac{(X-\mu)^4}{(n\sigma^4)} - 3$. The kurtosis is a measure of "super-Gaussian" or how spiky the probability density is. The use of the constant 3 ensures that Gaussians have zero kurtosis, super-Gaussians have positive kurtosis, and sub-Gaussians have negative kurtosis. A typical example for super-Gaussians is the Laplace density $p(\mathbf{X}) = \frac{1}{\sqrt{2}}\exp(\sqrt{2}|\mathbf{X}|)$. A non-Gaussian density in the context of ICA can be shown to mean independence. ICA estimation involves seeking for best super-(non) Gaussians projections that approximate the original and independent sources.

The extent to which a random variable is non-Gaussian can alternatively be assessed using negentropy. The entropy H for a random variable $\mathbf{X}$ is $H(\mathbf{X}) = -\int p(\mathbf{X})\log p(\mathbf{X})d\mathbf{X}$. It measures to what degree $\mathbf{X}$ is random and determines its minimum description length (MDL) code. Recalling that the Gaussian variable has the largest entropy among all the random variables of equal variance (and is thus least interesting) one concludes that spiky densities characteristic of non-Gaussians should display low entropy. Think of two vertical but separable clouds of points. PCA seeks for maximum variance using Gaussian assumptions. It finds the vertical axis as optimal for projection, which clearly fails to separate the clusters. ICA, similar to projection pursuit, finds the correct solution, the horizontal separation, while searching among super - Gaussian directions. Towards that end, one defines the negentropy $J(\mathbf{X})$ as $J(\mathbf{X}) = H(\mathbf{X}_{\mathbf{Gauss}}) - H(\mathbf{X})$ and its approximations (Hyvarinen et al., 2001), where $\mathbf{X}_{\mathbf{Gauss}}$ is a Gaussian that shares the same covariance matrix with $\mathbf{X}$.

ICA starts with preprocessing, similar to PCA. This consists of centering (using mean subtraction), whitening (uncorrelated components with unit variance), and possibly band-pass filtering or PCA for dimensionality reduction. One of the methods proposed for ICA estimation is the FastICA algorithm [2]. It is based on a fixed-point iteration scheme to find a maximum for an approximation of the negentropy

$$J(\mathbf{X}) \cong [E\{f(\mathbf{X})\} - E\{f(\mathbf{g})\}]^2 \qquad (5.23)$$

where $\mathbf{g} \sim \mathbf{G}(0, \mathbf{I})$ and f is some non-quadratic function. Useful choices for f are

$$f_1(u) = \frac{1}{a_1} \log \cosh(a_1 u) \quad \text{and} \quad f_2(u) = -\exp\left(-\frac{u^2}{2}\right) \qquad (5.24)$$

The road to independence can also be reached by minimizing the mutual information I for the given sources

$$I(\mathbf{S}_1, \mathbf{S}_2, \cdots, \mathbf{S}_m) = \sum_{j=1}^{m} H(\mathbf{S}_i) - H(\mathbf{S}) \qquad (5.25)$$

The mutual information corresponds to the Kullback-Leibler (KL) divergence or distance between the joint density of the source and the product of its marginal densities. It is always non-negative, and it is zero if and only if the variables composing the source are independent. The use of mutual information, in particular its minimization, leads again in the context of ICA to searching for non-Gaussian directions. The corresponding ICA method is based on the original algorithm proposed by Comon (1994). Using Comon's algorithm, Liu and Wechsler (2003) have described the derivation of independent Gabor features (whose dimensionality has first been reduced using PCA) for face recognition. The rationale behind integrating the Gabor wavelets and ICA is twofold. On the one hand, the Gabor transformed face images exhibit strong characteristics of spatial locality, scale and orientation selectivity, similar to those displayed by Gabor wavelets. Such characteristics produce salient local features surrounding the eyes, the nose and the mouth. On the other hand, ICA further reduces the redundancy among those features and represents the independent features explicitly. Independent features are most useful in the context of reliable face recognition for pattern discrimination and associative recall.

ICA achieves redundancy reduction (versus merely dimensionality reduction for PCA) by using factorial or sparse codes in which the probability of observing a particular face is a product of independent factors or "interesting" projections, e.g., the features that code for the face. Furthermore, if the strength of the factorial code output is proportional to its information content, the code can directly represent not only the sensory signal itself, but also its likelihood, and the detection of "suspicious coincidences," i.e., events or patterns, becomes easier (Barlow, 1989b). When the independent sources are found searching for super-Gaussians or high kurtosis, their distributions are clustered around zero and implement the factorial or sparse code mentioned earlier.

5.5 Feature Selection

Features are the coordinate axes that define the face space and affect recognition. Features, once derived, provide the opportunity to choose from in order to make

---

[2] http://www.cis.hut.fi/projects/ica/fastica/

recognition more reliable and efficient. Feature selection is the result of explicit dimensionality reduction transformations or it is managed using some objective function without the benefit of such transformations. The latter case is the one addressed in this section.

The objective functions used for feature selection come in two flavors, filter and wrapper methods. Starting with n features the goal is to find out the best subset of m features among the $\binom{n}{m}$ possible candidates. Exhaustive search is not feasible and one needs some search strategy to sift through. Strategies are defined in terms of the objective function used, how the fitness returned by such strategies for some candidate subset advances the search, and specific stopping criteria. The filter approach sets its objective function in terms of information contents, while the wrapper approach sets for its objective function the ultimate goal of (predictive) face recognition. Characteristic of the filter approach are abstract and intrinsic measures thought to be relevant to important properties for good feature sets, e.g., orthogonality, low variance, or class separability. The measures used also reveal the extent to which the features are correlated. Features that depend on other features can be eliminated without any loss. The filter approach is suboptimal in practice because the abstract measures used do not necessarily correlate well with good classification performance. The wrapper approach requires access to classification methods. The specific classifier used makes the wrapper approach biased and constitutes one of its limitation. Another limitation for wrapper methods comes from slow execution.

The search strategies used for feature selection are based on combinatorial optimization, e.g., branch and bound, beam search (Fukunaga, 1990) or greedy search, where features are added or removed in a sequential fashion, e.g., sequential forward, backward or floating selection. Branch and bound algorithms assume monotonicity, which "is not particularly restrictive and merely implies that a subset of features should not be better than any larger set that contains the subset." Beam search is like best-first search but bound in scope. Sequential Forward Selection (SFS) iteratively adds the most informative feature, while Sequential Floating Forward Selection (SFFS) on each iteration backtracks to remove the least useful feature (Kudo and Sklansky, 2000). The filter and wrapper methods can be merged in a hybrid approach such that subset evaluation and selection is driven by both features' intrinsic qualities and their potential for good classification performance. RELIEF, another generic feature selection approach proposed by Bins and Draper (2001), first filters out irrelevant and redundant features and then chooses among the relevant features left those deemed best using SFFS driven by the Mahalanobis distance. Irrelevant features are those that fail to discriminate between hits and misses, while redundant features are those found using K-means clustering, where the similarity distance measures correlation. More recent strategies characteristic of stochastic search, e.g., evolutionary computation and genetic algorithms, expand on hybrid approaches. They take advantage of random perturbations in order to avoid getting trapped in local minima. They are discussed next.

Evolutionary computation represents an emerging methodology for stochastic optimization. Its motivation comes from natural selection. Evolution takes place by maintaining one or more populations of (candidate solution) individuals ("chromosomes"), which compete for rewards like mating and placing off-springs in future generations. The competition is implemented via selection mechanisms that can choose from ever changing populations, which result from the birth and death of individuals. The selection mechanisms evaluate the fitness value of individuals based on specific figures of merit criteria. The population (of candidate solutions) evolves through the use of genetic operators that reflect the concepts of mating and inheritance (off-springs resemble their parents). When the fitness lacks an analytical form suitable for gradient descent or the computation involved is prohibitively expensive, as it is the case when the solution space is too large to be searched exhaustively, the alternative left is to use (directed) stochastic search methods for non-linear optimization and variable selection. The unique exploration (along variations farther away from an existing population) and the exploitation (of minor variations of the better fit parents) ability of evolutionary computation, guided by fitness, makes possible that very complex search face spaces can be searched for feature selection, in general, and the face space definition, in particular. The search for "optimal" bases that define the face space using stochastic/genetic optimization is addressed next.

The problem addressed is that of learning the face space from large and diverse populations using evolution as the driving force. The basis for the face space is found using Genetic Algorithms (GA). The basis' fitness is determined by both its "wrapper" like ability for face recognition and its "filter" like intrinsic qualities. The "hybrid" aspect comes from the interplay between performance, on one side, and the (categorical) density and class separation of the face space, on the other hand. The proper mix of wrapper and filter contributions is achieved using Evolutionary Pursuit (EP) (Liu and Wechsler, 2000). In analogy to (exploratory) pursuit methods from statistics, EP seeks to learn an optimal face space for the dual purpose of low dimensionality and pattern classification. The challenges that EP has successfully met are related to sparse functional approximation and predictive learning. Similar to structural risk minimization (SRM), evolutionary pursuit increases the generalization ability of face recognition (and thus reduce the guaranteed risk during testing) by handling the trade-off between minimizing the empirical risk encountered during training ("performance accuracy") and narrowing the predicted risk ("confidence interval").

EP explores the space of possible dimensions or coordinate axes and their layout in order to determine the optimal projection basis for the face space. It starts by projecting the original face images $\mathbf{X} = \{\mathbf{X}_i\}$ into a lower dimensional PCA space $\mathbf{Y}$ such that $\mathbf{Y} = \phi^T \mathbf{X}$. This is followed by a whitening transformation Γ such that $\mathbf{V} = \Gamma \mathbf{Z}$. Random rotations $\mathbf{Q}$ of pair wise and whitened basis vectors defining $\mathbf{U} = \mathbf{Q}\mathbf{V}$ are confined to $\left(0, \frac{\pi}{2}\right)$ and are evaluated by GA. Evolution is driven by a fitness objective defined in terms of performance accuracy ("empirical risk") and class separation ("confidence interval") (see Sect. 3.4). Note that the whitening transformation Γ can lead to a non-orthogonal basis for the face space. To see that this is indeed the case consider the overall transformation matrix $\Psi = \phi \Gamma \mathbf{Q}$ and assume that the basis vectors of Ψ are orthogonal, i.e., $\Psi^T \Psi = \Delta$ where Δ is a diagonal matrix. It follows that $\Gamma^2 = \Delta = c\mathbf{I}$ with c a constant and $\mathbf{I}$ the unit matrix. This holds, however, only when all the eigenvalues are equal; otherwise, the basis vectors in Ψ are not orthogonal. Informally, the 'unit' vectors after whitening are now of unequal length and rotating 'unit' vector of unequal lengths leads to non-orthogonality.

Learning the face space requires EP to search through all the possible subsets of m axes (rotated by $\mathbf{Q}$) in the whitened PCA space. Using ten bits (resolution) to represent each angle makes the discretized (angle) interval less than 0.09 degrees. The rotation angles (represented by strings of bits) and the axes' indicators (indicating whether the axes are chosen or not) define the search space. This requires $10 \cdot \left\lceil \frac{m(m-1)}{2} \right\rceil$ bits to represent the range for angles and another m bits to indicate if the axes are selected or not. The size of the genospace, $2^{**}5m(m-1)+m$, is too large to be searched in an exhaustive fashion. This suggests stochastic search instead using GA, which maintain a constant sized population of candidate solutions. The search underlying GA is such that breadth and depth - exploration and exploitation - are balanced according to the observed performance of the individual ("basis") solutions evolved so far. As GA search the genospace, exploration is helped by genetic operators using a wheel of fortune driven by fitness. The genetic operators are selection, crossover (or recombination), and mutation. There is proportionate selection according to fitness, two chromosomes exchange genetic material between the crossover points, and small but fixed mutations flip the bits. By allocating more reproductive occurrences to above average individual solutions, the overall effect is to increase the population's average fitness. Evolution is driven by the fitness $\chi(\mathbf{B})$

$$\chi(\mathbf{B}) = \chi_A(\mathbf{B}) + \lambda \cdot \chi_R(\mathbf{B}) \tag{5.26}$$

where the basis $\mathbf{B}$ is defined in terms of the number of axes, their identity, and the corresponding angles of rotations starting from the whitened PCA space, $\chi_A(\mathbf{B})$

records performance accuracy, i.e., the empirical risk, $\chi_R(\mathbf{B})$ is the generalization (or risk) index, i.e., the confidence interval, and λ is a positive constant that indicates the relative importance of the generalization term vs. the accuracy or empirical risk term. The risk index $\chi_R(\mathbf{B})$ is estimated for L face classes of mean $\mathbf{M}_i$ and grand (population) mean $\mathbf{M}_0$ as

$$\chi_R(\mathbf{B}) = \left[\sum_{i=1}^{L} (\mathbf{M}_i - \mathbf{M}_0)^T (\mathbf{M}_i - \mathbf{M}_0) \right]^{0.5} \tag{5.27}$$

Accuracy indicates the extent to which evolution has been successful, while the generalization index or risk indicates the expectation for future performance. The net result is that GA can evolve solutions that show both good recognition performance and generalization abilities. The fitness has a similar form to the cost functional used by regularization theory and to the cost function used by sparse coding. The cost functional for regularization compromises between the solution's closeness to data and its overall quality. The particular cost function for sparse coding strikes a balance between information preservation and the sparseness of the derived code.

Starting from a 30 dimensional (whitened) PCA space EP derives the face space using 26 eigen (rotated) axes (see Fig. 5.5). Note that while for PCA the basis vectors have a natural order this is not the case with the projection basis derived by EP due to the rotations involved during the evolutionary process. The natural order characteristic of the principal components reflects the representational aspect of PCA and its relationship to spectral decomposition. The very first principal components encode global image characteristics, in analogy to low-frequency components. EP, on the other hand, is a procedure geared primarily towards recognition and generalization. It is also worth pointing out that while PCA derives orthogonal basis vectors, EP's basis vectors are usually non-orthogonal. Orthogonality is a constraint for optimal signal representation, but not a requirement for pattern recognition. Actually, non-orthogonality has been shown to have great functional significance in biological sensory systems (Daugman, 1990). The use of EP for face identification is discussed in Sect. 6.2.

The scope for the EP framework is wide open. In particular, EP can search for optimal locations, bandwidth and orientations in the case of Gabor wavelets. The stochastic search framework is not limited to GA. It can use other modes of evolutionary computation, e.g., tabu search, particle swarm optimization (PSO), and ant colonies. Tabu search is a meta-heuristic that, unlike simulated annealing and GA, "avoids entrainment in cycles by forbidding or penalizing moves which take the solution, in the next iteration, to points in the solution space previously visited (hence 'tabu'). New courses are not chosen randomly. Instead the search proceeds according to the supposition that there is no point in accepting a new (poor) solution unless it is to avoid a path already investigated. This insures new regions of a problems solution space will be investigated with the goal of avoiding local minima and ultimately finding the desired solution" (Glover, 1986).

Particle swarm optimization (PSO), population based and driven by information sharing, draws insights from self-organizing processes, e.g., bird flocking and fish schooling (Kennedy et al., 2001), for solving continuous optimization problems. The candidate solutions or particles, as they are known, "swarm" through the search space by 'flying' closer to the 'best' particles found so far. Any discoveries and past experience are shared across the population and drive the velocity at which individual particles fly toward each other. Sharing has the effect that complex relationships can be captured among features leading to global rather than local solutions. Ant colony optimization (ACO) (Dorigo et al., 1999) focuses on discrete optimization problems. Yan and Yuan (2004) starting with PCA have applied ACO for optimal subset eigen feature selection using a wrapper approach based on SVM. Sharing of information among ants takes place by combining their pheromone intensities, which evaporate over time unless reinforced to prevent accumulation of trails. ACO-SVM results were

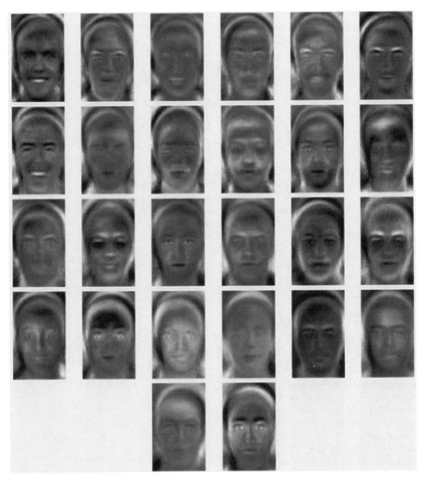

Fig. 5.5. Evolutionary Pursuit Faces (Reprinted from Liu and Wechsler, Evolutionary Pursuit and Its Application to Face Recognition, *IEEE Transactions on Pattern Analysis and Machine Intelligence*, ©2000 IEEE).

shown to be better than SVM alone and kernel PCA on both the ORL and Yale facial databases.

5.6 Caricatures

Face representations need to be distinguishable one from the other before recognition can succeed. Starting from some basic representation one can enhance or exaggerate its discrimination index using the caricaturing process (Rhodes, 1996). "A caricature is a portrait in epigram. It exaggerates a few distinctive features, often for witty effect, and it has pinked the pompous for centuries. Caricatures work by making us identify a real person with a comic image. In the Poetics, Aristotle mentions one artist who improves faces, another who copies them, and a third who worsens them. They are the flatterer, the realist, and the caricaturist." (McNeill, 1998). Caricaturing is different from morphing, where a smooth sequence of frame (face) images interpolates between two given (face) images. People appear to be faster in face identification using caricatures compared to complete and accurate line drawings. It is not known, however, if this finding is confined to familiar faces the media showers us with or if it applies to large galleries of faces too. "A good caricature, like every other work of art, is more true to life than life itself" according to Carracci (1550-1609).

Mauro and Kubovy (1992) have shown that pictorial rather than symbolic [not part of the facial anatomy] caricatures appear to be "super-portraits capable of eliciting recognition better than veridical depictions." Distinctive features are emphasized or exaggerated and they indicate what needs to be encoded and stored for subsequent face retrieval and recognition. The peak shift effect is one possible explanation for discrimination tasks, in general, and the role caricatures play in face recognition, in particular. The peak shift effect appears when an animal (or a human being) is trained to distinguish between two stimuli. The learning process rewards the subject when the first (positive) stimulus S^+ is present, while it penalizes the subject when the second (negative) stimulus S^- is used. It has been experimentally shown that subjects trained to each possible stimulus (ranging from S^- to S^+) respond strongest for an extreme version of the positive stimulus, i.e., for a value larger than S^+. (Dynamic) discriminative rather than (fixed) generative models support peak shift like phenomena. Execution and relevance of caricatures is further driven by face space paradigms as explained next.

Memory-based reasoning defines the face space in terms of face exemplars; this is known as Absolute-Based Coding (ABC). ABC corresponds to a learned base shared by all the faces with the norm playing no role. Driven by clustering and density measures, ABC regards typicality, e.g. for ethnicity, as depending on the local density surrounding some exemplar face(s) whose ethnicity is known. Sparsification, driven by caricatures, becomes important as it leads to a lesser number of misclassification errors. Support for the ABC exemplar model comes from Lewis and Johnston (1999) who have argued that faces tessellate the face space and are encoded into a multi-dimensional Voronoi diagram (see below) based on normally distributed face-space representations. The locations at which faces are encoded in the face space are used to partition the space into discrete identity regions or tiles. The identity/categorical tiles are such that their center is further from the boundary than the veridical exemplar that induced the boundary. The net result is that a slight caricature for the veridical exemplar (toward the center) stands better chances to be identified, authenticated and/or categorized.

The abstractive alternative, Norm-Based Coding (NBC), which defines typicality in terms of the distance from an average prototype that abstracts the faces exposed to, draws from cognitive research on schemata. Note that the typical prototype or the mean ignores both the variance of the features and their relevance. "Caricatures are effective because they exaggerate this norm deviation information" and "other race faces are coded relative to the (only available) own race norm" (Byatt and Rhodes,

1998). Latency in recall is indeed less for distinctive, i.e., atypical faces. If one subscribes to NBC, the follow-up question is why using only one prototype? Edelman (1999) takes up this very question to advance the concept of a chorus of prototypes. Categorization for Edelman calls for pattern representation of similarity instead of representation by similarity and it provides for both generalization and shape constancy. Such an approach is related to RBF classifiers (see Sect. 9.2) for which the prototypes or modules result from K-means clustering or estimation-maximization (EM)-like methods (see Sect. 3.1). Brennan's (1985) caricature generator was the first to generate caricatures using the equivalent of the NBC model. A line drawing defined the frontal mean shape and its vertices were displaced by a constant factor from the mean shape.

Experiments reported by Rhodes et al. (1998) seem to suggest that the ABC model compares favorably with the NBC model, even though it may not provide a complete account of race effects for face recognition. The other-race effect acknowledges the fact that people recognize faces belonging to their own race better than faces from other races. The contact hypothesis, which is the standard explanation for this effect, conjectures that it is the greater experience one has with her own race that accounts for such effects. Furl et al. (2002), however, suggest instead a refined contact hypothesis, where "a developmental learning process warps the perceptual space to enhance the encoding of distinctions for own-race faces." Warping is similar to caricatures when idiosyncrasies are emphasized for increased discrimination, possibly using LDA. The advantage observed does not carry over to the case where the representation is optimized for faithful reconstruction, e.g., Principal Component Analysis (PCA), when "experienced based algorithms recognize minority-race faces more accurately than majority-race faces." The minority faces are more distinctive to start with and PCA preserves their advantage for subsequent matching and recognition.

Leopold et al. (2001) have conducted a series of experiments to assess the role that high-level configural (holistic) short lived aftereffects, induced by adaptation, play in face recognition. Aftereffects are perceptual distortions traced to extended periods of exposure to some visual stimulus. A few 3D idealized faces generated using morphing were positioned in the (multi-dimensional) NBC face space. The faces span an identity trajectory that visits the original face, the average face for the NBC space, and anti-faces, i.e., faces lying on the same axis but on the opposite side of the average face. Caricatures lie further from the average face and beyond the original faces but on the same identity trajectory, while anti-caricatures lie between an individual face and the average face. Leopold et al. (2001) report that "not only does [anti-face] adaptation alters sensitivity, but it actually spurs the visual system to create a new identity for the average face." In particular, adaptation was shown to "lead to misperceptions in face identity that were very precise, biasing perceptions along an identity trajectory away from the adapting stimulus." Prototypes are formed by averaging but change with experience.

The ABC code explains the above finding by "shifts in sensitivity to certain exemplars, which would ultimately shift the population code" (Hurlbert, 2001). Distortion aftereffects to "squashed" faces, when subjects after five minutes of adaptation saw normal images as unnaturally expanded, were also reported. Most interesting and relevant to the face space structure is that the aftereffects discussed above point to two different but complementary roles for prototypes. They support both basic-level or categorical recognition for classes of faces (see Sect. 6.7) and subordinate-level and identity recognition. The aftereffects observed are now accounted for using standard (face-) opponent neural mechanisms. The average prototype for the face space is both mutable and induces anti-faces. As an example, "exposure to the 'anti-Adam' prototype shifts the prototype toward 'anti-Adam' and weak versions of Adam now appear more like Adam than like the new prototype. Compared to the 'anti-Adam' prototype, weak versions of Jim also seem more like Adam and thus are harder to recognize as Jim" (Hulbert, 2001).

Pujol and Wechsler (2002) provide a unified account on face modeling suitable for caricatures. It includes data compression, detection, tracking, and recognition. The proposed computational approach includes (i) conspicuous valley and ridge feature representations, (ii) Voronoi exemplar-based face models driven by Self-Organization Feature Map (SOFM) and using valley and/or ridge feature representations, and (iii) caricature effects obtained by increasing the acuity (number of receptive fields) for the most conspicuous parts of the SOFM face models using Hebbian learning and warping (Pujol et al., 2001).

Valley and ridge filters (Lopez et al., 2000), tuned as attention mechanisms, encode the face conspicuity and yield robust local feature descriptors with respect to illumination changes. The Hausdorff distance, which measures proximity rather than exact superposition (Huttenlocher et al, 1993; Takacs, 1998; Takacs and Wechsler, 1998b; Santini and Jain, 1999), provides for flexible and robust similarity estimation during the self-organization process. The modified Hausdorff distance (MHD) measures the similarity $MHD(A, B)$ between two sets of points A and B,

$$MHD(A, B) = \max(h(A, B), h(B, A)) \qquad (5.28)$$

using the direct (but not symmetric) Hausdorff $h(A, B)$ distance

$$h(A, B) = \max_{a \in A}(\min_{b \in B}(d(a, b)) \qquad (5.29)$$

with $d(a, b)$ (usually) being the Euclidean distance. Fig. 5.6 shows the raw face images used (top row) from the AR face data base, together with their responses for the ridge (second row), valley (third row), and Canny edge detector (bottom row), respectively. The columns are labeled (a) through (g), where each label denotes a different face acquisition (expression and illumination) condition: (a) neutral expression, (b) smile, (c) angry, (d), (e) and (f) changes of illumination, and (g) image acquired during a photo session held two weeks later than the one for columns (a) through (f). Visual inspection reveals that both ridges and valleys are more robust to illumination changes than Canny edges (see condition (d), (e) and (f)). Experimental results showed the hit recognition rates computed using valleys indeed outperform those computed using edges. Ridges are comparable to valleys except when the illumination is frontal.

The Self-Organization Feature Map (SOFM) (Kohonen, 1989) is one of the basic connectionist methods (see Sect. 3.2) available for data compression, feature selection, and the formation of topological preserving maps. The conspicuous features of the face images, which correspond to major valleys and ridges, need to be efficiently encoded. The goal is to reduce the dimensionality of the face representation while preserving as much as possible of its original information contents, i.e., the location of the conspicuous features. Given a set of samples $X = \{\mathbf{X}_1, \mathbf{X}_2, \cdots, \mathbf{X}_n\}$ from $\mathbf{R}^N$, the SOFM is a connectionist structure that consists of a k-dimensional lattice of nodes. SOFM maps each sample $\mathbf{X}_i$ to one of the lattice nodes. Each node corresponds to a codebook vector $\mathbf{m}_{ij} \in \mathbf{R}^N$ with (i, j) indexing the position of the node within the 2D lattice for $N = 2$. The SOFM iterative learning algorithm, also known as vector quantization (VQ) can be summarized as

(i) for each sample $\mathbf{X}$ find its nearest lattice node $(i, j) = \arg\min_{(i,j)} ||\mathbf{X} - \mathbf{m}_{ij}||$ where $|| \cdot ||$ stands for the similarity distance used and the node (i, j) is called the winning node;

(ii) the codebook entries are updated ("displaced") (in the original $\mathbf{R}^N$ space) according to the Hebb rule $\mathbf{m}_{kl}(t) = \mathbf{m}_{kl}(t-1) + \alpha(t)G(|(i, j) - (k, l)|)||\mathbf{X} - \mathbf{m}_{ij}(t-1)||$

where $\alpha(t)$ is the learning or elasticity/decay rate, and G is usually a bell shaped (Gaussian) function that decreases according to the distance from the winning node (i, j). SOFM is initialized over an array whose dimensions are smaller than those of the input (face) image. The codebook entries $\mathbf{m}_{ij}$ correspond to face locations (x, y) where conspicuous face features show up. The learning algorithm adapts the codebook vectors such that the mapping of conspicuous image points across the SOFM lattice preserves the original face topology and also yields a compressed face representation. The codebook entries define their own basin of attraction and together induce the

Voronoi tessellation referred to earlier. SOFM or its equivalent VQ is characteristic of unsupervised learning methods used for clustering and/or grouping. Note that unsupervised learning underlies most of biological learning. Quoting from Hume (1740, Part III, Sect. III) "All kinds of reasoning consist in nothing but a comparison and a discovery of those relations, either constant on inconstant, which two or more objects bear to each other," Edelman and Intrator (2004) argue that "both philosophical (ontological) and psychological (developmental) considerations support a radical Empiricist stance, according to which object representations and the features they rely on should be learned, initially in an unsupervised fashion."

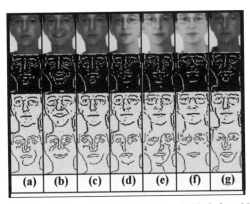

Fig. 5.6. Valley and Ridge Filter Outputs (Pujol and Wechsler, 2002).

Similar to topographic or retinotopic maps, the number of units or neurons allocated (across the face) is not uniform but rather proportional to the relevance that the area mapped serves for (face) recognition. This is similar to biological systems where lateral inhibition and redistribution of synaptic resources drives their self-organization. As SOFM depends on the order of presentation, conscience mechanisms occasionally interject suboptimal nodes as winners to avoid premature clustering (Hecht-Nielsen, 1990). Several top winners rather than only the winner take all (WTA) get updated according to their relative performance in order to smooth the map and speed up its realization. One expands on SOFM by considering the classification label for each of the samples $\mathbf{X}$. This leads to the supervised learning vector quantization (LVQ) algorithm where the codebook entries are moved around according to the winning node sharing the correct label or not with the sample $\mathbf{X}$. Adaptive updates are made such that the prototype for the winning node is moved closer or farther away from its present placement if its label is compatible or not with the label for sample $\mathbf{X}$. The size of the update depends on the decay rate and the distance between the winning node and the sample $\mathbf{X}$.

The prototype entries in the SOFM codebook are suitable for different face processing tasks. Such tasks include *face detection*, when the prototypes (see Fig. 5.7) are trained using faces of different subjects, *face categorization*, when the prototype is learned for different races, genders or ages, *face recognition* when different prototypes (see Fig. 5.8) are derived for different subjects, using for training set face images of the subject under different image acquisition conditions (face expression, illumination, shadows, $\cdots$), and *face tracking* (see Fig. 5.11).

SOFM induces a mapping between the conspicuity map coordinates (x, y) and the node lattice coordinates (i, j). The mapping (M_x, M_y) is used to caricature the input images $f(x, y)$ (from which the conspicuity maps have been constructed) into new images $f'(i, j)$ of the same size as the node lattice, i.e., $f'(i, j) = f(M_x(i, j), M_y(i, j))$. Fig. 5.9 shows warped face images obtained using the codebook entries of SOFM

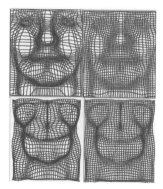

Fig. 5.7. SOFM Using Different Learning (Elasticity) Factors. Left column shows the SOFM obtained when nodes are strongly attracted to valleys (top row) or moved away from valleys (bottom row). Right columns show the SOFM obtained when a smaller learning coefficient is used (Pujol and Wechsler, 2002).

trained with $\alpha = 0.05$ (top row), 0.025, 0.015, 0.007, -0.007, -0.015, -0.025, and -0.05 (bottom row). The first six columns in Fig. 5.9 show face images obtained when the gray level images for three different subjects (two columns per subject, each column corresponds to a different face expression) are warped, using the SOFM codebooks' position, into new face images. The two rightmost columns show the caricatures obtained when the conspicuity map (using valleys as salient feature) from two different face images for the same subject are warped in a similar fashion.

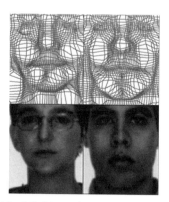

Fig. 5.8. SOFM for Individual Subjects (Pujol and Wechsler, 2002).

One notices (see top row of Fig. 5.8) that during Hebbian learning (positive learning rates), the size or the number of pixels dedicated to the main facial features (the mouth, eyes and nose) for caricatured faces increases compared to the original face images. During anti-Hebbian learning and using negative learning rates, facial features are deployed in increasingly reduced areas and restricted to the same position for all the face images. This effect is a direct consequence of the SOFM construction algorithm, which tends to increase the density of codebook entries around those places where conspicuous features are expected, and reduce the density for those places where a conspicuous feature is never expected. Hebbian learning provides a

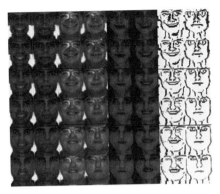

Fig. 5.9. Caricatures Driven by SOFM and Different Elasticity Factors that Range from Strong Attraction (top row) to Strong Repulsion (bottom row) Using Valley Image Representations (Pujol and Wechsler, 2002).

face representation (warped images) where more acuity is used for the most conspicuous locations of the face (mostly for the mouth, eyes, and nose). As a result of changes in acuity, stronger positive learning factors (Fig. 5.9 top row), the difference between two warped images is enhanced compared to the original images. On the other hand, if stronger negative or repulsive learning rates are used (Fig. 5.9 bottom row) the difference between two warped images decreases, thus increasing the similarity between face images. Hebbian and anti-Hebbian learning yield the equivalent of caricatures and anti-caricatures, respectively. As expected, when the differences between the gallery and probe images are due to changes in face expressions, i.e., experiment (b) (smile and neutral images), the hit rates obtained with anti-caricature (negative learning rates) images outperform those obtained using original face image. On the other hand, if variability is due mostly to differences between subjects rather than to face expressions, caricatures enhance the differences between subjects and the hit rates go up accordingly.

The face model developed so far assumes equal strength for the lateral connections that link among the nodes. Lateral connections, however, can be dynamically changed using Hebbian learning. Two nodes showing strong activations have their connection stronger. The nodes within the different parts of the face (chin, mouth, nose, eyes) show strong activations while the connections between different facial landmarks are weak. The result is a natural partition of the face where the main facial landmarks emerge and self-organize (see Fig. 5.10).

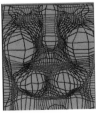

Fig. 5.10. Caricatures Using Dynamic Lateral Connections (Pujol and Wechsler, 2002).

The caricature based method tracks faces using the Condensation algorithm (Isard and Blake, 1998) (see Sect. 7.7). The state variables, including the location of conspicuous features, are estimated using a drift process and lock on the conspicuous (valley) features. The face regions where more detail is available, e.g., the eyes, nose and mouth, are tracked at increased spatial accuracy. The beneficial role lateral connection strengths play is revealed during the diffusion process, when displacements from one node propagate in a stronger or weaker way to its neighbors according to the weight of their lateral connection. This makes the displacements experienced by the mouth or the eyes less sensitive to the displacement experienced by irrelevant features. Most important, the nodes linked by strong lateral connections move together according to the overall face shape model. The average face shape model (see Fig. 5.7), derived using SOFM and trained on large face populations, is located automatically and initialized for the first frame of an image sequence. The location stage corresponds to face detection and is implemented using MHD for the distance (similarity) transform (DT) (Borgefors, 1984) (see Introduction to Ch. 6). The human subject that appears in the time-varying image makes a 90 degrees head rotation. Tracking results are shown in the bottom row. It becomes apparent that both face detection and face tracking are robust to shadows (see Fig. 5.11). SOFM adapts during tracking to the sequence of conspicuity features (2nd row of Fig. 5.11).

Fig. 5.11. Tracking Faces Using SOFM (Pujol and Wechsler, 2002).

5.7 Kernel Methods

The initial layout of patterns and their separation affect the search for optimal classifiers. Statistical learning theory seeks for linear classifiers and approaches non-separability using soft margins. Better performance can be expected from using non linear classifiers in a higher dimensional space. The justification is traced to Cover (1965) who argued that non-linearly separable patterns become linearly separable with high probability if the input space is mapped in a non-linear fashion to a high dimensional feature space. Non-linearity and a sparse high-dimensional space provide flexibility for tracing the boundary. The price to pay is a significant and sometimes prohibitive amount of increased computation. The kernel methods are the medium that makes non-linearity and higher dimensions computationally feasible. The basic paradigm is relatively straightforward. The original (raw) or transformed (PCA, $\cdots$) input space $\mathbf{X}$ is mapped to a higher dimensional feature space $\mathbf{Z}$ by Ψ such that $\mathbf{Z} = \Psi(\mathbf{X})$. The computation involved in the higher dimensional space consists of inner products that are directly and efficiently computed by inner products but in the original input space characterized by a much lower dimension. The non-linear boundaries for $\mathbf{X}$ are derived from the linear boundaries found by support vector machines (SVM) in $\mathbf{Z}$. The generic use of kernels methods using regression as a case study is summarized below. The treatment follows Shawe-Taylor and Cristianini (2004), Cherkassky and Mulier (1998), and Scholkopf and Smola (2002), and is complementary to the discussion on regularization (see Sect. 3.3) and filter banks (see Sect. 10.6).

Linear regression, for whom classification is just a discrete special case, seeks a real valued linear function $f(\mathbf{x}, y)$ to approximate $g(\mathbf{x}) = \langle \mathbf{w}, \mathbf{x} \rangle = \mathbf{w}'\mathbf{x} = \sum_{i=1}^{m} w_i x_i$ for (n dimensional) examples $\mathbf{X} = \{\mathbf{x}_i\}$ with corresponding (continuous) labels $\mathbf{y} = \{y_i\}$ and $'$ the transpose matrix operator. An exact solution for $\mathbf{Xw} = \mathbf{y}$ exists only when there are exactly n independent points $(\mathbf{x}, y)$. The (primal) least squares solution, due to Gauss, involves the normal equations $\mathbf{X}'\mathbf{Xw} = \mathbf{X}'\mathbf{y}$ and yields $\mathbf{w} = (\mathbf{X}'\mathbf{X})^{-1}\mathbf{X}'\mathbf{y}$. The prediction for new patterns $\mathbf{x}$ is $\hat{y} = g(\mathbf{x}) = \langle \mathbf{w}, \mathbf{x} \rangle$. The dual solution is found as $\mathbf{w} = \mathbf{X}'\boldsymbol{\alpha} = \sum_{i=1}^{m} \alpha_i \mathbf{x}_i$. When not enough data is available to make $\mathbf{X}'\mathbf{X}$ invertible or when there are more patterns than dimensions and there is noise, minimum norm and small error approximations are sough instead. The approximations are found using ridge regression as a particular case of penalized optimization or regularization (see Sect. 3.3). The problem that has to be solved now is to minimize $L_\lambda(\mathbf{w}) = ||\mathbf{w}||^2 + \sum_{i=1}^{m}(y_i - g(\mathbf{x}_i))^2$ and the (primal) solution found is $\mathbf{w} = (\mathbf{X}'\mathbf{X} + \lambda \mathbf{I}_m)^{-1}\mathbf{X}'\mathbf{y}$ with $(\mathbf{X}'\mathbf{X} + \lambda \mathbf{I}_m)$ always invertible for $\lambda > 0$. The dual solution solves for the weight vector $\mathbf{w}$ as a linear combination of the examples $\mathbf{x}_i$ and finds $\mathbf{w} = \lambda^{-1}\mathbf{X}'(\mathbf{y} - \mathbf{Xw}) = \mathbf{X}'\boldsymbol{\alpha} = \sum_{i=1}^{m} \alpha_i \mathbf{x}_i$ where $\boldsymbol{\alpha} = (\mathbf{G} + \lambda \mathbf{I}_m)^{-1}\mathbf{y}$. $\mathbf{G}$ is the Gram matrix such that $\mathbf{G} = \mathbf{XX}'$ with $\mathbf{G}_{ij} = \langle \mathbf{x}_i, \mathbf{x}_j \rangle$. The prediction using the dual solution on new (pattern) examples involves inner products $k_i = \langle \mathbf{x}_i, \mathbf{x} \rangle$ in the original space

$$g(\mathbf{x}) = \langle \mathbf{w}, \mathbf{x} \rangle = \sum_{i=1}^{m} \alpha_i \langle \mathbf{x}_i, \mathbf{x} \rangle = \mathbf{y}'(\mathbf{G} + \lambda \mathbf{I}_m)\mathbf{k} \qquad (5.30)$$

The dimensions for both $\mathbf{G}$ and $(\mathbf{G} + \lambda \mathbf{I}_m)$ are $(m \times m)$. The dimension $(n \times n)$ of $(\mathbf{X}'\mathbf{X} + \lambda \mathbf{I}_m)$, in the original feature space $\mathbf{R}^n$ is much larger when $n >> m$.

Non-linear solutions are sought using mappings Ψ and $\mathbf{Z} = \Psi(\mathbf{X})$ when linear solutions are not feasible. Similar arguments (see above) apply to the transform feature space $\mathbf{Z}$ leading to dual but still linear solutions where $\mathbf{G}_{ij} = \langle \Psi(\mathbf{x}_i), \Psi(\mathbf{x}_j) \rangle$ and $k_i = \langle \Psi(\mathbf{x}_i), \Psi(\mathbf{x}) \rangle$. The inner products can be computed efficiently in the original pattern space. It thus avoids the explicit computation of Ψ and the corresponding high dimensional costs associated with inner products in the feature space $\mathbf{Z}$. This calls for the use of proper kernel functions, $\kappa(\mathbf{x}_i, \mathbf{x}_j) = \langle \Psi(\mathbf{x}_i), \Psi(\mathbf{x}_j) \rangle$, leading to a computational complexity proportional to the number of patterns m rather than the usually much higher dimension of $\mathbf{Z}$. The non-linear prediction in the original space using kernel functions is then found using $g(\mathbf{x}) = \sum_{i=1}^{m} \alpha_i \kappa(\mathbf{x}_i, x)$.

The indirect evaluation of inner products in the high-dimensional space $\mathbf{Z}$ makes use of positive semi-definite (non-negative eigenvalues and symmetric) kernel functions $\kappa(\mathbf{x}_i, \mathbf{x}_j)$ defined for $\mathbf{x} \in [\mathbf{a}, \mathbf{b}]$ and input patterns (or support vectors in the case of SVM) $\mathbf{x}_i$ and $\mathbf{x}_j$. The (kernel trick) justification comes from the definition of inner products $\langle \mathbf{x}_i, \mathbf{x}_j \rangle$ in the Hilbert space (see below) using the (Gram) kernel matrix $\mathbf{K} = \kappa(\mathbf{x}_i, \mathbf{x}_j)$ and positive coefficients γ_l

$$\mathbf{G}_{ij} = \langle \Psi(\mathbf{x}_i), \Psi(\mathbf{x}_j) \rangle = \kappa(\mathbf{x}_i, \mathbf{x}_j) \quad \text{where} \quad \kappa(\mathbf{x}_i, \mathbf{x}_j) = \sum_{l=1}^{\infty} \gamma_i \Psi_l(\mathbf{x}_i)\Psi_l(\mathbf{x}_j) \qquad (5.31)$$

and the necessary and sufficient Mercer conditions (for $\mathbf{K}$ to be positive semi-definite)

$$\int_a^b \int_a^b \kappa(\mathbf{x}_i, \mathbf{x}_j)\Psi_l(\mathbf{x}_i)\Psi_l(\mathbf{x}_j)dx_i dx_j \geq 0 \quad \text{and} \quad \int_a^b \Psi^2(\mathbf{x})dx < \infty \qquad (5.32)$$

The **Hilbert space** is an inner product (infinite) space that is separable and complete with respect to the norm defined by the inner product $||\mathbf{x}|| = \langle \mathbf{x}, \mathbf{x} \rangle^{\frac{1}{2}}$. It is isomorphic to $\mathbf{R}^n$ and L_2 for finite and infinite n, respectively. The Cauchy-Schwartz inequality holds as $\langle \mathbf{x}_i, \mathbf{x}_j \rangle = ||\mathbf{x}_i||^2 ||\mathbf{x}_j||^2$. Hilbert spaces generalize on the concept of (infinite) Fourier expansion. The family of (inner product) kernels includes (1) polynomials of degree ν, $\kappa(\mathbf{x}_i, \mathbf{x}_j) = [\langle \mathbf{x}_i, \mathbf{x}_j \rangle + 1]^\nu$, (2) Gaussian kernels $\kappa(\mathbf{x}_i, \mathbf{x}_j) = \exp\left(-\frac{|\mathbf{x}_i - \mathbf{x}_j|^2}{\sigma^2}\right)$ when $f(\mathbf{x}) = sign\left[\sum_{i=1}^n \chi_i \exp\left(-\frac{|\mathbf{x} - \mathbf{x}_i|^2}{\sigma^2}\right)\right]$ (see Sect. 9.2 on RBF); and (3) sigmoid kernels $\kappa(\mathbf{x}_i, \mathbf{x}_j) = \tanh\{a\langle \mathbf{x}_i, \mathbf{x}_j \rangle + b\}$ with $a > 0$ and $b < 0$ when $f(\mathbf{x}) = sign\left(\sum_{i=1}^n \chi_i \tanh\{a\langle \mathbf{x}_i, \mathbf{x}_j \rangle + b\}\right)$.

Traditional subspace methods (see Sect. 5.4) can be extended using kernel methods for the purpose of extracting non linear features and capturing higher order statistics. This is described next using the Kernel PCA (KPCA) as a case study (M. H. Yang, 2002b). KPCA is an extension of the standard PCA that corresponds to polynomial kernels of first degree. The original eigenvalue problem $\Sigma\Phi = \Phi\Lambda$ becomes in the high dimensional feature space $\mathbf{Z}$ (with Σ^Ψ as the covariance matrix) $\Sigma^\Psi \mathbf{W}^\Psi = \mathbf{W}^\Psi \Lambda$. The solutions for $\lambda \neq 0$ lie in the span of $\Psi(\mathbf{x}_1), \cdots, \Psi(\mathbf{x}_m)$ and are solved for as $\mathbf{w}^\Psi = \sum_{i=1}^m \alpha_i \Psi(\mathbf{x}_i)$. Using the kernel (Gram) matrix $\mathbf{K}$ and assuming that the mapped exemplars $\Psi(\mathbf{x})$ are centered in $\mathbf{Z}$, the KPCA problem becomes $m\lambda\mathbf{K}\alpha = \mathbf{K}^2\alpha$ or equivalently $m\lambda\alpha = \mathbf{K}\alpha$. The non linear (kernel eigenvalues) projections in the original space $\mathbf{X}$ are found as $\mathbf{w}^\Psi \Psi(\mathbf{x}) = \sum_{i=1}^m \alpha_i \kappa(\mathbf{x}_i, \mathbf{x})$ and are ordered according to the (non-increasing) eigenvalues found. Similar kernel methods are available for the other subspace methods, e.g., Kernel (Fisher) Linear Discriminant Analysis (KLDA) (Mika et al., 2001), Kernel Independent Component Analysis (KICA) (Bach and Jordan, 2002, Liu et al., 2004)), and Kernel [Self-Organization Feature Maps] Learning Vector Quantization (KLVQ) (Andras, 2002; Tan et al., 2004). M. H. Yang (2000b) reports that "Kernel eigenfaces and Kernel Fisherfaces methods achieve lower error rates than ICA, eigenfaces and Fisherfaces on the small ATT (formerly Olivetti) and Yale data bases. The performance achieved by the ICA method also indicates that face representation using independent basis images is not effective when the images contain pose, scale or lighting variation." Shen et al. (2004) subject Gabor filters (see Sect. 5.2) to KPCA and KLDA for both dimensionality reduction and increased class separability. Gabor-KLDA achieved best results on face (recognition and verification) authentication compared to PCA, Gabor-PCA, and KLDA using FERET and BANCA data bases and showed reliability against variability in expression, illumination and pose.

The kernel methods described so far are limited in that they can handle only global rather than local features. Wallraven et al. (2003) have addressed this limitation and proposed local kernels as described next. Given a set of face images $I = \{I_i\}_{i=1}^m$ one derives the corresponding set of local features $\mathcal{L} = \{\mathbf{L}_i\}_{i=1}^m$ such that $\mathbf{L}_i = \{f_j(I_i)\}_{j=1}^{n_i}$ for some feature extraction set $\{f_j\}_{j=1}^{n_i}$. Consider for all pairs $(\mathbf{L}_h, \mathbf{L}_k) \in \mathcal{L}$ the kernel $K_L(\mathbf{L}_h, \mathbf{L}_k) = \frac{1}{2}\left[\widehat{K}(\mathbf{L}_h, \mathbf{L}_k) + \widehat{K}(\mathbf{L}_k, \mathbf{L}_h)\right]$ with $\widehat{K}(\mathbf{L}_h, \mathbf{L}_k) = \frac{1}{n_h}\sum_{j_h}^{n_h} \max\{K_f(f_{j_h}(L_h), f_{j_k}(L_k))\}$ where the maximum is evaluated over $\{j_k = 1, \cdots, n_k\}$. Wallraven et al. (2003) prove that if $K_f(f_{j_h}, f_{j_k})$ is a Mercer kernel, then $K_L(\mathbf{L}_h, \mathbf{L}_k)$ is a Mercer kernel too. They consider then the jet features (see Sects. 5.2 and 6.5) $\mathbf{x}$ and $\mathbf{y}$ and measure their similarity using the Mahalanobis distance $d_M(\mathbf{x}, \mathbf{y}) = [\langle \mathbf{x} - \mathbf{y} | \Sigma^{-1} | \mathbf{x} - \mathbf{y} \rangle]^{0.5}$ with Σ for the covariance matrix. The distance d_M is mapped to the Euclidean distance d_E via the SVD decomposition $\Sigma^{-1} = \mathbf{A}'\mathbf{D}\mathbf{A}$, with $\mathbf{A}$ orthogonal and $\mathbf{D}$ diagonal, to yield $d_M(\mathbf{x}, \mathbf{y}) = d_E(\sqrt{\mathbf{D}}\mathbf{A}\mathbf{x}, \sqrt{\mathbf{D}}\mathbf{A}\mathbf{y})$. This leads to the following local Mercer kernels

$$K_p(\mathbf{x}, \mathbf{y}) = \left(\left(\sqrt{\mathbf{D}}\mathbf{A}\mathbf{x}, \sqrt{\mathbf{D}}\mathbf{A}\mathbf{y}\right) + c\right)^p, \quad p \in N, \ c \in \mathbf{R}^+ \quad (5.33)$$

$$K_{Gauss}(\mathbf{x}, \mathbf{y}) = \exp\left\{-\rho d_E\left(\sqrt{\mathbf{D}}\mathbf{A}\mathbf{x}, \sqrt{\mathbf{D}}\mathbf{A}\mathbf{y}\right)\right\} \quad (5.34)$$

5.8 Color

Even though the spectral content of illumination is dimensionally infinite, three dimensions are thought enough to adequately represent color. Judd et al. (1964) showed
using PCA and daylight illumination that 99% of the variance found in color can be accounted for with only three principal components. Furthermore, 85% of the variance
was captured using only two color channels. Pigmentation information provides an
important cue for face recognition (Russell et al., 2004). "Evidence that color is part
of the perceptual representation of individual faces is based on the finding that the
relative degree of red and green in a face correlates with sex in both humans and non-
human primates" (Johnson and Tarr, 2004). Furthermore, changes along the R(ed)/
G(reen) [but not Blue-Yellow (B/Y)] color dimension affect memory for faces and their
recognition. This prediction made by Johnson and Tarr (2004) is supported by their
psychophysical experiments. Our own experiments using PCA have also shown that
the Red and Green channels contain most of the information related to face identity.
While explaining trichromacy using comb-filtered spectra, Barlow (1989a) reported
that the spectral sensitivity curves for Red and Green overlap and peak very close at
570 and 545 nm, respectively. This is in contrast to the Blue sensitivity curve that
peaks at 440 nm and is well separated from both the R and G ones. The conclusion
drawn by Barlow is that "because the two curves [R and G] are so close together, they
can be treated alike for problems of spatial resolution." Note that the RGB space is
sensitive to viewing condition, e.g., luminance and surface orientation.

Swain and Ballard (1991) have shown that "color histograms [are stable representations in the presence of occlusion and over change in view] and provide an efficient
cue for indexing into a large database of models." Color appears to be most relevant in
identifying skin patches for face detection (see Sect. 7.1) and face tracking (see Sect.
7.7). The use of color for identification and authentication, if at all, is complementary
to cues such as luminance, shape and texture. Skin color, mostly determined [in controlled environments] by the reflectance and absorption characteristics of a thin surface
layer called the epidermis, changes according to the dopa melanin concentration and
varies among human races (Stoerring et al., 1999). The usefulness of skin color for
face biometrics comes from its rotation and scale invariance properties. Uncontrolled
environments and thus the lack of color constancy, however, require reliable modeling
and adequate learning to capture the invariance properties of skin color. Modeling
includes physics-based vision and mixtures of Gaussians. Angelopoulou et al. (2001)
"to explain skin color (and its variations) and to discriminate between skin and dyes
designed to mimic human skin" argue that "skin reflectance can be best approximated
by a linear combination of Gaussians or their first derivatives. [Regarding optical acquisition devices] the entire visible spectrum of skin reflectance can now be captured
with a few filters of optimally chosen central wavelengths and bandwidth." Outdoor
(video) surveillance, sensitive to color blurring due to motion, has access to the temporal dimension. It employs estimation and prediction across consecutive frames in order
to adapt to changes in the skin color perceived (Sigal and Sclaroff, 2000; McKenna et
al., 2000).

The majority of skin color models takes the form of Red-Green-Blue (RGB) tuples
even that most of the information is encoded by the Red-Green (RG) channels (Gutta
et al., 2001). The tristimulus color space is, however, affected by "color distortions and
metameric colors, i.e., colors with the same tristimulus values but with distinct spectral
power distributions. To counteract such effects one should use spectrophometers that
capture the ratio of the amount of reflected light divided by the amount of incident
light over a continuum of wavelengths and at very high resolutions (often finer than 0.3
nm)" (Angelopoulou et al., 2001). The trade-offs between approximation (in terms of
accuracy, computational efficiency and discrimination), on one side, and psychophysics
and rendering, on the other side, showed that a five-chromatic model based on linear
combination of Gaussians performs better than both wavelets and PCA.

Shih and Liu (2005) have undertaken an extensive comparative assessment of
different color spaces for face image retrieval using PCA on FERET data to show

that both chromatic and achromatic (intensity or luminance) information are needed. They showed that "the R and the RG color configurations in the RGB color space, the $(I_1\ I_2)$ color configuration in the $(I_1\ I_2\ I_3)$ color space, the V and the HV color configurations in the HSV color space, the YI color configuration in the YIQ color space, the YV color configuration in the YUV color space, the YCb, the YCr, and the YCbCr color configurations in the YCbCr color space, and the X and the XY color configurations in the XYZ color space all perform better than intensity images when applied to content-based face image retrieval." The formal definitions of the above color spaces are given next. The $(I_1\ I_2\ I_3)$ color space (Ohta, 1985) decorrelates the RGB space for stabilization purposes using the Karhunen-Love (KL) transform, which is similar to PCA

$$I_1 = \frac{1}{3}(R+G+B), \quad I_2 = \frac{1}{2}(R-B), \quad I_3 = \frac{1}{2}(2G-R-B) \tag{5.35}$$

The HSV color space, with H, S, and V standing for hue, saturation and brightness, MAX $=$ max(R, G, B), MIN $=$ min(R, G, B) and $\tau =$ MAX $-$ MIN for $R, G,$ and B coordinates scaled to $[0, 1]$ is defined as $H = 60\left(\frac{G-B}{\tau}\right)$ if MAX $= R$, $60\left(\frac{B-R}{\tau}+2\right)$ if MAX $= G$, $60\left(\frac{R-G}{\tau}+4\right)$ if MAX $= B$, -1 (undefined) if MAX $= 0$ and $H + 360$ if $H < 0$; $S = \frac{\tau}{\text{MAX}}$ if MAX $\neq 0$ and 0 otherwise; and V $=$ MAX. The YUV, YIQ and YCbCr (video) color spaces (see Sect. 4.3) are defined for $R, G,$ and B scaled to $[0, 1]$ as

$$\begin{bmatrix} Y \\ U \\ V \end{bmatrix} = \begin{bmatrix} 0.2990 & 0.5870 & 0.1140 \\ -0.1471 & -0.2888 & 0.4359 \\ 0.6148 & -0.5148 & -0.1000 \end{bmatrix} \begin{bmatrix} R \\ G \\ B \end{bmatrix} \tag{5.36}$$

$$\begin{bmatrix} Y \\ I \\ Q \end{bmatrix} = \begin{bmatrix} 0.2990 & 0.5870 & 0.1140 \\ 0.5957 & -0.2745 & -0.3213 \\ 0.2115 & -0.5226 & 0.3111 \end{bmatrix} \begin{bmatrix} R \\ G \\ B \end{bmatrix} \tag{5.37}$$

$$\begin{bmatrix} Y \\ C_b \\ C_r \end{bmatrix} = \begin{bmatrix} 65.4810 & 128.5530 & 24.9660 \\ -37.7745 & -74.1592 & 111.9337 \\ 111.9581 & -93.7509 & -18.2072 \end{bmatrix} \begin{bmatrix} R \\ G \\ B \end{bmatrix} \tag{5.38}$$

Note that for the YIQ color space, I and Q stand for the *hue* and *saturation* (depth of color). The G component, for the YUV color space, contributes most to the luminance, and the chrominances U and V are found by subtracting the luminance from the R and B components. The I and Q components in the YIQ color space can be found via clockwise rotation $(33°)$ from the corresponding U and V coordinates in the YUV color space. The YCbCr is a scaled and offset variant for the YUV color space. The CIE color space and its variants are derived from the standard XYZ color space

$$\begin{bmatrix} X \\ Y \\ Z \end{bmatrix} = \begin{bmatrix} 0.607 & 0.174 & 0.200 \\ 0.299 & 0.587 & 0.114 \\ 0 & 0.066 & 1.116 \end{bmatrix} \begin{bmatrix} R \\ G \\ B \end{bmatrix} \tag{5.39}$$

The RGB color space can be (approximately) recovered from the YUV and YIQ color spaces using the following inverse transformations

$$\begin{bmatrix} R \\ G \\ B \end{bmatrix} = \begin{bmatrix} 0.30 & 0.59 & 0.11 \\ -0.15 & -0.29 & 0.44 \\ 0.61 & -0.52 & -0.10 \end{bmatrix} \begin{bmatrix} Y \\ U \\ V \end{bmatrix} \tag{5.40}$$

$$\begin{bmatrix} R \\ G \\ B \end{bmatrix} = \begin{bmatrix} 1.00 & 0.96 & 0.62 \\ 1.00 & -0.27 & -0.65 \\ 1.00 & -1.10 & 1.70 \end{bmatrix} \begin{bmatrix} Y \\ I \\ Q \end{bmatrix} \tag{5.41}$$

One big challenge for face recognition that still waits for a reliable solution is invariance to temporal changes. FRVT2002 results have shown that face recognition performance for probes acquired at time intervals that exceed 6-12 months stands an even chance to be authenticated. Pan et al. (2003) approached the temporal challenge when they acquired 31 hyper spectral bands over the near-infrared $(0.7\mu m - 1.0\mu m)$ spectrum. The results reported indicate better performance than current face recognition systems "over several week time intervals [and] in the presence of a wide range of changes in facial pose and expression." The benefits reported accrued from "sensing of subsurface tissue structure which is significantly different from person to person, but relatively stable over time." Further improvements in accuracy and efficiency are expected from using spatial information and subspace methods.

6. Face Recognition

Vision without abstraction is blind; abstraction without vision is empty (Kant)

Face recognition includes both identification and verification/ authentication. It involves matching the biometric signatures derived during enrollment against those derived for some unknown face probes. The biometric signatures consist of representations induced by the face space used. Matching requires access to distance functions to measure for similarity between the above signatures and a priori thresholds for making decisions regarding either verification or identification. Such decisions include acceptance or rejection for 1-1 verification, and (a) rejection or (b) detection and classification for 1-M identification (see Sect. 1.1 and Fig. 1.2). Verification checks if the biometric signature presented is genuine and belongs to the identity declared by the client. Identification usually corresponds to closed set face recognition and is implemented as iterative verification. It always finds a mate for identification, the most similar one, even if there is none. Rejection, an option available only during open set face recognition, is appropriate for the case when there is no enrolled mate for the unknown probe.

6.1 Metrics

Face recognition requires metrics to measure for similarity. Basic and straightforward matching employs then minimum nearest neighbor (NN) distance classification. Distance functions are directly related to similarity functions and their effectiveness on classification performance can be quite different (Santini and Jain, 1999). The impact of the distance function used on performance is complementary to the impact of the loss function used during training (see Introduction to Ch. 3). A large distance indicates small similarity. Several well-known distance measures (see below) were assessed to evaluate their efficacy using different face representations, e.g., PCA and Fisherfaces, for face recognition using NN matching. Given two n-dimensional vectors $\mathbf{X}, \mathbf{Y} \in \mathbf{R}^n$, the similarity distances d used were

$$d_{L1}(\mathbf{X}, \mathbf{Y}) = |\mathbf{X} - \mathbf{Y}| = \sum_{i=1}^{n} |x_i - y_i| \qquad (6.1)$$

$$d_{L2}(\mathbf{X}, \mathbf{Y}) = ||\mathbf{X} - \mathbf{Y}||^2 = (\mathbf{X} - \mathbf{Y})^T(\mathbf{X} - \mathbf{Y}) \qquad (6.2)$$

$$d_{\cos}(\mathbf{X}, \mathbf{Y}) = -\frac{\mathbf{X}^T\mathbf{Y}}{||\mathbf{X}||||\mathbf{Y}||} \qquad (6.3)$$

$$d_{Dice}(\mathbf{X}, \mathbf{Y}) = -\frac{2\mathbf{X}^T\mathbf{Y}}{||\mathbf{X}||^2 + ||\mathbf{Y}||^2} = -\frac{2\mathbf{X}^T\mathbf{Y}}{\mathbf{X}^T\mathbf{X} + \mathbf{Y}^T\mathbf{Y}} \qquad (6.4)$$

$$d_{Jaccard}(\mathbf{X}, \mathbf{Y}) = -\frac{\mathbf{X}^T\mathbf{Y}}{||\mathbf{X}||^2 + ||\mathbf{Y}||^2 - \mathbf{X}^T\mathbf{Y}} = \frac{\mathbf{X}^T\mathbf{Y}}{\mathbf{X}^T\mathbf{X} + \mathbf{Y}^T\mathbf{Y} - \mathbf{X}^T\mathbf{Y}} \qquad (6.5)$$

$$d_{Mah+L2}(\mathbf{X}, \mathbf{Y}) \quad = \quad (\mathbf{X} - \mathbf{Y})^T \Sigma^{-1}(\mathbf{X} - \mathbf{Y}) \tag{6.6}$$

$$d_{Mah+\cos}(\mathbf{X}, \mathbf{Y}) \quad = \quad -\frac{\mathbf{X}^T \Sigma^{-1} \mathbf{Y}}{||\mathbf{X}||||\mathbf{Y}||} \tag{6.7}$$

with Σ as the covariance matrix of the training data. Σ is diagonal for PCA and the diagonal elements are the (eigenvalue) variances of the corresponding components. The Mahalanobis $+L_1$ distance, defined only for PCA, is

$$d_{Mah+L1}(\mathbf{X}, \mathbf{Y}) = \sum_{i=1}^{n} \left(\frac{|x_i - y_i|}{\sqrt{\lambda_i}} \right) \tag{6.8}$$

L_1 defines the city-block distance, while L_2 defines the Euclidean distance. Cosine, Dice, Overlap and Jaccard measure the relative overlay between two vectors. The L_1, L_2 and cosine distances can also be weighted by the covariance matrix of training data, leading to Mahalanobis related distances. Our empirical findings have shown that Mahalanobis related distances are superior to others when expressive features (driven by PCA) are used; while overlay related similarity distances are superior when discriminating (Fisherfaces) features are used. Russell and Sinha (2001), while comparing the L_1 and L_2 metrics, have come to conclude that the L_1 metric may capture human notions of image similarity better. Nearest neighbor completes the recognition process using any of the distances described above.

Matching is not limited to the similarity functions listed above. One of the alternatives available is to use chamfer or flexible matching, e.g., Direct Transform (DT) and the Hausdorff distance (Barrow et al., 1977; Huttenlocher et al., 1993). Flexibility makes matching reliable and robust to missing or degraded facial data that might otherwise influence the match score and miss recognition. The DT distance $D_p(\mathbf{X})$ for some distance metric $|| \cdot ||$ and set of points P is

$$D_P(\mathbf{X}) = \{d(i,j)\} = \min_{\mathbf{Y} \in P} [||\mathbf{X} - \mathbf{Y}|| + \mathbf{1}_P(\mathbf{Y})] \tag{6.9}$$

to allow for occlusion and disguise when some $\mathbf{Y} \in P$ are missing. The indicator $\mathbf{1}_P(\mathbf{Y})$ is 0 when $\mathbf{Y} \in P$ or is equal to some penalty λ otherwise. The Hausdorff distance is an instantiation of DT that maximizes its value for $h(A, B) = \max_{a \in A} D_B(a)$ (see Sect. 5.6).

Pigeon and Vandendorpe (1997) have proposed using chamfer matching for face profile authentication. The shape of the profile is directly used to avoid deriving and selecting features. Edges are found and the weak or noisy ones discarded. Chamfer matching seeks the best match between some reference ("gallery") face and a given candidate ("probe") face. Chamfer matching works well when the model and image probe do not have scaling and rotation differences. The chamfer distance approximation using DT (Borgefors, 1988) "starts from an image where each pixel is set to zero if it belongs to the profile, [and] infinity otherwise. The DT map is obtained by applying the macro code shown below, from left to right/top to bottom first, and right to left/bottom to top afterwards (two passes are enough)"

```
for i = 2 to #rows - 1
for j = 2 to #cols - 1
   d(i, j) = min {d(i - 1, j - 1) + 4, d(i - 1, j) + 3,
               d(i - 1, j + 1) + 4, d(i, j - 1) + 3, d(i, j)}
   for i = #rows - 1 downto 2
   for j = #cols - 1 downto 2
      d(i, j) = min {d(i, j), d(i, j + 1) + 3, d(i + 1, j - 1) + 4,
                  d(i + 1, j) + 3, d(i +1, j + 1) + 4}
```

Takacs and Wechsler (1998b) have shown using the Hausdorff distance, augmented by neighborhood functions with associated (local) penalties, that fast and accurate face screening of large facial databases becomes feasible even when less than 1% of the original gray scale face image information is available. This is achieved without the explicit need of point-to-point correspondence and tolerates non-rigid distortions. The use of local neighborhoods allows for further matching flexibility and weights accordingly the match scores. Faces were represented using (binary) edge images that discount changes in illumination. Jesorsky et al. (2001) have used the Hausdorff distance for robust face detection (see Sect. 7.1). Concepts similar to the Hausdorff distance can apply to faces encoded using gray scale and/or feature representations (through subspace methods).

Good metrics are critical for face recognition. The metrics can be actually learned to achieve specific objectives. Some algorithms, e.g., Multidimensional Scaling (MDS) (see Sect. 6.8) and Locally Linear Embedding (LLE) (see Sect. 7.6), learn an embedded metric implicitly. Alternatively, a semi-supervised learning framework provides some labeled exemplars and the metrics chosen optimize the recognition objectives and/or satisfy the constraints given in terms of similar pairs of faces. The metric found is explicit and is expected to show large similarity for faces that share the same ID, and small similarity for faces that belong to different subjects. Learning the right metric helps with temporal processing as faces spaced in time share similar ID. The choice of representative exemplars can be active rather than passive as it is the case with active learning (see Sect. 7.4). The metrics derived are used to enhance the unsupervised component, e.g., clustering. Xing et al. (2003) show how to learn the metric $d(\mathbf{X}, \mathbf{Y}) = \|\mathbf{X} - \mathbf{Y}\|_{\mathbf{A}}$, with positive semi-definite $\mathbf{A}$ to satisfy non-negativity and triangle inequality, between points $\mathbf{X}$ and $\mathbf{Y}$ such that the similarity constraints between some of the points hold true. "Setting $\mathbf{A} = \mathbf{I}$ gives Euclidean distance; if we restrict $\mathbf{A}$ to be diagonal, this corresponds to learning a metric in which the different axes are given different "weights"; more generally, $\mathbf{A}$ parameterizes a family of Mahalanobis distances over $\mathbf{R}^n$" (Xing et al., 2003). Both labeled and unlabeled exemplars are used by Hertz et al. (2004) to learn distance functions for image retrieval. The scheme proposed combines boosting ("weak learners") hypotheses (see Sect. 9.3) over the original product $(\mathbf{X}, \mathbf{Y})$ space. The optimal distance learned, over alternative partitions of the product space, is a (strong) hypothesis that yields maximum margin (see Sect. 3.3).

6.2 Verification and Identification

The standard face recognition methodology (see Fig. 1.2) calls for feature extraction to precede matching. The face space methods discussed in the previous chapter provide adequate means for creating biometric signatures suitable for matching and recognition. Valentin et al. (1994), while reviewing connectionist models of face processing, have suggested that (a) both linear and non-linear auto-associative networks, and multi-layer networks trained using back propagation can serve the dual purpose of compression and feature selection; and that (b) features emerge naturally from image-based codes. This is similar to using self-organization for codebook derivation (see Sect. 5.6), back propagation for color compression (see Sects. 3.2 and 5.8), and distributed and associative memories (DAM) for overcoming occlusion and disguise (see Sect. 10.7). Samaria and Young (1994), drawing analogies from speech recognition, have proposed Hidden Markov Models (HMM) for face identification. Facial regions were associated with the states of a continuous HMM once the 2D face images are converted to 1D sequences using face symmetry. "This allows the boundaries between regions to be represented by probabilistic transitions between states and the actual image within a region to be modeled by a multivariate Gaussian distribution." HMM are formally modeled by some (finite) set of hidden states H and triplet $\Omega = \{P, E, \pi\}$ that describes a Markov process. Each hidden state has a probability distribution over its output tokens according to the emission matrix E. Transitions between the hidden states take place according to P, while the initial hidden state probability distribution is given by π. The HMM parameters are learned using the Baum-Welch algorithm.

The algorithm computes ML estimates using EM. The algorithm, referred to as the forward-backward algorithm (Rabiner, 1989), learns the HMM (hyper) parameters using the emissions E observed on training data T. The algorithm seeks the maximum likelihood (ML) solution $\hat{\Omega}$ that maximizes the likelihood $P(T|\Omega)$ given training data T. The optimal but hidden state sequence, which best explains the observations E witnessed and finds the ID of the subject, is found using the Viterbi dynamic programming (DP) algorithm. HMM are representative of recognition-by-parts models with the states and transitions corresponding to parts and relations among them (see Sect. 6.5). Extensions of HMM to 2D suffer from exponential growth and 1D (horizontal and vertical) approximations are used instead. Eickeler et al. (2000) have shown that ORL JPEG compressed images can be recognized using pseudo-2D HMM.

The probabilistic (Bayesian) face recognition PCA - difference approach proposed by Moghaddam and Pentland (1997) is a straightforward application of the orthogonality principle (see Sect. 3.2) using the PCA space for representation. Assume a multivariate Gaussian density for human faces and the Mahalanobis distance to measure the similarity between faces. According to the orthogonality principle, the similarity distance can be approximated using the sum of the (within) distance in the PCA feature space and the distance from the feature PCA space

$$d(\mathbf{X}) = \sum_{i=1}^{M} \frac{y_i^2}{\lambda_i} + \frac{1}{\rho} \left(||\mathbf{X}|| - \sum_{i=1}^{M} y_i^2 \right) \tag{6.10}$$

where λ_i are the largest M eigenvalues, $M < N$, ρ is the mean of the residual eigenvalues, Φ^T is the PCA transformation, and the transformed data $\mathbf{Y}$ is $\mathbf{Y} = \Phi^T \mathbf{X}$. This approach "relies on similarity metrics which are invariably based on Euclidean distance or normalized correlation, thus corresponding to standard 'template matching' - i.e., nearest-neighbor based recognition. Such a simple metric suffers from a major drawback: it does not exploit knowledge of which types of variation are critical (as opposed to incidental) in expressing similarity" (Moghaddam et al., 2000). To compensate for such apparent shortcomings, the authors use the Bayesian framework and introduce a probabilistic measure based on the belief that the image intensity differences, $\Delta = I_1 - I_2$, are the ones that capture the features most essential for authentication. *Intrapersonal* variations Ω_I (corresponding, for example, to different facial expressions) and *extra personal* variations Ω_E (corresponding to variations between different individuals) complete the proposed difference model. The similarity measure becomes $S(I_1, I_2) = P(\Delta \in \Omega_I) = P(\Omega_I|\Delta)$. A posteriori probabilities are sifted through to seek for the MAP solution among

$$S(I_1, I_2) = P(\Delta|\Omega_I)P(\Omega_I)[P(\Delta|\Omega_I)P(\Omega_I) + P(\Delta|\Omega_E)P(\Omega_E)]^{-1} \tag{6.11}$$

The priors $P(\Omega_I)$ and $P(\Omega_E)$ reflect specific operating conditions. This particular Bayesian intra/extra personal classifier formulation "casts the standard face identification task (essentially an M-ary classification problem for M individuals) into a *binary* pattern classification with Ω_I and Ω_E. This simpler problem is then solved using MAP or equivalently if $S(I_1, I_2) > \frac{1}{2}$." The simpler alternative, based only on the interpersonal likelihood $S = P(\Delta|\Omega_I)$ (and thus equal priors) and leading to maximum likelihood (ML) rather than MAP recognition, was also used and it proved to be almost as effective.

Perronnin and Dugelay (2003) and Perronnin et al. (2005) have addressed the problem of increased discriminative information for the purpose of enhanced face recognition. Discriminative information is either made available to the face representation or it becomes part of the deformable model used to match among faces. Using FERET, the authors conclude that "the discrimination of the deformable model should be preferred and can result in a 25%-40% relative error reduction compared to the baseline system." The general framework proposed entails a new measure of "distance" between faces. "This measure involves the estimation of the set of possible transformations between face images of the same person. The global transformation, which is assumed to be too complex for direct modeling, is approximated by a patchwork of local transformations, under a constraint imposing consistency between neighboring local transformations. The proposed system of local transformations and neighboring constraints is embedded within the probabilistic framework of 2D HMM." The intra class variability models variations in facial expressions and illumination. The above approach proposed by Perronnin et al. (2005) outperforms methods that trace their ancestry to Moghaddam and Pentland (1997) Bayesian intra/extra personal classifier. The explanation comes from the fact that "the proposed system of local transformations and neighboring constraints is embedded within the probabilistic framework of a 2D HMM" that enforces consistency and takes advantage of it. The emphasis on consistency is closely related to the coherent but unique spatio-temporal trajectories that each face spans across space and time.

Support Vector Machines (SVM) are one of the most widely methods used for classification. Jonsson et al. (2000) have carried out a series of experiments using SVM for face verification and recognition using M2VTS data that included 295 subjects. They reported an equal error rate (EER) of 1% for verification and a rank one error rate of 2% for identification. Their empirical findings suggest that "SVM are robust against changes in illumination provided theses are adequately represented in the training data." Most interesting, however, and in line with comments made earlier that representation supersedes classification in terms of relevance for classification, the above authors also report that "when the representation space already captures and emphasizes the discriminatory information, SVM loose their superiority." Radial Basis Functions (RBF) (see Sect. 9.2) is the other major classifier used for face recognition. An efficient hybrid method for high-speed face recognition based on the discrete cosine transform (DCT), LDA and RBF was proposed by Chen and Wu (2005). The dimensionality of the original face image is reduced using DCT, illumination changes are handled by discarding the first few low-frequency DCT coefficients, while LDA provides the discriminant features used by RBF.

Kotropoulos et al. (2000) have proposed a dynamic link architecture (DLA) (see Sect. 6.5) using dilation and erosion morphology rather than Gabor (wavelets) for feature extraction. Both the morphological and Gabor features describe and implement the scale space concept. The authors motivate the use of morphological features for reasons such as "scale space morphological techniques are able to find the true size of the object in an image smoothed to a particular size, the scale parameter has a straightforward interpretation, since it is associated with the area of the domain of the structuring function, dilation and erosions can be computed very fast and deal with the local extremes in an image. They are well suited for facial feature representation, because key facial features are associated either to local minima (e.g., eyebrows/eyes, nostrils, end-points of lips, etc) or to local maxima (e.g., the nose tip)." Feature selection using PCA and/or LDA is done prior to elastic graph matching (EGM).

Evolutionary pursuit (EP) (see Sect. 5.5) provides an adaptive alternative to the more traditional PCA and Fisherfaces subspace representations used for face recognition. The FERET data used to evaluate EP consisted of 1,107 face images, cropped to 64×96 size, captured from 369 subjects with three frontal images for each of them. The variety of the data used comes from the fact that for the first 200 subjects the third image is acquired at low illumination, while for the remaining 169 subjects the face images, referred to as duplicates, are acquired during different photo capture sessions. The background is uniform and the face images are not masked in order to preserve valuable face outline information. Two images of each subject are used for training with the remaining face image used for testing such that the training and test sets include 738 images and 369 images, respectively. The recognition performance using the EP subspace was found to compare favorably (using the McNemar's test) against both eigenfaces and Fisherfaces methods (Liu and Wechsler, 2000).

Oriented PCA (OPCA) (Diamantaris and Kung, 1996) is yet another example (in addition to EP) where the cost function balances between complementary requirements. While PCA is characteristic of unsupervised learning, OPCA has now instant access to class information. Rather than including the class labels during the LDA stage (that follows PCA) as it is the case with Fisherfaces, OPCA expands on the original cost function of PCA by including a penalty term that accounts for misclassification errors. OPCA thus trades fidelity in reconstruction for classification accuracy. The "orientation" aspect is such that the PCA axes are iteratively rotated or steered to bring the directions for maximum variance and maximum class separation margin in close alignment. One could further expand on the quality of the transformed subspace by combining EP and OPCA using a cost function that includes fidelity in reconstruction, empirical risk, and predicted risk. Jang et al. (2004) combine PCA and Quantum-inspired Evolutionary Algorithm (QEA) (Han and Kim, 2004) for face verification. The problem addressed in particular is that of threshold selection. Using the probabilistic (Bayesian) approach discussed earlier, QEA seeks to evolve "the optimal weight factors in the distance measure for a predetermined threshold value that distinguishes between face images and non face images." The QEA inspired fitness function can learn ahead of time, i.e., a priori, the threshold (across ROC) most likely to yield the best recognition performance.

6.3 Open Set Recognition

Open set face recognition expands the scope of traditional face identification. It involves both detection and recognition (Li and Wechsler, 2003; Li and Wechsler, 2004; Li and Wechsler, 2005) (provisional patent #60/623064 filed by Li and Wechsler) (see Fig. 6.1a). Detection means familiarity rather than finding faces in an image or tracking them in a crowd. When detection fails, the face is rejected using the "none of the above" option rather than be misclassified as the most similar face ID (in the gallery) as closed set face recognition does. Failing the "detection" test should be caused by a face that has never been enrolled and thus is unknown and novel. Rejection can also be caused by a deliberate attempt made by an impostor to penetrate a secure facility. Watch list (see Sect. 6.4), a special instance of open set face recognition, corresponds to the case when the overlap between the gallery and probe sets is the gallery (watch list) itself and the probe set size is much larger than the gallery (see Fig. 6.1b). Watch list corresponds to the case when subjects are matched for negative identification against some WANTED list.

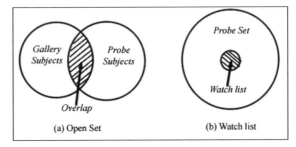

Fig. 6.1. Open Set Face Recognition and Watch List (Reprinted from Li and Wechsler, Open Set Face Recognition Using Transduction, *IEEE Transactions on Pattern Analysis and Machine Intelligence*, ©2005 IEEE).

Transductive inference (see Sect. 3.5) is most appropriate for face recognition when either some of the faces available for training lack proper ID labels or when one has to handle open set face recognition. The missing labels during enrollment are annotated using assignments consistent with those for similar faces that are already enrolled. The challenge is to choose among several (tentative) classification labels, each of them leading to different partitionings of the ID(entity) face space, the one that is most consistent with the training set composing the gallery. The latter case, about standard open set face recognition and watch list, is addressed here and in the next section, respectively. Towards that end, the original scope for transductive inference is augmented to cope with (a) detection in addition to mere identification using a priori setting of rejection thresholds; and (b) the ability to cope with multi-class rather than two-class classification.

There is a strong connection between transductive inference and Kolmogorov complexity. Let $\#(z)$ be the length of the binary string z and $K(z)$ be its Kolmogorov complexity, which is the length of the smallest program (up to an additive constant) that a Universal Turing Machine needs as input in order to output z. The randomness deficiency $D(z)$ for string z (Li and Vitanyi, 1997; Vovk et al., 1999) is

$$D(z) = \#(z) - K(z) \qquad (6.12)$$

$D(z)$ measures how random the binary string z is. The larger the randomness deficiency, the more regular and more probable the string z is (Vovk et al., 1999). Another connection between Kolmogorov complexity and randomness can be made using MDL (minimum description length) modeling. Transductive inference seeks to find from all the possible labeling available the one that yields the largest randomness deficiency, i.e., the most probable labeling. This choice models the working ("test") exemplar set W in a fashion most similar to the training set T that would minimally change the original (predictive) model learned from and for T or alternatively expand it to accommodate learning from the augmented set $T \bigcup W$. "The difference between the classifications that induction and transduction yield for some working exemplar approximates its randomness deficiency. The intuitive explanation is that we disturb a classifier (driven by T) by inserting a new working exemplar in a training set. A magnitude of this disturbance is an estimation of the classifier's instability (unreliability) in a given region of its problem space" (Kukar and Kononenko, 2002).

Randomness deficiency is, however, not computable (Li and Vitanyi, 1997). One has to approximate it instead using a slightly modified Martin-Löf test for randomness. The values taken by such randomness tests are referred to as p-values (to be distinguished from those used in statistics where they measure how well the data support or discredit the null hypothesis). The p-value construction used here has been proposed by Gammerman et al. (1998) and Proedrou et al. (2001). Given a sequence of distances from exemplar i to other exemplars, the strangeness of i with putative label y is defined as

$$\alpha_i = \frac{\sum_{j=1}^{k} d_{ij}^{y}}{\sum_{j=1}^{k} d_{ij}^{-y}} \qquad (6.13)$$

The strangeness measures the uncertainty for a data point or (face) pattern with respect to its assumed or putative identity label and the labels for all the other face patterns. Formally, the strangeness measure α_i is the ratio of the sum of the k nearest distances d from the same class y divided by the sum of the k nearest distances from all the other classes ($\neg y$). The strangeness of an exemplar increases when the distances from the exemplars of the same class become larger and/or when the distances from the other classes become smaller. The smaller the strangeness, the larger its randomness deficiency is. Note that each new test exemplar e with putative label y (and strangeness α_{new}^{y}) requires to recompute, if necessary, the strangeness for all the training exemplars when the identity of their k nearest neighbors exemplars changes due to the location of (the just inserted new exemplar) e.

The standard p-value construction shown below, where l is the cardinality of the training set T, constitutes a valid randomness (deficiency) test approximation (Melluish et al., 2001) for some transductive (putative label y) hypothesis. The standard p-value is

$$p_y(e) = \frac{\#\{i : \alpha_i \geq \alpha_{new}^y\}}{l+1} \qquad (6.14)$$

An alternative valid randomness (deficiency) test approximation (Vovk et al., 1999) and the one used here for open set face recognition, defines the p-value for a working exemplar e (with putative label y) as

$$p_y(e) = \frac{f(\alpha_1) + f(\alpha_2) + \cdots + f(\alpha_l) + f(\alpha_{new}^y)}{(l+1)f(\alpha_{new}^y)} \qquad (6.15)$$

where f is some monotonic non-decreasing function with $f(0) = 0$, e.g., $f(\alpha) = \alpha$. Empirical evidence shows that the alternative randomness (deficiency) approximation yields better performance than the standard one, which may suffer from "distortion phenomenon" (Vovk et al., 1999). If there are c classes in the training data, there are c p-values for each working exemplar e according to its putative membership in each one of the classes. Driven by p-values, one chooses the particular labeling that yields the largest randomness deficiency for some specific class membership, i.e., the putative label y that appears the least strange and for whom the p-value is the largest. This largest p-value also defines the *credibility* for the label chosen, which is a measure of information quality. The associated *confidence* measure, which is derived as the 1st largest p-value (or one) minus the 2nd largest p-value, indicates how close the first two assignments are. The confidence value indicates how improbable face classifications other than the predicted ID label are, while the credibility value shows how suitable the training set is for the classification of that particular face exemplar.

The transductive inference approach uses the whole training set T to infer a classification rule for each new exemplar. Based on the p-values defined above, Proedrou et al. (2001) have proposed the TCM-kNN (Transduction Confidence Machine - k Nearest Neighbors) to serve as a formal transduction inference algorithm for classification purposes. TCM-kNN has access to a distance function d that measures the similarity between any two exemplars. Given a new (test/probe) working exemplar e, the p-values derived by TCM-kNN record the likelihoods that the new exemplar comes from each putative subject in the gallery. If some p-value p is high enough and significantly outscores the others, the probe is mated to that putative subject ID with credibility p. If the top ranked (highest p-values) choices are very close to each other and outscore the other choices, the top choice can still be identified but its recognition is questionable due to ambiguity. The probe is accepted but identified with low confidence.

Biometric systems in general, and face recognition engines, in particular, require significant calibration and tuning, for setting the detection thresholds before any "plug and play" takes place. Setting thresholds is not easy to automate due to their strong dependency on image quality and the composition of the gallery. Note that "much more is known about the population, [or genuine customers,] of an application than is known about the enemies, [i.e., the imposters that have to be rejected]. Consequently, the probability of a false alarm rate (FAR), a false match [for screening and positive identification], is hard to estimate. Hence, the false reject rate (FRR), that concerns open set negative identification, is easier to estimate than the false alarm rate, because the biometric samples of the enemy population are not available" (Bolle et al., 2004). The thresholds needed for field deployment and operation have to be set up ahead of time, i.e., **a priori**, and without resorting to additional client, i.e., impostor data. The alternative of setting the thresholds **a posteriori** using the ground truth available from the aggregate similarity scores recorded for matching the probe set against the gallery set is not appropriate because the ground truth is not available during system operation.

TCM-kNN does not address the detection (decision) aspect needed for open set face recognition. The proposed Open Set TCM-kNN solution includes first a detection stage that uses the PSR (peak-side-ratio) to characterize the distribution of p-values

$$PSR = \frac{(p_{max} - p_{mean})}{p_{stdev}} \qquad (6.16)$$

where p_{mean} and p_{stdev} are the mean and standard deviation for the p-value distribution without the p_{max} value. PSR implements the equivalent of the likelihood ratio (LR) used in detection theory and hypothesis testing, with LR the ratio between the null hypothesis H_0 that the unknown face is enrolled in the gallery, and the alternative hypothesis H_1 that the face has never been seen or enrolled before. PSR serves here to determine optimal thresholds for accepting or rejecting the null hypothesis H_0 concerning the particular working exemplar e. Towards that end, one has to (re)label the training exemplars, one at a time, with all the putative labels except the one originally assigned to them. The PSR distribution derived in such a manner is characteristic of negative identification or rejection. Implementation wise, each training exemplar $\mathbf{X}$ has its mates first removed from the training set and treated as a probe to derive its p-value and corresponding PSR. The PSR values found for such exemplars are low - since they play the role of impostors and lack mates - compared to the PSR values derived for legitimate subjects. Low PSR values call thus for rejection. The PSR distribution obtained over the training set provides a robust method for deriving the rejection threshold without exposure and training with negative examples, characteristic of impostors. The threshold for rejection can be learned a priori using only the composition and structure of the training data set at enrollment time. Such type of constrained learning corresponds to semi-supervised learning. The PSR distribution (and its tail) for presumed impostors provides a robust method for deriving a priori the rejection threshold Θ for detection as

$$\Theta = PSR_{mean} + 3 \times PSR_{stdev} \qquad (6.17)$$

where PSR_{mean} and PSR_{stdev} are characteristic of the PSR distribution for presumed impostors. The test face is rejected if $PSR_{test} < \Theta$ holds true. Authentication takes place only for (large) values that exceed Θ.

There are conceptual similarities between the use of PSR to approximate the likelihood ratio and score normalization methods (see Sect. 12.2) used in speaker verification (Furui, 1997; Reynolds et al., 2000). The alternative hypothesis H_1 is modeled there using either the cohort or the universal background model (UBM). The cohort approximates H_1 using speech specific (same gender impostor) subjects, while UBM models H_1 by training a single speaker background model. The PSR measure is conceptually related to the cohort model, as both implement the LR using local estimation for H_1. The ability of the cohort model to discriminate the speaker's speech from those of similar, same gender impostors, is much better than that offered by UBM (Mak et al., 2001) and it leads to improved security at lower FAR (false acceptance rates). Similar arguments hold for other modalities, including human faces whose authentication is sought. The same cohort model leads to an alternative definition for strangeness that was successfully used to implement and combine weak learners for recognition-by-parts (see Sect. 9.7).

The experimental design and results on open set face recognition using transduction follow Li and Wechsler (2005). The data set from FERET consists of 750 frontal face images from 250 subjects - see Fig. 6.2 where each column corresponds to one subject. 200 subjects come from the difficult FERET batch #15 that was captured under variable illumination and/or facial expressions, while the other 50 subjects are drawn from other FERET batches. There are three normalized (zero mean and unit variance) images of size 150×150 with 256 gray scale levels for each subject. The normalized 300 face images from 100 subjects are used to learn the PCA and Fisherfaces face bases. Towards that end, 50 subjects are randomly selected from batch #15, while the other 50 subjects are drawn from other batches. The remaining 450 face images from 150 different subjects are used for enrollment and testing. The faces are projected on the face bases derived ahead of time to yield 300 PCA coefficients and 100 Fisherfaces using LDA on the reduced 300 PCA space (Liu and Wechsler, 2002). For each subject, two images are randomly selected for training and one image for testing. Several well known similarity measures (see Sect. 6.1) are used to evaluate different (PCA and Fisherfaces) face representation in conjunction with Open Set TCM-kNN (for $k = 1$). Our empirical findings indicate that Mahalanobis related similarity distances are better when expressive features (driven by PCA) are used; while overlay related similarity distances are better when discriminating (Fisherfaces) features are used. The nearest neighbor classifier completes the identification process using Mahalanobis $+ L_2$ and cosine distances for PCA and Fisherfaces, respectively.

Fig. 6.2. Face Images for Open Set Face Recognition.

Comparative performance of Open Set TCM-kNN against Open Set {PCA, Fisher-faces} is presented next. The detection thresholds for Open Set TCM-kNN are derived ahead of time, while for Open Set {PCA, Fisherfaces} the thresholds are found as explained next. The Open Set {PCA ("eigenfaces") and Fisherfaces} classifiers derive their rejection threshold from the intra- and inter- distance (similarity) distribution of training exemplars in a fashion similar to that used by FRVT2002. The statistics of intra- distance ("within") distribution set the lower bound of the threshold, while the statistics of inter- distance ("between") distribution set the upper bound. As the minimum distance of the new (test/probe) exemplar to the prototypes for each class becomes closer to or larger than the upper bound, the more likely it is that the test exemplar will be rejected.

The recognition rate reported below for Open Set {PCA and Fisherfaces} is the percentage of subjects whose probe is either correctly rejected or accepted and recognized. From the 150 subjects available, 80 subjects are randomly selected to form a fixed gallery, while another 80 subjects are randomly selected as probes such that 40 of them have mates in the gallery. The gallery and probe sets overlap thus over 40 subjects. The gallery consists of two (out of three) randomly selected images; the probes consist of the remaining image for faces that belong to the gallery and one (out of three) randomly selected image for faces that do not belong to the gallery. During testing different distance measurements are used and the threshold varies from the lower to the upper bound as explained above. The same experiment was run 100 times with different probe sets. The distance measurements d for Open Set {PCA, Fisherfaces} that yield the best results are Mahalanobis $+L_2$ and cosine, respectively. When ground truth is available, the thresholds Θ are optimally set to yield maximum performance; rejection occurs when min $d > \Theta$. The best average recognition rates (over 100 experiments), i.e., correct rejection and identification, for Open Set {PCA, Fisherfaces} classifiers at FAR = 7% were

- 74.3% (s.d. = 3.06%) for PCA representation and

$$\Theta \sim \frac{(Intra_{mean} \times Intra_{stdev} + Inter_{mean} \times Inter_{stdev})}{(Inter_{stdev} + Intra_{stdev})} \qquad (6.18)$$

- 85.4% (s.d. = 2.30%) for Fisherfaces representation and

$$\Theta \sim \frac{(Intra_{mean} \times Inter_{stdev} + Inter_{mean} \times Intra_{stdev})}{(Inter_{stdev} + Intra_{stdev})} \qquad (6.19)$$

For Open Set PCA, the results are quite similar when the number of components used varies from 150 to 300, while for Open Set Fisherfaces, the results are quite similar when the number of components used varies from 55 to 90. More experiments have been done by randomly varying the gallery set and the results obtained were similar. The optimal threshold, however, varies with the gallery and probe sets, and is hard to determine it a priori. Attempts made to learn the threshold a priori without access to ground truth were unsuccessful.

The same Open Set experiment was run then using Open Set TCM-kNN for $k = 1$. The only difference now is that the rejection threshold Θ is computed a priori as explained earlier. Detection requires large PSR. The average recognition (correct rejection and identification) rates for FAR $= 6\%$ are

- 81.2% (s.d. $= 3.1\%$) for PCA using $\Theta = 5.51$ and the Mahalanobis $+ \ L_2$ distance
- 88.5% (s.d. $= 2.6\%$) for Fisherfaces using $\Theta = 9.19$ and the cosine distance

Using PCA, the results for Open Set TCM-kNN are quite similar when the number of components used varies from 170 to 300, while using Fisherfaces the results for Open Set TCM-kNN are quite similar when the number of components used varies from 55 to 80. More experiments were done in a random fashion by varying the gallery but the results obtained were similar. The threshold varies with the chosen gallery but it is always determined a priori. This is different from Open Set {PCA, Fisherfaces} where the threshold is derived a posteriori using ground truth. Keeping this significant difference in mind, Open Set TCM-kNN outperforms the Open Set {PCA, Fisherfaces} classifiers both in performance and functionality.

The next experiment described assessed how the overlap size between the gallery and probe sets affects open set face recognition performance and the role different face representations play. Fig. 6.3 shows the mean detection and identification rates, labeled as recognition rates, for Open Set TCM-kNN using PCA and Fisherfaces representations with the Mahalanobis $+ \ L_2$ and cosine distances, respectively. There are 150 subjects, the size for both the gallery and the probe sets is 75 (subjects), and the overlap between the gallery and the probe set varies from 0 to 75 subjects. The average results reported were obtained over 100 randomized (over gallery and probe composition) runs. The performance goes down, almost linearly, as the overlap size increases. Fisherfaces representations yield overall much better performance when compared to PCA representations, except for a very small overlap size when the performance observed is close but still better for Fisherfaces compared to PCA. The explanation for the performance observed is that as the size of the overlap increases, it becomes more difficult to detect and identify subjects from the overlap set. The performance for the Open Set {PCA, Fisherfaces} classifiers was found to be very poor. In addition, Open Set TCM-kNN provides measures of credibility and confidence concerning the recognition decisions made, which facilitate data fusion.

6.4 Watch List and Surveillance

The gallery of wanted individuals is now very small compared to the number of subjects expected to flood the biometric system (see Fig. 6.1b). Negative identification takes place for subjects not listed on the watch list for surveillance. Again there are 150 subjects, three images from each subject, for a total of 450 face images. Open Set {PCA, Fisherfaces} and Open Set TCM-kNN classifiers are compared on small watch lists ("galleries"), whose size varies from 10 to 40 subjects. The mean (average) performance (detection and identification) rates obtained over 100 randomized runs are reported. Let the watch list size be n subjects, each of them having 2 (two) images in the gallery. There are $(450 - 2n)$ face images in the probe set, n stands for the number of subjects on the watch list and $(3 \times (150 - n))$ stands for the number of face images that come from subjects that are not on the watch list. The small size of the watch list requires that the threshold for rejection is derived from larger populations

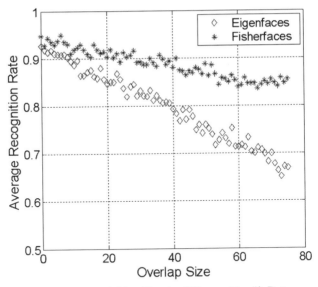

Fig. 6.3. Mean Detection and Identification("Recognition") Rates vs. Overlap Size Using Open Set TCM-kNN (Reprinted from Li and Wechsler, Open Set Face Recognition Using Transduction, *IEEE Transactions on Pattern Analysis and Machine Intelligence*, ©2005 IEEE).

for stability purposes. The decision thresholds Θ are found in a manner similar to that used by cohort models for speaker verification. Towards that end, the gallery is augmented with different subjects randomly drawn from other FERET batches that include illumination and facial expression variation. The intra- and inter- distance distributions and the PSR distributions determine as before the rejection thresholds for Open Set {PCA, Fisherfaces} and Open Set TCM-kNN, respectively. The size of the gallery used to determine the threshold is kept constant at 80 throughout the runs so the number $(80 - n)$ of different subjects needed to augment it varies according to the size of the watch list.

Table 6.1 and 6.2 show the mean performance of Open Set {PCA, Fisherfaces} and Open Set TCM-kNN for different sizes of the watch list. When the watch list size is n, the accuracy (detection and identification rate) is (average correct rejection + average correct recognition)/$(450 - 2n)$. The results obtained are interpreted as follows. Since the watch list size is much smaller than the number of subjects that should be rejected, the (detection and identification rate) accuracy will be very high even if all the probes are rejected. As a consequence, the average correct reject number, average correct recognition number, and the detection and identification accuracy are shown for comparative performance evaluation. The average results are better the closer the correct rejection number is to $(3 \times (150 - n))$, the closer the correct recognition number is to the watch list size, and the higher the accuracy is. The Fisherfaces representations outperform PCA regarding both rejection and identification decisions. As the watch list size increases, the performance drops as expected.

Table 6.2 shows the average performance of Open Set TCM-kNN for different watch list sizes. PCA and Fisherfaces representations yield similar performance when using Open Set TCM-kNN. The Fisherfaces are somewhat better than PCA when identification decisions are involved. Open Set TCM-kNN is better than Open Set {PCA, Fisherfaces}, when the correct rejection, correct recognition, and the accuracy

Table 6.1. Mean Performance on Watch List for Open Set {PCA, Fisherfaces} (Reprinted from Li and Wechsler, Open Set Face Recognition Using Transduction, *IEEE Transactions on Pattern Analysis and Machine Intelligence*, ©2005 IEEE).

Watch List Size	eigenfaces (Mahalanobis + L_2)			Fisherfaces (Cosine distance)		
	Average Correct Reject	Average Correct Recognition	Accuracy	Average Correct Reject	Average Correct Recognition	Accuracy
10	369.03	6.68	87.37%	389.16	7.93	92.35 %
15	355.67	9.82	87.02%	373.86	12.39	91.96 %
20	343.81	12.43	86.89%	359.92	17.04	91.94 %
25	331.40	15.09	86.62%	345.11	20.60	91.43 %
30	319.50	17.79	86.48%	330.70	24.93	91.18 %
35	305.43	20.42	85.75%	315.15	29.04	90.58 %
40	292.97	23.19	85.45%	300.95	32.99	90.25 %

are taken into account, especially when the watch list size is large. The overall performance for Open Set TCM-kNN, which stays almost constant as the watch list size increases, is more stable than the performance observed for Open Set {PCA, Fisherfaces}. The difference in performance between Fig. 6.3 and Table 6.2 suggests that the gallery size affects algorithmic performance. In Fig. 6.3 the gallery (watch list) size is always 75 subjects and only the overlap size between the gallery and probe sets changes, while in Table 6.2 the gallery size (watch list) varies.

Table 6.2. Mean Performance on Watch List for Open Set TCM-kNN (Reprinted from Li and Wechsler, Open Set Face Recognition Using Transduction, *IEEE Transactions on Pattern Analysis and Machine Intelligence*, ©2005 IEEE).

Watch List Size	eigenfaces (Mahalanobis + L_2)			Fisherfaces (Cosine distance)		
	Average Correct Reject	Average Correct Recognition	Accuracy	Average Correct Reject	Average Correct Recognition	Accuracy
10	389.74	7.64	92.41%	393.08	8.48	93.62 %
15	376.28	11.72	92.38%	380.24	12.16	93.43 %
20	364.18	14.12	92.27%	365.28	16.16	93.03 %
25	350.24	18.26	92.13%	351.84	19.56	92.85 %
30	336.94	21.62	91.94%	335.72	25.52	92.63 %
35	322.96	25.22	91.63%	322.28	29.36	92.54 %
40	309.24	27.98	91.14%	308.64	33.28	92.41 %

The availability of rejection for both open set face recognition and watch list and surveillance handles random or deliberate changes in appearance. It corresponds to outlier detection (for clustering) and novelty detection (for learning). The comparative advantages of transduction for open set face recognition using strangeness come from the non-parametric implementation and the deterministic a priori threshold selection. No assumptions are made regarding the underlying PDF responsible for the observed data clusters, i.e., the face ID. Feature selection for enhanced pattern recognition can be further achieved using strangeness and p-values (see Sect. 9.7).

The acquisition and/or generation of additional exemplars for each class (to increase k in Open Set TCM-kNN) should lead to better performance. Additional venues worth pursuing would take advantage of the linkage between transductive inference, active learning and evidence accumulation (see Sect. 7.4), co-training and semi-supervised learning and score normalization methods. The active learner decides whether or not to request labels ("classification") for unlabeled data in order to reduce the volume of computation and the human effort involved in annotation (Tong and Koller, 2001). Active learning selects, one by one, the most informative face patterns from some working set W, such that, after labeling by an expert ("classifier"), the patterns selected guarantee the best improvement in the classifier performance. The use of unlabeled data, independent of the learning algorithm, is characteristic of co-training (Blum and Mitchell, 1998; Nigam et al., 2000). The idea behind co-training is to learn two classifiers which bootstrap each other using labels for the unlabeled data (Krogel and Scheffer, 2004). Co-training leads to improved performance if at least one classifier labels at least one unlabeled instance correctly for which the other classifier currently errs. Unlabeled exemplars which are confidently labeled by one classifier are then added, with labels, to the training set of the other classifier. Semi-supervised learning, driven by labeled constraints, derives optimal metrics and thresholds, and guides transduction.

6.5 Recognition-by-Parts

Recognition-by-parts is treated separately due to its growing importance for object recognition, in general, and face processing, in particular. Face processing includes both face detection (see Sect. 7.1) and face identification and authentication (see Sect. 6.2). Recognition-by-parts is the structural and compositional alternative to holistic recognition methods. Its origins go back to the seminal work of Fischler and Elschlager (1973) whose goal was "given some description of a visual object, find that object in an actual photograph." The philosophy surrounding recognition-by-parts, however, goes much further back according to Edelman et al. (2002). They quote from Plato's Theaetetus (360 BC), in which Socrates points out the circularity in treating syllables as combinations of letters, if the latter are to be defined merely as parts of syllables "What might seem to be the most ingenious of all:- that the elements or letters are unknown, but the combination or syllables known [· · ·] can he be ignorant of either singly and yet know both together?"

The parts or nodes characteristic of such structural methods are also referred to as components, landmarks or patches, and are held together or connected by linkages or strings (see Fig. 6.4). The parts together with the link connecting them define graphs known as constellations. The painter Cézanne refers to patches and the strings holding them together when he says that "to read nature is to see it · · · by means of color patches, following upon each other according to a law of harmony." Statistical decision theory, e.g., template matching using correlation, applies only when "we possess a precise description of the noise and distortion process which defines the mapping between the reference and its image in the sensed scene" according to Fischler and Elschlager (1973). Their solution "bypasses" the need for such requirements and instead includes a "combined descriptive scheme and decision [embedded] metric." The matching algorithm for implementing the proposed solution is analog to a "transparent rubber sheet" that can be stretched, and "uses a procedure similar to dynamic programming in order to cut down on the vast amount of computation otherwise necessary." The rubber sheet distortions were limited in scope and range, and their relative costs varied. The structural components need to be adequately defined and modeled to facilitate their robust detection and subsequent discrimination. Mohan et al. (2001) detects pedestrians with the face, legs and arms serving as parts. Manual annotation of the parts is sensitive to noise as "the salience of facial features is different for unfamiliar and famous faces and subtle changes in the relative position of facial features can have a dramatic effect on the appearance of a face" (Valentine, 2001). The reference descriptive scheme matches that for an unknown probe when the corresponding (local) components are (almost) congruent and not much stretching is needed to make the corresponding (global) graphs or constellations similar. The smaller the amount of stretching needed, the better the overall fit is. The matching score is a weighted combination of the local and global evaluation costs.

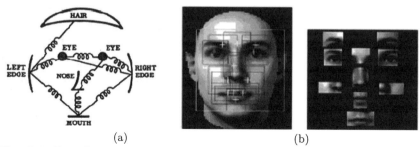

(a)   (b)

Fig. 6.4. Face Components and Their Linkages (a) Reprinted from Fischler and Elschlager, The Representation and Matching of Pictorial Structures, *IEEE Trasactions on Computers*, ©1973 IEEE; (b) Reprinted from *Computer Vision and Image Understanding*, Vol. 91, Heisele et al., Face Recognition Component-Based Versus Global Approaches, 2003, with permission from Elsevier.

Recognition-by-parts came in response to image variability, in general, and pose changes, in particular. The holistic approach solution for coping with variability requires point correspondence using precise alignment. This is quite hard to be met in practice. One way around the correspondence problem for the holistic approach is to cluster the views and build a corresponding family of (view specific) classifiers indexed by pose. Recognition-by-parts makes it easier. It does not seek for invariance. Instead, it handles variability using flexible geometric modeling and morphing to compensate for pose changes and possibly for limited occlusion and distortions (see Sect. 9.7). Representative of recognition-by-parts are the related methods of Dynamic Link Architecture (DLA) and Elastic ⟨Bunch⟩ Graph Matching (E⟨B⟩GM) (Lades et al., 1993; Wiscott et al., 1997). Elastic graph matching is a minimum distance classifier with respect to (a) scale space representation; and (b) some non-rigid string geometry connecting the nodes across the face. The string geometry is flexible enough to tolerate small changes in appearance, e.g., facial expressions, and to provide limited invariance. Recall that the parts or nodes define a set of landmarks, e.g., the pupils, the corners of the mouth, the tip of the nose et al. The landmarks are coarsely represented using Gabor jets $J_i = a_i \cdot \exp(j\Phi_i)$ with amplitude $a_i(\mathbf{x})$, which vary slowly with position $\mathbf{x}$, and phase $\Phi_i(\mathbf{x})$ (see Sect. 5.2). Iterative matching seeks the minimum for an energy function $S(\mathbf{J}, \mathbf{J}')$ that compares jets $\mathbf{J}$ and $\mathbf{J}'$ for amplitude preservation, on one side, and estimates the relative displacement of jets' locations, for geometry preservation, on the other side.

$$S(\mathbf{J}, \mathbf{J}') = \sum_i -\frac{\langle \mathbf{J}, \mathbf{J}' \rangle}{||\mathbf{J}||||\mathbf{J}'||} + \lambda \sum_{\mathbf{x}} d(\mathbf{J}, \mathbf{J}') \qquad (6.20)$$

Note that a phase sensitive similarity function can substitute for or augment the first component (for motivation see Sect. 5.2). Minimizing the energy function is computationally expensive. An approximate solution, which decouples the above computation, is found in two stages (Lades et al., 1993). Rigid matching, similar to template matching, first scores for jets' compatibility using local neighborhoods surrounding the jets' location $\mathbf{x}$. The second stage stretches (in a non-rigid fashion) the grid used for mapping the face using local perturbations in order to find ways to decrease the energy S. Orders of magnitude faster computation can be achieved using the power spectrum of the discrete wavelet transform (DWT) (see Sect. 7.2) rather than Gabor jets.

Face recognition using EGM requires first to find the landmarks and place them in correspondence. To find the landmarks, one needs some general face representation that accounts for image variability due to age, gender and diversity among the subjects, e.g., human eyes can be shaped differently. Wiscott et al. (1997), aware that "it would be too expensive to cover each feature combination by a separate graph," decided to "instead combine a representative set of individual model graphs into a stack-like structure, called a face bunch graph (FBG)" and proposed elastic bunch graph matching (EBGM). Each face model still enjoys the same grid structure like EGM but is now spanned by landmarks, which are represented using a bunch of jets instead and are connected by springs or edges that take the average distance among them for value. "An eye bunch, for instance, may include jets from closed, open, female, and male eyes etc. to cover these local variations." The minimization of the energy function includes now also searching, independent of each other, for the best jets or local experts, among the bunch dedicated to each landmark. Both EGM and EBGM lack when they assume that the jets are connected using similar strings disregarding the scale they were acquired at. Alternatively, the bunch for a landmark part can be reliable found using the golden ratio template (see Fig. 6.5), scale space, and clustering driven by strangeness (see Sect. 9.7).

Active shape models (ASM) (Lanitis et al., 1997) are flexible models similar in concept to the original model proposed by Fischler and Elschlager (1973). The standard frame of reference is the average face exemplar $\bar{\mathbf{X}}$, and deviations from the average face are computed from training data. Principal PCA directions for the deviations define the modes of variation. Any training exemplar $\mathbf{X_i}$ can be approximated and/or searched for using $\mathbf{X_i} = \bar{\mathbf{X}} + \mathbf{Pb}$ where $\mathbf{P}$ is a matrix of unit eigenvectors for the covariance matrix of deviations , while $\mathbf{b}$ is a vector of eigenvector weights that accounts for the model's parameters, $\mathbf{b} = \mathbf{P}^T(\mathbf{X_i} - \bar{\mathbf{X}})$. Flexibility is achieved by varying the model parameters starting from $\mathbf{b}$ but keeping them for plausibility within $\pm 3\sigma$ (standard deviations).

Recognition-by-parts was recently shown to outperform a holistic system on a very small, dense and thus redundant video sequence data base. Training had access to about 10,000 gray level face images of only ten subjects, from which about 1,400 were frontal views and the rest were acquired with rotations in azimuth up to about $\pm 40^o$. The test set, including 1,544 images of all the ten subjects, also acquired with rotation in depth up to about $\pm 40^o$, was recorded with the same camera but on a separate day, under different illumination, and with different background (Heisele et al., 2003). One of the concepts that recognition-by-parts has proposed is to dedicate individual classifiers for each of the face components and to combine accordingly their responses. Ivanov et al. (2004) have explored different strategies for classifier combination, e.g., voting, sum of outputs, and product of outputs. All the strategies mentioned showed a marked improvement compared to the scenario when "the gray values of the facial components are concatenated to a single feature vector which is fed into the face recognition classifier." Further improvements in performance were reported by using a Bayesian method that "weights the classifier outputs prior to their combination."

Recognition-by-parts requires choosing and learning the components, and locating and extracting them. The location of face components or their fragments calls for image segmentation which is a hard nut to crack, if at all possible, due to clutter. The components are expected to be low dimensional and relatively easy to extract and describe. Towards that end, Mikolajczyk et al. (2004) have proposed a generic framework for human detection, e.g., head or body, based on a probabilistic assembly of robust part detectors. The relative positions or object structure is modeled by a probabilistic framework using Gaussian densities. The parts code for co-occurrences of local features and "capture the spatial layout [and context] of the part's appearance." The body, head or for that matter any object, can be described using a joint likelihood Bayesian model that drives the search and scores the quality of recognition. The proposed model induces "a part assembly strategy [that] reduces the number of spurious detections and the search space" [using the appearance of parts and their relative position]. Assume features F, body B, and the body part relations encoded by geometric parameters R. The geometric relations R between parts are represented using Gaussians indexed by position and relative scale. The likelihood decision for some body B is

$$\frac{P(B|R,F)}{P(\neg B|R,F)} = \frac{P(R|F,B)}{P(R|F,\neg B)} \cdot \frac{P(F|B)}{P(F|\neg B)} \cdot \frac{P(B)}{P(\neg B)} \qquad (6.21)$$

The above approach is deficient because it requires precise (manual) annotation for parts and extensive training to approximate the Bayesian model. There is no common framework for basic modeling that can be shared, and learning each new category starts from scratch. Fergus et al. (2004) used a similar approach that models the constellation of parts in terms of descriptions D, locations $\mathbf{x}$, and scales S. The parts model the appearance ("texture") or the geometry ("curves") of a region. The relative locations $\mathbf{x}$ for the parts are modeled using a joint Gaussian distribution. Learning the model parameters requires expensive EM, heavily dependent on initialization, while the large number of parameters leads to overfitting unless large image sets are used for training. Such requirements are hard to meet in practice and the models are narrowly defined. Note that the above methodology is suitable for detection/categorization rather than multi-class face recognition.

Fei-Fei et al. (2006) have questioned recognition-by-parts algorithms regarding (i) their stringent requirements that images of each exemplar object are geometrically normalized and aligned with a prototype; and (ii) the huge size of training data required. This can become "expensive and tedious as 10^4 training exemplars are needed using a well-known rule-of-thumb that says that the number of training exemplars has to be 5 to 10 times the number of object parameters." Incremental and unsupervised learning can mitigate training requirement based upon "a much smaller training set using priors [and models] derived from previously learned classes" (Fei-Fei et al., 2003) (see analogy to UBM ⟨universal background models⟩). This is reminiscent to the way children continuously learn new categories from their relatively limited exposure to objects. Competitive learning enables the faces to share how the parts that compose the facial landscapes are described. What is shared across incremental semi-supervised learning is some generic but constrained domain knowledge about objects, in general, and faces, in particular. Variability co-exists with generic but common face characteristics. To implement such an approach for learning object categories, Fei-Fei et al. (2006) have proposed one-shot learning, which involves heavily parameterized Bayesian models and marginalization over the full set of parameters θ and training (image) data T,

$$\begin{aligned} p(\text{object}|\text{test}, \text{train}) &\cong p(\text{test}|\text{object}, \text{train})p(\text{object}) \\ &= \int p(\text{test}|\theta, \text{object})p(\theta|\text{object}, \text{train})d\theta \\ &= \int p(\text{test}|\theta, \text{object})p(\text{train}|\theta, \text{object})p(\theta)d\theta \qquad (6.22) \end{aligned}$$

Note the similarity between eqs. 6.21 and 6.22. The motivation for approximation rather than equality (using the chain rule for probability in eq. 6.22) comes from the assumption that the term $p(\text{T}\,|(\text{foreground})\,\text{object})/p(\text{T}\,|\text{background (clutter)}\,\text{object})$ is constant, and that the corresponding odds are somehow incorporated in the threshold used for decision-making. The assumptions behind eq. 6.22 are, however, quite restrictive. They include closed set recognition (over the training set T), pre-segmented and complete images, Gaussian (rather than uniform) background that does not include any of the categories learned. The odds are, however, not constant. The likelihood that a face is present varies. The odds are not the same when the background for the face comes from your cluttered office rather than from outdoors, e.g., an empty field or the forest. It is not obvious how to define, extract, and select the invariant features needed to account for large number of objects and/or background types, and their variability in terms of geometry and illumination. Since it is almost impossible to estimate the parameters needed to define full-fledged features, one-shot learning assumes the posterior and priors have the same functional form, the Norm-Wishart distribution, which leads to close integration. Such an assumption makes the computation simpler and feasible to implement but may be invalid for the problem. Learning employs variational Bayesian EM and assumes that the priors of the parameters for all the categories are the same. This is one of the reasons for using one-shot learning and explains why learning does not have to start from scratch. Such an assumption may be valid for several classes but is questionable when the number of classes is large.

The Bayesian framework for one-shot learning detects a category C when its likelihood ratio R_C is greater than some given threshold, with $R_C = p(\text{object}|\text{query, T})/p(\text{background (clutter) object}|\text{query, T})$. One-shot learning, which corresponds to marginalization (to integrate out redundant variables such as θ), is an example of Bayesian inference for estimating unknown probability density functions (see Sect. 3.1). The estimator is a weighted sum of all possible predictive models, with weights determined by priors and the accrued evidence (or posterior probability) that each model is correct. "However, multidimensional integration (due to the large number of parameters), presents a challenging problem. Standard numerical integration is impossible, whereas analytic evaluation may be possible only under restrictive assumptions when the posterior density has the same form as a prior (typically assumed to be Gaussian) and the density is linear in parameters θ; marginalization fails when the true model does not belong to the set of approximating functions" (Cherkassky and Mulier, 1998). Last but not least, one shot learning is limited because it is intended for detection rather than multi-class recognition.

The basic questions for face recognition-by-parts concern the "real (face) estate" support the parts draw their descriptive information from, the representation used for parts, the geometric (retinotopic) language that connects the face components, and last but not least the specific combination of descriptive and relational information. Kim et al. (2005) have proposed using LS (local salient) ICA (architecture I) for face recognition. Similar to recognition-by-parts methods, LS ICA employs local and salient facial information. This provides limited immunity against local distortion and partial occlusion. The proposed method derives the LS ICA base images using kurtosis maximization to "remove residual non-local modulation." The base images are sequenced in "the decreasing order of class separability as to maximize the recognition performance." Experimental results suggest that LS ICA, implemented using FastICA (rather than InfoMax) performs better than PCA, (architecture I and II) ICA (see Sect. 5.4 and Ch. 15), LFA, and LNFM. FastICA computes independent components by "maximizing non-Gaussianity of whitened data distributions using a kurtosis maximization process [to trigger sparse face representations]." Assume that $\mathbf{S}$ stands for unknown source signals, $\mathbf{A}$ is the unknown mixing matrix, $\mathbf{X}$ is the mixed model such that $\mathbf{X} = \mathbf{AS}$. FastICA estimates the independent source signals $\mathbf{U}$ by computing the separating matrix $\mathbf{W}$ such that $\mathbf{U} = \mathbf{WX} = \mathbf{WAS}$.

The support grid that guides the parts' location can come from competitive or unsupervised learning (see Sect. 5.6 and Fig. 5.10), golden ratio face templates (see Fig. 6.5), or attention schemes that lock on the major facial landmarks (Takacs and Wechsler, 1998; Walther et al., 2005). This preempts the need for image segmentation, which is NP-hard (Gurari and Wechsler, 1982). One of the suggestions made is that the parts are described by features that encode for both shape ("what") and location ("where") (Edelman and Intrator, 2000). Neuropsychological evidence suggests that "face recognition based on holistic information can occur in isolation from recognition based on local feature cues [i.e., parts]. [Furthermore], local features provide insufficient information to ensure the accurate discrimination of identity and, thus, holistic processing of the face is also necessary (McKone et al., 2001). The corollary is that the whole face should be used as one of the components that face recognition-by-parts has access to (see Sect. 10.6), and that both shape (outlines) and texture are used to describe the parts.

Feature selection is critical for recognition-by-parts. Versatility and efficiency are achieved when recognition-by-parts is model free and non parametric, the parts are automatically learned by grouping similar features, enrollment and recognition do not require prior segmentation, and clutter, occlusion, and/or pose can be accommodated.

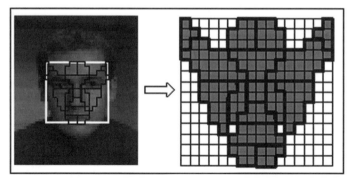

Fig. 6.5. Golden Ratio Face Template (Reprinted from *Computer Vision and Image Understanding*, Vol. 95, Anderson and McOwan, Robust Real-Time Face Tracker for Cluttered Environments, 2004, with permission from Elsevier).

Such requirements are met by competitive data fusion methods driven by transduction and boosting (see Sect. 9.7). Conceptual support for a unifying and competitive approach for recognition-by-parts comes from Edelman et al. (2002). They argue for learning parts, referred to as fragments, from unsegmented raw images of structured objects. Frequently occurring fragments "tend to be treated as a whole" and facilitate the authentication of occluded and/or disguised faces. Learning, in search of a sparse and joint code "that resemble the 'what + where' receptive fields found in the ventral visual stream", is incremental and unsupervised. "Fast imprinting of parts with lateral interactions" are claimed to "support the systematic treatment of structured objects."

6.6 Face Selection

Face selection expands on the traditional role of face recognition. It assumes that multiple image sets for each enrollee are available for training, and that sequences of face images, possibly acquired from CCTV, are available for testing. The goal is to identify the (CCTV) frames where each enrolled subject shows up. Subjects can appear and disappear as time progresses so the presence of any face is not necessarily continuous across (video) frames. Faces belonging to different subjects can appear in a sporadic fashion across the sequence. Some of the CCTV frames could actually be void of any face, while other frames could include occluded or disguised faces from different subjects. Face selection is different from key frame selection using change detection as practiced during video processing for archival and retrieval (see Sect. 7.5).

The formal problem statement for face selection goes as follows. Given a (training) set T of face exemplars $\mathbf{X}$ from one or several subjects y where $y \in \{1, \cdots, N\}$ and an unstructured (working or test video) set W of faces find the best subset (of size k) from W, if any, for each enrolled subject y from T. The relevance of face selection for security applications is straightforward. Given descriptions of wanted subjects the challenge consists of finding across the (CCTV) sequence the faces, if any, which match each subject. Most if not all of the faces from W fail to match the faces from the wanted list T. It is apparent that W should be consistent with T for face selection to take place and that transduction plays a major role. Consistency means that because W and T are drawn independently from the same distribution of the face population, the error distributions observed, e.g., leave-one-out cross-validation, are consistent over $T \bigcup W$. This is quite similar to co-training (Blum and Mitchell, 1998) where the classifiers learned over T and W have to agree on their putative labeling assignments.

Kleinberg and Tardos (2005) have originally addressed the multi-class case for selection and have provided non-trivial polynomial approximation algorithms for solving it. The goal is to assign one of k (class) labels to each one of n objects, in a way that is consistent with the training data available. Using pair wise relationships among the objects to be classified one seeks to find a classification that optimizes a (combinatorial) function consisting of the costs to assign labels to each object, and separation costs - based on the pair of choices one makes for two "related" objects. The resulting labeling problem is viewed by the authors as "a substantial generalization of the multi-way cut problem, and equivalent to a type of uncapacitated quadratic assignment problem." Both the assignment and separation costs could be defined in terms of strangeness. Active rather than passive access to pairwise relationships, characteristic of semi-supervised learning for pairwise constrained clustering (Basu et al., 2004), is a possible approach. The pairs are chosen in an active fashion during stream-based face selection. The optimization index seeks in an iterative fashion those pairs (i, j) with $i \in T$ and $j \in W$ whose strangeness driven transductive predictions are close to each other.

Blum and Chawla (2001) used the binary rather than the more general multi-way setting for selection. They show how to find exact solutions using polynomial time algorithms, where minimum cuts are used to learn from labeled and unlabeled data. Minimum cuts minimize the sum over some connecting edges and are an indicator for the least disruptive partitions or alternatively label assignments. The minimum cuts for the binary case are found, using the max-flow algorithm, over the adjacency matrix $\mathbf{A}$ of the graph G whose nodes come from T and W and are linked by edges that measure their similarity. Max-flow can be computed with the Ford-Fulkerson method, which is usually implemented using the Edmonds-Karp algorithm. The proposed framework is similar to that used for grouping or image segmentation, on one side, and image restoration and noise suppression, on the other side. The optimization goal is to smooth the data while making the minimal number of changes. Further computational analogies are possible, e.g., Ising spin systems, fluid dynamics and Markov random fields (MRF). Joachims (2003) has proposed spectral graph partitioning (SGP) for transductive learning, in general, and selection and co-training, in particular. To avoid unbalanced splits and degenerate results, the average [weight of the] cut, $ACut$, rather than the sum of the weights, is minimized. One formally seeks for $\min_y cut(\mathbf{A}, y)/[|\{i : y_i = 1\}| \, |\{i : y_i = -1\}|]$. Alternatively, one can use the normalized cut, $NCut$ and seek to trade between balance and separation. Spectral relaxation was proposed to get around the fact that both $Acut$ and $Ncut$ are NP-complete problems. The challenges left involve outliers and open set face recognition to accommodate unknown classes. Note that learning to enroll the signatures for each class y during face selection requires taking advantage of negative or counter examples. The near counter examples are most important and include the cohort (negative) samples characteristic of impostors. The negative examples used are the faces whose appearance looks like y while their actually come from a different class y. The strangeness can rank the examples in terms of class membership while at the same time supports graph cuts for selection purposes. The negative examples are selected in an active fashion using the closeness of their (strangeness driven) p-values for different putative labels (see Sect. 7.4).

6.7 Categorization

Categorization is different from familiarity and is hard to solve. One can recognize specific subordinate classes and still fail to model the category they belong to or recognize other subordinate classes from the same category. Human screeners use category-level knowledge to screen for targets and people. Smith et al. (2005a; 2005b) report on cognitive studies related to the apparent constraints and limits on humans' categorization abilities when they face visual complexity, and the direct implications for aviation security. Familiarity inflates true performance as it is limited to known targets, what Smith and his colleagues refer to as specific-token effects. Participants in the studies reported were found to have "enormous difficulty. Despite intensive and ongoing category training, they detect targets at near-chance levels unless displays are extremely simple or target categories extremely focused." General category knowledge to compensate for unfamiliarity has a hard time to emerge, if at all. Possible remedies, but not a panacea, are extensive and varied training. Weakly learning, modeled after recognition-by-parts using boosting and strangeness (see Sect. 9.7), aims to overcome specific-token effects.

There is evidence that basic level categorization precedes identification and helps it. Categorization takes place along two complementary dimensions, those of appearance and functionality. It involves abstraction and sharing of common characteristics among the members the category is made of. In a similar fashion, face categorization, e.g., gender and ethnicity, can help with face recognition. What kind of information is needed for categorization tasks? Mangini and Biederman (2004) designed a series of experiments whose purpose is to make "the ineffable explicit." The observers were unaware that the underlying face (which was midway between each of the classes) was identical throughout a task, with only the high levels of noise rendering it more like one category value or the other. The subjects had to perform on (male vs. female) gender, (happy vs. unhappy) expression, and (Tom Cruise vs. John Travolta) individuation tasks. The difference between the average of noise patterns for each task provided a linear estimate for what it takes to choose one category rather than the other. The reverse correlation method used estimated what "is in the subject's (rather than the experimenter's) head." The explanations for such "superstitious perceptions" make explicit how categorization might take place. As expected the experimenters found that "whereas gender and expression can be conveyed by low frequency information, individuation is carried in higher frequency channels."

A "fundamental question about cognition concerns how knowledge about a category is acquired through encounters with examples of the category" (Knowlton and Squire, 1993). Gender and ethnicity categorization are obvious examples in the context of face recognition, and they induce a categorical rather than identity face space. In practice, categorization helps with binning by reducing the fraction of the data base that has to be matched for identification or authentication, e.g., on the average the face for a male has to be matched only against half of the data base. The obvious dichotomy for encoding categories provides for their corresponding regions of identity be induced by either specific exemplars or their abstracted representations. Memory-based reasoning, characteristic of the exemplar approach to categorization (similar to ABC), supports the view that categorical concepts are implicitly defined in terms of some of the exemplars encountered; it does not call for stored abstractions and/or prototypes (Estes, 1993). This view is shared by Knowlton and Squire, who suggest that "category-level knowledge has no special status but emerges naturally from item memory," and that a novel probe "would be endorsed as belonging to a particular category as a function of the similarity between the new item and the exemplars of that category already stored in memory." The abstractive (NBC) approach, on the other hand, defines regions of identity in terms of prototypes (see Sect. 5.6 on ABC and NBC.)

McNeill (1998) suggests that help for categorizing gender comes from "the clues scattered across the countenance. Men in general have craggier features. Their brows and chins jut out more. Their foreheads often slope more steeply, and their eyes lie in deeper sockets. They have longer cheeks and greater overall depth of face. Women, on the other hand, have smaller faces, usually about four-fifth the size of men's. Their face seems wider and their eyes appear much bigger. Their eyelashes are longer and thicker. Their mouths are smaller, their upper lips relatively shorter, and their cheeks stick out more than men's, because of their smaller nose. The nose also sets the sexes apart. Women have smaller, wider, and more concave noses. Men's are bigger and more protrusive, possibly because men need a larger respiratory system overall, from lungs to breathing passages to nose."

Our hybrid approach for gender and ethnicity categorization involves ensembles of radial basis functions (ERBF) (see Sect. 10.5) and decision tress (DT) (see Sect. 7.1) (Gutta et al., 2000). The data for our experiments included a very large set of 3,006 frontal images (from FERET) that corresponds to 1,009 human subjects (see Fig. 6.6). The faces were normalized to a standard resolution of 64 × 72. The ground truth label for gender or ethnic origin was determined by visual inspection and human consensus. The labels for gender are male and female, while the ethnic labels used were Caucasian, South Asian, East Asian, and African. The total number of images for the 'male' and 'female' gender labels is 1,906 and 1,100, respectively, while the total number of face images for ethnicity categorization is 1932 Caucasian, 362 South Asian, 474 East Asian, and 238 African , respectively.

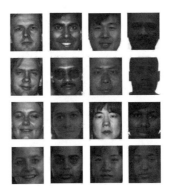

Fig. 6.6. Gender and Ethnicity.

The interface for numeric to categorical data conversion required by decision trees (DT) is provided by Ensembles of Radial Basis Functions ERBF. The hybrid ERBF/DT categorization approach is beneficial in several ways. First, query by consensus (provided by ERBF) copes with the inherent variability of the image formation and data acquisition process. This is accomplished by employing different topologies for the RBF networks and training them on different data sets corresponding to variations on the original data. Second, flexible and adaptive thresholds are derived using the entropy as opposed to ad-hoc and hard thresholds. Third, categorization rules (provided by DT) are available. The cross-validation results reported by Gutta et al. (2000) yield on the average an accuracy rate of 96% for gender classification and 92% for ethnic classification. Twenty cross-validation cycles were performed and averaged for gender categorization using for each cycle 60 face images for training and the remaining 2,946 images for testing.

6.8 Morphometrics

The chapter started with a brief discussion on the role similarity plays in face recognition. Similarity is most affected by the representations and distances used for matching. The distances used are mostly deterministic with the exception of some flexible methods like chamfer matching and the Hausdorff distance. An alternative for the direct similarity metrics discussed earlier is statistical shape analysis, which refers to the geometrical study of random objects where location, rotation and scale information can be removed through proper registration or equivalently through shape growth and/or deformations. Characteristic of statistical shape analysis is morphometrics, in general, and procrustean methods, in particular.

The term procrustean comes from Greek mythology. It refers to the giant Procrustes who would capture people, tie them to an iron bed and stretch them to make their bodies adjust to the one size fits all bed in his house. (Procrustes was eventually met the same fate by Theseus.) Morphometrics, a more encompassing term, comes also from Greek, where *morph* means shape. It is about the taxonomy of organisms and *allometry* - how growth changes the (relative) proportions of body parts. Geometric morphometrics, which goes beyond multivariate statistical analysis, focuses on the coordinates of (facial) landmarks and the preservation of their relative spatial layout (Rohlf and Marcus, 1993). One immediate forensic application for geometric morphometrics is in phylogeny estimation. This helps with locating missing children as they grow older. The fundamental geometric construction underlying geometric morphometrics is the Kendal's shape space. "Each point in this shape space represents the shape of a configuration of points in some Euclidean space, irrespective of size, position, and orientation. In the Kendal's shape space, scatters of points correspond to scatters of entire landmark configurations, not merely scatters of single landmarks. Most multivariate methods of geometric morphometrics involve linearizations of statistical analysis of distances and directions in this underlying space" [1]

Procrustes analysis, characteristic of superimposition methods, seeks to eliminate the non-shape variation element for constellations of landmarks by overlaying them according to some optimization criterion and using least square (MSE) estimation. After the optimal superimposition is found, shape differences, if any, tabulate the residuals in the transformed coordinates between the shape under scrutiny and the model it is compared against. Alternatively, "the thin plate spline can be used to map the deformation in shape from one object to another (Bookstein, 1991). Differences in shape, represented in this fashion, are a mathematically rigorous realization of D'Arcy Thompson's (1917) idea of transformation grids, where one object is deformed or "warped" into another. Differences in shape among objects can then be described in terms of differences in the deformation grids depicting the objects" (Adams et al., 2004). Subspace methods can describe and/or summarize the deformations taking place. Towards that end, Nastar (1998) has used deformable matching for face recognition. The intensity for the face image is modeled as a deformation in a 3D mesh $(x, y, I(x, y))$ that obeys Lagrangian dynamics. Matching two faces (in terms of the analytic modes of vibration) yields a dense correspondence field (or 3D warp). Valid deformations and/or their principal PCA directions are learned to provide a priori knowledge about the subspace used for face deformations (similar to the active shape models introduced in Sect. 6.5). The deformation grids can also be the result of competitive learning, similar to the way caricatures are generated (see Sect. 5.6).

Procrustes analysis (Dryden and Mardia, 1998) seeks to align two sets of (face) points A and B that belong to (test) data $\mathbf{D}$ and model (gallery) $\mathbf{M}$, respectively, and lie in a single image plane. Following Carcassoni and Hancock (2002), $A = \{\mathbf{u}_i, \forall\, i \in D\}$ and $B = \{\mathbf{v}_j, \forall\, j \in M\}$, while $\mathbf{D}$ and $\mathbf{M}$ are coordinate matrices that have $\mathbf{u}_i$ and $\mathbf{v}_j$ for their columns. The data and model share the same cardinality or number of facial landmarks. The matrix $\mathbf{DM}$ is factorized as $\mathbf{DM} = \mathbf{U}\Delta\mathbf{V}$ using SVD. Δ is a diagonal matrix whose elements are greater or equal than zero, while $\mathbf{U}$ and $\mathbf{V}$ are orthogonal matrices that define the rotation matrix $\mathbf{R} = \mathbf{VU}$, which aligns the directions of $\mathbf{D}$ and $\mathbf{M}$. The alignment has to be further refined in order to maximize the correlation between $\mathbf{D}$ and $\mathbf{M}$. Towards that end, the centroids of $\mathbf{D}$ and $\mathbf{M}$ are brought into correspondence, and the transformed data points $\mathbf{D}$ are scaled to display similar variance to that shown by model $\mathbf{M}$. The overall optimal transformation that aligns $\mathbf{D}$ onto $\mathbf{M}$, using covariance matrices Σ and $\hat{\nu}_i$ serving for new data coordinates is

$$\hat{\nu}_i = \mu_{\mathbf{M}} + \left[\frac{(trace\Sigma_{\mathbf{M}})}{(trace\Sigma_{\mathbf{D}})}\right]^{0.5} \mathbf{VU}'(\mathbf{u}_i - \mu_{\mathbf{D}}) \tag{6.23}$$

---

[1] http://life.bio.sunysb.edu/morph/glossary/gloss1.html

Carcassoni and Hancock show that multidimensional scaling (MDS) offers "the advantage over conventional Procrustes analysis that it extends the range of rotational angles over which is effective. Moreover, it does not require separate, and explicit, centering, scaling and rotation steps. It also proves robust under severe levels of point-set noise and corruption." MDS (see below) is applied to the inter-point distance matrix with "alignment the result of transforming different [data and model] point-sets into a common embedding (sub) space, and correspondences located on a nearest neighbor basis."

Multidimensional Scaling (MDS) transforms data to lie on a lower dimensional manifold embedded in the original but higher dimensional space (Kruskal, 1964; Borg and Groenen, 1996) (see Sect. 7.6 for manifolds). Given numerical similarities between pairs of abstract entries, MDS maps them as vectors in the Euclidean space. The mapping is such that the dot-products or distances between the vectors match the given similarities or differences between their corresponding entities. The match for each pair-wise difference is done using the standard Euclidean distance. MDS facilitates the interplay between visual exploration and data analysis through the emergence of hidden but meaningful structure. The difference matrix $\mathbf{D}$ or similarity matrix $\mathbf{B}$ for $\mathbf{B} = \mathbf{X}^T\mathbf{X}$ are given. Assume that x is zero-mean and that $\mathbf{B}$ encodes the covariance matrix $\mathbf{B}(i,j) = \mathbf{x}_i^T\mathbf{x}_j$. $\mathbf{D}$ and $\mathbf{B}$ are related as

$$\mathbf{D}(i,j) = (\mathbf{x}_i - \mathbf{x}_j)^T(\mathbf{x}_i - \mathbf{x}_j) = \mathbf{B}(i,i) + \mathbf{B}(j,j) - 2\mathbf{B}(i,j) \tag{6.24}$$

$$\mathbf{B}(i,j) = -\frac{1}{2}(\mathbf{D}(i,j) - \mathbf{D}(\bullet,j) - \mathbf{D}(i,\bullet) + \mathbf{D}(\bullet,\bullet)) \tag{6.25}$$

where $\bullet$ denotes the average over the corresponding index. The right side of this equation is called "double-centering matrix." The MDS derivation seeks the (transformed) matrix $\hat{\mathbf{X}}$ that minimizes the STRAIN cost function

$$\rho_{STRAIN}(\mathbf{D}, \hat{\mathbf{D}}) = ||\mathbf{J}^T(\mathbf{D}^2 - \hat{\mathbf{D}}^2)||_F^2 \tag{6.26}$$

where $\mathbf{J}$ are weighting factors, $\mathbf{D}^2$ is the matrix of squared-distances (element-wise product), and $|| \bullet ||$ is the Frobenius norm, which for some matrix $\mathbf{A}$ is defined as

$$||\mathbf{A}||_F^2 = \sum_{i=1}^{m}\sum_{j=1}^{n}|a_{ij}|^2 = trace(\mathbf{A}\mathbf{A}^*) = \sum_{i=1}^{\min\{m,n\}} \sigma_i^2 \tag{6.27}$$

with $\mathbf{A}^*$ the conjugate transpose of $\mathbf{A}$, and σ_i the singular values of $\mathbf{A}$. The top ranked q eigenvectors capture the largest component of variation for $\mathbf{J}^T\mathbf{D}^2\mathbf{J}$. In analogy to PCA, and using SVD for implementation, one finds that $\mathbf{J}^T\mathbf{D}^2\mathbf{J} = \mathbf{R}\mathbf{S}\mathbf{R}^T$, $\mathbf{S} = \mathbf{Q}\mathbf{Q}^T$, and finally $\hat{\mathbf{X}} = (\mathbf{R}\mathbf{Q})^T$. The above method is called metric MDS. In case of ordinal data, one seeks to recover the order of proximities using non-metric MDS. The fitness STRESS measure for non-metric MDS is minimized while searching for optimal coordinates (parameter estimation) and then searching for optimal monotonic transformation of the data (optimal scaling). Phillips et al. (1999) have used MDS to assess the qualitative accord between several face recognition algorithms and human perceivers.

7. Face in a Crowd

The apparition of these faces in the crowd:
Petals, on a wet, black bough
(Ezra Pound, 1911-1912, Haiku-like
inspired by a journey on the Paris Metro)

Marco [Polo] enters a city; he sees someone in a square living a life or an instant that could be his; he could now be in that man's place, if he had stopped in time, long ago; or if, long ago, at a crossroads, instead of taking one road he had taken the opposite one, and after long wandering he had come to be in the place of that man in the square. By now, from that real or hypothetical past of his, he is excluded; he cannot stop; he must go on to another city, where another of his pasts awaits him, or something perhaps that has been a possible future of his and is now someone else's present. Futures not achieved are only branches of the past: dead branches. (Italo Calvino, Invisible Cities)

We have considered so far face recognition in isolation. The face, already captured, was available to identification or authentication. This is characteristic of controlled situations, e.g., security applications using machine readable travel documents (MRTD). It does not come as a big surprise to find that real life is much more complicated. The real challenge thus is to automatically identify a person without her active cooperation. The face has to be detected first and tracked before any attempt is made to identify or authenticate it. This problem, usually referred to as *Face in a Crowd*, is most challenging. There is much more variability, e.g., clutter, illumination, pose, and scale, compared to what one encounters during standard face recognition applications. The news are not all that bad because at the cost of increased variability one gains access to the temporal dimension, to accrue and smooth evidence that helps to disambiguate among alternative facial interpretations. Evidence accumulation, always watchful for change and ready to integrate it, is both progressive and adaptive. It is progressive because it is selective about what to look for and in what order, on one hand, and how to process it, on the other hand. It is adaptive because it learns how to combine exploration and exploitation in order to be effective and nimble. In addition, and perhaps most important, the temporal dimension begets coherence across spatial-temporal manifolds to constrain what is feasible and probable from what is either impossible or unlikely. Coherence supports invariance and makes tracking and recognition complementary to each other. This chapter addresses the time dimension and how to take advantage of it (see Sect. 8.4 on the complementary use of 3D for similar purposes). Time connects sensing and perception, anticipation and control, exploration and exploitation, and adaptation and learning.

7.1 Face Detection

Face detection is the first stage for any automated face recognition system, since a face has to be located before it can be recognized. As detection is just a particular case of recognition, the methods described in the preceding chapter apply here too. The natural way to approach the face detection problem belongs to two class pattern recognition, where one $(+)$ class corresponds to human faces, and the other $(-)$ class includes everything else. The fly in the ointment is how to define everything else. One approach is to use the strangeness and the mechanisms proposed for open set face recognition (see Sect. 6.3). Another alternative employs a voting scheme like AdaBoost in conjunction with cascade learning (see Sect. 9.3). AdaBoost is a mixture of weak classifiers, which are simple stump functions whose odds are only better than chance. It is the combination of such weak classifiers that yields reliable and strong classifiers. Viola and Jones (2004) have shown robust real-time face detection based upon AdaBoost and cascade classifiers using simple features reminiscent of the Haar basis functions. The rectangular features used are computed fast using integral images as an intermediate representation. The integral image $\mathbf{I}(x, y)$ for the image at location (x, y), $\mathbf{I}(x, y) = \sum_{x' \leq x, y' \leq y} f(x', y')$, is computed in one pass over the original image. Sochman and Matas (2004) have proposed an extension to AdaBoost that reduces the upper bound on the training error by correcting, during each cycle, the coefficients for the weak classifiers learned so far. Similar detection and false positive rates were achieved but the detector was 20% faster and included only a quarter of the weak classifiers found using standard AdaBoost.

Face detection is difficult because the whole range of image variability has to be now confronted. This includes both geometry and illumination, most of which are uncontrolled. As pose and scale are unknown, search, sometimes exhaustive over their Cartesian product, becomes necessary. Statistical methods are characteristic of generative methods. They estimate the face and non-face distributions and apply pattern classification methods to search over a range of scales and locations. Connectionist methods, characteristic of discriminative methods, bypass the estimation stage. They train instead on the implicit distributions for face and non-face patterns and learn to discriminate among them.

Hjelmas and Low (2001) and Yang et al. (2002) provide good surveys on face detection. The latter survey categorizes the approaches used for face detection as knowledge-based, e.g., rules about how the human face is structured, feature invariance, e.g., texture, color, and multiple cues, template matching, e.g., predefined or deformable templates, and appearance-based methods, e.g., subspace methods. Additional approaches for face detection include SVM (see Sect. 3.4), SNoW (see Sect. 9.3), HMM (see Sect. 6.5), naïve Bayes (see below) and information-theoretical methods, e.g., decision trees (DT) and Kullback-Leibler (KL) divergence (see below). Naïve Bayes assumes that the m attributes x_i are independent for variable $\mathbf{X}$ within each class c, and estimates the conditional probability as $P(\mathbf{X}|c) = \prod_{i=1}^{m} P(x_i|c)$. The naïve Bayes classifier estimates (for computational expediency) the joint probability for appearance-based methods assuming that there is no statistical dependency between specific events or occurrences. Faces are successfully detected when the likelihood (face vs. non-face) ratio is larger than the ratio of prior probabilities for each detection outcome.

Decision trees (DT) are one of the basic non-parametric methods used for pattern classification. DT make use of induction to learn concepts, and to construct implicit decisions rules for classification. The object classes are described by a fixed collection of attributes, each of them characterized by a domain of possible values. Starting from the root of the tree, and at each node thereafter, one has to answer questions related to the values some specific attribute can take. The iterative inductive process used by DT learns the optimal order in which the attributes are queried for their value. According to the way the queries are answered, one moves along different branches until a terminal leaf, whose class identity is known, is reached. The unknown pattern shares the same identity with the leaf node reached. The sequence of queries asked provides the explanation for how the decision on classification was reached. The strategy used to learn DT is characteristic of greedy search. The pool of records available for training is split at each node to favor homogeneous or pure class distributions. The C4.5 DT (Quinlan, 1993) employs an information theoretical approach based on entropy.

C4.5 builds the decision tree using a top down, divide and conquer approach. Select an attribute, divide the training set into subsets characterized by the possible interval values of the attribute, and recursively follow the same partitioning step with each subset. Stop the iteration for nodes where the large majority of instances come from a single class, define them as leaves, and label them with the identity of the majority class. The optimal criterion for selecting the query attribute and the corresponding split at each iteration is gain ratio maximization using the entropy. Assume S is any set of objects and let $freq(C_i, S)$ stand for the number of objects in the set S that belong to class C_i, while $|S|$ is the total number of objects in S. Define message m as one that corresponds to the case when one object is selected at random from S and belongs to some class C_j. The message m has the probability $p = \frac{freq(C_i, S)}{|S|}$ and the information it conveys is $-\log_2 p$ bits. The expected information or entropy H for messages coming from k classes, $info(S)$, is defined as

$$H = info(S) = -\sum_{i=1}^{k} p_i \log_2 p_i \qquad (7.1)$$

Let A be now a possible query test (for attribute A selection) with n outcomes that partitions the set T of training records into subsets $T_1, T_2, \cdots, T_n$ and define

$$info(A, T) = \sum \left(\frac{|T_i|}{|T|} \right) info(T_i) \text{ and } gain(A) = info(T) - info(X, T) \qquad (7.2)$$

The gain criterion selects that query A for whom the $gain(A)$ is maximized. This criterion, however, suffers from a strong bias that favors those attributes that yield many but irrelevant outcomes when tested for, e.g., the ID. The bias is rectified by normalization where gains, due to tests that display many outcomes, are properly adjusted. Towards that end, one defines *split info(A)* as the entropy of a message where information is defined in terms of outcomes, rather than classes as it was the case with *info(S)*. The updated and better criterion, *gain ratio(A)*, is

$$gain\ ratio(A) \quad = \quad \frac{gain(A)}{split\ info(A, T)}$$

$$\text{with } split\ info(A, T) \quad = \quad -\sum \left(\frac{|T_i|}{|T|} \right) \log_2 \left(\frac{|T_i)|}{|T|} \right) \qquad (7.3)$$

The *split info* for many but equally probably classes k grows as $log_2 k$. The *gain ratio* prefers small splits all other things being equal. An alternative way to build the DT is to use the Gini index $g(S) = 1 - \sum_{i=1}^{k} p_i^2$ rather than the entropy H. Both the entropy and the Gini index reach their minimum and maximum when the training records belong to one class or are equally distributed among all the classes, respectively. The entropy grows faster than the Gini index to reach its maximum.

A simple but effective face detection method using DT is described next (Huang, Gutta and Wechsler, 1996). The method is suitable for machine readable travel documents, and FERET and FRVT type of evaluations. The accuracy reported, on face detection for MRTD like images, for 2,340 face images from FERET was 96%. The approach is quite efficient because it does not require multiple scale templates. It involves three main stages, those of location (using histogram equalization, edge detection, and profile/projection analysis to roughly box the approximate location of the face), cropping (using DT to find face like windows within the box), and post-processing (using profile analysis, window counting and aggregation for face like appearance, and normalization) (see Fig. 7.1). Each 8×8 window and its corresponding four quadrants yield thirty features that are used to learn DT for cropping faces. The features, entropy, mean, and standard deviation, are derived using the raw image and its Laplacian. Accuracy, based on visual observation, requires that the face box found

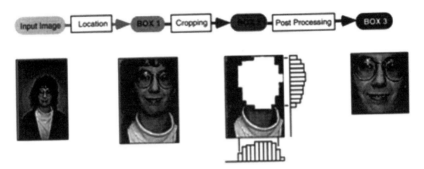

Fig. 7.1. Face Detection Using Decision Trees.

includes both eyes, nose, and mouth, and that the top side of the box is below the hairline.

Characteristic of information-theoretical methods and useful for face detection is the Kullback-Leibler (KL) divergence or relative information (see Sect. 9.4). Lew (1996), while addressing face detection, motivates the use of KL as follows. Assume n observations, each of which is distributed according to $p_1(x)$ if the null hypothesis H_1 is true, and $p_2(x)$ if the alternative hypothesis H_2 holds true. The Neyman-Pearson lemma asserts that all useful information about differentiating between H_1 and H_2, e.g., face and non-face, is contained in the likelihood ratio or its logarithms. This is similar to the use of discriminative (rather than generative) methods for pattern classification. Face detection amounts to finding the most informative pixels (MIP) that maximize KL (Lew, 1996). The mutual information $I(X, Y)$, which measures the statistical dependence between two random variables, is defined for two events X and Y as $I(X, Y) = H(X) + H(Y) - H(X, Y) = H(X) - H(X|Y) = H(Y) - H(Y|X)$ where $H(X, Y)$ is the joint entropy $H(X, Y) = -\sum_{x,y} p(x, y) \log p(x, y)$ and $H(X|Y)$ is the entropy of X conditioned on observing Y. The mutual information amounts to the uncertainty in X that is discarded from observations of Y and vice versa. Mutual information is closely related to the log-likelihood ratio test in the context of contingency tables and Pearson's χ^2 test used to assess the independence for a pair of variables.

Terrillon et al. (2000) detect human faces fusing information on skin color and invariant Fourier-Mellin (FM) moments. Hsu et al. (2002) approach face detection using lighting compensation and a non - linear color transformation for skin tone detection. Jesorsky et al. (2001) have proposed flexible matching for face detection using the Hausdorff distance. The Hausdorff distance operates on binary edge images where the edges provide quasi invariance to illumination. Similar to active shape models (ASM) and the joint manifold distance (MD) (see Sect. 9.4), face detection using the Hausdorff distance seeks the parameters $\theta \in P$ for transformation T that minimize the expression

$$d = \min_{\theta \in P} MHD(A, T_P(B)) \tag{7.4}$$

where MHD is the modified Hausdorff (forward and reverse) distance between the image A and model B. MHD averages over single point distances and reduces the impact of outliers, while the inclusion of forward and reverse distances acknowledges the dual roles played by data and the face model. The choice of transformations T, e.g., scale and translation, and the corresponding parameter space used is context dependent. The edge based model B can be evolved using genetic algorithms (Kirchberg et al., 2002).

Smeraldi (2003) has introduced a family of multiscale, orientation selective, and non-parametric ranklet features, modeled on the Haar wavelets for face detection.

Ranking simply means a permutation on a given set of observations. A connection is made between non-parametric methods and statistical methods based on rank, to take advantage of the fact that the rank statistics are robust to outliers and invariant under monotonic transformations, e.g., brightness and contrast changes. The rank transform (RT) measures relative local brightness and assigns to each pixel the value of its rank. RT, closely related to the Wilcoxon rank-sum test for the comparison of two treatments, is its equivalent when only one treatment observation is given. The analogy between the Wilcoxon test and RT "can be carried further by devising new image descriptors that correspond to a number of "treatment" pixels n greater than 1." The ranklet descriptors, which can be efficiently computed using Mann-Whitney statistics, are shown to compare favorably against the Haar wavelets, SNoW, and linear SVM on face detection using the MIT-CBCL face database. Huang et al. (2005) describe a robust face detection scheme using Gabor filters whose output is fed to a face vs. non-face classifier. The classifier, a polynomial neural network, takes its input from the PCA subspace derived using Gabor filters. The detection performance reported is competitive with existing schemes on complex scenes. The performance is better when both the magnitude and phase of the Gabor filters are used compared to the use of magnitude only.

Interesting findings regarding the comparative merits of SVM (see Sect. 3.4) and SNoW (see Sect. 9.3) with respect to their ability for generalization have been reported in the context of face detection. Alvira and Rifkin (2001) have reported that SNoW performs about as well as linear SVM, and substantially worse than polynomial (kernel) SVM. Yang et al. (2002) compared the relative performance of SVM and SNoW. SVM implements an additive update Perceptron-like (dual) rule, while SNoW implements a multiplicative update rule. SNoW was shown to be better than SVM concerning generalization for face detection, while SVM was more suitable when the efficiency of feature representations is of concern. The key feature of the Winnow update rule (for SNoW) is that the number of exemplars needed to learn the linear discriminant (function) scales linearly with the number of relevant features and only logarithmically with the total number of features. Yang et al. (2002) argued that SNoW is suitable for data that is L_∞ norm bounded and can be separated with a small L_1 norm hyper-plane, while SVM is more appropriate for data that is characterized by a small L_2 norm. In order to fully exploit the nice generalization properties of SNoW one should learn and use a sparse feature representation.

7.2 Eye Detection

Eye detection is important for both face detection and face normalization. The presence of the eyes, with or without other facial landmarks, is a strong indicator for a face. The jitter characteristic of eyes serves as an important cue that determines if the face belongs to a live person or not, and it preempts deception. Once the face has been detected, the inter-ocular distance between the eyes and its orientation serve for scale and in plane rotation normalization. Riopka and Boult (2003) have argued that "correct measurement of eye separation is more important than correct eye location, highlighting the critical role of eye separation in the scaling and normalization of face images."

Yuille (1991) locates facial landmarks such as the eyes, using the concept of deformable templates. The template is a parameterized geometric model of the face or part of it (mouth and/or eyes) that needs to be located. Eye location amounts to measuring how well the eye template fits image data, where variations over the parameter space correspond to legal deformations. Yeshurun et al. (1991) developed a generalized symmetry operator for eye detection. Subspace methods help with defining subspace features useful for both detection and recognition, e.g., PCA and eigen features for eigen eyes (Pentland et al., 1994). Lam and Yan (1996) extended Yuille's method by using corner locations inside the eye windows, which are obtained using average anthropometric measures once the head boundary is located. Takacs and

Wechsler (1998) detect facial landmarks, including the eyes, using a dynamic and multi-resolution model of visual attention. The method proposed employs a non-linear sampling lattice of oriented Gaussian filters to extract conspicuous features that lock on small oscillatory ("jitter") movements. The method then integrates the features found to determine their saliency, which guides exploratory saccades that scan the facial landscape for landmarks. Huang et al. (1998) implement eye detection on FERET data and report that SVM using polynomial kernels of second degree performed best. Huang and Wechsler (1999) have approached eye detection using optimal wavelet packets for eye representation, and radial basis functions (RBF) for classification of facial areas as eye vs. non-eye regions. Experimental data shows that eye images reconstructed using optimal wavelet packets (see below) lead to improved and robust RBF performance compared to the case where original raw images are used.

Wavelets and optimal wavelet packets, characteristic of the scale space, in general, and optimal and conjoint spatial-spatial frequency representations, in particular, are fundamental blocks for image representation. The wavelet basis functions (Mallat, 1989), a self-similar and spatially localized code, are spatially localized frequency/orientation tuned kernels that tessellate the conjoint spatial-spectral signal domain. One derives a wavelet pyramid using (orientation-tuned) iterative decompositions at a dyadic (powers of two) sequence of scales. The wavelet representation W of the function $f(x)$ requires the "mother" wavelet $\Psi(x)$, the scale parameters a_x and a_y, and the shift parameters s_x and s_y. The wavelet representation implements multi-resolution analysis through the orthogonal decomposition of a function along basis functions that correspond to translations and dilations of the mother wavelet function, e.g., the Haar basis $\Psi(x) = \{1 \text{ for } 0 \le x \le 0.5 \text{ and } -1 \text{ for } 0.5 \le x \le 1\}$. Continuous wavelets, defined using a pair of functions (scaling function) ϕ and Ψ ('mother'-wavelet function), satisfy

$$\phi_{a,b}(x) = |a|^{\frac{1}{2}} \phi(ax - b) \tag{7.5}$$

$$\psi_{a,b}(x) = |a|^{\frac{1}{2}} \psi(ax - b) \tag{7.6}$$

with a, b real numbers, while $\phi_{a,b}$ and $\Psi_{a,b}$ are the scaling and mother wavelet functions dilated by a and translated by b. The discrete wavelet transform (DWT) results for $a = a_0^{-m}, b = nb_0$, with m, n integers, and the corresponding scaling and mother wavelet functions

$$\phi_{m,n}(x) = |a|^{-\frac{m}{2}} \phi(a_0^{-m} x - nb_0) \tag{7.7}$$

$$\psi_{m,n}(x) = |a|^{-\frac{m}{2}} \psi(a_0^{-m} x - nb_0) \tag{7.8}$$

For the choice $a_0 = 2$, $b_0 = 1$ one obtains

$$\phi_{m,n}(x) = 2^{-\frac{m}{2}} \phi(2^{-m} x - n) \tag{7.9}$$

$$\psi_{m,n}(x) = 2^{-\frac{m}{2}} \psi(2^{-m} x - n) \tag{7.10}$$

The dilation equation, relating the mother wavelet to the scaling function is

$$\psi(x) = \sqrt{2} \sum_k h_1(k) \phi(2x - k) \tag{7.11}$$

with $h_1(k) = (-1)^k h_0(1 - k)$. The wavelet coefficients and the corresponding wavelet decomposition for DWT are

$$c_{m,n} = \int_{-\infty}^{\infty} f(x) \psi_{m,n}(x) dx \tag{7.12}$$

$$f(x) = \sum_{m,n} c_{m,n} \psi_{m,n}(x) \tag{7.13}$$

Daubechies (1988) derives the low h_0 and high h_1 pass filters needed to design families of scaling and mother wavelet functions. Mallat (1989) proves that for any orthonormal wavelet basis, the sequences of two-channel filter banks can compute the DWT with perfect reconstruction. The self-similar Gabor basis functions, a special case of non-orthogonal wavelets, correspond to sinusoids modulated by a Gaussian and are thus redundant. Better performance is expected using such redundancy compared to a dictionary consisting only of orthogonal bases (Daugman, 1990).

Optimal sampling can be approached using different fitness criteria. As an example, Wilson (1995) mentions the requirement for more complex and adaptive approaches to signal representation. Similar to model selection, the quest is for an approach that can automatically adjust the resolution of the representation, i.e. its reconstruction ability. The goal is to provide the best fit to a given data set rather than use a fixed representation, whose resolution is merely a compromise between space-time and frequency. The wavelet packets (Coifman and Wickerhauser, 1992), with the wavelet dictionary derived using maximal energy concentration and/or minimal Shannon entropy (see below), implement the above approach. Once the coefficients of the discrete wavelet transform (DWT) are derived, one chooses an optimal subset, with respect to some reconstruction criteria for data compression purposes. Towards that end, Coifman and Wickerhauser (1992) defined the Shannon entropy μ as

$$\mu(\nu) = -\sum_i ||\nu_i||^2 \ln ||\nu_i||^2 \qquad (7.14)$$

where $\nu = \{\nu_i\}$ is the corresponding set of DWT coefficients. The Shannon entropy measure is the cost function used to find the best subset of wavelet coefficients. Note that minimum entropy corresponds to less randomness ("dispersion") and helps with shaping data clusters (see Sect. 6.3 for analogies to transduction using strangeness and p-values). If one generates the complete wavelet representations (wavelet packets) as a binary tree, the selection of the best coefficients is done by comparing the entropy of wavelet packets corresponding to adjacent tree levels (father-son relationships). One compares the entropy of each adjacent pair of nodes to the entropy of their union, and the sub tree is expanded further only if it results in lesser entropy. For a signal whose size is n the DWT yields n coefficients and the search for optimal coefficients yields that set (still of size n) for whom the Shannon entropy is minimized. Data compression, subject to the same entropy criteria, ranks the optimal coefficients according to their magnitude, and picks up subsets consisting of m coefficients where m is less than n. The optimal wavelet packets are over complete and thus redundant. They are expressed using a library of redundant bases with arbitrary resolution that is more expressive for non-stationary signals compared to DWT. Another apparent benefit encountered during tracking, from using optimal wavelet packets (compared to DWT), concerns an increased expressive power at high spatial frequencies and low temporal frequencies. Optimal wavelet packets provide an alternative face representation that supports the design of classifiers, e.g., wavelet networks (Zhang and Benveniste, 1992), or weak learners and their combination using AdaBoost (see Sect. 9.7).

Huang and Wechsler (2000) developed visual routines for navigation across the facial landscape for the purpose of eye detection. The visual routines for face exploration and eye detection are adaptive. They are derived using learning and evolution rather than being handcraft ahead of time. The role for exploration is to seek for salient objects and determine their identity. The saliency for the *where* map is derived using the consensus found between navigation routines encoded as FSA (finite state automata). FSA animats explore the facial landscape and are evolved using genetic algorithms (GA). The classification *what* stage implements a wrapper approach that selects the best features over salient regions for DT classification using GA.

7.3 Uncertainty

Intelligence does not run along fixed and predetermined paths. "[The] human brain is not a Von Neumann computer, running through well defined algorithms to reach certain conclusions. Rather it is, like all complex biological systems, a hodge-podge of quasi-independent sub-systems, which normally are mutually constraining. The mutual constraints enable the system to arrive, under normal circumstances, at answers that are good enough for most purposes - or, anyway, good enough for evolution purpose" (Westbury, 1999). Uncertainty, always present when one engages in face recognition, has to be reduced using evidential reasoning. As evidence accrues, the priors change. Thinking is statistical rather than deterministic and involves chance and exploration. Handling uncertainty is complementary to data fusion (see Ch. 9). The two basic methodologies addressed here for handling uncertainty include Bayesian or Belief Networks (BN), also referred to as graphical models, and Dempster-Shafer (DS) interval logic.

Kevin Murphy, quoting from Michael Jordan on Bayesian networks [1], writes that "they are a marriage between probability theory and graph theory. They provide a natural tool for dealing with two problems that occur throughout applied mathematics and engineering - uncertainty and complexity - and in particular they are playing an increasingly important role in the design and analysis of machine learning algorithms. Many of the classical multivariate probabilistic systems studied in fields such as statistics, system engineering, information theory, pattern recognition and statistical mechanics are special cases of the general graphical model formalisms - examples include (Gaussian) mixture models, factor analysis, HMM, Kalman filters, and Ising models." The motivation for BN, beyond dealing with uncertainty, comes from the fact that inference is not "one-way", i.e., it does not proceed from a predefined input to a given output. Bayesian networks (Jensen, 2001) provide the means to assess the potential impact of additional or changing evidence on the beliefs presently held, and accordingly seek for such evidence to advance both exploration and interpretation. As an example, BN implement the Wizard for MS Office. Bayesian networks, originally proposed by Pearl (1988), are realized using dynamic programming (DP) and/or approximation algorithms using variational methods, e.g., mean field, and sampling methods, e.g., Monte Carlo. BN act as a generative classifier when the class variable is an ancestor of some or all the features. They act as a discriminative or diagnostic classifier when the class variable has none of the features as descendants (Cohen et al., 2003). Temporal models suitable for stochastic processes exist and are refereed to as dynamic Bayesian networks.

Bayesian networks are directed graphs where the nodes stand for random variables and the lack of arcs indicates conditional independence. One can see the arc from node A to node B as an indicator for causality to distinguish from mere correlation (Pearl, 2000). BN, which model joint probability distributions for their variables, earned their name from using the Bayes' rule for inference. The (directed acyclic) graph structure for discrete variables is augmented by a Conditional Probability (Distribution) Tables (CPT) at each node, while continuous variables are treated using Gaussian and/or softmax distributions. CPT lists the probability for a child node to assume its different values (on its attributes) when considering all the possible combinations of values for its parents. The graph structure is given or has to be learned using maximum likelihood, while CPT are estimated (Heckerman, 1995). The chain or product rule that defines the joint probability to observe n attributes A_i is

$$P(A_1, A_2, A_3, \cdots, A_n) = P(A_1)P(A_2|A_1)P(A_3|A_1A_2) \cdots P(A_n|A_1A_2 \cdots A_{n-1}) \quad (7.15)$$

Conditional independence in a Bayesian network means that a node is independent of its ancestors given its parents. The chain or product rule simplifies significantly when it updates beliefs according to the specific ancestry relationships encoded by

---

[1] http://www.ai.mit.edu/ murphyk/Bayes/bnintro.html

the particular graph structure and CPT. Examples of using Bayesian networks are described next.

Pham et al. (2002) have used aggregate (forest structured) BN classifiers for face detection. The search is for a network structure that maximizes the Kullback-Leibler (KL) divergence, which is known to be effective for discrimination, in general, and detection, in particular. Symmetry is embedded in the network model. Nefian (2002) has proposed an embedded Bayesian network (EBN) for face recognition. An EBN is "defined recursively as a hierarchical structure where the "parent" node is a BN that conditions the EBN or the observation sequence that describes the nodes of the "child" layer." Liu et al. (2003) use BN on multi-modal fusion for robust and real time face tracking. The BN integrates a prior on second order system dynamics, and likelihood cues from color, edge, and face appearances. Cohen et al. (2003) learn BN (generative) classifiers for facial expression recognition (from video) using both labeled and unlabeled data.

Learning the Bayesian network for objects, in general, and faces, in particular, is NP-complete as the search takes place in a high dimensional space. The apparent sparse structure of statistical dependency for such cases suggests, however, that it might be still feasible to learn the BN but using a divide-and-conquer approach instead. Similar to recognition-by-parts using the dynamic link architecture (see Sect. 6.5), Schneiderman (2004) has approached learning the BN as a search that "optimizes two cost functions: a localized error in the log-likelihood function (for a large number of candidate sets of variable parts) to restrict and guide the final BN structure, and a global classification error to choose the final structure using empirical classification on cross-validation images." The approach trained detectors of frontal faces, eyes, and iris, and reports state of the art performance on the MIT-CMU test set for face detection.

Dempster-Shafer (DS) interval logic (Shafer, 1976) takes for its decision space the power set of some domain Ω that consists of hypotheses θ which are not necessarily disjoint. There is a belief assignment (BA) or mass probability (MP) associated with each authentication decision θ such that $m : 2^\Omega \to [0,1]$ where $\sum_{\theta \in 2^\Omega} m(\theta) = 1$ with $\emptyset$ the empty set and $m(\emptyset) = 0$. As the belief $m(\theta)$ can be committed to a set rather than a singleton, recognition can linger over a number of identities before locking on one of them. One of the decisions θ proposed can be an inconclusive or non-committal one ζ, whereby some mass probability $m(\zeta)$ is kept available for later distribution according to the evidence accrued. Interval logic derives its name from the way confidence is defined and the way it accrues. Rather than arbitrarily deciding on some fixed probability $p(\theta)$ the Dempster-Shafer methodology defines an interval of confidence $[SP(\theta), PL(\theta)]$ with SP and PL as support and plausibility, respectively. The residual $PL(\theta) - SP(\theta)$ indicates the initial ignorance or reluctance to make a firm commitment to some specific interpretation. The support draws the evidence leading one to believe in θ with certainty, while plausibility includes the evidence accrued so far that does not preclude θ, i.e., $PL(\theta) = 1 - SP(\neg\theta)$. The true probability for θ lies somewhere between $SP(\theta)$ and $PL(\theta)$. As evidence accumulates, the residual (of uncertainty) shrinks and the beliefs become more certain. Given two mass probabilities distributions one seeks their conflicting evidence Y (whose probability mass gets redistributed) and defines the new probability mass distribution $MP(\theta) = MP_1(\theta) \oplus MP_2(\theta)$

$$MP(\theta) = \frac{1}{1-Y} \sum_{A \subseteq \theta} MP(A) \qquad (7.16)$$

where A are compatible entries such that $A \subseteq MP_1 \bigcap MP_2$. The intersection between some event E and the unknown/unassigned event ζ is E and it becomes more specific. Conclusions can be drawn about events for which their conflicting evidence is suppressed. When there is evidence that confirms some conflicting hypotheses H and $\bar{H}$ to degree d, interval logic will reduce its support for the two hypotheses and their new mass probability becomes $\frac{d}{1+d}$. Foucher and Gagnon (2004) have used Dempster-Shafer for face recognition from real (video) films. Faces are detected and identified independently of each other in each frame without using any temporal information. Statistical evidence accumulates and is then integrated using DS.

7.4 Active Learning and Evidence Accumulation

Active learning and evidence accumulation are complementary to each other and expand on the uncertainty framework described in the previous section. Changes, continuously detected and analyzed, determine how and what to learn, on one side, and how to update the beliefs held in possible interpretations Training is active rather than passive, and choices are made about the patterns most relevant to face recognition. Evidence threads between (key) frames over time to decrease uncertainty, and locks eventually on some specific decision(s) regarding face recognition. Active learning and evidence accumulation are the result of exploration and exploitation, and are driven by the performance observed and spatiotemporal constraints. Conspicuity and saliency, the driving forces behind active and selective vision, determine *what* and *where* to search for relevant information, and *when*. The temporal dimension is crucial to face recognition. Challenging face instances also get boosted during training leading to strong face classifiers (see Sect. 9.3).

Evidence accumulation involves steady progression in the way the biometric information is analyzed. The motivation for progressive transmission and processing comes from bandwidth requirements and the need for an early and fast impression, categorization or recognition of the input. "Event-related potentials (ERP) [for reaction time] show that target [or face] detection, which involves go/no-go [YES and NO] categorization [for unseen photographs flashed on for just 20 ms], peak at about 200 ms but may start as early as 140 ms after stimulus onset. Much of the processing required to achieve such a phenomenal amount of computation in such a short time must be based on essentially feed-forward mechanisms" (Thorpe et al., 1996). Asynchronous spike propagation and rank order (rather than rate) coding are some of the means proposed to explain the speed with witch "neurons in the monkey temporal lobe can respond selectively to the presence of a face" (Rullen et al., 1998) (see Sect. 7.5 for relationships between exchangeability, martingale, and rank order). The most strongly activated neurons or processing units fire first, greater impact is assigned to the spikes with shortest latency to stimulus onset, and the order and relative strength in which this takes place is the [temporal] code used for recognition. Furthermore, "since neurons in the attended regions will tend to reach threshold and fire earlier, they will tend to dominate later stages of processing [possibly using shunting inhibition]" (Rullen and Thorpe, 1999). Such processing squares well with sparse coding driven by suspicious coincidences (Barlow, 1989a,b) and has been shown to "generalize well to novel views of the same face [for identification] and to be remarkably resistant to image noise and reduction in contrast" (Delorme and Thorpe, 2001).

Intensity-to-time (adaptive) processing to sort and index information (Brajovic and Kanade, 1999) and analog VLSI retina with steering filter capabilities and temporal output coding (Barbaro et al., 2002), are examples of latency driven (progressive) processing. Progressive transmission and analysis lead to savings in computation and shorter latency in resolving queries. Low and medium resolution "previews" provide versions of only moderate quality. They are, however, good enough for browsing large biometric databases when time or small bandwidth make full fledged face representation and recognition impractical. First "impressions" are followed by higher fidelity versions and /or guide additional attempts, if any, for identification and authentication. When the face obtained is not the one sought after, transmission is terminated and authentication against another face is initiated. Progressive transmission, using wavelet decomposition, would thus start by sending the lowest frequency components for early decompression and reconstruction. Progressive transmission is usually evaluated using objective mean-squared error (MSE) and peak signal-to-noise-ratio (PSNR) criteria or subjective ratings. Much better is, however, to evaluate according to functionality and performance. Towards that end, Schilling and Cosman (2002) suggest "an experimental and statistical framework for comparing progressive coders using the correctness of the answers as well as the response times for fast image browsing applications. The subjects have now to respond questions about the images as they become recognizable." The results reported indicate that "a multi-resolution decoding is recognized faster than a single scale decoding [most likely due to priming and temporal coding], and at the same PSNR, global blurriness slows down recognition more than do localized "splotch" [distortion] artifacts." The contributions due to specific psychophysical effects further enhance progressive coding schemes and assess their relative performance.

The standard framework in machine learning, in general, and pattern classification, in particular, presents the learner with a randomly sampled data set. There has been, however, a growing interest in active learning where one has the flexibility to choose the data points that seem most relevant for the learning task, and include them in the training set. One analogy for active learning is that a standard passive learner is a student who sits and listens to a teacher, while an active learner is a student that asks the teacher questions, listens to answers and asks further questions based upon the teacher's response (Tong and Koller, 2000) (see sequential importance sampling (SIS) for an analogy). The setting most relevant for face recognition is stream-based because labels for some face patterns but not the others are requested on the fly, and the amount of information available to answer the active learner is limited compared to the pool-based setting.

Ho and Wechsler (2006a) have recently proposed a novel method for stream-based active learning using transduction. The data points, e.g., patterns that are observed in sequence, are chosen according to their p-values, which are determined using their corresponding Lagrange multipliers derived using kernel SVM. The p-values provide a measure of diversity and controversy/disagreement regarding the true identity - face ("Y") vs. non-face ("N") - of unlabeled patterns. The patterns $\mathbf{X}$ relevant for face detection are those for whom their p-values are close to each other, i.e., $p_Y(\mathbf{X}) \approx p_N(\mathbf{X})$. The method proposed is different from alternative active learning methods, which select the examples that are as close as possible to the dividing hyper plane. The advantages of stream-based active learning are less annotation and manual effort during training, better performance, and smaller variance in performance. In addition, active learning using transduction can help with face selection (see Sect. 6.6) and with finding video breaks and key frames during video processing (see Sect. 7.5).

A simple architecture for automatic video based person authentication (AVBPA) suitable for face surveillance and driven by evidence accumulation was described by Wechsler et al. (1997). The AVBPA architecture proposed (see Fig. 7.3) involves preprocessing, difference methods or optical flow analysis to detect the moving subject, projection analysis and decision trees (DT) for face location, and Radial Basis Function (RBF) for face recognition. Preprocessing saves computation by skimming the video sequence to sample six rather than all the thirty frames per second available. Subject and face detection correspond to video break and key frame detection, respectively, while recognition corresponds to identification. Video break is implemented using optical flow or frames' difference according to the signal-to-noise (SNR) ratio measured for the video frames sampled. Face detection iterates until a (key) video frame is found for whom the face is properly located and boxed for RBF identification. Simple data fusion of RBF scores using relative confidence and temporal voting determine the recognition outcome. Low confidence requires seeking for another key frame and repeating the same process.

We describe only the implementation for video break (see also Sect. 7.5) while the RBF component is described elsewhere (see Sect. 9.2). Two video break methods have been implemented and the choice made is done according to SNR. The first method, the frame difference, is cheaper, but works only on those video sequences that display a relatively high SNR. The second method, optical flow, becomes necessary when the SNR falls below an acceptable value, and is described next. Image motion results from the projection of an object's 3D motion onto a 2D image plane. Optical or image flow, the apparent motion of an image pattern in the image plane, corresponds to a velocity field. The perception of visual motion involves two types of computations, those of temporal changes and spatial integration. The well known intensity gradient model applies differential operators to both the spatial and temporal dimensions. Since natural images are not always differentiable, the intensity gradient model usually requires pre-smoothing. The intensity gradient model thus includes a spatial smoothing filter followed by time differentiation. Assuming that velocities vary smoothly everywhere, one solves the optical flow constraint equation $E_x u + E_y v + E_t = 0$ using a global smoothness constraint. The spatial (E_x, E_y) and temporal E_t derivatives are estimated from the video sequence. The over determined optical flow constraint equation is solved by minimizing the error function $Error(u, v) = ||E_x u + E_y v + E_t||^2$ subject to global smoothness. To detect (smaller) moving objects like faces it is better to consider just the error map $Error(u, v)$ rather than computing explicitly the optical flow (Tsao and Chen, 1993). For the case of moving objects, the image is usually not differentiable around the locations of the objects and the intensity gradient method may generate large errors for the optical flow. The error map serves thus as an indicator for moving objects, bodies and/or faces. The errors due to clutter and noise are mostly removed and only the large errors due to the moving bodies remain. This method works very well at very low SNR when the frame difference method fails.

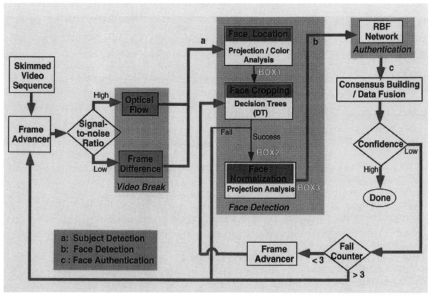

Fig. 7.2. Architecture for Automatic Video Based Person Authentication (AVBPA) (Reprinted from Wechsler et al., Automatic Video-Based Person Authentication Using the RBF Network, ©1997 Springer).

The above AVBPA architecture was tested on FERET video sequences acquired under different (controlled and uncontrolled) illuminations (see Fig. 7.4). The first sequence shown (one subject) was taken indoors, while the second sequence (two subjects) was acquired outdoors. The third (outdoor) sequence captured during stormy conditions (the trees in the background are no longer stationary) displayed low SNR and required optical flow computation to locate video breaks. Positive and negative identification (with respect to the database used) for the probe is indicated using the + and − signs, respectively. The probe for the first sequence belongs to the gallery, for the second sequence, the left person belongs to the gallery but the right person does not, while for the third sequence the probe does belong to the gallery. The stepwise (b, c, and d) decisions for (detection, location, and identification) are marked (using an arrow) above that frame when a reliable decision can be first made regarding detection, location, and identification, respectively. All the identification decisions made by RBF were correct and were achieved with high confidence.

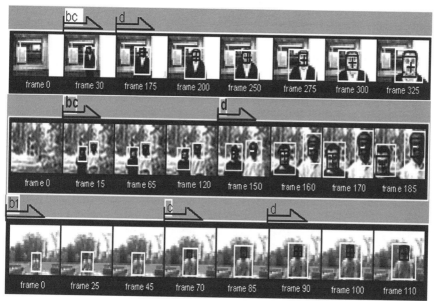

Fig. 7.3. Positive and Negative Authentication Using Automatic Video-Based Person Authentication (AVBPA) (Reprinted from Wechsler et al., Automatic Video-Based Person Authentication Using the RBF Network, ©1997 Springer).

Characteristic of evidence accumulation during tracking is also the condensation algorithm (Isard and Blake, 1998) and its particle filtering (PF) variants that estimate the posteriors for specific identifications taking place over time (see Sect. 7.7). Condensation employs sequential importance sampling (SIS), where the probability of possible (face) interpretations is represented by a randomly generated set. It "uses learned dynamical models [motion equation], together with visual observations [observation equation], to propagate the random set [identity equation] over time. The probability density propagation occurs in three phases, drift due to the deterministic component of object dynamics, diffusion due to the random component, and reactive reinforcement due to observations." Marginalization (see Sect. 3.1) over the motion vector yields the posterior distribution for the identity distribution, while degeneracy in the posterior probability of the identity variable(s) locks on recognition (Zhou et al., 2003). Condensation iterates SIS over the (select, predict, and measure) cycle using Markovian and independence assumptions. The algorithm accrues evidence in an incremental fashion, and matches it against existing (gallery) models using the Bayesian framework. Exploration or equivalently tracking and identification are guided by both priors and observations. The tracker can be taught to follow several targets at once and to switch accordingly between face models. Performance is determined to a large degree by the accuracy with which the target is initialized and locked on first. Other relevant factors affecting performance include the ability for recovery when the target is lost due to occlusion or being outside the field of view, on one side, and the correctness of the dynamical model, on the other side. In addition to merely locking on the target one has to handle the possibility that the probe sequence is out of (natural) order or does not match the motion and expected appearance models. Learning arbitrary dynamics (beyond simple and consistent second-order processes) is difficult. The actual observations models and target distributions could be highly non-linear and non-Gaussian. Marginalization and thus particle filters are not applicable when the true motion and identity models do not belong to the set of approximating functions used.

Not all the evidence is equal in helping with tracking and identification, and some evidence might be even detrimental (see Sect. 10.1 for human biases). Evidence that repeats itself does not add much. Evidence is useful only to the extent it is new and of high quality. Evidence does not accumulate in proportion to the number of frames, but rather in proportion to the amount of information the new frames add to those already observed. The active interpreter seeks frames that are informative enough to decrease the uncertainty rather than observing from the same vantage point over and over again. Different clusters of evidence, for both the gallery and the probe sequences, their strength, and the extent to which they complement already existing evidence are thus most important in changing the mind of the interpreter. This depends on context and inter alia on the anchoring effect, i.e., first interpretations tend to be decisive, and also on the stubbornness one shows in abandoning "cherished beliefs." Mistakes made early on tend to persist. Effective evidence accumulation, similar to what control systems are tasked for, alternates between exploration and exploitation. Charting alternative identification manifolds helps to sift among alternative interpretations. The following discussion, due to Stephen McKenna, elucidates some of the pitfalls involved in the use of evidence and its accumulation.

Face recognition from video involves estimating the posterior probability (mass) distribution density function $p(n|z_{1:t})$ where n denotes the (discrete) identity and $z_{1:T}$ is the probe sequence $[z_1, z_2, \cdots, z_T]$ received up to the current time T, and z_t denotes (some appropriate representation of) frame t. Assume each identity is equally probable a priori. Then it is sufficient to estimate the class conditional densities for the probe video $p(z_{1:T}|n)$. Assume *identity constancy*, i.e., all the probe frames are of the same person's face. Assume that motion is fairly unconstrained, i.e. one cannot expect that the probe facial motion will be similar to the facial motion observed in the training data. The frame rate is low relative to the speed at which a person might move their head so that the relying dynamic models will not help that much. Any number of representation and matching algorithms developed for face recognition from stills could be used to estimate $p(z_t|n)$ for any given frame. One naïve approach is to compare the distribution (or manifold) of the observations in the feature space with distributions (or manifolds) similarly estimated from training examples for each class, and choose the class with the most similar distribution (e.g. based on small divergence measure) or manifold (using some inter-manifold similarity measure). This does not work in general because motion is unconstrained so that the gallery and probe data are drawn from different distributions (i.e. carve out different manifolds in the feature space) even if they belong to the same person! Another naïve approach is to estimate $p(z_t|n)$ for each frame and for each class and seek to combine these values to estimate the class -conditionals for the probe video, $p(z_{1:T}|n)$. The problem with this approach (as with the other naïve approaches listed above) is that the video frames are not independent (not i.i.d.) and not equally useful. Here is a toy example to convince anyone in doubt. Let $N = 2$ and $T = 10$ and suppose one computes the following values for $p(z_t|n)$:

t	1	2	3	4	5	6	7	8	9	10
$p(z_t|n = 1)$	.01	.01	.1	.1	.1	.1	.1	.1	.1	.1
$p(z_t|n = 2)$	.1	.1	.01	.01	.01	.01	.01	.01	.01	.01

Based on the above information alone, the more probable identity would seem to be $n = 1$, and this holds for nearly any such algorithm one might consider (e.g. assume independence and multiply conditional probabilities, or use another (voting) rule like the sum, or bias more recent frames more heavily $\cdots$). But there are in fact many situations in which this could be suboptimal and $n = 2$ might be the better decision, e.g.,

- *Frame 1 is a frontal view, frame 2 is a $\frac{3}{4}$ view and frames 3-10 are all the same profile view (so most of the information is in frames 1 and 2).*
- *The poses/expressions/illumination during frames 3-10 are poorly modeled (due to lack of training data or an inadequate modeling scheme) whereas the conditions in frames 1 and 2 are well represented in the training data and are adequately modeled.*
- *The illumination conditions deteriorate between frames 3 and 5*
- *The person is moving away from the camera and by frame 3 the resolution has become very low*

Recognition from video therefore has to take into account

- *The similarity (lack of conditional independence) between frames and the extent to which some frames essentially add no new information*
- *The extent to which the estimated individual likelihoods $p(z_t|n)$ can be relied upon, i.e., how credible they are given the model, the training data and the probe data.*

To address the first point one might try an online clustering algorithm as a first attempt. Intuitively, the idea is that rather than treat frames as independent (a very poor approximation), one should cluster the frames instead and treat the "clusters" as independent samples (a much better approximation). As new frames arrive, they clustered sequentially in the feature space. At time T one has K clusters, $C_1, \cdots, C_K$. MAP recognition finds then for the class n that maximizes the following log-likelihood function

$$\log p(z_{1:T}|n) \approx \sum_{k=1}^{K} \log \frac{1}{C_k} \sum_{z_t \in C_k} p(z_t|n) \qquad (7.17)$$

7.5 Video Break Detection and Key Frame Extraction

Video processing includes video break detection and key frame extraction. Video breaks identify and separate relatively homogeneous video segments. The segments are archived and later on retrieved or interpreted using their characteristic key frames. Video segmentation and the extraction of key frames, complementary to each other, help with video analysis and management. Video segmentation is performed in the temporal domain by seeking for shot changes. Key-frame extraction seeks for the best representative(s) from each video segment. Many algorithms (Lefevre et al., 2003; Zhai and Shah, 2005) have been proposed to perform video shot change detection. The range of existing methods includes pixel- or histogram- based difference methods, and motion based methods, e.g., optical flow. The decision thresholds required for shot change are learned using similarity scores and ground truth. Threshold selection, a critical step for successful change detection, has access to methods based on global and local thresholds or their combination. For video sequences with clear and distinct shots, a single global threshold is sufficient. For video sequences that have both abrupt and gradual changes between shots, however, a global threshold cannot be found. To address such concerns local thresholds are employed. The use of local thresholds requires choosing the appropriate window size. Alternatively, Zhai and Shah (2005) have recently proposed that video breaks should be detected using the deviation from some current model. Setting the local threshold requires knowledge of the assumed model and its underlying distribution.

A new machine learning method based on the martingale framework was recently proposed to detect changes in the data generating process for data streams. The method was shown to be robust (Ho, 2005) and theoretically sound (Ho and Wechsler, 2005). The method proposed assumes that the data points are labeled. This assumption does not hold for multimedia video streams that are composed of unlabeled image data. The extended martingale method for video shot change detection, briefly described here, is driven by exchangeability concepts, including rank ordering. The martingale method is driven by a strangeness measure and p-values, which together characterize the extent to which the image characteristics vary (Ho and Wechsler, 2006b). To accommodate unlabeled data, the strangeness measure, however, has been reformulated using clustering concepts that operate on image representations that include color and edge histograms. Unlike existing video shot change detection methods, the martingale method uses a priori thresholds based on the probability bound on the martingale value computed. The proposed non-parametric method is efficient and robust, and is suitable for video shot change detection. A key frame extraction method is implemented based on the least strange image frame identified by the maximum p-value during the computation of the martingale value.

Let $\{Z_i : 1 < i < \infty\}$ be a sequence of random variables. A finite sequence of random variables $Z_1, \cdots, Z_n$ is exchangeable if the joint distribution $p(Z_1, \cdots, Z_n)$ is invariant under any permutation of the indices of the random variables. The satisfaction of the exchangeability condition indicates that there is no change in the distribution the sequence of random variables is drawn from. Vovk et al. (2003) introduced the idea of testing exchangeability on-line using the martingale. A martingale is a sequence of random variables $\{M_i : 0 < i < \infty\}$ such that M_n is a measurable function of $Z_1, \cdots, Z_n$ for all $n = 0, 1, \cdots$ (in particular, M_0 is a constant value) and the conditional expectation of M_{n+1} given $M_0, \cdots, M_n$ is equal to M_n, i.e.

$$E(M_{n+1}|M_1, \cdots, M_n) = M_n \qquad (7.18)$$

After each new data point received, an observer outputs a positive martingale value reflecting the strength of evidence found against the null hypothesis of data exchangeability. Testing for exchangeability can be used to detect changes in time-varying data streams for labeled data (Ho, 2005). Exchangeability is closely related to transduction when testing for data stability and consistency. Exchangeability is a necessary condition for a stable data stream. The absence of exchangeability suggests the occurrence of change.

To apply the martingale method, one needs to rank the data points according to their differences. Towards that end, one defines a strangeness measure that scores how much a data point is different from the other data points. Consider the set of data points $Z = \{z_1, \cdots, z_{n-1}\}$ and the new data point z_n. To compute a valid strangeness value for each data point, the method must satisfy the simple assumption, that at any time instance, the strangeness value of each data point seen so far is independent of the order the data points are used in computation (Vovk et al., 2005). A statistic is constructed to rank the strangeness value of the new data point z_n with respect to the strangeness values of all the observed data points. The statistic, the p-value of z_n, is defined as

$$\text{p-value} = V(Z \bigcup\{z_n\}, \theta_n) = \frac{1}{n}\{\#\{i : s_i > s_n\} + \theta_n \#\{i : s_i = s_n\}\} \qquad (7.19)$$

where s_i is the strangeness measure for the examples $z_i, i = 1, 2, \cdots, n$, and θ_n is randomly chosen from $[0, 1]$. The random number n ensures that the p-values for function V are distributed uniformly in $[0, 1]$, provided that the input examples are generated by an exchangeable probability distribution (Vovk et al., 2003).

A family of martingales, indexed by $\epsilon \in [0, 1]$, and referred to as the *power martingale*, is defined as

$$M_n^{(\epsilon)} = \prod_{i=1}^{n} \left(\epsilon p_i^{\epsilon-1}\right) \qquad (7.20)$$

where the p_i are the output p-values for function V, with the initial martingale $M_0^\epsilon = 1$. One also notes that $M_n^{(\epsilon)} = \epsilon p_i^{\epsilon-1} M_{n-1}^{(\epsilon)}$ and that there is no need to store the previous p-values. The following theorem (Ho and Wechsler, 2005) is applicable to both labeled and unlabeled data streams. Let $\{M_i : 0 < i < \infty\}$ be a martingale sequence constructed using p-values based on a valid strangeness measure for a given data stream. Then (1) the martingale test [MT] to verify if no change occurs in the given data stream is $P(\max_k M_k \geq \lambda) = \frac{1}{\lambda}$ where $\lambda > 0$; (2) let α be the size of the test deciding in favor of the alternative hypothesis "change occurs in the data stream" when the null hypothesis "no change occurs in the data stream" is true, and let $1 - \beta$ be the power of the test deciding in favor of the alternative hypothesis when it is true. The martingale test is an approximation of the sequential probability ratio test (SPRT) $\lambda \leq \frac{1-\beta}{\alpha}$. The mean delay time $E(m)$, i.e., the expected number of data points observed before a change is detected is $E(m) \approx \frac{(1-\beta)\log\lambda}{E\left(\log \epsilon p_i^{\epsilon-1}\right)}$. λ is found in a deterministic fashion using (α, β) for some false positive rate. To estimate the start of the shot change one employs $E(m)$.

Video streams are unlabeled data streams consisting of a sequence of image frames. Testing for exchangeability using the martingale requires to handle unlabeled data streams. The first question one needs to answer is how to redefine the strangeness measure for unlabeled data points. The strangeness measure is derived using clustering, e.g., K-means for $K = 1$. The strangeness value for a data point, i.e., video frame, is high when the frame is further away from the cluster representation, e.g., the median for the cluster. The unlabeled data points are image representations based on color and edge histograms (Ho and Wechsler, 2006b). The video sequence (see Fig. 7.5) shows the use of martingale for shot change detection and key frame extraction. The human figure starts to appear in frame 98 and completes her appearance around frame 150 (see Fig. 7.5a). The strangeness and p-values, computed as intermediate steps in the computation of martingale values, are useful in extracting key frames from a video sequence. With the availability of the strangeness values for all previous images frames, one can extract key frames based on the least strange image frame before a shot change is detected. An image frame is thus the least strange when the p-value is one. The last frame in the segment that achieves the maximum p-value of one before a shot change is detected becomes the key frame for the corresponding segment. The last frame is the preferred one because it is representative of more frames. The shot change found at frame 158 defines two consecutive video segments. The frames 111 and 171 are found as key frames because they are the last frames for their corresponding segments that achieve the p-value of one (see Fig. 7.5b). The martingale approach compares favorably against alternative methods using recall and precision measures for performance evaluation. In addition, the martingale provides a sound theoretical basis for setting thresholds a priori without any learning or prior models, compared against existing a posteriori empirical methods and heuristics. Last but not least, the martingale method is an efficient one pass algorithm.

7.6 Pose Detection and Manifolds

Face identification and authentication usually access only frontal and still images. Face in a crowd, however, has access to time varying (video) sequences where the head moves and the 2D frontal view is just one possibility among many. As the head rotates, pose variation in 3D rather than in plane rotation takes place. Different views or (out of plane) poses, including up-and-down nodding rotations, become apparent and self-occlusion and self-shadowing are possible. The views or poses cluster to build user profiles, while biometric learning and recognition takes place separately for each cluster. When a face is detected, its pose is estimated, and one proceeds by normalizing the face image and recognizing it using the classifier that is indexed by the corresponding pose. The order in which the views can follow each other is not arbitrary but rather lawful. As the rotating head makes the views available for inspection,

(a)

(b)

Fig. 7.4. Shot-Change Detection and Key Frame Extraction (Ho and Wechsler, 2006b).

a manifold is charted. Manifolds are topological space that provide for connectedness and continuity. Alternatively, one can visualize the path traced by a rotating head using the concept of a phase space where dynamical variables that describe the changes incurred, as the pose changes, are plotted against each other. A simple example for a manifold is that of a single particle moving in one dimension. There are two degrees of freedom, e.g., position and velocity, and the phase diagram provides qualitative information about the internal dynamics. In a similar fashion, each degree of freedom or parameter for the rotating head becomes now an axis for a multidimensional space. The succession of plotted points corresponds to the transitions taking place over time or equivalently to how the manifold evolves over time. The phase diagram constraints the shape such evolution takes, and can be used to make predictions and recognize among different rotating heads. Pose detection comes first before any manifold can be charted and it is addressed next. Clusters and manifolds are alternative ways to handle pose variation. One can contemplate to cluster across the manifold using geodesics.

As pose estimation is basically a multi-class discrimination task, any of the classification methods described in this book could be used. The basic architecture for pose estimation includes a combination of pose detectors for specific ranges, e.g., view-specific eigen spaces, K-means clustering for training, and maximum likelihood. Clustering is important to determine the optimal views and their range. Stereo for head pose and gaze estimation has also been proposed. The active shape models and alignment are yet another possibility for pose estimation but are impractical because they require precise correspondences and some manual annotation. An early example for pose detection using SVM is described by Huang et al. (1998). FERET data, which included frontal and 33.75 (rotated) left and right poses for both training and testing, was used. Perfect accuracy was reported using both polynomial of degree 3 and RBF kernels. The quantization of the pose space and the accuracy with witch the pose can be estimated affect the recognition performance. Li et al. (2001) used kernel machine based learning for multi-views face detection and pose estimation.

Shakhnarovich et al. (2003) have proposed fast pose estimation using parameter sensitive hashing and local regression. Pose estimation, depending on the precision use, can become quite complex and requires a large number of exemplars for training. Such concerns are addressed using an extension of local hashing, which is sensitive to the similarity displayed in the original parameter space and finds approximate neighbors in sub-linear time with respect to the number of exemplars. Li et al. (2004) review pose estimation and suggest using a combination of PCA for input and support vector regression (SVR). Two pose estimators, one for tilt (elevation), and the other for yaw (azimuth), are used. The view space is partitioned into eight (overlapping) segments and model based strategies, including symmetry, are used. We describe next *Isomap* and *Locally Linear Embedding (LLE)* methods for charting manifolds in low dimensional spaces and their application to the exploration of video sequences when the pose and/or the dynamics vary. The goal for both methods is to find low dimensional structures hidden in the original high dimensional observations that render themselves to relatively simple analysis and interpretation.

Isomap (isometric feature mapping) makes reference to a geometric framework that consists of a single global coordinate system for non-linear dimensionality reduction (Tenenbaum et al., 2000) (but see Balasubramanian and Schwartz (2002) for earlier references.) Isomap can discover the non-linear degrees of freedom that underlie complex natural observations. It combines the major algorithmic features of PCA and MDS - computational efficiency, global optimality, and asymptotic convergence - with the flexibility to learn a broad class of non-linear manifolds. Isomap builds on classical MDS but seeks to preserve the intrinsic geometry of the data, which is captured using the geodesic (shortest) manifold rather than Euclidean distance for pairs of data points. The geodesic is the shortest distance between two points on a mathematically defined surface. e.g., a straight line on a plane or an arc of a great circle on a sphere. The use of the geodesic is motivated "by its ability to reflect the true low-dimensional geometry of the manifold" (Tennenbaum et al., 2000). The input space distance provides a good approximation to the geodesic distance for neighboring points. The Euclidean distance between "near by" points in 3D, however, can be small while the geodesic distance on the intrinsic 2D manifold can be quite large. Isomap starts by constructing a neighborhood graph that connects each point to all the points within a sphere of radius ϵ in the input space, or to all its k nearest neighbors. For far away points, the geodesic distance can be approximated by adding up a sequence of "short hops" between neighboring points, which can be computed efficiently by finding the shortest paths in a graph with edges connecting neighboring data points (Floyd's algorithm). MDS (see Sect. 6.7) is then applied using the approximations found for the geodesic distances. The summary of the Isomap algorithm proposed by Tenenbaum et al. (2000) is

1. *Construct the neighborhood graph*: Define the graph G over all data points by connecting point i and j if [as measured by $d_k(i,j)$] they are closer than ϵ (ϵ-Isomap), or if i is one the k nearest neighbor of j (K-Isomap). Set the edge lengths equal to $d_k(i,j)$.

2. *Compute shortest paths*: Initialize $d_G(i,j) = d_k(i,j)$ if i and j are linked by an edge; $d_G(i,j) = \infty$ otherwise. Then for each value of $k = 1, 2, \cdots, N$ in turn, replace all entries $d_G(i,j)$ by $\min(d_G(i,j), d_G(i,k) + d_G(k,j))$. The final values $D_G = d_G(i,j)$ will contain the shortest path distance between all pair of points in G (Floyd-Warshall algorithm).

3. *Construct d-dimensional embedding*: Let λ_p be the pth eigenvalue (in decreasing order) of the matrix $\tau(\mathbf{D}_G)$, ν_p^i be the ith component of the pth eigenvector, and set the pth component of the d-dimensional vector $\mathbf{y}_i$ equal to $\sqrt{\lambda_p}\nu_p^i$. Here $\tau(\mathbf{D}_G) = -\frac{\mathbf{HSH}}{2}$ where $\mathbf{S}$ is the matrix of squared distance ($\mathbf{S}_{ij} = \mathbf{D}_{ij}^2$), and $\mathbf{H}$ is the "centering matrix" ($\mathbf{H}_{ij} = \delta_{ij} - \frac{1}{N}$).

Finally the coordinate vectors $\mathbf{y}_i$ for points in Y are chosen to minimize the cost function

$$E = \|\tau(\mathbf{D}_G) - \tau(\mathbf{D}_Y)\|_F \qquad (7.21)$$

where $\mathbf{D}_y$ denotes the matrix of Euclidean distances and F is the Frobenius norm. The operator τ converts distances to inner products for efficient optimization. The global minimum for the above minimization is achieved by setting the coordinates $\mathbf{y}_i$ to the top d eigenvectors of the matrix $\tau(\mathbf{D}_G)$ similar to multidimensional scaling (MDS). The true dimensionality of the data can be estimated from the decrease in error as the dimensionality of Y is increased (compared to fixing d ahead of time for techniques such as self-organization feature maps). Tenenbaum et al. (2000) apply Isomap to canonical dimensionality reduction where the input consists of a sequence of 4,096 dimensional vectors, representing the brightness values of 64×64 pixel images of a face rendered with different poses and lighting directions. Isomap ($K = 6$) learns a 3D embedding of the intrinsic geometric structure of the face data. Each coordinate axis for the embedding space was found to highly correlate (R) with the original data: left-right pose (x axis, R = 0.99), up-down pose (y axis, R = 0.90), and lighting direction (R = 0.92). Pless (2003) has used Isomap to explore and analyze video sequences for the purpose of classifying video clips. The video trajectories, charted by changing frames, index the original clips in a lower dimensional space for classification and/or cluster them according to their similarity. The geodesic distance and connectivity for real data may often be approximated inaccurately using neighboring data points. Balasubramanian and Schwartz (2002) have argued that "[the Isomap] approach is topologically unstable and can only be used after careful preprocessing of the data [and proper choice of ϵ or K]." In addition, they claim that "the nearest Euclidean neighbors in the high dimensional space are vulnerable to short circuit errors if the neighborhood is too large with respect to the folds in the manifold on which the points lie or if noise in the data moves the points slightly off the manifold."

Locally Linear Embedding (LLE) shares similar aims with Isomap but captures the local geometry for complex embedding manifolds using a set of linear coefficients that best approximate each data point based upon its neighbors in the input space (Roweis and Saul, 2000). LLE, which is local and non-iterative, discovers non-linear manifolds and can capture context. LLE seeks for a set of low dimensional points that are similarly approximated using the same set of coefficients found initially for the higher dimensional space. Isomap and LLE have complementary strengths: Isomap handles holes well but can fail if the data hull is non-convex; and vice versa for LLE (Brandt, 2002). The LLE algorithm computes a low-dimensional embedding with the property that "nearby points in the high dimensional space remain nearby and similarly co-located with respect to one another in the low dimensional space" (Saul and Roweis, 2003). The embedding is optimized to preserve the local configurations of nearest neighbors without considering the relationship between far away data points maps. The outline for LLE follows Saul and Roweis (2003). Assume now that the data consist of n real valued vectors $\mathbf{X}_i$ with dimensionality d. The points are well sampled from a smooth underlying manifold such that each point has on the order of $2d$ neighbors that define a roughly linear patch on the manifold with respect to some metric. The local geometry of each point $\mathbf{X}_i$ is characterized by the coefficients or weights $\mathbf{W}_{ij}$ that linearly reconstruct the data point from its neighbors using the k nearest neighbors for each data point and the Euclidean distance. The reconstruction errors are quantified by the cost function

$$E(\mathbf{W}) = \sum_i \left| \mathbf{X}_i - \sum_j \mathbf{W}_{ij} \mathbf{X}_j \right|^2 \tag{7.22}$$

The weights $\mathbf{W}_{ij}$ are found by minimizing the above cost function subject to two constraints: a *sparseness* constraint and an *invariance* constraint. The sparseness constraint is that each data point $\mathbf{X}_i$ is reconstructed only from its neighbors, enforcing $\mathbf{W}_{ij} = 0$ if $\mathbf{X}_j$ is outside of the immediate neighborhood. The invariance constraint requires that the rows of the weight matrix sum to one $\sum_j \mathbf{W}_{ij} = 1$. For any data point, the constrained weights are invariant to rotations, rescaling and translations of that data point and its neighbors. Therefore, the reconstruction weights characterize geometric properties that do not depend on a particular reference frame. There is no invariance to local affine transformation. The constrained weights can be computed in closed form. Consider a data point $\mathbf{X}$ with k nearest neighbors η_j and the corresponding weights w_j. The reconstruction error can be written as

$$\epsilon = \left| \mathbf{X} - \sum_j w_j \eta_j \right|^2 = \left| \sum_j w_j (\mathbf{X} - \eta_j) \right|^2 = \sum_{jk} w_j w_k \mathbf{C}_{jk} \qquad (7.23)$$

using the fact that the weights sum to one and introducing the local covariance matrix $\mathbf{C}_{jk} = (\mathbf{X} - \eta_j)(\mathbf{X} - \eta_k)$. Using Lagrange multiplier, the problem is reformulated to minimize

$$\Phi = \left| \sum_j w_j (\mathbf{X} - \eta_j) \right|^2 + \alpha \sum_j w_j \qquad (7.24)$$

Let $\mathbf{e}$ be the vector of all ones. Solving this problem one obtains

$$\frac{\partial \Phi}{\partial w_k} = 2 \sum_j w_j \mathbf{C}_{jk} + \alpha = 0 \text{ and } \mathbf{CW} = -\alpha \mathbf{e} \qquad (7.25)$$

The optimal weights are found as

$$\mathbf{w}^T = \frac{\mathbf{e}^T \mathbf{C}^{-1}}{\mathbf{e}^T \mathbf{C}^{-1} \mathbf{e}} \text{ and } \mathbf{w}_j = \frac{\sum_k \mathbf{C}_{jk}^{-1}}{\sum_{lm} \mathbf{C}_{lm}^{-1}} \qquad (7.26)$$

The above problem can be dealt more efficiently by solving the linear system $\sum_k \mathbf{C}_{jk} w_k = 1$ and then rescaling the weights so that they sum to one. If the local covariance matrix is singular or nearly singular, it can be conditioned by adding a small multiple of the identity matrix. Since the weights reflect the local geometric properties of the data, one expects those properties to be preserved after the data is mapped into the lower d dimensional space. The same weights $\mathbf{W}$ that reconstruct the input in d dimensions should also reconstruct the embedded manifold coordinates in d dimensions. This is done by choosing the d-dimensional coordinates of each output $\mathbf{Y}_i$ to minimize the cost function

$$\Phi(\mathbf{Y}) = \sum_i \left| \mathbf{Y}_i - \sum_j \mathbf{W}_{ij} \mathbf{Y}_j \right| \qquad (7.27)$$

The embedding is determined entirely by the geometric information encoded by the weights $\mathbf{W}_{ij}$. The cost function now has a quadratic form

$$\begin{aligned} \Phi(\mathbf{Y}) &= tr\left((\mathbf{Y} - \mathbf{WY})(\mathbf{Y} - \mathbf{WY})^T \right) \\ &= tr\left(\mathbf{Y}^T (\mathbf{I} - \mathbf{W} - \mathbf{W}^T + \mathbf{W}^T \mathbf{W}) \mathbf{Y} \right) \\ &= \sum_{ij} \mathbf{M}_{ij} (\mathbf{Y}_i \cdot \mathbf{Y}_j) \end{aligned} \qquad (7.28)$$

where $\mathbf{M}_{ij} = \delta_{ij} - \mathbf{W}_{ij} - \mathbf{W}_{ji} + \sum_k \mathbf{W}_{ki} \mathbf{W}_{kj}$ and δ_{ij} is 1 if $i = j$ and 0 otherwise. To avoid the degenerate solution, two constrains are used: centering the embedding vectors and using the identity matrix for the covariance matrix $\sum_i \mathbf{Y}_i = 0$ and $\frac{1}{N} \sum_i \mathbf{Y}_i \mathbf{Y}_i^T = \mathbf{I}$, respectively. The first constraint allows the coordinates $\mathbf{Y}$ to be translated without affecting the cost, while the second constraint expresses the assumption that the reconstruction errors for different coordinates in the embedding space should be measured on the same scale.

According to the Rayleigh-Ritz theorem (Horn and Johnson, 1990), the cost function $\Phi(\mathbf{Y})$ is minimized by composing $\mathbf{Y}$ of the eigenvectors pertaining to the lowest $(d + 1)$ eigenvectors of the Hermitian matrix $\mathbf{M}$. The bottom eigenvector, the unit vector with all components equal, which represents a free translation model that corresponds to a zero eigenvalue, is discarded. The remaining d non-zero eigenvectors form the d embedding coordinates found by LLE, which discovers the global structure of the data by integrating information from overlapping local neighborhoods. LLE is affected by the number of nearest neighbors used to approximate the local structure. "Why does one need to care about this problem? The reason is that a large number of nearest neighbors causes smoothing or eliminating small structures in the manifold. In contrast, too small neighborhoods can falsely divide the continuous manifold into disjoint sub-manifolds" (Kouropteva et al., 2002). The solution is driven by the fact that "the lower the residual variance is, the better high-dimensional data are represented in the embedding space." LLE can be used for matching (presegmented) local parts or patches. It fails short, however, from serving as a weak learner for boosting (see Sect. 9.7).

Yang (2002a) makes reference to subspace methods and points out that they belong to two categories, reconstruction, e.g., PCA and MDS, or classification, e.g., LDA. Using this as an analogy, Yang argues that "Isomap and LLE in their original form are only suitable for finding the embedding manifolds that best describe the data points with minimum reconstruction error. The same methods are, however, suboptimal from the classification viewpoint." To address this, Yang extends Isomap with LDA for classification purposes where each data point is represented by a feature vector of its geodesic distance to all the other points. The extended Isomap "consistently performs better than or equally well as some best methods in the face recognition literature." Other embeddings, e.g., the Lipschitz embedding (Bourgain, 1985) or the Locally Preserving Projections (LLP) (He et al., 2005) have been proposed for charting manifolds. The Lipschitz embedding works well with clusters of image data; LLP, linear and defined everywhere [vs. LLE that is nonlinear and defined only for training data], preserves the local structure [for some adjacency graph] by deriving Laplacianfaces as approximations to the eigen functions of the Laplace Beltrami operator.

Chang et al. (2004) have used the enhanced Lipschitz embedding (Johnson and Lindenstrauss, 1984) together with Isomap for probabilistic video based facial expression recognition on manifolds. The recognition of facial expressions is driven by the fact that the images for all the possible facial deformations of an individual "make a smooth manifold embedded in a high dimensional image space. In the embedded space, a complete expression sequence becomes a path on the expression manifold, emanating from a center that corresponds to the neutral expression. Each path consists of several clusters. A probabilistic model of transition between the clusters and paths is learned through training videos in the embedded space. The likelihood of one kind of facial expression is modeled as a mixture density with the clusters as mixture centers. The transition between different expressions is represented as the evolution of the posterior probability of the six basic paths." Preprocessing to reduce the variation due to scaling and face poses employs Active Wavelets Networks (AWN) (Hu et al., 2003) on the image sequence for face registration and facial feature localization.

He et al. (2005) used the Laplacianfaces, which are related to spectral clustering, for face manifold analysis in order to "eliminate or reduce unwanted variations resulting from changes in lighting, facial expression, and pose." A weighted graph G is constructed for each data point using ϵ-neighborhoods or k nearest neighbors, the weights W are chosen using a heat kernel similar to the Gaussian, D is a diagonal and symmetric weight matrix whose entries are column sums of W, and $L = D - W$ is the Laplacian matrix. The Laplacianfaces y_i are the solution for the generalized eigenvector problem $Ly = \lambda Dy$. LLP finds a 2D linear (manifold) embedding of face images that induces a partition between faces with open mouth and faces with closed mouth, where the pose and expression change continuously and smoothly. The Laplacianfaces were shown to perform much better than eigenfaces and better than Fisherfaces. The same LLP can be used on face recognition for unknown probes that are projected across the manifold [to reflect their proper pose and expression] and then identified using nearest neighbor information. Matching sets of images when both sets undergo various distortions, such as viewpoint and illumination changes, is a particular case for data fusion from multiple samples and has been addressed using the Joint Manifold Distance (JMD) (Fitzgibbon and Zisserman, 2003) (see Sect. 9.4), which "may be seen as generalizing invariant distance metrics such as tangent distance" (Vasconcelos and Lippman, 1998). Charting manifolds is closely related to tracking and recognition from video, which is discussed in the next section.

7.7 Tracking and Recognition from Video

Face tracking and recognition from video means that the probe data come from video. The gallery data, on the other hand, might consist of still images, videos or even a combination. As in the case of recognition from still images, applications will vary according to the extent to which data capture is controlled. For example, a broadcast talking head clip might have well controlled illumination, pose and image quality. However, CCTV video surveillance might exhibit large variations in pose, including scale and resolution, and illumination. Within a short time scale, such as that of a video clip of a person, face image variations will tend to occur primarily due to face movement relative to the camera, illumination changes and occlusion. The former can be decomposed into global head motion (six degrees of freedom) and local motion due to facial expression change, speech, opening and closing of the eyes and mouth, and movement of hair. Over longer time scales, such as might occur between video clips of a person being acquired, significant variation can also take place due to aging effects, changes of hair style or disguise, for example. Research on face recognition from video has only been gathering momentum for a decade or so; the literature on it is consequently far smaller compared to that of face identification and authentication from stills. Zhao et al. (2003) surveys some of the work on recognition from video up until 2001. The book by Gong et al. (2000) also focuses on face recognition from video. Zhou and Chellappa (2005) review some recently proposed approaches to face recognition from multiple still images and video. The treatment of video tracking and recognition that follows comes from Stephen McKenna.

Video is a richer source of information than stills and should therefore expedite both learning and recognition. Such information can be gainfully combined using data fusion methods (see Ch. 9). Image sequences provide multiple images with which to cope with the sources of image variability. They also provide temporal information useful for tracking and recognition. It makes sense to utilize this extra information where available. The case in which both gallery and probes consist of video data is especially interesting. It should be particularly amenable to adaptive learning, in which probe data augments existing gallery data over time using transduction. It also introduces a new source of variability between gallery and probe instances not present in the case of recognition from stills: that of motion. No two videos of a face are likely to be of the same relative motion. One expects that such variability can differentiate among individuals. Face recognition in which both gallery and probe are spatial-temporal is presumably also the formulation of face recognition for which evolution has honed our abilities. Indeed, psychophysical experiments provide evidence for the role of temporal information in learning and recognition of faces (Hill et al., 1997; Christie and Bruce, 1998; Pike et al., 1997; Bruce and Valentine, 1988; Knight and Johnston, 1997; Lander et al., 1999; Roark et al., 2003). There are three ways in which gallery videos for face representation and learning can be distinguished:

- Unordered multiple images: ignoring temporal labelling, treat the images as an unordered set of multiple stills (see Sect. 9.4).
- Stored image sequences: use temporal information to assist in batch (pool-based) learning to characterize faces from image sequences (see Sect. 7.8).
- Sequential learning: perform on-line learning, updating representations as new frames arrive, without the need to store all the images (see Sect. 7.5).

Once visual face recognition is formulated using image sequences, fusion with audio for learning and recognition suggests itself (Choudhury et al., 1999; Song et al.,

2004). Audio-visual approaches are promising and clearly worthy of further research. Nevertheless, attention is restricted here to visual recognition. It is instructive to consider the tracking and recognition from video as one of probabilistic learning and inference (see Sect. 7.4 for condensation and particle filtering). While methods are often not formulated this way, at least not explicitly, the probabilistic approach provides insight into the simplifying assumptions being made by the various methods. It is a general and complete framework with which to categorize and compare methods. It also suggests novel alternatives to existing methods.

Let us consider closed set recognition in batch mode. Let $n \in \{1, 2, \cdots, N\}$ denote the set of gallery identities. Given video probe data $\mathbf{z}$, we want to compute a probability mass function (PMF) $p(n|\mathbf{z})$. A recognition decision can then be made, if necessary, simply by choosing the identity with the largest probability mass. We also distinguish the case of sequential recognition. In this case, $p(n|\mathbf{z}_{1:t})$ should be estimated at time t as the image data arrive. It is helpful to introduce hidden variables, here denoted generically as $\mathbf{x}$, and to estimate the desired PMF using marginalization (see Sect. 3.1)

$$p(n|\mathbf{z}) = \int p(n, \mathbf{x}|\mathbf{z})d\mathbf{x} = \int p(n|\mathbf{x}, \mathbf{z})p(\mathbf{x}|\mathbf{z})d\mathbf{x} \qquad (7.29)$$

For example, $\mathbf{x}$ could be the parameters of an affine image transformation, perhaps specifying the translation, rotation and scale of the face in the image plane for each frame of video. Alternative schemes could use hidden variables $\mathbf{x}$, which also capture out of plane rotation (up to six degrees of freedom rigid motion), or parameterize facial shape (in 2D or 3D), facial image texture, or both, for example. The above equation suggests the following strategy. A generic face tracker is used to compute $p(\mathbf{x}|\mathbf{z})$. A face recognizer subsequently computes $p(n|\mathbf{x}, \mathbf{z})$ using $\mathbf{x}$ to perform affine alignment of $\mathbf{z}$. A rather crude approximation is to use only the single value of $\mathbf{x}^*$ which is the maximum of $p(\mathbf{x}|\mathbf{z})$. The recognizer then simply needs to compute $p(n|\mathbf{x}^*, \mathbf{z}) \propto p(\mathbf{x}^*, \mathbf{z}|n)p(n)$. The likelihood $p(\mathbf{x}^*, \mathbf{z}|n)$ can be further simplified by assuming independence between frames in which case your favorite still image method can be applied to compute it.

If the face tracker generates a point estimate $\mathbf{x}^*$, relatively small errors in this estimate can significantly degrade recognition. Rather than use a point estimate, adopting a Bayesian strategy of marginalization of $p(n|\mathbf{x}, \mathbf{z})$ over $\mathbf{x}$ should yield better results, even if $p(\mathbf{x})$ is modeled as a simple Gaussian. Nevertheless, it is standard practice to use a point estimate from a tracker although the potential of performing such a marginalization has been noted recently in the context of face recognition (Zhou and Chellappa, 2004).

As mentioned above, it is common practice to decompose face recognition from a video probe into two stages. The first stage is responsible for detecting, extracting and aligning face image data from each frame in the sequence. The second stage takes the resulting aligned face sequences as input, each assumed to contain exactly one person's face, and performs identification. One approach is to scan each image with a static face detector without using previous detections to produce temporal priors in order to crop face images. Tracking, on the other hand, should make use of temporal information. Tracking systems that have been used to provide face sequences for identification typically estimate image plane translation, rotation and scale for cropping and alignment (McKenna et al., 1997). Choudhury et al. (1999) used a tracker that estimated 3D pose and attempted to normalize for it. Alternatively, face texture and 2D shape changes due to factors such as rotation in depth, non-rigid deformations and partial occlusion have been tracked (Gross et al., 2004a). Li et al. (2001) fitted a learned 3D shape and shape free texture model to face image sequences using temporal continuity to constrain fitting. This two stage decomposition, while convenient, is suboptimal. Several attempts to more closely couple tracking and recognition have been made and are discussed later. Recognition from aligned face sequences treated as unordered image sets is discussed next.

There are many examples in the face recognition literature in which multiple images are available for each person in the gallery as training data. Usually, however, these images are treated as unordered sets. In some cases, the images are labeled with parameters such as pose and this information is used to help learn identity models. For example, Li et al. (2003a, b) estimate the pose in a face space from pose labeled training data. If aligned probe face sequences are to be treated as unordered sets of images, two common approaches to recognition are

- compute similarities of each probe image to the faces in the gallery separately and then combine these similarities over the probe sequence.
- directly compute a similarity between the probe image set and each of the gallery faces.

Although these approaches are amenable to open set identification, they have generally only been applied to closed set batch mode recognition (Choudhury et al., 1999; McKenna et al., 1997; Senior, 1999) or verification (Choudhury et al., 1999; Yamaguchi et al., 1998) (see also Sect. 9.4). In the first class of methods, McKenna et al. (1998) used Gaussian or constrained Gaussian mixtures to estimate a PDF for each person in a PCA space. Recognition then consisted of computing a likelihood for each probe image and combining these likelihoods. Senior (1999) and Choudhury et al. (1999) used Gaussian PDF, estimated in a Gabor feature jet space and a PCA subspace, respectively. One simple fusion rule is to compute the identity with maximum likelihood in each frame and treat it as a vote for that identity (McKenna et al., 1997; Yamaguchi et al., 1998; Huang and Trivedi, 2002). Another method is to select only the most confidently aligned frame and use its likelihood (Senior, 1999). Choudhury et al. (1999) used a confidence measure based on the ratio of the best match to the average of the other likelihoods to select the most confident frame and based recognition on that frame's likelihood. Matsui et al. (2004) used a Metropolis-Hastings method to match deformable templates incorporating Gabor feature jets. The resulting likelihoods appear to have been combined assuming independence between frames.

The second class of methods adopts the alternative approach of computing similarity between a probe set and each of the gallery sets. Notions of similarity are based on subspaces or probability distributions estimated from these data sets. Yamaguchi et al. (1998) computed a PCA subspace for each person directly from tracker aligned image sets. These subspaces did not define PDF although probabilistic interpretations could have been made. Yamaguchi et al. (1998) used a measure of similarity between subspaces based on the angle between the subspaces. Wolf and Shashua (2003) describe a more general similarity measure between sets based on kernel principal angles. The kernel trick was used to enable efficient matching of non-linear surfaces rather than linear subspaces. Senior (1999) used Bhattacharyya and d' as measures of similarity between PDF. Shakhnarovich et al. (2002) use a Gaussian model of appearance distribution and performed matching based on the Kullback-Leibler divergence between densities estimated from the probe image set and each of the gallery sets. Arandjelovic and Cipolla (2004) computed a non - linear similarity between face image sets which achieved more accurate recognition by avoiding the Gaussian assumption. Given a gallery and a probe image set, kernel principal components analysis was applied to their union. After projecting the data onto the kernel principal components, the resistor average distance (a symmetric dissimilarity measure based on Kullback-Leibler divergence) was used.

The adequacy of modeling a face's gallery and probe data as i.i.d. samples from some fixed probability distribution will depend to a great extent on existing image capture conditions. Where factors such as illumination, viewpoint, expression and pose vary similarly during gallery and probe acquisition, such an approach can be well motivated. However, where these factors vary differently, such a model is likely to give poor results. Sequences will be relatively short and their frames will be far from independent. The second important aspect for video processing is that of learning. Face image sequences have been used to construct 2D or 3D spatial face models for use in subsequent identification either from stills or video. Learning these models from video can potentially take advantage of temporal information to either perform batch learning or sequential learning in which only the most recent images are stored.

Structure from motion (SfM) algorithms can be used to reconstruct 3D models from video. General purpose SfM algorithms tend to give reconstructions of insufficient quality for reliable recognition. Better results can be obtained by initializing SfM using a generic face model (Fua, 2000). Chowdhury et al. (2002) argue that this tends to lead to convergence to results close to the generic model. They propose an alternative method in which the result of an SfM algorithm is combined with a generic model by comparing local regions in the two models. Krueger and Zhou (2002) describe a sequential clustering algorithm to learn a set of aligned exemplars from a gallery sequence. Rather than store a face representation from every frame, aligned face representations from a subset of the frames are stored along with weights indicating the fraction of the frames which they best approximate.

Models learned from video can potentially capture temporal dependencies and these can be generic or identity specific in nature. Such temporal regularities can be helpful for tracking and recognition. Lee et al. (2003) applied K-means clustering to exemplar images from gallery videos and modeled each cluster as a linear subspace using PCA. Transitions between these clusters were counted in order to estimate transition probabilities. The clusters tended to correspond to different head poses and the transition probabilities thus encoded temporal information about pose change. For example, it is more likely that a left profile will transition through a frontal view than directly to a right profile view. The model is a first order Markov process over a piecewise linear structure. A related method involves training an HMM for each person in the gallery by compressing each cropped face image using PCA to obtain observation sequences for training. Recognition of a probe video then consists of selecting the HMM with the highest likelihood (Huang and Trivedi, 2002; Liu and Chen, 2003). Continuous density HMM were found to give more accurate recognition than discrete HMM or a simple majority vote scheme (Huang and Trivedi, 2002).

The assumption underlying the above approaches is that gallery and probe data both contain similar transitions in appearance. Such an assumption is most useful in situations in which the acquisition set-up, illumination and human activity are constrained. The models can then capture activity specific temporal information. However, under less constrained conditions, there is a danger of insufficient generalization since transitions in the training data are unlikely to be representative of those encountered in the probe data. Aggarwal et al. (2004) model a moving face as a linear dynamical system. They use a first-order autoregressive and moving average (ARMA) model for each person in the gallery. The model is estimated from cropped face images and captures variations in appearance due to head pose, for example. Identification is then based on computing distance measures between the probe ARMA model and gallery ARMA models.

The most intuitive, efficient and reliable way for performing face recognition from video is combining tracking and recognition so that they feed to and reinforce each other. Edwards et al. (1998) attempted to integrate tracking and identification using active shape (appearance) models (ASM) of faces (see Sect. 6.5). Linear discriminant analysis was used to separate ASM into components for identity and other variations. Person-specific variation was estimated and used to enhance tracking assuming identity constancy over time. If the posterior $p(n|\mathbf{x}, \mathbf{z})$ could be computed, the identity PMF could be obtained by marginalization. Estimating these posterior amounts to solving both tracking and identification tasks together. Let $\mathbf{s}_t = (n_t, \mathbf{x}_t)$ denote the estimate at time t of the state, comprising both the identity and the tracking parameters. Note that this is a mixed distribution of discrete and continuous variables. Bayesian (particle) filtering can recursively compute the posterior by making a Markov assumption so that the posterior propagated using a dynamic model from the previous frame becomes the prior

$$p(\mathbf{s}_t|\mathbf{z}_{1:t}) \propto p(\mathbf{z}_t|\mathbf{s}_t) \int_{s_{t-1}} p(\mathbf{s}_t|\mathbf{s}_{t-1})p(\mathbf{s}_{t-1}|\mathbf{z}_{1:t-1})d\mathbf{s}_{t-1} \qquad (7.30)$$

This propagation can be implemented using particle filters in which the densities are represented as sets of weighted samples termed particles.

Krueger and Zhou (2002), Zhou and Chellappa (2002), and Zhou et al. (2003) used versions of condensation to compute the above equation. Earlier work used particle filtering but did not include identity in the state (Li and Chellappa, 2002). Instead, the probability of the motion parameters was propagated and the verification probability approximated by marginalizing over a region of the state space redefined at each time step. The dynamic model was decomposed as $p(s_t|s_{t-1}) = p(n_t|n_{t-1})p(\mathbf{x}_t|\mathbf{x}_{t-1})$. The identity was assumed to be constant over time, so $n_t = n_{t-1}$. Samples for the identity variable were thus kept fixed. The other component of the state $\mathbf{x}_t$, consisted of affine motion parameters. In the modified condensation algorithm, a random sample of the marginal motion distribution $x_t^{(i)}$, gives rise to N particles $\{(n, x_t^{(i)}, w_{t,n}^{(i)})\}_{n=1}^{N}$. Various likelihood functions were employed. Given a gallery of still images, a truncated Laplacian likelihood function based on a single image template for each person in the gallery was used. Alternatively, a probabilistic PCA representation was used. Given a video gallery, the likelihood used a mixture model for each person in which exemplar face representations were used as mixture component centers. Adaptive Gaussian mixture appearance models were subsequently incorporated into this scheme (Zhou et al., 2004). In order to make an identification decision from a probe sequence, the identity PMF was reset to a uniform prior after convergence. At the end of the sequence, the identity which most often had the highest probability mass after convergence was selected. Zhou and Chellappa (2004) discuss replacing the discrete identity variable n, with a continuous variable α, with invariance to location, illumination and pose variations. Given suitably strong invariance, such a variable can be treated as encoding identity. Identification could then be performed by comparing densities $p(\alpha|\mathbf{z})$ estimated from different gallery and probe sequences. When α is high dimensional, computing the required integrals becomes computationally demanding. However, Monte Carlo methods might be able to yield tractable approximations.

Tracking and recognition amount to parsing images and understanding them. Tu et al. (2003) suggest a general framework for parsing images into regions and objects such that "detection and recognition [of faces] proceed simultaneously with image segmentation in a competitive and cooperative manner [to explain the image]. This method makes use of bottom-up proposals combined with top-down generative models using Data Driven Markov Chain Monte Carlo (DDMCMC). The proposals for a face are learned using AdaBoost." Such an approach is similar to performing cycles of analysis and synthesis that feed each other. Two recent methods go beyond particle filters and stand out in pointing to fruitful directions for future research. They combine tracking and recognition using methods characteristic of statistical learning and model selection. Avidan (2004) has proposed Support Vector Tracking (SVT) that integrates the SVM classifier into an optic flow based tracker. Rather than tracking by minimizing the standard sum of squared differences (SSD), which makes no assumptions about the class of the tracked object, and using the tracker and classifier sequentially, SVT tries to maximize the SVM classification score over neighborhoods and space tessellation of the (affine) transform space. The intensive search required by SVT is mitigated by using pyramids and coarse to fine processing. (The disadvantage of tracking first and matching later is that "the tracker is not guaranteed to move to the best location (the location with the best classification score) but rather find the best matching image region. Furthermore, such an approach relies heavily on the first frame and its proper initialization. Even if a better image for classification purposes were to appear later in the sequence, the tracker will not lock on it as it tries to minimize the SSD error with respect to the first image which might have a low classification score.) Prior knowledge needs to be integrated directly into the tracking process in order "to leverage the power of the classifier for tracking." The combined tracker and classification SVT is thus more reliable because training (to different object or face appearances) can overcome the noise and the affine transformations that the face undergoes during tracking. SVT can, however, mistakenly switch from one face to another one in case of two nearby faces unless context and reasoning are taken into account.

One limitation for SVT is that SVM is applied to each video frame independently of other frames. Williams et al. (2005), aware of the benefits that can accrue from using temporal fusion, address this limitation. One possibility, later dismissed due to its frailty, was training SVM to discriminate motion rather than perform direct verification. The state of a Euclidean 4D similarity [2D translation, zoom, and rotation] transformation is inferred [over each test region] using SVM operating on each dimension independently and fusing the results using multiple regression. The better alternative is using "the [single stage] regression form of a fully probabilistic Relevance Vector Machine (RVM) to generate observations with Gaussian distributions that can be fused over time. [RVM recasts basic SVM using the Bayesian framework and Gaussian processes.] A classification SVM is [now] used in tandem, for object [or face] verification, and this provides the capability of automatic initialization and recovery." Given a test region, RVM estimates the errors [with respect to some previous region] or change in states using an output probability distribution and traces their origin to a full fledged rather than partitioned 4D similarity space. RVM tracks using Kalman filtering. The probabilistic output or observations about changes in the current state are expressed using [Gaussian] noise and kernel functions that measure the similarity between relevance vectors and the current image region. The dynamical process behind motion is modeled as a second order autoregressive process (ARP) that augments the state equations to incorporate two previous observations. RVM is more complex than SVT, and its performance will depend heavily on the adequacy of the specific assumptions made. RVM estimates error bars (Gaussian posterior). In regions of input space not well represented by training data the variance estimates produced by RVM decreases! It should of course increase because uncertainty is greater given fewer points. This problem arises due to the conflict between Bayesian inference and sparseness (Rasmussen and Quinonero-Candela, 2005). Tracking and recognizing faces might still fare better using SVT.

Ultimately, what is needed for many applications is adaptive learning in which the biometric templates are updated in an incremental fashion based on incoming probe data. This should reduce the need for labeled data, increase system autonomy, and help longer term changes due to aging to be better accommodated. Memory-based (exemplar-based) face recognition algorithms, employing non-parametric methods such as nearest neighbor classification, can be incrementally trained on-line by adding probe exemplars with known (or assumed known) identity to the gallery. Sukthankar and Stockton (2001) describe an application in which users are notified of the arrival of a visitor and can provide feedback to the system when the visitor is wrongly identified. Thus, labeled data created during operation becomes available for incremental gallery update. Okada and von der Malsburg (1999) describe another memory-based system but perform gallery updating in an unsupervised manner without feedback from a human supervisor. Whenever a person is recognized by the system, using a nearest mean classifier, their probe data are added to the gallery. If a person is not recognized, a new gallery identity is initialized. The danger with such an approach is that any identification errors made by the algorithm lead to learning with incorrectly labeled data, potentially leading to reduced accuracy over time. These methods did not otherwise exploit temporal information for recognition. Liu and Chen (2003) modeled each person using an HMM and used probe data to update the HMM when a person was recognized with confidence above a predetermined threshold. The difference between the highest and second highest likelihood was used as a measure of recognition confidence. Model update was performed using MAP adaptation (Gauvain and Lee, 1994). Liu et al. (2003) performed PCA on the faces of each person in the gallery to obtain an eigenspace representation for each person. They proposed using video frames recognized with high confidence as a person to update that person's eigenspace. Confidence was the difference between the lowest and second lowest residual (reconstruction error). The update algorithm used decay parameters ("forgetting factors") to place more emphasis on recent samples. Several such methods for updating PCA eigenspaces have been proposed. For example, Li (2004) proposed a robust, incremental algorithm and demonstrated successful adaptation under large head pose change.

Unsupervised recognition of images extracted from video is useful for certain applications such as automatic indexing of archive film footage. The goal here is to find clusters so that each person in the video has one cluster. Eickeler et al. (2001) represented face images using pseudo-2D HMM and performed clustering using the K-means algorithm. Face sequences were treated as unordered sets of images so temporal information was not used. They were able to automatically extract clusters of images, with each cluster corresponding to one of four people in a TV broadcast news sequence. Raytchev and Murase (2002, 2003) argued that clustering algorithms such as K-means are inappropriate for face representation schemes in which inter-person distances are often greater than intra-person distances. Non-linear manifolds due, for example, to head pose change, are responsible for such occurrences. Instead, Raytchev and Murase used pairwise (unsupervised) clustering methods such as the normalized cut algorithm and minimal spanning tree (MST), and clustering by attraction and repulsion algorithms. Inter-set similarity was based on either minimal distance or a modified Hausdorff distance. Alternatively, they proposed vector quantization (VQ) faces to operate on data streams and handle both frontal and side-view faces, and temporal constraints to cluster the different sequences into face categories using combinatorial optimization. This is quite similar to the phonetic maps suggested by Kohonen (1988). Fitzgibbon and Zisserman (2002) clustered face images extracted from movies by a face detector. They used a hierarchical mediod-based clustering algorithm and successfully extracted clusters containing individual, principal members of the cast. Clustering was performed using a distance function that contained priors on the affine transformations between face images and on the affine motion between contiguous frames. In subsequent work, Fitzgibbon and Zisserman (2003) used the infimum of manifold distance between points in two subspaces as a measure of distance for clustering.

Most methods for identification from video assume that face image subsequences have been reliably extracted by some previous module performing face detection and/or tracking. Furthermore, it is assumed that each such subsequence contains only images of a single person's face. Decoupling of recognition from video in this way is suboptimal (McKenna and Gong, 1998) as was noted earlier. Information about probable identity can be used to enhance tracking, for example. One way in which identity information can help is in disambiguating occlusions. Lee et al. (2003) proposed dealing with temporary, partial occlusions using an image mask in which each element denotes the probability that the corresponding pixel is occluded. This mask was updated using a temporal prior propagated from previous frames. The mask elements were then used as weights during matching. Zhou et al. (2004) used a robust likelihood formulation to down-weight outlier pixels. Given a high proportion of such outliers, appearance model updating was also suspended. The presence of a large and varying number of targets leads to complex interactions and ambiguity regarding occlusion and/or appearance and disappearance. To address such problems, recognition from video can be enhanced by exploiting contextual visual information. For example, human body tracking provides strong context for face tracking and alignment. Fig. 7.6 illustrates a situation in which body tracking, using adaptive appearance models, allows people to be tracked through occlusions, maintaining correspondence between identities. A system based solely on face tracking could not have reliably extracted and linked face subsequences of a single person through the grouping behavior. Contextual information, in this case adaptive body color models, helped to disambiguate identity and enabled correspondence over time to be established through temporary occlusions.

Whilst spatial-temporal models have been learned from gallery sequences, it seems likely that the temporal information captured has been rather generic in nature. For example, a left profile does not usually transition to a right profile without a more frontal view in between. However, there is also information in facial motion patterns, both rigid and non-rigid, which can help discriminate between different people. This

Fig. 7.5. Tracking People through Grouping Behaviour (Reprinted from *Computer Vision and Image Understanding*, Vol. 80, McKenna et al., Tracking Groups of People, ©2000 with permission from Elsevier).

type of temporal information has yet to be fully exploited for identification. Formulation of face recognition as probabilistic inference from video suggests that the application of state of the art probabilistic learning and inference methods to enable principled spatial-temporal fusion will yield improved performance. Ultimately, face recognition and active learning need to be unified. Learning should be an ongoing process during recognition with the face models efficiently initialized and adapted. Such sequential learning is usually not fully supervised, and some of the data are unlabeled. Partial information or feedback on identity may be available from other sources or sensory modalities, with learning likely to be semi-supervised in many situations. Automatic initialization and adaptation of facial models require further research. In particular, sequential learning with fixed computational resource implies forgetting. Certainly, models need to be updated to account for temporal processes such as aging. How to update the face models in a robustly and efficient fashion is an open issue. Recognition as a temporal process involves accumulation of evidence over time and, hopefully, also accumulation of certainty. It is clear, however, that not all images should contribute equally to such a process. The new availability of a particularly informative view even after extended observation of a subject might justifiably prompt the system to "change its mind." Face recognition from video has only been applied to relatively small data sets. Quantitative evaluation on large video sets is needed in order to properly compare methods. Evaluation becomes even more challenging when sequential learning and adaptation are considered.

7.8 Spatio-Temporal Subspace Analysis Using 3D ICA

Independent component analysis (ICA) was originally developed for blind source separation (Bell and Sejnowski, 1995). It decomposes (linearly) mixed signals into interesting and not necessarily orthogonal super (non) Gaussian components, i.e., a basis whose components are statistically independent and display high kurtosis (see Sect. 5.4). Independent events must be uncorrelated, but uncorrelated events may not be independent. Principal Component Analysis (PCA) requires that the components are only uncorrelated and Gaussian. ICA can account for higher order statistics and is suitable to derive localized features, e.g., nose, mouth, eye, forehead, jaw-line or cheek-bone from 2D faces. Most applications of the ICA are related to spatial analysis. For image sequences, where the 2D spatial features vary over time, temporal ICA may be used to find independent components over time. Using fMRI as an example, "spatial ICA (sICA) seeks a set of mutually independent component (IC) source images and a corresponding (dual) set of unconstrained time courses. In contrast, temporal ICA (tICA) seeks a set of ICA source time courses and a corresponding (dual) set of unconstrained images" (Stone et al., 2002). While "the images extracted by sICA are approximately independent, their corresponding dual time courses can be [however] highly correlated" (McKeown, 2000). Spatio-temporal ICA (stICA) "permits a trade-off between the mutual independence of images and the mutual independence of their corresponding time courses" (Stone et al., 2002).

Joint spatio-temporal ICA, which maximizes the degree of independence over both space and time, has been proposed for analyzing natural image sequences (Van Hateren and Ruderman, 1998). A unifying framework for natural image sequences, referred to as bubbles, was proposed by Hyvarinen et al. (2003). They argue that "contrary to earlier ICA results on static images, which gave only filters at the finest possible scale, the spatio-temporal analysis yields filters at a range of spatial and temporal scales. Filters centered at low spatial frequencies are generally tuned to faster movements than those at high spatial frequencies." The "bubbles" combine properties related to sparseness, temporal coherence, and energy correlations. "Positive correlation of energies means that the cells tend to be active, i.e., have nonzero outputs, at the same time, but the actual values are not easily predictable from each other." The spatio-temporal ICA models claim that the subspace derived could be the output of simple cells in the primary visual cortex (see Fig. 7.7), e.g., 3D Gabor filters of different frequency and orientation.

To decompose a sequence of 2D images over time, spatio-temporal ICA maximizes the degree of independence over space and time. Instead of using a set of 2D spatial features, a set of 3D space-time cubes, i.e., stacks of 2D spatial features over time, is used to find a set of spatio-temporal independent components (IC) (see Fig. 7.8) such that

$$\mathbf{X}_k(x, y, t) = \sum_{n=1}^{N} a_n \cdot IC_n(x, y, t) \qquad (7.31)$$

The use of 3D here refers to time rather than depth as the third dimension. Similar arguments apply, however, to (x, y, z) volumes and to (x, y, z, t) volumes that vary over time in 4D. The $\{IC_n\}$ independent components define the basis for the spatiotemporal subspace (see top of Fig. 7.7), while the coefficients $\{a_n\}$ for the biometric signature are derived during enrollment. The topographic features found using ICA are local, sparse (and thus robust to noise), and low-dimensional, and yield a minimum entropy code (Barlow, 1989b). Similar to local feature analysis (LFA) (Penev and Attick, 1996) the features are useful for head segmentation and face recognition. Recognition proceeds the standard way by matching 3D test probe sequences (after their projection onto 3D ICA subspace) against the gallery composed of the biometric signatures captured during enrollment.

One additional challenge now is to search the spatio-temporal 3D IC subspace when temporal coherence does not hold. This might be the case when the face images are captured at different times, from different view angles, express different local distortions, or when whole faces are not available due to occlusion and/or disguise and face patches or parts define 2D slices instead. Spatio-temporal manifolds charted by such 3D image sequences could help with face recognition. The weighting matrix

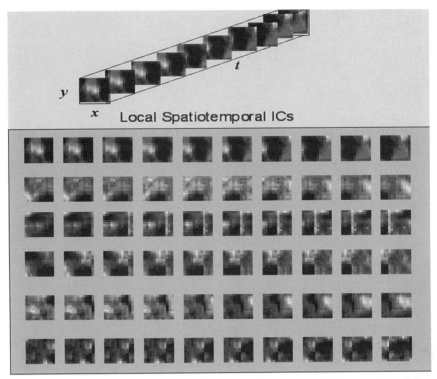

Fig. 7.6. Local Spatio-Temporal Independent Components (Chen and Wechsler, 2006).

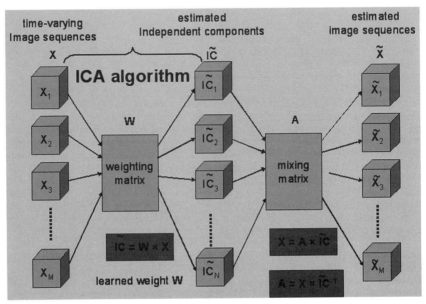

Fig. 7.7. 3D Spatio-Temporal ICA (Chen and Wechsler, 2006).

$\mathbf{W}$ is learned using fast ICA [2] and faces from the ORL database. The face images come from 40 subjects and were captured when temporal coherence does not hold. A patch image sequence that shows low temporal coherence and is made up of local patches can be projected onto the IC subspace to yield its biometric signature (see Fig. 7.9) (Chen and Wechsler, 2006). Compared to 2D spatial IC, the 3D spatio-temporal IC decomposition can change its phase from time to time (Hyvarinen and Hoyer, 2000).

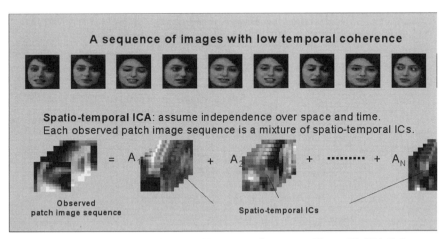

Fig. 7.8. Enrollment and Derivation of Biometric Signatures Using 3D ICA Subspace (Chen and Wechsler, 2006).

Another possible venue for addressing the lack of temporal coherence is the use of skewed (rather than high kurtosis) spatio-temporal ICA probability density functions (Stone et al., 2002). The motivation is similar to that proposed for fMRI, where source images are likely to consist of spatially localized features surrounded by an homogeneous background and the source images have skewed [rather than high kurtosis for speech] PDF (Suzuki et al., 2002). Processing should first normalize the data and transform it using whitened PCA, filter the whitened PCA subspace using Gabor filters, and feed the results to skewed spatio-temporal ICA. Morphology and/or spectrum analysis would then learn "optimal" bubbles and use them to extract local features for biometric enrollment and recognition. The bubbles could constitute the building blocks of weak learners for spatio-temporal recognition-by-parts, with boosting providing the mechanisms for accruing the evidence needed for reliable face recognition (see Sect 9.7). The ultimate challenge here would be a unified theory of space and time that has access to "elementary particles" that define the corresponding dimensions for face appearance and event occurrence.

---

[2] http://www.cis.hut.fi/projects/ica/fastica/

8. 3D

People only see what they are prepared to see (Ralph Waldo Emerson).

Much of the existing face recognition systems operate in 2D. As the search for improved recognition performance intensifies, alternative methods, e.g., 3D, are under consideration. Head and face modeling using 3D could also benefit novel applications related to animation, digital film technology, game development, and medicine. The perceived advantage for 3D comes from its ability to provide depth information, and at the same time yield a better grasp on the overall shape of the head the face belongs to. One could also seek and chart manifolds in 3D that capture the intrinsic characteristics of the spatial-temporal trajectories traced together by the head and face. Another perceived advantage comes from the perception that "working in 3D overcomes limitations due to viewpoint and illumination" (Medioni and Waupotitsch, 2003). More is not always better if attention is not paid to the new imaging medium regarding enrollment and variability. 3D data acquisition, while not dependent on surrounding illumination depends, however, on the illumination source used for image capture. 3D enrollment considers [easy] availability [of imaging devices for capture purposes], capture and costs, on one side, and consistency, on the other side. Consistency concerns repeatability of the measurements obtained. Depth varies, however, according to facial expression, head size, stress, diet, physiological state, and aging. The face is quite complex both in appearance and the way it changes in 3D. The spatial and temporal challenges still persist and have yet to be met. The context for both challenges needs to include large scale data sets, in the thousands, rather than small and limited galleries. The gallery's composition should also display diversity. The two challenges could possibly be addressed together using spatial-temporal analysis (see Sect. 7.8).

Bowyer et al. (2006) review approaches for 3D face recognition. The early methods modeled the range data, for matching purpose, using the surface curvature. Convex regions were found using the sign of the mean and Gaussian curvature. An Extended Gaussian Image (EGI) (Horn, 1984), which is not sensitive to changes in object size, is created for each convex region. The surface normal vector for any object, extracted using plane fitting, is mapped onto the unit Gaussian sphere and assigned a weight according to the area of the surface where it came from. EGI uniquely identifies only convex objects, while an infinite number of non-convex objects can possess the same EGI. In addition, faces that are similar in shape but different in size yield the same EGI. The EGI models are stored as a surface vector histogram and matched using correlation or appearance graphs that incorporate relational constraints (Lee and Milios, 1990). Kang and Ikeuchi (2003) introduced the complex EGI for the purpose of 3D pose determination. Another general approach employs multi-modal recognition based upon the (weighted) contributions from 3D and 2D (Beumier and Acheroy, 2001). Wang et al. (2002) use Gabor filter responses in 2D and "point signatures" in 3D for joint modeling and authentication. Gao et al. (2003) proposed a significance based multi-view Hausdorff distance approach to fuse multiple views of faces using non-rigid flexible matching. Chang et al. (2003) report on PCA-based 2D and 3D recognition results. Multi-modal 2D and 3D, using a simple weighting scheme, performed better than 2D alone or multi sampled 2D images. One of the major limitations perceived so far with respect to 3D comes from dealing with the variation in expression. The non rigid aspect of the face suggests local analysis, in general, and recognition-by-parts, in particular. 3D appears to be affected by face expressions more than 2D, and the "illumination invariance" appears to be just a myth (Bowyer et al., 2006).

Pose, illumination and expression (PIE) is still a challenge for face recognition. Jiang et al. (2005) review different strategies for coping with the PIE challenge in 3D for reliable face recognition as described next. The normalization methods, which lack the 3D head and face model, render 2D face images to a unified PIE space or extract invariant features for generalization and training purposes, on one side, and testing, on the other side. Alternatively, alignment algorithms work in 3D to recover the shape and texture parameters for a 3D morphing model. Other methods aim to expand the training set for the purpose of analysis by synthesis. The warping or the directed morphing approach guides how a different geometry and/or illuminations should be simulated for synthesis purposes. Shape from shading (Attick et al., 1996), illumination cones (Georghiades et al., 2001), quotient images (Raviv and Shashua, 2001) and the plenoptic function or (eigen) light fields (Gross et al., 2004a) are characteristic of such an approach. The quality of synthesis is affected by the similarity in geometry or head structures between the training and test images, annotation and correspondence, alignment, and speed of execution.

8.1 Sensing

Depth recovery from 3D is achieved using a variety of passive methods, e.g., stereo, and active methods, e.g., structured light or range finders using lasers. Depth recovery for stereo relies entirely on visual cues and requires correspondences, hard to establish, and triangulation. There is no requirement for special illumination. Correspondence requires detection and matching of similar feature points. Correspondence is difficult because the face does not show much texture and there is not much of an opportunity to find dense correspondences. *FaceVision* from *Geometrix* makes use of stereo and multi-resolution (pyramid) processing to sense the 3D facial shapes including the face's absolute size and to compare them (Medioni and Chen, 2001). The two cameras are calibrated, both internally and externally. This leads to true metric reconstruction that is rendered in the end as a 3D mesh of triangles with an associated texture map. Geometrix claims that the "3D facial images [that produce 2.1 Mpixels color images in the proposed face recognition data format M1/04-0041] can be then processed and viewed from any orientation, under any [front, side, or behind] lighting conditions, to matching those of a surveillance camera and eliminating ambiguity." The mean and median errors observed after alignment between Geometrix and *Cyberware* Head & Face Color 3D Scanner Model 3030RGB/PS (see below), were 0.93mm and 0.92mm, respectively. The acquisition time for Geometrix is fast, the costs involved are low, and there is operational flexibility.

Photometric or multiple stereo, an extension of standard stereo, generates a (textured) 3D (mesh) model of the face from a sequence of images taken by a single (uncalibrated) camera and a generic face model (Fua, 2000). A simpler and more robust alternative gets rid of the generic face model using instead an internally calibrated camera (Medioni and Pesenti, 2002). The approach proposed by Medioni and Pesenti has the subject move her head from one side to the other while 4-5 seconds of biometrics at 15 frames per second are recorded. The features between adjacent frames are matched to produce an initial estimate for motion, reject outliers using robust statistics, e.g., RANSAC, and refine the matches with triplets of frames using global bundle adjustment. Sets of adjacent views are treated as stereo pairs and (partial) depth maps are iteratively generated, refined and integrated into a single 3D model in about 15 minutes.

Structured light takes advantage of the physics of ambient illumination and the image formation process. It acts as an intelligent filter that discards details and enhances the signal in order to increase SNR with noise referring to background clutter. Structured light is implemented using active sensing. Range acquisition using structured light projects light patterns [on the object of interest, here the head] and takes advantage of shape from texture gradients and/or their density. Depth and/or the face geometry are derived using distortions that are easily registered between the coded light pattern and the final scanned pattern, simple triangulation, and mesh interpolation. Structure light can yield higher accuracy than that obtained using passive stereo. An example of structured light is the Moiré patterns that result when the illumination of two gratings interfere on the surface (in depth) of some object [head]. Depth is derived using the light and dark fringe contours created by the Moiré patterns. *A4 Vision* captures 3D [from ear to ear] facial images [and a standard color image] and registers them as digital data in less than 10 seconds. The subject stands still, while characteristic of structured light, a projector beams an invisible coded light pattern onto her face that is scanned using a digital camera. Bronstein et al. (2003) used bending invariant canonical representations or isometric invariant transformations to cope with head orientations, makeup, and facial expressions. Range (using structured light) and texture are captured, the range image is then converted to a (sub sampled) mesh, geodesic distances between sampled points are computed, and finally canonical signatures used for authentication are extracted. Bronstein et al. (2005) have modeled the facial surface as a deformable and non-rigid object using the Riemannian geometry. They report on a 3DFACE approach that performs 3D face recognition without explicit surface reconstruction and is able to distinguish between identical twins. Last but not least, a strong case is made that "the human visual system uses mainly 2D information for face recognition. The individuality of the subject concealed in the 3D geometry of his face is lost. This reveals the intrinsic weakness of all the 2D face recognition approaches: the face is a 3D object, and using only 2D projection can be misleading."

Range finders use lasers and time of flight to derive depth and ultimately shape. They can yield very high precision without need for hard to implement correspondences. The disadvantage for range finders comes from the relatively long time it takes to capture a sequence of images while the subject stays still. This makes image capture for moving subjects, who are not cooperative, difficult. Another problem is alignment when both 3D and color images are extracted. Safety is also a concern when using lasers and could prompt subjects to close their eyes during data capture. Laser scanners work on the same principle of triangulation but introduce constraints that make the reconstruction process more accurate, yet much slower. Instead of projecting a complete pattern at a time, a single laser beam is shot at the target and a dedicated camera captures its reflection. Since laser is coherent and well focused, it is possible to scan very accurately, row-by-row and column-by-column, any 3D surface. Furthermore, depending on the color of the laser beam (typically red), a special filter can be designed to make detection highly reliable. As these systems image one pixel at a time, the problem of feature matching goes away. Yet, to obtain a full scan takes considerable time as the target face, or the imaging system, must be rotated around or tied to a relative coordinate system.

Characteristic of laser scanners is the *Cyberware 3030PS* scanner [1]. It includes *DigiSize*, a set of software tools for anthropometric measurements of the whole body and head & face 3D data sets, e.g., craniofacial proportions. Scans are stored in cylindrical coordinates relative to a vertical axis. In angular steps ϕ and vertical steps h, at a spacing of $0.7°$ and $0.615mm$, respectively, the device measures the radius r, along with the red, green, and blue components of surface texture R, G, B (Blanz et al., 2002)

$$I(h, \phi) = (r(h, \phi)), R(h, \phi)), G(h, \phi)), B(h, \phi))^T \qquad (8.1)$$

---

[1] http://www.cyberware.com/

The sampling speed is 14,580 points per second digitized to (X, Y, Z) and (R, G, B) components using eight bits for each color. Cyberware also provides the M7G Ear Impression 3D Scanner. Another range finder is the NEC (High-end) Range Finder *Fiore* [2] that captures two raw images from both right and left, prepares 3D montage for both images and models them using masks, and connects the points for the two sides to generate the 3D model. Multiple 3D views, generated through control software, include full color texture mapping with natural skin tones, polygonal data, and a wire frame model. The accuracy and resolution specifications are $0.2mm$ and $0.6mm$, respectively, and the calculation time for (W × H × D) = ($300mm$ × $400mm$ × $300mm$) is $0.6sec$. Simultaneous comparison of live 2D against 3D facial representations and Geodesic Illumination Basis (GIB) descriptors for differences in skin texture is done using Fiore and the *Mugshot Matching Processor*. Processing is sped up using an Ideal Optical Flow (IOF) method for registration. Konica Minolta [3] *VIVID 910* scanner is yet another example of 3D scanners. Software for editing scans and their composition, available from Minolta, e.g., Polygon Editing Tool (PET) or from Geomagic [4], can interface with 3D Virtual Reality Modeling Language (VRML) to produce 3D head models.

Bowyer et al. (2006) argue that "successful practical applications of 3D face recognition would be aided by various improvements in 3D sensor technology. Among these are reduced frequency and severity of artifacts; increased depth of field; increased spatial and depth resolution; and reduced acquisition time." Artifacts such as holes and spikes are due to missing data, and occlusion and errors, respectively. The nostrils, the ears and under the chin areas are rather vulnerable and can be hardly imagined from a single point of view. The above artifacts can be dealt with limited success using hole filling or interpolation and robust statistics, respectively. Alternatively, one would use multiple shots and viewing angles to provide good coverage. Reduced acquisition time is needed to prevent additional motion artifacts for non-cooperative subjects. The specific issues affecting 3D reconstruction are discussed below.

Whatever the physical principle for 3D reconstruction is, any 3D cameras solution must address four basic issues according to Barnabas Takacs from Digital Elite. The first one is the accurate *reconstruction of shape*, meaning a set of 3D points in space that characterize the facial surface. In essence this is a measurement task where the accuracy, due to the nature of triangulation, depends on the relative geometry (baseline) of imaging components, the precision with which pairs of feature points captured from different points of views can be matched up, and the resolution of the camera itself. In general, the wider the base line, i.e., the further apart the projector and the receiving camera are, the more accurate the resolution is. However, if the baseline is too long, the same facial feature can not be seen from both cameras; just think of the nose shadowing a portion of the face, resulting in gaps in the reconstruction process.

The second basic problem is that of *surface generation*. Surface generation takes the 3D point cloud measured by the sensor and represented as a set of individual points in XYZ space, and fits a polygonal mesh (most typically) or parametric surface (like NURBS) that captures its characteristic with minimal error. Due to inherent imaging problems, such as holes caused by non-visible regions or measurement errors caused by lost data, lack of reflection or incorrect values, the algorithm used must approximate the surface locally until it arrives at a consistent representation. The method of choice to fill in smaller holes in most cases relies on local surface curvature and gradients. In more complex or larger areas one may use statistical shape models or preferably integrate information from other sensors. Redundancy can be introduced by using multiple cameras that cover the face from angles below the chin, the front, and the sides as well. The problem with such an arrangement, however, is two folds. First it requires the integration of multiple 3D surfaces, and second, for active imaging systems, the cameras can not be fired at the same time as the projected patterns would

---

[2] http://www.de.nec.de/productfiles/551_Fiore_3D_e.pdf
[3] http://kmpi.konicaminolta.us/vivid/products/vi910-en.asp
[4] http://geomagic.com/products/studio

otherwise interfere. As a result, depending on the time elapsed between any two shots, the subject may slightly move. Thus, integrating two surfaces, called patches, often results in ambiguities that can be difficult to resolve.

The third basic problem of a 3D facial imaging system is *texture* generation. The texture obtained is a 2D image that when back projected on the reconstructed 3D surface creates the appearance of the object, a face in our case. For a generic 3D facial surface the 2D texture is an unwrapped image showing views from left to right. This 2D representation is a one to one mapping of each 3D point (or triangle) to corresponding 2D pixels that contain the color of each surface element. This mapping is generally described using UV coordinates. Obtaining a high resolution texture map has its own set of problems. Laser scanners, for example, do not automatically produce a color image, thus separate snapshots must be taken of the subject and UV mapped onto the surface later. At a first glance camera based solutions do not suffer from this drawback. However, as described before, the shape reconstruction process often requires projecting a pattern (on the subject) that may interfere with the creation of a clean texture. Consequently, most solutions proposed take two consecutive shots in quick succession, one with the pattern ON, and one with OFF. Others will use a single shot but high resolution cameras, and remove the projected grid pattern using image filtering techniques. This degrades the quality of the texture resulting maps, but gains on capture speed. This leads us to the fourth and final problem of 3D imaging, specifically issues related to speed.

The fourth, and in many cases the most limiting, parameter of a 3D imaging system is its *speed of acquisition*. The capture speed must be in synch with the kind of facial events the system needs to image. As an example, obtaining a neutral expression for entry to a secured facility should take only a few seconds. On the other hand when building a large and varied representative data set that captures facial expressions and even non-verbal facial actions, such as micro expressions, faster imaging techniques are required. Ranked relative to speed, the slowest technique is laser scanning. It may take up to several minutes to obtain a good quality scan (however, that will be at very high resolution). The speed of photographic methods largely depends on how fast the imaging camera and the projector's flash can repeatedly recharge and strobe again. For ideal imaging, two shots from each camera angle are required to obtain separate shape and texture shots. To cover the complete facial area, one needs at least five cameras: one full frontal, one below the chin, two profile or $\frac{3}{4}$ profile ones on the sides, and one from the back, if required. In practical terms this means ten high resolution images per each static expression. Using standard cameras working at the capture speed of 30 or maximum 60 frames per second (fps) leads to an effective 3D frame rate of 3-6 fps. While holding the neutral expression is relatively easy, extreme muscle activity and involuntary facial actions occur only for a fraction of a second and are difficult to produce "on cue" even by professional actors. The best way to build a representative 3D facial data set would record a person's facial actions at least with 30fps. This requires approximately ten times the capture speed current digital cameras have to offer. Another problem with continuous 3D facial capture is that the faster the shutter speed, the less time the camera has for integrating the photons arriving at its sensor, i.e. forming the image. Thus, higher speeds require stronger and more perfect lighting as well as uncompressed storage, especially if dense correspondence based tracking algorithms, such as optic flow, are used.

8.2 Analysis by Synthesis

Analysis by synthesis is a generative or transformational methodology that captures and employs generic 3D face model, which are morphed to estimate 2D images of novel faces from non-frontal input images and match them for the purpose of face recognition (Blanz and Vetter, 2003). Face images captured from any angle are projected or morphed to simulate the appearance of the subject in a frontal pose or any other pose. Given a sufficiently large database of 3D face models, any arbitrary 2D frontal face, at a standard illumination, can be generated by morphing the faces enrolled in the database. The 3D shapes can be compressed using PCA in a method reminiscent of Active Shape (Appearance) Models (ASM) (Lanitis et al., 1997). Slow speed and the manual interaction required for semi-automatic 3D correspondences affect both training and recognition. Alternatively, matching takes place in the space of morphing parameters, which is invariant to illumination and viewpoint. FRVT2002 showed that the performance of the top ranked systems on very small data sets increases on non-frontal images using 3D morphing.

Blanz et al. (2002) and Romdhani et al. (2002) describe how analysis by synthesis works on the CMU-PIE database using a generative approach, which takes advantage of 3D morphing face models. The general strategy proposed is "to fit the generative model to a novel image, thereby parametrizing it in terms of the model." Some manual interaction was required for initializing the fitting process. The morphing face model is based on a vector space representation of faces, where any combination of shape or texture vectors for a set of exemplars describes a realistic human face (Ullman and Basri, 1991; Vetter and Poggio, 1997). The shape and texture parameters thus identified, along with pose, illumination, camera characterization such as color and contrast, and the residuals observed, point to an image similar to the input image and are used for face recognition. The model coefficients of the probe image are compared with the coefficients for all the face images in the gallery. The fitting scores, in terms of residuals, attach confidence to recognition. For fitting the model to an image, the approach requires approximate prior information about external conditions including but not limited to specular reflections and cast shadows. As an example, synthesis with different PIE (pose, illumination, and expression) for the purpose of face recognition requires rotating the 3D face model, domain dependent illumination models, and MPEG-4 based facial animation parameters (FAP) for expressions (Jiang et al., 2005).

Huang et al. (2003) combine 3D morphing models and component-based recognition for pose and illumination invariant face detection and recognition. A 3D morphing model computes 3D face models, rendered under varying pose and illumination, from three (frontal, half profile, and a profile) high resolution input images for each subject in the gallery. The synthesized images are used to train a component-based face recognition system. The positive training data for the face detectors was generated from 3D head models, with a pose range of $\pm 45^{\circ}$ rotations in depth and $\pm 10^{\circ}$ rotations in the image plane. The negative training set initially consisted of randomly selected non-face patterns augmented in an iterative fashion by difficult to detect face patterns. Similar arguments hold for training, when the 3D face models are rendered under varying pose and illumination. Variability in pose comes from simulating rotation in depth from 0° to 34° in 2° increments, while variability in illumination is achieved using ambient light or ambient light and a directed light source pointed at the center of the face for rendering purposes. Second degree polynomial SVM classifiers were trained in a one-vs.-all approach using labeled face exemplars for which the components extracted are concatenated. Testing included 200 images, of varying pose and illumination, for each of ten subjects. The maximal recognition rate of 88%, using a posteriori ground truth to set optimal thresholds, was approximately 20% higher than that obtained for a holistic recognition system. Changes in the head position were accommodated by the inherent flexibility offered by using face components rather than whole faces.

8.3 Animation

Similar to caricatures and analysis by synthesis, 3D recognition could operate using flexible matching of gallery and probe face image sets, which have been augmented through plausible transformations, e.g., expressive hints (facial expressions and speech). Such transformations are generative in nature and increase face separation. Dynamic in nature, such transformations are found using learning and adaptation.

This is different from searching for and using transformations whose role is to facilitate image alignment or registration (Christensen, 1999), e.g., for anatomical and/or medical purposes, or interpolation, e.g., using views of different faces and past experience for face interpolation (across different poses and/or illumination) (Beymer and Poggio, 1995; Georghiades et al., 2001). While analysis by synthesis reconstructs the equivalent of neutral faces, possibly rendered using varying illumination for matching purposes and recognition, animation seeks to generate expressive rather than neutral faces with the belief that faces are more likely to look different when their appearance changes. There is still scope for synthesis but much broader, e.g., a talking head (Parke and Waters, 1996). The synthesis aspect, rather than seeking for mere static invariance, explores and takes advantage of the spatial temporal coherence that makes human faces different from each other.

Support for a 3D approach using animation is provided by the neuroplasticity of the brain to rewire itself. The brain is wired with innate abilities that shape, though never determine, the way people perform in response to their environment (Pinker, 2002). Unlike the ape, which Kohler (1925) tells us is "the slave of its own visual field, [even] children acquire an independence with respect to their concrete surroundings; they cease to act in the immediately given and evident [perceptual] space." This is characteristic of mediated behavior, where one modifies the stimulus situation as part of the process required to respond to it. Vygotsky (1978) has further suggested that "for the young child, to think means to recall; but for the adolescent, to recall means to think." To think means to reason and to make plausible but valid inferences. It is through both anticipation and planning that animation, rather than being merely reactive to "photographic" (eidetic) memory traces, helps face recognition to handle contingencies and to become accurate and efficient. Animation acknowledges the fact that both form and functionality are essential for face recognition. Form corresponds to the (raw) face patterns, while functionality corresponds to transformed faces driven by expressions, e.g., FACS and/or Abstract Muscle Actions (AMA), and/or activities the face is engaged in, e.g., speech. Moving and distorted faces are used to create a database of prototypes for different groups of people. Once this is done, a new face can be added to the database from a single 3D scan. The face is animated to talk, smile or frown using the (chorus of) prototypes stored. The "talking heads" are useful to generate mug shots from eye witnesses. They also expand the training set for enhanced generalization and identification.

MPEG-4 provides many of the ingredients needed for animation (Pandzic and Forchheimer, 2002). It renders human avatars for both data compression (suitable for teleconferencing) and digital animation. MPEG-4 standards are defined in terms of Face Definition Parameters (FDP) [5], responsible for the face appearance, and Facial Animation Parameters (FAP), responsible for describing the movements of the face starting from a neutral face. The displacements are expressed by means of specific FAPU units that represent a fraction of a key distance on the face. The neutral face, defined using some predefined mesh of arbitrary resolution, e.g., number of polygons, and a few FDP, finds the remaining FDP to track and/or animate the face (Parke and Waters, 1996). MPEG-4 employs FIT (Facial Interpolation Table) to define and encode inter-FAP dependencies in polynomial form. Face characteristics, e.g., symmetry, co-articulation and FAP trajectories, complement each other to yield significant data compression rates and chart discriminative trajectories for facial animation. Pockaj and Lavagetto (2001) have shown, based upon correlation analysis, that a subset of only ten FAP, chosen from the complete set of 66 FAP, can be used to guarantee the efficient encoding of MPEG-4 facial animation sequences and significantly reduce the FAP bit rate. The quality of the "compressed" animation was much better than if one were to try to subject the FAP to coarse quantization. The explanation is that movements of the head are among those most sensitive to quantization noise, and that the reproduction of head movements must be sufficiently smooth to avoid severe subjective artifacts, e.g., annoying jerky head motion. Additional processing similar to active shape (appearance) models using PCA, could further exploit the a

[5] http://mpeg.telecomitalialab.com/

priori knowledge of the geometry and dynamics of human faces for data compression and interpolation purposes (Kshirsagar et al., 2001). Long and short term interval FAP animation could also be subject to spatial temporal ICA analysis for better interpretation and recognition. Interpolation and blending ("composition") functions, which are required to animate the vertices that are not part of the FDP set (and are not defined using FAP) across (local) space and time, could be then learned and actively sought for discrimination and recognition purposes. 3D face recognition using animation could consist of a database of face prototypes, active learning for training and augmenting the gallery, and probe sets that employ animation, flexible matching, and data fusion using evidence accumulation, to reduce uncertainty or alternatively increase the confidence in the recognition decisions made. This is discussed in the next section.

8.4 Modeling and Recognition

Static 3D scans provide only a partial solution as they can model view point changes and different illuminations but only for a limited set of facial expressions. Despite these limitations, 3D scans can efficiently be used to derive 3D feature sets that complement the 2D information already available from a camera and provide a more reliable recognition platform for cooperative subjects willing to have their 3D image captured as part of the access control protocol. However, in applications such as airport security and remote screening of large numbers of people, face recognition solutions will still have to use 2D cameras as input devices. Thus, a more generic but complementary 3D solution would start from a prototype set of 3D facial scans, and derive a morphing face model by transforming the shape and texture of the exemplars into a vector space representation that can be freely parameterized and used to generate an infinite set of appearances, expressions and viewing conditions for matching and recognition. Such a 3D based solution meets the needs and requirements for the next generation of facial recognition engines by addressing the following critical tasks

TASK1   Derive a universal face set (prototypes) and distortions to define, match and cluster facial images by building a mathematical face space (morphing, compression, animation);

TASK2   Provide advanced tracking solutions that help accumulate evidence in order to reduce uncertainty during training and recognition;

TASK3   Develop matching algorithms that support flexible and non-rigid deformations between video A ("gallery") and video B ("probe"), i.e., matching between (individual) collections of images, some partially occluded or varying in pose;

TASK4   Choose relevant prototype images for gallery and probes by means of active learning.

To utilize the power of 3D spatial information and address the training and recognition tasks, one must start by building a representative parametric head, face, and expression database that can be readily used to synthesize new appearances that match a given input sequence. 3D facial modeling and recognition systems rely on their ability to capture the characteristic 3D facial appearances of a given gallery and create non-rigid deformations and expressions to find the best match to an input photograph. This matching process works by animating a 3D normalized head shape and expression model in a low dimensional shape space, while minimizing an error function that compares the current state of the model (texture and shape) with that of the input image. To achieve this goal, advanced computer vision techniques can be deployed to provide a set of tools for reconstructing the 3D shape of a curved surface such as a face, to extract features and track them in a sequence, and - using these temporal cues - analyze expressions characteristic of a given individual. Furthermore, high performance animation methods can be deployed to convert the raw 3D scanned data sets to photo-real digital replicas of each person in the database. These *digital facial clones* can then be used to model and carry out flexible matching in 3D, thereby significantly reducing the size of the data set required to get positive identification.

The above approach involves analysis and synthesis, on one side, and animation, on the other side. The "transformational" solution proposed by Barnabas Takacs [6] and described here relies on an advanced automatic modeling and animation process (see Fig. 8.1). It corresponds to the approach proposed throughout the book (see Ch. 7 and Epilogue) and it can be implemented using a pipeline that includes five major stages: (1) 3D facial modeling, (2) a deformation system, (3) animation, (4) photo-real rendering, and (5) facial tracking.

1. **3D Facial Models:** Human faces have a particular way of deforming that should be reflected in the topology of the surfaces. Local resolution and orientation of model surface elements (patches) dramatically affect the quality for the final animation and therefore the convergence of the matching procedure. Thus, a facial model, in this context, not only needs to be of high resolution and accurate in terms of head shape but also needs to be suitable for natural looking deformations.

2. **Deformation System:** The second step in the 3D face recognition process is to link the face model to a control network of morph shapes and or bone based deformers of about 40 bones and 15 muscles, which enable the algorithms to manipulate not only identity but expressions as well. The muscles acting on top of this bone structure are designed to create common facial expressions such as eye blink, smile, or jaw down.

3. **Animation/Controlling Deformations:** To match a probe (an input photograph or scanned 3D head shape) to the gallery, the system employs a series of deformations and converges to the best matching solution via a minimization procedure. In each step of this convergence a composite error function containing coefficients from shape differences as well as texture differences is evaluated to determine how to update the face model during the next step. The output of this iterative process is a series of facial shapes and expressions that gradually appear to be more similar to the probe.

4. **Photo-Real Rendering:** Once the head shape and facial expressions are updated, a new output image of the digital face is created using photo-realistic rendering techniques. The higher the quality of this output, the easier it is to compare texture features of the model to that of the input photograph using image based metrics.

5. **Facial Tracking:** Finally, to accumulate data over time and thereby simplify the complex pattern matching and recognition problem, and reduce uncertainty, a facial feature tracking solution is required.

The modeling process starts by capturing high resolution 3D images. Typically two or three cameras take a frontal and $\frac{3}{4}$ left/right images from which a textured 180° head model is reconstructed. This 3D head scan is stored in a central *facial database* and is used as a reference for subsequent stages. Next, a series of modeling phases, including facial region identification, feature extraction, tracking and non-rigid elastic deformations, turn this reference scan into a high resolution *standardized model*. All the faces and their respective expressions in the database use this standardized mesh designed specifically to meet the demand of high quality facial deformation, i.e., sufficient resolution in areas of high curvature deformations and shape change, while minimal resolution elsewhere for manageability. The advantage of having a standardized model is that each new head in the database is represented as a set of fixed number of 3D coordinate triplets and associated texture elements, which can be freely transformed from one another, by simple vector arithmetic, to create new faces, views and expressions at will. This capability is at the very heart of the recognition algorithms that iteratively deform this standard mesh to match the likeness and thus the identity of a person shown in a specific photograph or video frame. When temporal information is available, this match can be used to form hypotheses regarding the likely identity

---

[6] http://www.digitalElite.net

of the pérson, hypotheses that can be gradually updated and made mode accurate as more evidence accumulates and eventually converges to a unique identity. Finally, the *deformation and appearance parameters* that transform the standard mesh model into a specific person's head are stored into the facial database.

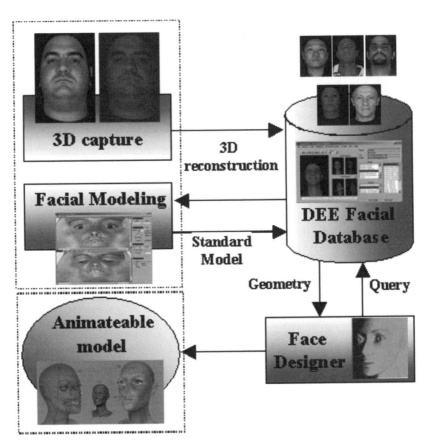

Fig. 8.1. Overview of a Facial Modeling System for Advanced Face Recognition Tasks (courtesy of Barnabas Takacs and Digital Elite).

When a large number of faces become available, the parameters form the *basis set* over which new faces can be expressed as a linear combination of deformation parameters. These parameters are subsequently modified automatically or interactively by the *face designer* module that creates novel faces of people that do not exist but appear to be plausible. At this point creating a new face becomes a *query* to the database that generates the appropriate geometry and its accompanying texture. For the database to be fully useable it must also store additional information tags that describe a vast range of information from ethnic origin, age, and skin tone, to weight, hair color and style, having a beard or wearing accessories like glasses. Facial expressions are further coded using *Facial Action Units* (FACS) (see Sect. 11.2) to provide a standardized basis for analysis and synthesis. This extensive set of augmented information helps with statistical analysis, clustering and grouping. As an example, one could create a new face by formulating a query that directly returns the geometry for ⟨ average, Caucasian, female, age between 20 and 25, body weight of ···⟩.

The framework described above provides the foundation to address the four basic tasks required for developing the next generation of face recognition systems. Namely, the parametric and deformable facial appearance database provides the mathematical foundation to derive a universal set of facial prototypes and distortions (TASK1). The ability to create new faces enables the design and evaluation of an optimal training set for classification algorithms that accrues evidence to reduce uncertainty and increase confidence (TASK2). Using the parametric facial deformation space results in non-rigid shape changes that can be used to design and objectively assess the performance of flexible matching algorithms (TASK3). Finally, statistical and data compression methods can be used to reduce the size of the head templates and choose relevant prototype images for the gallery (TASK4).

The overall architecture of a *Face Tracker Module* for evidence accumulation is presented in Fig. 8.2. The facial tracking low-level interface (API) consists of multiple layers starting from a set of basic 2D and 3D tracking algorithms and camera motion trackers. On top of this general purpose API, a set of application specific routines extract highly detailed 3D data of head motion (yaw, pitch, roll, 3D position) and facial features such as eyes (pupils, eyelids), mouth corners, lips or nose. The system may also detect and track a number of details such as wrinkles and/or miscellaneous points that only occur occasionally and indicate the onset of certain expressions. Once all subtle facial movements are extracted, the tracker proceeds to generate animation data for high fidelity expression analysis and photo-real rendering.

Low level tracking is implemented using region based tracking algorithms, such as normalized correlation, texture based trackers, and optical flow based estimators of physically plausible 3D deformations. Low level trackers exhibit serious limitations in a real world environment due to lack of context. Higher level implicit structural models are thus required for accurate registration. To overcome these problems, a hybrid tracking algorithm may be used that combines the advantages of each low level method while minimizing the overall sensitivity to noise and variations in imaging conditions. Fig. 8.3 demonstrates this concept. The *Point Tracker* adaptively selects the best method for each tracking point in a given frame. The image is then processed multiple times and the results are integrated. As time goes by and the tracking process progresses, more and more evidence emerges supporting a consistent interpretation of the underlying data. Higher level 2D/3D trackers use these raw inputs and impose a simple geometric model on the tracking process and subsequently correct for inaccuracies from the lower API layers. This geometric correction layer operates on top of region based Gabor jets and optical flow tracking algorithms. The second layer in this architecture implements a set of structural trackers that, instead of following individual points in the image plane, take advantage of the underlying model geometry to which these (individual) points belong to. Thus, one can track point groups, 2D structures, and/or splines, as well as true 3D objects, imported using geometry description files. The 3D tracker can also be set to maintain rigid shape or accommodate non-rigid deformations.

One of the most important benefits of using morphable facial representations, as opposed to simply storing facial scans, is that such representations can be used to create an automatic *analysis-synthesis* loop that addresses facial recognition tasks very efficiently. Fortunately, many of the basic algorithms required have been developed for video conferencing and facial animation applications (Terzopoulos and Waters, 1993). Such a 3D recognition system works by identifying people from any point of view and illumination condition using only a small number of well designed head samples. This form of automatic face recognition employs a search technique whereas the parameters controlling the shape and texture of a 3D rendered model of the standardized head are gradually adapted to a facial image (probe) representing the person to be matched against the gallery. This process, called *fitting*, is carried out in an iterative fashion until the system arrives at a minimal error of shape and texture between the original input and the final rendered 3D head model. As a result of this

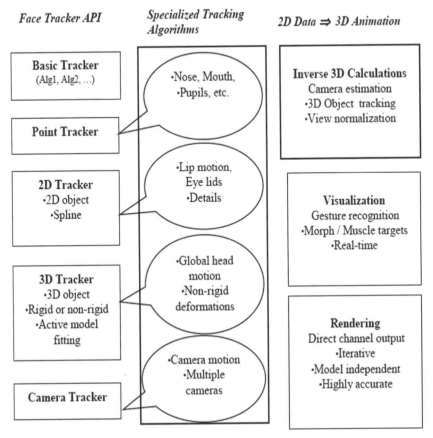

Fig. 8.2. High Fidelity Face Tracker Architecture for Evidence Accumulation and Expression Analysis (courtesy of Barnabas Takacs and Digital Elite).

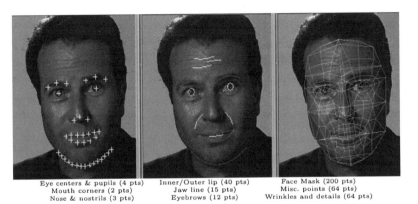

Fig. 8.3. Tracked Facial Points, Fitted Splines and Global Head Model (courtesy of Barnabas Takacs and Digital Elite).

fitting process the final shape and texture coefficients define the identity of the person as a linear combination of base shapes from the face basis. Identification of a novel face image is similar to 2D face recognition, by matching the coefficients recovered from the image with the coefficients recovered from the image of a known individual computed before (Romdhani et al., 2002).

In addition to identification, the technique described above can also be efficiently used to evaluate *facial expression analysis* software. The complete methodology is shown in Fig. 8.4. At the top left of the image the preparation process, i.e. the construction of the 3D database, is shown. It involves recording a large number of 3D scans of different people and multiple different expressions. These scans are subsequently converted to a standardized morphing 3D model, which can be parametrically controlled to create the required facial deformations. The specific control parameters are connected to a Disc Controller unit that maps the shape and texture parameters representing the appearance constraints into the domain of a normalized unit circle. Training and testing data sets are created by smoothly varying the expression parameters of the 3D head model and rendering the resulting facial surface using a given set of viewing conditions (pose, lighting conditions, etc.). The final output from this step is passed directly to the facial tracker unit to extract a set of facial feature points as needed for recognition. Two additional parallel data paths provide ground truth for the training algorithm. The data used are the $[0,1]$ normalized coordinates that represent the ideal output of the classification algorithm, and the coordinates of the true feature points without tracking error. This latter information allows for training and evaluating classification algorithms to operate independently from the noise and error characteristics of the facial feature tracking algorithms used. As a complete, integrated solution, this analysis-synthesis system has paramount importance for standardization and assessment. It can help derive optimal facial evaluation test beds as well as objective performance measures and evaluation criteria for advanced facial information processing systems.

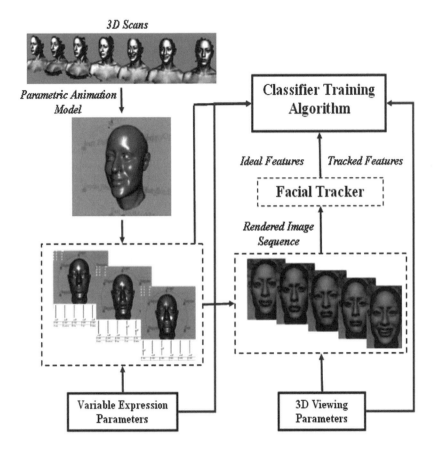

Fig. 8.4. 3D Face Animation for Training and Evaluation (courtesy of Barnabas Takacs and Digital Elite).

9. Data Fusion

Divide et Impera

To paraphrase Churchill, certainty in face recognition [rather than oil] lies in variety and variety alone. Variety comes in several forms and drives the way fusion takes place. Fusion can include raw or transformed data and their cues, on one side, and the face classifiers and the voting schemes that combine them, on the other side. A voting scheme implements the equivalent of a gating network that arbitrates among the scores made available by the Cartesian product of classifiers and face representations used (Poh and Bengio, 2006). The data originates from one or several modalities using different sensors, e.g., audio and video or 2D and 3D, and/or one or several image domains, e.g., face and ear. The modality itself can be further defined along specific channels, e.g., the RGB space for color. Each modality can be sampled over space and/or time. This leads to multi sample fusion, using parts and/or (temporal) multi-image sets. The cues used are drawn from one modality, e.g., shape and texture from 2D, or from several domains, e.g., face and fingerprints or face, voice, and lip movement. What makes the face attractive or not could be used for face recognition too. Particulars like moles, acne and birthmarks are great cues for identification and are used by soft biometrics. Augmented cognition, which expands on soft biometrics (see Ch. 11), accesses mental models and reasons about how biometric events unfold and the reasons behind. Data fusion ultimately operates across a multi-dimensional Cartesian product whose bounds and dimensions are only set by experts' imagination and technical innovation. The basic motivation for data fusion is the justified belief that the biometric dimensions, relatively independent of each other, should accrue and integrate circumstantial evidence leading to better recognition. *Divide et Impera* and the Gestalt that *the whole is more than the sum of its parts* are a succinct description of what data fusion thrives to achieve. Last but not least, data fusion implements a convoluted architecture, similar to that found in the neocortex, where the activity at the lower levels is primed by projections or cortical feedback from the higher levels. The level of data fusion at the lower levels is reduced when the higher levels can explain or predict the input (Mumford, 1992; Rao and Ballard, 1999). This is similar to the analysis by synthesis framework used in image understanding.

9.1 Multiple Cues

The cues and their possible combinations for face recognition are many (see Ch. 2). The human face is characterized by both its contents/texture, and the (head) shape/outline it is embedded within. Liu and Wechsler (2001) have used a variation of LDA, the Enhanced Fisher linear discriminant Method (EFM), to integrate shape and texture features. Shape describes the geometry of the face, while the texture supplies a normalized shape-free image and corresponds to the full anti-caricature. The texture is a normalized and shape-free face image that is warped to the mean shape, which is the average of aligned training shapes. The dimensionality for both the shape and texture cues is reduced using PCA but constrained for enhanced generalization by EFM. This is achieved by maintaining a proper balance between the spectral energy requirements of PCA for proper representation, and the LDA requirements that the eigenvalues of the within-class covariance matrix do not include small trailing values, which stand mostly for noise and show up in the denominator of the Fisher discriminant. Experimental results for 200 subjects, whose face images display varying illumination and facial expressions, have shown that the integrated shape and texture features carry the most discriminating information followed in order by texture only, masked images, and shape images. Both proper annotation, of internal and face boundary points, and alignment are required before shape and texture undergo fusion. The reduced shape Y_1 and texture Y_2 subspaces, of dimension m_1 and m_2, are integrated using concatenation. The new (fused) space Z is found then as

$$Z = \left(\frac{Y_1^T}{||Y_1||} \ \frac{Y_2^T}{||Y_2||} \right)^T \tag{9.1}$$

where $Z \in \mathbf{R}^m$ and $m = m_1 + m_2$. Normalization commensurates the lower dimensional shape and texture subspaces. Alternatively, one could use a diagonal weight matrix to combine the shape and texture subspaces according to their relative importance. The weights can be found using cross-validation or (the supervised mode of) radial basis functions (RBFs) (see Sect. 9.2).

Terrillon et al. (2000) have proposed using skin color and invariant Fourier-Mellin (FM) moments for face detection in complex scenes. Color segmentation is done in a normalized hue-saturation color space, where the color variability of human skin and the dependency of chrominance on illumination changes are reduced. Translation, scale and in plane rotation invariant FM moments, calculated for the clusters identified by color segmentation, are fed to a MLP network for final detection. Chang et al. (2005) evaluated the use of 2D and 3D face biometrics. PCA subspace methods are used separately for both 2D and 3D. Best performance was obtained when the 2D and 3D scores are combined using the sum rule with linear score transformation and confidence weighting. 2D and 3D were found to have similar performance when used individually, and the 2D and 3D combination was reported to outperform both multi-sample 2D results or the individual use of either 2D or 3D.

The scale space provides many cues or complementary image representations for data fusion. Different channels, whose bandwidth varies, are known to carry complementary information. The specific choice and integration of harmonics, usually referred to as multi - resolution analysis, is quite challenging. Zhang and Blum (1999) suggest a number of data fusion methods for multi level resolution image decomposition (MLD). The basic strategy is to select and merge coefficients, say of the Discrete Wavelet Transform (DWT), using their activity level and neighborhood relationships. The first decomposition level consists of four frequency bands: low-low (LL), low-high (LH), high-low (HL), and high-high (HH). MLD iterates on the "coarse" sub image LL to create the equivalent of a pyramid with N levels. Fusion is carried out only at the same resolution level on the high frequency bands. Alternatively, grouping and merging takes place using MLD relationships across the pyramid.

Another interesting approach for fusion comes from graphics. Raskar et al. (2004) have proposed to capture images under different illuminations and to fuse them for context enhancement. Art proved again fertile ground for inspiration. The authors were motivated by "surrealism [which] is the practice of producing incongruous imagery by means of unnatural juxtapositions and combinations." The low information contents of poor quality videos is increased using high quality images, which have been acquired ahead of time, and proper registration. Face images could be thus acquired under different controlled and uncontrolled conditions, and blended for better viewing and identification. This is yet another example of hallucinations (see Sect. 10.4).

9.2 Multiple Engines

One simple method to fuse multiple engines is the Winner-Take-All (WTA) combination strategy. It can be argued that WTA "wastes" those "expert" biometric engines that lost the competition. Instead of choosing a single "best" expert, a mixture of several experts may produce better recognition. Simple methods like majority rule, average, sum, and product are used to integrate the scores supplied by the experts. Consensus can be also reached using elections-like strategies where each voter or classifier rank orders the candidates [1], e.g., the Borda count or the Condorcet winner. The Borda count for n candidates is such that the first place candidate on a ballot receives $(n-1)$ points, the second place candidate receives $(n-2)$, and in general the candidate in the ith place receives $(n-i)$ points. The candidate ranked last on the ballot receives zero points. The points are added up across all the ballots, and the candidate with the most points is declared the winner. The Condorcet winner is the candidate who, when compared in turn with each of the other candidates, is the preferred over the other candidate. Note that a Condorcet winner will not always exist in a given set of votes. More elaborate voting procedures consist of a two stage process. In the first stage, the training data are used to separately estimate a number of different models. The parameters of these models are then held fixed. In the second stage, these models are (linearly or non-linearly) combined, mixed or gated, to produce the final predictive model. One way to combine evidence and probably the best one is to weight the contributions according to their confidence. Past performance, experts' acumen, the (normalized) scores themselves, and credibility and confidence (see transduction) can be used for such purposes. The mixing weights for evidence can be also found using RBF as explained next.

RBF networks are hybrid connectionist classifiers whose architecture is very similar to that of a traditional three layer network. The RBF input consists of normalized (face) images. Connections between the input and the middle layer have unit weights and do not require training. The (hidden) nodes in the middle layer, called basis functions (BF) nodes and modeled as localized receptive fields (RF), produce a localized response to (face) images using Gaussian kernels that approximate the input face pattern. The hidden layer, trained using (unsupervised) K-means clustering or equivalently using expectation and maximization (EM), yields the basis for the face space, where each cluster node encodes some common characteristics/dimension shared across the face space by some or all the faces. The activation level y_i for each hidden node i spanned by some Gaussian basis function is given by

$$y_i = \Phi_i(||\mathbf{X} - \boldsymbol{\mu}||) = \exp\left[-\sum_{k=1}^{D} \frac{(x_k - \mu_{ik}^2)}{2h\sigma_{ik}^2 o}\right] \qquad (9.2)$$

where h is a proportionality constant for the variance, x_k is the kth component of the input vector $\mathbf{X} = [x_1, x_2, \cdots, x_D]$, μ_{ik} and σ_{ik}^2 are the kth components for the mean and variance vectors, for the basis function node i, and o is the common overlap factor between nodes. The outputs of the hidden units lie between 0 and 1 and code for the degree of node membership; the closer the input is to the center of the Gaussian node, the larger the response of the hidden node is. The activation level Z_j for an output unit is

$$Z_j = \sum_i w_{ij} y_i + w_{0j} \qquad (9.3)$$

where Z_j is the output of the jth output node, y_i is the activation of the ith BF node, w_{ij} is the weight connecting the ith BF node to the jth output node, and w_{0j} is the bias or the threshold for the jth output node. There are M output nodes, each of them corresponding to some face ID class. The unknown face $\mathbf{X}$ is authenticated with the ID corresponding to the output node j that yields the largest output

---

[1] http://en.wikipedia.org/wiki/Voting_system

Z_j. The weights or synapses w_{ij} are derived using closed analytical solutions that implement memory associations using mean-square error (MSE) minimization. RBF learning amounts to solving $\mathbf{w} = \mathbf{R}^{-1}\mathbf{B}$ where $\mathbf{R}$ is the correlation matrix for the BF outputs, $\mathbf{B}_{lj} = \sum_l y_j(l)d_j(l)$ for j and l indexes running over the number of classes $(1, \cdots, M)$ and number of patterns $(1, \cdots, n)$ in the training set, respectively. The objective for supervised learning, which takes place on the connections between the hidden and output layers, is to map face patterns to their corresponding ID class. The same connections, once found, can also serve to weight the contributions made by different data partitions, each of them the result of unsupervised or competitive aggregation. The "data" corresponds to different combinations of sensors, cues, representations, and/or scores, which would cluster according to their similarity, intrinsic identity or functionality. The overall goal is to learn the confidence placed on aggregates $\mathcal{A}(\mathbf{X})$ from their relative performance, i.e., $p(\mathbf{X}|\mathbf{w}_j, \mathcal{A}_j(\mathbf{X}))$ for class j and its weight $\mathbf{w}_j$ together with the "channel" induced group $\mathcal{A}_j(\mathbf{X})$. The weights are adaptive and can be set through a process of iterative adjustment using softmax activation functions.

Bengio et al. (2002) seek to find the confidence that results when the scores for different algorithms are fused. Individual confidence measures are integrated to improve on overall performance and to produce reliable confidence levels for the fusion decisions made. This is applied in particular to multi-modal (see Sect. 9.5) identity verification using speech and face information from XM2VTS but its scope for data fusion is wide open. Similar to the RBF approach, the data fusion methods proposed by Bengio et al. (2002) require the selection of one or more hyper-parameters using cross-validation. The networks used include multilayer perceptrons (MLP) (trained using BP), (kernel) support vector machines (SVM), and Bayes classifiers modeled using Gaussian mixture models (GMM). Examples of hyper-parameters include the number of hidden units for MPL, the kernel and its specific realization for SVM, and the number of Gaussians for GMM and their characterization. Confidence estimation for scores is achieved using Gaussian hypotheses to approximate the score distributions for genuine subjects and impostors.

Consider now the problem of learning a classification mapping whose form varies for different regions of the input space. Although a single homogeneous network could be applied to this problem, one expects that the task would be made easier if different expert networks are assigned to each of the different regions, while a "gating" network, which also sees the input data, decides which of the experts should determine the classification output (Bishop, 1995). Such networks, based on the "divide and conquer" modularity principle (Jacobs et al., 1991), train the expert networks and the gating network together. Jordan and Jacobs (1994) extend this approach by considering a hierarchical system in which each expert network can itself consist of a mixture-of-experts network, complete with its own gating network. A similar concept using corrective training, and driven by an active learning scheme, was suggested by Krogh and Vedelsby (1995). The active learning scheme takes advantage of the obvious observation that combining the outputs from several networks is useful only if the networks disagree on some inputs. The disagreement, called the ensemble ambiguity, can reduce the generalization error of the network ensemble. Gating networks as described above can be shown to have conceptual similarities to mixture estimation and the EM algorithm (Jordan and Jacobs, 1994).

Partitioning the data space and calling for different experts is further motivated when the faces are sorted out in terms of their perceived difficulty to be recognized. Not all the faces are alike in terms of distinctiveness, and the ones ranked most difficult require special attention. Such ranking can be based on methods similar to those discussed for caricaturing (see Sect. 5.6), on credibility and confidence measures developed for open set face recognition using transduction (see Sect. 6.3), and on pattern specific error inhomogeneities (PSEI) methods for error analysis (see Sect. 13.3). Open Set TCM-kNN {PCA and Fisherfaces} classifiers do not completely overlap in the recognition decisions they make. In addition, some faces are more prone to recognition errors than others or equivalently the face patterns are not homogeneous in terms of their ability to be recognized. As an example, faces showing "goats" behavior (see Sect. 13.3) represent only 11% from the faces represented using PCA, but their share of errors is much larger. In particular, the same faces contribute 23% and 21% of the false reject and false accept errors, respectively. The same holds true for "goat" like faces represented using Fisherfaces. Their share in the population is only 9%, but they contribute 32% and 29% of the false reject and false accept errors, respectively. The above observations suggest that fusing the outputs of different face recognition engines could lead to better identification. Data fusion of multiple engines like Open Set TCM-kNN {PCA and Fisherfaces} driven by PSEI analysis has been shown to yield better face recognition performance for subjects that are rejected by one classifier (engine) but accepted by another classifier (Li and Wechsler, 2005). This is described next in terms of specific scores and the decisions proposed for data fusion using the PSEI framework.

Assume that during Open Set TCM-kNN the thresholds Θ, the PSR standard training deviations, the probe PSR values and confidences for PCA and Fisherfaces are Θ_{PCA} and Θ_{Fisher}, σ_{PCA} and σ_{Fisher}, PSR_{PCA} and PSR_{Fisher}, C_{PCA} and C_{Fisher}, respectively. The first case to consider occurs when the probe is accepted with both $PSR_{PCA} > \Theta_{PCA}$ and $PSR_{Fisher} > \Theta_{Fisher}$. The identification of the probe is then determined as follows: (i) If Open Set TCM-kNN {PCA and Fisherfaces} yield the same ID for their largest (credibility) p-values, then the decision taken is to authenticate the ID no matter what the confidences found are; and (ii) If the Open Set TCM-kNN {PCA and Fisherfaces} yield different ID for their largest p-values, then choose that ID that yields larger confidence. In the case when the two confidences are very close to each other, choose the label coming from Open Set TCM-kNN Fisherfaces classifier because it yields overall better performance than the Open Set TCM-kNN PCA classifier.

The second case occurs when the probe is rejected with both $PSR_{PCA} < \Theta_{PCA}$ and $PSR_{Fisher} < \Theta_{Fisher}$. The third possible case occurs when $PSR_{PCA} \geq \Theta_{PCA}$ and $PSR_{Fisher} < \Theta_{Fisher}$, i.e., the two engines disagree on rejection. One has now to consider how far the probe's PSR are away from the thresholds Θ and the relative location of the "barnyard" class predicted by the Open Set TCM-KNN PCA in the "zoo" (see Sect. 13.3). When the label predicted by Open Set TCM-kNN PCA is a (reliable) "sheep", the probe is accepted and its ID is the original one. If the label predicted by Open Set TCM-kNN PCA is not "sheep" compare the distances $\alpha = \frac{(PSR_{PCA} - \Theta_{PCA})}{\sigma_{PCA}}$ and $\beta = \frac{(\Theta_{Fisher} - PSR_{Fisher})}{\sigma_{Fisher}}$. If $\min(\alpha, \beta) < T_0 = 2$ (standard deviations), then if $\alpha > \beta$ the ID that Open Set TCM-kNN PCA predicts is accepted; otherwise the probe is rejected. If $\min(\alpha, \beta) > T_0$, the probe is rejected using the decision the Open Set TCM-kNN Fisherfaces classifier made. Similar arguments apply for the last case when $PSR_{PCA} < \Theta_{PCA}$ and $PSR_{Fisher} \geq \Theta_{Fisher}$. The open set face recognition experiments (see Sect. 6.3) were redone using the data fusion procedure described above. The results are now 91.55% accuracy at only 3.1% false alarm compared to the previously reported results of 81% and 88% correct accuracy (with a much larger false alarm of 6%) for PCA and Fisherfaces, respectively. The increased accuracy is obtained without excluding any error prone exemplar. Note that PCA and Fisherfaces are, however, not independent representations. Some "animals" were observed to continue to be error prone after the LDA step (of Fisherfaces) once they were found to be "bad" for PCA. In our data set, only 33 subjects were labeled "sheep" for both PCA and Fisherfaces components, while 64 subjects were labeled "sheep" using either the PCA or Fisherfaces components. Note that the "barnyard" representation is characteristic of data partitioning (with overlap).

Intuition seems to suggest that the combination of different engines must improve performance but the user better beware. Daugman (2000) has shown that for unbalanced systems a strong biometric is better used alone than in combination with a weaker one. According to Daugman, the key to "the apparent paradox is that when two tests or [equivalently] engines are combined, one of the resulting new error rates, false alarm (FAR) or false reject (FRR), depending on the combination rule used, becomes *better than that of the stronger of the two tests*, while the other error rate becomes *worse even than that of the weaker of the tests.* If the two biometric tests differ significantly in their power, and each operates at its own cross-over point where $P(FAR) = P(FRR)$, then combining them actually results in significantly worse performance than relying solely on the one, stronger, biometric."

9.3 Voting Schemes

"It is time to stop arguing over what is best because that depends on our context and goal. Instead we should work at a higher level of organization and discover how to build managerial systems to exploit the different virtues and evade the different limitations of each of these ways of comparing things" (Minsky, 1986). Mind architectures, similar to those proposed by Minsky, are modular. "No single model exists for all pattern recognition problems and no single technique is applicable for all problems. Rather what we have in pattern recognition is a bag of tools and a bag of problems" according to Leveen Kanal. It is localization, specialization, and combination of expertise that lead to hybrid systems or mixtures of learning experts.

SNoW (Sparse Network of Winnows), bagging, boosting and random forests are some of the better known voting schemes available. SNoW (Littlestone, 1988) is an early voting scheme that learns in an incremental fashion a sparse and simple feature space. The output (target) nodes are modeled as linear units that are trained to recognize examples of specific concepts. The target nodes t and the corresponding active features i are linked using weighted edges w_i^t, such that the target is active or equivalently the concept is detected when $\sum_i w_i^t > \theta_t$. Training updates the weights for each target concept, which is expressed as a binary vector using the global pool of features available, by promoting or demoting features when mistakes are made. For the binary (detection) case, promotion has the weights multiplied by $\alpha > 1$ when the target misses the concept, while demotion has the weights decreased when a false detection occurs by multiplying them using $0 < \beta < 1$. The number of examples required grows logarithmically with the (quite large) number of features in the pool. Alvira and Rifkin (2001) report that SNoW performed about as well as linear SVM, but substantially worse than polynomial (kernel) SVM.

Bagging is a **B**ootstrap **AGG**regat**ING** method where the training set T is randomly resampled with replacement to generate independent bootstrap replicates. Classifiers are developed based on each replicate and combined (Breiman, 1996). Given the training set $T = \{(\mathbf{x_1}, y_1), \cdots, (\mathbf{x_n}, y_n)\}$ one samples L sets T_i from T with replacement $\{T_1, T_2, \cdots, T_L\}$ and trains the corresponding binary classifiers C_i whose outputs are $f_i(\mathbf{x})$. The final aggregate, $H(\mathbf{x}) = majority \left(\sum_{i=1}^{L} sign(f_i(\mathbf{x})) \right)$, is expected to reduce the overall variance. Ensembles of SVM (Vapnik, 2000) are a variation on bagging. They involve standard bagging, different kernels and/or features, and different hyper-parameters (ϵ and C) for optimization.

The most popular voting scheme today is boosting. The basic assumption behind boosting is that "weak" learners can be combined to learn any target concept with probability $1 - \eta$. Weak learners, usually built around simple features, learn to classify at better than chance (with probability $\frac{1}{2} + \eta$ for $\eta > 0$). AdaBoost (Freund and Shapire, 1996) serves as the exemplar boosting algorithm. It works by adaptively and iteratively resampling the data to focus learning on those samples that the previous weak (learner) classifier has failed on. Towards that end the relative weights of misclassified samples are increased after each iteration. There are two parts to AdaBoost: (a) choosing T effective features to serve as weak classifiers; and (b) construction of the separating hyper-plane. The pseudo-code for the binary case classification is

AdaBoost: Given sample training pairs $(x_1, y_1), \cdots, (x_n, y_n)$ such that $x_i \in X$ and $y_i \in Y = \{0, 1\} = \{-, +\}$ for a negative ("0") and b positive ("1") examples such that $n = a + b$

Initialize sampling (weight) distributions $D_t = \{w_t(i)\} = \{w_t^-(i) = \frac{1}{a}, w_t^+(i) = \frac{1}{b}\}$

(Iterate) for $t = 1 \cdots T$

1. Normalize the weights D_t to become a probability distribution $w_t(i) = \frac{w_t(i)}{\sum_{j=1}^n w_t(j)}$

2. Train (and validate) weak (learner) classifiers h_k (for some feature k) using D_t where $h_k : x \to \{0, 1\}$ and evaluate the error e_k with respect to the weights $w_t(i)$ such that

$$e_k = P_{i \sim D_t}[h_k(x_i) \neq y_i] = \sum_i w_t(i)|h_k(x_i) - y_i| \qquad (9.4)$$

3. Choose the best weak classifier $h_t(x) = h_j(x)$ such that $e_j < e_k$, $\forall k \neq j$ and $e_t = e_j$. If $e_t \geq 0.5$ set $T = t - 1$ and terminate the loop.

4. Set $\gamma_t = \frac{e_t}{(1-e_t)}$.

5. Update the weights $w_{t+1}(i) = w_t(i)\gamma_t^{1-\epsilon_i}$ where $\epsilon_i = 0$ if sample x_i is classified correctly and 1 otherwise. "Easy" examples that are usually correctly classified have their weight decreased while "hard" examples that tend to be misclassified have their relative weight increased.

6. Set $\alpha_t = -\log \gamma_t = -\log \left[\frac{e_t}{(1-e_t)}\right] < 1$.

The mixture of experts or final boosted (stump) strong classifier H is

$$H(x) = \sum_{t=1}^T \alpha_t h_t(x) > \frac{1}{2} \sum_{i=1}^T \alpha_t \qquad (9.5)$$

The constant $\frac{1}{2}$ comes in because the boundary is located mid-point between 0 and 1. If the negative and positive examples are at -1 and $+1$ the constant used is 1 rather than $\frac{1}{2}$. The training error incurred using H drops exponentially and is (Freund and Shapire, 1997)

$$e \leq \exp\left[\frac{1}{2}\sum_{i=1}^T \beta_t^2\right] \quad \text{where } \beta_t = \frac{1}{2}e_t \qquad (9.6)$$

The goal for AdaBoost is margin optimization with a large margin viewed with confidence for its predictive ability. Despite existing (and qualitative) proofs of convergence, AdaBoost has been recently shown to converge to a solution whose margin is significantly below the maximum value (Rudin et al., 2004). In particular, it was shown that AdaBoost "exhibits cyclic behavior", which is common when there are very few support vectors. Margin based ranking, RankBoost, was proposed instead for convergence to a maximum margin solution. AdaBoost and RankBoost yield similar performance when AdaBoost maximizes the exponential loss associated with the Area Under the Curve (AUC). Several comments are in order here. First, the availability of only a few support vectors would suggest that the pattern space was not learned well. Second, the loss function, as expected, affects learning and convergence. Last but not least, ranking is reminiscent of selection problems and active learning (see Sects. 6.6 and 7.4). Relative rather than absolute scores are all what is sometimes available. Ranking avoids normalization, and is more intuitive and easy to use.

The weights taken by the data samples are related to their margin and explain the AdaBoost's generalization ability (Shapire et al., 1998). AdaBoost minimizes (using greedy optimization) the risk functional

$$R(\mathbf{w}) = E\{\exp[-yf(x, w)]\} = \sum_i D_t(i)\exp(-y_i h(x_i)) \qquad (9.7)$$

where E stands for expectation and its minimum defines logistic regression (Hestie et al., 2001). AdaBoost converges to the posterior distribution of y conditioned on x, and the strong but greedy classifier H in the limit becomes the log-likelihood ratio test. The margin can be also implemented relative to the strangeness used to define weak learners (see Sect. 9.7). As AdaBoost is characteristic of greedy optimization, one could possibly revisit the weak learners (and the decisions made) from previous iterations and, similar to feature selection, backtrack and update them using FloatBoost (Li et al., 2004). Early stopping (thought of as a penalty on the solution length using regularization) and cross-validation improve boosting with respect to convergence and consistency (Zhang and Yu, 2005).

The multi-class extensions for AdaBoost are AdaBoost.M1 and AdaBoost.M2 (Freund and Shapire, 1996). The final hypothesis of AdaBoost.M1 for $y_i \in Y = \{1, \cdots, k\}, h_t : x \rightarrow Y$, and $\gamma_t = \frac{e_t}{(1-e_t)}$ is

$$H(x) = \arg\max_{y \in Y} \sum_{i=1}^{T} \left(\log \frac{1}{\gamma_t} \right) [t : h_t(x) = y] \tag{9.8}$$

$H(x)$ outputs the label y that maximizes the sum of weights for the weak learners that predict that label. The weight for each hypothesis, $\log \frac{1}{\gamma_t}$, weights more the hypotheses with lower error. Freund and Shapire further note that "if the weak [but simple] hypotheses [learners] have error only slightly better than $\frac{1}{2}$, then the training error of the final hypothesis $H(x)$ drops to zero exponentially fast. The difference between training and test errors can be theoretically bound for "simple" hypotheses and the number of iterations T "not too large". The use of features for the weak learners is justified by their apparent simplicity. The drawback for AdaBoost.M1 comes from its expectation that the performance for the weak learners selected is better than chance, i.e., $e_t = \frac{1}{2}$. When the number of classes is $k > 2$, the condition on error is, however, hard to be met in practice. The expected error for random guessing is $1 - \frac{1}{k}$; for $k = 2$ it works because the weak learners need to be just slightly better than chance. AdaBoost.M2 addresses the above problem by allowing the weak learner to generate now instead a set of plausible labels together with their plausibility (not probability), i.e., $[0,1]^k$. The AdaBoost.M2 version focuses on the incorrect labels that are hard to discriminate. Towards that end, AdaBoost.M2 introduces a pseudo-loss e_t for hypothesis h_t such that for a given distribution D_t one seeks $h_t : x \times Y \rightarrow [0,1]$ that is better than chance

$$e_t = \frac{1}{2} \sum_{(i,y) \in B} D_t(i,y)(1 - h_t(x_i, y_i) + h_t(x_i, y)) \tag{9.9}$$

$$H(x) = \arg\max_{y \in Y} \sum_{t=1}^{T} \left(\log \frac{1}{\gamma_t} \right) \cdot h_t(x, y) \tag{9.10}$$

for $B = \{(i,y) : i \in \{1, \cdots, n\}, y \neq y_i\}$. "The pseudo-loss [e.g. (9.9)] is computed with respect to a distribution over the set of all pairs of examples and incorrect labels. By manipulating this distribution, the boosting algorithm can focus the weak learner not only on hard-to-classify examples [i], but more specifically, on the incorrect labels [y] that are hardest to discriminate" (Freund and Shapire, 1996). Opelt et al. (2004) have compared boosting with SNoW. The bits for the target concepts in SNoW are seen as outcomes of weak learners, one weak classifier for each position in the binary vector. "Thus for learning it is required that the outcomes of all weak classifiers are calculated a priori. In contrast, boosting only needs to find the few weak classifiers which actually appear in the final classifier and the optimal threshold can be determined efficiently when needed. This substantially speeds up learning."

An interesting extension for AdaBoost is a voting scheme known as the cascade classifier (Viola and Jones, 2004). There are many situations where the distribution of class labels is highly skewed, e.g., face detection (see Sect. 7.1), when there are very few faces to be found in the image relative to the number of windows that have to be searched, i.e., $P(y=1) << P(y=0)$. Concerns related to prevalence and fallacies become thus paramount (see Sect. 13.2). The challenge is to be very fast and still achieve very low false negative rates, i.e., almost never miss a face. Early rejection of non-faces leads to computational efficiency. An input window has to pass each cascade node in order to be labeled as a face. Deeper nodes can correct false positives. Assume now that the stage-wise hit or detection and false positive rates are h and f, respectively. The ultimate detection and false alarm rates for a cascade that consists of N classifier stages are h^N and f^N, respectively. Training at each stage must meet prespecified hit and false alarm rates, e.g., $h = 0.995$ and $f = 0.5$ in order to reach expected rates of performance upon completing the cascade. Stage wise weak learners are generated using asymmetric AdaBoost, which goes beyond mere minimization of the classification error. It also minimizes the number of false positives by increasing the weights for positive examples in order to penalize more the false negative rate, i.e., missing a face, compared to the false positive rate. Resampling, which takes place after training each stage of the cascade, is conditioned by the possible imbalance in the population. As an example, when intra-personal and extra-personal are used as positive and negative examples for verification or detection purposes, there are many more negative than positive examples. The solution proposed at each stage is to use a negative example that has passed all the previous stages (Viola and Jones, 2004). Yang et al. (2004) have proposed and showed better performance when resampling includes as negative examples those that pass just the current (cascaded) strong classifier. Due to the imbalance referred to earlier, all the positive examples are used in each stage.

Random forests are voting schemes that generate random vectors (from a fixed PDF rather than an adaptive one as done for AdaBoost) for decision trees (DT) classifiers. "The generalization error for forests converges asymptotically strong to a limit as the number of trees in the forest becomes large. The generalization error of a forest of tree classifiers depends on the strength of the individual trees in the forest and the correlation between them. Their accuracy indicates that they act to reduce bias. Using a random selection of features to split each node yields error rates that compare favorably to AdaBoost but are more robust with respect to noise" (Breiman, 2001). Random forests benefit from their flexible interplay between features ("filters") and classifiers ("wrappers") and could help with the face selection problem (see Sect. 6.6). CCTV faces (from the working set W) are first assigned a PDF that indicates the label distribution induced by the random forest that was trained using enrollment data. Credibility and confidence measures, similar to those derived during open set face recognition, rank the faces accordingly. The top ranked faces are then clustered using proximity distances based on strangeness or the similarity observed on the pathways followed by DT. Cluster homogeneity and thus viability are determined using the entropy, the group label induced by random forest, and the components ranked according to their original confidence and credibility. The best k members from each cluster are then the solution to the face selection problem. Clustering and selection are thus the result of active learning and transduction using the strangeness (De Barr and Wechsler, 2006).

9.4 Multiple Samples

Data fusion accumulates evidence across sensors, representations, and algorithms. Data fusion traces its origin, among others, to multimodal sensory integration. The multiple samples can, however, originate from only one source and have their multiplicity occur over time. The Face Recognition Grand Challenge (FRGC) (Phillips et al., 2005) is an attempt in this direction. FRGC ver2.0 [2] has collected a very large

---

[2] http://www.biometricscatalog.org/documents/Phillips%20FRGC%20-%20Feb%202005-5.pdf

multi-frame data corpus of 50,000 still images but from a relatively small number of subjects. In particular, FRGC has enrolled only 466 subjects compared to close to 40,000 subjects for FRVT2002 or 1,400 subjects for FERET (see Sect. 13.4). The empirical resolution of the conjecture made by FRGC that "using 4 or 5 well chosen 2D faces is more powerful for recognition than one 3D face image or multi-modal 3D + 2D face" will thus have to wait to be properly tested for a time when it has access to a large and significant number of enrolled subjects. Questions on how to choose and match 2D faces, and on the feasibility and practicality of acquiring huge collections of stills for each enrollee, have yet to be addressed. The more likely avenue for progress in addressing the face recognition challenge would be to start with collecting short face biometric videos during both enrollment and testing, and to require periodic reenrollment whose frequency should vary according to the age of the enrollee.

The modes of operation for multiple sample fusion discussed here include both video and stills. The former takes advantage of space-time manifolds and their apparent coherence and/or 3D modeling. The latter considers the multiple still samples as points drawn from some PDF and matches them in a selective fashion. Multiple sample fusion of still images can be modeled using recognition-by-parts and treated using boosting driven by strangeness (see Sect. 9.7). The parts, the weak learners are tuned for, trace their origin under such a scenario to different biometric samples in order to overcome clutter, occlusion, and disguise. Prior to boosting, the multiple samples could be brought in registration and/or clustered for better match and recognition.

The basic recognition method for multiple sample fusion (Zhou and Chellappa, 2005) is to combine the (distance or similarity) match scores from multiple samples for the query (probe) Q, gallery candidates g^n for $n = 1, \cdots, N$, and samples $i, j = 1, \cdots, M$

$$ID = \arg \min_n d(Q_i, g_j^n) \qquad (9.11)$$

Simple voting schemes are available to fuse the pairwise distance functions d, e.g., minimum arithmetic or geometric mean, minimum median or majority voting. The similarity distances available (see Ch. 6) map the Cartesian product $Q \times g^n$ for each enrollee n. Better use of computational resources is achieved when the frames are summarized or clustered prior to applying some voting scheme. Another possibility is to assume that the samples are independent of each other, and to model them using PDF or manifolds. The identity is found using the distance between PDF, e.g., Chernoff and Bhattacharyya distances or Kullback-Leibler (KL) divergence, or transformation invariant metrics between manifolds using the tangent distance (TD) (Vasconcelos and Lippman, 2005). As an example of PDF distances, the relative entropy or the KL divergence between two normal (multiple samples) distributions is

$$KL(p1||p2) = \int_x p_1(x) log \frac{p_1(x)}{p_2(x)} dx \qquad (9.12)$$

Another example, this time concerning manifolds, is the joint manifold distance (JMD) proposed by Fitzigibbon and Zisserman (2003). The space of parametrized images S, similar to active shape models (ASM) (Lanitis, 1997) and learned using subspace models, is specified using the mean image m, a set of basis vectors M, i.e., $S = \{m + Mu | u \in U\}$ with the vector u used to linearly parametrize any image in the space induced. The distance $d(x_1, S)$ between a query point x_1 and the set S is

$$d(x_1, S) = \min_{y \in S} d(x_1, y) = \min_u ||m + Mu - x_1||^2 \qquad (9.13)$$

Consider now the case when y is subject to unknown transformations $T(y, a)$ with priors on a and u. The above distance becomes now using $\log p(y)$ for priors on y

$$
\begin{aligned}
d(x_1, S) &= \min_{u,a} ||T(m + Mu; a) - x_1||^2 + E(a) + E(u) \\
&= \min_{u,a} ||T(y; a) - x_1||^2 + E(a) - \log p(y) \qquad (9.14)
\end{aligned}
$$

The joint manifold distance $d(S, R)$ between the manifolds S and R measures the extent that (face) images subject to given transformations are similar and can be clustered together despite the image variability (described by their corresponding parametrizations a and b) that was experienced (using T) during data capture. The JMD for two subspaces $S = \{m + Mu | u \in U\}$ and $R = \{n + Nv | v \in V\}$ is defined as

$$d(S, R) = \min_{x \in S, y \in R} (S, R)$$
$$= \min_{u,v,a,b} ||T(m + Mu; a) - T(n + Nv; b)||^2$$
$$+ E(a) + E(b) + E(u) + E(v) \tag{9.15}$$

9.5 Multimodal Sensory Integration

Biometric information for authentication can come from more than one sensory channel. The channels are expected to be mostly independent of each other, and complementary in their coverage. Data fusion of such information amounts to "expert conciliation," and is expected to yield better results than each channel on its own (Bigun et al., 1997). The benefits include not only enhanced performance but extra security against spoofing. The use of multimodal biometrics requires that the outcomes from multiple engines are integrated. Methods similar to those described in Sect. 9.2 are available for integration. The gating network used for integration needs to uncover the relative sensitivity for each face vis-à-vis the multimodal biometrics used, and weight accordingly the scores returned before combining them.

The factors that need to be considered when designing a multimodal biometric system include "the choice and number of biometric traits; the level in the biometric system at which information should be integrated; the methodology adopted to integrate the information; and the cost versus performance trade-off" (Jain and Ross, 2004). The traits include but are not limited to fingerprints, hand geometry, ear, iris, retina, voice, and 3D. Sensory integration can happen at the feature level, at the match score computation level, or at the decision making stage. Access and compatibility requires that the match scores are normalized first. The individual scores are concatenated or fed to a voting scheme. Examples of normalization and specific voting schemes for multimodal integration are described next.

Brunelli and Falavigna (1995) have used the hyperbolic tangent for normalization, and weighted geometric average for combining the face and voice biometrics. Kittler et al. (1999) report that the simple sum rule outperforms the product, minimum, median, and maximum voting schemes when integrating face and voice biometrics. Ben Yacoub et al. (1999) report that the Bayes classifier performs better compared to decision trees, SVM, and MLP, for multimodal integration of face and voice biometrics. Wang et al. (2003) have proposed a hybrid scheme for fusing the face and iris biometrics, which consists of LDA and RBF. Ross and Jain (2004) combine fingerprints, hand geometry and face biometrics using the weighed sum rule and show, using ROC, the gains that accrue relative to the individual use of each of the biometrics mentioned. The sum rule was reported to outperform decision trees and linear discriminant functions. The choice for weights, complementary to the rule used, requires corrective training, e.g., boosting. Snelick et al. (2005) combine score normalization with multimodal biometric fusion. The scope for normalization is limited to make the scores compatible. This is achieved by mapping the scores to the $[0, 1]$ interval (see Sect. 12.2 for full fledged score normalization driven by the true clients' and impostors' distributions using cohort and world background models). Score normalization for s includes min-max (MM), Z-score (ZS), and hyperbolic tangent (TH)

$$n_{MM} = \frac{s - \min(S)}{\max(S) - \min(S)} \tag{9.16}$$

$$n_{ZS} = \frac{s - mean(S)}{\sigma(S)} \qquad (9.17)$$

$$n_{TH} = \frac{1}{2}\left[\tanh\left(0.01\frac{(s - mean(S))}{\sigma(S)}\right) + 1\right] \qquad (9.18)$$

where S is the set of original scores, and n is the normalized score for s. Note that the Z-score defined above is different from the Z-norm used in signal and speech processing for normalization purposes (see Sect. 12.2). Snelick et al. (2005) have also proposed adaptive (AD), another score normalization method that is inspired by the T-norm used for speaker verification. The scope for AD is to decrease the overlap between the genuine and impostor distributions. AD is implemented using two-quadrics (QQ), logistic (LG), or quadric-line-quadric (QLQ). Multimodal biometric fusion includes traditional simple-sum, min- and max- scores, matcher (MW) and user (UW) weighting. The last two methods weight the multimodal evidence based on training and user preferences, respectively. The best (score normalization, voting scheme) pairs for multimodal fusion were found to be (min-max, simple-sum) and (QLQ, UW) for open [airport] and closed [office] populations, respectively. The same study by Snelick et al. (2005) concludes that higher accuracy COTS systems leave less room for improvement using data fusion. This concurs with the comments made earlier by Daugman (2000).

Alternative voting schemes based on the management of uncertainty and iterative evidence accumulation were proposed. Choudhury et al. (1999) combine unconstrained audio and video using Bayesian networks. Teoh et al. (2004) have proposed a ternary (accept, reject, inconclusive) decision scheme to integrate face and voice biometrics. Data fusion is based on k-nearest neighbors and Dempster-Shafer (DS) theory of evidence (see Sect. 7.4). Credibility and plausibility measures for DS serve as relative measures of confidence in the decisions proposed. The space of training examples for DS, using the k-nearest neighbors to measure uncertainty, is bimodal. Uncertainty management can address the class imbalance problem (for whom the class distributions are quite different) using different figures of merit (FOM) for metrics, cost sensitivity and corrective learning, and sampling-based approaches (Tan et al., 2006). Additional examples of multimodal biometrics are described next.

Pigeon and Vandendorpe (1998) combine frontal face, profile face, and voice. Frischholtz and Dieckmann (2000) have developed BioID, a commercial system that combines face, voice, and lip movement biometrics. They claim that the use of a dynamic feature, i.e., lip movement, provides more security against fraud, e.g., checking for aliveness, than systems using only static features. Socolinsky et al. (2003) present a comprehensive study on face recognition using visible and thermal long wave infrared (LWIR) imagery. Their findings indicate that "under many circumstances, using thermal infrared imagery yields higher performance, while in other cases performance in both modalities is equivalent." The apparent improved performance of LWIR, as a stand alone, is attributed to newly developed methods to register visible/LWIR data. There is agreement, however, with Chen et al. (2003) that performance improves when the outcomes of algorithms operating on visible and thermal infrared imagery are fused. An advantage from using LWIR is illumination invariance. Thermal emission compared to skin reflectivity can be isolated from external illumination. 3D range information has been used together with 2D data. Tsalakanidou (2003) has used depth and color eigenfaces on XM2VTS facial data. Multimodal fusion of 2D intensity appearance, shape and depth from 3D, and heat from infrared (IR) is reported by Chang et al. (2004) on a gallery set of 127 images/subjects and an accumulated time-lapse probe set of 297 images. Pairwise combination of the multimodal biometrics performs better than each of the three unimodal biometrics taken alone. 100% recognition is achieved when the three multimodal biometrics are combined. This seems to suggest to Chang et al. that "the path to higher accuracy and robustness in biometrics involves use of multiple biometrics rather than the best possible sensor and algorithm for a single biometric." Chen et al. (2005) report that for scenarios that involve time lapses between gallery and probe, and relatively controlled lighting, PCA based recognition using visible images outperforms PCA based recognition using infrared images but the combination of PCA based recognition using visible and infrared imagery significantly outperforms either one individually. The ear as a biometric and its multimodal fusion using 3D and 2D images are discussed next.

Hurley et al. (2005) explore the use of ear biometrics (Iannarelli, 1989; Burge and Burger, 1999) for personal authentication because "Ears have certain advantages over the more established biometrics; as Bertillon pointed out, they have a rich and stable structure that is preserved from birth well into old age. The ear does not suffer from changes in facial expression, and is firmly fixed in the middle of the side of the head so that the immediate background is predictable, whereas face recognition usually requires the face to be captured against a controlled background. The ear is large compared with the iris, retina, and fingerprint and therefore is more easily captured." Gravity, however, can cause ear stretching at early and late stages of life and the ear can be covered with hair or a hat. Chang et al. (2003) report similar performance for face and ear biometrics using (eigenfaces and eigenears) PCA, 70.5% and 71.6%, respectively, but much higher, 90.9%, when the masked ear and face images of a subject are concatenated to form a combined face-plus-ear image. Hurley et al. (2005) represent the ear as an array of Gaussian attractors that act similar to a force field transform. This is equivalent to a powerful low pass filter "that obliterates all fine detail such as edges, yet preserves all the image information" and provides increased immunity to noise. The divergence operator extracts peaks and ridges across the Gaussian force field as features. Personal authentication done using cross-correlation completes the Force Field Extraction (FFE) method. The ear database used for experiments came from the XM2VTS face database. FFE outperforms PCA but proper registration is expected to significantly improve on the PCA results.

Yan and Bowyer (2005b) describe an extensive study on ear biometrics using their 2D and 3D images. 2D preprocessing includes geometric normalization and histogram equalization for proper registration and to mitigate lighting variation. 3D preprocessing is more complex and includes 3D pose normalization, pixel size normalization for the range images, and hole filling. 3D Iterative Closest Point (ICP) and 2D PCA were found to be the best authentication methods for 3D and 2D ear biometrics, respectively. ICP finds for a set of source points P and a set of model points X the rigid transformation T that best aligns P with X (Besl and McKay, 1992). 3D ICP outperforms 2D PCA on large galleries that consisted of 100 to 300 subjects. 3D ICP was also shown to be better than either 3D PCA or Hausdorff matching using edge-based 3D. Multimodal 2D PCA together with 3D ICP achieved the highest performance. The fusion rule, based on the interval distribution between rank 1 and rank 2, reached a rank one recognition rate of 91.7% with 302 subjects enrolled. Multiple sample fusion further improves on performance. The highest rank one recognition rate reached 97% with 3D ICP and min rule for recognition, when a two image per person probe is matched against a two image for gallery subjects.

9.6 Soft Biometrics

Standard identification and authentication work by using the physical or external appearance made available by cooperating subjects. There is, however, complementary information that can facilitate and enhance face recognition. First there is information, sometimes even carried on travel or identity documents, which records human characteristics that can distinguish between people. Examples include simple traits such as age, height and weight, eye color, hair color and texture, skin tone and color, body frame, scars and blemishes, and the list goes on. The traits are not limited to the visual domain and could include speech accent and smell. The characteristics, commonly referred to as soft biometrics, provide additional information that can be fused with what is presently and routinely captured for biometric identification and authentication. Most of the soft biometrics could be automatically captured to augment enrollment data. Additional soft biometrics related to demographics, e.g., ethnicity and gender, can be automatically determined using categorization (see Sect.

6.7). Context and behavior are also strong clues that can alter our confidence in what the face recognition engines have determined based solely on physical appearance and soft biometrics. They help recognition and/or counter denial and deception using augmented cognition (see Ch. 11), which is the equivalent of a "sixth" sense that gets fused with the data sensed and the soft biometrics. Estimating some of the soft biometrics using automated means is described next.

Lanitis et al. (2004) evaluated automatic age estimation methods and report an average absolute error of 3.82 years for the top ranked method, the appearance-and age-specific quadratic classifier method. This is similar to the human performance observed on similar benchmark studies. The methods used include quadratic functions that model existing relationships between face parameters, a shortest distance classifier to predefined "age" prototypes, and supervised and unsupervised neural networks, e.g., MLP and SOFM. Age estimation can also proceed in a hierarchical fashion from some rough value to a more refined and accurate estimate. Ben-Abdelkader et al. (2002) have estimated the height of (upright) people first by segmenting their body from the background and then fitting their apparent height to a time-dependent (phase walking) model. "The apparent height of a walking person was modeled as a sinusoidal curve, whose maximum occurs at the mid-stance phase of walking, when the legs are closest together, and is slightly smaller than the person's stature, typically within less than 1 cm. The minimum height occurs at the mid-swing phase of walking, when the legs are furthest apart." Ailisto et al. (2004) have shown simple data fusion through the unobtrusive use of (Salter model 984 scale) weight, height and (Omron Body Fat Monitor BFM306) body fat. Such soft biometrics, referred to as light biometrics, are reliable and easy enough to capture for low security applications and/or where a small number of subjects are under scrutiny. The weight, height, and body fat percentage when taken alone produce total error rates of 11%, 15%, and 35%, respectively for verification. Fusion of weight and height using the AND rule decreased the total error rate to 2.4%.

Soft biometrics are not persistent, e.g., weight can change, and some of them are easy to forge. In addition, they do not carry much distinctiveness and can be expensive to implement. The "soft" hedge for such biometrics comes as an acknowledgement to their limited role when used alone. The soft biometrics taken together with the primary face appearance and/or multimodal biometrics, however, can sometime make the difference and help to gain confidence in the recognition decisions made. Ailisto et al. (2006) have shown that fusing fingerprint biometrics with soft biometrics, e.g., weight and fat percentage, decreases the total error rate (TER) from 3.9% to 1.5%, in an experiment with 62 clients. Some of the soft biometrics are a throw back to the dawn of biometrics when anthropometric measures such as the length and breadth of the head were proposed by Bertillon, or reminiscent of early automatic biometric methods, e.g., the feature based approach.

9.7 Boosting and Strangeness

Data fusion is ultimately about integrating bits and pieces of biometric information. The bits and pieces include everything about what, how, and when the information was acquired. Training and learning are tasked to integrate the information available in a proper and reliable fashion. Data fusion is concerned here with evidence accumulation and the iterative removal of uncertainty and/or ambiguity. Towards that end, we propose here that the strangeness can implement the interface between face representation and boosting using the recognition-by-parts paradigm. The proposed interface combines the merits of filter and wrapper methods using the strangeness measure, and leads to efficient and reliable personal identification and authentication (see pending patent #60/623064 filed by Li and Wechsler in 2004 on the merits of using the strangeness for feature selection, voting schemes, and outlier detection). The parts, clusters of local patches described using similar features, are modeled using an exemplar based representation. Multi-resolution patches can be represented using

SIFT features, with coding of higher order relations recommended. The model-free and non-parametric weak learners correspond to parts and compete in building the strong classifier. The relative (confidence) weighting and order (ranking) for the weak learners is determined according to their strangeness. We first reacquaint ourselves with some of the characteristics of the strangeness measure, which was introduced earlier in the context of open set face recognition (see Sect. 6.3). We argue that the strangeness is intimately related to the classification margin and can thus induce weak learners, which are characterized by large classification margin and lead to good generalization.

The strangeness, for some given feature description, measures its uncertainty with respect to the label it carries. A face part is strange when its description is similar to those for parts labeled otherwise but different from parts labeled the same way. The higher the strangeness, the higher is the uncertainty associated with the label the part carries. At the same time, the usefulness of such a part for accurate recognition decreases (see Fig. 9.1a). The k-nearest neighbor strangeness is redefined (compared to Sect. 6.3) to account for the frequency of each class in the neighborhood of the part. The motivation, empirically validated, comes from cohort models where the likelihood ratio can be modeled to discriminate against a specific impostor class (see Fig. 9.1c) compared to universal background models where the likelihood ratio models discrimination against everyone else (see Fig. 9.1b). The revised definition used for the strangeness of exemplar j with putative class label c (see Fig. 9.1c) is

$$\alpha_j = \frac{\sum_{l=1}^{k} d_{jl}^c}{\min_{C, n \neq c} \sum_{l=1}^{k} d_{jl}^n} \tag{9.19}$$

with class n the most 'frequent' in the neighborhood of class c among all the C classes. The strangeness can be alternatively defined using the Lagrange multipliers associated with (kernel) SVM classifiers but this would require a significant increase in computation relative to the simple definitions proposed.

The Cover and Hart (1967) theorem proves that asymptotically, the generalization error for the nearest neighbor classifier exceeds by at most twice the generalization error of the Bayes optimal classification rule. The same theorem also shows that the k-NN error approaches the Bayes error (with factor 1) if $k = O(\log n)$. The optimal piecewise linear boundary should include samples for whom the strangeness α is thus constant. Li (2005) has made several empirical connections between the standard k-NN, strangeness k-NN, margin, and posteriors. In particular, Li has shown for binary classification, using data generated independently by 2D Gaussian distributions with equal covariance matrices, that if the two classes are well separated then the boundaries constructed by k-NN and strangeness k-NN are very close to each other even when the number of samples s and the number of neighbors k are small; when both s and k increase, both types of boundaries converge to the optimal Bayes boundary. In reality, however, two classes are rarely well separated and their data are usually drawn from a very high dimensional space. The advantage for the strangeness k-NN against standard k-NN shows up here. One can observe that the boundaries induced by the strangeness k-NN are smoother and closer to the optimal boundary compared to the boundary induced by k-NN, with the corresponding errors and their standard deviations also lower. As a consequence, one expects from the strangeness k-NN to provide better generalization within the regularization framework using penalty terms for smoothness. The mean strangeness and classification margin were found to be related via a monotonically non-decreasing function (see Fig. 9.2). The margin is $-y \log \alpha(\mathbf{x})$, when the mapping function $f(\mathbf{x})$ for the prediction rule $y = sign(f(\mathbf{x}))$ is $f(\mathbf{x}) = -y \log \alpha(\mathbf{x}) = 0$. It is similar to the (hypothesis) margin used by AdaBoost (Freund and Shapire, 1997) and corresponds to minimizing the risk/loss $R(\mathbf{w})$ (see Sect. 9.3). The margin of a hypothesis with respect to an instance is the distance between the hypothesis and the closest hypothesis that assigns an alternative label to that instance. An alternative definition (Bachrach et al., 2004) for the hypothesis margin, similar in spirit to the strangeness definition used here, is

$$\phi(x) = \frac{1}{2} \left(||\mathbf{x} - nearmiss(\mathbf{x})|| - ||\mathbf{x} - nearhit(\mathbf{x})|| \right) \tag{9.20}$$

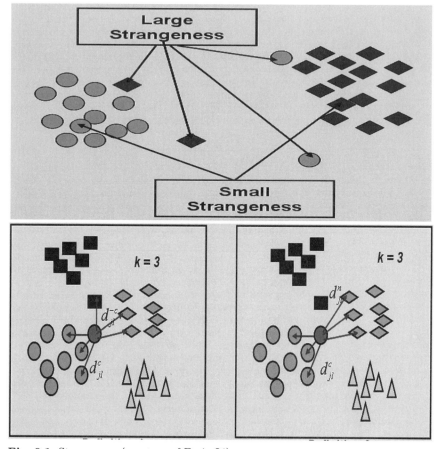

Fig. 9.1. Strangeness (courtesy of Fayin Li).

with $nearhit(\mathbf{x})$ ad $nearmiss(\mathbf{x})$ the samples nearest to $\mathbf{x}$ that carry the same and a different label, respectively. Li has also shown that the strangeness is not only related to the margin but it also participates in a one-to-one relationship with the posterior probability $p(c|\mathbf{x})$. Last but not least, the strangeness leads to more than bare predictions as it also provides credibility and confidence in the decisions made (see Sect. 6.3 and 6.4). The above characteristics make the strangeness ideally suited to realize the weak learners needed for boosting.

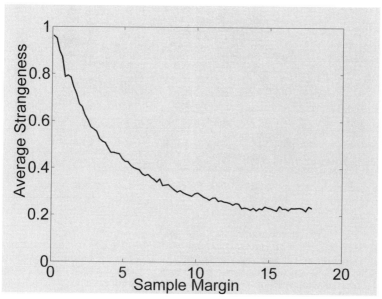

Fig. 9.2. Strangeness vs. Margin (courtesy of Fayin Li).

Face recognition-by-parts can start with extracting and representing face patches using SIFT features (or alternatively using Gabor jets). As the face is a highly non-rigid object and it shows big local distortions, due to facial expressions, the golden ratio template (see Fig. 6.5), suitable for processing MRTD, e.g., passports, is chosen as the geometrical frame where patches are looked for and detected. (The way parts are found for Face in a Crowd is discussed later.) The template provides a rough spatial map of the facial features, and it is quite informative about the relative importance of facial regions for recognition. Instead of computing the ratio of the average gray values from different regions to represent the face, as is done by Anderson and McOwan (2004), each region center (within the template) is treated as a feature point where face patches at different scales and of different bandwidth/resolution are extracted. Given the positions of the eyes, the center o_i and the minimal width/height or scale r_i of each face patch is determined by the size of each region in the golden ratio template. In order to encode for both local and some global information, multiple face patches are extracted at different scales for each feature center position. The k-th patch of region i has the scale $r_{ik} = s^{k-1}r_i$ for $s = \sqrt{2}$ and the corresponding Gaussian pyramid is built using blurring. Given that the golden ratio template consists of 16 regions, there are $16N_sN_b$ first order patches for N_s scales and N_b blurring levels starting from the original non-blurred image with $b = 0$. Motivated by the suspicious coincidences conjecture (Barlow, 1989b), 27 higher second order patches are also computed but only for neighboring regions due to the computational costs involved. The total number of patches is thus equal to $43N_sN_b$. SIFT descriptors (Lowe, 2004) are computed for each patch and normalized to unit length to reduce their sensitivity to contrast and brightness changes during testing (see Fig. 9.3 for the patches extracted at their initial scale). The patches (and their SIFT feature representation), are equivalent to the parts modeling golden ratio embedded faces. Each face is thus represented using $P = 43N_s = 215$ parts (for $N_s = 5$), and each part has five (SIFT) feature (vector) instances (for $N_b = 5$).

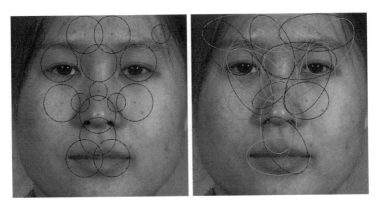

Fig. 9.3. First and Second Order Face Patches.

The Face in a Crowd scenario for face detection against background/clutter or object categorization with the face just one of the possible objects, finds the parts as follows. Patches are still described using SIFT vectors as was the case for golden ratio embedded faces. Patch selection corresponds now to (discriminative) feature selection, which is implemented using iterative backward elimination given local features $\{g_i\}$ in $\mathbf{R}^d$ and class labels for whole images with the location of the object unknown. Features characterized by high strangeness are iteratively discarded and the strangeness of the remaining features is updated given that objects, among them generic faces together with background/clutter, are properly labeled as whole images. Backward elimination terminates when the strangeness for all the features is less than some predetermined optimal threshold. The strangeness could have been used for both feature (patch) selection and variable selection, with the latter responsible for the selection of the most predictive feature (SIFT) components. The patches selected are aggregated into parts using K-means clustering for Face in a Crowd, or alternatively, relative locations for golden ratio templates. Clustering serves to accommodate redundant features left after patch selection in close-by locations. The parts are conceptualized using an exemplar-based representation that includes patch elements (see Fig. 9.4 for some of the parts and their constitution using patches). The feature vectors that define the patches self-organize and construct the parts.

The parts serve as weak learners for boosting. The motivation comes from the earlier discussion regarding the strangeness' characteristics and the merits one accrues from its use to combine filter/feature selection and wrapper/boosting methods for object recognition, in general, and face recognition, in particular. The strangeness based multi-class weak learner (classifier) selected at each iteration corresponds to the most discriminant part. The confidence and thresholds required for the strangeness based weak learners are found using a cross validation regime similar to that used during open set face recognition to determine rejection thresholds (see Sects. 6.3 and 6.4). The same approach works for golden ratio templates or when the object or face of interest, e.g., a face in a crowd, shares the image space with clutter (Li et al., 2006). Segmentation, a hard-NP problem (Gurari and Wechsler, 1982), is not a prerequisite for learning the face characteristics or using them later on during testing and recognition. The explanation comes from the fact that the parts are found as clusters of non-accidental structures. The parts are thus more likely to define "semantic" objects rather than clutter, and "parts" most likely traced to clutter are discarded.

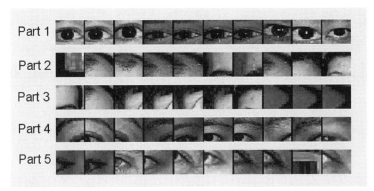

Fig. 9.4. Face Parts.

The strangeness driven weak learners are trained and validated as follows. Each class or category is represented by P parts in terms of their patches and corresponding features. Assume now C classes for whom there are N validation images. For each part of class c $(c = 1, \cdots, C)$ one obtains N positive examples for the strangeness value - corresponding to each validation face image from the same class c, and $N(C-1)$ negative examples for the strangeness value - corresponding to all the validation images from the other classes. The strangeness values are ranked for all the parts available and the best weak learner i is the one that maximizes the recognition rate over the whole set of validation images for some threshold θ_i (see Fig. 9.5). On each similar iteration another part is chosen as a weak learner. Upon completion, boosting yields the strong classifier $H(\mathbf{x})$, which is a collection of discriminative parts that play the role of weak learners.

The strangeness weak learner for categorization using boosting (Li et al., 2006a) follows closely the transduction method described for open set face recognition and watch list (see Sects. 6.3 and 6.4). It is described next using the notation introduced above. During *initialization*, the training gallery is $\{G_j^c\}_{j=1}^P$, with G_j^c the feature instance set of jth part of class c, the validation images are $V_i, i = 1, \cdots, NC$ and their associated features are $\{g(V_i)_k\}$. The *strangeness computation* seeks for each part j of class c the feature $\hat{g}(V_i)_j$ that best matches G_j^c and $g(V_i)_k$. The strangeness is computed according to eq. 9.19 with the putative class label c of V_i. Each part of class c has now NC strangeness values $\{\alpha_k^c\}_{k=1}^{NC}$, N of which are positive and $N(C-1)$ which are negative. The next step is that of *strangeness sorting*. For each part j of class c, let $\pi(1), \cdots, \pi(NC)$ be that permutation such that $\alpha_{\pi(1)}^c \leq \alpha_{\pi(2)}^c \leq \alpha_{\pi(3)}^c \leq \cdots \leq \alpha_{\pi(NC)}^c$. *Threshold selection* is the next step (see Fig. 9.5). For each part j of class c, find the best position s that maximizes the classification rate, rate $(j) = \max_s \sum_{k=1}^s w_{\pi(k)} h(\alpha_{\pi(k)})$, with $w_{\pi(k)}$ the relative weights for each part and $h(\alpha_{\pi(k)})$ equal to one if $\alpha_{\pi(k)}$ is positive and zero otherwise. The threshold for the current weak learner is $\theta(j) = \frac{1}{2} \left(\alpha_{\pi(s)} + \alpha_{\pi(s+1)} \right)$. Finally the *selection of the best weak learner* takes place. The best part found to serve as the weak learner for this iteration cycle is the mth part for whom $m = \max_j \text{rate}(j)$, and the threshold is $T_m = \theta(m)$. The (distribution) weights w_k are updated and the AdaBoost coefficients α_t are computed according to the error $(1- \text{rate}(m))$. The weak (classifier) learner and backward feature elimination are complementary wrapper and filter approaches used for the selection of discriminative parts. The parts are ranked, their coefficients

α_t normalized so their sum is one, and the strong classifier for each object/category or client $H_c(x)$ is derived accordingly.

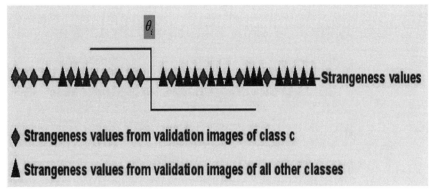

Fig. 9.5. Learning Weak Learners as Stump Functions (courtesy of Fayin Li).

Testing is similar to validation. Given some query using probe Q, one extracts patches and represents them using SIFT features. Patches then aggregate or are indexed by the golden ratio template to form parts. Resolving the query Q is a process that iterates over an ensemble that consists of C classes. For each class $c \in C$ and part $i \in c$ one has to find the closest feature (and thus part) in Q. The weak "stump" learner $h_i(Q)$ outputs 1 when the part is recognized and 0 otherwise. The part is recognized if the strangeness α_i for the weak learner is less than the threshold learned (see Fig. 9.5), i.e., $\alpha_i < \theta_i$. In a similar fashion one finds and matches the remaining parts for query Q with those for the putative class label c and determines the score for the strong classifier $H_c(Q)$. The ID for the face is the label c that maximizes $H_c(Q)$.

Biometric experiments using strangeness and boosting (see above) were performed on frontal faces from the University of Notre Dame (UND) collected during 2002-2003, and now part of the FRGC face image database (Phillips et al., 2005). The experiments are similar in functionality to those using multiple samples (see Sect. 9.4). The face images were acquired under different and sometimes uncontrolled lighting conditions and/or with different facial expressions. There is also temporal variation as the face images were acquired during different sessions over a one year period. We sampled 200 subjects from the data base; for each one there are 48 images of which 16 were acquired in an uncontrolled environment. Each face image is normalized at 289×289 with 256 gray scale levels (see Fig. 9.6).

The number P of parts used was 215 for $N_s = 5$, while the number of feature instances for each part is $N_b = 4$. Considering the symmetry of the frontal face [but preserving the whole nose area] there are only 130 parts for each face with $P = 26N_s$. Each subject owns 48 images. In a random fashion, 12 images were selected for training, 12 images for validation, and the remaining 24 images for testing. The Euclidian distance is used to compute the strangeness. Our strangeness-based (AdaBoost.M2) boosting approach using symmetry yields 97.8% and 98.9% using only first-order or both first and second order patches, respectively (Li et al, 2006b). The results are much better than those obtained using an alternative voting approach that implements the Transductive Confidence Machine (TCM) (Proedrou et al., 2002; Li and Wechsler, 2005) or decides on recognition simply from the number of matched parts (Ivanov et al., 2004). The corresponding results for TCM were 88.1% and 89.2%, respectively. The distribution of coefficients for the weak learners also shows the relative importance of local regions to identify or authenticate subjects. The contribution of the patches around the nose is on the average the largest when symmetry was not used.

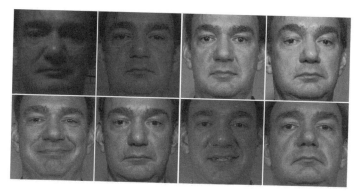

Fig. 9.6. Face Images from FRGC.

This is in agreement with our findings when using asymmetric faces for recognition (see Sect. 10.5). One also finds that for each location on the face, median size regions tend to be more important for recognition than the small and large sized regions.

The strangeness and boosting approach was finally evaluated with respect to occlusion. Face images were modified to simulate occlusion in the following way. Occlusion occurs when a circle region with a radius of r pixels is randomly chosen, and its contents are set at 0 or filled with random pixel values in the range $[0, 255]$ (see Fig. 9.7). The top one rank recognition, when the radius is less than 10 pixels, stays above 90% disregarding the way occlusion was simulated. The average top one rank recognition rates show that the use of symmetry improves on performance. The recognition rate decreases on the average when the radius of the occluded region increases but it does not drop too much. The performance is also very stable when the occluded regions are not too large. Even when the radius is 30 pixels the top one rank recognition stays at 80%, disregarding the way occlusion was simulated. The recognition rate for TCM, much lower than that for strangeness and boosting, drops dramatically with respect to r. The next experiment considered the case when the occluded regions are fixed, e.g., eyes, nose, and mouth, and symmetry is used. The results obtained confirmed that the occlusion of the nose affects the performance more than that for either the mouth or the eyes.

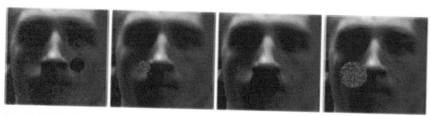

Fig. 9.7. Occluded Face Images.

The golden ratio template captures the recognition-by-parts structure only implicitly. The alternative, for the case when the layout grid is not available, is to use the fully connected constellation model whose complexity is $O(N^P)$ for N features and P parts. To address such computational concerns, Fergus et al. (2005) have proposed a star model of lower complexity $O(N^2P)$. The star model is a tree of depth one that factors the joint probability of the configuration. Less dependencies and thus parameters are now needed without the danger for overfitting, a larger number of features and parts can be dealt with, and less training is needed. One way to conceptualize the star model is to think about some important landmark on the face, e.g., the nose, which becomes the root for the tree, and other facial characteristics referred to as non-landmarks, which are independent of each other and become the leaves for the same tree.

The same boosting approach using parts for weak learners was tested on categorization using the Caltech database [3]. The selected features come from objects with most background features discarded. The particular data set included motorbikes, faces, airplanes, and cars (side). Categorization proceeds in two stages. First the choice is between background and all the other objects, and second the choice is among objects when the background hypothesis has been rejected. The ROC equal error rate for faces was 94.4% using $P = 30$ parts and $k = 5$ (Li et al., 2006a). Boosting performance was stable when the number of parts P is in the range $[25, 50]$. When P is small, there is not enough evidence and the final strong classifier lacks enough discriminative power. When P is too large, similar features are shared across clusters leading to redundancy between weak hypotheses, and the final strong classifier overfits.

Our approach to capture the facial layout is to expand on our face recognition approach (see above) using again the strangeness to construct weak learners that code for structure and implicit order among the parts using their sequencing in the strong classifier. Boosting would now learn also the most discriminative dependencies between parts and propose them as weak learners. The parts and dependencies, i.e., appearance and structure, compete against each other to have their corresponding weak learners included in the strong classifier $H_c(\mathbf{x})$, which can be thought of as a "bag of features." Learning structural weak learners depends on how reliable the appearance nodes or parts are, in addition to the connection or dependencies linking the parts themselves. The proposed framework, model free, non-parametric, and working in an unsupervised fashion with images that do not require pre-segmentation, is discriminative in nature due to the boosting component that minimizes the validation error. The generative component responsible to describe the parts is much simpler and makes training efficient. The boosting approach driven by strangeness is more effective and more efficient than the Bayesian framework. It is more effective because it makes no assumptions about underlying PDF and avoids marginalization. It is more efficient because it is model free, non-parametric, and discriminative. The proposed approach provides for reliable face recognition despite clutter, noise and occlusion. Last but not least, the scope for pattern recognition, in general, and face recognition, in particular, is now much wider because both training and testing can take place using incomplete or camouflaged/disguised patterns from single and/or multiple image sets.

---

[3] http://www.vision.caltech.edu/feifeili/Datasets.htm

10. Denial and Deception

The percept is always a wager. Thus uncertainty enters at two levels, not merely one: the configuration may or may not indicate an object, and the cue may or may not be utilized at its true indicative value (James Gibson)

Denial, which stands for occlusion, and deception, which stands for masking, affect biometric analysis. Biometrics should not assume that the personal signatures are complete and reliable. Occlusion and disguise are not necessarily deliberate. They can take place in crowded environments, e.g., CCTV when only parts of the face are visible from time to time. Temporal changes can easily deceive current face recognition engines. Examples of phenomena, with deceptive impact, include bags under the eyes and wrinkles from aging, changes in appearance due to the use of cosmetics, medical condition (injuries and allergies), fatigue, hair style and facial hair. "Our face reflects the lifelong pull of gravity, which lengthens the jaws and deepens orbital bags. In addition people develop fat pads under the eyes, shadows fall differently on the upper and lower eyelid" (McNeill, 1998). Current face recognition systems are ineffective when temporal (involuntary or not) changes occur. In addition, the working hypothesis for the large evaluations carried out so far, e.g., FRVT2002, has not been particularly concerned with the very possibility that subjects would seek to deny and/or foil their true biometric signatures. Most clients are legitimate and honest. They have nothing to hide, and have all the incentives to cooperate. The very purpose of biometrics, however, is to provide security from impostors and those seeking to breach security. It is quite obvious that such subjects are well motivated to interfere with the proper acquisition of their biometric signatures, and will attempt to hide and/or alter information that is needed for their identification.

Another dimension of deception comes when assessing the emotive aspect that the face presents. Wearing internal and/or external masks, e.g., falsify or hide emotions, on one side, or alter and embellish appearances (see M. Butterfly and Phantom of the Opera), on the other side, are examples of emotive deception. The challenge here is to detect if emotive disguise took place, e.g., using lie detectors, and to overcome false appearances in order to reveal the original facial information. Direct gaze and eye contact are usually taken as signs for honesty. Signs for deceit coming from being physiologically aroused, e.g., rapid blink rate and dilated pupils, are not always a true reflection of the internal state of the subject. They can reflect instead the equivalent of false confessions due to fear and apprehension. According to Sharon Begley from the Wall Street Journal, "making the suspect anxious about his denials, challenging inconsistencies (a taste of what he would face at a trial) and justifying the offense all induce confessions. Those most likely to confess to a crime they didn't commit are compliant, suggestible, young, mentally retarded, mentally ill, or afraid of confrontation and conflict." The polygraph used in law enforcement for lie detection most likely locks on arousal rather than deception. How are lies spotted and genuine emotions distinguished from the false ones? McNeill (1998) suggests that the lower face is more prone to deception because we have greater control. He claims that the smile, however, is the key. "Felt smiles last too long, animate only the mouth, are abrupt and asymmetric. In addition there is a mismatch between the upper face, e.g., eyes, and the lower face. When uncertain, the information coming from the eyes should prevail. The potential and scope for deception varies, e.g., mischievous, benign or nefarious, and suggests different methods for detection." Both actors in the cat and mouse game of deception, the perpetuator and the detector, have to continuously hone their skills and/or learn new methods. Success at deception or avoiding it depends on the correctness of the assumptions made regarding mutual abilities and limitations, on one side, and the capability to deal with uncertainty, on the other side.

This chapter describes some of the means available to detect and overcome denial and deception within the context of biometrics. Denial and deception are complementary to security and privacy (see Ch. 14). Some of the conceptual motivation and treatment of denial/occlusion, and disguise/deception, is related to military and intelligence analysis. The shared objective is awareness and/or responsiveness to "signal" coupled with "noise" suppression in order to ultimately increase SNR. Overcoming denial and deception is relevant across the board for face recognition. It is thus complementary to the discussion in Chaps. 6 and 7 on face detection (in a crowd), identification and authentication, and tracking.

10.1 Human Biases

Similar to military deception, one has to contemplate both perceptual and cognitive biases and aliasing. The perceptual and cognitive dimensions are related to the sensory and reasoning/inference mechanisms employed. Biases are preferences that sway the abilities of the face recognition engine. Beauty marks or skin texture are some of the means used to bias recognition. In signal processing, aliasing results when sampling is not properly done. Aliasing is caused by limited resolution or low sampling rate, i.e., lack of enough data for analysis. The signal processing explanation for aliasing is quite simple. When the sampling rate is less than twice the bandwidth of the signal, i.e., the Nyquist frequency, translated versions of the spectrum overlap in the frequency domain. Failing to distinguish between different states or signatures, one ends up by confounding them. In the context of face recognition, aliasing can take place when the grid used to sample the face does not reflect the relative importance of the facial landscape being scanned. Varying rather than uniform resolution is helpful with the eyes sampled at a higher resolution than the cheeks. Biases and aliasing come from both the deceiver perpetuating deception and the counter deceiver trying to spot deception. Our discussion on perceptual and cognitive biases for deception purposes and the quotes follows Heuer's (1981) exposition on strategic military deception.

Perception is active. It is neither necessarily objective nor accurate. It involves inference according to Helmholtz such that the face recognition engine "constructs its own version of "reality" on the basis of information provided by the senses. This sensory input is mediated by processes that determine which information to attend to and how to organize it. Thus what is perceived is strongly influenced by past experience and requirements." Experience and training drive our expectations, assumptions, and preconceptions, with all of them affecting what is ultimately sensed. In other words *seek and ye shall find.* "Patterns of expectation become so deeply embedded that they continue to influence perceptions even when one is alerted and tries to take account of the existence of data that do not fit preconceptions." Expectations also affect causality and inference, in general, and the relative importance assigned to observations or features, in particular. The unexpected is usually dismissed or given short thrift and false positive rates skyrocket. The mind-set and the facts are always on a collision course, and biases are unavoidable. "There is a grain of truth in the otherwise pernicious maxim that an open-mind is an empty mind." The alternative is our inability to process large amounts of data and/or the consequent large variance in results due to bias-variance trade offs.

Perceptions "are quick to form but resistant to change. New information is assimilated to existing images [and expectations]. This principle explains why gradual, evolutionary change often goes unnoticed. First impressions are persistent and are hard to change." Mistakes tend to persist. Initial hypotheses bear a large impact on subsequent processing. It takes more evidence to dislodge expectations and preconceptions than to confirm them. Initialization, when expectations and priors are missing, is required but difficult to make. Losing track and reinitializing the search is hard too. An outsider may generate better and more accurate perceptions "overlooked by experienced [but biased] analysts." This might explain why a mixture of weak classifiers (see Sects. 9.3 and 9.7) builds a strong classifier that works so well. Expectations are most harmful when there is a large degree of blur or uncertainty surrounding the events of interest. "The greater the initial blur, the clearer the [face] has to be before [people] could recognize it. The longer time that [people] were exposed to a blurred [face], the clearer the picture has to be made before they could recognize it." People are "quick to reject new information that does not conform to their preconceptions." How can one resist the temptation for making hasty decisions? Latency and progressive processing (see Sect. 7.4) seek first strong signals in order to discount the pernicious effect of blur and expectations. Another solution for dealing with the effects of ambiguous data is the principle of least commitment that "suspends [early] judgment." Alternative interpretations can be carried forward and disambiguated only when enough evidence becomes available as it is the case with sequential importance sampling.

Cognitive biases affect "the estimation of probabilities, the evaluation of evidence, and the attribution of causality" (Heuer, 1981). As an example, "the anchoring bias, keeps the final estimate closer to the starting point." People are more likely to confirm rather than disconfirm initial estimates. Another bias is that of simplicity. Occam's razor argues that when two explanations compete, the simpler one wins. (see Sect. 3.4 for structural risk minimization) There is beauty in simplicity, and counterfactual information that interferes with simplicity is easily dismissed. As Thomas Huxley observed "The great tragedy of science: the slaying of a beautiful hypothesis by an ugly fact!" Absence of evidence is another example of evaluation biases. Gaps in evidence are "out of sight, out of mind." Discredited or invalidated evidence are glossed over rather than analyzed. "Perceptual tendencies and cognitive biases strongly favor the deceiver as long as the goal of deception is to reinforce a target's preconceptions, which is by far the most common form of deception." Access to the FERET data base and knowledge of how the face space is computed helps thus a potential impostor with deception. More information is not always better as it can lead to overconfidence. As more information becomes available the amount of noise increases. The focus for counter deception should be "primarily on problems of analysis, only secondarily on collection" (Heuer, 1981). Such cognitive biases are the reason tracking and recognition can fail. Human biases often surface as machine biases. Model-free, non-parametric, and unsupervised methods are the proper means to counter such biases and handle denial and deception. Parceling the biometric information into parts, and combining the parts using boosting, makes face recognition more reliable and less prone to human and/or machine biases and errors.

10.2 Camouflage

Deception is ubiquitous but diverse in nature. Essential for survival, it is one of the forces that drives natural selection. "Among all [these] evolutionary achievements, perhaps none are more important, more widely used, and more highly developed, than those characteristics which serve to elude, to attract, or to deceive the eye, and facilitate escape from enemies or the pursuit of prey" (Cott, 1966). The discussion on crafting deception and defending against it follows Gerwehr and Glenn (2002) using the language of perception and adaptation. Perception, because it deals with sensory inputs, and adaptation, because there is a continuous "arm race" between the practice of deception and the means to defend against it. Deception, like camouflage, is most effective in cluttered environments when it becomes easier to hide, thanks to the many distracters available.

Deception "engenders inaccuracy in the perceptions of the foe (be it attacker or defender)." This tends to be highly advantageous and leads to "erroneous action that so often follows an inaccurate perception." The inaccuracies referred to are the result of degraded biometric signatures and/or manipulated perceptions. Degraded perceptions involve blur and/or increase in noise. Manipulated perceptions are induced by distorted views on reality. Gerwehr and Glenn have identified three axes along which to measure individual deception, and at least three means by which individual deceptions may be aggregated. The dimensions for individual deception include,

- Sophistication (static, dynamic, adaptive, and premeditative)
- Effects (masking or concealing signature, decoy or misleading, decrease in SNR for confusion)
- Means (form/morphological and behavioral)

Camouflage usually takes advantage of the basic dimensions of the face space, e.g., color, shape, and texture. Commingling with people in crowds is one easy way to mask both presence and identity. Camouflage results from confused recognition because the target blends with the surrounding environment. Many people do not want to stand out but rather wish to assume what might be called an average appearance. Morphing the face appearance toward some average appearance, and/or mimicry for anonymity serve such a purpose. Crypsis, complementary to mimicry, displays a pattern of spots and lines to break up the outline of the face. It can be quite effective against CCTV and makes face detection and location hard. Recognition-by-parts is one approach to address crypsis and fight anonymity. Other aspects related to the effectiveness of camouflage include "parameters, variability, and longevity."

According to Gerwehr and Glenn, masking a signature in motion appears to be much more difficult than when at rest. This is yet another reason why video processing is useful for face recognition. The coherent changes taking place over space and time are multi-faceted and are much more difficult to mask. A more effective way to deceive is to combine various tactics. Referred to as "nesting," this might include the use of mask(s) and decoys, e.g., face and/or head ornaments. Local face analysis, characteristic of recognition-by-parts, and data fusion are possible means for dealing with nesting. Motion camouflage (Srinivasan and Davey, 1995), different from masking the biometric signature in motion, is a "stealth behavior that allows a predator [or human] to conceal its apparent motion on approaching a moving prey [camera]" (Anderson and McOwan, 2003). Motion camouflage is of interest to tracking, in general, and human identification from distance (HID), in particular. The deception strategy would be to position oneself directly between the current position of the camera and some starting hypothetical point in order to emulate a distant stationary object. The target of deception, or the camera, "perceives no lateral motion (retinal slip) of the subject's [face and/or body] relative to the environment and is less likely to notice the approach."

Deception can be detected first and/or countered using robust means for recognition. Pavlidis et al. (2002) claim that deception can be detected on the fly using thermal facial screening. Deception, associated with stress and the corresponding "fight or flight" syndrome, leads to "an instantaneous increase of blood flow around the eyes of a subject." Question marks, similar to those raised about polygraph investigations, raise a red flag here too. Tankus and Yeshurun (2000) propose camouflage breaking using direct (3D) convexity estimation. Edge-based region of interest (ROI) detection methods, characteristic of attention mechanisms, are defeated by faces camouflaged using stripes in natural environments. The striped faces and the environment blend to produce uniform edge maps and conceal human presence. Humans can be detected, however, using convexity rather than edge maps.

Counter deception needs to be an integral component to any biometric system. It should be considered early on, starting with the design phase and proceeding with development, implementation and deployment. Counter deception should be adaptive, dynamic, allow for flexible matching, and should consider data fusion. Deception and counter deception play a cat and mouse game. Sophistication increases on both sides as a result of adaptation and/or co-evolution. Proper timing is of essence.

10.3 Aliveness Detection

The first line of attack for deception is the front end of the biometric system. It concerns *spoofing* or impersonation. It can happen when biometric access is remote or unattended. Spoofing using a fake signature is usually referred to as a replay attack. It takes place using biometric data that was previously acquired, e.g., the face image. The counter deception methods of choice are aliveness detection, which is discussed here, and multimodal biometrics, e.g., speech and fingerprints. Aliveness detection works by looking for change detection. The change looked for concerns the whole face, e.g. head movements, but much of the time, most attention is paid to the eyes. Eye detection and analysis precedes aliveness detection and is discussed next.

The eye parameters can be derived using high resolution color images (Heishman et al., 2001). Data collection takes place using Sony DFW - VL500 progressive color scan camera. Image processing consists of Gaussian smoothing, color edge detection, and the Hough Transform (HT) for iris and pupil detection. Color edges are detected by combining the gradients in the red, green, and blue color bands (Jahne, 2002); the edges are thinned using non-maxima suppression. Irises and pupils (see Fig. 10.1) are located via the HT using multiple size templates and assuming that their shapes are circular with varying radius **r**. The HT searches for disrupted (by noise) or otherwise incomplete curves by mapping the data space to a parameter $\{a, b, r\}$ space that corresponds to a circle described by $(x-a)^2 + (y-b)^2 = r^2$. An accumulator array gathers supporting evidence for each one of the possible curves according to the strength of the edge components and constrained by the curve equation and symmetry. The HT is conceptually nothing more than a match filter (MF). It can be derived from the Radon transform (Deans, 1981) and operates by accruing evidence for alternative model interpretations. The edges in the vicinity of irises are the candidates used to search for eyelids and eyebrows. The list of derived parameters includes $P1$ and $P2$, the pupil and iris diameters, $P3$ and $P4$, the distances from the center of the iris, which coincides with the center of the pupil, to the upper and lower eyelids, respectively, and $P5$, the distance from the center of the iris to the eyebrow. The parameters P_1 through P_5 are always positive; P_3 and/or P_4 become small when the eyes are almost closed. Other parameters, such as the density of lines around the eyes and the curvature of the eyelids and the eyebrows, can be derived for better performance.

Ji and Yang (2001) have proposed a real time system for pupil detection and tracking. Once the face and eyes are detected, pupil detection proceeds with background removal via subtraction of the image obtained with only ambient light from the image obtained with both ambient and IR light. Localization of the initial pupils position takes place by seeking bimodal distributions of two regions, background and pupil, which satisfy certain size, shape, and distance constraints. Validation, complementary to localization, ensures that what was found are pupils rather than "glint, the small bright spot near the pupil, produced by corneal reflection of IR, or glares of glasses." One can further estimate the gaze direction based on the relative positions of the pupil and the glint (Ebisawa, 1989). Pupil tracking takes place using the Kalman filter (KF). Pupil detection can be hampered by eye closure or occlusion, and illumination interference. Pupil detection does not have to assume that the eyes have been detected but rather help with eye detection in a complementary fashion.

Tsuda et al. (2004) have proposed photometric stereo for liveliness detection. Two IR LED are installed on both (left and right) sides of the camera for this purpose. The direction of the surface created by the photometric stereo is used to distinguish between a planar surface, i.e., a photograph, and a non-planar surface, i.e., a real person. Liveliness detection can also be based on the light absorbing properties of living (vs. non-living) tissue, red-eye effect, specular reflections at the optical interfaces of the eye known as the Purkinje reflections, and pupil oscillations. The pupil is never at rest. It undergoes spasmodic and rhythmical dilations and constrictions, independent of illumination or psychic stimuli. The variation in the size of the pupil is caused by iris tremors and is referred to as hippus. Expression challenge and response mechanisms, motivated by human behavior and physiology, can trigger eyelid blinks and/or eye

Fig. 10.1. Pupil and Iris (courtesy of Massimo Tistarelli).

saccades for liveliness detection. Some eye responses, e.g., pupil dilation, are correlated with cognitive load and the interest value of the visual stimuli (Hess and Polt, 1964).

10.4 Hallucinations

There is an obvious need to increase the SNR in order to cope with both occlusion and disguise, e.g., human identification from distance (HID). "Faces often appear very small in surveillance imagery because of the wide fields of view and resolution enhancement techniques are therefore generally needed" (Baker and Kanade, 2000). This requires super resolution imagery that is reminiscent of hallucination, which is similar to mental anticipation. The specific techniques for hallucination usually engage in exemplar-based learning of the priors needed for pixel substitution. Alternatively, the pixels needed can be drawn from image distributions, indexed by demographic and age characteristics. Baker and Kanade (2003) describe a nearest neighbor learning algorithm that is able "to predict the gradient prior and show a huge improvement over existing interpolation and super-resolution algorithms. A small number of [merely] 12×16 images of a human face can be fused into a single 96×128 pixel image that closely resembles the original face." The benefits from hallucination were limited to appearance and did not extend to recognition performance.

Hallucination overcomes some of the limits imposed by the standard super-resolution algorithms. Large magnification factors "provide less and less useful information" because "any smoothness prior leads to overly smooth results with very little high-frequency contents" (Baker and Kanade, 2002). The lack of high-frequency or details, however, due to quantization, is detrimental to face recognition. The better alternative is to learn the priors (see above) ahead of time, using local estimation methods, and during HID processing detect local features and hallucinate them at the highest resolution needed. Wu et al. (2004) use hallucination to synthesize face images after eyeglasses are removed. This requires learning how to map the area uncovered after removing the eyeglasses using information from similar face images without eyeglasses. The limitations for using hallucination are obvious. It is not only the eye appearance that needs to be properly mapped but rather the whole state of the face including her inner state or personal disposition and the expressions displayed momentarily. Wang and Tang (2004) have proposed the eigen transformation as the means for hallucination. High resolution "is rendered by replacing the low-resolution training images with high-resolution ones, while retaining the same combination coefficients." The non-face like distortions are reduced by using known correlations between the high and low-frequency bands that correspond to the principal components identified. The correspondence holds because the power spectrum is related to the Fourier transform of the autocorrelation function. The advantage over super-resolution algorithms, which encode dependencies as homogeneous Markov Random Fieds (MRF), comes from the explicit inclusion of high-frequency details. Dedeoglu et al. (2004) expand hallucination to video by exploiting spatial-temporal regularities. Significant improvements were reported with respect to both video flicker and the mean-square error.

10.5 Asymmetric Faces

Humans can detect and identify faces with little or no effort even if only partial views (due to occlusion) are available. This skill is quite robust, despite changes in the visual stimulus due to viewing conditions and expression. Much of the research on face recognition has focused so far on the use of full frontal images. Partial faces, however, are all what is sometimes available for training and/or testing (see Face in a Crowd). The scant attention given so far to occlusion is reviewed next. Gross et al. (2000) address occlusion using eigen subspaces derived using a sliding window and model the ID references as a sequence of signatures. A face of unknown identity is compared against the stored reference sequences using Dynamic Space Warping (DSP), similar to Dynamic Programming (DP) used for speech recognition. The images considered were small and vary in size between 15×20 and 40×54. The occlusions considered were limited in scope. The data base included a very large number, about 60 pictures, for each ID reference. The large number of pictures is explained by the need to accommodate parameter estimation for DSW but it is impractical for real life face recognition.

Martinez (2002) suggests a (Gaussian or mixture of Gaussians) probabilistic approach that attempts to model the variation in image appearance due to poor face (or facial landmarks) localization and partial occlusion. To resolve the occlusion problem, each face is divided into six local but contiguous regions which are then analyzed in isolation. One major drawback for this method, which makes it impractical for real use as readily acknowledged by the author, is that "the ground-truth data (i.e., the correct localization of every feature that has to be detected on each face) is needed in order to estimate the localization error of a given localization algorithm. The problem with this is that the ground-truth data has to be obtained manually, which is a cost to be considered." The ground-truth problem is more general, and affects most performance evaluation studies carried so far. Even more challenging is the fact that ground truth is required for both training and test data. Martinez (2002) working on the synthetic (1/6 to 1/3) occlusion problem reports different recognition rates for the left and right face images. Tan et al. (2005) expand on the approach used by Martinez using Self-Organized-Feature-Maps (SOFM) instead of the mixture of Gaussians. Their method requires manual annotation and needs to be told about occlusions and their location.

Faces can be recognized from either their left or right half images when the face recognition engine is trained on full faces and tested on (hallucinated) asymmetric faces constructed from either the left or right half augmented by their mirror image (Gutta and Wechsler, 2003; 2004). Liu et al. (2002; 2003) have proposed to extend the use of facial asymmetry measures, a critical factor in the evaluation of facial attractiveness (Thornhill and Gangstead, 1999) and expression (Richardson et al., 2000), to human identification. Facial attractiveness for men is inversely related to recognition accuracy and asymmetrical faces are found less attractive. The explanation comes from the simple observation that asymmetrical faces are more distinctive and thus easier to remember and recognize. In particular, Liu et al. (2003) have argued that asymmetric faces can be further exploited if combined with either eigenfaces or Fisherfaces representations. Building asymmetric faces required a face midline defined in terms of two canthi and a philtrum, fiducial landmarks marked manually under consistent lighting. The asymmetric faces, the Density Difference D-Face and the Edge Orientation Similarity S-Face, are then derived using reflection with respect to the face midline. Using a random set of 110 subjects from the FERET data base, a 38% classification error reduction rate was obtained. Error reduction rates of 45%-100% are achieved on 55 subjects from the Cohn-Kanade AU-Coded Facial Expression

Database. The expressions produced on demand are likely to be more asymmetric than those elicited by real emotions. Our approach, characteristic of mixture of experts and voting schemes, employs an Ensemble of Radial Basis Functions (ERBF), which is described next.

ERBF is a mixture of RBF "expert" classifiers (see Sect. 9.2 for RBF). Rather than building a strong classifier as AdaBoost does (see Sect. 9.3), ERBF induces direct invariance to small affine transformations and/or blur using hints. A connectionist network is successful to the extent that it can generalize, i.e., cope with the variability that characterizes the data acquisition process. Our solution to this problem using ERBF is characteristic of *committee networks* or *query by consensus* (see Fig. 10.2). Both original face patterns and their distorted exemplars, hinted by small geometrical changes and/or blur, are used for robust learning. The RBF nodes vary in terms of their defining characteristics and are trained on original images or on their transformed images using either Gaussian noise or a small degree of rotation. The hidden (unsupervised) RBF layer, implements an enhanced K-means clustering procedure, where both the number of BF Gaussian cluster nodes F and their variance are dynamically set. The number of clusters varies, in steps of 5, from $\frac{1}{5}$ of the number of training images to n, the total number of training images. The width of the Gaussian for each cluster, is set to the maximum of (the distance between the center of the cluster and the member of the cluster that is farthest away - within class diameter, the distance between the center of the cluster and the closest face pattern from all other clusters) multiplied by an overlap factor o. The intermediate nodes $C1$, $C2$, and $C3$ act as buffers for the transfer of the normalized face images to the various RBF components. Training (for the hidden layer) is performed until almost perfect recognition is achieved for each RBF node. During testing, the nine output vectors generated by the RBF nodes are passed to a judge who decides to what particular class the face probe ('input') belongs to. The majority or consensus decision used by the *judge* requires that the average of any five of the nine network (class) outputs be greater than some (empirically found) threshold for the probe to be assigned to that class. Similar to open set face recognition, no recognition is made when the above rule fails.

ERBF implementation involves a simple and fully automated method using asymmetric faces (for either training or testing) and yields excellent results on a larger data set (compared to the methods mentioned earlier) that consists of 150 subjects whose face images were acquired under varying illumination. The recognition rate obtained was in excess of 90%. The asymmetric right face performance (96%) was slightly better than the asymmetric left face performance (92%) when the corresponding asymmetric faces were matched against the full face. One possible explanation for the right asymmetric face performing slightly better comes from the fact that, since the appearance for the nose is not symmetric, the asymmetric left face has a more pronounced nose or sometimes a "double" nose is present. The relative higher importance of the nose for face identification concurs with our additional findings using transduction and boosting (see Sect. 9.7). Training on the left asymmetric faces and testing on the full face or training on the right asymmetric face and testing on the full face yield similar performance (92%) and compares favorably against matching complete faces (Gutta and Wechsler, 2004). Finally, there is the case when both training and testing have access only to asymmetric faces. Training, done using ERBF, copes with both the inherent variability in the image formation process and the missing half of the face. The same data base as before includes 150 subjects for whom the pose rotation ranges across $\pm 5°$ and yields 3,000 face images. The k-fold cross-validation face recognition rates obtained using the same type (Left or Right) of asymmetric faces during both training and testing was around 92%. The recognition rate falls to about 80% if training and testing take place using different (Left vs. Right or vice versa) asymmetric faces.

Data collection for the asymmetric face experiment proceeds as follows. The distance from the subject and the camera is approximately 3 feet. Each subject was asked to first look at the camera for approximately 5 seconds and turn his/her head $\pm 5°$. The images were acquired at a resolution of 640×480 pixels and encoded using

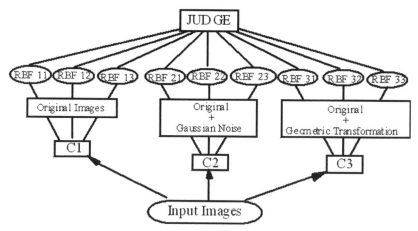

Fig. 10.2. ERBF Architecture.

256 gray scale levels. The images are then passed to the face detection module, and subsequently normalized to account for geometrical and illumination changes using information about the eyes' location. The face obtained at the end of the detection and normalization stage is encoded using 64 × 72 resolution. Since the location of the eyes is known from the detection module, one can create the partial faces by cutting the normalized facial image vertically at the point where the distance from one end of the image to the center is half the inter ocular distance. The mirror image of the partial face is constructed by flipping the partial face image from left to right or vice versa. The asymmetric face image is obtained by combining the partial (half) face image with its mirror image. A set of face images, their half face images and corresponding asymmetric faces are shown in Fig 10.3.

The role of asymmetric faces goes beyond coping with frontal occlusion. Poor illumination can be handled using asymmetric faces too. Here one would choose the half face not affected by poor illumination and construct the corresponding asymmetric face. Similar arguments apply to faces seen only from profile.

10.6 Adaptive and Robust Correlation Filters

The face recognition-by-parts paradigm is realized here using Adaptive and Robust Correlation Filters (ARCF). The filter banks are optimized match (correlation) filters for the face components including the whole face as one of the components. ARCF enjoy optimal characteristics compared to existing correlation filters, on one side, and are useful for efficient face recognition subject to occlusion and disguise, on the other side (Lai and Wechsler, 2006). Occlusion corresponds to missing parts, while disguise is the result of purposeful or temporal changes in facial appearances. The approach proposed enables that (i) the face parts record both representation and location across the face (Edelman and Intrator, 2000); and that (ii) hybrid image representations combine part-based and holistic components such as the whole face and its half sides (see Sect. 6.5). The inclusion of whole and/or half faces benefits the face recognition-by-parts paradigm only when occlusion does not occur.

ARCF expand on MACE filters and adaptive beam forming from radar and sonar. Characteristic of recognition-by-parts, they seek for the best constellation of face components in terms of both similarity and configuration. The identification or authentication of an unknown face is signaled by strong correlation peaks, which correspond

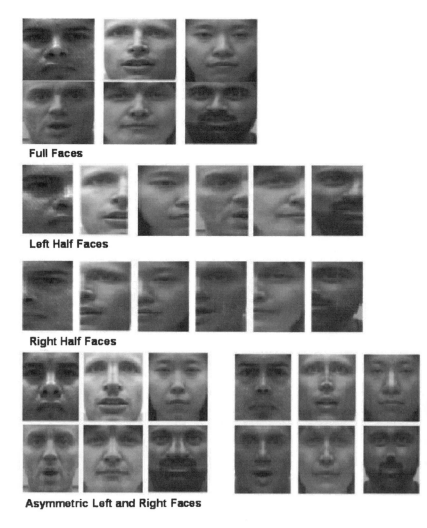

Full Faces

Left Half Faces

Right Half Faces

Asymmetric Left and Right Faces

Fig. 10.3. Half Face Recognition Using Asymmetric Faces.

to matched (patch-based and/or holistic) components. The peaks have to line up and be centered (in the response/transform domain) in order to indicate that a correct configuration with the proper alignment was found. If the individual face components for the probe match some gallery face but the relative locations for the components are different, the correlation peaks do not align but rather scatter, and recognition fails. The cluster and strength of the ARCF correlation peaks are a measure of confidence in the recognition decision made, if any. Note that the ARCF approach does not require expensive graph matching. Occluded or disguised components, which show up as missing or weak correlation peaks, are interpreted as such. Information on peaks and clusters can be used to train weak learners and combine their outputs using boosting (see Sect. 9.7). The adaptive aspect of ARCF comes from their derivation using both training and test data, while the robust aspect comes from optimizing ARCF to withstand distortions. The "world" is its own representation, and test data is used as additional training data in a fashion similar to transduction. What better source to learn about variations in face structure and noise than the probe face itself? Reliability and robustness come from the close similarity between the ARCF design using correlation filters and Tikhonov regularization. Experimental evidence shows the feasibility and utility of ARCF for face recognition-by-parts, in general, and occlusion and disguise, in particular. ARCF and their application are described next.

Correlation filters (CF) display nice properties that are suitable for implementing recognition-by-parts using template matching. The strength of the correlation peak indicates how well the training and test images match, while the location of the peaks indicates the relative dislocation between training and test images. Recognition-by-parts involves matching the corresponding parts for similarity, and expecting their aligned location to be close to the origin of the response domain (see rightmost box in Fig. 10.4). One maintains for this purpose the relative locations of the parts during training and testing in order to check for their alignment. This is easily accomplished by using masks that expose only the parts and zero out the rest of the face. Three masks are applied to the training face to extract out the face parts corresponding to the right eye (RE), left eye (LE), and nose (N), with the area outside the mask zeroed out (see Fig. 10.4). The masks consist of boxes that surround the training face parts as shown in the left image. The three face parts are used to design three Match Filters (MF) (see below) that are used for recognition-by-parts. In the first example, the test image (middle box) is from the same subject. The matching scores (correlation peaks) for the face components are high and the peak locations are aligned near the center.

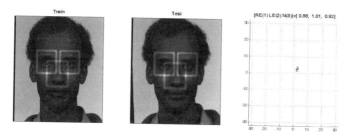

Fig. 10.4. Match Filter for Same Subject.

The next example (see Fig. 10.5) illustrates the case of parts that match but miss proper alignment. The training and test images come again from the same subject. The test image has been artificially cut at the middle and pulled apart so the interocular distance has increased and the nose is now split. MF indicates a good match for the eye components, poor match for the nose component, and that the peak locations for the eyes components do not align. The net result is that authentication fails.

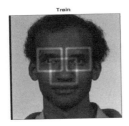 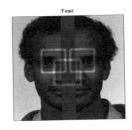 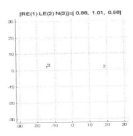

Fig. 10.5. Match Filter for Same Subject when Face Parts Are Distorted.

The last example illustrates the case for different subjects (see Fig. 10.6). The peaks for MF are weak and misaligned. Authentication fails.

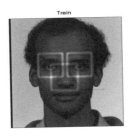 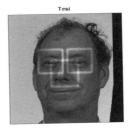 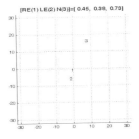

Fig. 10.6. Match Filter for Different Subjects.

We briefly review in a comparative fashion various but related correlation filters, beginning with the simple Match Filter (MF) and ending with the Optimal Trade-off Filter (OTF), to justify later on the novel design proposed for ARCF. The following convention on notation is used. Vector **b** will be in lower case and bold, matrix **B** will be upper case bold, and scalar b will be in lower case. **s** refers to a training vector, **n** to additive noise, **x** to test vector, **d** to the desired response vector and **h** to the filter weight. $\mathbf{D_x}$ refers to a matrix containing the power spectrum of **x** on the diagonal and zeros elsewhere, and ^{H} refers to conjugate transpose.

Match Filter

minimize $\mathbf{h}^H\mathbf{h}$

subject to $\mathbf{s}^H\mathbf{h} = \mathbf{d}$

Solution: $\mathbf{h} = \mathbf{s}(\mathbf{s}^H\mathbf{s})^{-1}\mathbf{d}$ (10.1)

MF is optimum for white noise and can train from only one exemplar **s**. Training with multiple exemplars requires using the Synthetic Discriminant Function (SDF) filter

Synthetic Discriminant Function (SDF) (Hester and Casasent, 1980)

minimize $\mathbf{h}^H\mathbf{h}$

subject to $\mathbf{S}^H\mathbf{h} = \mathbf{d}$

where $\mathbf{S} = [\mathbf{s_1} \cdots \mathbf{s_M}]$ and $\mathbf{d} = \mathbf{1_M}$ (vector of M ones)

Solution: $\mathbf{h} = \mathbf{S}(\mathbf{S}^H\mathbf{S})^{-1}\mathbf{d}$ (10.2)

SDF is robust to white noise. Robustness to general non-white noise leads to the Minimum Variance Synthetic Discriminant Filter (MVSDF)

Minimum Variance SDF (Kumar, 1986)

> minimize $h^H Q_n h$
>
> subject to $S^H h = d$ where $S = [s_1 \cdots s_M]$ and $d = 1_M$
>
> Solution: $h = Q_n^{-1} S (S^H Q_n^{-1} S)^{-1} d$ (10.3)

where Q_n is defined as a diagonal matrix that contains the average training exemplars' noise power spectrum. When the noise power spectrum is not known, it is typically assumed to be spectrally white, $Q^n = \sigma_n^2 I$, and the MVSDF filter reduces to the SDF filter. Like SDF and MF, MVSDF suffers from the presence of side lobes which are secondary peaks away from the true correlation peak on the correlation surface, even when training and testing with the same image. This problem is addressed using the Minimum Average Correlation Energy (MACE) filter

MACE Filter (Mahalanobis et al., 1987)

> minimize $h^H D_s h$
>
> subject to $S^H h = d$ where $S = [s_1 \cdots s_M]$ and $d = 1_M$
>
> Solution: $h = D_s^{-1} S (S^H D_s^{-1} S)^{-1} d$ (10.4)

where D_s is defined as a diagonal matrix that contains the average training exemplars' power spectrum. The MACE filter minimizes the correlation side lobes for the training images. It is, however, extremely sensitive to noise typically present in the test image. To improve MACE robustness to noise and distortion one should use instead the Optimal Trade-off filter (OTF) filter

Optimal Trade-off Filter (Refregier, 1991)

> minimum $\{h^H D_s h, h^H Q_n h\}$
>
> subject to $S^H h = d$ where $S = [s_1 \cdots s_M]$ and $d = 1_M$
>
> Solution: $h = T^{-1} S (S^H T^{-1} S)^{-1} d$ (10.5)

where $T = (\alpha D_s + \sqrt{1 - \alpha^2} Q_n)$. OTF is designed to trade off, using α, between correlation side lobe suppression and noise robustness. $\alpha = 1$ results in the MACE filter (maximum side lobe suppression), while $\alpha = 0$ results in the MVSDF filter (maximum noise robustness). $\alpha = 0$ with white noise assumption results in the SDF filter. OTF has been used on face verification (Kumar et al., 2004).

The correlation filters described so far do not take advantage of the information provided by test data, e.g., noise and distortions. Similar to beam forming (Cox et al., 1987), the correlation filter should be designed to adapt and automatically tune out the actual noise/distortion observed in test data without making any arbitrary assumptions about the structure of the noise. The immediate result is an adaptive correlation filter whose output correlation surface has an optimally low average side lobe level. The correlation peak, however, is still sensitive to noise/distortion. To make the correlation peak robust to noise/distortion, an adjustable loading parameter, which can be derived using an approach motivated by beam forming or Tikhonov regularization, is introduced. This leads to a robust filter constrained by a loading parameter and based on the magnitude of the match filter weight (Lai and Wechsler, 2006). The adaptive (A) and robust (R) components for the new adaptive and robust correlation filter (ARCF) are formally explained below.

Adaptiveness. If the noise/distortion in test data can be measured then it can be directly minimized. This approach is used by both MVSDF and OTF when Q_n, the noise power spectrum or covariance, is known. When $\mathbf{Q_n}$ is not known, it is assumed to be white. A different approach, motivated by adaptive beam forming, learns about the noise/distortion in test data, and automatically adjusts the correlation filter in order to minimize it. This is accomplished by minimizing the output correlation energy due to test data subject to a unit response to unit training data

$$\text{minimize} \quad \mathbf{h}^H \mathbf{D_x} \mathbf{h}$$

$$\text{subject to} \quad \mathbf{S}^H \mathbf{h} = \mathbf{d} \text{ where } \mathbf{S} = [\mathbf{s}_1 \cdots \mathbf{s}_M] \text{ and } \mathbf{d} = \mathbf{1}_M \quad (10.6)$$

where $\mathbf{D_x}$ is a diagonal matrix that contains the power spectrum of the test exemplar. The (still non-robust) adaptive correlation filter solution, $\mathbf{h} = \mathbf{D_x}^{-1}\mathbf{S}(\mathbf{S}^H \mathbf{D_x}^{-1}\mathbf{S})^{-1}\mathbf{d}$, is similar to the MACE filter, except that $\mathbf{D_s}$ is now replaced by $\mathbf{D_x}$. The use of test data $\mathbf{D_x}$, in addition to training data $\mathbf{S}$, in the design of the filter, is different from previous approaches to correlation filter design. The filter tunes itself to the noise present in the test data in order to reject it. The output correlation surface has an optimally low side lobe level, irrespective of the actual structure of the noise. This is different from MACE, which lacks an optimization criterion to reject the noise from test data. It is also different from MVSDF and OTF where the noise information $\mathbf{Q_n}$ must be known or has to be assumed to be white even when the actual noise/distortion is not.

Robustness. A robust CF should produce a stable correlation peak that changes very little even when there is a large change in the strength of distortion/noise. To minimize the sensitivity of the correlation peak to noise/distortion, the rate of change of the squared correlation peak with respect to the strength of the noise/distortion is now minimized. Let the squared correlation peak be $p = E\{|\mathbf{h}^H \mathbf{x}|^2\}$

$$
\begin{aligned}
p &= E\{\mathbf{h}^H \mathbf{x}\mathbf{x}^H \mathbf{h}\} \\
&= E\{\mathbf{h}^H(\mathbf{s}+\mathbf{n})(\mathbf{s}+\mathbf{n})^H \mathbf{h}\} \\
&= E\{\mathbf{h}^H(\mathbf{s}\mathbf{s}^H + \mathbf{s}\mathbf{n}^H + \mathbf{n}\mathbf{s}^H + \mathbf{n}\mathbf{n}^H)\mathbf{h}\} \\
&= \mathbf{h}^H \mathbf{s}\mathbf{s}^H \mathbf{h} + \mathbf{h}^H E\{\mathbf{s}\mathbf{n}^H + \mathbf{n}\mathbf{s}^H + \mathbf{n}\mathbf{n}^H\}\mathbf{h} \\
&= \mathbf{h}^H \mathbf{s}\mathbf{s}^H \mathbf{h} + \mathbf{h}^H \mathbf{Q}\mathbf{h} \\
&= \mathbf{h}^H \mathbf{s}\mathbf{s}^H \mathbf{h} + \zeta \mathbf{h}^H \mathbf{N}\mathbf{h} \quad (10.7)
\end{aligned}
$$

where the covariance $\mathbf{N}$ is normalized so that the average of the diagonal elements is 1, and ζ is the strength parameter. One seeks to minimize $\frac{dp}{d\zeta} = \mathbf{h}^H \mathbf{N}\mathbf{h}$. When the noise/distortion is not known, it is typically assumed to be white, $\mathbf{N} = \mathbf{I}$. The ARCF formulation becomes

$$\text{minimize the output correlation energy} \quad \mathbf{h}^H \mathbf{D_x} \mathbf{h}$$

$$\text{subject to unit response to training signal} \quad \mathbf{S}^H \mathbf{h} = \mathbf{d}$$

$$\text{subject to sensitivity constraint} \quad \mathbf{h}^H \mathbf{I}\mathbf{h} \le \alpha \quad (10.8)$$

The solution is $\mathbf{h} = (\mathbf{D_x} + \epsilon \mathbf{I})^{-1}\mathbf{S}[\mathbf{S}^H(\mathbf{D_x} + \epsilon \mathbf{I})^{-1}\mathbf{S}]^{-1}\mathbf{d}$ for ϵ chosen to satisfy the constraint $\mathbf{h}^H \mathbf{I}\mathbf{h} \le \alpha$ (Lai and Wechsler, 2006).

The solution for $\epsilon = 0$ is $\mathbf{h} = \mathbf{D_x}^{-1}\mathbf{S}[\mathbf{S}^H \mathbf{D_x}^{-1}\mathbf{S}]^{-1}\mathbf{d}$. Similar to the MACE filter, it is sensitive to noise and distortion. The solution $\mathbf{h} = \mathbf{S}[\mathbf{S}^H \mathbf{S}]^{-1}\mathbf{d}$ is found when $\epsilon = \infty$. This is the same solution as the SDF filter and the correlation peak displays maximum robustness to white noise. The magnitude of the SDF weight is the smallest among the adaptive correlation filters that are robust to white noise. The choice for ϵ thus satisfies the constraint $\mathbf{h}^H \mathbf{h} \le k|\mathbf{h}_{SDF}|^2$ where $k \ge 1$.

Tikhonov Regularization. The derivation of ARCF can also be done using Tikhonov regularization. Suppose some objective function $f(\mathbf{h})$ that has to be minimized is very flat, which makes it difficult to find its minimum. Tikhonov regularization approximates the minimum by adding a quadratic term to force the new objective function to be strongly convex and to have a unique solution. Rather than minimizing $f(\mathbf{h})$ one minimizes instead $f(\mathbf{h}) + \epsilon|\mathbf{h}|^2$. ARCF is derived using Tikhonov regularization as shown next. The objective function $f(\mathbf{h}) = \mathbf{h}^H \mathbf{D_x} \mathbf{h}$ may not have a unique minimum when $\mathbf{D_x}$ is ill-conditioned. One adds the quadratic term $\epsilon \mathbf{h}^H \mathbf{h}$ in order to make the new objective (correlation energy) function $\mathbf{h}^H \mathbf{D_x} \mathbf{h} + \epsilon \mathbf{h}^H \mathbf{h} = \mathbf{h}^H (\mathbf{D_x} + \epsilon \mathbf{I}) \mathbf{h}$ strongly convex so it has a unique solution. ϵ is a positive number that controls the degree of regularization. ARCF formulation using Tikhonov regularization yields the same solution as the one (eq, 10.8) derived earlier

$$\text{minimize} \quad \mathbf{h}^H (\mathbf{D_x} + \epsilon \mathbf{I}) \mathbf{h}$$

$$\text{subject to unit response} \quad \mathbf{S}^H \mathbf{h} = \mathbf{d}$$

$$\text{solution} \quad \mathbf{h} = (\mathbf{D_x} + \epsilon \mathbf{I})^{-1} \mathbf{S} [\mathbf{S}^H (\mathbf{D_x} + \epsilon \mathbf{I})^{-1} \mathbf{S}]^{-1} \mathbf{d}$$

$$(10.9)$$

Fig. 10.7 shows how different correlation filters compare when matching the left eye component in terms of both representation and location. One can see that ARCF outscores MF, MACE, and OTF in terms of its ability to discriminate between the true peak corresponding to the left eye and the false peak caused by the right eye. In addition, one notes that ARCF displays the lowest average side lobe, which indicates robustness to noise. The advantage of ARCF over competing CF becomes even more pronounced when noise is added. The false peak for OTF shows up as the strongest one (see Fig. 10.8).

The architecture for recognition-by-parts is shown in Fig. 10.9. The face parts for an enrolled subject and their counterparts from test data claiming the same identity are combined on a part-by-part basis to build corresponding ARCF filters. The outputs from ARCF are combined here in a simple and straightforward fashion using LDA, which learns the optimal direction for separation. An alternative worth to be pursued is to use the strangeness and combine matching and configural information using boosting (see Sect. 9.7). ARCF outputs are projected on the LDA direction axis to find the overall score. ROC at FAR = 1% using scores from both authentic and impostor claims determines the optimal decision threshold. It was feasible to learn the optimal LDA direction and the corresponding decision threshold from one facial data base population, e.g. FERET, and use them for a different population, e.g., AR.

ARCF processing proceeds as follows. Faces are rotated and scaled first for the eye centers to align. A common full-face mask is applied to the image to extract the full face, and the face is normalized by its mean and standard deviation to have zero mean and unit variance. A mean face is also computed from the whole training population. The final preprocessed face is the normalized face from whom the mean face is subtracted. A single but complete training face image yields multiple face parts by applying different masks to expose the important face components. Seven face parts that correspond to left eye, right eye, nose, mouth, left half-face, right half-face, and the full face without the hair, are used. The relative location of these parts is maintained in the mask such that their overlay reconstructs the original whole face. When the face parts are perfectly correlated with the original whole face the components come from, the correlation peaks align at a single point in the correlation surface. The strength of the correlation peaks indicates how similar the individual face components are. Tight clustering of the locations for those correlation peaks indicates proper alignment.

The face model consists of a collection of ARCF filters, one for each face part. Each ARCF filter corresponds to one of the parts and is derived using both the training/enrolled face and the corresponding part from the test face. Multiple training and/or test faces are allowed. The output of the ARCF filter bank is a vector that contains the correlation peak strengths and their distances from the origin. The vector consists of 14 components corresponding to seven correlation peaks' strength and seven distances. The ARCF filter bank could be expanded to include filters that correspond

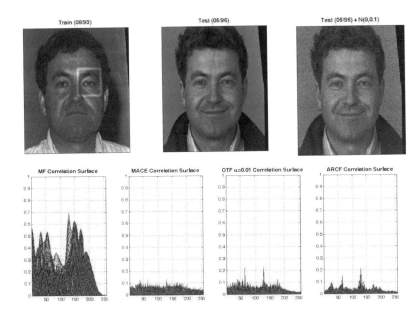

The left eye component is matched against the whole face using various CF. The true peak is at the center of the horizontal axis. Note that MF has the strongest true peak, but it also has significant false peaks. MACE correlation peak is sensitive to distortion and is barely visible. OTF has a good true peak but also an equally strong false peak. Of the four CF, ARCF shows the largest separation between the true peak and the much weaker false peak and has the lowest average side lobe level.

Fig. 10.7. Distortion Effects on MF, MACE, OTF and ARCF.

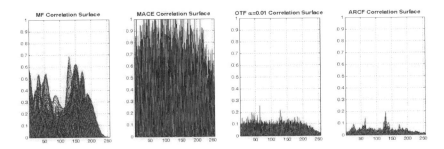

Fig. 10.8. Additive White Noise Effects on MF, MACE, OTF, and ARCF.

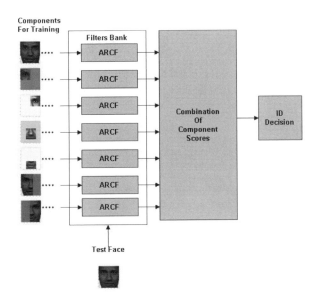

Fig. 10.9. ARCF Recognition-by-Parts Architecture.

to additional parts extracted using the golden ratio template. The distance information is used to enforce proper alignment by eliminating false peaks using an empirically found threshold. By having a bank of ARCF filters, where each filter is trained on a single face component, instead of a single ARCF filter trained on all seven face components, the intermediate outputs for each face components can be monitored and interpreted individually. The intermediate outputs can be also combined non-linearly to exploit face symmetry as described next.

Face symmetry is exploited using non-linear processing of the individual correlation peaks. For symmetric face components, such as the left and right eyes, or left and right half faces, the most dominant correlation peak is used. One computes three similarity scores for full-face (F), half-faces (H), and face parts (P), with H the maximum score for the left and right half-faces and P a linear combination of [max (left eye, right eye), nose, mouth] using the weight $\mathbf{w}$ derived using LDA on training data drawn from FERET. In particular, $\mathbf{w}$ is the optimal projection that separates the authentic class from the imposter class. If any of the three similarity scores exceeds its respective threshold, authentication succeeds (Accept). If all three similarity scores are below their respective threshold, authentication fails (Reject). Experimental results have shown the feasibility and usefulness of ARCF for reliable face recognition using face images from both FERET and AR.

ARCF succeeds to uncover the identity behind disguise. Test images were obtained from those used for training by applying face blush and sunglasses (see the middle box in Fig. 10.10). In both cases, the parts similarity score P was the strongest among the three similarity scores and exceeded the threshold. The notation used inside the "match" boxes is F, H, h, E, e, N and M for the full face, right and left half-face, right and left eye, nose, and mouth, respectively. The next experiment addressed occlusion. The faces, both for training and testing, come from the AR database (see the rightmost box in Fig. 10.10). The strong correlation peaks for parts that are not occluded are aligned such that the similarity score P is the strongest among the three similarity scores and exceeds the a priori threshold. Authentication succeeds to uncover the identity behind occlusion. The weak correlation peaks for the full face and eyes (see Test1 with sunglasses), and mouth (see Test2 with scarf) cannot distract ARCF from locking on the correct identification in both cases. The same experiment has also shown that holistic components do not help with recognition for occluded faces.

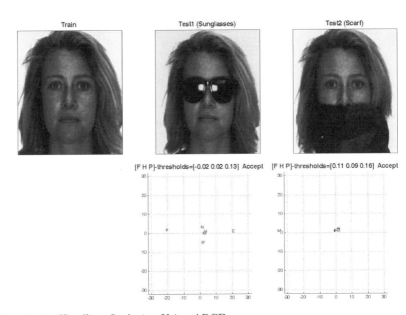

Fig. 10.10. Handling Occlusion Using ARCF.

The next experiment addressed the effects of varying illumination on ARCF. The face images used for training and testing came again from AR (see Fig. 10.11). The test images are different from the training ones in terms of varying illumination. The correlation peaks for the face seen below are strong and are all aligned, the similarity scores exceed the thresholds, and authentication succeeds.

The effects of temporal change on ARCF were analyzed last. The face images used for training and testing came from FERET (see Fig. 10.12). The test images were acquired two years later than the face images used for training. The correlation peaks for the face seen below are strong and are all aligned, the similarity scores exceed the thresholds, and authentication succeeds again.

10.7 Associative, Distributed and Holographic Memories

Matching for similarity can be implemented using template correlation or projections implemented as a vector dot product. The latter approach, discussed in this section, is closely related to the filter banks discussed in the preceding section. Some of the motivation for using such projections comes from Kohonen (1987), who has shown that "orthogonal projection operations have the property of correcting and standardizing incomplete key patterns towards "memorized" reference patterns." One hundred reference face patterns, of size 54×54 and using eight gray levels, were learned using the

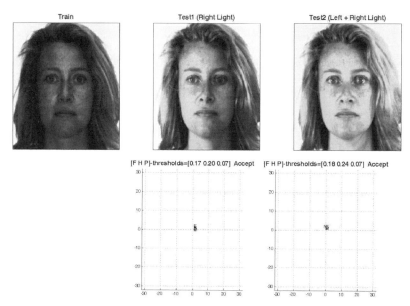

Fig. 10.11. Varying Illumination Using ARCF.

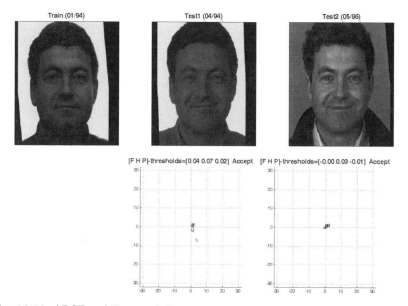

Fig. 10.12. ARCF and Temporal Change.

auto-associative memory (AM) model. Noise suppression that withstands 25% masking was also demonstrated. Distributed associative memories (DAM), a generalization of AM and similar to holographic memories, can learn stimuli-response associations and have shown resilience to noise, partial occlusion, and (random or continuous) memory faults (Wechsler and Zimmerman, 1988; Wechsler, 1990). As matching by projection is sensitive to shift, invariance has to be explicitly encoded for, e.g., using conformal (polar) maps.

The mapping $\mathbf{M}$ learned by the DAM is $\mathbf{MS} = \mathbf{R}$, where $\mathbf{S}$, e.g., face patterns, and $\mathbf{R}$, e.g., face patterns or face identity for $\mathbf{R} = \mathbf{I}$, correspond to stimuli $\{\mathbf{s}\}$ and response $\{\mathbf{r}\}$ matrices, respectively. The stimuli $\{\mathbf{s}\}$ are different versions for the same face. The optimal mapping $\mathbf{M}$ is the least-square solution for

$$\min \|\mathbf{MS} - \mathbf{R}\|^2 \tag{10.10}$$

The solution is $\mathbf{M} = \mathbf{RS}^+$, with $\mathbf{S}^+$ the pseudo-inverse of $\mathbf{S}$ where $\mathbf{S}^+ = \mathbf{S}'(\mathbf{SS}')^{-1}$ and $\mathbf{S}^+\mathbf{S} = \mathbf{I}$. The auto-associative case, when $\mathbf{R} = \mathbf{S}$, yields $\mathbf{M} = \mathbf{S}(\mathbf{S}'\mathbf{S})^{-1}\mathbf{S}'$ for independent stimuli $\{\mathbf{s_i}\}$. Note that the mapping $\mathbf{M}$ and the SDF filter $\mathbf{h}$ (see Sect. 10.6) are closely related, i.e., $\mathbf{h} = \mathbf{S}(\mathbf{S}'\mathbf{S})^{-1}\mathbf{d} = \mathbf{P_S}\mathbf{d}$ vs. $\mathbf{M} = \mathbf{S}(\mathbf{S}'\mathbf{S})^{-1}\mathbf{S}'$ with $\mathbf{S}'$ substituting for the filter response $\mathbf{d}$. One defines the projection matrix $\mathbf{P}$ such that $\mathbf{P} = \mathbf{P_S}\mathbf{S}' = \mathbf{SP}_{S'}$. The columns of $\mathbf{P_S}$ form the basis of the subspace spanned by $\mathbf{S}$.

When there is no cross-talk between the stimuli learned, i.e., $\mathbf{s_i s_j} = \delta_{ij}$, the pseudo-inverse matrix becomes the transpose matrix, i.e., $\mathbf{S}^+ = \mathbf{S}'$, and the auto-associative mapping yields $\mathbf{M} = \mathbf{SS}'$ for $\mathbf{S} = \mathbf{R}$. Alternatively, the optimal mapping $\mathbf{M}$ can be found using the recursive Widrow-Hoff delta rule, i.e., least-mean square (LMS). The solution found is $\mathbf{M}(t + 1) = \mathbf{M}(t) - \epsilon(t)[\mathbf{M}(t)\mathbf{s}(t + 1) - \mathbf{r}(t + 1)]\mathbf{s}(t + 1)$, where t stands for cycle or iteration, and $\epsilon(t)$, the decay factor used for convergence and stabilization, behaves like $\epsilon(t) \to 0$. When the stimuli and response matrices are the same, i.e., $\mathbf{S} = \mathbf{R}$, the memory reduces to $\mathbf{M} = \mathbf{SS}^+$. The last case applies when faces are associated with themselves for authentication and retrieval purposes. The same mapping $\mathbf{M}$ can be expressed in terms of novelty or residual filters $(\mathbf{I} - \alpha\mathbf{S}'\mathbf{S})$. The solution is the von Neumann expression

$$\mathbf{M} = \alpha\mathbf{R}\sum_{k=0}^{\infty}(\mathbf{I} - \alpha\mathbf{S}'\mathbf{S})^k\mathbf{S}' \tag{10.11}$$

where $0 < \alpha < \frac{2}{c}$, c is the largest eigenvalue for $\mathbf{S}'\mathbf{S}$, and $\mathbf{M_0} = \alpha\mathbf{RS}'$. The von Neumann expansion is similar to the projection operators $\mathbf{P}$. For $y \in \mathbf{R}^n$ there exist a symmetric and idempotent matrix/projection operator $\mathbf{P}$ that derives $y = \{\hat{y}, \tilde{y}\}, \hat{y} \in \mathbf{L} \subset \mathbf{R}^n, \hat{y} = \mathbf{P}y, \tilde{y} \in L^{\perp} \subset \mathbf{R}^n, \tilde{y} = (\mathbf{I} - \mathbf{P})y$ such that $\mathbf{P} = \mathbf{SS}^+$ and $(\mathbf{I} - \mathbf{P}) = (\mathbf{I} - \mathbf{SS}^+)$. The decomposition shown reflects the geometric interpretation of the well-known orthogonality principle. The novelty filters show the extent to which the recall is different from the pattern that encodes the true identity.

The memory recall for some face pattern $\mathbf{s_i}$ is $\hat{s}_i = \mathbf{Ms_i} = \mathbf{R}(\mathbf{S}^+\mathbf{s_i}) = \sum h_j \mathbf{r_i}$. The weights h_j indicate the similarity between the stimuli $\mathbf{s_i}$ and each response $\mathbf{r_j}$ learned (see SDF). One significant peak, while all the other returns are small, is a clear indication that the face or identity has been properly retrieved. The quality of the face reconstructed can be measured by computing the cosine of the angle between $\mathbf{s_i}$ and $\hat{s}_i$. Perfect recall or reconstruction occurs when the cosine value is one. Cross talk between stimuli becomes apparent when the recall histogram $\mathbf{h}$ has more than one significant peak. The best case occurs when the only significant weights are those that belong to different versions of the same face while the weights that correspond to similar or negative examples are small. Such an occurrence most likely comes from a face that belongs to the same distribution as the one that was encoded by the original stimuli. The small weights merely remind of insignificant similarities to other faces. Memory recall can take place for a set of face probes $\{\mathbf{s_i}\}$ rather than merely one face. This is the case when authentication takes places between sets or video segments. DAM can serve as a filter, an indexing/hashing scheme, and/or a base that defines the individual face space. DAM can return whole patterns, while ARCF only returns the pattern's identity. The fault tolerance property for DAM transpires from

$$\frac{\sigma_{output}^2}{\sigma_{input}^2} = \frac{1}{m}\text{trace}(\mathbf{MM}') = \frac{n}{m} \tag{10.12}$$

where n and m are the number of associations learned and the stimuli dimension, respectively, $n << m$, and the DAM is auto-associative, i.e., $\mathbf{S} = \mathbf{R}$. The smaller the number of associations and the larger the dimension of the stimuli, the better the recall is.

Associative mappings and linear regression are also closely related. $\mathbf{S}$ and $\mathbf{R}$ play now the role of the independent and dependent variables for regression. The weight histogram $\mathbf{h}$ corresponds to regression coefficients whose significance for both rejection and novelty can be assessed using the *student t-test*. Additional relations between DAM, ARCF and model selection show up using regularization. In particular, when the training data is highly correlated, the matrix $\mathbf{SS}'$ becomes near singular and smaller eigenvalues or noise dominate the computation of the inverse $(\mathbf{SS}')^{-1}$ matrix. The solution, based upon regularization, defines the ridge regression risk (RRR) using the original objective function whose minimization is sought and a penalty constraint on the norm of the solution

$$RRR = ||\mathbf{MS} - \mathbf{R}||^2 + \lambda||\mathbf{M}|| \tag{10.13}$$

The regularized solution is $\mathbf{M}_\lambda = \mathbf{S}(\mathbf{S}'\mathbf{S} + \lambda\mathbf{I})^{-1}\mathbf{S}'$. Ridge regression for $\lambda = 0$ is equivalent to the pseudo-inverse solution, while for $\lambda = 1$ ridge regression becomes constant and predicts the average face pattern. The optimal value for λ is found using cross-validation.

DAM and likewise ARCF can function beyond the standard feed-forward mode. The outputs coming from either DAM or ARCF, possibly augmented by further contextual information or face residuals, can be fed back to percolate through as additional inputs. The residuals could guide exploration similar to active and selective perception. Attention preempts segmentation and makes the whole recognition process more efficient and more effective. DAM and ARCF continue to iterate until there are no further changes in the recall.

11. Augmented Cognition

I keep six honest [W5+] service men
(They taught me all I knew):
Their names are:
WHO *and* **WHAT**
WHEN *and* **WHERE**
WHY *and* **HOW**
(Just So Stories, Rudyard Kipling, 1902)

Augmented cognition extends users' abilities in order to improve their performance and to provide for graceful degradation. "At the most general level, the field of Augmented Cognition has the explicit goal of utilizing methods and designs that harness computation and explicit knowledge about human limitations to open bottlenecks and address the biases and deficits in human cognition" (Schmorrow and McBride, 2004) [1]. Here, it is the computer rather than the human user that needs to have its cognition augmented in order to overcome biases and enhance its performance. Towards that end, one seeks a closed loop and reliable face recognition system, which is aware of subjects' intentions and emotions, and processes faces accordingly. There is feedback, the interface is adaptive, and anticipation is driven by predictions. Both context and the subjects' (mental states) models are attended to or inferred to leverage the connections between personal appearance, cognitive state, and behavior, for enhanced identification and authentication. Facial expressions are usually considered a nuisance for face recognition, but not here. Augmented cognition can parse both covert and overt communication, supports switching among contexts, and helps in counter deception. In summary, augmented cognition provides the upper management layer needed by data fusion to (a) make appropriate choices for bandwidth, context, and specific functionality; (b) adapt, prioritize and coordinate; (c) reduce the effects of cross - talk ("modal") interference; and (d) handle in a flexible way time-varying inputs.

The questions augmented cognition addresses are not limited to human identity. The questions are also about what the (face) messages convey and the reasons behind them, the place and time (sequence), and the channels of communication used. $W5+$ is a succinct framework to handle such queries. It bears a close relationship to several new disciplines focusing on human computer intelligent interaction (HCII), including aware computing, cognitive prostheses, human-centered computing, and pervasive and ubiquitous computing. Yet another emerging discipline, socially aware computing (Pentland, 2005), takes into account the social context in support of group activities. The goal for social computing (and intelligence) is to analyze and predict human behavior. It includes, among others, categorization, hierarchies, and group cohesion. Collaboration and team work, distant learning, and teleconferencing benefit from reflection on attitudes and/or opinions that can be inferred from face expressions and mental models. Belief networks are the method of choice to model and implement augmented cognition. The belief networks play the "what if" anticipation game based upon bidirectional sensitivity analysis for data changes using both causality

---

[1] http://www.augmented.cognition.org/overview

and abduction modes of reasoning. Semantic and pragmatic (re)alignment for optimal decision making takes place using profiles, preferences, desired functionalities, and observed behaviors. The profiles are built using case-based learning (Kolodner, 2004). Paralanguage, part and parcel of augmented cognition, refers to any (nonverbal) communication that goes beyond spoken words and includes inflection, emotions, and gestures. Sadness, according to Knapp and Hall (2005), is communicated when "the inner corners of the eyebrows are drawn up. The skin below the eyebrows is triangulated, with the inner corner up. The upper-eyelid inner corner is raised." The medium of paralanguage or non-verbal face (and body) display plays a major role in face recognition and avatars' design. There are several conversational levels including the arm, face, and head. Face communication includes gestures to modify and/or help with understanding, e.g., nodding or shaking the head, frowning for puzzlement, and raising the eyebrows for questioning (Bruce and Young, 1998). Gaze direction reveals mental state and social contact, e.g., intimacy, directness, and honesty (Baron-Cohen and Cross, 1992). Marshall McLuhan's "the medium is the message" underlies augmented cognition.

11.1 Paralanguage

Emotions have an affective valence, i.e., a positive or negative feeling. Surprise is considered to be valence neutral, before giving way to happiness or sadness, whose valences are positive and negative, respectively. Interest, however, is an inner or cognitive state rather than just an emotion (Cole, 1998). The face, however, is more than just an expression of thoughts and emotions. The genetic narrative for facial displays, modulated by specific survival needs, led Panksepp (1982) and Gray (1982) to suggest specific biological drives that explain the "basic" emotions witnessed. Rather than merely serving as the means for communication, the drives are special routines or programs that provide an indication for intention and predict human behavior. Examples of such early but important drives for survival include fight and flight, which signals fear and horror, and inhibition, which communicates anxiety. Ortony and Taylor (1990) model anger as a mix of several drives "The furrowed brow might accompany frustration or puzzlement; the open set mouth, pre adapted attack; the compressed lips, resolve; the raised upper eyelids, increased vigilance and attention" (Cole, 1998). Men are generally less sensitive to emotions than women with the exception of spotting anger. Williams and Mattingley (2006) have recently shown that "angry male faces are found more rapidly than angry female faces by both men and women. In addition, men find angry faces of both genders faster than women, whereas women find socially relevant expressions (for example, happy or sad) more rapidly." Anger signals potential threat, captures attention, and therefore "stands out" in a crowd. Such an enhanced ability, according to evolutionary psychology, allowed men faster reaction times for appeasement, attack or defense, and had and still has survival advantages for defusing potential threats. The explanation that evolutionary psychology would suggest that to defuse threat such ability led men to faster reaction times for appeasement, attack or defense, and had and still has survival advantages. The drives themselves can be further decomposed or assembled from sub-drives and so on. Facial display and emotional state are not necessarily equivalent (Friedlund, 1991). There are, however, many possible associations, e.g., the intention to fight and the display of anger. Staring, usually rude, is used for control and power. Medusa's look petrifies humans. People "face off" and "face down," when competing. "Saving face" and "losing face" are related to dignity. Expressions affect or reinforce emotions. Smile, and you'll feel much better.

Fernandez-Dols et al. (2001) discuss inconsistencies in the way emotions and facial expressions are linked. The same ambiguities, which affect natural language processing, hamper paralanguage too. The domain of discussion must first make the distinction, regarding behavior, between thoughts and emotions, and their consequences. The consequences are observed by all but the intentions are hidden. The observables are expressed using communication via either regular language or paralanguage. The search or inference, for the physiological processes behind the observed or expressed behavior, is similar to that undertaken by Hidden Markov Models (HMM). The problem raised by Fernandez-Dols et al. (2001) is that "emotions are particularly opaque to and challenge language." The solutions proposed to lock on the meaning of emotions vary according to the "ontological status of emotions" and can be best described "as lying along a continuum between two extreme ontological perspectives. At one extreme, which could be labeled as Idealism (or Platonic realism) [intangible] emotions are universal, real entities that can shape what people say about emotions but are independent of language. At the other end, which could be labeled as Nominalist, emotions are mere labels, i.e., words that lack a universal, real denotation, and summarize the sameness of some psychological events. Psychological events labeled as emotions are specific and idiosyncratic; there are no universal realities such as emotions."

The empirical but standard approach for studying emotions goes back to Darwin's (1872) *The Expression of the Emotions in Man and Animals*. The approach, more recently associated with Izard (1971) and summarized by Ekman (1992) (see Sect. 11.2), has been idealistic in its belief in universal emotions. According to the idealistic view, there are basic emotions, whose production (modulated by culture) and (innate) recognition has been regulated by evolutionary needs. Today, however, one is constantly aware about and seeks individual (rather than universal) profiles and preferences. Emotions are further driven by context and motivation. Human behavior is situated, and above all, sequenced or time dependent rather than static. As an example, "most of the smiles found in the [classical painting] works from the Prado [museum in Madrid] are displayed by vulgar, drunk or crazy models, or by children. Smiling was not linked, as it is today, with beauty; a fixed, open smile was a sign, not of happiness, but of simpleness." Evidence that "patterns of facial movements" are not the same, that attribution of emotion is not universal, and that the actual expression of emotion can vary, are brought by Fernandez-Dols. et al (2001) in support of the Nominalist approach.

According to Ginsburg and Harrington (1996), "emotion is action in context." Blank or neutral faces involve no facial movements but can still convey emotions. Action amounts here to being left speechless and doing nothing. Emotions are controlled and pragmatic rather than merely unique and universally determined. They play out according to (social) context and are further mediated by the constant feedback received. The alternative view ultimately espoused by Fernandez-Dols et al. (2001) is that "facial expressions are not [persistent] objects or concepts but [rather experienced only once and not unique] events." Facial expressions cannot be recognized but rather have to be categorized. According to this view, the facial expression is an icon, which suggests similarity rather than a pointer to some static and unique emotions.

11.2 Face Expressions

According to the idealistic approach, at least some facial expressions are not culturally determined, but appear to be universal and thus presumably biological in their origin. The expressions the idealistic approach finds to be universal include anger, disgust, fear, joy, sadness and surprise (see Fig. 11.1). "These signals emerge in infancy and on a reliable timetable. They are almost certainly unlearned. The smile and surprise appear [first] at birth. Thalidomide babies born blind, deaf, and armless show them" (McNeill, 1998). A global survey sponsored by the National Geographic Magazine is now underway [2] to help scientists understand how people identify human facial expressions. The computer study of face expressions traces its origins to the Facial Action Coding System (FACS), which is based on measurements of facial actions (Ekman and Friesen, 1978). FACS defines a repertoire of Action Units (AU) that is driven by the complex interplay between the skull/cranium and bones, the soft

---

[2] www.ngm.com/Survey2005

tissue/flesh, and the muscles. The face expressions are the result of the collective activity of the face muscles. Forehead muscles are most important and are usually most difficult to dissemble.

There are thousands of facial expressions and their combinations of AU vary in intensity, level of control, and genuineness (from feigned to real). "The most easily recognized expression on earth is the smile, the flare of happiness. It employs two muscles. The *zygomatic major* curves the mouth and the *orbicularis oculi* hoist the cheek, pressing skin toward the eye in a squint of joy. In a wider smile, the teeth flash and the eyes glisten. Not every smile indicates pleasure, but the true smile is unmistakable" (McNeill, 1998). Smiles can get quite complex and convey a wide range of meanings including agreement and contempt. There is no unique emotion linked to a smile. :) signals good will in our email communications but not yet in official documents :).

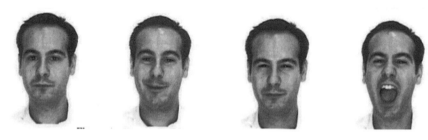

Fig. 11.1. Face Expressions from the AR Data Base.

The Cohn-Kanade AU (Action Units)-Coded Facial Expression Database from CMU includes approximately 2000 image sequences from over 200 subjects [3]. Subjects were instructed by an experimenter to perform a series of 23 facial displays that included single action units (e.g., AU 12, or lip corners pulled obliquely) and combinations of action units (e.g., AU 1 + 2, or inner and outer brows raised). Subjects began and ended each display from a neutral face. Before performing each display, an experimenter described and modeled the desired display. Six of the displays were based on descriptions of prototypic emotions (i.e., joy, surprise, anger, fear, disgust, and sadness). These six tasks and mouth opening in the absence of other action units were coded by a certified FACS coder.

The analysis of face expressions serves several purposes. Among them, indexing of inner states and emotion displayed, either spontaneous or deliberate, for augmented cognition. Similar to pose detection, which leads to subsequent face recognition indexed for that particular pose, one would train for recognizing faces constrained by the specific face expressions displayed. Face expression analysis requires image acquisition, image representation, and classification. The methods used to represent face expressions involve the aggregation of deformations starting from some neutral state. The methods are similar to those employed to define and encode the face space or those used to transform and warp faces for animation and virtual reality. The latter capture the dynamic aspect and bear resemblance to motion analysis, e.g., (dense) optical flow and tracking. MPEG-4-SNHC (Koenen, 2000), characteristic of such methods includes analysis, coding, and animation (of talking heads) (see Sect. 8.4). Recognition and interpretation are interchangeable.

As discussed earlier, facial expressions are deformations that result from the contractions of facial muscles. "Typical changes of muscular activities are brief, lasting for a few seconds, but rarely more than $5s$ or less than $250ms$. Of importance is the

---

[3] http://vasc.ri.cmu.edu/idb/html/face/facial_expression/

location of facial actions, their intensity as well as their dynamics. [Timing of] facial expressions can be described with the aid of three temporal parameters: onset (attack), apex (sustain), and offset (relaxation)" (Fasel and Luettin, 2003). Demographics, factors related to denial and deception, and the geometry and ambient lighting experienced during the image acquisition process, affect the analysis of face expressions. The representations used are local, e.g., Gabor filters, or global, e.g., PCA. Classification aggregates and relates among temporal information, e.g., HMM or (recursive) neural networks. Evidence accrues using the type of deformations, and temporal evolution. The net result is that tracking and interpretation of face expressions are intertwined and become feasible. Time is of the essence, and is most important for disambiguating between alternative face interpretations. A note of interest is that aphasics, people who show deficit in understanding spoken language, are "unusually sensitive to deceitful behavior and significantly more accurate at detecting lies," possibly from "the growth of compensatory skills" (Etkoff et al., 2000). Representative studies on face expression analysis are reported next.

Donato et al. (1999) report on an extensive study concerning the automatic classification of facial expressions from image sequences. The methods used include the analysis of facial motion through estimation of optical flow; holistic spatial analysis, such as PCA, independent component analysis (ICA), local feature analysis (LFA), and LDA; and methods based on the outputs of local filters, such as Gabor wavelet representations and local PCA. Best performance on classifying twelve facial actions of the upper and lower face were obtained using Gabor wavelets and ICA. Local filters, high-spatial frequencies, and statistical independence were found most important for classifying the facial actions. Cohn et al. (2002) have measured facial expressions over intervals from four to twelve months, and found that individual differences were stable over time and "sufficiently strong that individuals were recognized on the basis of their facial behavior alone at rates comparable to that for a commercial face recognition system." They conclude that "facial action units convey unique information about person identity that can inform interpretation of psychological states, person recognition, and design of individual avatars." The classification and/or interpretation of facial expression are quite difficult and prone to error due to the many factors, known and unknown, which affect and drive our emotive expressions. Diogene, the Greek philosopher, did not fare much better using a lantern at night in his search for an "honest" face.

Fidaleo (2003) describes a new approach that integrates analysis and data-driven synthesis for emotive gesture and speech analysis, on one side, and 3D avatar animation, on the other. This is essential for the development of intelligent human-machine interfaces. The abstract parameters that interface between the control signals and the animated character allow model and animation independence. Such use of indirect or decoupling methods contributes to significant savings in computation. There is less realism, which the authors claim is not necessarily the goal of animation, but expensive 3D facial motion capture and tracking is avoided as a result. Standard 3D employs stereo and takes advantage of epipolar geometry, with or without markers. This is, however, expensive, difficult to calibrate and synchronize, and quite sensitive to noise. Fidaleo and Neumann (2002) have the face partitioned into local regions of change labeled as co-articulation (CoArt) regions. Each of the local CoArt regions displays its own texture while actuated by a limited number of facial muscles or degrees of freedom, and the coupling between such regions is limited. Significant reduction in the dimensionality of the facial gesture data can be further achieved using PCA. This avoids the combinatorial complexity of existing methods that have to analyze the whole face. One of the important innovations made comes from using Gesture (second-order) Polynomial Reduction (GPR) to model and learn the G-manifolds or trajectories that correspond to different facial gesture movements and/or speech (viseme) sequences. GPR overcomes the limitations of the discrete face space defined by CoArt. Both the input and output space for GPR are continuous. GPR is behind 2D muscle morphing animation, with a mass-spring muscle system that drives the control points. Synthesis for direct animation, driven by GPR modeling, is achieved by using a single camera and varying the settings in terms of user models, context, and lighting. An added advantage of GPR comes from the use of intensity for the gestures analyzed. This goes beyond universal face expressions for which the answer for existing systems is usually binary. The flexibility to distinguish nuances of emotive expressions is still important for interactive and intelligent HCI.

11.3 $W5+$

Imagine a computer interface that could predict and diagnose whether the user was fatigued, confused, even alive, frustrated or momentarily distracted by gathering a variety of non-verbal information including papillary responses, eye fixations, facial expressions, upper-body posture, arm movements, and keystroke force. Further imagine that the interface could adapt itself -simplify, highlight, or tutor- to improve the human-computer interaction using similar diagnoses and predictions. Such smart interfaces meet specific needs, while users' preferences and profiles change over time, and provide for a richer, more versatile and effective environment for human activities. Non-verbal information or paralanguage facilitates now a special type of communication, where the ultimate goal is to probe the inner (cognitive and affective) states of the mind before any verbal communication has been even contemplated and/or expressed. The existing work on facial processing can be extended to task relevant expressions rather than the typical arbitrary set of expressions identified in face processing research. This is characteristic of the nominalistic approach and leads incrementally to $W5+$ (who, what, when, where, why and how)(Duric et al., 2002) and Human Computer Intelligent Interaction (HCII) via traditional Human Computer Interaction (HCI) and dynamic Bayesian (belief) networks (DBN) approaches as described next.

Human-Computer Interaction (HCI) has mostly developed along two competing methodologies: direct manipulation and intelligent agents (also known as delegation) (Shneidermann and Maes, 1997). These methodologies can be contrasted as the computer sitting passively waiting for input from the human vs. the computer taking over from the human. Another dimension for HCI is that of affective computing (Picard, 1998), which is concerned with the means to recognize "emotional intelligence." Most HCI studies elicit emotions in relatively simple settings, whereas emotional intelligence includes both bodily (physical) and mental (cognitive) events. Recognition of affective states focuses now on their physical form (e.g., blinking or face distortions underlying human emotions) rather than implicit behavior and function (their impact on how the user employs the interface or communicates with others). There are many interacting but hidden factors behind the display of expressions, and a probabilistic approach that includes uncertainty in their interpretation is required. The usual approach involves Bayesian networks, in general, and Hidden Markov Models, in particular.

Pentland et al. (2005) have proposed the coupled-HMM framework for modeling face-to-face interactions. The factors taken into account are the interaction features, e.g., paralanguage, the participants themselves, the context, and the contents. The human dynamics, once revealed and analyzed, contribute to collaboration, e.g., sharing expertise and social networking, and to pervasive and wearable computing. Zhang and Ji (2005) have explored the use of multimodal sensory data fusion for facial expression understanding using DBN. The face expressions are modeled using FACS. The input comes from image sequences, and evidence accumulates. Ambiguity, possibly due to occlusion, is resolved using sensitivity analysis and active perception along the temporal dimension. Relevant information is actively sought and integrated for reliable and robust reading of face expressions. Ji and Yang (2001) have used a similar approach for real time eye, gaze, and face pose tracking to monitor driver vigilance.

Human-centered design and implementation is problem-driven, activity-centered, and context-bound. It employs computing technology as a tool for the user, not as a substitute. The emphasis is on supporting human activities rather than on building fully autonomous systems that mimic humans. Human-centered systems seek to make HCI components "team players" in the context of human activity, so people and computer technology interact to achieve a common purpose. The ultimate goal for smart interfaces is to expand and complement the human perceptual, intellectual, and motor activities. The old debate between direct manipulation and delegation using software agents has led to the realization that what is really needed is to look at people, to understand them, and to adapt to them (Cipolla and Pentland, 1998). The gap between evaluation and execution, so important for better interfaces, can be bridged by integrating perceptual and cognitive modeling. This leads to HCII (see Fig. 11.2) in general, and $W5+$, in particular, which are adaptive and smart (Wechsler et al., 2005). Multimodality includes cognition, which provides an additional channel of information to mediate processing.

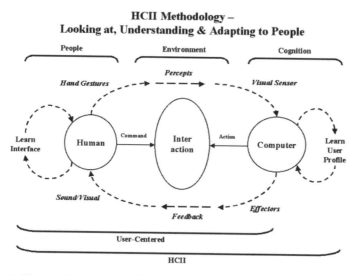

Fig. 11.2. Human-Computer Intelligent Interaction.

$W5+$ makes the transition from HCI to HCII. It allows people and computers to augment each other's capabilities and work as a team. $W5+$ integrates parsing and interpretation of non-verbal information with a computational model of the user, which in turn feeds into processes that adapt the interface to enhance user performance and provide for rational decision-making. HCII uses computer intelligence to further increase the bandwidth through which humans interact with computers. Non-verbal information such as facial expressions, posture, and point-of-gaze is parsed and interpreted by the computer to iteratively construct and refine a model of human cognitive and affective states. The availability of users' embodied cognitive models is used in an adaptive fashion to enhance human-computer interactions and to make them appear intelligent, i.e., causal, to an outside observer. HCII promotes human activity and creativity. It combines the (computational) ability to perceive multimodal affordance (input) patterns, reasoning and abstraction, learning and adaptation, and meaningful communication. These concepts, akin to perceptual intelligence (Pentland, 2000), echo those of Kant, for whom perception without abstraction is blind, while abstraction without perception is empty.

DBN "meter" only external behavior. To reach the sophistication characteristic of HCII, one needs to **(a)** perceive users' behaviors; **(b)** infer users' cognitive and affective states on the basis of those behaviors; **(c)** adapt in real-time to help the users achieve their goals; and **(d)** improve the quality of interactions for users. Adaptive interfaces are especially needed in situations where the user may become confused and frustrated in carrying out tasks with a computer application. Time stamped records for both explicit and implicit user behaviors are maintained for dynamic modeling purposes. Examples of explicit behaviors include (saccadic) eye movements, while examples of implicit behaviors include facial expressions and eye measurements. These behaviors are natural forms of non-verbal communication that signal particular affective states such as confusion, frustration, fatigue, stress, and boredom. The record of explicit and implicit behaviors serves as input to a computational model of embodied cognition, e.g., ACT-R/PM cognitive architecture (Byrne and Anderson, 1998). ACT-R/PM is a framework to create models of cognitive processing out of fundamental building blocks of cognition, perception and motor control. The outputs from ACT-R/PM drive HCII to align itself with the user's task and cognitive states, subject to the affective states mentioned above. The range of adaptations includes (i) presentation of pertinent tutorial information; (ii) reduction or enhancement of visual and auditory stimulation; (iii) emphasis of the most relevant information and de-emphasis of secondary information (for the subtask at hand); (iv) acceleration or deceleration of the pace of interaction; and (v) dynamic adjustment of the reactivity of the input devices in response to transient physical motor problems. ACT-R/PM enables HCII to react to a problem or specific need after it occurs, i.e., reactive adaptation, as well as to anticipate an upcoming problem or need and act before it occurs, i.e., proactive adaptation.

A cognitive model solves the same tasks as humans do using similar cognitive steps. An embodied cognitive model is endowed with affective states to match the user's states, and with the ability to perceive and interact with an external world in a similar way as the user does. During model tracing, the model is aligned with the task and behavioral choice data (i.e., what the state of the world is, and what the human has chosen to do) such that one can infer the internal cognitive steps the human must have taken in order to produce the observed behavior. Embodied cognition uses affective sub-symbols and their degree of belief, derived earlier by the perceptual and behavioral processing modules. Building models of embodied cognition calls for a specific cognitive architecture, e.g., ACT-R, Soar, EPIC, 3CAPS, which includes a relatively complete and well validated framework for describing basic cognitive activities, possibly at a fine granularity. Currently the framework that works best for building models of embodied cognition appears to be ACT-R/PM, a system that combines the ACT-R cognitive architecture (Anderson and Lebire, 1998) with a modal theory of visual attention (Anderson, Matessa and Lebire, 1997) and motor movements (Kieras and Meyer, 1997).

ACT-R/PM is a hybrid production system architecture, which represents knowledge at both a symbolic level (declarative memory elements and productions) and subsymbolic level (the activation of memory elements, the degree of association among elements, the probability of firing productions, etc). ACT-R/PM contains precise (and successful) methods for predicting reactions times and probabilities of responses that take into account the details of and regularities in motor movements, shifts of visual attention, and capabilities of human vision. The task for the embodied cognition module is to build a detailed mapping of interpretations, i.e., motion/affective states, for parsed sensory-motor data within the ACT-R/PM model. One can extend ACT-R/PM to make it a true model of embodied cognition by incorporating the effects of affect on performance. For example, in addition to handling the interactions between memory, vision, and motor movements, the model can become fatigued and distracted when there is too much to attend to. ACT-R/PM can model the effects of fatigue and distraction on memory, vision, and motor behavior, and thereby on performance as well. Similar to people, as the model becomes fatigued several changes occur. First, the model slows down (increasing the interval between physical actions and shifts in visual attention, as well as increasing the time needed to store or retrieve information from memory). The model also becomes distracted, losing its focus of attention, and running the risk of applying the "right" response to the "wrong" object or the "wrong" response to the "right" object.

The scope for $W5+$ and HCII extends beyond cognitive and affective states and includes understanding and/or ascribing intentions. The tentative narrative for such an expansion comes from the discovery of mirror neurons in Broca's and pre-motor cortical areas of the brain, which fire when performing an action or when observing the same action performed by another subject (Fogassi et al., 2005; Nakahara and Miyashita, 2005). Such neurons, a kind of mind readers making predictions on others' expected behavior, appear to be important for imitation learning and for encoding the intentions behind particular actions. Lack of the mirror neurons is conjectured to be responsible for autism. $W5+$ parsing is interactive and helps with face recognition. $W5+$ involves structure, meaning, and pragmatics, which are duly conscribed by context and functionality.

12. Performance Evaluation

The right to search for Truth implies also a duty; one must not conceal any part of what one has recognized to be true (Einstein)
The role of the scientist is to falsify theories and not to verify them. The focus should be on refutation rather than confirmation (Karl Popper)

Testing and evaluation are important tools used to assess the quality of face recognition systems. Blackburn (2001) provides a structured approach to a complete evaluation, which moves the user through three major steps: a technology evaluation, a scenario evaluation, and an operational evaluation. Each type of evaluation requires a different protocol and produces different results. To avoid conflict of interest, evaluations need to be administered by "independent groups that will not reap any benefits should one system outperform the other" (Orlans et al., 2003). The perception that overall technological advances are made can justify otherwise further R&D investments leading to yet additional evaluations. An organization should thus not be in charge of both R&D and evaluations (Orlans et al., 2003). The evaluations should use sequestered data, i.e., data that none of the face recognition systems being tested have previously seen. In addition, the evaluations must not be too easy nor too difficult, the results should be properly spread out to differentiate among systems' abilities, and adequate documentation should be made available for sharing and reuse. Last but not least, the evaluations have to be driven by realistic requirements suitable to assess whether the results show that further technology investment is warranted or not.

The evaluations have predictive value, if at all, only indirectly. Additional statistical analysis is required for making predictions on confidence intervals regarding future performance (see Sects. 13.1 and 13.2). The formal and large face recognition evaluations carried out so far (see Sect. 13.4), mostly technological in nature rather than operational, were tested on specific algorithms rather than complete operational systems. Testing was not performed at the actual site intended for future use, the decision-making steps, e.g., a priori setting of thresholds, were missing, score normalization (see Sect. 12.3) was sometimes allowed and misinterpreted, and face variability due to disguise, e.g., cosmetics and/or beard, is not accounted for at all.

The figure of merits used to characterize the performance observed, match score normalization and a priori setting of decision-making thresholds, the very reliability and uniqueness of biometric signatures, and a brief survey on some of the data bases available to benchmark face recognition performance, are among the topics discussed in this chapter. Error analysis is deferred to the next chapter.

12.1 Figures of Merit

The heart of the matter concerning performance evaluation is illustrated in Fig. 12.1 (for positive identification). The subjects are mostly legitimate and honest, but there is always a minority of impostors. The similarity match scores (see Sect. 1.1 on Tasks and Protocols) are compared against some threshold (see Sect. 12.3) for either acceptance or rejection. High similarity scores suggest genuine subjects. The genuine and imposter score distributions, however, overlap and mistakes are thus made. False accept and false reject errors, FA and FR, respectively, happen when impostors are let through while genuine users are denied access, respectively. The corresponding error rates are FAR and FRR. Identification, which is basically the result of repeated verification, can consider both positive and negative scenarios that bear on how the above errors are defined. ATM, an example of positive verification, seeks to distribute cash to legitimate users. The false reject amounts here to denying services to genuine customers. Surveillance, which seeks to find those subjects who appear on some watch list, corresponds to negative identification. Subjects that appear on the watch list but can gain access by mistake represent false rejects under the negative identification scenario. FAR and FRR are also referred to as FPR (false positive rate) and FNR (false negative rate), respectively.

The purpose for the Figures of Merit (FOM) discussed here (but see also Sect. 13.2 for alternative FOM) is to tabulate the results and make inferences about the relative biometric performance observed. This becomes the subject for detailed risk analysis driven by specific loss and cost functions. The optimal choice for operational thresholds is related to the Bayes minimum error if the score distributions were known (see Sect. 3.1). In practice, however, the distributions are only estimated and are usually biased, much more so the distributions for impostors because there are fewer of them.

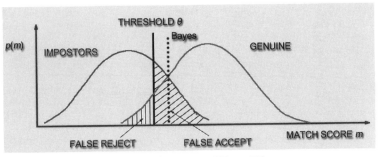

Fig. 12.1. Positive Authentication (courtesy of Fayin Li).

Receiver Operating Characteristic (ROC) curves are routinely used to report on the detection performance for verification tasks. They express the tradeoff between FAR and $1 - $ FRR or equivalently between FAR and FRR (see Fig 12.2). Note that the Hit Rate (or True Positive Rate) is HR $= 1 - $ FRR. ROC measures how well some biometric engine can detect signal from noise. Alternative references to the terms introduced above are available. FAR is referred to as the significance level α for a test, while the hit rate is referred to as the sensitivity or power $1 - \beta$ of the test. Operating points on ROC trade-off security for convenience. Negative identification for high security, associated with low FAR but low convenience, requires high value thresholds $\theta = T_{max}$ when comparing the similarity match scores. Positive identification, for high user convenience at ATM, on the other hand, requires low FRR (at the expense of increasing FAR) that is obtained for low value thresholds when comparing the similarity match scores.

Different thresholds yield different operating points (FAR, FRR) on the ROC curve. A single number that sometimes is used to express the performance of a biometric system is EER (Equal Error Rate) when EER $=$ FAR $=$ FRR. The operating point "does not necessarily need to be static. For example, screening processes such as airports can be multimodal, in the sense that demographics, text, sound, image and video can all be used. Depending on demographic match, biometrics authentication can operate at different operating points on the ROC curve" (Bolle et al., 2004). Using different operating points is characteristics of adaptive and dynamic authentication protocols. Two face recognition engines, A and B, are compared at specific operating points using hypothesis testing rather than using their ROC curves (unless one ROC curve dominates the other one). This is done by fixing the false accept rate FAR for both face recognition engines, say FAR = 1% and testing for the null hypothesis H_0 {FRR(A) = FRR(B)} against the alternative one-sided hypothesis H_1 {FRR(A) < FRR(B)}.

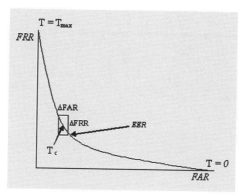

Fig. 12.2. ROC and Operational Points.

The alternative figures of merit (FOM) for ROC are DET (detection error trade-off) curves and Tippet plots. DET plots type I error vs. type II error. Type I error counts the false hypotheses accepted and aggregates them as FAR or the false match rate (FMR). Type II error counts the true hypotheses rejected and aggregates them as FRR or the false non-match rate (FNMR). DET gives uniform treatment to both types of errors, I and II, and chooses to plot errors (on both axes) rather than accuracy. "The reason is that error lends itself to better intuition than does accuracy. For example, it is easy to see that reducing the error rate from 10 percent to 5 percent is in a very real sense a doubling of performance, which is of course the same as increasing the accuracy from 90 percent to 95 percent" (Doddington et al., 2000). DET are graphed using logarithmic axes to spread out the plot and to better differentiate between systems that are extremely close in performance (Martin et al., 1997). DET enlarges the upper left corner of the ROC curve with nonlinear (normal) Gaussian deviates, rather than using the probabilities themselves, to allow an almost linear representation for system performance. Fig. 12.3 illustrates how ROC and DET compare against each other on two popular face recognition methods, Fisherfaces and Eigenfaces. Testing took place for a particular but difficult data set from FERET that has been acquired under significant variability in illumination. One can see that relative performance shows much better for DET compared to ROC. Fig. 12.3 also illustrates how comparative assessment of competing algorithms (see Sect. 12.4) can be carried out. Note that if the DET curve is close to a straight line, one can verify that the underlying likelihood distribution is close to normal. The diagonal DET curve $y = -x$ suggests random performance.

Yet another alternative used to report the evaluation results for competing algorithms is the use of Tippet plots (Tippet et al., 1968) (see Fig. 12.4). The likelihood ratio (LR) for two competing hypotheses is an indicator of the discriminating power of the classifier algorithm, e.g., the face recognition engine (see Sect. 3.6). The a posteriori odds, which are equal to the product between the LR and the prior odds, are the ones that should determine the authentication decision made. The prior odds en-

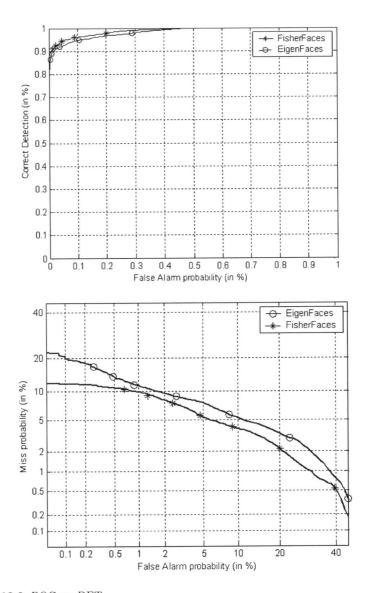

Fig. 12.3. ROC vs. DET

compass the policy being enforced based on risk analysis considerations. Tippet plots represent the proportion of cases with LR values greater than θ. The use of Tippet plots for forensics and/or biometrics is discussed next.

Classical forensic reporting provides only "identification" or "exclusion/elimination" decisions, which results in a very high percentage of non-reporting cases. It has two main drawbacks. The first one is related to the use of subjective thresholds. If the forensic scientist is the one choosing the thresholds, he will be ignoring the prior probabilities related to the case, disregarding the evidence under analysis and usurping the role of the Court in taking the decision, "··· the use of thresholds is in essence a qualification of the acceptable level of reasonable doubt adopted by the expert" (Champod and Meuwly, 2000). The second drawback is the large amount of non-reporting cases that this identification/exclusion process induces. The Bayesian approach's use of the likelihood ratio avoids such drawbacks. The roles of the forensic scientist and the judge/jury are now clearly separated. What the Court wants to know are the posterior odds in favor of the prosecution proposition (C)

$$\text{posterior odds} = \text{LR} \times \text{prior odds} \qquad (12.1)$$

The prior odds concern the Court (background information relative to the case), while the likelihood ratio, which indicates the strength of support from the evidence, is provided by the forensic scientist. The forensic scientist cannot infer the identity of the probe from the analysis of the scientific evidence, but gives the Court the likelihood ratio (LR) for the two competing hypothesis (C and $\neg C$). LR serves as an indicator of the discriminating power of the forensic system, e.g., the face recognition engine, and can be used to comparatively assess the rejection performance of Open Set TCM-kNN algorithm for Eigenfaces and Fisherfaces face representations (see Sects. 6.3 and 6.4). The analysis for negative verification proceeds as follows. For any exemplar face $\mathbf{X}$, the likelihood ratio (LR) is defined as

$$LR = \frac{P(\mathbf{X}|\neg R)}{P(\mathbf{X}|R)} \qquad (12.2)$$

$P(\mathbf{X}|R)$ is the likelihood that (non-target) exemplar $\mathbf{X}$ does not belong to the gallery and that rejection R is the right decision, while $P(\mathbf{X}|\neg R)$ is the likelihood that (target) exemplar $\mathbf{X}$ belongs to the gallery and rejection would be the wrong decision. One can assume that $P(\mathbf{X}|R) \propto PSR(\mathbf{X}|R)$ and $P(\mathbf{X}|\neg R) \propto PSR(\mathbf{X}|\neg R)$, where PSR stands for peak-to-side ratio (PSR) (see Sect. 6.3). $PSR(\mathbf{X}|R)$ is the PSR value derived using Open Set TCM-kNN, while $PSR(\mathbf{X}|\neg R)$ is the PSR value derived using Open Set TCM-kNN when $\mathbf{X}$ is added as another class into the gallery and thus should not be rejected. The above analysis is post-mortem and has access to ground truth. The procedure was run 100 times for different sampling realizations. The corresponding Tippet plots are displayed in Fig. 12.4.

The rightmost curve corresponds to target exemplars (hypothesis C) and records high LR values, while the leftmost curve corresponds to non-target exemplars (hypothesis $\neg C$) and records low LR values. The greater the separation between the two curves, the higher the discriminating power and the better the face recognition engine are. In an ideal system, the curves should lie close to the upper right and lower left margins of the plot. In addition, good performance from both curves around LR = 1 is desired, i.e., the proportion of targets with LR > 1 and non-targets with LR < 1 should be as small as possible. The Tippet plots shown illustrate that (solid line) Fisherfaces have higher discriminating power than (star point) Eigenfaces for the face data they were tested on.

Identification is different from verification in both functionality and implementation. The closed set case is 1-MANY rather than 1-1 and it retrieves, using repeated 1-1 verification a rank - based list of candidates ordered according to their similarity to the unknown test probe. Rank one corresponds to the gallery image found most similar to the test probe. The percentage of probes for which the top ranked candidate is the correct one defines the probability for rank one. The probabilities for rank "k"

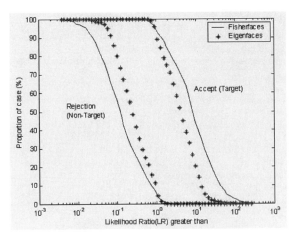

Fig. 12.4. Tippet Plots for Eigenfaces and Fisherfaces.

record the likelihood that the correct gallery image shows up at rank "k" or lower. The probability points trace the Cumulative Match Curve (CMC). CMC are useful tools for (ranked) identification only when there is exactly one mate for each probe query, i.e., the gallery sets are singletons. The presence of more than one mate for some or all of the probes, e.g., Smart Gate and now FRGC, can be handled in several ways. One way is to declare a probe matched at rank k if at least one of its mated gallery images shows up at that rank. Other possibilities could include retrieving all the mates or a fraction thereof at rank k or better and/or using a weighted metric that combines the similarity between the probe and its mates. Recall and precision are additional indexes that can be used for this task (see Sect. 13.2). There is also the possibility that the test probe itself consists of several images and/or that both the gallery and the probe sets include several image for each subject (see Sect. 9.4).

Additional FOM, related to overall system design, record the Failure to Enroll Rate and Failure to Acquire Rate, referred here together as the FTA error. Such type of errors are overcome by repeated attempts at data capture. If acceptance ("verification"), however, depends on a single successful match then

$$FAR = PEN \times FMR \times (1 - FTA) \tag{12.3}$$

$$FRR = FTA + (1 - FTA) \times BER + (1 - FTA) \times (1 - BER) \times FNMR \tag{12.4}$$

FAR and FRR are the false accept and false reject rates, respectively, while FMR and FNMR are the false match and false non-match rates, respectively. FTA stands for the failure to acquire rate, while BER and PEN are the binning error rate and the penetration, in a manner that depends on the decision policy implemented. FTA can be further split to make explicit the failure to enroll from the failure to acquire rate. The penetration rate is defined as the expected proportion of the template data to be searched against. Binning, related to and constrained by categorization, e.g., demographics, focuses the search for match (see Sect. 6.7). The more partitioned the database is, the lower the penetration rate and the greater the probability of binning error are.

It is not only performance that is assessed for evaluation purposes but also the relative costs involved in making specific type of errors. This requires choosing some loss function that reflects operational expectations and constraints. As an example, the NIST 2003 speaker recognition evaluation protocol defines the verification cost C_V (for negative verification) as a weighted sum of FRR ("miss") and FAR ("false alarm") error probabilities

$$C_V = C_{FRR} \times P_{FRR|T} \times P_T + C_{FAR} \times P_{FAR|NT} \times P_{NT} \tag{12.5}$$

where T and NT stand for target and non-target, respectively. The parameters for the verification cost are the relative costs of detection errors, C_{FRR} and C_{FAR}, e.g., 10 : 1 ratio when security is most important, and the a priori odds of the specified target (impostor) speaker, P_T, e.g., 0.01. The role that the prior or odds play is quite important as it affects the effectiveness of the biometric system. This is discussed next.

12.2 Score Normalization

Score normalization is practiced to counter subject/client variability during verification. It is used to draw sharper class or client boundaries for better authentication and to make the similarity scores compatible. The emphasis in this section is the former rather than the latter, which was already discussed in Sect. 9.5. Score normalization is concerned with adjusting both the client dependent scores and the thresholds needed for decision - making as part of post-processing. The context for score normalization includes clients S and impostors $\neg S$. One should not confuse post-processing score normalization with normalization implemented during preprocessing, which is used to overcome the inherent variability in the image acquisition process. Such preprocessing type of normalization usually takes place by subtracting the mean (image) and dividing by the standard deviation. This leads to biometric data within the normalized range of $[0, 1]$. Score normalization during post-processing can be adaptive or may be empirical, and requires access to additional biometric data prior and/or during the decision-making process.

Z-norm normalization is characteristic of adaptive post-processing score normalization. It is supposed to account for input variability and can provide relatively stable subject independent decision thresholds. Z-norm normalization, characteristic of client-centric score normalization, makes use of the LR, S, $\neg S$, and Ω concepts introduced earlier. Local and global information, referred to as anti-faces or impostors $\neg S$ and generic faces Ω, respectively, are used. Boundaries are outlined using the likelihood ratio (LR). Given the face PDF for some client S, which consists of one or several faces, anti-faces $\neg S$, which are most similar to the class defined by S, are found as negative examples for S. The anti-faces are used to define the cohort model for impostors and serve similar functionality to hypothetical support vectors for $\neg S$ or as validation during transduction. Alternatively, one models the "other" faces using some hypothetical generic world distribution Ω. Generative models, e.g., Gaussian Mixture Models (GMM), can define S, $\neg S$, and Ω. The maximum likelihood (ML) approach, e.g., expectation maximization (EM), is used to derive the parameters for GMM.

The generative model $P(S_i|\mathbf{X})$ for client S_i given her face $\mathbf{X}$ is

$$P(S_i|\mathbf{X}) = \frac{P(\mathbf{X}|S_i)P(S_i)}{P(\mathbf{X})} \tag{12.6}$$

The cohort model $P(\mathbf{X}|S_i)$ is defined in a similar fashion for anti-faces. The log-likelihood ratio test authenticates subject S_i if

$$LR = \log P(\mathbf{X}|S_i) - \log P(\mathbf{X}|\neg S_i) > \log \theta_i = \Delta \tag{12.7}$$

with the global threshold Δ adjusted for different operating costs using context-driven risk analysis. Rather than starting from scratch to learn the model $P(\mathbf{X}|S_i)$ for each subject S_i, one can instead "tweak" the universal background model (UBM) $P(\mathbf{X}|\Omega)$ to learn $P(\mathbf{X}|S_i)$ in a fashion similar to one-shot learning (see Sect. 6.5).

Z-norm is client dependent and makes the impostors distributions compatible by assuming they come from the same Gaussian distribution $N(0, 1)$. It updates the likelihood ratio LR test for S_i as

$$LR^+ = \frac{(LR - \mu_{S_i})}{\sigma_{S_i}} > \Delta \tag{12.8}$$

The use of LR^+ requires, however, significant access to client data. To overcome such needs, Poh and Bengio (2006) suggest to normalize the score for the client using the mean and standard variation (μ_I, σ_I) of impostors instead of $(\mu_{S_i}, \sigma_{S_i})$. The pair (μ_I, σ_I) is learned off line from simulated impostors. The T-norm, similar to Z-norm, derives the pair (μ_I, σ_I) on line from the impostors found for other clients. The analysis gets more involved if real rather than casual impostors are used to train the system.

The other alternative for post processing score normalization is using empirical methods, similar to Z-score normalization, or access to actual enrollment ("gallery") and/or test data. Post processing empirical normalization was used during FRVT2002 but not for earlier major evaluations, e.g., FRVT 2000. Post processing normalization changes the mode of operation for verification from 1-1 to 1-MANY because additional data and scores are now needed before one settles on the final verification score for the original 1-1 verification task. Cognitec, the top ranked vendor for FRVT 2002, has argued this obvious point and went on to say that "We strongly believe that an evaluation based primarily on the non-normalized scores is more appropriate for real-world problems" (Phillips et al., 2003). Verification is basically hypothesis testing and each of the hypotheses should be independently judged as "true" or "false". Empirical post-processing score normalization enhances and spreads the differences between a given probe image, whose verification one is seeking, against a "pre-selected" but actual gallery of images that it has access to. Performance has been shown by FRVT 2002 to increase, using post processing empirical score normalization, by about 6% on the average but exceptions were observed. Post processing empirical score normalization skews the results and is not a viable option for real life operations where access to additional data is not readily available. Score normalization changes the distribution of results in terms of both absolute and relative values and thus both ROC and CMC figures of merit are likely to change.

The basic concept behind empirical score normalization during testing is context dependent and can be deceptive. Empirical score normalization requires that the face probe queries both the target face and a normalization set drawn from the same gallery the probe is querying. All the scores are then used to compute the normalized score for the query. Pooling among test data results amounts to ad hoc a posteriori inference and is not deterministic. This is the reason why NIST 2003 speaker verification evaluation [1] specifically requires that "each decision is to be based only upon the target speaker. Neither normalization over multiple target speakers nor the use of evaluation data for impostor modeling is allowed."

An appreciation for the inner works of empirical score normalization and its effects can be gained from Adler (2003). Assume that the PDF of match ("similarity") scores is available for both genuine transactions (for the same client), i.e., $P_g(m)$, and impostor transactions (between different clients), i.e., $P_i(m)$. Such information can be gleaned from sets maintained during enrollment or gained during the evaluation itself. One way to calculate the normalized similarity score ns for a match score m is to use Bayes' rule

$$ns = P(g|m) = \frac{P(m|g)P(g)}{P(m)} \tag{12.9}$$

where $P(g)$ is the a priori probability of a genuine event and $P(m|g) = P_g(m)$ is the conditional probability of match score m for some genuine event g. The probability of m for all events, both genuine and impostor transactions, is

$$P(m) = P(g)P_g(m) + (1 - P(g))P_i(m) \tag{12.10}$$

The normalized score ns is then

---

[1] http://www.nist.gov/speech/tests/spk/2003/doc/2003-spkrec-evalplan-v2.2.pdf

$$ns = \frac{P(g)P_g(m)}{[P(g)P_g(m) + (1 - P(g))P_i(m)]} \tag{12.11}$$

The accuracy for the match similarity scores depends on the degree to which the genuine and impostor PDF approximate ground truth. Bayesian theory can determine optimal decision thresholds for verification only when the two (genuine and impostor) PDF are known. To compensate for such PDF estimation errors one should fit for the "overall shape" of the normalized score distribution, while at the same time seek to discount for "discrepancies at low match scores due to outliers" (Adler, 2003). The normalized score serves to convert the match score into a more reliable confidence value.

The motivation behind empirical score normalization using evaluation data can be explained as follows. Evaluation data available during testing attempts to overcome the mismatch between the estimated and the real conditional probabilities referred to above. New (on-line) estimates are obtained for both $P_g(m)$ and $P_i(m)$, and the similarity scores are changed accordingly. As a result, the similarity score between a probe and its gallery counterpart varies. The estimates for the genuine and impostor PDF should be obtained at enrollment time and/or during training rather than during testing.

One of the innovations advanced by FRVT 2002 was the concept of virtual image sets. The availability of the similarity (between queries Q and targets T) matrix enables one to conduct different "virtual" experiments by choosing specific query P and gallery G sets as subsets of Q and T. Examples of virtual experiments include assessing the influence of demographics and/or elapsed time on face recognition performance. Performance scores relevant to a virtual experiment correspond to the $P \times G$ similarity scores. Empirical score normalization compromises, however, the very concept of virtual experiments. The explanation is quite simple. Empirical score normalization has no access to the information needed to define the virtual experiment. As a result, the updated or normalized similarity scores depend now on additional information whose origin is outside the specific gallery and probe subsets.

12.3 Decision Thresholds

The ultimate goal for any operational biometric system is reliable and robust decision-making. "Yet, the actual decision making process, specifically the setting of decision thresholds, has often been neglected in speaker recognition research. Making these decisions has often been dismissed as an unchallenging problem to be addressed during application development. Yet for those who actually have had to deploy real operational systems, the problem has been found to be quite challenging, indeed. The important point here is that actual decision process must be considered to be part of any comprehensive speaker recognition research program and that the ability of a system to make good decisions should be an integral part of the evaluation" (Doddington et al., 2000). Decisions must be also made without the artificial luxury of having access to ground truth. The same arguments hold true for face recognition and are discussed next.

BEM [2], which stands for Biometric Evaluation Methodology, provides "a common criteria scheme for Information Technology Security Evaluation that is mutually recognized by organizations in several countries." The match component compares the biometric information extracted from probes against signatures stored in reference templates. "It will typically include comparing an output score with a predefined threshold value. The comparison may be against a single template (for verification), or against a list of candidate templates (for identification). The threshold may be configurable by the administrator, or it may be fixed by the biometric system. Clearly, the security assurances related to the setting of this value, the protective means within

---

[2] http://www.cesg.gov.uk/site/ast/biometrics/media/BEM_10.pdf

the biometric system to safeguard the threshold setting, and the internal decision process to decide a match are some of the most critical components of a biometric system and their vulnerabilities should be carefully assessed." Sliding thresholds in search of optimal performance, while deriving ROC during formal evaluations such as FERET and FRVT2002 is, however, not feasible during real time biometric operation when ground truth is lacking. As Doddington et al. (2000) succinctly state "Knowledge of the best decision thresholds is inadmissible information - decisions must be made without the artificial luxury of knowing the answers. Inference of the best decision thresholds from the test data is false knowledge - random sampling produces the illusion of good decision points that do not really exist." Biometrics systems in general, and face recognition engines, in particular, require thus significant tuning and calibration (for setting thresholds) before myths such as "plug and play" (Bolle et al., 2004) can happen, if at all.

Threshold selection is difficult to automate due to the diversity and variability of the data corpus collected. Note also that "much more is known about the population, [or genuine clients,] of an application than is known about the foes, [i.e., the impostors]. Consequently, the probability of a false alarm rate, a false match [for screening and positive identification], is hard to estimate. Hence, the false reject rate (FRR) for a particular decision is easier to estimate than the false alarm rate (FAR) for that decision, because the biometric samples of the enemy population are not available" (Bolle et al., 2004). The sliding thresholds employed to derive the (FAR, FRR) operating points used to plot ROC curves (for verification) were found a posteriori by FRVT2002 with the hindsight benefit of ground truth and aggregate similarity scores. Neither of them, however, is available during operational deployment. "A real-world application, however, is only realistic with a priori thresholds that should be determined during enrollment" (Zhang et al., 1999). The thresholds therefore need to be set up a priori [to use] rather than a posteriori, and without resorting to additional client data as empirical score normalization does. Formal evaluations carried out by NIST in 2003 have shown that there is a large displacement [discrepancy] between the ROC curves derived during enrollment and those derived during actual operation when using the thresholds locked at enrollment time.

There are several ways to choose thresholds using the ROC framework. This is detailed next, while complementary information related to confidence intervals on performance is presented in Sect. 13.1. One way to find operating points for ROC is using the Neyman - Pearson method (Fukunaga, 1990). The power or sensitivity of interest is chosen first and one maximizes then the specificity subject to the chosen sensitivity constraint (or vice versa). Additional analysis on the decision thresholds and operating points would check if the power or sensitivity $(1 - \beta)$ of the test can be further increased with little loss in specificity $(1 - \alpha)$ (Bradley, 1997), where α is the significance or confidence of the test.

Another typical method to derive optimal thresholds computes the distribution of inter- and intra- ID [client] biometric similarities and then chooses that EER threshold that equalizes the overlapping FAR and FRR areas (see Fig. 12.1). "The average of FAR and FFR can be about 3 to 5 times larger than the EER, which suggest that the EER is an over optimistic estimate of the true system performance" (Pierrot et al., 1998). Maximum likelihood usually models the inter- and intra-score PDF as Gaussians and takes advantage of the fact that approximately 99.7% of the samples drawn from them should be located within the interval $(\mu - 3\sigma, \mu + 3\sigma)$. The success of this method relies on whether the estimated PDF are indeed Gaussian and match the client- and impostor- PDF, and if the session-to-session PDF variability is limited. Chen (2003) suggests that the means to improve on the above methods include better estimates for the usually unreliable variance of the intra-PDF, and incremental and adaptive thresholds.

We conclude this section with a short discussion on the complementary role that the odds play in decision-making relative to that of setting thresholds. "Jurists interpret the threshold as an expression of the criminal standard "beyond reasonable doubt." Would jurists accept that the concept of reasonable doubt on the identifica-

tion of a suspect escapes their province and that the scientist imposes the threshold
onto the court? It is the utility function of the court that is appropriate, not the utility
function of the statistician" (Champod and Meuwly, 2000). Such concerns are easily
addressed if what are sought after are the posterior odds instead. The supporting
evidence, i.e., the likelihood ratio LR and the prior odds are provided by the face
recognition engine and the security policy, respectively. The fuzzy linguistic equivalent of LR could be limited support, moderate support, strong support, and excellent
support for ratio intervals (1, 10), (10, 20), (20, 50) and over 50. The security policy
is ultimately driven by risk analysis and logistics. To really appreciate the role that
the odds play in verification assume that $P(+)$, the probability, driven by the similarity score, for positive identification, is around 0.99. According to Bayes' theorem,
$P(ID|+)$ depends then on both the evidence $P(+)$ and the prior probability $P(ID)$:

$$P(ID|+) = \frac{P(+)P(ID)}{[P(+)P(ID) + P(-)(1 - P(ID))]}$$
$$= 0.99 \cdot \frac{P(ID)}{[0.99 \cdot P(ID) + 0.01 \cdot (1 - P(ID))]} \quad (12.12)$$

The validity of the conclusion depends critically on the prior odds used. The statement
that $P(ID|+) > 0.99$ is correct only if $P(ID) \geq 0.50$!

12.4 Comparative Assessment

Competing algorithms are evaluated to determine statistical significant differences in
their performance, if any, and their relative rankings. Statistical significance means
that the observed differences, if any, are larger than what could have occurred by
chance only. The web site [3] at Colorado State University (CSU) is a resource for
researchers developing and comparing face recognition algorithms (Beveridge et al.,
2005). The site provides a standard set of well known algorithms together with well-
established experimental protocols. The goal is to provide a solid statistical basis for
drawing conclusions about the relative performance and observed behavior of different
algorithms. Some of the statistical evaluations for Human ID algorithms (Beveridge et
al., 2001) have produced results that go counter to common knowledge. In particular,
they have shown, using McNemar's test (see below), that PCA is significantly better
than ICA; and have shown, using bootstrap, that a standard PCA classifier performs
better than PCA followed by the LDA classifier, i.e., Fisherfaces. Martinez and Kak
(2001) have confirmed that when the training dataset is small, PCA is better than
LDA, and appears to be less sensitive to different training datasets. The contradictory
claims on the relative performance of ICA algorithms has been recently elucidated and
shown to depend on the specific task statement (see Ch. 15).

Comparative assessment of two competing algorithms on classification starts with
confusion matrices (see Sect. 13.2). There are two classification algorithms 1 and 2
and the confusion or contingency 2×2 matrix C tabulates for them the outcomes
c_{00}, c_{01}, c_{10}, and c_{11} that correspond to the number of faces misclassified by both
algorithms, the number of faces misclassified by algorithm 1 but not by algorithm
2, the number of faces misclassified by algorithm 2 but not by algorithm 1, and the
number of faces correctly classified by both algorithms, respectively. The background
and implementation of the comparative assessment are described next.

Assume Bernoulli trials or equivalently independent random variables X whose
outcome is either success 1 or failure 0. Assuming that p is the probability for success,
the expected value and variance for X are p and $p(1-p)$, respectively. When N identical and independent Bernoulli trials take place, the random variable Y, which stands
for the number of successes observed, is binomially distributed and the probability
that it scores s successes is

[3] http://www.cs.colostate.edu/evalfacerec/

$$P(Y = s) = \left(\begin{array}{c} N \\ s \end{array} \right) p^s (1 - p)^{N-s} \qquad (12.13)$$

The expected value and variance for Y are Np and $Np(1-p)$, respectively. The extent to which the binomial distribution fits with the way the evaluation is conducted can be, however, questioned with regard to sampling with and without replacement, and the very probability of success. If the target population is relatively large, sampling with or without replacement are about the same. The fixed probability of success is actually the more problematic item because some subjects are harder to identify than others (see Sect. 13.3).

The binomial distribution is approximated by the Gaussian (normal) distribution $\mathcal{N}(Np, Np(1-p))$. The null hypothesis H_0 corresponds to the two classification algorithms being similar in performance relative to their error rates c_{01} and c_{10}. The McNemar's test determines whether the number of correct vs. incorrect classifications are "similar" for the two competing algorithms. The entries in the contingency matrix tabulate for each operational point and corresponding threshold on similarity the true and predicted (positive and negative) class outcomes for $c = 2$. The pairs $c_{01}(n+)$ and $c_{10}(n-)$ are binomially distributed with $p = 0.5$ and $N = (n+) + (n-)$. The entries in the confusion matrix where both algorithms yield similar results are discarded. The McNemar's test computes exact p-values (to be distinguished from the p-values computed during transduction using the strangeness)

$$\text{p-value} = \sum_{i=0}^{\min(n+,n-)} \left(\begin{array}{c} N \\ i \end{array} \right) 0.5^N + \sum_{\max(n+,n-)}^{N} \left(\begin{array}{c} N \\ i \end{array} \right) 0.5^N \qquad (12.14)$$

or alternatively tests for differences that are statistically significant using the chi-square χ^2 test with one degree of freedom

$$\chi_1^2 \sim \frac{(|c_{01} - c_{10}| - 1)^2}{(c_{01} + c_{10})} \qquad (12.15)$$

Chi-squared variables are sums of normally distributed variables. The χ^2 test accepts the hypothesis that algorithms 1 and 2 are comparable at significance level α or equivalently with confidence $1 - \alpha$ if $\chi_1^2 < \chi_{\alpha,1}^2$ where $\chi_{0.05,1}^2 = 3.84$ for $\alpha = 5\%$. "χ^2 tests the null hypothesis that the confusion matrix was obtained by random selection. Low χ^2 values support the null hypothesis. If the value of the χ^2 test exceeds certain bounds the evidence to reject the null hypothesis is called significant ($\chi^2 > 3.84$; at the 5% level), highly significant ($\chi^2 > 6.63$; 1%) or very highly significant ($\chi^2 > 7.88$; 0.5%). The actual χ^2 value can be used as a guide to select an operating point [or decision threshold] on the ROC curve" (Bradley, 1996). Note that biometric tests are not Bernoulli trials because they are usually not independent and their behavior follows specific operational rules, e.g., test completion. In particular, the McNemar's test cannot be used when the gallery contains multiple images for the same subject or when one needs to account for within-subject variability using binning or penetration methods. The independence assumption among outcomes does not hold any more and the binomial model is not suitable. In such situations non-parametric resampling methods and/or confidence intervals are required (see Sect. 13.2). Examples of resampling methods include Monte Carlo methods (Micheals and Boult, 2001; Beveridge et al., 2001).

Analysis of variance (ANOVA) compares M candidate classification algorithms for $M > 2$ (Alpaydin, 2005). The classification algorithms are trained on k partitions to define k (fold) full fledged classification algorithms. The algorithms are then run on the k (fold) validation partitions and yield $M \cdot k$ accuracy scores. Some of the algorithms may use the same basic approach and differ only in terms of their specific parameterization. ANOVA compares the M sets of k accuracy or error rate values X_{ij} to find significant statistical differences, if any. Formally,

$$X_{ij} \sim \mathcal{N}(\mu_j, \sigma_2), \quad j = 1, \cdots, M, \quad i = 1, \cdots, k \tag{12.16}$$

The M algorithms are found similar if the null hypothesis

$$H_0 : \mu_1 = \mu_2 = \cdots = \mu_M \tag{12.17}$$

holds true. ANOVA estimates σ^2 differently for each hypothesis. Assuming that m_j and m are the means for the k fold partitions and the overall mean, respectively, the first estimator under H_0 is

$$\sigma_0^2 = k \sum_{j=1}^{M} \frac{(m_j - m)^2}{(M-1)} \text{ and } X_0 = \sum_{j=1}^{M} \frac{(m_j - m)^2 k}{\sigma_0^2} \sim \chi_{M-1}^2 \tag{12.18}$$

The second estimator σ_1^2 under H_1 is

$$\sigma_1^2 = \sum_j \sum_i \frac{(X_{ij} - m_j)^2}{M(k-1)} \text{ and } X_1 = \sum_j \sum_i \frac{(X_{ij} - m_j)^2}{\sigma_1^2} \sim \chi_{M(k-1)}^2 \tag{12.19}$$

The ratio of two independent chi-square random variables divided by their respective degrees of freedom yields a random variable that is F distributed

$$\frac{[X_0/(M-1)]}{[X_1/M(k-1)]} \sim F_{M-1,M(k-1)} \tag{12.20}$$

If the hypothesis H_0 is accepted then the competing algorithms and/or their parameterized versions are comparable in terms of performance. Otherwise, there are significant statistical differences and some guided subset analysis using McNemar's test is warranted.

Comparative assessment of competing algorithms on verification can be simply done by comparing the corresponding figures of merit, e.g., ROC, DET and/or Tippet plots. The comparison is easy to make as long as one plot dominates over the competing one. The ROC, DET and Tippet plots can be further compared using relative locations, separation and/or percentage of the area under the curve. As an example, the diagonal line for ROC indicates random prediction, while ROC area percentages of 0.9 to 1.0 indicate almost perfect performance. When the plots intersect each other, a deeper but more meaningful comparison, which takes into consideration the relative costs incurred at different operational points, is called for. Rather than visualizing and comparing ROC curves one could summarize ROC using the area under the receiver operating characteristic curve (AUC). Bradley (1997) discusses AUC and claims that "it displays increased sensitivity to ANOVA tests, it is not dependent on the decision threshold chosen, it gives an indication on how well separated the negative and positive classes are for the decision index, and it is invariant to prior class probabilities."

An important consideration for biometric evaluations is the choice made for the loss function. Yet another consideration during comparative assessment is the inclusion of the reject option. This corresponds to open set face recognition, when it can be cheaper to withhold a decision rather than making a poor one. In the latter case, the tradeoffs can be resolved using a rule proposed by Chow (1970). The rule, which minimizes the error rate for a given reject rate, or vice versa, rejects a customer if the maximum a posteriori probability (over c classes) is less than some value $1 - t$, where the rejection threshold $t \in \left[0, 1 - \frac{1}{c}\right]$. The rule is optimal in the sense that for some reject rate specified by t, no other rule can yield a lower error rate. Recall also the fact that it is variability rather than similarity that most affects face verification. It is easier to reject impostors than to accept legitimate clients. This observation is important when resolving tradeoffs between security and convenience and comparing figures of merit.

Martinson et al. (2005) raised serious questions about ethical habits for the scientific community. Some of the habits listed were failing to present data that contradict one's own previous research or changing the design, methodology or results of a study in response to pressure from a funding agency. Many times a researcher will report top performance 95+% for a new algorithm A against other phantom algorithms. The same researcher then comes a year or so later with yet another top notch new algorithm B that again displays 95+% against other phantom algorithms while any comparison against her previous algorithm A is missing. What face recognition needs to assess real progress is a set of biometric protocols set up by disinterested third parties like ISO, and implemented for easy access using open-source and e-science (see Ch. 15).

12.5 Data Bases

Training and evaluation requires more and better quality data than is easily available today. Training, which is involved in building the face space that is needed to generate the biometric signatures, requires data independent of that used to create the actual individual signatures or templates at enrollment time. Li and Tang (2004) have shown experimentally that "LDA-based face recognition performance depends more on the mix of the right variety of images in the training data than on the size of the training set." Training data coming from different sessions, e.g., video, captures more of the intra-personal variations and makes recognition more reliable. The effort required for data collection is tedious but is essential. There are two ways to satisfy the requirements for larger and more diverse data bases. One way is to physically acquire them, while the second is to artificially synthesize them by expanding and/or morphing from some original data set. Note that synthesis is useful to the extent that it properly approximates the face appearance. This is not easy when one considers how difficult it is to interpret and/or discount face expressions. Data acquisition is discussed here. Large scale evaluations and the protocols used are deferred to Sect. 13.4. The generation of virtual samples and face synthesis are discussed in the next section, while 3D face synthesis is addressed in Ch. 8.

The web site for information and resources on face recognition [4] points to some of the public facial data base collections [5]. One of the earliest data bases is from ATT (formerly from and referred to as Olivetti ORL). It contains a set of face images taken between April 1992 and April 1994 at ORL [6] (see Fig. 12.5). There are ten different images for each of forty distinct subjects. For some subjects, the images were taken at different times, varying the lighting, facial expressions (open/closed eyes, smiling/not smiling) and facial details (glasses/no glasses). All the images were taken against a dark homogeneous background with the subjects in an upright, frontal position (with tolerance for some side movement). The size of each image is 92×112 pixels, with 256 grey levels per pixel.

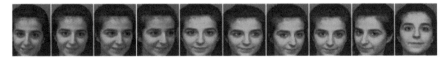

Fig. 12.5. Faces from ATT/ORL Data Base.

---

[4] http://www.face-rec.org/

[5] http://www.face-rec.org/databases/

[6] http://www.uk.research.att.com/facedatabase.html

The Yale Face Database (size 6.4MB), another of the earliest and small data bases but still widely used, contains 165 grayscale images in GIF format of 15 individuals (see Fig. 12.6). There are eleven images per subject, one for each of several but different facial expression and/or configurations: center, left, and right illumination, w/without glasses, happy, normal, sad, sleepy, surprised, and wink [7].

Fig. 12.6. Faces from Yale Data Base.

The largest and most varied facial data base available is FERET (see Fig. 12.7). The design and collection for FERET took place at George Mason University under the direction of Harry Wechsler between 1994 and 1997 (Phillips et al., 1998). FERET [8] was used for large scale evaluations, e.g., FERET and FRVT2000 (see Sect. 13.4), and has become the standard facial data base for benchmark biometric evaluation studies. The gallery for FERET includes 1,199 subjects for whom a total of 14,126 face images were acquired and stored in raw or TIFF format. The data collected originally in color has been made available in both B/W and color. Face images were acquired in sets of five to eleven images, collected under relatively unconstrained conditions. Two frontal views were taken (**fa** and **fb**); a different facial expression was requested for the second frontal images. Images were also collected at the following head aspects: right and left profile (**qr** and **ql**), and right and left half profile (**hr** and **hl**). Additionally, five extra locations (**ra, rb, rc, rd**, and **re**) irregularly spaced among the basic images, were collected if time permitted. Sometimes, a second set of images of a person was taken at a later date; such a set of images is referred to as a duplicate set. In total FERET acquired 1,564 sets of images including 365 duplicate sets. Such duplicate sets record variations in scale, pose, expression and illumination of the face, w/without glasses and hair style changes (see Fig. 1.1c). For some subjects, there was a lag of eighteen months between the first and last sitting, with some individuals being photographed multiple times.

Fig. 12.7. Faces from FERET Data Base.

The extended XM2VTS project captured a large multimodal database onto high quality digital video. The XM2VTS database contains four recordings of 295 subjects taken over a period of four months. Each recording contains a speaking head shot and a rotating head shot. Sets of data taken from this database are available including high quality color images, 32 KHz 16-bit sound files, video sequences, and a 3D model [9]. The follow-up for XM2VTS is the BANCA multimodal (face and voice) data base. It addresses security concerns for network and e-commerce applications [10]. BANCA had 208 subjects enrolled for whom 6,240 images at relatively high 720 × 576 resolution were acquired over 12 sessions.

The AR face database was created by Aleix Martinez and Robert Benavente at the Computer Vision Center (CVC) in Barcelona. It contains over 4,000 color images corresponding to 126 people's faces (70 men and 56 women). The images feature frontal view faces with different facial expressions (see Fig. 11.1), illumination conditions, and occlusions (sun glasses and scarf) (see Fig. 10.10). The images were captured under strictly controlled conditions. No restrictions on wear (clothes, glasses, etc.), make-up, hair style, etc. were imposed. Each subject participated in two sessions, separated by two weeks time. The conditions recorded by AR include neutral expression, smile, anger, scream, left and right light on, all side lights on, wearing sun glasses or scarf, and wearing sun glasses or scarf and right or left light on [11].

Two data base collections important for their variability come from Carnegie Mellon University (CMU). They are the CMU Hyperspectral data base, collected under the DARPA Human Identification (at a) Distance (HID) program, and the CMU Pose, Illumination, and Expression (PIE) data base. The gallery for the hyperspectral data base consists of 54 subjects for whom the faces were captured at a spectral range of 0.45-1.1 μm [12]. The CMU PIE gallery has 68 subjects enrolled for a total of 41,368 images whose resolution is 640 × 486 [13]. Another hyperspectral data base is the Equinox infrared face data base using the following co-registered modalities: broadband-visible/LWIR (8-12 microns), MWIR (3-5 microns), SWIR (0.9-1.7 microns), and a spectral range of 8-12 μm at a resolution of 240 × 320 [14] (see Fig. 12.8).

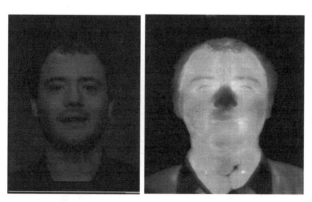

Fig. 12.8. Faces from Equinox Data Base.

---

[9] http://xm2vtsdb.ee.surrey.ac.uk/
[10] http://www.ee.surrey.ac.uk/Research/VSSP/banca/
[11] http://web.archive.org/web/20030602180713/rvl1.ecn.purdue.edu/ aleix/aleix_face_D
[12] http://www.ri.cmu.edu/pubs/pub_4110.html
[13] http://www.ri.cmu.edu/projects/project_418.html
[14] http://www.equinoxsensors.com/products/HID.html

The Max Planck Institute of Biological Cybernetics has collected a 3D data base using a Cyberware laser scanner [15]. The database contains images of seven views of 200 laser scanned (Cyberware TM) heads without hair. The 200 head models were newly synthesized by morphing real scans to avoid close resemblances to individuals who might not want to appear on a computer screen or in scientific publications. Multimodal (visible, range, and IR) and temporal collections are available for (⟨ frontal, quarter and side views ⟩ face, hand, and ear) biometrics from Univ. of Notre Dame [16]. The 3D collection [17] is currently maintained at Ohio State University. Specialized data bases also exist for face detection and face expression studies. Frontal and profile face images for face detection are available from Carnegie Mellon University (CMU) [18]. The Cohn-Kanade AU-Coded Facial Expression Database includes approximately 2,000 image sequences from over 200 subjects [19].

Complementary to the European and American face image data bases there is now available a well annotated Korean Face Data Base (KFDB) that provides Asian faces (Hwang et al., 2004) (see Fig. 12.9). KFDB contains 52,000 face images taken from 1,000 subjects with their description, ground truth information, and the locations for 26 feature points. There are 52 conditions for imaging, including illumination, expression, and pose change. It would be worth (i) to evaluate the extent to which the face spaces developed for Caucasian faces work for KFDB and vice versa; and (ii) to undertake a comparison between the norm and absolute base coding schemes and their alternatives (see Sect. 5.1) using data drawn from FERET and KFDB. Another data base from Asia is the CAS-PEAL Chinese data base [20]. CAS-PEAL contains currently 99,594 images of 1,040 individuals (595 males and 445 females) with varying Pose, Expression, Accessory, and Lighting (PEAL). For each subject, nine cameras spaced equally in a horizontal semicircular shelf are set-up to simultaneously capture images across different poses in one shot. Each subject was asked to look-up and down to allow an additional 18 images to be captured using two extra shots. There are 5 kinds of expressions, 6 kinds of accessories, and 15 lighting directions. This facial database has been made only partly available as CAS-PEAL-R1.

Fig. 12.9. Faces from Korean Face Data Base.

FRGC (Face Recognition Grand Challenge) is the latest large scale face recognition evaluation effort in terms of the number of images per subject (see Sect. 13.4). FRGC is, however, relatively limited in the number of subjects compared to previous evaluations, e.g., FRVT2002. The corpus collected consists of 3D images, and high resolution controlled and uncontrolled stills. The data is divided into training and validation partitions, with the standard still-image training partition consisting

[15] http://faces.kyb.tuebingen.mpg.de
[16] http://www.nd.edu/%7Ecvrl/UNDBiometricsDatabase.html
[17] http://sampl.eng.ohio-state.edu/%7Esampl/data/3DDB/index.htm
[18] http://vasc.ri.cmu.edu/idb/html/face/
[19] http://vasc.ri.cmu.edu/idb/html/face/facial_expression/
[20] http://www.jdl.ac.cn/peal/index.html

of 12,800 images, and the validation partition consisting of 16,028 controlled still images, 8,014 uncontrolled stills, and 4,007 3D scans. It becomes difficult to assess the extent to which the face recognition algorithms have improved, if at all. Better performance can simply be the result of better image quality and/or more data available for training and testing on each subject. Last but not least, one has to question the extent to which such relatively high image quality and its consistency, due to one collection/enrollment site only, can be actually replicated during extended biometric operation and diversity of sites.

12.6 Virtual Samples

The variability and in particular, the size of the data base, affect training and learning, and ultimately the very performance of the deployed face recognition system. The small size problem challenges in particular LDA in terms of singularities and/or can bias the results leading to large variance. What about augmenting the size of data bases by populating them with virtual samples? We have already seen such examples in the preceding sections and/or chapters. Hallucinations (see Sect. 10.4) fill in for missing information or provide super-resolution using priors. Asymmetric faces complete the face, when only half of it is available, and are an important tool to overcome denial, i.e., occlusion (see Sect. 10.5). Asymmetric faces can also be synthesized by computing the average between the original face image and its vertical mirrored image leading to improved performance on authentication (Marcel, 2004). Subspace adaptation for incremental face learning is another way to augment the data base at a low cost and without starting from scratch. During the initial learning stage, "a set of MKL ("multi-PCA") subspaces is created for each individual, starting from the feature vectors extracted through a bank of Gabor filters." Then, "during the normal system operation, an incremental updating technique can be applied to adjust the subspaces without recalculating the face models from scratch; this makes the method able to cope with gradual changes [aging] that occur over time" (Cappelli et al, 2002).

Inductive principles can incorporate domain knowledge as useful hints (Abu Mostafa, 1995a) to guide and constrain ("bias") training and learning. Hints are essential for semi-supervised learning (Chapelle et al., 2006). Most common type of hints are supplied as virtual exemplars. Recognizing a face from any angle becomes easier with a symmetry hint and it leads to generalization from a smaller number of presentation angles. Simard et al. (1992) have shown the advantages of using selective hints such as invariance to small rotations or scaling. Animals may rely on an innate understanding of such a hint. Monkeys can be taught to recognize a face more reliably if they memorize it first from an oblique angle rather than a frontal view. According to Abu Mostafa (1995b) "hints are auxiliary information about the target function and are known independently of the training examples; like regularization, hints would not be needed if an unlimited supply of proper exemplars (and unlimited computation) could be secured."

Face variability can be artificially induced by augmenting the data available for training through perturbations, e.g., (Gaussian) noise and/or simple geometrical distortions using in-plane linear transformations (see ERBF training in Sect. 10.5). Thian et al. (2003) have shown that the mean of N face images, generated using simple geometric transformations and fed through a trained neural network, decreases the variance of the merged scores. The flexible active shape models (ASM) proposed by Lanitis et al. (1997) to code face images could provide the means to describe face variability and generate virtual samples. Given training data, any training exemplar X_i can be approximated as $X_i = \bar{X} + Pb$, where $\bar{X}$ is the average exemplar, P is a matrix of unit eigenvectors for the covariance of deviations, and b is a weight vector referred to as the model parameters (see Sect. 6.5 for ASM). "By modifying b, new instances of the model can be generated; if the elements of b are kept within some limits (typically $\pm 3\sigma_k$, where σ_k is the standard deviation of b_k over the training set) the corresponding model instances are plausible examples of the modeled [faces]." To further mitigate illumination changes, beyond what has already been achieved using a "factorization method that separates albedo from illuminant" and "contrast limited adaptive histograms," Torre et al. (2005) have proposed "several linear [e.g., Prewitt, Sobel, Laplacian, Gaussian et al.] and non-linear filters [e.g., morphological and diffusion operators] to be applied to illumination normalized images. The representations produced play the role of virtual samples and many of them while redundant still "introduce different types of robustness against different types of noises and appearance changes."

One potential drawback from using perturbations comes from the possibility that the generated face images are highly correlated (Martinez, 2002). To avoid such correlations one should learn instead the space of feasible transformation for the synthesis of virtual exemplars (Beymer and Poggio, 1995; Poggio and Beymer, 1995). Another approach used is that of resampling with replacement. Towards that end, Breiman (1996) has proposed resampling of pattern exemplars for aggregation using bagging, while Ho (1998) applies resampling to the feature space using random forests. Training data is resampled with replacement to simulate expected data variability. This generates independent bootstrap replicates, which once trained yield different classifiers. Voting schemes (see Sect. 9.3) combine the results from each classifier into a global and stronger decision rule. Note that the similarity distances used affect the effectiveness of any synthesis method and the range of the virtual samples generated.

Virtual samples can be generated using known distortions or can be learned and evolved. Towards that end, Chen et al. (2004) have introduced a genetic algorithm based method to "swell" face data bases through resampling from existing faces. Original faces are aligned and preprocessed for uniform treatment and are then divided into training and validating sets. The intermediate solutions or populations are evaluated as faces and non-faces by the Sparse Network of Winnows (SNoW) classifier (see Sect. 9.3) using the validation set. SNoW is retrained during each generation using the initial and present population and non-faces samples collected using bootstrap. Crossover breaks down parents into non-overlapping parts corresponding to the main face components before exchanging genetic material. Mutation simulates image variability and includes sharpening, blurring and/or lighting. Evolution, driven by face fitness as determined by SNoW, ends when the difference between two successive populations is negligible.

Another way to generate additional face images and to account for image variability is through interpolation and extrapolation. Given two distinct prototype features z_{c1} and z_{ck} for some class c one constructs corresponding feature lines L_{lk} as span$(z_{c1} - z_{ck})$. The nearest feature line (NFL) seeks for class labels according to the nearest feature line pair wise distances. The declared winner is that class for whom NFL yields the minimum distance between the feature point of the query and the feature lines connecting any two prototype feature points (Li and Lu, 1999). NFL was shown to yield better performance than the nearest neighbor method it expands on. NFL could be further augmented such that both gallery and probes take advantage of NFL extensions and/or whole virtual prototypes are constructed and matched against each other. Note that NFL is not without problems. All the virtual exemplars are limited to lie on the feature lines (a severe restriction that makes close by faces to fail matching if they are not aligned. This led Chien and Wu (2002) to suggest the nearest feature plane (NFP) as a higher order interpolation and extrapolation method that augments the capacity for the virtual prototype features. At least three linearly independent feature vectors are needed to span NFP. To cover sufficient facial variations without much overhead the geometrical concept can be generalized from plane, i.e., NFP, to space, i.e., NFS. The latter corresponds to the case when there are several exemplars for each class and the identity of the probe is resolved by finding the nearest feature space among all classes. The space extension corresponds to matching multi (gallery and probe) sets of faces (see Sect. 9.4).

13. Error Analysis

Precision is not truth (Matisse)

Performance evaluation, discussed in the previous chapter, was mostly about the comparative evaluation of competing face recognition systems. Error analysis explores here complementary objectives. First, for operational purposes, there is the acute need to predict performance in order to properly assess the utility in deploying a particular face recognition system. This is in sharp contrast to a technological evaluation that has access to ground truth and merely records the results. Bounds on expected performance and how the results scale up for larger data sets are also sought. Second, the errors have to be analyzed and their source understood. In particular, it is important to know not only what works and to what extent it works, but also to know what does not work and why (Pankanti et al., 2002). Anecdotal evidence suggests that 90% of errors are due to only 10% of the face patterns. The faces that can be easily remembered are not necessarily those that are easily rejected when they have not been seen previously. The correlation between the hit rate and the false positive rate is zero (Bruce and Young, 1998). "Our current understanding of the performance evaluation facilitates a comparative assessment of the candidate solutions on a particular dataset but does not permit us to objectively predict the system performance in the real world. Neither do we have the capability of objectively describing the existing databases nor any means of quantifying/comparing their complexities independent of a fully implemented matching system. Acquisition of these capabilities will indicate a level of understanding of the data that will instill end-user trust and result in a more widespread acceptance of the [biometrics] system" (Jain and Pankanti, 2001).

Error analysis requires a good grasp of facts and understanding their implications. There has been much interest to characterize the error margin for FAR and FRR. Assume that the face recognition engine yields a set of M match score pairs and a set of N mismatch score pairs. Here $M < N$ because there are always going to be more mismatched than matched similarity pairs. It follows that the false alarm rate can be estimated more accurately than the false rejection rate. There has been much interest to extrapolate the results for hypothetical large-scale evaluations. The conjecture advanced by FRVT2002 is that the identification performance decreases linearly with respect to the logarithm of the database size; the decrease was claimed to be approximately 2% - 3% for every order of magnitude increase in gallery size. The assumptions used by FRVT 2002, that similarity scores and real face images are i.i.d (identical and independently distributed) are, however, not warranted. The model suggested fits only one of the participants (out of more than ten) who participated in FRVT2002. Does the log-linear performance for such a model continue indefinitely or does it change at some point? FRVT2002 does not answer this question. For the (18-22) and (23-27) age groups top rank identification for FRVT2002 yields about 63%. Increase the size of the data base for those important age groups to 300,000 and the average top rank identification performance falls below 50%. The conjectures made by FRVT2002 regarding comparative performance evaluation driven by demographics are deficient because "within-bin comparisons may have higher false match rates than

random comparisons due to the similarities that caused the patterns binned together"
(Mansfield and Wayman, 2002).

13.1 Confidence Intervals

Confidence is concerned here with confidence in results, bounds on accuracy, effects
due to unbalanced distributions, and errors' behavior. We have shown earlier that
transduction provides confidence measures based on p-values, e.g., credibility in the
recognition choice made and its confidence relative to the next best choice available
(Li and Wechsler, 2005) (see Sect. 6.3). The scope for confidence here is different, with
the goals now inferential. The specific questions addressed are about predictive power
and confidence intervals, and how would performance fare when the biometric system
scales up. The confidence interval $CI = (L, U)$ bounds the range for some parameter
or result $\mathbf{x}$ and confidence level $(1 - \alpha)$, such that $P(\mathbf{x} \in CI) = (1 - \alpha)$. As the size
of the data corpus becomes larger, the confidence interval or uncertainty shrinks and
the bounds on future results become tighter and more useful. Confidence intervals
are more informative than simple hypothesis testing since they provide a range of
plausible values.

A good way to start the discussion on confidence intervals is to introduce the
concepts of bias and variance and the tradeoff they induce. The error involved in
approximation, e.g., regression, can be decomposed into bias and variance components.
Bias comes from the mismatch between the approximation and target functions, while
the variance is simply the estimation error due to finite samples. Bias occurs when
the approximation functions are not representative of the data they are supposed to
model, e.g., the mix of faces or their diversity used to approximate the face space is
not representative of the enrolled population. Variance comes from sampling errors
and underlying variability. The tradeoffs between bias and variance are modeled, in a
fashion similar to that used in constrained optimization and using relative weighting,
e.g., MSE = bias $+\lambda\cdot$ variance. Increasing λ tends to decrease the variance during
MSE minimization. It will increase, however, the bias, because more data are used (to
lower the variance) and incorrect assumptions are made about how to approximate
the target function, e.g., cumulative matching curves (CMC). On the other hand,
decreasing λ tends to lower the bias and increase the variance because the model
found is strongly dependent on the training data, i.e., is biased. One can't thus find
a single class of approximating functions to provide superior estimation accuracy for
all the learning problems encountered (Friedman, 1994).

The most critical issue in the biometric community, with respect to the deployment
of face recognition engines, is the uncertainty surrounding their performance. Modeling
and prediction are not suitable here because one lacks functional specifications for
the face recognition engines used. Rather than providing merely observational post
mortem results using ground truth, e.g., ROC (Receiver Operating Characteristic)
and/or CMC (Cumulative Matching Curves), the face recognition engines need to
be informative about their expected levels of performance and what the best way
to reach them is. Some results concerning confidence intervals on performance are
discussed next. They provide lower bounds on the size of the data corpus required or
alternatively on the number of trial needed to reach a given level of accuracy.

The *Rule of 3* states that $\frac{3}{n}$ is an upper 95% confidence bound for the binomial
probability p when in n independent trials no error events occur (Jonanic and Levy,
1997; Wayman, 1999). So, for example, a test of 3,000 independent samples returning
no errors can be said with 95% confidence to have an error rate of 0.1% or less. Another rule, the *Rule of 30* states that there must be at least 30 errors to achieve 90%
confidence that the true error rate is within ±30% of the observed error rate (Doddington et al., 2000). So, for example, if there are 30 false non-match errors in 3,000
independent legitimate trials, one can say with 90% confidence that the true error
rate is between 0.7% and 1.3%. The *Rule of 30* is derived for the binomial distribution
assuming independent trials. The rules discussed above are, however, over-optimistic

because they assume that (**i**) the error rates are due to a single source of variability; and that (**ii**) i.i.d trials rather than cross-validation might actually reduce uncertainty. As the trial size increases, the expected decrease in the variance of estimates is limited by the non-homogeneous composition of the population. "Ten enrollment-test sample pairs from each of a hundred people is not statistically equivalent to a single enrolment-test sample pair from each of a thousand people, and will not deliver the same level of certainty in the results" (Mansfield and Wayman, 2002). Similar over-optimistic assumptions are made by FRVT2002 for building confidence intervals for the ROC results derived. Furthermore, "by decoupling data collection and signal processing subsystems, off-line technical evaluations using a standardized corpus may not give a good indication of total system performance" (Mansfield and Wayman, 2002).

One problem that is quite intriguing but highly important is to make predictions about large scale biometric performance from past operating (FAR, $1 - $ FRR) points observed during relatively small scale formal biometric evaluations. The approach proposed here is that of model selection (see Sect. 3.4). In particular, one has to choose the "best" among a class of approximating functions, given a set of ROC operating points. For the identification task one models the identification rate at rank one (dependent variable y) as a function of the data base size (the independent variable x). In a similar fashion, for verification, one keeps the FAR fixed and models the hit rate (1-FRR) as a function of the data base size. Both scenarios correspond to model selection for regression and are discussed next.

The goal for regression is to estimate an unknown (target) function $g(\mathbf{x})$ in the relationship $y = g(\mathbf{x}) + \epsilon$ where the random error (noise) is zero mean, $\mathbf{x}$ is a $d-$dimensional vector and y is a scalar output. A learning method (or estimation procedure) selects the "best" model $f(\mathbf{x}, \mathbf{w_0})$ from a set of (parameterized) approximating functions (or possible models) $f(\mathbf{x}, \mathbf{w})$ specified *a priori*, where the quality of an approximation is measured by the loss or discrepancy $L(y, \mathbf{f}(\mathbf{x}, \mathbf{w}))$. A common loss function for regression is the squared error. Learning corresponds to the problem of finding the regression function $\mathbf{f}(\mathbf{x}, \mathbf{w_0})$ that minimizes the prediction risk functional $R(\mathbf{w}) = \int (y - \mathbf{f}(\mathbf{x}, \mathbf{w_0}))^2 p(\mathbf{x}, y) d\mathbf{x} dy$ using training data $(\mathbf{x}_i, y), (i = 1, \cdots, n)$, that is generated according to some (unknown) joint PDF $p(\mathbf{x}, y) = p(x)p(y|\mathbf{x})$. $R(\mathbf{w})$ measures the accuracy for predictions made on the unknown target function $g(\mathbf{x})$. The problem is ill-posed since the prediction risk functional is unknown (by definition). Most learning methods implement empirical risk minimization (ERM), and choose the model that minimizes the empirical risk or the average loss experienced for training data

$$R_{emp}(\mathbf{w}) = \frac{1}{n} \sum_{k=1}^{n} (y_k - f(\mathbf{x}_k, \mathbf{w}))^2 \qquad (13.1)$$

The ERM approach is only appropriate when the parametric form for the unknown dependency is known. In most practical applications, parametric assumptions do not hold true, and the unknown dependency is estimated using a wide class of possible models of varying complexity. The goal for learning, minimal prediction risk, is achieved by choosing a model of optimal complexity. Existing methods for model complexity control include penalization (regularization), weight decay (in neural networks), and various greedy procedures, e.g., growing and pruning methods.

Classical methods for model selection are based on asymptotic results for linear models. Non-asymptotic (guaranteed) bounds on the prediction risk for finite-sample settings have been proposed in VC-theory (Vapnik, 1998). There are two general approaches for estimating prediction risk for regression problems with finite data: analytical and data-driven or empirical (Cherkassky and Mulier, 1998; Wechsler et al., 2004). Data driven methods are implemented using cross-validation and/or bootstrap (see below). Analytical methods are discussed first. They use analytical estimates of the prediction risk, which is modeled in terms of the empirical risk (training error) penalized (adjusted) by some measure of model complexity. The model chosen is the one that minimizes the estimated prediction risk. In the statistical literature, various analytic prediction risk estimates have been proposed for model selection (for linear regression). These estimates take the form of

$$\text{estimated risk } = r\left(\frac{d}{n}\right)\frac{1}{n}\sum_{i=1}^{n}(y_i - \hat{y}_i)^2 \tag{13.2}$$

where r is a monotonically increasing function of the ratio of model complexity (degrees of freedom) d and the training sample size n (Hardle et al., 1988). The n samples correspond to the data base size used for evaluation. The function r is often called a penalization factor because it inflates the average residual sum of squares for increasingly complex models and small sized training sets. Functional forms of r for $p = \frac{d}{n}$ that trace their origin to statistics include

$$\text{Final Prediction Error } (fpe)\text{: } r(p) = (1+p)(1-p)^{-1} \tag{13.3}$$

$$\text{Schwartz' criterion } (sc)\text{: } r(p,n) = 1 + \frac{\ln n}{2}p(1-p)^{-1} \tag{13.4}$$

$$\text{Generalized Cross-Validation } (gcv)\text{: } r(p) = (1-p)^{-2} \tag{13.5}$$

$$\text{Shibata's Model Selector } (sms)\text{: } r(p) = 1 + 2p \tag{13.6}$$

The above approaches are motivated by asymptotic arguments for linear models and therefore work well only for very large training sets. In fact, for large n, the prediction estimates provided by fpe, gcv, and sms are asymptotically equivalent. The fpe risk follows the Akaike Information Criterion (AIC) (Hastie et al., 2001).

Structural risk minimization (SRM) (see Sect. 3.4) is an alternative analytical approach. SRM provides analytic upper bounds on the prediction risk that can be used for model selection (Vapnik, 1998). To make practical use of such bounds for model selection, one still has to choose practical values for the theoretical constants involved (Cherkassky and Ma, 2003; 2004). This yields the penalization factor, $r(p, n)$

$$r(p,n) = \left(1 - \sqrt{p - p\ln p + \frac{\ln n}{2n}}\right)^{-1} \tag{13.7}$$

where $p = \frac{h}{n}$, h denotes the VC-dimension of an estimator (and corresponds to the number d of degrees of freedom), n is the training sample size and $(x)_+ = 0$ for $x < 0$. For linear estimators with m degrees of freedom, the VC-dimension is $h = m$. The model that provides minimal prediction risk $r(p, n)$ is chosen. Our experimental results show that the Vapnik induced measure $vm = r(p, n)$ compares favorably against the alternative model selection methods listed above, regarding the confidence they offer on model selection problems related to change (Wechsler et al., 2004).

What are the bounds on future performance for the mean accuracy μ given an approximation model, when the mean and standard deviation measured for the results are m and σ? Given N samples drawn from a Gaussian (normal) distribution G, their sample average $m \sim G(\mu, \frac{\sigma^2}{N})$, and $Z = \frac{(m-\mu)}{\sigma} \sim G(0,1)$, the two-sided 95% confidence interval for $Z_{0.025}(-1.96, 1.96)$ is

$$P\left\{-1.96 < \sqrt{N}\frac{(m-\mu)}{\sigma} < 1.96\right\} = 0.95 \tag{13.8}$$

The confidence interval shrinks as the sample size N gets larger. Confidence intervals can also be built around the standard deviation to assess variability. The sample variance s^2 is

$$s^2 = \frac{1}{N-1}\sum_{i=1}^{N}(x_i - m)^2 \text{ and } (N-1)\frac{s^2}{\sigma^2} \sim \chi^2_{N-1} \tag{13.9}$$

and the confidence interval for the variance becomes

$$P\left\{(N-1)\frac{s^2}{\chi^2_{N-1,\frac{\alpha}{2}}} \leq \sigma^2 \leq (N-1)\frac{s^2}{\chi^2_{N-1,1-\frac{\alpha}{2}}}\right\} = 1 - \alpha \qquad (13.10)$$

The sample size that yields some specified confidence interval is found in a way similar to the confidence intervals found for parameter estimation (Hastings, 1997). Assume again a binomial random variable X, which stands for the false accept or reject rate, $X = \frac{\#y}{N}$, where $\#y$ is the count of relevant events and N is the sought after sample size. The relationship between N and the confidence interval $[\frac{\#y}{N} - \epsilon, \frac{\#y}{N} + \epsilon]$ of size 2ϵ built around $\frac{\#y}{N}$ is

$$\epsilon = Z_{\frac{\alpha}{2}} \cdot \left[\frac{\left(\frac{\#y}{N}\right)\left(1 - \frac{\#y}{N}\right)}{N}\right]^{\frac{1}{2}} \text{ for } N \approx \left(\frac{Z_{\frac{\alpha}{2}}}{\epsilon}\right)^2 \left(\frac{\#y}{N}\right)\left(1 - \frac{\#y}{N}\right) \qquad (13.11)$$

Confidence intervals and bands for ROC curves were derived by FRVT2002 with the thresholds being swept across similarity match scores to generate (elliptic) confidence bounds around (FAR, $1 - $ FRR). Alternatively, one swept around the FAR rates to generate vertical [averaging] confidence bands. Mackassy et al. (2003) have argued that the above approach yields bounds that are too tight and are not realistic. They have recently proposed means to generate and evaluate more realistic confidence $(1-\alpha)$ bands [from confidence intervals] on ROC curves and how to gauge their relative fit. Previous 1D methods for creating confidence intervals for ROC, such as vertical averaging for $(1-$FRR) rates at successive FAR rates, or freezing threshold and averaging (FAR, $1-$FRR) pairs, make unwarranted assumptions, e.g., normal distribution, and/or are very complex and not tractable. Additional drawbacks for standard ROC confidence intervals methods are due to the fact that the vertical bands will tend to be much wider for smaller FAR (due to the initial sharp rise in the slope). The realization that the corresponding points for cost sensitive classification on different ROC curves are those points where the tangent lines to the curves have the same slope led Mackassy et al. (2003) to propose the opt-radial approach. The three basic steps for the approach are listed below with its *innovations* highlighted in *italic*:

- Create a distribution of ROC curves [from several training and/or test sets using cross-validation or bootstrap]
- Generate 1D confidence intervals using
  1. [normal | binomial | empirical] distribution assumption
  2. [1D vertical | 1D threshold | *2D radial ⟨innovation⟩*] sweep method
- Create confidence bands from the confidence intervals and optimize them for better containment with respect to some objective function that is suitable for the problem domain ⟨*innovation*⟩].

The opt-radial methodology was shown to yield performance that is significantly better than both the standard threshold and vertical sweeping methods.

"If the apparent [observed] error rate were a good estimator of the true error, the problem of classification and prediction will be automatically solved. Basing the estimate of performance on the apparent error leads to overspecialization or *overfitting*" (Weiss and Kulikowski, 1991). If unlimited cases for training and tuning are available, the apparent rate becomes the true error rate. This is, however, not the case in practice. Learning the true error rate from limited data requires resampling tools, e.g., cross-validation and/or bootstrapping, characteristic of data driven or empirical methods.

Cross-validation (CV) involves resampling and randomized (virtual) experiments. The advantage of CV is that all the cases in the data corpus are used for both training and tuning/validation. For the basic k-fold CV the cases ("faces") are randomly divided into k mutually exclusive partitions of approximately equal size. The faces not found in the tuning partition are independently used to estimate the model's parameters. Once found, the parameters complete the definition for the face recognition engine, and the engine is evaluated on tuning data. The same process, iterated k times, yields (mean, standard deviation) statistics on accuracy and determines the optimal choice of parameters. There are a number of enhancements to the CV scheme described above that are of interest. First and foremost is to keep the size of the training partitions fixed but to enlarge the size of the tuning partition. This becomes important for determining how biometric performance scales up. The other issue of concern is to choose an optimal value for k. Hastie et al. (2002) comment that "if the learning curve has a considerable slope at the given training size, five or tenfold cross-validation will overestimate the true prediction error. Whether this bias is a drawback in practice depends on the objective. On the other hand, leave-one-out [size one for all partitions] cross-validation has low bias but can have high variance. Overall, five or tenfold cross-validation are recommended as a good compromise."

For small samples, the method of choice for obtaining a low variance estimate is bootstrap. This estimator resamples from the original data set but *with replacement*. Bootstrap reduces the need to make unrealistic assumptions about the underlying distribution of the observed error rates and dependencies between trials. The (empirical) distributions and possible dependencies are inferred from the sample (with replacement) itself. The probability, that each face out of N is sampled is $\frac{1}{N}$, and the probability that it is not sampled is $1 - \frac{1}{N}$. The probability that the face has not been sampled after N attempts is $\left(1 - \frac{1}{N}\right)^N \approx e^{-1} = 0.368$. The probability that a given sample shows up in the bootstrap sample of size N is .632. The tuning set is composed of items that were not sampled into the bootstrap sample used for training. The prediction error ϵ_0 for a (leave-one-out) sample not included in the bootstrap will likely be larger since less is known about it. The .632 estimator (Hastie et al., 2001) predicts the error pe as

$$pe = .368 \cdot \epsilon_1 + .632 \cdot \epsilon_0 \qquad (13.12)$$

where ϵ_1 is the empirical or apparent error rate observed using the bootstrap sample, while ϵ_0 is the leave-one-out bootstrap estimate.

13.2 Prevalence and Fallacies

Figures of merit (FOM) relevant to error analysis and possible pitfalls are discussed here (see also Sect. 12.1). Confusion matrices, in particular, are suitable for hypothesis testing and/or two class discrimination, e.g., legitimate vs. impostor classification (see Fig. 13.1). The confusion matrix tabulates all the information needed for error analysis on the verification task when the total number of events or subjects to be verified is $n = a + b + c + d$. Ground truth markers True and False corresponds to legitimate clients and impostors, respectively. TP, FP, FN, and TN, stand for True Positive, False Positive, False Negative, and True Negative, respectively.

Sensitivity and specificity, and their related concepts of recall and precision, come from information retrieval and are alternative FOM (to ROC) for verification. Based on the entries listed above in the confusion matrix one defines the following FOM

$$\text{Accuracy} \quad = \quad \frac{(a+d)}{(a+b+c+d)} \qquad (13.13)$$

$$\text{Sensitivity} \quad = \quad \frac{a}{(a+c)} \qquad (13.14)$$

$$\text{Specificity} \quad = \quad \frac{d}{(b+d)} \qquad (13.15)$$

$$\text{1 - Specificity} \quad = \quad \frac{b}{(b+d)} \qquad (13.16)$$

Ground Truth

	T	F
Predict: T	a (TP)	b (FP)
Predict: F	c (FN)	d (TN)

Fig. 13.1. Confusion Matrix.

$$(1 \text{ - Specificity, Sensitivity}) \quad = \quad \left[\frac{b}{(b+d)}, \frac{a}{(a+c)} \right] \qquad (13.17)$$

$$\text{Precision} = \text{PPV (+ predictive value)} \quad = \quad \frac{a}{(a+b)} \qquad (13.18)$$

$$\text{NPV (- predictive value)} \quad = \quad \frac{d}{(c+d)} \qquad (13.19)$$

$$\text{Prevalence (P)} \quad = \quad \frac{(a+c)}{(a+b+c+d)} \qquad (13.20)$$

$$\text{Recall} \quad = \quad \frac{a}{(a+c)} \qquad (13.21)$$

$$(\text{Recall, Precision}) \quad = \quad \left[\frac{a}{(a+c)}, \frac{a}{(a+b)} \right] \qquad (13.22)$$

The (Sensitivity, Specificity) and (Recall, Precision) pairs serve as useful FOM for information retrieval. In the context of face recognition, such FOM characterize the behavior of the face recognition engine when it is possible for the gallery to include more than one mate for each probe. A face recognition engine with constant sensitivity of 99.9% and specificity of 99.9% would appear to provide excellent performance. Assume that the face recognition engine screens for negative identification a population of one million subjects at some point of entry (POE) where just 1% or 10,000 out of 1,000,000 clients are impostors. Since the face recognition engine is 99.9% sensitive, it will detect 9,990 ⟨TP⟩ impostors and miss 10 ⟨FN⟩ impostors. To continue the analysis, recall that out of one million subjects, 990,000 are not impostors. If the specificity is also 99.9%, one can see that 989,010 legitimate ⟨TN⟩ customers are let through, while 990 legitimate customers, or approximately 0.1% of the original population, are labeled as ⟨FP⟩ impostors and denied entry. What is still needed to complete a meaningful analysis is the prevalence of impostors in the general population, which was referred to earlier as the prior odds. Assume now that the prevalence for impostors is 0.1% rather than 1%, i.e., there are 1,000 rather than 10,000 impostors. At 99.9% sensitivity, the face recognition engine will pick up 999, leaving only one impostor to slip through. Of the 999,000 genuine subjects, the face recognition engine lets through 998,001 of them, and falsely labels 999 of them as impostors. The evaluation yields now the same number of false positive as true positive, and the PPV (+ predictive value) for impostors is now only 50%. Each other subject labeled as an impostor is a mistake! When the prevalence goes up to 1%, the POE decision is worth much more because the PPV goes up to 90%, i.e., only one tenth rather than half of clients are denied entry by mistake. PPV is further affected by sensitivity and specificity changes that are related to the differences in the populations trained on and then screened at POE. This type of analysis has been suggested by the diagnosis of infections and epidemiologist studies [1] (Kraemer, 1992).

Similar arguments as those discussed above apply to intrusion detection. Effectiveness is now defined as the extent to which detectors can correctly classify intrusions and avoid false alarms. Axelsson (1999) has claimed that "for a reasonable set of assumptions, the false alarm rate is the limiting factor for the performance of an intrusion detection system. This is due to the base rate fallacy phenomenon, which says that, in order to achieve substantial values for the Bayesian detection rate $P(intrusion|alarm)$, one has to achieve - a perhaps unattainably low-false alarm rate."

A related performance index to PPV and biometric system effectiveness is the lift. It measures the ratio between the percentage of impostors found and the percentage of individuals in the general population labeled as impostors

$$\text{Lift} = \frac{\text{Recall}}{\text{Prevalence}} = \frac{\text{PPV}}{\text{P}} = \frac{\left[\frac{a}{(a+c)}\right]}{\left[\frac{(a+b)}{(a+b+c+d)}\right]} \tag{13.23}$$

The target could be to detect 50% of imposters while labeling only 5% of the population as impostors for a lift of 10. The lift measures how much better is the observed performance compared to random guess.

Identification for an unknown subject is basically an N-class verification task, where N is the number of distinct subjects enrolled. As N becomes arbitrarily large, the probability of correctly identifying the subject becomes arbitrarily small. Note, however, that "in most cases, the speaker identification task appears to be more of a scientific game than an operationally useful capability. This is especially true for security system applications, because here the speaker has good reason to cooperate with the system by proffering an identity, thus reducing the N-class task down to a 2-class task. Even for forensic type applications, the problem most often is one of evaluating each candidate separately rather than choosing one from among many candidates. Thus it seems that, although the speaker identification task may garner considerable scientific interest, it is the speaker verification task that has the greatest application potential" (Doddington et al., 2000). The same reasoning carries over to face recognition. Some easy number crunching makes the point that identification is, at least for the time being, impractical for large data bases (Daugman, 2000). Assume that P_1 is the probability of false accept (FAR) for each 1 : 1 verification trial and that N is the size of the data base that has to be exhaustively searched for identification. The false accept probability P_N for a data base of size N using repeated verification and closed world assumptions is

$$P_N = 1 - (1 - P_1)^N \tag{13.24}$$

Consider now a biometric verifier that achieves 99.9% correct rejection, i.e., its FAR is as low as 0.001. This would indicate higher accuracy than what state-of-the art face recognition can achieve today. The P_N values for relatively small data bases given by $N = 200, N = 2,000$, and $N = 10,000$ are 18%, 86%, and 99.995%, respectively. Once the enrolled data base size "reaches only about 7,000 persons, the above biometric actually becomes more likely (99.91%) to produce a false accept in identification trials than it is to produce a correct reject (99.9%) in verification trials. A false accept rate of merely 10^{-4} on verification trials yields a false acceptance rate of 92% for identification against a data base that consists of 50,000 people. Merely good verifiers are of no use as identifiers. Observing the approximation $P_N \approx N \cdot P_1$ for small $P_1 << \frac{1}{N} << 1$, when searching a data base of size N, an identifier needs to be roughly N times better than a verifier to achieve comparable odds against a false

---

[1] http://www.musc.edu/dc/icrebm/sensitivity.html

accept" (Daugman, 2000). The above numbers are definitely not comforting for mass screening. Alternatively, one seeks for the probability of making i false accepts among N comparisons P_N^i instead

$$P_N^i = C_N^i P_1^i (1 - P_1)^{N-1}, \quad i = 0, 1, \cdots, N, \quad C_N^i = \frac{N!}{i!(N-i)!} \qquad (13.25)$$

The probability $P_N^{\geq i}$ of making at least i false accepts among N comparisons is

$$
\begin{aligned}
P_N^{\geq i} &= \sum_{k=1}^{N} P_N^k \\
&= \sum_{k=1}^{N} C_N^k P_1^k (1 - P_1)^{N-k} \\
&= 1 - \sum_{k=0}^{i-1} P_N^k \\
&= 1 - \sum_{k=0}^{i-1} C_N^k P_1^k (1 - P_1)^{N-k} \qquad (13.26)
\end{aligned}
$$

Equations for false-match and false-non match error prediction for the general M-to-N biometric identification, under simplifying but limiting assumptions of statistical independence for all the errors, were derived by Wayman (1999). Errors are, however, not independent and depend, among other things, on clients' characteristics (see Sect. 13.3). Both the gallery and the probe sets can consist of one or more samples in the above equations.

Similar analysis for watch list using repeated verification but open world assumptions is described next. The watch list task involves both detection and identification (see Sect. 6.4). A hit is declared only if the corresponding similarity match score m exceeds a threshold θ. Assume now N independent trials, v is the FAR for (m, θ), and w is the FAR for watch list. The above watch list case is analyzed by Sherrah (2004) to yield

$$w = P(\text{at least one false alarm}) = 1 - P(\text{no false alarm}) = 1 - (1 - v)^N \qquad (13.27)$$

Similar to the case discussed earlier, "if $v << \frac{1}{N}$ then $w \approx Nv$, and one needs a low v to achieve the required w for high values of N, say 1,000,000. w varies roughly linearly with N for small v. For larger values of v, however, there is a rapid non-linear increase in w with N, again emphasizing the need to keep v very low. For verification with v greater than about 1 in 1,000, the watch list classifier would be practically useless" (Sherrah, 2004). The preceding analysis shows again that the false alarm rate is a critical performance measure for face recognition.

13.3 Pattern Specific Error Inhomogeneities

It is a well established fact that biometric artifacts can hamper face recognition and negatively affect performance. The temporal lag between enrollment and testing is preeminent among the factors leading to inaccurate recognition. Performance is also known to be affected by the very composition of the population. Older people are easier to recognize than the younger ones because everyone ages in a different way. The effects listed above are categorical rather than individual effects. There has been little error analysis, however, on assigning personal responsibility regarding the errors encountered and dealing with them. Pattern Specific Error Inhomogeneities (PSEI) analysis (Doddington et al., 1998) recognizes the fact that the error rates indeed vary across the population and seeks to discriminate among clients according to their propensity to cause errors. PSEI has led to the jocular characterization of the target population as being composed, among others, of "*sheep*" and "*goats*". In this characterization, the *sheep*, for which authentication systems perform reasonably well, dominate the population, whereas the *goats*, though in a minority, tend to determine the comparative performance of the biometric system through their disproportionate contribution of false reject errors. Similar to targets, the impostors also get barnyard appellations. There are impostors who have unusually good success at impersonating many different targets. These are called "*wolves*". There are also some targets that are easy to imitate and thus seem unusually susceptible to many different impostors. These are called "*lambs*". Performance can be improved if some of the most difficult data (e.g., the "*goats*", the hard to match subjects) were excluded and/or processed differently. In general, if the tails of the ROC curve do not asymptote at zero FAR and zero FRR, there is probably some data that could be profitably excluded and maybe processed off-line. The trick is to find automatic means for detecting such "poor" data items (Bolle et al., 2004) and to adopt biometric solutions different from "one size fits all."

The PSEI approach described here divides the clients' faces into corresponding "barnyard" classes (Li and Wechsler, 2005). The analysis of the error structure in terms of rejection and acceptance decisions follows that of Pankanti et al. (2002) for fingerprints but is driven here instead by transduction using the paradigm of open set face recognition (see Sects. 6.3 and 6.4). Recall that a (new) probe is rejected if the relationship $PSR_{new} \leq \Theta$ holds true, and that authentication takes place for (large) PSR values that exceed Θ. There are low peak-to-side ratio PSR scores X that, in general, do not generate false rejects, and there are high PSR scores Y associated with clients that, in general, do not generate false accepts. The corresponding "rejection/mismatch" and "acceptance/match" cumulative distributions for some rejection threshold $T = \Theta$ are F^T and G^T

$$F^T(x) = \frac{\#(PSR \leq x | PSR \leq T)}{\#(PSR \leq T)} \quad (13.28)$$

$$G^T(y) = \frac{\#(PSR \geq y | PSR > T)}{\#(PSR > T)} \quad (13.29)$$

As the scores X and Y are samples of ordinal random variables, the Kolmogorov-Smirnov (KS) test compares the individual score distributions $F_i(x)$ and $G_i(y)$ (see below) for client/subject i with the (typical) distributions F^T and G^T, respectively

$$F_i(x) = \frac{\#(PSR \leq x | PSR \text{ from rejected subject } i)}{\#(PSR \text{ from rejected subject } i)} \quad (13.30)$$

$$G_i(y) = \frac{\#(PSR \geq y | PSR \text{ from accepted subject } i)}{\#(PSR \text{ from accepted subject } i)} \quad (13.31)$$

The distances between the typical and individual distributions used by the KS test are $|\Delta_i^F|$ and $|\Delta_i^G|$, respectively. They quantify the variance in behavior for subject i from typical behavior. The unsigned Δ_i^F and Δ_i^G quantities (see Fig. 13.2a), however, are those used instead for PSEI analysis, because they show how well the PSR scores for subject i "agree" with the scores originating from well behaved subjects and corresponding thus to easy but correct rejection or recognition, respectively

$$\Delta_i^F = F_i(x_{\max}) - F^T(x_{\max}) \text{ where } x_{\max} = \arg\max |F_i(x) - F^T(x)| \quad (13.32)$$

$$\Delta_i^G = G_i(y_{\max}) - G^T(y_{\max}) \text{ where } y_{\max} = \arg\max |G_i(y) - G^T(y)| \quad (13.33)$$

Negative (positive) Δ indicates that the average population score characteristic of some subject i is lower (higher) than the average (well-behaved) overall population. The identities left (right) of the y-axis display undesirable (desirable) intra-pattern similarity. Identities above (below) the x-axis display desirable (undesirable) inter-pattern similarity. Many identities clustered along the coordinate axes imply that sharing both the (un)desirable match score property and the (un)desirable non-match property is very unlikely. Most of the population shows either a central (near origin) tendency or a tendency to deviate along one of the axes. For rejection, positive (negative) Δ_i^F implies that the average rejection PSR for subject i is higher (lower) than the average rejection PSR for the whole population. For acceptance, negative (positive) Δ_i^G implies that the average acceptance PSR for subject i is higher (lower) than the average acceptance PSR for the whole population. The different types of barnyard animals are displayed in Fig. 13.2a using a four-quadrant diagram induced by the 2D scatter plot of (Δ_i^F, Δ_i^G). In general, the more negative Δ_i^F is, the more the false acceptance rate the subject i is responsible for; the more positive Δ_i^G is, the more the false rejection rate the subject i is responsible for.

A threshold has to be ultimately chosen for deciding what counts as desirable or undesirable biometric behavior. If one assumes that the well-behaved set of subjects is responsible for only 1% false rejection or false acceptance, one sorts Δ_i^F and Δ_i^G and determines the thresholds T_F and T_G such that (i) all subjects for whom $\Delta_i^F \geq T_F$ account only for 1% false acceptance; and (ii) all subjects for whom $\Delta_i^F \leq T_G$ account only for 1% false acceptance. Most of the *sheep* occupy the forth quadrant and are characterized by desirable rejection behavior when Δ_i^F is greater than T_F and desirable acceptance behavior when Δ_i^G is less than T_G. Note that if the PSR value of the probe is far away from the threshold, the decisions are easy to make; only the parts of the distributions near thresholds are likely to contribute to errors and need to be considered.

The first quadrant (see the zoo in Fig. 13.2a) is characteristic of subjects that display desirable rejection behavior (when they should be indeed rejected) but also of subjects showing undesirable rejection behavior (when they should be accepted) (*wolves/lambs*). The second quadrant includes subjects that are difficult to label in terms of rejection or recognition (*goats*). The third quadrant is characteristic of subjects that display desirable acceptance behavior (when they should be accepted) but also of subjects showing undesirable acceptance behavior when they should be instead rejected (*goats*). Finally, the fourth quadrant represents subjects with good performance (*sheep*).

PSEI error analysis, using the approach described above, has shown that only a small number of face patterns are indeed responsible for much of the error observed. Open Set TCM-kNN using either PCA or Fisherfaces components was run 1,000 times to yield corresponding PSR scores. The overlap, of size $m = 40$, between the gallery and test sets, each of size 80, is randomly chosen. The 2D scatter plots of (Δ_i^F, Δ_i^G) for Open Set TCM-kNN using PCA and Fisherfaces are shown in Figs.13.2b and 13.2c. Most of the subjects show a central (near origin) tendency with good performance. Several subjects show the tendency to deviate along one of the axes. Only few subjects show undesirable characteristics along both axes. The average false rejection and false acceptance rates for Open Set TCM-kNN using PCA components are 13.36% and 8.29%, respectively. The subjects with the top 10(20)Δ_i^G values contribute 24.76% (50.09%) of the total false rejection rate. The subjects with top 10 (20) $-\Delta_i^F$ values contribute 28.54% (49.85%) of the total false acceptance rate. The average false rejection and false acceptance rates for Open Set TCM-kNN using Fisherfaces are 8.33% and 4.37%, respectively. The subjects with top 10(20)Δ_i^G values contribute 32.19% (62.64%) of the total false rejection rate, and the subjects with top 10(20)$-\Delta_i^F$ values contribute 38.74% (68.83%) of the total false acceptance rate.

The knowledge gained from PSEI error analysis helps with face recognition. The decision threshold for determining "bad" face patterns, which are prone to errors, is determined using the individual (Δ_i^F, Δ_i^G) characteristics for both PCA and Fisherfaces components. For PCA, there were 52 (34.67%) subjects identified as sheep or

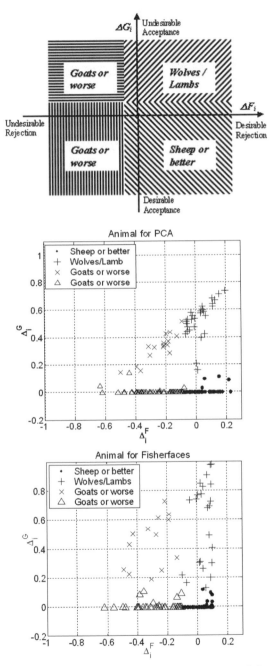

Fig. 13.2. PSEI Error Analysis (Reprinted from Li and Wechsler, Open Set Face Recognition Using Transduction, IEEE Transactions on Pattern Analysis and Machine Intelligence, ©2005 IEEE).

better, 28 (18.67%) subjects identified as wolves/lambs, and 54 (36%) subjects identi-fied as goats or worse (in the third quadrant). Only 16 (10.67%) of the subjects were identified as goats or worse in the second quadrant, and they contributed to both 22.92% false rejection and 20.94% false acceptance. 37% of the subjects were identi-fied as error prone animals (not sheep) and they contributed about 98.2% and 98.9% of the total false rejection and false acceptance errors, respectively. For Fisherfaces, there were 78 (52%) subjects identified as sheep or better, 24 (16%) subjects identified as wolves/lambs, and 35 (23.3%) subjects identified as goats or worse (in the third quadrant). Only 13 (8.67%) of the subjects were identified as goats or worse (in the second quadrant), and they contributed to both 32.1% false rejection and 29.0% false acceptance. 48% of the subjects were identified as error prone animals (not sheep), and they contributed about 98.9% and 98.5% of the total false rejection and false acceptance errors, respectively. All the error prone animals contribute to either false rejection or false acceptance for both PCA and Fisherfaces components. If some of the error prone animals were removed from the test set, the performance for Open Set TCM-kNN improves. As an example, if all *Goats* or worse in the second quadrant are removed from PCA and Fisherfaces recognition, and the watch list experiments (see Sect. 6.4) are redone, Open Set TCM-kNN performance scores now 85.69% and 91.63% accuracy (at FAR = 3%) for PCA and Fisherfaces, respectively, vs. the earlier results of 81% and 88% accuracy (but at higher FAR = 6%).

13.4 Large Scale Biometric Evaluations

Large scale biometric evaluations require that significant amounts of data are se-questered for testing. It is customary to provide the results using ROC and CMC curves built using score normalization and sliding thresholds. The large scale bio-metric evaluations carried out so far have more to do with testing algorithms rather than with decision-making full-fledged operational systems geared for mass screening (in the absence of ground truth). The discrepancy observed in performance between the relatively small but real face recognition evaluations (at Logan airport and Super Bowl) and the large scale face recognition evaluations shows that real operations are much more exacting than "clean room" competitions.

The large scale face recognition evaluations are recounted here to mark algorith-mic progress and list their highlights. The basic face recognition tasks and protocols (see Sect. 1.1) detail the framework used to conduct such evaluations. Figures of merit, virtual experiments, and the major facial data bases available were discussed earlier (see Ch. 12) and throughout this chapter. The evaluations recounted here in-clude FERET, FRVT2000, XM2VTS, BANCA, FRVT2002, and HumanID. FRGC and FRVT2006 are on-going face recognition evaluations. The evaluations listed do not render themselves to an easy comparison because the size, diversity, and the qual-ity of the data bases used are different. XM2VTS and BANCA evaluations are geared for authentication, and include a priori setting of decision thresholds.

Face Recognition Technology (FERET) evaluations were carried out between Au-gust 1994 and March 1997 using the FERET data base (Wechsler et al., 1998; Phillips et al., 2000) [2]. The face representations used were PCA, LDA, and Gabor Jets/DLA and their variants, the similarity measures employed were standard or (Mahalanobis) weighted L_1 and L_2, and elastic graph matching (EGM), and the baseline to compare against was PCA or correlation. Some algorithms were fully automated, while some only partially automated required the eyes' coordinates. Best CMC performance at rank 1 for face images captured during the same session using similar camera and lighting (FERET **fa** vs. **fb**) was 95% using partially automated PCA-difference space (see Sect. 6.2). Best CMC performance at rank 1 for duplicate images or images ac-quired during the same day but using a different camera and/or illumination were 60% and 80% using DLA and LDA, respectively. When the time lag between duplicates

---

[2] see also http://www.frvt.org/FERET/default.htm

was one year or more the best CMC at rank 1 yields 50% using DLA. The performance for fully automatic algorithms on corresponding tasks was much worse.

BANCA (Biometric Access Control for Network and e-Commerce Applications) (Bengio et al., 2001) evaluates face verification and fusion algorithms using audio tracks and images from XM2VTS. The objective was to optimize EER on the evaluation set. Training builds the client models, validation computes the decision by estimating optimal thresholds, and testing evaluates the whole system. There were 200 clients, 25 impostors for validation, and 70 impostors during testing and evaluation. Best performance, obtained using LDA and a client-specific threshold, was (FAR, FRR) = (2.3%, 2.4%). The client-specific threshold was found by projecting the probe to its specific LDA subspace learned during training and ensuring, using validation data and some desired operating ROC point, that the projection is far enough from the class of impostors.

Face Recognition Vendor Test 2000 (FRVT2000) was the first major technology evaluation to assess the functional capabilities for commercially available facial recognition systems (Blackburn et al., 2001). This included the determination of specific strengths and weaknesses for such systems and an overall assessment of the state-of-the art in face recognition in order to answer *Quo Vadis* (where do we go) type of questions. Vendors were provided with 13,872 face images from the FERET data base that were previously sequestered, and were asked to provide the full similarity matrix for them. Virtual experiments were administered to test for experimental conditions such as compression, distance, expression, illumination, pose, resolution, and temporal lag. Major weaknesses were identified. The results on the distance experiments were quite poor as expected. Even when the gallery was acquired indoor, under ambient lighting and with the camera at a distance of $1.5m$ from subjects (vs. $2m$ for the probe images), the best identification performance, in terms of CMC at rank 1, was only 43%. Temporal lag experiments on relatively small size ($\sim 1,000$) subsets showed a significant decrease in performance with the best CMC performance on identification at rank 1 hovering around 50%.

FRVT2002 was designed to measure technical progress since FRVT2000 and to evaluate performance on real-life large scale data bases (Phillips et al., 2003). It included both medium and high computation intensity evaluations, MCINT and HCINT, respectively. The number of clients available went up from 1,196 for FERET (and FRVT2000) to 37,437 for FRVT2002. The number of signatures enrolled for FRVT2000, FRVT2002-MCINT and FRVT2002-HCINT were 13,872, 7,500, and 121,589, respectively. The number of corresponding comparisons went up accordingly, from $\sim 192 \times 106$ (~ 72 hours with minimum 742 comparisons per second) for FRVT2000 to $\sim 15 \times 109$ (~ 264 hours with minimum 15,555 comparisons per second) for FRVT 2002 HCINT. The data corpus for HCINT was relatively homogeneous in terms of its composition.

The results from FRVT2002 for HCINT show that, given reasonable controlled indoor lighting, the best operating points (FAR, FRR) for ROC on verification using score normalization are (0.1%, 82%) and (1%, 90%). The top ranked 1 CMC identification rate was 85% on a data base subset of 800 people, 83% on a data base of 1,600, and 73% on the whole HCINT data base of 37,437 subjects. One of the conjectures advanced by FRVT2002 was that the identification performance decreases linearly with respect to the logarithm of the data base size. In particular, it was conjectured that for every doubling of the data base size, performance would decrease by 2%-3% points. Outdoor imagery was found to be a major challenge. The corresponding ROC operating point for faces captured outdoors was only (1%, 50%), i.e., about the same as that recorded earlier for FERET and thus practically useless. Temporal lag performance, still a challenge, appeared to degrade approximately 5% per lapsed year. This suggests that frequent updates or reenrollment are necessary for better security. Demographic information, e.g., age and gender, was found to significantly affect performance. Recognition rates for males were higher (by about 6% - 9%) than for females (see Sect. 2.2). Older people were easier to recognize than younger people, because time works differently on human faces and transforms, i.e., "caricatures", them in a unique way. For every ten years increase in age, the recognition rate increased by approximately 5%. One should not misinterpret this as superseding the decrease observed in temporal lag performance.

The Human Identification at a Distance (HumanID) program (2000-2003) aimed at developing automated biometric technologies to detect, recognize and identify humans at great distance. Such technologies are needed to provide critical early warning support for force protection and homeland defense against suspected threats. HumanID was expected to determine critical factors that affect performance, to identify the limits of feasible range and reliability, and the benefits expected to accrue for face recognition from the complementary use of gait analysis. HumanID was supposed to cover

- Operational evaluation of a long range (25-150 feet) face recognition system
- Development of a multi-spectral infrared and visible face recognition system
- Development of a low power millimeter wave radar system for wide field of view detection and narrow field of view gait classification
- Gait analysis performance characterization from video for human identification at a distance

HumanID found that gait analysis is not reliable and as one would expect, it becomes harder to identify people from increasing distances. Larger distances act as low pass filters and blur details. Geoffrey Loftus, a psychologist from the University of Washington, explains this in the context of eyewitness identification as follows "At 10 feet you might not be able to see individual eyelashes on a person's face. At 200 feet you would not even be able to see a person's eyes. At 500 feet you could see the person's head but just as one big blur. There is the equivalence between size and blurriness. By making something smaller you lose the fine detail." Better cameras with high resolution and zoom could overcome some of the distance handicap.

The Face Recognition Grand Challenge (FRGC) is the most recent attempt to rethink and recharge face recognition (Phillips et al., 2005). The main contenders for FRGC are high resolution images and 3D. In terms of resolution, the data made available by FRGC is such that the distance between the eyes is about 140 to 260 pixels rather than 40 to 60 pixels for previous evaluations and MRTD. 3D is expected to provide some of the means for coping with changes in lighting and pose. The overall objective is to ultimately reduce the error rate by an order of magnitude for verification. At the desired false acceptance rate of 0.1%, the goal is to leapfrog from the current 20% error experienced by FRVT2002 to a much lower 2% rejection error rate and reach a 98% hit rate. Even such low error rates, if achieved at all, would still be a hindrance for security when considering the number of people screened on a daily basis (see Sect. 13.2). FRGC serves as a pilot program for trying new technologies. The size of the FRGC population is much smaller compared to previous evaluations. The number of enrolled subjects is smaller by orders of magnitude compared to FRVT 2002. The FRGC population is even smaller than that of FERET, which still remains the de facto data base used for standard face recognition evaluations. Last but not least, the temporal lag for the corpus of data used for FRGC is smaller than that used during FRVT2002.

The large and still training set for FRGC consist of 222 subjects whose images were captured during 9 to 16 sessions (2002-2003) for a total of 12,776 recordings. Experiments are conducted on a validation set collected during 2003-2004 that consists of 466 subjects for whom data comes from 1 to 22 sessions for a total of 50,000 recordings that required 70 GB of storage. The three modes for processing are high resolution, 3D, and multiple images from the same person. The FRGC ver2.0 distribution consists of three parts. The first part is the FRGC ver2.0 data set. The second part is the FRGC Biometric Experimentation Environment (BEE). The BEE distribution includes all the data sets for performing and scoring the six ver2.0 experiments. The baseline or control algorithm to comparatively evaluate the FRGC evaluation results employs whitened PCA for face space, and the cosine of the angle between two whitened PCA representations for the similarity distance used by a nearest neighbor classifier. Data fusion (see Experiment 2 below) control algorithm employs the average of similarity scores.

A client set for FRGC consists of all the images captured for that client during a given session. The set consists of four controlled still images, two uncontrolled still images, and one 3D image. The controlled face images, captured in a studio-like setting, are frontal and were acquired under two lighting conditions and with two facial expressions (smiling and neutral). The uncontrolled images were captured under varying illumination conditions; e.g., hallways, atriums, or outdoors. Each set of uncontrolled images contains two expressions, smiling and neutral. The subject is cooperative under both the controlled and uncontrolled collection mode. The 3D image was captured under controlled illumination conditions. The 3D images consist of both a range and a texture image. The 3D images were acquired by a Minolta Vivid 900/910 series sensor [3].

FRGC ver2.0 consists of six experiments. In experiment 1, the gallery consists of a single controlled still image of a person and each probe consists of a single controlled still image. Experiment 1 is the control experiment. Both the target and query sets are of size 16,028. Note that the size refers to the number of different images rather than clients. Experiment 2 studies the effect on performance from the use of multiple still images from the same subject. Each biometric sample consists of the four controlled images captured in one session. This corresponds to data fusion for multiple image sets. Experiment 3 measures the performance of 3D face recognition by fusing texture and shape information. The gallery and probe sets consist of 3D images of a subject. The target and query sets are both of size 4,007. Experiment 4 measures the recognition performance for uncontrolled face images. The gallery consists of a single controlled still image, and the probe set consists of a single uncontrolled still image. The target and query sets are of size 16,028 and 8,014, respectively. Experiments 5 and 6 examine matching 3D and 2D images. In both experiments, the gallery consists of 3D images. In experiment 5, the probe set consists of a single controlled still face image. In experiment 6, the probe set consists of a single uncontrolled still face image. The BEE baseline verification performance, using PCA, for Experiments 1 through 4, at FAR = 0.1% were found to be 85%, 75%, 50%, and 15%, respectively. FRVT2006, the large scale face recognition evaluation that follows in the steps of FRGC, plans to assess commercial systems and their relative progress since FRVT2002.

FRGC addresses only verification. While it involves a much smaller number of subjects compared to FRVT 2002, it significantly increases the number of images available for each subject. Less subjects means less diversity, while more and better quality data helps with variability and supports data fusion. All in all, FRGC should be much easier than previous face recognition biometric evaluations, e.g., FRVT2002. As many factors can affect the results it will be difficult to ferret out to what extent the new generation of algorithms is better than the ones it tries to replace, if at all. One way to answer that question would have been to test the new algorithms on the legacy but larger data bases, in terms of subjects enrolled and their demographics, and compare their results against those obtained during earlier evaluations. Some of the conjectures advanced by FRGC based on some preliminary results, are

- the shape channel of one 3D image is more powerful for face recognition than one 2D image (Bowyer's)
- one high resolution 2D image is more powerful for face recognition than one 3D image (Phillips')
- using 4 or 5 well-chosen 2D face images is more powerful for recognition than one 3D face image or multi-modal (one image) 3D + (one image) 2D fusion
- the most promising aspect of 3D addresses the case where the known images of a person are 3D biometrics samples and the samples to be recognized are uncontrolled stills.

Large scale biometric evaluation share similar prediction interests with epidemiological (see Sect. 13.2) or financial evaluations. Bill Alpert has recently written an

---

[3] see http://www.frvt.org/FRGC/

article that reviews *The Little Book that Beats the Market* by Joel Greenblatt (see the March 27, 2006 issue of *Barron's*), a book that claims to describe a "magic formula" for picking stocks. The article, *The Little Book's Little Flaw*, raises several question marks on the way predictions are made and evaluated. Bill Alpert questions in particular the practice of spurious back-testing and lack of "out-of-sample" evaluations using several different data bases. Spurious back tests "are a hazard now that computers allow finance researchers to try formula after formula, until they get one that performs well on the data. If such a formula subsequently bombs out in the real world, it's said to have fallen prey to a problem known as over-fitting, data mining or data snooping. Score normalization and a priori threshold selection (see Sects. 12.2 and 12.3) are examples of back-testing used by FRVT2002. The conjecture advanced by FRVT2002, that the identification performance approximately decreases in a linear fashion 2%-3%, for every order of magnitude increase in gallery size, is yet another example of back testing used by FRVT2002. Last but not least, "physical scientists can repeat an experiment over and over, to generate data on hundred of independent trials." The large scale face recognition evaluations performed so far are limited by the (independence) assumptions made, back-testing using ground truth knowledge, the technological rather than scenario and field operation scope, and the scarcity of the data used with only one data base actually employed. Recent testimony by Dr. Martin Herman from NIST before the House of Representatives [4] in 2005 that "face images are not recommended by NIST for large scale applications," is partly motivated by the shortcomings observed during the large scale evaluations undertaken so far for face recognition.

Last but not least more reliable and realistic face recognition evaluations are urgently needed. Some of the shortcomings associated with the FERET (and FRVT) methodology were discussed throughout the book. The most problematic aspect of the FERET methodology (Phillips et al., 2000) is the use of ROC to report the absolute and relative performance for the top ranked biometric systems. ROC is based on sliding thresholds using ground-truth knowledge and score normalization. Ground-truth and gallery access are not available, however, during field operation. This makes the use of a priori thresholds and score normalization as practiced by FERET and FRVT not feasible in practice. The error analysis surrounding ROC using ellipses for confidence intervals used by FERET and FRVT is also not realistic (Mackassy, 2003) (see Sect. 13.1). The proper way to undertake large scale evaluations requires the use of data driven or empirical methods, in general, and cross-validation, in particular (see Sect. 13.1) rather than unrealistic "plug and play" methods (Bolle et al., 2004). A straightforward evaluation would employ k-fold cross-validation, with the empirical results partitioned in training (and possibly tuning) and testing sets. Optimal thresholds are iteratively learned (and possibly tuned) and frozen, and then used on the sequestered partition. The overall performance is reported in terms of the mean and variance observed for k-fold cross-validation. The same methodology holds for experiments geared to assess the effects of co-variants, e.g., gender and age. Another aspect that any new methodology should consider and evaluate is the effect that denial and deception plays on performance.

---

[4] http://hsc.house.gov/files/TestimonyHerman.pdf

14. Security and Privacy

Quis custodiet ipsos custodes? (Who shall guard the guardians?) (Juvenal)

The reliability concerns for face recognition go beyond mere performance accuracy. Reliability also addresses security and privacy with respect to the storage and distribution of biometric information. It concerns potential attacks, threats and vulnerabilities, and the means to thwart them. Security ensures authentication, non-repudiation, confidentiality, authorization and delegation, and data integrity. The face itself can become the means used to verify in a secure fashion other types of information. Face recognition can be remote or direct. The biometric system can be attacked at the client site, during communication, or at the host (server). Privacy safeguards the biometric details from unauthorized entities and/or fraudulent use, e.g., phishing and identity theft. Justice Louis Brandeis described privacy as "the right to be left alone." According to Crews (2002) "the challenge of the biometric future is to prevent mandatory national IDs [and unwelcome surveillance possibly using CCTV and/or RFID], ensure Fourth Amendment protections with respect to public surveillance, and avoid the blurring of public and private data bases [that] will undercut a presumptive right to maintain anonymity." Privacy and anonymity are potentially undermined because the face biometrics can be used as unprotected "cookies" for covert tracking. Looser matches undercut privacy too because they lead to an increase in the false positive error rate and place undue suspicion on innocent bystanders.

User authentication is split into object-, knowledge-, and ID- based categories. Standard authentication methods, e. g., physical possession of ID cards and passwords, are implemented using physical possession of tokens/objects or what you have and/or secret knowledge (of passwords) or what you know, and require an exact match. Tokens can be stolen, while passwords need to be memorized and can be easily forgotten. Due to sharing and/or improper capture, standard biometric methods lack the means for repudiation. Biometrics, in general, and face recognition, in particular, are driven by individual physical and behavioral characteristics or who you are, accrue the advantages of long passwords, and are hard to refute (but see Sect. 14.1). The matches for biometric authentication are never perfect and have to be adjudicated by decision policies using the similarity score for the match and the number of attempts initiated. Biometrics are overall more suitable for authentication purposes because they can't be forged, lost, or forgotten as it might be the case with ID cards, pins or passwords. Smart cards, physical tokens that include memory and often a processor, are some of the means used for enhanced security. The biometric template stored on the smart card is matched against the live biometrics presented by the user for authorization purposes. The smart cards are ideally suited for anonymity and privacy (see Sect. 14.5) because they do not require centralized storage, and because they include internal safeguards against tampering with the biometric data stored or its covert acquisition.

The threats affecting a biometric system are linked to its basic architecture and define specific points of attack and vulnerabilities. The threats are visualized around a pattern recognition system (see Fig. 1.2) further augmented by means for sensing, (networked and compressed) communication, and storage (Bolle et al., 2002; Bolle et al.,

2004). The biometric sub-tasks vulnerable to such threats include enrollment, feature extraction, template construction, matching, and decision-making. The transmission of information provides further opportunities for attackers to insert and/or intercept communication traffic and/or highjack the connection from legitimate clients. The threats and the corresponding vulnerability points (see Fig. 14.1) are the results of collusion, fraud and circumvention, e.g., Trojan horses that generate false results using disguise. They comprise injecting fake biometrics (see Tom Cruise in Minority Report for futuristic eye transplants to conceal his identity) including impersonation or coercive submission of biometrics ("1A"), lack of cooperation during enrollment ("1B"), covert acquisition and biometric replays or brute - force attacks using hill climbing to regenerate raw face images ("2") (see Sect. 14.2), capturing or subverting information ("3A"), e.g., the eigenspace and/or the means used to extract features, Trojan horses that consist of preselected features ("3B"), snooping/eavesdropping and/or replacing the biometric signatures before they reach a physically separated matcher ("4"), corrupting the matcher ("5"), improper access and use of stored templates ("6A") or tampering with stored templates ("6B") and their distribution to matching stations ("7"), and overriding the final biometric decision ("8") possibly by inserting a Trojan horse (Ratha et al., 2001). The wide availability of FERET from NIST and its use by many vendors to derive almost similar eigenfaces introduce additional vulnerabilities for privacy (image regeneration at attack point "2" using hill-climbing methods), and hacking geared to subvert the base representations and feature extraction ("3A") and ("3B"), respectively.

Replay attacks, another threat shared by both physical possession and biometrics, bypass the capture device using previously acquired passwords or templates, and are usually met using challenge/response pairs to validate the integrity of the signal captured. The response to guided challenges depends on both the challenge string and the signal acquired after the challenge was issued. This ensures freshness and authenticity against mere substitution and/or replay by the attacker. Interactive proofs [1] implement such challenge-response schemes and are the foundation for designing digital signature protocols [2]. In an interactive proof, the prover has to prove some fact, e.g., identity, to the verifier, i.e., the other party. Messages are exchanged between the prover and the verifier for the latter to eventually either accept or reject the "proof". Interactive proofs are expected to be complete and sound. Complete, to accept the proof if it is true, and sound to reject it if it is false. Another important characteristic of interactive proofs is that the verifier learns nothing about what has just been proved, e.g., identity. The proof can not be repeated without the prover participation and replay attacks are thus prevented. Zero knowledge protocols, e.g., Feige-Fiat-Shamir or Guillou-Quisquater proofs of identity, are useful cryptographic realizations for smart cards and embedded applications because they are faster than RSA (see below).

Replay attacks against biometrics can also be challenged and/or fought against using techniques similar to those used to enforce copyrights. Hidden data placed as digital watermarks in either (JPEG) compressed or uncompressed images can check for authenticity at the source (see Sect. 14.3 on steganography). Yet another scenario for replay attacks would decompress and decrypt the signal broadcast first. Spoofing or masquerading using fake biometrics, a variation on replay attacks, is a threat specific to biometrics (see Sect. 10.3 for checking on aliveness to counter spoofing). Some subjects are also better than others to succeed as imposters (see Sect. 13.3 on pattern specific error inhomogeneities). Last but not least, while physical possession once compromised can be easily cancelled and replaced, it is not obvious how to handle and/or replace compromised biometrics. One of the solutions proposed to prevent templates from being compromised and to safeguard confidentiality distorts (after proper alignment) in a unique and non-invertible fashion either the raw biometric signal and/or the features extracted during both enrollment and authentication. This yields multiple

---

[1] http://www.rsasecurity.com/rsalabs/node.asp?id=2178
[2] http://www.rsasecurity.com/rsalabs/node.asp?id=2182

but different biometric versions for the same client and prevents access to the original raw data and/or biometrics. Cancellation then "simply requires the specification of a new distortion transform" (Bolle et al., 2002). Teoh and Ngo (2005) have proposed to cancel biometrics using a "realization approach based on the iterated inner products between the tokenized pseudo-random number and the face features to produce a set of user-specific compact binary code, coined as FaceHash. Revocation of FaceHash is straightforward via token replacement and there is no deterministic way to reveal FaceHash without having both tokenized random number and face features."

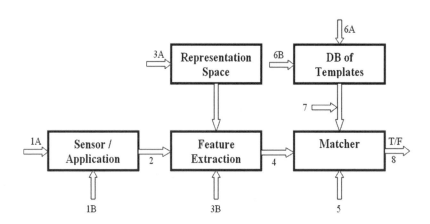

Fig. 14.1. Threats to Biometric Systems (Adapted from Bolles et al., Biometrics, ©2004 Springer).

A functional terminology for the threats enumerated so far would include *denial of service* when the biometric system becomes corrupted and is out of service, *circumvention* for attacks aimed at gaining access to unauthorized data, *repudiation* of ownership for specific biometrics using theft and/or improper match as ruses, *contamination* or *covert acquisition* of biometric imprints, and *collusion* or *coercion* for illegal acquisition of personal biometrics to gain unauthorized access and privileges to the authorization system (Jain et al., 1999; Maltoni et al., 2003). In summary, "biometrics work well only if the verifier can verify two things: one, that the biometric came from the person [owning them] at the time of verification, and two, that the biometric matches the master biometric on file. If the system can't do that, it can't work. Biometrics are unique identifiers, but they are not secrets. [They] don't handle failure well. Once someone steals your biometric, it remains stolen for life; there's no getting back to a secure situation. Biometrics are powerful and useful, but they are not keys. They are not useful when you need the characteristics of a key: secrecy, randomness, the ability to update or destroy" (Schneier, 1999).

An intriguing security application for face biometrics is related to CAPTCHA [3] (Von Ahn et al., 2003). CAPTCHA protects web sites and/or services from malicious computer programs impersonating humans. Completely **A**utomated **P**ublic **T**uring test to tell **C**omputers and **H**umans **A**part (CAPTCHA), text or image based, are based on hard interactive challenges known as Human Interactive Proofs (HIP) that differentiate between humans and smart programs or crawling agents like (soft) bots.

---

[3] see http://www.captcha.net

Most humans but not current bots are expected to pass such tests. Rui and Liu (2004) proposed ARTiFACIAL, which stands for Automated Reverse Turing test using FACIAL features, for a HIP algorithm. It is similar to a Turing test but it aims to differentiate bots from humans (rather than proving that the bots are as intelligent as humans.) ARTiFACIAL synthesizes an image with a distorted face embedded in clutter. The user is asked to find the face and click on six points (four eye corners and two mouth corners). Human users have no difficulty to complete the task whereas just the detection rate (without feature detection) for bots, using the best face detectors, is very poor. Another interesting CAPTCHA challenge will be to test potential bot impostors on face verification. Start from one face image and create two alternative versions using different transformations. The challenge is to authenticate the same identity for the two versions.

Another intriguing biometric application for human faces is to use them as passwords. *PassFaces*, from Real User Co., replaces traditional passwords with a logon made up of several faces, which are chosen at random from a large library of anonymous faces the user is presented with. Familiarization with the PassFaces is claimed to be fast. Authentication asks the user to identify the faces chosen ahead of time for her logon from consecutive displays, where each 3×3 grid of faces includes at some random location one of the chosen faces, while the other eight faces are used as decoys. The challenge-response succeeds once the whole logon is successfully identified. Davis, et al. (2004), however, dispute the reliability professed by PassFaces. In particular, they showed that the users tend to choose the most attractive faces or those representing the user's ethnicity making the logon not difficult to guess. The bias in the case of men was "so severe as to render the scheme fatally flawed." Ten percent of the passwords could be guessed within two attempts. This rendered the whole scheme insecure. The flaws observed are simply due to the fact that the passwords used have "entropy far below the theoretical optimum and, in some cases, that [they] are highly correlated with the race or gender of the user." The alternatives proposed to mitigate such threats are "to prohibit or limit user choices of passwords, to educate users on better approaches to select passwords, or to select images less prone to these types of [attraction and race] biases."

14.1 Diversity and Uniqueness

There is a lot of organic diversity including the human face. According to Dobzhansky (1951), one of the giants of modern genetics, "experience shows that every person whom one meets differs from all met before. Every human individual is unique, different from all others who live or lived." What is diversity after all? Again, according to Dobzhansky, diversity is "the discontinuity of the variation among organisms. The observed variation does not form any kind of continuous distribution. Instead, a multitude of separate, discrete distributions are found." Diversity also induces categorization and leads to the emergence of hierarchical order.

The conjecture under consideration here is that of biometric uniqueness, diversity notwithstanding. The conjecture claims says that no two individuals share the same (extracted) biometric characteristics. Note that the conjecture on uniqueness is concerned here with extracted and/or processed biometrics rather than the original client data. The validity for the conjecture advanced is highly relevant because it affects both security and privacy. There has been scrutiny of and challenge to this conjecture, in particular concerning the biometric signatures extracted and used for authentication. The US Supreme Court heard in 1993 the case of Daubert versus Merrell Dow Pharmaceuticals, Inc. One of the concerns raised was about the reliability of evidence. The Supreme Court did list several criteria for qualifying expert testimony:

- whether the particular technique or methodology in question has been subject to a statistical hypothesis testing
- whether its error rate has been established

- whether the standards controlling the technique's operation exist and have been maintained
- whether it has been peer reviewed and published
- whether it has a general widespread acceptance

In the context of face recognition, reliability requires signatures that are both original, i.e., uncorrupted, and that they can be traced to a unique individual, something that has never been done. There are studies on the individuality of iris codes (Daugman, 2003) and fingerprints (Pankanti et al., 2002), but none yet for human faces. Daugman (2000) has investigated the role of statistical decision theory, in general, and combinatorial complexity, in particular, to analyze decision landscapes, e.g., ROC, and to measure the uniqueness of biometric signatures. For biometrics that do not compare lists of distinct features but rather use a simple analogue measure such as correlation, using more (features) is not better. The basic but obvious observation made by Daugman is "how likely it is that some proportion of the features will be matched by chance by different people, and some proportion will fail to be matched even by the same person, that really determines the shape of the decision landscape. The goal of biometric feature encoding is to maximize the number of degree-of-freedom that will belong to the score distribution [arising from comparing different people], while minimizing the number [of degrees-of-freedom] that will belong to the authentic ["sameness"] distribution." One metric suggested by Daugman (2000) to gauge uniqueness is data size divided by its mean correlation. It corresponds to Hartley's classic definition of the number of degrees-of-freedom or the number of resolvable cells in the information diagram proposed by Gabor.

The key to iris recognition proposed by Daugman (2001) is "the failure of a test of statistical independence, which involves so many degrees of freedom such that this test is virtually guaranteed to pass whenever the [binary] phase codes for two different eyes are compared, but it uniquely fails when any eye's phase code is compared with another version of itself." The test of statistical independence is simply implemented using XOR applied to the 2048 bit phase vectors that encode any two iris patterns, masked (ANDed) by both of their corresponding mask bit vectors to prevent non-iris artifacts from influencing iris comparisons. The fractional Hamming distance (HD) implements the above test for statistical independence as it measures the dissimilarity between any two iris patterns. The number of degrees of freedom can be estimated by the number of seemingly independent yes/no questions the biometric signature queries about. Assume N to stand for the size of the subset of independent questions that can be answered by simple matching, and let the probability p for each match to hold true be the same, i.e., assume independent Bernoulli trials. The probability that some fraction $X = \frac{m}{N}$ of the questions has its answers matched by chance between unrelated signatures is binomially distributed with parameters (p, N)

$$P\left(X = \frac{m}{N}\right) = \left(\begin{array}{c} N \\ m \end{array}\right) p^m (1-p)^{(N-m)} \tag{14.1}$$

Exhaustive pairwise comparisons are made to estimate the disagreement or distance between unrelated biometric signatures. The mean p and standard deviation σ found are used to estimate N, the number of degrees of freedom, as $N = \frac{p(1-p)}{\sigma^2}$. As expected, the mean for uncorrelated irises was found to be close to 0.5, while the standard deviation estimate found, larger than what the theory predicts, was $\sigma = \left[\frac{p(1-p)}{N}\right]^{\frac{1}{2}}$. This indicates that the Bernoulli trials are correlated (but still binomially distributed) and leads to a corresponding decrease in the number of effective degrees-of-freedom. Note that the HD distribution is similar for both genetically identical and different irises in pairwised eyes suggesting that "the iris patterns are epigenetic, arising from random events and circumstances in the morphogenesis of this tissue" (Daugman, 2001). The uniqueness of failing the test for statistical independence corresponds to the case when the match HD found is less than the minimum HD observed for unrelated biometric signatures.

Diversity and uniqueness, in general, and flexibility and privacy, in particular, are further enhanced using different biometrics and fusing them. Woodward (1997) claims that "biometric balkanization, or the use of multiple biometric technologies deployed for multiple applications, provides greater privacy protections than does biometric centralization, or the use of one dominant biometric technology for multiple applications."

14.2 Regeneration of Face Images from Biometric Templates

The stored biometric templates are considered non-identifiable data, similar to a password hash, and are claimed to be immune to hacking. Soutar et al. (1999) and Adler (2003) have shown, however, that hill climbing can do "reverse engineering" and estimate source face images from their biometric templates using perturbations. Hill climbing, similar to stochastic search and genetic algorithms, requires "access to match score values for comparisons between an arbitrary image and the template of the target image. Beginning with a generic [best guess] initial image, such an algorithm makes small modifications, and measures the resulting changes in the match score value. Modifications, which increase the match score are retained, and, eventually, the modified image will resemble the unknown source image" (Adler, 2004). The restored images, shown to display much of the essential features needed for face discrimination, e.g., eyebrows and eye shape, nose and head shape, but not hair and moustache, could be used to masquerade legitimate users or visually identify them.

Hill climbing, the hallmark of brute-force attacks, e.g., Trojan horses, are immune to template encryption but can be thwarted first by limiting the number of sequential attempts (not necessarily consecutive). To prevent hill climbing attacks, BioAPI ANSI/INCITS 358 Version 1.1 specification from 2001 [4] recommends that match scores are quantized before release such that small changes to an image will normally not result in a change in the match score. Quantized levels significantly diminish the number of successful (random) perturbations the hacker can use to lock on the target. The scope for quantization is limited, however, by security applications that require accurate match scores for high confidence decisions. Knowledge of the face library used to derive the base representation for feature extraction, e.g., FERET, speeds up hill climbing and makes it more accurate and efficient against face recognition applications developed using FERET. Standard and modified hill climbing to restore source face images from their templates is described below.

Standard hill climbing based on eigenfaces includes both (i) *preprocessing* to normalize the "local" image database, e.g., FERET, and to calculate for each face its eigenface representation; and (ii) *regeneration* to restore source face images (Adler, 2003). Such processing involves searching for that image in the database that yields the maximum match score against the target template. Regeneration works [to optimize the image estimates and reflect the information stored by the template] by selecting at each iteration k an eigenface EF image, finding that value c that minimizes the match score $m(image[k] + c \cdot EF, target)$, updating the estimate $image[k + 1] = image[k] + c \cdot EF$, and cropping the image values to stay within legal bounds, if necessary. The iterations end when no further improvements are observed. Score normalization (see Sect. 12.2) starting from several initial guesses and averaging their estimates can improve on basic hill climbing performance.

The modified hill climbing algorithm described next "works separately on [A, B, C, and D] quadrants of an image. [From each EF image calculate the part for each quadrant, e.g., EF_A.] Because the quantized match score will not normally give information to allow hill climbing, a carefully chosen level of [degradation] [Gaussian] noise is introduced into the opposite image quadrant [to make it appear worse], in order to

---

[4] http://www.bioapi.org/BIOAPI.1.pdf

force the quantized score [below the threshold and] into a range where its information can once again be used" (Adler, 2004). The modified hill climbing algorithm loops as it selects a quadrant eigenface, e.g., EF_A, selects a degraded image in the opposite quadrant DI_D, finds k such that $m(image[k] + k \cdot DI_D, target)$ is one [discrete] score lower, finds c to maximize the score $m(image[k] + k \cdot DI_D + c \cdot EF_A, target)$, updates the estimate image $[k + 1] = image[k] + c \cdot EF$ and crops the image values to stay within legal bounds, if necessary.

14.3 Cryptography

Cryptography employs encryption for both confidentiality and data integrity. It keeps messages, in general, and authentication information, in particular, out of eavesdropping and snooping by hackers. The process of recovering the original message from the encrypted one is called decryption. The larger the key used for encryption is, the more difficult guessing the key and decryption are. Biometrics provide large keys for encryption, are relatively difficult to forge, and prevent repudiation. Similar to passwords in their use, the biometric template can be secured using a non-invertible "hash" transform expected to be collision free (but see birthday attacks). The same biometric template can be also bound to the cryptographic key during the generation process such that the latter will not be revealed without successful biometric authentication (Udulag et al., 2004). The perceived deficiency for using biometrics as passwords comes from their variability. As a consequence, inexact or flexible matching is required for authentication. This makes the generation of unique but identical cryptographic keys at both encryption and decryption difficult. Flexible matching can be performed using raw biometrics but becomes impractical for encryption. Encryption and quantization of matching scores are complementary to each other in mitigating replay and hill climbing attacks.

Encryption employs symmetric and asymmetric key algorithms. The symmetric key algorithm shares (via some type of communication and/or distribution) the same private and secret key for both encryption and decryption, e.g., DES. The asymmetric key scheme uses two different but related keys, a public one for encryption and a private one for decryption, e.g., RSA (Hellman, 1978; Adelman and Rivest, 1978). Communication involves now only the (trusted and authenticated) public keys while there is no sharing or communication of the private keys. The message sent by A to B is encrypted using B's public key and decrypted by B's using its own private key. The use of a public key is immune to brute force attacks because breaking it requires computationally expensive modulo arithmetic, solving discrete logarithms for large numbers, and factoring large numbers into two or more large (hundred of bits) primes. Digital signatures, which use asymmetric encryption schemes and trusted third parties, ensure non-repudiation and data integrity, and are essential for applications such as e-commerce. The sender A "digitally" signs using the message and her private key, and encrypts the message using destination B's public key. At the other end, the message is decrypted by B using her private key, and authenticated using A's public key. Digital signatures cannot be repudiated. This is different from secret-key authentication using Kerberos (see below) where copies for the secret keys are centrally stored and could be thus easily compromised on a large scale. Public-key cryptography can still be vulnerable to impostors attacking the certification authority and impersonating public identities. Public-key cryptography can be slow. Digital envelopes combine the speed of symmetric secret-keys with the security of asymmetric public-keys. The public-key secures the relatively short secret-key and thus handle the key management problem, while the secret-key encrypts the relatively long message.

The key distribution or management protocols vary according to their implementation. The same protocols can be shared by both user authentication and machine-machine authentication for ensuring secure and trusted sites (and against Trojan Horses), e.g., secure sockets layer (SSL) protocol for browser-server communication. Examples of specific protocols include shared and centralized authentication, e.g.,

RADIUS, cryptographic symmetric key distribution for network authentication, e.g., Kerberos, the latter requiring some public key infrastructure (PKI) [that is not easy to use and hard to deploy], and single "password" for multiple (internet) access, e.g., [biometrics as a personal] SSO [device] (O'Gorman, 2003). Host side attacks, at the server, are thwarted using non-invertible mappings such as one-way hash functions, e.g., SHA or MDA-5. Hashing, however, is not suitable alone because the biometrics are matched merely by closeness. Biometrics are better suited for use with smart cards rather than remote servers due to the latters' potential for large scale privacy and security subversion. The biometrics should always be encrypted, particularly if stored on a remote server. Last but not least, the biometrics are more reliable when used as part of a multi-strategy biometric authentication and cryptographic scheme.

Cryptography relies on randomness. It starts with one-way initial authentication but it can proceed during subsequent communication with two-way challenge and response authentication protocols that thwart suspected replay attacks. Challenge and response protocols in effect "time stamp" the input to ensure its immediacy. The protocols require that the host, after initial user U identification, sends the user some random number r that identifies the session, a hash function h, and a challenge f. The response expected from the user $f(r', h(P'))$ for the password and random number returned P' and r', respectively, should match $f(r, h(P(U)))$ at the host (O'Gorman, 2003). The protocol involves the biometric itself and some additional challenge that the user has to respond to.

14.4 Steganography and Digital Watermarking

Rather than encrypting messages for security purposes as cryptography does, steganography is "the art of hiding information in ways that prevent the detection of hidden messages" (Johnson and Jajodia, 1998). The term steganography, which comes from Greek where it means "covered writing," goes back to antiquity and medieval libraries where, for authors' safety, the real text was obscured under beautiful floral or more recently under invisible inks and microdots masquerading as periods. The message, e.g., the biometric signature, rather than being subject to encryption (and subsequent decryption) is dissimulated or hidden to prevent interception and replay attacks, on one side, and tampering, on the other side. Digital watermarking (Hartung et al., 1999), yet another security method characteristic of information hiding (Petitcolas et al., 1999), dissimulates a mark using a (public) key and it is particularly useful for forensics. It ensures the integrity of face images (or paper currency) while in traffic and thwarts forgery attempts to alter face images or their templates. Digital watermarks can be used to enforce and verify ownership (or copyrights). The concealed information that is added can be related to the biometric cover and remains secure even after decryption. "Traditional steganography conceals information; watermarks extend information and become an attribute of the cover image. Steganography's niche in security is to supplement cryptography, not to replace it" (Johnson and Jajodia, 1998). Steganography by definition arouses less suspicion than cryptography does. Digital watermarks are either visible or invisible, and their reproduction is usually quite difficult. The secret watermark, whose existence is not known, is not hidden in a fixed location but rather is placed in locations dependent on the structure of the face. Different watermarks are embedded in different face images according to their contents. The watermarks control the use of biometric information and prevent or track its illicit distribution. The rights that digital watermarks entail can be simply renewed, changed, and/or revoked.

An example for the use of steganography using acrostic is a message sent during WWI by a German spy "Apparently neutral's protest is thoroughly discounted and ignored. Isman hard hit. Blockade issue affects pretext for embargo on by $\cdots$" (Kahn, 1967). Taking the second letter in each word the following message emerges "Pershing sails from NY $\cdots$" Similar to cryptography, steganography can access some private but shared key K. Using a cover C, it embeds in a non-apparent fashion a hidden message

M to create a *stego-image* that is then ready for communication or use. The recipient or user recovers M using K, which for the German spy above meant to assemble the hidden message using each second letter from consecutive words. The steganography methods in use with digital images are either spatial or spectral (frequency), e.g., least significant bit insertion (LSB), change or replace small compression coefficients in some transformed space, e.g., DCT using LSB, masking and filtering, and spread spectrum, i.e., the hidden data is concealed across the whole cover that the spectrum provides. LSB is simple and fast to implement but vulnerable to cropping and compression. It is fragile and can become conspicuous with color images when the number of bits used is small. One can, however, tamper with face images without altering the LSB. The distinction between fragile and robust watermarks is that the fragile ones are destroyed when the message is tampered with, while the robust ones, once removed and/or defanged, would damage and even destroy the message itself. Spread spectrum (Cox et al., 1995) works in the frequency domain and is arguably more robust than the spatial domain methods. One of the transforms used is DCT or its block variation. The watermark is embedded within preselected frequencies, usually of higher amplitude to limit image alteration, and the amount of change chosen is less than just noticeable differences. Ruanaidth and Pun (1998) described a method for self-synchronization for watermarking that is based on the Fourier-Mellin transform and is thus invariant to scale, translation, and rotations (see also Alghoniemy and Tewfik (2000) and Lin et al. (2001) on invariance to geometric distortions).

Digital watermarks can alternatively be inserted using masking constrained by notions of non-visibility and sensitivity of the human visual system (HVS). Bas et al. (2002) proposed content insertion based on similarities using fractal coding. The detection of the watermark is done by seeking for similarities between related areas. The salient feature points provide the self-references needed for self-synchronization. Bogumil (2004) improves watermark robustness against both local and global (bilinear) geometric distortions (e.g., StirMark attacks to de-synchronize watermarking algorithms) using template self-referencing and autocorrelation features. Distortions are estimated and reversed to the extent possible in order to maximize watermark recovery. Criteria used to assess steganography and digital watermarking include fidelity and imperceptibility, capacity or information rate, reliability against detection (using statistical analysis or searching for repeated patterns and/or anomalies), immunity against unauthorized removal or insertion, robustness with respect to noise and image processing transformations, e.g., quantization, image conversion, (affine) geometric or bilinear distortions, cropping and (JPEG) compression, blur and/or enhancement, and costs (for embedding and extraction).

Steganography is also concerned with detecting hidden messages and thwarting removal attacks, e.g., median filters and contents screening. Digital watermarking shares similar criteria with steganography, e.g., imperceptibility, robustness (to survive distortions and/or attacks), and fragility to tampering. Faces can be either protected using steganography and digital watermarking or used for digital watermarking to protect other data. Modern steganography and digital watermarking model information hiding as a noisy channel for communication and treat it accordingly. Moulin and Koetter (2003; 2005) view hiding as a game between two (embedding/decoder and attacking) teams and develop practical codes for optimal data hiding and attack strategies. The main challenges listed are "(1) The watermarking process should introduce limited distortion in the host signal. Likewise, the attack should introduce limited distortion. (2) While the host signal is known to the information embedder, it may be unknown to the decoder (blind watermarking/data hiding). Additional side information (such as a cryptographic key) may be shared by the encoder and decoder. (3) The communication channel is under control of the attacker." The dual goals for game theory under the above scenario are for the embedding/decoder team to minimize the probability of error and for the attacker to maximize it.

Biometric data, even if it is watermarked, can still be attacked during transmission, e.g., cellular and wireless, altered (or eavesdropped) and then retransmitted to its final destination. In this context, Jain (2000) is interested in "determining whether the correct [face] image has in fact been sent and that it has been transmitted without alteration requires use of [exclusive] data the owner would prefer not to transmit (namely the [invisible] watermark itself or the original image). Therefore a different key needs to be used by the receiver for authentication." The key proposed, a matrix of local averages, is compact and can pinpoint if and where tampering took place. The key is only semi-unique because different alterations, if any, can still yield the same key. Face alterations that were handled successfully included smudges, compression at 70% or less, (Wiener) filtering for smoothing purposes. Note that "minor" alterations can also be traced to channel noise. Nikolaidis and Pitas (2000) proposed embedding and detecting a chaotic (trajectory) watermark in the digital spatial domain of color face images based on localized salient facial features. The watermarks so produced are non-invertible, while the feature make-up constitutes the equivalent of "fingerprints minutiae" and can withstand geometrical distortions. Cox et al. (2002) has taken an information theoretical perspective and proposed a communication channel using ICA for watermarking. For Bounkong et al. (2003) ICA "allows the maximization of the information content and minimization of the induced distortion by decomposing the cover text (in this case the [face] image) into statistically independent sources. Embedding information in one of these independent sources minimizes the emerging cross-channel interference." One can actually show that the information hiding capacity of statistically independent sources is maximal (Moulin and O'Sullivan, 2003). The factorized sources make Bayesian decoding efficient. Jain and Uludag (2005) describe how to hide faces in fingerprint images ("cover") using amplitude modulation-based watermarking. The watermark data, which consists of the eigenface coefficients of a user's face, can be used in authenticating the host fingerprint image.

Last but not least, the reader should be fully aware that there is an escalating race between defense and offence, e.g., jitter against spread spectrum-based methods, inversion attacks that insert additional watermarks to generate ambiguity and confusion, lack of synchronization, or signal denoising. Recall that steganography can be used as a means of covert communication, while steganalysis aims at detecting steganography. Methods are continuously devised to detect and disable both licit and illicit hidden information and to develop the means to thwart such attacks. StirMark [5] are 'fault analysis' tools that assess (robustness) and benchmark digital watermarks (Petitcolas, 2000). The best defense can still be to attack. Both steganography and digital watermarking apply to both 2D face images and (3D) video images.

14.5 Anonymity

A basic criticism of biometrics from the standpoint of privacy is that "we, as individuals, lose our anonymity whenever biometric scanning systems are deployed. Controlling information about ourselves includes our ability to keep other parties from knowing who we are. Biometrics can establish our identity almost instantaneously in unexpected, unwelcome, or unforeseen future circumstances, and in combination with related technologies would enable the state to monitor the actions and behavior of its citizenry" (Woodward, 1997). Drawing analogies from George Orwell's *1984*, while worrying about function creep [for biometrics] that would reduce the individual's reasonable expectation of privacy, Clarke (1994) writes that "any high-integrity identifier [such as biometric scanning] represents a threat to civil liberties, because it represents the basis for a ubiquitous identification scheme, and such a scheme provides enormous power over the populace. All human behavior would become transparent to the State, and the scope for non conformism and dissent would be muted to the point envisaged by the anti-utopian novelists." The above concerns can be addressed using a Code of Fair Information Practices (CFIP) and an outright legal prohibition of any kind of transactions in the secondary biometrics market (Woodward, 1997). Rather than "succumbing to the criticisms of biometrics as privacy's foe, the counter case needs to

---

[5] http://www.petitcolas.net/fabien/watermarking/stirmark/

be made: biometrics is privacy's friend [because it] protects information integrity in both the private- and public-sector context. By restricting access to personal information, biometrics provides effective privacy protection [and safeguards against fraud]" (Woodward, 1997). To what extent can anonymity be nevertheless preserved while using biometrics? This is discussed next.

Anonymity (see 6A and 6B in Fig. 14.1) is safeguarded if the authentication system does not store the original biometrics. Protection of templates from both outsiders and insiders can be achieved using private biometrics (Davida et al., 1998), fuzzy commitments (Juels and Wattenberg, 1999), cancelable biometrics (Ratha et al., 2001), and fuzzy vault architectures (Juels and Sudan, 2002) that use *helper data* for verification tasks (Tuyls and Goseling, 2003). Davida et al. (1998) have suggested using the biometric (iris) template as the information bits of an error correcting code. Protection for privacy is ensured when only the error correction bits rather than the template itself are physically stored. Assume that the binding authorization information, which includes $NAME$ and other public attributes $ATTR$ to increase the entropy, i.e., cryptographic strength, is linked to the template on some smart card or token. Assume also that the check digits for the biometric template T are C, and that their concatenation is simply $T||C$. Private and public keys are established and the latter distributed to biometric readers. Authentication for a newly captured biometric template T' succeeds when a match can be established between the (digitally) signed messages $SIGN(Hash(NAME, ATTR, T||C))$ and $SIGN(Hash(NAME, ATTR, T''||C))$ after error correction is performed on $T'||C$ to recover $T''||C$. Biometric identification correctly accepts a legitimate client whose T' has less than $\frac{d}{2}$ errors for a $[n, k, d]$ coding scheme of n bit code words (vectors), where k is the number of information digits, d is the minimum distance of the code, and algebraic decoding has been applied. Anonymity is preserved when only the error correcting bits C are stored in the database.

Fuzzy commitment (Juels and Wattenberg, 1999) expands on the scheme proposed by Davida et al.(see above) by using the template itself (without the check bits) as a code word that serves the role of witness and can vary, i.e., is fuzzy. Biometrics are used as private keys during both encryption ("commitment") and decryption ("decommitment"). The proposed scheme makes reference to the original biometric T as $T = s + \delta$ and stores an encrypted version $F(s, T) = (h(s), \delta) = (\alpha, T - s)$ using some secure (one-way) hash function h, e.g., $SH - 1$, and leaving δ in the clear. To decommit $F(s, T) = (T', \delta)$ using a newly captured template T', which is close to T and comes from the same client, the biometric reader computes $s' = f(T' - \delta) = f(s + (T' - T))$ using the error decoding function f. If $\alpha = h(s')$ holds true authentication succeeds. Fuzzy commitment works to the extent that T and T' are properly aligned and ordered. All the schemes proposed, sensitive to variability and distortions, are likely to yield unacceptably high false reject rates. This is formalized next.

The threats to the original biometrics are ineffective when "(1) the information that is stored in the database does not give sufficient information to make successful impersonation possible and (2) the information in the database provides the least possible information about the original biometrics, in particular it reveals no sensitive information" (Tuyls and Goseling, 2003). Towards that end, one could simply store the biometrics in a cryptographically (non-invertible) hashed form and match the hashed value rather than the original biometrics. This is infeasible, however, because the biometrics are noisy to start with and the hashed value will fail to match. Decryption becomes then necessary and vulnerabilities crop up. Biometric authentication can still be combined with cryptography using helper data derived during enrollment (see above). "The helper data [stored in the database and publicly available] guarantees that a unique string can be derived from the biometrics of an individual during authentication as well as during the enrollment phase" (Tuyls and Goseling, 2003). The proposed (quantization) scheme by Tuyls and Goseling employs at enrollment some mapping M to generate secret reference data s [from the biometric B possibly using significant PCA components], which is statistically independent [in terms of mutual information I] of the helper data W [generated from B too], and stores it in hashed form $h(s)$ together with the helper data W. The helper data W could consist of residuals that complete B according to a scheme driven by the secret s. During authentication, a noisy version B' of the biometric is captured, and a secret s' is generated by M using B' and W such that $s \approx s'$. Using error correction on the secret bits of s and s', an exact match is required between the hashed versions $h(s)$ and $h(s')$ for verification to succeed without any uncertainty [in terms of entropy H]. Brute force attacks are prevented when the set of secrets $S = \{s\}$ is sufficiently large. The proposed scheme works when W depends on B and

$$P(M(B + \text{ noise}, W) \neq M(B, W)) \leq \delta \qquad (14.2)$$

$$I(W; s) \leq \epsilon \qquad (14.3)$$

$$H(s|B, W) = H(s'|B', W) = 0 \qquad (14.4)$$

Dodis et al. (2004) combine randomness and error-correction to expand on the fuzzy and helper data schemes. They describe how to generate keys from noisy data, e.g., biometrics B, and the means to reliably and securely authenticate them. The "noisy" keys are "neither reproducible precisely nor distributed uniformly," which are basic requirements for cryptography but hard to be met in practice by biometrics. The cryptographic primitives proposed include "a fuzzy extractor that extracts nearly uniform [and error-tolerant] randomness R from its biometric input; and a [public] secure sketch about [error prone] B without revealing it [but] helping with its exact recovery for close examples." Practical constructions for secure sketches and fuzzy extractors are provided in three metrics: Hamming distance, set difference, and edit distance. Chang and Li (2005) argue that set difference is insufficient to model noise and propose point set differences instead for small but secure sketches.

Biometric anonymity can draw further insights from network communication. Pfitzmann and Köhntopp (2000) define anonymity as "the state of being not identifiable within a set of objects, the anonymity set" and refine the concept using metrics like "anonymity is the stronger, the larger the respective [cardinality of the k] anonymity set is and the more evenly distributed the sending or receiving, respectively, of the subjects within that set is." Serjantov and Danezis (2002) make the obvious observation that "the potentially different probabilities of different members of the anonymity set actually having sent or received the message are unwisely ignored. Yet they can give a lot of extra information to the attacker [and increase apparent vulnerability]." This carries over to biometrics where the users engage differently in authentication, e. g., time, roles, protocols, and routing. As a first step, anonymity should thus be measured using entropy rather than cardinality. More sophisticated metrics that use knowledge-based vulnerabilities for mix-based biometric systems should be explored (Serjantov and Danezis (2004).

Newton et al. (2003) made the interesting suggestion of de-identifying facial images in the context of sharing video surveillance data for the purpose of "limiting automatic persistent recognition of populations whose images are captured on video but who have done nothing suspicious" and protecting privacy. Many facial characteristics are left in place but the face cannot be reliably recognized. Effective de-identification, related to denial and deception (see Ch. 10) and perturbations (see cancelable biometrics above), should meet both security and privacy concerns. The method proposed "determines similarity between faces based on a distance metric and creates new faces by averaging image components, which may be the original k-same image pixels or k-same eigenvectors." Ad-hoc de-identification methods, e.g., masking (of eyes), were shown deficient with respect to thwarting face recognition software.

Alexander and Smith (2003) are also concerned with protecting privacy in public and defeating perceived threats, e.g., Human ID at a Distance (HID). The thread for the methods considered is to confound the face recognition software, e.g., denying the ability to locate the eyes for normalization purposes. The goal for the "disguise" countermeasures proposed is to keep as many correct identifications as possible out of the top N ranks. The countermeasures used were concealment behind an opaque object, or overloading the camera's sensory apparatus with a bright light source. The degree to which those two broad classes of methods appear to work "can be summed up in a single word: *contrast*, i.e., large color difference between adjacent pixels. That is, the single most important factor seems to be to add as much contrast as possible, contrast that the system cannot predict based solely on the training photographs, or else to conceal or distract from a contrast that the system expects to find." The explanation for such findings is simply that proper contrast usually leads to discriminating features and thus to recognition. Playing with contrast is similar to deploying camouflage and/or distracters. Alexander and Smith point out that privacy protection could be modeled using the noisy channel concept from information theory where a non-cooperative subject would be involved with both transmission (of biometric data) and jamming. The most effective means for privacy protection would require targeted rather than random noise.

14.6 Photofits

Photofits are face resemblances constructed from images of remembered facial features using manual or computerized recall systems. The sketch artists were the first to try to reconstruct face images from witnesses' verbal recall. Verbal description, however, "overshadows" and interferes with reconstruction and identification. As sketches contain mostly shape information and little texture, if any, they are poor candidates for reliable authentication. Early photofit systems were manual, e.g., *Idenkit* using line drawings printed on transparencies or *Photofit* using photos of individual features. The manual process, which had access to a limited range of relatively rigid features, is slow. The result is not very life-like, and target identification from memory, about 12.5%, is quite low (Ellis, Sheperd, and Davis, 1975). Familiarity, context, exposure time, delay, target distinctiveness, illusory causation (see below), emotion, stress, and age play an important role in the quality and usefulness of the photofits assembled. The presence of the target helps with recall. Current computerized photofit systems are much faster and more consistent with helping witnesses choose from a wide range of photographed features to montage them. Examples of computerized systems include Mac-A-Mug Pro, E-FIT, FACES, Idenkit2000, and PROfit. Morphing, warping, multi-views (frontal and $\frac{3}{4}$), aging, accessories such as spectacles and hats, and last but not least a diverse and large database of more than 20,000 features, are used to further improve on the quality of the photofits by *PROfit* [6] from ABM UK. Features can be resized, repositioned, lightened or darkened and enhanced to reflect witnesses' recall. It has been reported that the naming performance for computerized photofits hovers around 20%. A forensically valid comparison of facial composite systems, which utilized only a 3-4 hour delay between encoding and cognitive interview, was reported by Frowd et al. (2005a).

Merely choosing features without any relation to the whole face is, however, lacking and inefficient. A pastiche of incongruous parts is not good enough. We have seen elsewhere in this book that for reasons of reliability and robustness, face recognition employs the recognition-by-parts paradigm where both the parts and their relative layout are important. The assembly of parts to make a face recognizable requires optimized search. Genetic algorithms, in particular, are suitable for the assembly task involved to create photofits using optimal design principles. The face should evolve in an iterative fashion until the resulting photofit is indeed "fit" enough to satisfy the user. *EigenFIT* (Solomon at Univ. of Kent, UK) and *EvoFIT* (Frowd and Hancock at Univ. of Sterling, UK) are software packages that work in similar ways to evolve photofits [7]. "Using the sex, race and hairstyle of the person the witness remembers, the genetic algorithm produces nine random faces, from which the witness chooses the one that seems the closest likeness. The [computer] algorithm then uses this face to mutate a new set of variants. The [non-verbal] cycle continues until the witness is happy with

---

[6] http://www.abm-uk.com/uk/pdfs/profit.pdf
[7] see electronic *NewScientist.com* at http://www.newscientist.com/article.ns?id=dn7143)

the likeness. Each generation can be calculated in seconds, making the process far quicker than retrieving facial features from databases and trying them one by one." But just what is being evolved? Similar to evolutionary pursuit (Liu and Wechsler, 2000) (see Sect. 5.5) each face is represented by an array of fifty principal components. "If [one] changes just one of these parameters it alters the face, albeit rather subtly. It might make the skin a bit darker, wrinklier, or move the nose up the face a bit." Once a feature, say the mouth, is correct it can be "locked," and the rest of the face evolved around it. The holistic regeneration of the raw face from witnesses bears close analogies to the regeneration of the face from biometric template by hackers (see Sect. 14.2). Face mutation can draw from one witness or a combination of them to obtain a better likeness. EvoFIT still is quite complex to use and its performance is rather poor (Frowd et al., 2005b).

The reliability of photofits as forensic evidence, has been recently questioned along lines similar to those discussed in the context of diversity and uniqueness (see Sect. 14.1). Lassiter (2002) has researched how people organize and comprehend the information contained in another person's ongoing stream of behavior, and the use of videotape technology to record and present confession evidence to mock juries. The goal was to determine more objectively whether a confession was voluntary or coerced. "Relative to other confession-presentation formats, e.g., audiotapes and transcripts, videotapes that are recorded with the focus on the confessor [compared with other points of view] tend to produce judgments of greater voluntariness and guilt. [The explanation is that] people attribute unwarranted causality (influence) to a stimulus simply because it is more noticeable or salient than other available stimuli."

Frowd et al. (2005a) assess the impact of a forensically-relevant target delay using a more realistic two day interval between seeing an "assailant" and constructing a composite. Composite naming was surprisingly low (3% overall), with sketches named best at 8%. The conclusions drawn suggest that "the computerized systems tested [E-FIT, PROfit (see above), and (human) sketch from UK, FACES [8] from USA and EvoFIT (see above), a system still under development from UK] perform equivalently but are poorer than the manually-generated sketches. Lastly, the data suggest that line-ups may be a poor instrument for evaluating facial composites." Photofits, in general, and sketches, in particular, can be used for automatic face recognition. Tang and Wang (2004) describe how sketches derived from photo images can be matched against manual sketches using eigenfaces.

---

[8] http://www.iqbiometrix.com/products_faces.html

15. e-Science and Computing

There are therefore two sorts of mind: one penetrates quickly and deeply the conclusions of principle, and that is the accurate mind; the other can grasp a large number of principles without mixing them up, and that is the mathematical mind. The first is a powerful and precise mind, the other demonstrates breadth of mind. Now it is quite possible for one to work without the other, for a mind can be powerful and narrow, and can be also broad and weak (Pascal).

The question addressed in this chapter is how to expand the scope for biometrics and how to add to existing knowledge and practice. Alternatively, the question addressed is how to combine the two kinds of minds Pascal talks about. The rapid increase expected in biometric data volumes is not matched by a commensurate increase in the quantity or quality of (data intensive) scientific research tools. To reach existing and future biometric challenges, we propose here the idea of agent-based middleware, driven by machine learning, to automate the process of data search, query formulation, workflow configuration and service composition, and collaborative reuse. This should permit biometrics to include a much larger volume and diversity of data in the discovery process than would otherwise be possible. The overall working theme here is moving from mere access to biometric data to information integration and scientific discovery, which should lead to more reliable face recognition systems. The end-user is faced with a seemingly inexhaustible search space of data collections and analysis tools. What this user needs is an intermediary (agent or middleware) architecture that recognizes the user's patterns of data usage and analysis, and then automatically assists the user with data discovery, navigation, retrieval, mining, fusion, and analysis. Precision and recall metrics validate the search and discovery capabilities of the proposed architecture.

The unabated exponential growth of data and information contents in biometric databases is a well documented challenge for researchers. This challenge is matched by the comparably daunting heterogeneity and distributed nature of data and analysis tools, which need to be integrated in order to solve the fundamental problems face recognition science, engineering, and technology have to cope with. It is often found that great advances in human knowledge occur when seemingly disconnected facts (perhaps from completely disparate disciplines or methodologies) are found to be intimately joined in some previously unexpected conceptual or physical unification. The nature of such connections for face recognition could reveal itself through further integration and fusion of knowledge drawn from disparate domains, e.g., data compression for image capture, strangeness for feature selection and outlier detection, transduction for open set face recognition, and voting schemes for data fusion .

As computational horsepower, network bandwidth and speed, algorithmic sophistication, and data storage capabilities continue to grow at prodigious rates, the problem of data and information integration becomes even more acute. Frequently, the semantic or contextual information that enables easy integration and co-analysis of disparate data sources, possibly acquired using different sensors and modalities, is missing from the face recognition data bases. This is a natural consequence of the fact that the primary end-users of these systems were envisioned and (through self-fulfilling prophecy) continue to be domain experts who have no need for the semantic [and pragmatic] context, e.g., age, gender and/or ethnicity, to be explicitly annotated. With the advent of worldwide high-speed networks, it is now possible for scientists and engineers to tap into a seemingly limitless plethora of databases for solving hard research problems in their domains. To solve the fundamentally novel interdisciplinary problems at the interface of different disciplines, researchers are increasingly probing territory that has not been yet chartered. Even within a single discipline, the data and information resources may reside in many places using different data base systems and/or image standards.. What is required to address such challenges is the use of electronic-science or e-science.

E-science refers to large scale science projects that are increasingly carried out through distributed global collaboration enabled by the Internet. This allows scientists to generate, analyze, and share their insights, experiments, and results in a more effective manner. It brokers virtual collaboration and leads to seamless automation. Typically, a feature of such collaborative scientific enterprises is the one that requires "access to very large data collections, very large computing resources and high performance visualization" [1]. The Grid architecture provides the generic middleware required to enable e-science and virtual organizations. The face recognition enterprise, characterized by similar characteristics, is expected to benefit from e-science too. In particular, face recognition would gain from access that goes beyond the facial data (bases) needed for performance evaluation. This includes access to the specific components needed to build up effective and transparent face recognition systems including proper evaluation and testing environments.

The main functionality of current face recognition R&D is to "search and find" (i.e., to provide a unified interface to assist users in efficiently locating relevant data sources in distributed heterogeneous data archives). The quest for the computational environment of the future - where *Web Services* meet the *Semantic Web* meets *The Grid* - is generating an enormous effort to develop agent-based virtual organizations that address the semantics/pragmatics - services/utilities interface. Such virtual organizations take into account specific tasks and functionalities, user profiles and interests, costs, utility, and ultimately the very availability of resources. The three components mentioned above are briefly reviewed next.

The term Grid was coined by Foster and Kesselman (1998) to "describe a set of resources distributed over wide area networks that can support large-scale distributed applications. The Grid is like the electrical power grid: access to computation and data should be as easy, pervasive, and standard as plugging in an appliance into an outlet." The connection between the Grid and pervasive or ubiquitous computing is straightforward. The Grid leverages distributed resources, and negotiates the sharing of those resources. Complementary but similar to the Grid are adaptive computing (HP Open View), on-demand autonomic computing (IBM), agile computing, and organic or dynamic computing (Sun and Microsoft). The ultimate objective is an autonomy that leads to self-{configuration, diagnosis, healing, optimization, and security} computing, and also to innovation. Open-source software posts *inter lingua* standards in order for different software packages, referred to as web services, to talk to each other without human participation. Alternatively, web services are a utility delivered over the net and paid for according to its use and economics. This is different from traditional application service providers (ASP) for whom the appropriate analogy is that of a dedicated rental for specific services. The Grid offerings include science portals, resource discovery, large-scale data analysis, computer - in the loop instrumentation for quasi-real-time analysis, collaborative work, access negotiation, software and hardware configuration, and data integrity and security.

There is a growing trend towards the convergence of Grid computing with so-called "peer-to-peer" (P2P) computing. P2P is generally defined as a class of applications that takes advantage of resources that are available at the edges of the Internet. P2P services sprung up from grass-roots user communities, especially those interested in file sharing, and avoid using centralized IP services. In contrast, the driving forces behind

---

[1] http://www.rcuk.ac.uk/science/

Grid computing are scientific and research communities. Despite these differences, both the Grid and P2P emphasize a decentralized and shared approach to distributed computing.

The Semantic Web is an extension of the current Web in which information acquires well-defined meaning, and facilitates human - machine communication. Data on the Web is now defined and linked in a way that leads to more effective discovery, automation, integration, and reuse across various applications. The Web can reach its full potential if it becomes a place where "data can be shared and processed by automated tools as well by people" [2]. "The Semantic Web is not a separate Web but an extension of the current one, in which information is given well-defined meaning, better enabling people and computers to work in cooperation" (Berners-Lee et al., 2001) in order for the web to understand its findings. The Semantic Web expands on the functionality of the Grid as it exists now. The key to this is "an infrastructure where all the resources, including services, are adequately described in a form that is machine-processed, i.e., knowledge becomes explicit. Semantic interoperability and seamless automation deliver semantic services for Grid-based large-scale science using easily deployed components whose utility transcends their immediate application" [3]. The Semantic Web includes tools for ontology building (DUET [DAML UML] and Protégé), annotation (UBOT [UML based]), learning (Corporum), and navigation and manipulation (DAML and Jena API) tools.

The Semantic Grid broadens the scope of virtual organizations and the services they provide by merging the Grid and the Semantic Web. Learning and adaptation are paramount and user profiles and interests drive the optimal (re)-configuration of the Grid to support workflow management and delivery of services. Open Source, which supports the Semantic Grid with software development, is characteristic of swarm intelligence and promotes peer collaboration through mass innovation and participation. "The collaboration is open to all and the source code is freely shared. Open source harnesses the distributive powers of the Internet, parcels the work to many, and uses their piecework to build a better whole putting informal networks of volunteer coders in direct competition with big corporations. It works like an ant colony, where the collective intelligence of the network supersedes any single contributor" [4]. The simple but clear ideals of Open Source are about sharing the common goals, the work, and the results. Sharing involves reuse, continuous improvement, and ever better quality and performance.

Web Services constitute an important emerging distributed computing paradigm different from DCE, CORBA and JAVA RMI in its focus on simple Internet based standards such as XML and AJAX. Web services are defined within W3C and form the basis for .NET (Microsoft), Dynamic e-Business (IBM) and ONE (Sun). The standards used include SOAP, WSDL, and WS-Inspection. This aligns Grid technologies with Web services while expanding Globus Toolkit, GT2, into the Open Grid Services Architecture (OGSA). In this environment, the term *architecture* refers to a well-defined set of basic interfaces from which one can construct interesting systems, while the term open source communicates extensibility, vendor neutrality, and a community standardization process. The architecture makes use of WSDL to achieve self-describing, discoverable services and interoperable protocols (Foster, 2002).

The Web, "once a repository for text and images, is evolving into a provider of information-providing services" (McIlraith et al., 2001). The web services referred to could include face recognition components, e.g., face detection, data compression and feature selection, classifiers, mixture of experts, and last but not least security and privacy services. In traditional closed environments "programmers manually configure their software systems so that the desired components can be linked and used. This task proves quite onerous in large-scale distributed systems, especially when the components are heterogeneous and autonomous" (Sreenath and Singh, 2004). Web

---

[2] http://www.w3.org/2001/sw/Activity
[3] http://www.semanticgrid.org/vision.html
[4] http://www.wired.com/wired/archive/11.11/opensource.html

services (WS) are "a [new] framework of software technologies designed to support interoperable machine-to-machine interaction over a network. WS are about accessing and connecting data and unlocking the value of that data" (Leavitt, 2004). Web services facilitate and enhance research into complex phenomena by addressing a broad range of interrelated challenges including (Ackerman et al., 2004)

- data integration using metadata, data dictionaries, and ontologies
- middleware that mediates data discovery and access, and enables exchanges between archives and data base repositories
- data acquisition and enrollment
- distributed computing
- large-scale analysis, e.g., service selection, composition, and reuse
- data summarization and mining
- software and hardware configuration
- data integrity and security

In summary, web services make the transition from closed systems to open information environments, which are able to handle both heterogeneity and autonomy. They provide a solid foundation for developing e-science and fostering seamless collaboration between physically separated people and resources.

The approach for achieving the above goals is to use a distributed intelligent agent environment. An agent is a semi-autonomous software process that works together with other agents. Agents are semi-autonomous in the sense that they are meant to be active, persistent software processes that perceive, reason, act, and communicate often without human intervention. Agents have been applied to data and information-rich environments, including cooperative information systems. Some agent-based systems are also mobile, in the sense that an agent can suspend execution, transport itself to another location, and resume execution. Agents share knowledge among and between themselves by using agent-processed ontologies. An ontology is a knowledge representation based upon a domain specific taxonomy that has been made available to all the agents in the system. Some of the biometric ontologies relevant here would describe the face space along social and psychological dimensions, categorize and bin populations of clients along gender and ethnicity, and include both generative and discriminative services for classification. The solution proposed for service selection and composition, on one side, and collaborative reuse, on the other side, is to combine the use of ontological representations with an agent communication language, while taking advantage of data mining, and (reinforcement) learning and prediction. Service selection and composition is highly flexible and much more than the standard stovepipe, where components are narrowly defined in terms of responsibilities, while their outputs and feedback "move" along an established path in the chain of command.

Imagine now playing some competitive game where the players choose their moves from some agreed upon repertoire while obeying specific rules. There are continuous board evaluations but ultimately there is just some (reinforcement) scalar to indicate the outcome (win, draw, or loss), characteristic of generic Constraint Satisfaction Problems (CSP). It is this outcome that teaches the players how to make wiser moves in future "games" using credit assignment strategies characteristic of reinforcement learning (see Sect. 4.3). Reinforcement learning consists of {select, score, and rate/rank}, and goes beyond merely (one) service selection (Sreenath and Singh, 2004). It addresses the more challenging task of selecting face recognition services and their proper composition. The compositional aspect is most important here. Individual face recognition services, e.g., face detection and face classification, could perform quite well on an individual basis for some given context but still fail to provide adequate service when sequenced for some specific task and field operation.

The agents combine evidence from other (referral) users searching for guidance and expert moves, and/or learn from their own experience gained after composing and executing a purposeful sequence of web services. Here learning involves two-tiered (short and long) term adaptation. Short-term adaptation is needed to learn enough about web services in order to "play," i.e., compose according to the rules and achieve average face recognition performance. Long-term adaptation is required to evolve novel strategies and tactics that beat seasoned "players," i.e., users and/or the agents composing face recognition systems on their behalf. Note the similarity to system engineering, which is concerned with requirements engineering, system prototyping and evaluation, architectural design and specifications, sub-system development (biometrics, communication, security/privacy and storage), system integration, and system validation (see Sect. 1.2).

The agent middleware architecture proposed, called Agent-based Virtual Biometrics Organization (AVBO), is an intelligent querying solution that understands the semantic context of tools, services, data, information, and metadata. The inclusion of the term "Virtual Organization" conveys an emphasis for using tools and techniques from Grid Computing. AVBO provides for dynamic (on-the-fly and on-demand) integration and interoperability of information using processes that handle workflow generation, execution, and reuse. In the current state of information glut, agents are needed to search, integrate, and analyze in a secure and private fashion the ever-growing flood of heterogeneous and distributed biometrics. The emphasis is to develop adaptive and intelligent distributed systems driven by e-science, where collaboration, sharing, and reuse lead to new strategies and tactics for face recognition. The use of agents in the Grid community has recently received a lot of attention. There has also been much recent interest in developing resource allocation tools and techniques for Grid oriented network-level multicasting, quality of service (QOS), and Grid based performance monitoring. Although not directly tied to Grid computing, there has also been much recent effort in agent-based service selection and composition. The scope for agents is somewhat broader then these efforts, including a light-weight agent communication language for cross-domain e-science.

The architecture proposed expands on the capabilities of today's virtual organizations (VO) to establish tomorrow's VO for enhanced biometric scientific research. What would it take to make the life for the biometric scientist easier and more productive? To answer this question, we provide a conceptual scenario involving the AVBO, where one can see the need and utility of the architecture (intelligent query formulation, data discovery, and automated workflow configuration of web services) proposed here. In particular, the user might be interested to find out to what extent some novel (invariant) features, e.g., the Scale Invariant Feature Transform (SIFT), affect the face recognition performance on some challenging data bases, compared to alternative feature derivation methods such as Gabor jets. The explicit goal for the user could be to assess if the performance can be improved under conditions of occlusion and/or clutter. The workflow configuration module is charged with planning for a sequence of executable modules. What makes web services selection and composition even harder is that the information is only partially available and is decentralized, and that the only interactions available are local. The configuration chosen should be faithful to the objectives the user has stated and reflect the fact that the module most likely to be affected by SIFT is that of face representation (see Sect. 9.7).

The user profile, from previous experimentation and/or stated preferences, together with recent results related to face detection and face recognition, would automatically assemble a workflow configuration that includes scale space, data compression, part-based constellations and probabilistic reasoning, and select reliable web services to implement them. Rather than manually searching and collecting data from multiple distributed heterogeneous sources, and then agonizing over how to integrate the numerous data and services available, the biometric scientist instead has now intelligent information tools to automate the experimental design, data retrieval, data integration, and data processing steps. Intelligent middleware brokers the services that are needed. AVBO eventually would find out experimentally that SIFT-PCA provides a more discriminative representation for local image descriptors (Ke and Sukthankar, 2004) or suggest Gabor-Kernel LDA (Shen et al., 2004) for PIE challenges.

The enabling infrastructure for AVBO is a general purpose layered Grid architecture, including a *fabric* layer, a *connectivity* layer, a *resource* layer and a *collective* layer. The purpose of the fabric layer is to provide low level access to shared resources, such as file storage or computing cycles. The connectivity layer provides basic core communication services such as TCP/IP, and security services, such as single user sign-on. The resource layer offers protocols for negotiation, initiation, monitoring, and control of individual resources. Finally, the collective layer offers basic global services such as directories, workload management and service discovery. One can build an agent oriented system using the Grid architecture.

The objective now is to support complex queries and collaborative biometrics via data mining and discovery operations, service composition, workflow management for processing activities, and collaborative reuse strategies. Towards that end, one builds a set of communicating agents that are capable of automating the previous functions. In order to accomplish this, several methodological questions have to be answered. For instance, a critical aspect of all general-purpose agent-based systems is interoperability. The basis for agent interoperability is the availability of an Agent Communication Language (ACL), which serves both as a formal language and as semantic specification. Instead of trying to use a general purpose ACL one can adopt a light-weight approach instead. Different AVBO sections, representing queries, data, and intermediate analysis and processing strategies are stored, exchanged and transformed by system agents. The key advantage of this approach is that multiple levels of system activity can be simultaneously expressed using AVBO. For instance, an AVBO data file may describe a particular scientists' approach to answer a type of query. It would describe the processing steps, data sources, and preferred visualization options. For collaborative reuse, portions of this file would be automatically copied and transformed in a way to answer a slightly different type of query. Encoding collaboration data and exchanges within AVBO language units supports both synchronous and asynchronous collaboration. AVBO language units are simply data files that are constructed, transformed, and exchanged by AVBO agents. To emphasize the machine readable and dynamic nature of these data structures, we refer to them as AVBO *dk-pages*, for dynamic knowledge pages. The basic research questions that need to be addressed and the approach to answer them were suggested by Robert Simon and are described next.

(a) What should the formal AVBO agent communication language include?

ACL makes extensive use of existing knowledge and service representation languages such as OWL, OWL-S and WSDL. The function of the AVBO ACL is to produce, exchange, and transform dk-pages. In addition to providing AVBO specific syntax and ontologies, each AVBO dk-page also incorporates other web-based markup languages, including DAML-S. AVOB dk-pages are used by AVBO to provide collaboration and query control, and to reuse the results of previous queries, intermediate results, processing steps, and answers. Further, AVBO agents use AVBO dk-pages in order to identify and take advantage of Grid based processing opportunities. This is achieved by decomposing a query into the necessary processing steps so the work to solve the particular problem can be parceled to the appropriate agents.

(b) How should the agent interconnection patterns be managed?

In the proposed agent based architecture for the AVBO system, there will be extensive multi-party data flows. The natural support mechanism for this is to use network level multicast. However, many existing networks do not offer native multicasting. This can be a problem for Grid based systems that assume the availability of efficient communication technologies to support distributed group communication. The approach proposed is to adopt a distributed agent architecture that can dynamically place agents on different end-hosts in the system (Simon et al., 2004). A specialized routing agent implements an adaptive routing policy that allows multiple paths between agents during the construction of the overlay routing tree. One has to optimize the overlay multicast tree and the placement of agents on different end-hosts. The optimization results in more efficient network resource usage through load balancing.

A novel and important part of the overlay multicasting approach is that multicast addressing is based upon both "who you are" and "what you are interested in". An *interest-oriented* multicast addressing scheme should enable scientists to dynamically communicate based upon shared interests, such as "who has data about SIFT?" To accomplish this, one could extend previous work using dynamic data management methods used in real-time Distributed Virtual Simulations (Simon et al., 2003). This enables multicast addressing to be formed based upon user-level characterizations of their own interests. This method has been quite effectively used in distributed simulation and war-gaming, and can be modified to fit the AVBO environment.

(c) How should discovery and composition be performed?

There is the capability to create hundreds or even thousands of agents and dk-pages if one wishes to. Service discovery can be done using both syntactic and semantic techniques. First, notice that all AVBO agents and services are represented by dk-pages. These pages are XML-based structures, using semantically rich keywords and concepts. Similarity based measures are used to discover information for dk-page treated as vectors (Simon et al., 2001). Similarity measurements by themselves are not powerful enough to perform highly precise discovery. As a consequence one would also incorporate recent results in collaborative filtering techniques. In this approach, users rank services. Based upon these rankings, as well as ratings of the users themselves (e.g., based upon area overlap), one can produce highly accurate service discovery and collaboration results.

(d) How should AVBO be built?

The approach proposed is to make maximal use of existing Grid and semantic web tools such as OWL-S for constructing agents and defining AVBO. Communication and dk-page storage and retrieval are achieved through a variety of overlay multicasting techniques, and yellow and white page directories such as UDDI. AVBO will operate in a fully distributed environment. The approach is to utilize existing Grid tools such as the Globus toolkit, as well as tools for Web Services and the Semantic Web. An important part of such an approach requires validating it both for performance and for the quality of results. Performance evaluation is accomplished via system tests for delay and throughput. Perhaps a more important measure is how well the system performs. In order to judge this, one adopts an information retrieval approach, and focuses on precision and recall metrics.

One can build AVBO using semi-autonomous light-weight agents. The agents are semi-autonomous in the sense that they can communicate with each other, can automatically produce new knowledge representations and can suggest alternative query strategies without human intervention, but overall are meant to be under the control and guidance of a human scientist. Light-weight agent-oriented design is meant to easily support collaboration and service composition in e-science for biometrics and to support scientist-directed processing strategies. The advantage of this approach is that it is simple to implement, off-loads a substantial amount of work to the underlying agents, but it still allows direct and indirect human control of processing strategies, thereby enhancing the confidence and understanding of how the results were produced.

The new intelligent middleware-enabled architecture proposed is driven by complex and powerful agents that provide general-purpose tools to integrate information from disparate sources and enable scientific discovery. In the end, combining several such intelligent information tools yields a community of smart agents that collaborate in an iterative fashion to plan experiments, seek and acquire relevant data, and analyze the results obtained. Biometrics in general, and face recognition, in particular, derive their newly found know-how from evaluating competing work-flows, with experimental design and context playing an important role. One also needs to explain the reasons for the choices made and the results obtained.

As an example of what web services selection and composition could achieve, consider comparing PCA and ICA (see Sects. 5.1, 5.4, 6.5, and 7.8) on face recognition. Draper et al. (2003) undertook this very task to resolve conflicting claims about the relative performance of PCA vs. ICA. Their findings indicate that the contradictory claims in the literature can be explained based on the task statement (face expression vs. face recognition), ICA architecture (I-local vs. II-global), ICA algorithm (Info Max vs. Fast ICA), and for PCA the subspace distance metric used (Mahalanobis vs. cosine). The ICA architecture I treats the input face images, $\mathbf{X}$, as a linear combination of statistically independent basis images, $\mathbf{S}$, combined by the mixing but unknown matrix $\mathbf{A}$. The coefficients obtained by projecting face images onto the statistically independent basis images are not statistically independent. The kurtosis maximization yields sparse codes for basis images, or alternatively localized edge filters. On the other hand, the ICA architecture II displays global characteristics and finds statistically independent coefficients that represent the face signatures. Systematic experimental design would have considered all the possible combinations listed above and found that Fast ICA configured according to the global ICA architecture yields best performance on face recognition, while InfoMax ICA configured according to the local ICA architecture is better on recognizing facial expressions. It would have been interesting to repeat the experiments performed by Kim et al. (2005) (see Sect. 6.5) and assess advantages, if any, for ICA architecture I using InfoMax relative to occlusion and disguise. In all the configurations considered, PCA fared worse than ICA. The specific results obtained by ICA could have been expected. Local information is most important for facial expression, while global information or Gestalt unity is most important for recognizing the face as a whole. Such constraints could have guided AVBO in web selection and service composition in the first place and reached similar conclusions.

Computing, in particular computer science rather than computers, is one of the "paradigm shift(s)" behind the current scientific revolution, as defined by Thomas Kuhn. The recent report [5] "Towards 2020 Science" from Microsoft Research Cambridge, UK, is concerned with "the synthesis of computing and sciences," and ultimately with the way computing will affect and change science. It states, among others, that computing will go much beyond being merely a supporting tool for doing science when "its concepts, tools, and theorems have become integrated into the fabric of science itself," and that computer science provides "an orderly, formal framework and exploratory apparatus for other sciences." Computing, mediated by e-science, has become paramount in the analysis and interpretation of data. Computing has also become responsible for preparing and running some of the large experiments needed to generate the data itself, and produce high value-added knowledge. The report envisions that "science-based innovation will supplant technology-based innovation." This large availability of computer power and bandwidth, and its distributed infrastructure "will have to support stream processing and advanced data mining/machine learning techniques. In the long run, an 'active learning' model [see Sect. 7.4] is envisioned which requests data sources autonomously and leads to 'autonomous experimentation'." Active and selective automation and computing are complimentary. They will provide the framework needed to collect, extract, and interpret data, gain insights, and bridge theory and experimentation through new hypotheses and testing. It will ultimately expand and revise the distributed knowledge and expertise available and increase creativity. This is true for science, in general, and biometrics and face recognition, in particular.

---

[5] http://research.microsoft.com/towards2020science/background_2020.htm

16. Epilogue

An imaginative conception of what might be true is the starting point of all great discoveries in science (Medawar)

Heraclitus of Ephesus (c. 500 B.C.) claimed that all things are in flux and that everything is constantly changing. One can not step into the same river twice since the river is never the same. Hence the variability of biometrics and the "permanent" challenge to handle in a reliable fashion the ever changing human faces. Parmenides of Elea (c. 515-450 B.C.) thought quite differently from Heraclitus. He sought what is permanent and never changing, and proposed a duality of appearance and reality. The changing world registered by our senses is merely an illusion. There are alternatives or hypotheses about illusory appearances and they have to be searched to ferret out the reality behind them. Parmenides claimed that it is only through reason that one can indirectly learn about "real" existence, which by itself is permanent, i.e., unchanging and unmoving. Continuous change, on one side, and a fixed reality, on the other side. How to navigate between those seemingly Scylla and Charybdis rocks of beliefs?

It was Democritus (c. 460-370 B.C.) who, while trying to reconcile between Heraclitus and Parmenides, came to claim that there is place for both permanence and change. What is permanent and unique, however, is the change itself. Permanence is found in the essence of things, while change comes from motion. According to David Hume there appear to be only three principles of connection among ideas, namely resemblance, contiguity (in time or place), and cause or effect. This corresponds to similarity across the face space, spatial-temporal coherence, and learning and inference. There is a growing realization that tracking and recognition, i.e., change and permanence, are complementary to each other. What is indeed unique to objects, in general, and faces, in particular, and constitutes their essence, is the particular way each human face changes. The spatial-temporal trajectories traced by faces are unique to each individual and should serve for their reliable identification and authentication. The difference between appearance or manifestation, and essence is crucial. It is the same difference that distinguishes the Turing test from John Searle's Chinese Room experiment.

Trajectories are narratives for story telling. The narrative form "is the only way they [psychologists] have of organizing the world, of organizing experience. They are not able to bring theories that organize things in terms of cause and effect and relationships, so they turn things into stories, and when they turn things into stories, and when they try to make sense of their life they use the storied version of their experience as the basis for further reflection. If they don't catch something in a narrative structure, it doesn't get remembered very well, and it doesn't seem to be accessible for further kind of mulling over" (Jerome Bruner, in Nelson, Katherine (ed.), *Narratives from the Crib*, Harvard Univ. Press, 1989). It is easier when the clues are placed in order but smart film editing makes one understand stories that are narrated in haphazard order or even in reverse.

There are two related paradigms that describe the means for reliable face recognition. The first paradigm captures prediction (Wechsler, 1990). The Perception-Control-Action-Learning (PCAL) cycle proposed by Wechsler argues that perception is directed and primed for prediction as a result of anticipation and learning. Predictions or anticipations fill in expectations that are then further explored and validated. Anticipation supports active perception and leads to reliable face recognition. Be it for need or curiosity, active perception explores and harnesses the rich but complex facial landscape to stimulate in a productive way its analysis and synthesis (or hallucination) for successful face identification and/or authentication. Predictions are planned and tested while discriminative evidence about suspicious coincidences and their plausible associations (Barlow, 1989b) accumulates. Similar and related, "feedback connections from a higher- to a lower-order visual cortical area carry predictions of lower-level neural activities, whereas the feed-forward connections carry the residual errors between the predictions and the actual lower-level activities" (Rao and Ballard, 1999). The residuals have to be accounted for or explained, or alternatively they spur further understanding and identification efforts. The recognition apparatus could also pursue a strategy where human faces are caricatured or transformed for the purpose of making them easier to distinguish from each other, and thus increase the residuals when the wrong hypothesis is proposed.

The predictive power for categorization and hierarchical coding comes from the fact that the expected features are suppressed while the unexpected ones have to be accounted for and explained (see Gombrich making similar comments about art in Sect. 2.4). Koch and Poggio (1999) recall from Arthur Conan Doyle's story *Silver Blaze* when Inspector Gregory from Scotland Yard asks Sherlock Holmes "Is there any point to which you would wish to draw my attention?," to which Holmes replies "To the curious incident of the dog in the night time. The dog did nothing in the night time. That was the curious incident." The dog did not bark because it knew the criminal and expected to see him. The stranger the features or feedback are, the more likely it is they convey useful information for recognition. Reliable face recognition involves similar cycles of synthesis and analysis. Synthesis requires predictions guided by learned invariances and intrinsic structure, while analysis calls for discriminative exploration and identification. Both prediction and exploration chart together the course for identification and authentication. The unexpected complements prior suspicions, and together they affect and alter the recognition odds. As an example, occlusion and disguise are incongruous but stand out in the context of face recognition.

The second paradigm encompasses the specific face representations used for detecting and recognizing human faces. The representations are sparse and statistically independent, on one side, and functional and purposeful, on the other side. Functionality and purpose are met when the local representations-by-parts proposed can cope with occlusion and structural noise using partial and flexible matching for recognition purposes. Picasso fragmented and faceted the human figure in a similar fashion leading to Cubism. Time and feedback are highly relevant for processing and interpreting biometric data streams. The time provides the glue or equivalently the invariance that links properly the parts, and makes their succession coherent across specific spatial-temporal trajectories. The more traditional biometric input used is static. The biometric input is now changing and has become augmented to include its natural temporal dimension together with the manifold of coherent transformations that are feasible across the joint spatial-temporal domain. Coherence is recast as spatial-temporal redundancy that makes predictions feasible and easier to make. Redundancy wastes channel capacity when communication is the main concern but improves the SNR, and most importantly it provides the structure needed by the "brain" to make sense and interpret the world surrounding us [e.g., biometrics] using its statistics and likelihoods (Barlow, 2001). The same redundancy was also deemed important for deductive reasoning and inference and thus for prediction by Watanabe (1960). Again it is Barlow (2001) to remind all that redundancy also makes possible associative learning. Barlow notes in particular that there is a "genuine sense in which all reinforcement learning is a response to statistical structure (of special kinds) in the sensory messages" and that "economy in the number of neurons used for representation of sensory information is a bad idea, and the reverse is what actually seems to happen. On the other hand economy in the number of active neurons would make redundancy manifest and explicit rather than hidden, and would make each impulse represent an important, informative, event." Coherence reduces the descriptive complexity of a human face. Murray et al. (2004) have suggested that "Feedback from high-level visual areas reduces activity in lower areas in order to simplify the description - consistent with both predictive coding models of perception and probabilistic notions of 'explaining away'." The biometric story, however, can be also narrated out of sequence, e.g., CCTV, but still be interpreted using the recognition-by-parts strategy with the strangeness playing the dual role of features and weak classifiers. Dimensionality reduction, feature selection, and exemplar-based abstract part representations make the representation sparse. The implementation of parts using local patches and their relative strangeness is simple. Open set (face) recognition becomes feasible, while impostors are rejected without having explicit access to them during enrollment and/or training. Open set recognition, similar to outlier detection, facilitates intrusion detection and surveillance. The scope for pattern recognition, in general, and face recognition, in particular, becomes much wider because recognition-by-parts enables training and/or testing to take place using incomplete or camouflaged/disguised patterns from single and/or multiple image sets.

Integral to transduction, the strangeness clues help with local estimation. Training is local in both spatial and temporal terms. Learning is continuous and the query or test data is used to retrain the very classifier that will be used for its own recognition. The strangeness clues, non-parametric and fast to estimate, correspond to the active neurons to which Barlow has referred earlier. The strangeness handles fragments or patches the parts consist of, and disregards clutter to preempt the need for pre-segmentation. The parts employ exemplar-based representations to cope with variability using flexible matching. Patches involve both information contents and spatial-temporal layout, or equivalently combine the *what* and *where* and *when* for reliable face recognition. Contents cover both representation and location, and are implicitly ordered. The weak classifiers or experts draw their sensory input from one or several modalities and are purposefully combined using mixture of experts and voting schemes such as boosting. The scope for the weak learners includes both the parts' joint spatial-temporal contents and the relevant dependencies that hold among them.

Objects, in general, and faces, in particular, are known to be processed sequentially over time (Delorme and Thorpe, 2001). The human faces are parsed into discrete and local units of space and time. The resulting parts are then shared by recognition models that compete to identify and/or authenticate faces in a progressive fashion similar to boosting. Parsing involves change and drift detection, on one side, and seeking for parts, on the other side. The parts, which make up the dictionary of local spatial-temporal units the human face chooses from to write its own script, are found using non-accidental co-incidence detectors and data mining techniques that seek for hidden regularities. Rather than simply crawling around to merely score and rank human faces, the progressive recognition-by-parts scheme, similar to Really Simple Syndication (RSS), could "ping" discrete parts and/or events to competing face recognition "browsers" to share, update, and plan on how to proceed with their biometric mission. The grand synthesis for recognition-by-parts takes place over a layered and hierarchical structure that consists of a "dictionary" of Gabor/SIFT elementary like particles, "phonemes" or parts using weak learners that assembly the elementary particles, meaningful "words" or objects that combine the parts or phonemes using strong classifiers, and coherent spatial-temporal speech, text, or visual imagery that includes "acting" faces among others. The scope of expression for such a language is bound only by imagination. Contrast such a discriminative (visual) language with one that is limited to draw from a few PDF, usually the normal distribution, and reasons using generative models and marginalization.

Transduction, active learning, co-training, and semi-supervised learning methods are complementary to each other. The active learner decides whether or not to request labels for the working samples. To improve on classification or selection, the active learning iteratively selects the most informative patterns among the working samples that are streaming. As an example, the active sampling strategy proposed by Juszczak and Duin (2004) is based upon the variation in label assignments (of the unlabeled working set) between the classifier trained on the (usually few) labeled samples and the one that also includes the stream-based unlabeled working samples. The use of unlabeled samples is characteristic of co - training (Blum and Mitchell, 1998; Nigam et al., 2000), when two independent classifiers bootstrap each other while labeling the working samples (Krogel and Scheffer, 2004). Co-training might lead to improved performance when one of the classifiers labels at least one unlabeled instance correctly for which the other classifier errs. Unlabeled samples, which are labeled by one classifier with relatively high confidence, augment the set of labeled samples available for training the other classifier. Co-training can be expanded to several classifiers using random forests.

The interplay between labeled and unlabeled examples is most appealing when there are plentiful of unlabeled data as it is the case with face recognition. The unlabeled faces provide additional information on the face distribution including constraints and hints about the meaningful relations and regularities affecting their discrimination. This perspective on the use of unlabeled data is the main motivation behind semi-supervised learning (SSL) (Chapelle et al., 2006). It is worth to explore the overlap and mutually beneficial relationships between semi-supervised learning and transduction, which lead to two-step learning algorithms suitable for both face recognition and face selection tasks. The assumptions proposed by SSL are straightforward. They include "smoothness" to yield similar outputs for similar inputs, "clustering" to express the fact that samples that can group together belong to the same class, and "low-density" to enforce that decision boundaries are traced in low-density regions and do not split well-formed clusters. Note that low-density separation corresponds to large margin and low strangeness.

Transduction is "always semi-supervised; they use information in the test points" and can achieve further gains if it operates simultaneously on the unlabeled samples. This works to the extent that the unlabeled samples share some meaningful structure with the labeled samples. The perceived overlap between SSL and transduction leads to two-step algorithms for transduction that take advantage of the constraints and/or hints uncovered by SSL regarding the unlabeled samples. The first step seeks for meaningful clusters and enforces the constrains and /or hints given, if any, while the second step involves transduction through local estimation for the still unlabeled samples. The locality aspect, already narrowed down by the explicit structure found during the first step, helps transduction with interpreting the unlabeled samples and eventually classifying them. A small but diverse number of clusters and hypotheses on the partitions generated with small training errors are characteristic of quality clustering and "guarantee" that the corresponding transductive test error will be small (El-Yaniv and Gerzon, 2005). The overall hypothesis chosen to label the test data is the one that minimizes the transductive error bound. Multiple image sets consisting of human faces and available for face selection (see Sect. 6.6) can be resolved using the above two-step approach.

Sir Isaiah Berlin recalls in his landmark *The Hedgehog and the Fox* (Simon & Schuster, 1953) that "There is a line among the fragments of the Greek poet Archilochus which says: 'The fox knows many things, but the hedgehog knows one big thing. For there exists a great chasm between those, on one side, who relate everything to a single central vision, one system less or more coherent or articulate, in terms of which they understand, think and feel - a single, universal, organizing principle in terms of which alone all that they are and say has significance - and, on the other side, those who pursue many ends, often unrelated and even contradictory, connected, if at all, only in some *de facto* way, for some psychological or physiological cause, related by no moral or aesthetic principle; these last lead lives, perform acts, and entertain ideas that are centrifugal rather than centripetal, their thought is scattered or diffused, moving on many levels, seizing upon the essence of a vast variety of experiences and objects for what they are in themselves, without consciously or unconsciously, seeking to fit them into, or exclude them from, any one unchanging, all-embracing, sometimes self-contradictory and incomplete, at times fanatical, unitary inner vision. The first kind of intellectual and artistic personality belongs to the hedgehogs, the second to the foxes." The clash is between "monist and pluralist," with the latter aware of the permanence of ambiguity and uncertainty.

Philip Tetlock's recent book on prediction, *Expert Political Judgment* (Princeton, 2005), recalls Isaiah Berlin to say that "hedgehogs are less prone to self doubt [and thus overconfident], extend the explanatory reach of that one big thing [they know] into new domains, more likely to dismiss evidence that contradicts their vision, and less likely to admit mistakes," while foxes, on the other hand, "are skeptical of grand schemes, draw from an eclectic array of traditions, and accept ambiguity and contradictions as inevitable." As uncertainty is a fact of life, reliable face recognition needs more foxes. Weak learners are looking for signs of coherent spatial-temporal to emerge and build-up consistent and meaningful objects. They are the "foxes" that boosting employs to build strong classifiers. Overspecialization is not better than boosting using weak learners because in Tetlock's words "we reach the point of diminishing marginal predictive returns for [such kind of] knowledge disconcertingly quickly." Similar arguments were made recently by James Surowiecki in his book *The Wisdom of Crowds* (Double-day, 2004) to the effect that "under the right circumstances, groups are remarkably intelligent, and are often smarter than the smartest people in them." Swarm or col-lective intelligence benefits from diversity, independence of opinion, and individual decision-making. Swarm intelligence corresponds in our book to recognition-by-parts using weak learners driven by strangeness and boosting.

Reliable face recognition requires much more than mere access to face images. As face recognition is an elaborate enterprise, its pursuit requires augmented cognition that situates everything within some specific context and explains senses and percepts through data fusion and grounded inferences. The foxes among us, through divide and conquer, help with reading faces, interpret the minds behind them, and overcome hu-man and machines biases. The foxes know that the face representation used is comple-mentary to if not more important than classification. As such, they seek to optimize the representations used for the purpose of facilitating meaningful sparse codes for associations, spatial-temporal coherence, distinctiveness, and non-orthogonality. Such representations buttress an all encompassing analysis and synthesis face recognition control loop. The analysis and synthesis components implement discriminative and generative methods, have access among others to statistical shape and texture analy-sis and animation, and complement each other by providing feedback, and anticipating and making predictions, respectively. Last but not least, one of the grand challenges for any research program, including the one advocated throughout this book, is to eventually verify that the faces shown below share the same identity despite the time lapsed between their capture.

References

[1] Y. S. Abu-Mostafa (1995a), Machines That Learn from Hints, *Scientific American*, April, 64–69.

[2] Y. S. Abu-Mostafa (1995b), Hints, *Neural Computation* Vol. 7, 639–671.

[3] T. P. Ackerman et al. (2004), Integrating and Interpreting Aerosol Observations and Models within the PARAGON Framework, *Bulletin of the American Meteorological Society*, Vol. 85, No. 10, 1523–1533.

[4] D. C. Adams, F. J. Rohlf, and D. E. Slice (2004), Geometric Morphometrics: Ten Years of Progress Following the 'Revolution', *Ital. J. Zool.*, Vol. 71, 5–16.

[5] L. M. Adelman and R. L. Rivest (1978), The Use of Public Key Cryptography in Communication System Design, *IEEE Communications*, Vol. 16, No. 6, 20–23.

[6] A. Adler (2003), Sample Images Can Be Independently Regenerated from Face Recognition Templates, http://www.site.uottawa.ca/~adler/publications/2003/adler-2003-fr-templates.pdf.

[7] A. Adler (2004), Images Can Be Regenerated from Quantized Biometric Match Score Data, *Can. Conf. Elec. Computer Eng. (CCGEI)*, Niagara Falls, Canada.

[8] G. Aggarwal, A. Chowdhury, and R. Chellappa (2004), A System Identification Approach for Video-Based Face Recognition, *17th Int. Conf. on Pattern Recognition (ICPR)*, Cambridge, UK, Vol. 4, 175–178.

[9] L. von Ahn, M. Blum, N. Hopper, and J. Langford (2003), CAPTCHA: Using Hard AI Problems for Security, *Eurocrypt*.

[10] H. Ailisto, M. Lindholm, S-M. Mäkelä, and E. Vildjiounaite (2004) Unobtrusive User Identification with Light Biometrics, *Proc. of the Third Nordic Conference on Human-Computer Interaction (NordiCHI)*, Tampere, Finland, 327–330.

[11] H. Ailisto et al. (2006), Soft Biometrics - Combining Body Weight and Fat Measurements with Fingerprint Biometrics, *Pattern Recognition Letters*, Vol. 27, 325–334.

[12] J. Alexander and J. M. Smith (2003), Engineering Privacy in Public: Confounding Face Recognition, *3rd Int. Workshop on Privacy Enhancing Technologies*, Dresden, Germany, 88–106.

[13] M. Alghoniemy and A. H. Tewfik (2000), Geometric Distortion Correction in Image Watermarking, *ICME*, New York, NY, 82–89.

[14] E. Alpaydin (2005), *Introduction to Machine Learning*, MIT Press.

[15] M. Alvira and R. Rifkin (2001), An Empirical Comparison of SNoW and SVMs for Face Detection, AI Memo 2001-004, MIT

[16] J. R. Anderson, M. Matessa, and C. Lebiere (1997), ACT-R: A Theory of Higher Level Cognition and Its Relation to Visual Attention, *Human-Computer Interaction*, Vol. 12, 439–462.

[17] J. R. Anderson and C. Lebiere (Eds.) (1998), *Atomic Components of Thought*, Erlbaum, Hillsdale, NJ.

[18] A. J. Anderson and P. W. McOwan (2003), Humans Deceived by Predatory Stealth Strategy Camouflage Motion, *Proc. R. Soc. London B (Suppl)* 270, S18–S20.

[19] K. Anderson and P. McOwan (2004), Robust Real - Time Face Tracker for Cluttered Environments, *Computer Vision and Image Understanding*, Vol. 95, 184–200.

[20] P. Andras (2002), Kernel-Kohonen Networks, *Int. J. of Neural Systems*, Vol. 12, No. 2, 117–135.

[21] E. Angelopoulou, R. Molana, and K. Daniilidis, Multispectral Skin Color Modeling, *Computer Vision and Pattern Recognition (CVPR)*, 635–642.

[22] O. Arandjelovic and R. Cipolla (2004), Face Recognition from Face Motion Manifolds Using Robust Kernel Resistor-Average Distance, *1st IEEE Workshop on Face Processing in Video*, Washington D. C.

[23] H. Arendt (1973), *The Origins of Totalitarianism*, Harcourt Brace Jovanovich.

[24] J. Attick, P. Griffin, and N. Redlich (1996), Statistical Approach to Shape from Shading: Reconstruction of 3D Face Surfaces from Single 2D Image, *Neural Computation*, Vol. 8, 1321–1340.

[25] S. Avidan (2004), Support Vector Tracking, *IEEE Trans. on Pattern Analysis and Machine Intelligence*, Vol. 26, No. 8, 1064–1072.

[26] S. Axelsson (1999), The Base-Rate Fallacy and Its Implications for the Difficulty of Intrusion Detection, *6th ACM Conf. on Computer and Communications Security*, Singapore, 1–7.

[27] F. R. Bach and M. I. Jordan (2002), Kernel Independent Component Analysis, *J. of Machine Learning Research*, Vol. 3, 1–48.

[28] R. G. Bachrach, A. Navot, and N. Tishby (2004), Margin Based Feature Selection - Theory and Algorithms, *21th Int. Conf. on Machine Learning (ICML)*, Banff, Canada.

[29] E. Bailly-Bailliere et al. (2003), The BANCA Database and Evaluation Protocol, *4th Audio-Video Based Person Authentication (AVBPA)*, 625–638.

[30] S. Baker and T. Kanade (2000), Hallucinating Faces, *4th Int. Conf. on Face and Gesture Recognition*, Grenoble, France.

[31] S. Baker and T. Kanade (2002), Limits on Super-Resolution and How to Break Them, *IEEE Trans. on Pattern Analysis and Machine Intelligence*, Vol. 24, No. 9, 1167–1183.

[32] M. Balasubramanian and E. L. Schwatz (2003), The Isomap algorithm and Topological Stability, *Science* 295, 7a.

[33] M. Barbaro, P.Y. Burgi, A. Mortara, P. Nussbaum, and F. Heitger (2002), A 100 x 100 Pixel Silicon Retina for Gradient Extraction with Steering Filter Capabilities and Temporal Output Coding, *IEEE Journal of Solid-State Circuits*, Vol. 37, No. 2, 160–172.

[34] H. B. Barlow (1989a), What Causes Trichromacy? A Theoretical Analysis Using Comb-Filtered Spectra, *Vision Res.*, Vol. 22, 635–643.

[35] H. B. Barlow (1989b), Unsupervised Learning, *Neural Computation*, 1, 295–311.

[36] H. B. Barlow (2001), Redundancy Reduction Revisited, *Network: Computation in Neural Systems*, Vol. 12, 241–253.

[37] H. B. Barlow, T.P. Kaushal, and G.J.Mitchison (1989), Finding Minimum Entropy Codes, *Neural Computation*, 1, 412–423.

[38] S. Baron-Cohen and P. Cross (1992), Reading the Eyes: Evidence for the Role of Perception in the Development of a Theory of Mind, *Mind and Language* 7, 182–186.

[39] R.J. Baron (1981), Mechanisms of human face recognition, *Int. J. Man, Mach. Stud.*, Vol. 15, 137–178.

[40] H. G. Barrow, J. M. Tenenbaum, R. C. Bolles, and H. C. Wolf (1977), Parametric Correspondence and Chamfer Matching, *5th Int. Joint Conf. on Artificial Intelligence (IJCAI)*, Cambridge, MA, 659–663.

[41] M. S. Bartlett, M. H. Lades, and T. J. Sejnowski (1998), Independent Component Representations for Face Recognition. *Proceedings of the SPIE, Conference on Human Vision and Electronic Imaging III*, Vol. 3299, 528-539.

[42] P. Bas, J. M. Chassery, and B. Macq (2002), Image Watermarking: An Evolution to Content Based Approaches, *Pattern Recognition*, Vol. 35, 545–561.

[43] S. Basu, A. Banerjee, and R. J. Mooney (2004), Active Semi-Supervision for Pairwise Constrained Clustering, *SIAM Int. Conf. on Data Mining*, Lake Buena Vista, FL, 333–344.

[44] P. N. Belhumeur, J. P. Hespanha, and D. J. Kriegman (1997), Eigenfaces vs. Fisherfaces: Recognition Using Class Specific Projection, *IEEE Trans. on Pattern Analysis and Machine Intelligence*, Vol. 19, No. 7, 711–720.

[45] A. J. Bell and T. J. Sejnowski (1995), An Information-Maximization Approach to Blind Separation and Blind Deconvolution, *Neural Computation*, Vol. 7, 1129–1159.

[46] A. J. Bell and T. J. Sejnowski (1997), The Independent Components of Natural Scenes are Edge Filters, *Vision Research*, Vol. 37, No. 23, 3327–3338.

[47] B. Ben-Abdelkader, R. Cutler, and L. Davis (2002), Person Identification Using Automatic Height and Stride Estimation, *16th Int. Conf. on Pattern Recognition (ICPR)*, Quebec-City, Canada.

[48] S. Bengio, J. Mariethoz, and S. Marcel (2001), Evaluation of Biometric Technology on XM2VTS, IDIAP Research Report 01-21, Martigny, Switzerland.

[49] S. Bengio, C. Marcel, S. Marcel, and J. Mariethoz (2002), Confidence Measures for Multimodal Identity Verification, *Information Fusion*, Vol. 3, No. 4, 267–276.

[50] S. Ben-Yacoub, Y. Abdeljaoued, and E. Mayoraz (1999), Fusion of Face and Speech Data for Person Identity Verification, *IEEE Trans. on Neural Networks*, Vol. 10, No. 5, 1065–1075.

[51] T. Berners-Lee, J. Handler, and O. Lassila (2001), The Semantic Web, *Scientific American*, May.

[52] P. Besl and N. McKay (1992), A Method for Registration of 3-D Shapes, *IEEE Trans. on Pattern Analysis and Machine Intelligence*, Vol. 14, No. 2, 239–256.

[53] C. Beumier and M. Acheroy (2001), Face Verification from 3D and Gray Level Cues, *Pattern Recognition Letters* Vol. 22, 129–136.

[54] J. R. Beveridge, K. She, B. Draper, and G. H. Givens (2001), Parametric and Non-parametric Methods for the Statistical Evaluation of Human ID algorithms, *3rd Workshop on Empirical Evaluation Methods in Computer Vision*, Kauai, HI.

[55] J. R. Beveridge, D. Bolme, M. Teixeira, and B. A. Draper (2005), The CSU Face Identification Evaluation System: Its Purpose, Features and Structure, *Machine Vision and Applications*, Vol. 16, No. 2, 128–138.

[56] D. Beymer and T. Poggio (1995), Face Recognition from One Example View, *5th Int. Conf. on Computer Vision (ICCV)*, Boston, MA, 500–507.

[57] I. Biederman (1987), Recognition by Components: A Theory of Human Image Understanding, *Psychology Review* Vol. 94, 115–147.

[58] E.S. Bigun, J. Bigun, B. Duc, and S. Fisher (1997), Expert Conciliation for Multimodal Person Authentication Systems Using Bayesian Statistics, *1st Int. Conf. on Audio and Video-Based Biometric Person Authentication (AVBPA)*, Crans Montana, Switzerland, 291–300.

[59] J. Bigun and J. M. H. du Buf (1994), N-Folded Symmetries by Complex Moments in Gabor Space, *IEEE Trans. on Pattern Analysis and Machine Intelligence*, Vol. 16, No. 1, 80–87.

[60] J. Bigun, K. Choy, and H. Olsson (2001), Evidence on Skill Differences of Women and Men Concerning Face Recognition, *3rd Int. Conf. on Audio- and Video-Based Biometric Person Authentication (AVBPA)*, Halmstad, Sweden, Springer, LNCS-2091, 44–51.

[61] J. Bins and B. A. Draper (2001), Feature Selection from Huge Feature Sets, *8th Int. Conf. on Computer Vision (ICCV)*, Vancouver, Canada.

[62] C. Bishop (1995), *Neural Networks for Pattern Recognition*, Oxford University Press.

[63] D. M. Blackburn (2001), Evaluation Technology Properly-Three Easy Steps to Success, *Corrections Today*.

[64] D. M. Blackburn, M. Bone, and P. J. Phillips (2001), Facial Recognition Vendor Test 2000, NIST.

[65] V. Blanz, S. Romdhani, and T. Vetter (2002), Face Identification Across Different Poses and Illuminations with a 3D Morphable Model, *5th Int. Conf. on Automatic Face and Gesture Recognition (FGR)*, Washington, D.C.

[66] V. Blanz and T. Vetter (2003), Face Recognition Based on Fitting a 3D Morphable Model, *IEEE Trans. on Pattern Analysis and Machine Intelligence*, Vol. 25, No. 9, 1063–1074.

[67] V. Blanz, P. Grother, P. J. Phillips, and T. Vetter (2005), Face Recognition Based on Frontal Views Generated from Non-Frontal Images, *Computer Vision and Pattern Recognition (CVPR)*, San Diego, CA, 454–461.

[68] W. W. Bledsoe (1964), The Model Method in Facial Recognition, Panoramic Research Inc., Tech. Rep. PRI:15, Palo Alto, CA.

[69] A. Blum and T. Mitchell (1998), Combining Labeled and Unlabeled Data with Co-Training, *Conf. on Computational Learning Theory (COLT)*, 92–100.

[70] A. Blum and S. Chawla (2001), Learning from Labeled and Unlabeled Data Using Graph Mincuts, *18th Int. Conf. on Machine Learning (ICML)*, 19–26.

[71] D. Bogumil (2004), Reversing Global and Local Geometrical Distortions in Image Watermarking, *6th Int. Workshop on Information Hiding*, Toronto, Canada, 25–37.

[72] R. M. Bolle, J. H. Connell, and N. K. Ratha (2002), Biometric Perils and Patches, *Pattern Recognition*, Vol. 35, 2727–2738.

[73] R. M. Bolle, J. H. Connell, S. Pankanti, N. Ratha, and A. W. Senior (2004), *Guide to Biometrics*, Springer.

[74] F. L. Bookstein (1991), *Morphometric Tools for Landmark Data: Geometry and Biology*, Cambridege University Press.

[75] I. Borg and P. Groenen (1996), *Modern Multidimensional Scaling: Theory and Applications*, Springer.

[76] G. Borgefors (1984), Distance Transformations in Digital Images, *Computer Vision, Graphics, and Image Processing*, Vol. 34, No. 3, 344–371.

[77] G. Borgefors (1988), Hierarchical Chamfer Matching, *IEEE Trans. on Pattern Analysis and Machine Intelligence*, Vol. 10, No. 6, 849–865.

[78] S. Bounkong, B. Toch, D. Saad, and D. Lowe (2003), ICA for Watermarking Digital Images, *Machine Learning Research*, Vol. 4, 1471–1498.

[79] J. Bourgain (1985), On Lipschitz Embedding of Finite Metric Spaces in Hilbert Space, *Israel J. Math.*, Vol. 52, Nos. 1–2, 46–52.

[80] K. W. Bowyer, K. Chang, and P. Flynn (2004), A Survey of Approaches to Three-Dimensional Face Recognition, *17th Int. Conf. on Pattern Recognition (ICPR)*, Cambridge, UK, 358–361.

[81] K. W. Bowyer, K. Chang, and P. Flynn (2006), A Survey of Approaches and Challenges in 3D and Multi-Modal 3D + 2D Face Recognition, *Computer Vision and Image Understanding*, Vol. 101, 1–15.

[82] A. P. Bradley (1996), ROC curves and the χ^2 test, *Pattern Recognition Letters*, Vol. 17, 287–294.

[83] A. P. Bradley (1997), The Use of the Area Under the ROC Curve in the Evaluation of Machine Learning Algorithms, *Pattern Recognition*, Vol. 30, No. 7, 1145–1159.

[84] V. Brajovic and T. Kanade (1999), A VLSI Sorting Image Sensor: Global Massively Parallel Intensity-to-Time Processing for Low-Latency Adaptive Vision, *IEEE Trans. on Robotics and Automation*, Vol. 15, No. 1, 67–75.

[85] M. Brand (2002), Charting a Manifold, *NIPS* 15, 661–668.

[86] N. Breen et al. (2000), Models of Face Recognition and Delusional Misidentification: A critical Review, *Cognit. Neuropsychol.*, Vol. 17, 55–71.

[87] L. Breiman (1996), Bagging Predictors, *Machine Learning*, Vol. 24, No. 2, 123–140.

[88] L. Breiman (2001), Random Forests, *Machine Learning*, Vol. 45, No. 1, 5–32.

[89] S. E. Brennan (1985), Caricature Generator: The Dynamic Exaggeration of Faces by Computer, *Leonardo*, Vol. 18, No. 3, 170–178.

[90] A. M. Bronstein, M. M. Bronstein, and R. Kimmel (2003), Expression-Invariant 3D Face Recognition, *4th Int. Conf. on Audio- and Video-Based Person Authentication (AVBPA)*, Surrey, UK, 62–70.

[91] A. M. Bronstein, M. M. Bronstein, and R. Kimmel (2005), Three-Dimensional Face Recognition, *Int. Journal of Computer Vision*, Vol. 64, No. 1, 5–30.

[92] V. Bruce, T. Valentine, and A.D. Baddeley (1987), The Basis of the Three-Quarter View Advantage in Face Recognition, *Applied Cognitive Psychology*, 1, 109–120.

[93] V. Bruce and T. Valentine (1988), When a Nod's as Good as a Wink. The Role of Dynamic Information in facial Recognition, in M. M. Gruneberg, P. Morris and R. N. Sykes (Eds.), *Practical Aspects of Memory: Current Research and Issues*, Vol. 1, Lawrence Erlbaum Associates, Chichester, UK, 169–174.

[94] V. Bruce et al., (1991), Recognizing Facial Surfaces, *Perception*, 20, 755–769.

[95] V. Bruce and A. Young (1998), *In The Eye of the Beholder*, Oxford Univ. Press.

[96] R. Brunelli and T. Poggio (1993), Face Recognition: Features vs. Templates, *IEEE Trans. on Pattern Analysis and Machine Intelligence*, Vol. 15, No. 10, 1042–1053.

[97] R. Brunelli and D. Falavigna (1995), Person Identification Using Multiple Cues, *IEEE Trans. on Pattern Analysis and Machine Intelligence*, Vol. 17, No. 10, 955–966.

[98] M. Burge and W. Burger (1999), Ear Biometrics, in A. Jain, R. Bolle and S. Pankanti (Eds.), *Biometric Identification in Network Society*, Kluwer, 273–286.

[99] G. Byatt and G. Rhodes (1998), Recognition of Own-Race and Other-Race Caricatures: Implications for Models of Face Recognition, *Vision Research*, Vol. 38, 2455–2468.

[100] M. D. Byrne and J. R. Anderson (1998), Perception and Action, in J. R. Anderson and C. Lebiere (Eds.), *Atomic Components of Thought*, Erlbaum, 167–200.

[101] R. Cappelli, D. Maio, and D. Maltoni (2002), Subspace Adaptation for Incremental Face Learning, *7th International Conference on Control, Automation, Robotics and Vision (ICARCV)*, Singapore, 974–979.

[102] M. Carcassoni and E. Hancock (2002), Point-Set Alignment Using Multidimensional Scaling, *16th Int. Conf. on Pattern Recognition (ICPR)*, Quebec, Canada, 402–405.

[103] C. Champod and D. Meuwly (2000), The Inference of Identity in Forensic Speaker Recognition, *Speech Communication*, Vol. 31, 193–203.

[104] E. C. Chang and Q. Li (2005), Small Secure Sketch for Point Set Difference (under review).

[105] K. I. Chang, K. W. Bowyer, S. Sarkar, and B. Victor (2003), Comparison and Combination of Ear and Face Images in Appearance-Based Biometrics, *IEEE Trans. on Pattern Analysis and Machine Intelligence*, Vol. 25, No. 9, 1160–1165.

[106] K. I. Chang, K. W. Bowyer, P. J. Flynn, and X. Chen (2004), Multi-Biometrics Using Facial appearance, Shape and Temperature, *6th Int. Conf. on Automatic Face and Gesture Recognition*, Seoul, Korea.

[107] K. I. Chang, K. W. Bowyer, and P. Flynn (2005), An Evaluation of Multi-modal 2D + 3D Face Biometrics, *IEEE Trans. on Pattern Analysis and Machine Intelligence*, Vol. 27, No. 4, 619–624.

[108] Y. Chang, C. Hu, and M. Turk (2004), Probabilistic Expression Analysis on Manifolds, *Computer Vision and Pattern Recognition (CVPR)*, Washington, D.C., 520–527.

[109] O. Chapelle, B. Schölkopf, and A. Zien (Eds.) (2006), *Semi-Supervised Learning*, MIT Press.

[110] R. Chellappa, C. L. Wilson, and S. Sirohey (1995), Human and Machine Recognition of Faces: A Survey, *Proc. IEEE*, Vol. 83, 705–740.

[111] J. Chen, X. Chen, and W. Gao (2004), Expand Training Set for Face Detection by GA Re-sampling, *6th Int. Conf. on Automatic Face and Gesture Recognition (FGR)*, Seoul, Korea.

[112] K. Chen (2003), Towards Better Making a Decision in Speaker Verification, *Pattern Recognition*, Vol. 36, 329–346.

[113] M. Chen and W. S. Wu (2005), High-Speed Face Recognition Based on Discrete Cosine Transform and RBF Neural Networks, *IEEE Trans. on Neural Networks*, Vol. 16, No. 3, 679–691.

[114] V. Chen and H. Wechsler (2006), Face Recognition Using Spatio-Temporal ICA (in preparation).

[115] X. Chen, P. J. Flynn, and K. W. Bowyer (2003), PCA-based Face Recognition in IR: Baseline and Comparative Studies, *Int. Workshop on Analysis and Modeling of Faces and Gestures*, 127–134.

[116] X. Chen, P. J. Flynn, and K. W. Bowyer (2005), IR and Visible Light Face Recognition, *Computer Vision and Image Understanding*, Vol. 99, 332–358.

[117] V. Cherkassky and F. Mulier (1998), *Learning from Data*, Wiley.

[118] V. Cherkassky and Y. Ma (2003), Comparison of Model Selection for Regression, *Neural Computation*, Vol. 15, No. 7, 1691–1714.

[119] V. Cherkassky and Y. Ma (2004), Comparison of Loss Functions for Robust Linear Regression, *Int. Joint Conf. on Neural Networks (IJCNN)*, Budapest, Hungary.

[120] V. Cherkassky and Y. Ma (2004) Practical Selection of SVM Parameters and Noise Estimation for SVM Regression, *Neural Networks*, Vol. 17, No. 1, 113–126.

[121] J. T. Chien and C. C. Wu (2002), Discriminant Waveletfaces and Nearest Feature Classifiers for Face Recognition, *IEEE Trans. on Pattern Analysis and Machine Intelligence*, Vol. 24, No. 12, 1644–1649.

[122] T. Choudhury, B. Clarkson, T. Jebara, and A. Pentland (1999), Multimodal Person Recognition Using Unconstrained Audio and Video, *2nd Int. Conf. on Audio and Video-Based Biometric Person Authentication (AVBPA)*, Washington, DC, 176–181.

[123] C. K. Chow (1970), On the Optimum Recognition Error and Reject Tradeoff, *IEEE Trans. on Inf. Theory* 16, 41–46.

[124] A. Chowdhury, R. Chellappa, R. Krishnamurthy, and T. Vo (2002), 3D Face Reconstruction from Video Using a Generic Model, *Int. Conf. on Multimedia and Expo*, Lausanne, Switzerland, 26–29.

[125] G. E. Christensen (1999), Consistent Linear-Elastic Transformations for Image Matching, *Inf. Processing in Medical Imaging*, LCNS 1613, Springer, 224–237.

[126] F. Christie and V. Bruce (1998), The Role of Dynamic Information in the Recognition of Unfamiliar Faces, *Memory and Cognition*, Vol. 26, No. 4, 780–790.

[127] R. Cipolla and A. Pentland (Eds.) (1998), *Computer Vision for Human-Machine Interaction*, Cambridge University Press.

[128] R. Clarke (1994), Human Identification in Information Systems: Management Challenges and Public Policy Issues, *Info. Technology People* 12.

[129] C. Clausen and H. Wechsler (2000a), Quad-Q-Learning, *IEEE Trans. on Neural Networks*, Vol. 11, No. 2, 279–294.

[130] C. Clausen and H. Wechsler (2000b), Color Image Compression Using PCA and BackPropagation Learning, *Pattern Recognition*, Vol. 33, No. 9, 1555–1560.

[131] C. Clausen and H. Wechsler (2004), Fractal Image Compression Using Reinforcement Learning, US Patent 6,775, 415 B1.

[132] I. Cohen, N. Sebe, F. G. Cozman, M. C. Cirelo, and T. S. Huang (2003), Learning Bayesian Network Classifiers for Facial Expression Recognition Using both Labeled and Unlabeled Data, *Computer Vision and Pattern Recognition (CVPR)*, Madison, WI

[133] J. Cohn, K. Schmidt, R. Gross, and P. Ekman (2002), Individual Differences in Facial Expression: Stability over Time, Relation to Self-Reported Emotion, and Ability to Inform Person Identification, *Int. Conf. on Multimodal User Interfaces*, Pittsburgh, PA, 491–496.

[134] R. Coifman and V. Wickerhauser (1992), Entropy-based Algorithms for Best Basis Selection, *IEEE Trans. on Information Theory*, Vol. 38, No. 2, 713–718.

[135] J. Cole (1998), *About Face*, MIT Press.

[136] J. Cole (2000), Relations Between the Face and the Self as Revealed by Neurological Loss, *Social Research*, Vol. 67, No. 1, 187-218.

[137] C. A. Collin, C. H. Liu, N. F. Troje, P. A. McMullen, and A. Chaudhuri (2004), Face Recognition Is Affected by Similarity in Spatial Frequency Range to a Greater Degree Than Within-Category Object Recognition, *J. of Experimental Psychology: Human Perception and Performance*, Vol. 30, No. 5, 975–987.

[138] P. Comon (1994), Independent Component Analysis, a New Concept?, *Signal Processing*, Vol. 36, 287–314.

[139] J. Cooney, J., W. Kelley, M. Miller, and M. Gazzaniga (2002), Interview with Endel Tulving, *J. of Cognitive Neuroscience*, Vol. 3, No. 1, 89–94.

[140] N. P. Costen, D. M. Parker, and I. Craw (1996), Effects of High-Pass and Low-Pass Spatial Filtering on Face Identification, *Perception & Psychophysics*, Vol. 58, 602–612.

[141] H. Cott (1966), *Adaptive Coloration in Animals* (3rd ed.), Methuen & Co, London.

[142] T. M. Cover (1965), Geometrical and Statistical Properties of Systems of Linear Inequalities with Applications in Pattern Recognition, *IEEE Trans. Elect. Comp.*, Vol. 14, 326–334.

[143] T. M. Cover and P. E. Hart (1967), Nearest Neighbor Pattern Classification, *IEEE Trans. on Info. Theory*, Vol. IT-13, 21–27.

[144] H. Cox, R.M. Zeskind and M.M. Owen (1987), Robust Adaptive Beamforming, *IEEE Trans. on ASSP*, Vol. 35, No. 10.

[145] I. J. Cox, J. Kilian, T. Leighton, and T. Shamoon (1995), Watermarking for Multimedia, NEC TR 95-10.

[146] I. J. Cox, M. L. Miller, and J. A. Bloom (2002), *Digital Watermarking*, Morgan Kaufmann.

[147] I. Craw (1995), A Manifold Model of Face and Object Recognition, in T. Valentine (Ed.), *Cognitive and Computational Aspects of Face Recognition: Explorations of Face Space*, Routledge, 183–203.

[148] C. W. Crews (2002), Human Bar Code - Monitoring Biometric Technologies in a Free Society, *Policy Analysis* 452, Cato Institute.

[149] J. Culham (2004), Functional Neuroimaging: Experimental Design and Analysis, in R. Cabezza and A. Kingstone (Eds.), *Handbook of Functional Neuroimaging of Cognition* (2nd. ed.), MIT Press.

[150] M. Cunningham (1986), Measuring the Physical in Physical Attractiveness: Quasy-Experiments on the Sociobiology of Female Facial Beauty, *J. of Personal & Social Psychology*, Vol. 50, 925–935.

[151] A. R. Damasio (1994), *Descartes' Error*, Avon.

[152] I. Daubechies (1988), Orthonormal Bases of Compactly Supported Wavelets, *Comun. on Pure and Appl. Math.*, 41, 909–996.

[153] J. G. Daugman (1980), Two-Dimensional Spectral Analysis of Cortical Receptive Field Profiles, *Vision Research*, 20, 847–856.

[154] J. G. Daugman (1990), An Information-Theoretic View of Analog Representation in Striate Cortex, in E. Schwartz (Ed.) *Computational Neuroscience*, MIT Press, 403–424.

[155] J. G. Daugman (1997), Face and Gesture Recognition: Overview, *IEEE Trans. on Pattern Analysis and Machine Intelligence*, Vol. 19, No. 7, 675–676.

[156] J. G. Daugman (2000), Biometric Decision Landscapes, TR 482, Univ. of Cambridge, UK.

[157] J. G. Daugman (2003), The Importance of Being Random: Statistical Principles of Iris Recognition, *Pattern Recognition*, Vol. 36, No. 2, 279–291.

[158] J. G. Daugman (2004), How Iris Recognition Works, *IEEE Trans. on Circuits and Systems for Video Technology*, Vol. 14, No. 1, 21–30.

[159] G. Davida, Y. Frankel, and B. Matt (1998), On Enabling Secure Applications through Off-Line Biometric Identification, *Symposium on Security and Privacy*, Oakland, CA, 148–157.

[160] D. Davis, F. Monrose, and M. Reiter (2004), On User Choice in Graphical Password Schemes, *12th USENIX Security Symposium*, San Diego, CA, 151–164.

[161] R. Dawkins (1976), *The Selfish Gene*, Oxford University Press.

[162] S. R. Deans (1981), Hough Transform from Radon Transform, *IEEE Trans. on Pattern Analysis and Machine Intelligence*, Vol. 3, No. 2, 185–188.

[163] D. DeBarr and H. Wechsler (2006), Face Selection Using Random Forests and Transduction (in preparation).

[164] G. Dedeoglu, T. Kanade, and J. August (2004), High-Zoom Video Hallucination by Exploiting Spatio-Temporal Regularities, *Computer Vision and Pattern Recognition (CVPR)*, 151–158.

[165] A. Delorme and S. Thorpe (2001), Face Identification Using One Spike per Neuron: Resistance to Image Degradations, *Neural Networks*, Vol. 14, 795–803.

[166] A. P. Dempster, N. M. Laird, and D, B. Rubin (1977), Maximum Likelihood from Incomplete Data via the EM algorithm, *Journal of the Royal Statistical Society*, B 39 (1), 1–38.

[167] K. I. Diamantaris and S. Y. Kung (1996), *Principal Component Neural Networks*, John Wiley and Sons.

[168] T. Dobzhansky (1951), *Genetics and the Origin of Species* (3rd ed.), Columbia Univ. Press.

[169] G. R. Doddington, W. Liggett, A. Martin, M. Przybocki, and D. Reynolds (1998), Sheep, Goats, Lambs, and Wolves: A Statistical Analysis of Speaker Performance, *5th Int. Conf. Spoken Language Processing*, 1351–1354.

[170] G. R. Doddington, G. R., M. Przybocki, A. F. Martin, and D. A. Reynolds (2000), The NIST Speaker Recognition Evaluation, *Speech Communications*, Vol. 31, 225–254.

[171] Y. Dodis, L. Reyzin, and A. Smith (2005), Fuzzy Extractors: How to Generate Strong Keys from Biometrics and Other Noisy Data, *Eurocrypt*, LNCS 3027, Springer-Verlag, 523–540.

[172] G. Donato, M. S. Bartlett, J. C. Hager, P. Ekman, and T. J. Sejnowski, Classifying Facial Actions, *IEEE Trans. on Pattern Analysis and Machine Intelligence*, Vol. 21, No. 10, 974–989.

[173] M. Dorigo, G. Di Caro, and L. M. Gambardella (1999), Ant Algorithms for Discrete Optimization, *Artificial Life*, Vol. 5, No. 2, 137–172.

[174] B. A. Draper, K. Baek, M. S. Bartlett, and J. R. Beveridge (2003), Recognizing Faces with PCA and ICA, *Computer Vision and Image Understanding*, Vol. 91, 115–137.

[175] I. L. Dryden and K. V. Mardia (1998), *Statistical Shape Analysis*, John Wiley and Sons.

[176] B. Duchaine, G. Yovel, E. Butterworth, and K. Nakayama (2004), Elimination of All Domain-General Hypotheses of Prosopagnosia in a Single Individual: Evidence for an Isoalted Deficit in 2nd Order Configural Face Processing, *Vision*, 4 (8), 214a.

[177] B. Duchaine and K. Nakayama (2005), Dissociations of Face and Object Recognition in Developmental Prosopagnosia, *J. of Cognitive Neurosciences*, Vol. 17, No. 2, 1–13.

[178] Z. Duric, W. D. Gray, R. Heishman, F. Li, A. Rosenfeld, M. J. Schoelles, C. Schunn, and H. Wechsler (2002), Integrating Perceptual and Cognitive Modeling for Adaptive and Intelligent Human-Computer Interaction, *Proc. IEEE*, Vol. 90, No. 7, 1272–1289.

[179] Y. Ebisawa (1989), Unconstrained Pupil Detection Technique Using Two Light Sources and the Image Difference Method, *Visualization and Intelligent Design in Engineering*, 79–89.

[180] G. M. Edelman (1987), *Neuronal Darwinism. The Theory of Neuronal Group Selection*, Basic Books, NY.

[181] S. Edelman (1998), Representation is Representation of Similarity, *Behavioral and Brain Sciences* 21, 449–498.

[182] S. Edelman (1999), *Representation and Recognition in Vision*, MIT Press.

[183] S. Edelman and N. Intrator (2000), Coarse Coding of Shape Fragments + Retinotopy $\sim$ Representation of Structure, *Spatial Vision*, Vol. 13, 255–264.

[184] S. Edelman, N. Intrator, and J. S. Jacobson (2002), Unsupervised Learning of Visual Structure, in H. H. Bülthoff, T. Poggio, S. W. Lee and C. Wallraven (Eds.), *Lecture Notes in Computer Science*, Vol. 2025, Springer, 629–643.

[185] S. Edelman and N. Intrator (2004), Unsupervised statistical Learning in Vision. Computational Principles, Biological Evidence, *Workshop on Statistical Learning in Computer Vision*, Prague, The Czech Republic.

[186] J. Edwards, T. F. Cootes, and C. J. Taylor (1997), Face Recognition Using Active Appearance Models, *5th European Conf. on Computer Vision (ECCV)*, Freiburg, Germany.

[187] S. Eickeler, S. Muller, and G. Rigoll (2000), Recognition of JPEG Compressed Face Images Based on Statistical Methods, *Image and Vision Computing*, 18, 279–287.

[188] S. Eickeler, F. Walho, U. Iurgel, and G. Rigoll (2001), Content-Based Indexing of Images and Video Using Face Detection and Recognition Methods, *Int. Conf. on Acoustics, Speech and Signal Processing (ICASSP)*, Salt Lake City, UT.

[189] P. Ekman and W. V. Friesen (1978), *Facial Action Coding System (FACS): A Technique for the Measurement of Facial Actions*, Consulting Psychologists Press, Palo Alto, CA.

[190] P. Ekman (1992), An Argument for Basic Emotions, *Cognition and Emotion*, 6, 162–200.

[191] H. D. Ellis, J. W. Shepherd, and G. M. Davies (1975). An Investigation of the Use of the Photofit Technique for Recalling Faces, *British Journal of Psychology*, Vol. 66, 29–37.

[192] H. D. Ellis and M. B. Lewis (2001), Capgras Delusion: A Window on Face Recognition, *TRENDS in Cognitive Sciences*, Vol. 5, No. 4, 149–156.

[193] El-Yaniv and L. Gerzon (2005), Effective Transductive Learning via Objective Model Selection, *Pattern Recognition Letters*, Vol. 26, 2104–2115.

[194] W.K. Estes (1993), Concepts, Categories, and Psychological Science, *Psychological Science*, Vol. 4, No. 3, 143–153.

[195] K. Etemad and R. Chellappa (1997), Discriminant Analysis for Recognition of Human Face Images, *J. Opt. Soc. Am. A*, Vol. 14, No. 8, 1724–1733.

[196] N. L. Etkoff, P. Ekman, J. J. Magee, and M. G. Frank (2000), Lie Detection and Language Comprehension, *Nature*, Vol. 405, 139.

[197] B. Fasel and J. Luettin (2003), Automatic Facial Expression Analysis: A Survey, *Pattern Recognition* 36, 259–275.

[198] L. Fei-Fei, R. Fergus, and P. Perona (2003), A Bayesian Approach to Unsupervised Learning of Object Categories, *9th Int. Conf. on Computer Vision (ICCV)*, Nice, France.

[199] L. Fei-Fei, R. Fergus, and P. Perona (2006), One-Shot Learning of Object Categories, *IEEE Trans. on Pattern Analysis and Machine Intelligence*, Vol. 28, No. 4, 594–611.

[200] R. Fergus, P. Perona, and A. Zisserman (2004), A Visual Category Filter for Google Images, *8th European Conference on Computer Vision (ECCV)*, Prague, the Czech Republic, Vol. 1, 242–256.

[201] R. Fergus, P. Perona, and A. Zisserman (2005), A Sparse Object Category Model for Efficient Learning and Exhaustive Recognition, *Computer Vision and Pattern Recognition (CVPR)*, San Diego, CA, Vol. 1, 380–387.

[202] J. Fernandez-Dols, P. Carrera, and C. Casada (2001), The Meaning of Expressions: Views from Art and Other Sources, in L. Anolli, R. Ciceri, and G. Riva (Eds.), *Say not to Say: New Perspectives on Miscommunication*, IOS Press.

[203] D. Fidaleo and U. Neumann (2002), Coart: Coarticulation Region Analysis for Control of 2D Faces, *Computer Animation*, 17–22.

[204] D. Fidaleo (2003), *G-Folds: An Appearance Based Model of Facial Gestures for Performance Driven Facial Animation*, PhD Thesis, University of Southern California.

[205] D. J. Field (1987), Relations Between the statistics of Natural Images and the Response Properties of Cortical Cells, *J. of Optical Society of America A* 4 (12), 2379–2394.

[206] M. A. Fischler and R. A. Elschlager (1973), The Representation and Matching of Pictorial Structures, *IEEE Trans. on Computers*, Vol. C-22, No. 1, 67–92.

[207] A. Fitzgibbon and A. Zisserman (2002), On Affine Invariant Clustering and Automatic Cast Listing in Movies, *7th European Conf. on Computer Vision (ECCV)*, Copenhagen, Denmark.

[208] A. Fitzgibbon and A. Zisserman (2003), Joint Manifold Distance: A New Approach to Appearance Based Clustering, *Computer Vision and Pattern Recognition (CVPR)*, Madison, WI, 26–36.

[209] L. Fogassi, P. F. Ferrari, B. Gesierich, S. Rozzi, F. Chersi, and G. Rizzolatti (2005), Parietal Lobe: From Action Organization to Intention Understanding, *Science* 308, 662–667.

[210] I. Foster and C. Kesselman (Eds.) (1998), *The Grid-Blueprint for a New Computing Infrastructure*, Morgan Kaufmann.

[211] I. Foster (2002), The Grid: A New Infrastructure for 21st Century Science, *Physics Today*, Vol. 55, No. 2, 42–47.

[212] S. Foucher and L. Gagnon (2004), Face Recognition in Video Using Dempster-Shafer Theory, *ICASSP*, Montreal, Canada.

[213] S. A. Fox, T. J. McKeeff, and F. Tong (2004), A Perceptual Basis for the Lighting of Caravaggio's Faces, *Vision*, 4 (8), 215a.

[214] Y. Freund and R. E. Shapire (1996), Experiments with a New Boosting Algorithm, *13th Int. Conf. on Machine Learning (ICML)*, 148–156.

[215] Y. Freund and R. E. Shapire (1997), A Decision-Theoretic Generalization of On-Line Learning and an Application to Boosting, *J. of Computer and Systems Sciences*, Vol. 55, No. 1, 119–139.

[216] A. J. Friedlund (1991), Evolution and Facial Action in Reflex, Social Motive and Paralanguage, *Biological Psychology* 32, 3–100.

[217] J. H. Friedman (1994), An Overview of Predictive Learning and Function Approximation, in V. Cherkassky, J. Friedman and H. Wechsler (Eds.), *From Statistics to Neural Networks*, NATO ASI Series F, 136, Springer.

[218] R. W. Frischholtz and U. Dieckmann (2000), BioID: A Multimodal Biometric Identification System, *Computer*, February, 2–6.

[219] C. D. Frowd, D. Carson, H. Ness, J. Richardson, L. Morrison, S. McLanaghan, and P. Hancock (2005a), A Forensically Valid Comparison of Facial Composite Systems, *Psychology, Crime and Law*, Vol. 11, No.1, 33–52.

[220] C. D. Frowd, D. Carson, H. Ness, D. McQuiston - Surret, J. Richardson, H. Baldwin, and P. Hancock (2005b), Contemporary Composite Techniques: The Impact of a Forensically - Relevant Target Delay, *Legal and Criminological Psychology* 10, 63–81.

[221] P. Fua (2000), Regularized Bundle Adjustment to Model Heads from Image Sequences without Calibration Data, *Int. J. of Computer Vision*, Vol. 38, No. 2, 153–171.

[222] K. Fukunaga (1990), *Introduction to Statistical Pattern Recognition* (2nd ed.), Academic Press.

[223] N. Furl, P. J. Phillips, and A. O. Toole (2002), Face Recognition Algorithms and the Other-Race Effect: Computational Mechanisms for a Developmental Contact Hypothesis, *Cognitive Science*, 26, 797–815.

[224] S. Furui (1997), Recent Advances in Speaker Recognition, *Pattern Recognition Letters*, Vol. 18, 859–872.

[225] S. Gablick (1977), *Progress in Arts*, Rizolli, New York.

[226] D. Gabor (1946), Theory of Communication, *J. IEEE* 93, 429–459.

[227] F. Galton (1883), *Inquiries into Human Faculty and Its Development*, Macmillan, London.

[228] F. Galton (1888a), Personal Identification and Description - I, *Nature*, 173–177.

[229] F. Galton (1888b), Personal Identification and Description - II, *Nature*, 201–203.

[230] F. Galton (1910), Numeralized Profiles for Classification and Recognition, *Nature* 83, 127–130.

[231] A. Gammerman, V. Vovk, and V. Vapnik (1998), Learning by Transduction. *Uncertainty in Artificial Intelligence (UAI)*, 148–155.

[232] Y. Gao, S. C. Hui, and A. C. M. Fong (2003), A Multiview Facial Analysis Technique for Identity Authentication, *Pervasive Computing*, Vol. 2, No. 1, 38–45.

[233] K. Gates (2004), The Past Perfect Promise of Facial Recognition Technology, *ACDIS*, University of Illinois at Urbana-Champaign.

[234] I. Gauthier and N. K. Logothetis (2000), Is Face Recognition Not so Unique After All? *J. of Cognitive Neuropsychology*, Vol. 17, No 1-3, 125–142.

[235] J. L. Gauvain and C. H. Lee (1994), Maximum a Posteriori Estimation for Multivariate Gaussian Mixture Observations of Markov Chains, *IEEE Trans. on Speech and Audio Processing*, Vol. 2, No. 2, 291–298.

[236] S. Geman, E. Bienenstock and R. Doursat (1992), Neural Networks and the Bias/Variance Dilemma, *Neural Computation*, 4, 1–58.

[237] S. Gerwehr and R. W. Glenn (2002), *Unweaving the Web-Deception and Adaptation in Future Urban Operations*, Rand.

[238] A. S. Georghiades, P. N. Belhumeuer, and D. J. Kriegman (2001), From Few to Many: Illumination Cone Models for Face Recognition under Variable Lighting and Pose, *IEEE Trans. on Pattern Analysis and Machine Intelligence*, Vol. 27, No. 6, 643–660.

[239] J. J. Gibson (1957), Survival in a World of Probable Objects, *Contemporary Psychology*, 2, 33–35.

[240] G. P. Ginsburgh and M. E. Harrington (1996), Bodily States and Context in Situated Line of Actions, in R. Harre and W. G. Parrot (Eds.), *The Emotions. Social, Cultural and Biological Dimensions*, Sage, London.

[241] F. Glover (1986), Future Paths for Integer Programming and Links to Artificial Intelligence, *Computers and Operations Research*, 5, 533–549.

[242] G. Golarai, D. L. Eberhardt, K. Grill-Spector, and G. D. D. Gabrieli, Representation of Parts and Canonical Face Configuration in the Amygdala, Superior Temporal Sulcus (STS) and the Fusiform "Face Area" (FFA), *Vision*, 4 (8), 131a.

[243] A. J. Goldstein, L. D. Harmon, and A. B. Lesk (1971), Identification of Human Faces, *Proc. IEEE*, 59, 748–760.

[244] B.A. Golomb, D.T. Lawrence, T.J. Sejnowski (1991), Sexnet: a Neural Netwok Identifies Sex from Human Faces, in D. S. Touretzky, R. Lipmann (Eds.), *Advances in Neural Computation Processing Systems (NIPS)*, Vol. 3, Morgan Kaufmann, 572–577.

[245] E. H. Gombrich (1972), The Mask and the Face: The Perception of Physiognomy Likeness in Life and Art, in M. Mandelbaum (Ed.), *Art, Perception, and Reality*, John Hopkins University Press.

[246] E. H. Gombrich (1984), *Art and Illusion* (7th ed.), Princeton University Press.

[247] S. Gong, S. McKenna, and A. Psarrou (2000), *Dynamic Vision: from Images to Face Recognition*, Imperial College Press, London.

[248] D. Goren and H. R. Wilson (2004), Differential Impact of Spatial Frequency on Facial Expression and Facial Identity Recognition, *Vision*, 4 (8), 904a.

[249] J. A. Gray (1982), *The Neuropsychology of Anxiety*, Oxford University Press.

[250] P. Griffin (2004), Face Recognition Format for Data Interchange, M1/04-0041, INCITS.

[251] P. Griffin (2005), Understanding the Face Image Format Standards, Identix, http://fingerprint.nist.gov/standard/workshop1/presentations/Griffin-Face-Std-M1.pdf

[252] R. Gross, J. Yang, and A. Waibel (2000), Face Recognition in a Meeting Room, *4th Int. Conf. on Automatic Face and Gesture Recognition (FGR)*, Grenoble, France.

[253] R. Gross, I. Matthews, and S. Baker (2004a), Appearance-Based Face Recognition and Light Fields, *IEEE Trans. on Pattern Analysis and Machine Intelligence*, Vol. 26, No. 4, 449–465.

[254] R. Gross, I. Matthews, and S. Baker (2004b), Constructing and Fitting Active Appearance Models with Occlusion, *1st IEEE Workshop on Face Processing in Video*, Washington, D. C.

[255] P. Grother (2004), Face Recognition Vendor Test 2002-Supplemental Report, NIST(IR) 7083.

[256] E. Gurari and H. Wechsler (1982), On the Difficulties Involved in the Segmentation of Pictures, *IEEE Trans. on Pattern Analysis and Machine Intelligence*, Vol. 4, No. 3, 304–306.

[257] S. Gutta, J. Huang, J. Philips, and H. Wechsler (2000), Mixture of Experts for Classification of Gender, Ethnic Origin, and Pose of Human Faces, *IEEE Trans. on Neural Networks*, Vol. 11, No. 4, 948–960.

[258] S. Gutta, J. Huang, C. J. Liu, and H. Wechsler (2001), Comparative Performance Evaluation of Gray Scale and Color Information for Face Recognition Tasks, *3rd Int. Conf. on Audio and Video-Based Biometric Person Authentication (AVBPA)*, Halmstad, Sweden.

[259] S. Gutta and H. Wechsler (2003), Analysis of Partial-Faces for Face Recognition, *10th Int. Conf. on Comp. Analysis of Images and Patterns (CAIP)*, Groningen, Netherlands, 630–637.

[260] S. Gutta and H. Wechsler (2004), Face Recognition Using Asymmetric Faces, *1st Int. Conf. on Biometric Authentication*, Hong Kong.

[261] E. Halgren, A. M. Dale, M. I. Sereno, R. B. H. Tootell, K. Marinkovic, and B. R. Rosen (1999), Location of Human Face-Selective Cortex With Respect to Retinotopic Areas, *Brain Mapping*, 7, 29–37.

[262] K. H. Han and J. H. Kim (2004), Quantum - Inspired Evolutionary Algorithms with a New Termination Criterion, *IEEE Trans. on Evolutionary Computation*, Vol. 6, 580–593.

[263] P. J. B. Hancock, R.. J. Baddeley, and L. S. Smith (1992), The Principal Components of Natural Images, *Network: Computation in Neural Systems*, Vol. 3, 61–70.

[264] W. Hardle, P. Hall, and J. S. Marron (1988), How Far Are Automatically Chosen Regression Smoothing Parameters from their Optimum, *J. Amer. Stat. Assoc.*, Vol. 83, 86–95.

[265] L.D. Harmon (1973), The Recognition of Faces, *Scientific American*, Vol. 229, No. 5, 71–82.

[266] L. D. Harmon and B. Julesz (1973), Masking in Visual Recognition: Effects of Two-Dimensional Filtered Noise, *Science*, 180, 1194–1197.

[267] F. Hartung and M. Kutter (1999), Multimedia Watermarking Techniques, *Proc IEEE*, Vol. 87, No. 7, 1079–1107.

[268] T. Hastie, R. Tibshirani, and J. Friedman (2001), *The Elements of Statistical Learning: Data Mining, Inference and Prediction*, Springer.

[269] K. J. Hastings (1997), *Probability and Statistics*, Addison-Wesley.

[270] J.H. van Hateren and D.L. Ruderman (1998), Independent Component Analysis of Natural Image Sequence Yields Spatio-Temporal Filters Similar to Simple Cells in Primary Visual Cortex, *Proc. R. Soc. Lond. B. Biol. Sci.* Dec. 7, 265 (1412), 2315–2320.

[271] J. Hawkins (with Sandra Blakeslee) (2004), *On Intelligence*, Times Books, Henry Holt and Co., NY.

[272] X. He, D. Cai, and W Min (2005), Statistical and Computational Analysis of Locality Preserving Projection, *22nd Int. Conference on Machine Learning (ICML)*, Bonn, Germany.

[273] X. He, S. Yan, Y. Hu, P. Niyogi, and H. J. Zhang (2005), Face Recognition Using Laplacianfaces, *IEEE Transactions on Pattern Analysis and Machine Intelligence*, Vol. 27, No. 3, 328 –340.

[274] R. Hecht-Nielsen (1990), *Neurocomputing*, Addison-Wesley.

[275] D. Heckerman, D. Geiger, and D. H. Chickering (1995), Learning Bayesian Networks: The Combination of Knowledge and Statistical Data, *Machine Learning*, Vol. 20, No. 3, 197–243.

[276] B. Heisele, P. Ho, J. Wu, and T. Poggio (2003), Face Recognition: Component-Based Versus Global Approaches, *Computer Vision and Image Understanding*, Vol. 91, 6–21.

[277] R. Heishman, Z. Duric, and H. Wechsler (2001), PUPILS - Enabling a Dialogue Between the Machine and the Brain, *Applied Imagery Pattern Recognition (AIPR)*, Washington, DC.

[278] M. E. Hellman (1978), An Overview of Public Key Cryptography, *IEEE Communications*, Vol. 16, No. 6, 24–32.

[279] T. Hertz, A. Bar-Hillel, and D. Weinshall (2004), Learning Distance Functions for Image Retrieval, *Computer Vision and Pattern Recognition (CVPR)*, Washington, DC., 570–577.

[280] E. H. Hess and J. M. Polt (1964), Pupil Size in Relation to Mental Activity During Simple Problem-Solving, *Science*, 143, 1190–1192.

[281] C. F. Hester and D. Casasent (1980), Multivariant Technique for Multiclass Pattern Recognition, *Applied Optics*, Vol. 19, 1758–1761.

[282] R. J. Heuer (1981), Cognitive Factors in Deception and Counterdeception, in Daniel and Herbig (Eds.), *Strategic Military Deception*, Pergamon Press.

[283] H. Hill, P. G. Schyns, and S. Akamatsu (1997), Information and Viewpoint Dependence in Face Recognition, *Cognition* 62, 201–222.

[284] H. Hill and A. Johnston (2001), Categorizing Sex and Identity from the Biological Motion of Faces, *Curr Biol* 11, 880–885.

[285] E. Hjelmas and B. K. Low (2001), Face Detection: A Survey, *Computer Vision and Image Understanding*, Vol. 83, 236–274.

[286] S.-S. Ho (2005), A Martingale Framework for Concept Change Detection in Time-Varying Data Streams, *22nd Int. Conf. on Machine Learning (ICML)*, Bonn, Germany, 321–328.

[287] S.-S. Ho and H. Wechsler (2005), On the Detection of Concept Change in Time-Varying Data Streams by Testing Exchangeability, *Uncertainty in AI (UAI)*, Edinburgh, Scotland, UK, 267–274.

[288] S.-S. Ho and H. Wechsler (2006a), Stream-based Active Learning Using Transduction, *Pattern Recognition Letters* (unde review).

[289] S.-S. Ho and H. Wechsler (2006b), Change Detection and Key-Frame Extraction Using Martingale (in preparation).

[290] T. K. Ho (1998), The Random Subspace Method for Constructing Decision Forests, *IEEE Trans. on Pattern Analysis and Machine Intelligence*, Vol. 20, No. 8, 832–844.

[291] B. K. P. Horn (1984), Extended Gaussian Images, *Proc. IEEE*, Vol. 72, 1671–1686.

[292] R. A. Horn and C. R. Johnson (1990), *Matrix Analysis*, Cambridge University Press.

[293] R.-L. Hsu, M. Abdel-Mottaleb, and A. K. Jain (2002), Face Detection in Color Images, *IEEE Trans. Pattern Analysis and Machine Intelligence*, Vol. 24, No. 5, 696–706.

[294] C. Hu, R. Feris, and M. Turk (2003), Active Wavelet Networks for Face Alignment, *British Machine Vision Conference (BMVC)*.

[295] M. K. Hu (1962), Visual Pattern Recognition by Moments Invariants, *IEEE Trans. Inf. Theory*, 8, 179–187.

[296] J. Huang, S. Gutta, and H. Wechsler (1996), Detection of Human Faces Using Decision Trees, *2nd Int. Conf. on Automatic Face and Gesture Recognition (FGR)*, Killington, VT, 248–252.

[297] J. Huang, D. Ii, X. Shao, and H. Wechsler (1998), Pose Discrimination and Eye Detection Using Support Vector Machines, in H. Wechsler et al. (Eds.), *Face Recognition: From Theory to Applications*, Springer, 528–536.

[298] J. Huang and H. Wechsler (1999), Eye Detection Using Optimal Wavelet Packets and Radial Basis Functions (RBFs), *Int. Journal of Pattern Recognition and Artificial Intelligence*, Vol. 13, No. 7, 1009–1025.

[299] J. Huang and H. Wechsler (2000), Visual Routines for Eye Location Using Learning and Evolution, *IEEE Trans. on Evolutionary Computation*, Vol. 4, No. 1, 73–82.

[300] J. Huang, B. Heisele, and V. Blanz (2003), Component-based Face Recognition with 3D Morphable Models, *4th Int. Conf. on Audio- and Video- Based Person Authentication (AVBPA)*, Surrey, UK, 27–34.

[301] K. Huang and M. Trivedi (2002), Streaming Face Recognition Using Multicamera Video Arrays. *16th Int. Conf. on Pattern Recognition*, Quebec-City, Canada, Vol. 4, 213–216.

[302] L. L. Huang, A. Shimizu, and H. Kobatake (2005), Robust Face Detection Using Gabor Filter Features (2005), *Pattern Recognition Letters*, Vol. 26, 1641–1649.

[303] P. J. Huber (2004), *Robust Statistics*, Wiley.

[304] D. Hume (1740), A Treatise of Human Nature (on line) http://socserv2.socsci.mcmaster.ca/~econ/ugcm/3ll3/hume/treat.html

[305] A. Hurlbert (2001), Trading Faces, *Nature Neuroscience*, Vol. 4, No. 1, 3–5.

[306] D. J. Hurley, M. S. Nixon, and J. N. Carter (2005), Force Field Feature Extraction for Ear Biometrics, *Computer Vision and Image Understanding*, Vol. 98, 491–512.

[307] D. P. Huttenlocher, G. A. Klanderman, and W. Rucklidge (1993), Comparing Images Using the Hausdorff Distance, *IEEE Trans. on Pattern Analysis and Machine Intelligence*, Vol. 15, No. 9, 850–863.

[308] B. W. Hwang, M. C. Roh, and S. W. Lee (2004), Performance Evaluation of Face Recognition Algorithms on Asian Face Database, *6th Int. Conf. on Automatic Face and Gesture Recognition (FGR)*, Seoul, Korea.

[309] A. Hyvarinen and P. O. Hoyer (2000), Emergence of Phase and Shift Invariant Features by Decomposition of Natural Images into Independent Feature Subspaces. *Neural Computation*, Vol. 12, No. 7, 1705–1720.

[310] A. Hyvarinen, J. Karhunen, and E. Oja (2001), *Independent Component Analysis*, Wiley-Interscience.

[311] A. Hyvarinen, J. Hurri, and J. Vayrynen (2003), Bubbles: a Unifying Framework for Low-Level Statistical Properties of Natural Image Sequences, *J. Opt. Soc. Am. A.* Vol. 20, No.7, 1237–1255.

[312] A. Iannarelli (1989), *Ear Identification*, Paramount Publishing Co., Freemont, CA.

[313] M. Isard and A. Blake (1996), Contour Tracking by Stochastic Propagation of Conditional Density, *4th European Conf. on Computer Vision (ECCV)*, Cambridge, UK, 343–356.

[314] M. Isard and A. Blake (1998), Condensation - Conditional Density Propagation for Visual Tracking, *Int. J. Computer Vision*, Vol. 28, No. 1, 5–28.

[315] Y. Ivanov, B. Heisele, and T. Serre (2004), Using Components for Face Recognition, *6th Int. Conf. on Automatic Face and Gesture Recognition*, Seoul, Korea, 421–426.

[316] C. E. Izard (1971), *The Face of Emotion*, Appleton-Century-Crofts.

[317] D. H. Jacobs et al. (1995), Emotional Face Imagery, Perception, and Expression in Parkinson's Disease, *Neurology* 45, 1695–1702.

[318] R. A. Jacobs, M.I. Jordan, S.J. Nowlan, and G.E. Hinton (1991), Adaptive Mixtures of Local Experts, *Neural Computation*, 3, 79–87.

[319] B. Jahne (2002), *Digital Image Processing*, 5th ed., Springer.

[320] A. K. Jain, R. M. Bolle, and S. Pankanti (Eds.) (1999), *Biometric: Personal Identification in Networked Society*, Kluwer.

[321] A. K. Jain and S. Pankanti (2001), Biometrics Systems: Anatomy of Performance, *IEICE Trans. Fundamentals*, Vol. E00-A, No. 1, 1–13.

[322] A. K. Jain and A. Ross (2002), Learning User-Specific Parameters in a Multibiometric System, *International Conference on Image Processing (ICIP)*, Rochester, New York, 57–60.

[323] A. K. Jain and A. Ross (2004), Multibiometric Systems, *Comm. of ACM*, Vol. 47, No. 1, 34–40.

[324] A. K. Jain and U. Uludag (2005), Hiding Biometric Data, *IEEE Trans. on Pattern Analysis and Machine Intelligence*, Vol. 25, No. 11, 1404–1498.

[325] S. Jain (2000), Digital Watermarking Techniques: A Case Study in Fingerprint and Faces, *ICVGIP*, Bangalore, India, 139–144.

[326] J. S. Jang, K. H. Han, and J. H. Kim (2004), Evolutionary Algorithm-based Face Verification, *Pattern Recognition Letters*, Vol. 25, 1857–1865.

[327] I.N. Jarudi and P. Sinha (2003), Relative Contributions of Internal and External Features to Face Recognition, AI Memo 2003-004, MIT AI Lab.

[328] T. Jebara (2002), *Discriminative, Generative, and Imitative Learning*, PhD Thesis, MIT.

[329] F. V. Jensen (2001), *Bayesian Networks and Decision Graphs*, Springer.

[330] O. Jesorsky, K. J. Kirchberg, and R. W. Frischoltz (2001), Robust Face Detection Using the Hausdorff Distance, in J. Bigun and F. Smeraldi (Eds.), *Int. Conf. on Automatic Video-Based Person Authentication (AVBPA)*, Halmstad, Sweden, 90–95.

[331] Q. Ji and X. Yang (2001), Real Time Visual Cues Extraction for Monitoring Driver Vigilance, *Int. Workshop on Computer Vision Systems*, Vancouver, Canada.

[332] Q. Ji and Y. Zhang (2002), Real-Time Eye, Gaze, and Face Pose Tracking for Monitoring Driver Vigilance, *Real-Time Imaging* 8, 357–377.

[333] D. Jiang, Y. Hu, S. Yan, L. Zhang, H. Zhang, and W. Gao (2005), Efficient 3D Reconstruction for Face Recognition, *Pattern Recognition* 38, 787–798.

[334] T. Joachims (1999), Transductive Inference for Text Classification Using Support Vector Machines, *16th Int. Conf. on Machine Learning (ICML)*, Bled, Slovenia.

[335] T. Joachims (2003), Transductive Learning via Spectral Graph Partitioning, *20th Int. Conf. on Machine Learning (ICML)*, Washington, DC.

[336] A. D. Johnson and M. Tarr (2004), Red-Green, but not Blue-Yellow Color Manipulations Affect Memory of Facial Identity (2004), *Vision*, 4 (8), 419a.

[337] N. F. Johnson and S. Jajodia (1998), Steganography: Seeing the Unseen, *Computer* 2, 26–34.

[338] W. Johnson and J. Lindenstrauss (1984), Extension of Lipschitz Mapping into a Hilbert Space, *Contemporary Math.*, Vol. 26, 189 - 206.

[339] R. A. Johnston, A. B. Milne, C. Williams, and J. Hosie (1997), Do Distinctive Faces Come from Outer Space? An Investigation of the Status of a Multidimensional Face-Space, *Visual Cognition*, 4, 59–67.

[340] B. D. Jonavic and P. S. Levy (1997), A Look at the Rule of Three, *American Statistician*, 51 (2), 137–139.

[341] K. Jonsson, J. Matas, J. Kittler and Y. P. Li (2000), Learning Support Vector for Face Verification and Recognition, *4th Int. Conf. on Automatic Face and Gesture Recognition (FGR)*, Grenoble, France, 208–213.

[342] M. I. Jordan (1995), Why the Logistic Function? A Tutorial Discussion on Probabilities and Neural Networks, Computational Cognitive Science TR 9503, MIT.

[343] M. I. Jordan and R.A. Jacobs (1994), Hierarchical Mixture of Experts and the EM Algorithm, *Neural Computation*, 6, 181–214.

[344] D. B. Judd, D. L. McAdam, and G. Wyszecki (1964), Spectral Distribution of Typical Daylight as a Function of Correlated Color Temperature, *Journal of the Optical Society of America A* 54: 1031–1040.

[345] A. Jules and M. Wattenberg (1999), A Fuzzy Commitment Scheme, *6th ACM Conf. on Computer and Communication Security*, Singapore, 28–36.

[346] A. Jules and M. Sudan (2002), A Fuzzy Vault Scheme, *Int. Symposium on Inf. Theory*, Lausanne, Switzerland.

[347] P. Juszczak and R. P. W. Duin (2004), Selective Sampling Based on the Variation in Label Assignment, *17th Int. Conf. on Pattern Recognition (ICPR)*, Cambridge, UK.

[348] D. Kahn (1967), *The Codebreakers*, Macmillan, New York.

[349] D. Kahneman and A. Tversky (2000) (Eds.), *Choices, Values, and Frames*, Cambridge Univ. Press.

[350] T. Kanade (1977), *Computer Recognition of Human Faces*, Birkhauser.

[351] S. B. Kang and K. Ikeuchi (1993), The Complex EGI: A New Representation for 3-D Pose Determination, *IEEE Trans. on Pattern Analysis and Machine Intelligence*, Vol. 15, No. 7, 707–721.

[352] N. Kanwisher, J. McDermott, and M. Chun, M. (1997), The Fusiform Face Area: A Module in Human Extrastriate Cortex Specialized for the Perception of Faces. *Journal of Neuroscience*, Vol. 17, 4302–4311.

[353] N. Kanwisher and M. Moscovitch (2000), The Cognitive Neuroscience of Face Processing: An Introduction, *J. of Cognitive Neuropsychology*, Vol. 17, No 1-3, 1-11.

[354] G. J. Kaufman, Jr. and K. J. Breeding (1976), The Automatic Recognition of Human Faces from Profile Silouhettes, *IEEE Trans. Syst. Man and Cybern.* 6, 113-121.

[355] Y. Kaya and K. Kobayashi (1972), A Basic Study on Human Face Recognition, in S. Watanabe (Ed.), *Frontiers of Pattern Recognition*, Academic Press, NY.

[356] Y. Ke and R. Sukthankar (2004), PCA-SIFT: A More Distinctive Representtaion for Local Image Descriptors, *Computer Vision and Pattern Recognition (CVPR)*, 506-513.

[357] M. D. Kelly (1970), Visual Identification of People by Computer, Tech. Rep. AI-130, Stanford AI Project, Stanford, CA.

[358] K. M. Kendrick, A. P. da Costa, A. E. Leigh, M. R. Hinton, and J. W. Pierce (2001), Sheep Don't Forget a Face, *Nature* 411, 165-166.

[359] D. Kennedy (2003), Forensic Science: Oxymoron?, *Science*, Vol. 302, No. 5651, p. 1625.

[360] J. Kennedy, R. C. Eberhart, and Y. Shi (2001), *Swarm Intelligence*, Morgan Kaufmann.

[361] B. Khurana and G. Hole (2004), Face Recognition: What's Sauce for the Goose Is Not Sauce for the Gander, *Vision*, 4 (8), 428a.

[362] D. E. Kieras and D. E. Meyer (1997), An Overview of the EPIC Architecture for Cognition and Performance with Application to Human Computer Interaction, *Human-Computer Interaction*, Vol. 12, 391-438.

[363] J. Kim, J. Choi, J. Yi, and M. Turk (2005), Effective Representation Using ICA for Face Recognition Robust to Local Distortion and Partial Occlusion, *IEEE Trans. on Pattern Analysis and Machine Intelligence*, Vol. 27, No. 12, 1977-1981.

[364] M. Kirby and l. Sirovitch, (1990), Application of the Karhunen - Loeve Procedure for the Characterization of Human Faces, *IEEE Trans. on Pattern Analysis and Machine Intelligence*, Vol. 12, No.1, 103-108.

[365] K. J. Kirchberg, O. Jesorsky, and R. W. Frischholtz (2002), Genetic Model Optimization for Hausdorff Distance-Based Face Localization, *Int. ECCV Workshop on Biometric Authentication*, Copenhagen, Denmark, 103-111.

[366] J. Kittler, M. Hatef, R. P. W. Duin, and J. Matas (1998), On Combining Classifiers, *IEEE Trans. on Pattern Analysis and Machine Intelligence*, Vol. 20, No. 3, 226-239.

[367] J. Kleinberg and E. Tardos (2005), *Algorithm Design*, Addison-Wesley.

[368] M. L. Knapp and J. A. Hall (2005), *Nonverbal Communication in Human Interaction*, 6th ed., Wadsworth.

[369] B. Knight and A. Johnston (1997), The Role of Movement in Face Recognition, *Visual Cognition*, Vol. 4, No. 3, 265-273.

[370] B.J. Knowlton and L. S. Squire (1993), The Learning of Categories: Parallel Brain Systems for Item Memory and Category Knowledge, *Science*, Vol. 262, 1747-1749.

[371] C. Koch and T. Poggio (1999), Predicting the Visual World: Silence is Golden, *Nature Neuroscience*, Vol. 2, No. 1, 9-10.

[372] J. J. Koenderink and A. J. van Doorn (1979), The Internal Representation of Solid Shape with Respect to Vision, *BiolCyb*, Vol. 32, 211-216.

[373] R. Koenen (2000), MPEG-4 Project Overview, ISO/IEC JTC1/SC29/WG11.

[374] W. Kohler (1925), *The Mentality of Apes*, Harcourt Brace.

[375] T. Kohonen (1988), The "Neural" Phonetic Typewriter, *Computer*, Vol. 21, No. 3, 11-22.

[376] T. Kohonen (1989), *Self-Organization and Associative Memories* (3rd ed.), Springer-Verlag.

[377] J. Kolodner (Ed.) (2004), *Case-Based Learning*, Kluwer.

[378] G. Kotonya and I. Sommerville (1998), *Requirements Engineering*, Wiley.

[379] C. Kotropoulos, A. Tefas, and I. Pitas (2000), Frontal FACE Authentication Using Morphological Elastic Graph Matching, *IEEE Trans. on Image Processing*, Vol. 9, No. 4, 555–560.

[380] O. Kouropteva, O. Okun, and M. Pietikainen (2002), Selection of the Optimal Parameter Value for the Locally Linear Embedding Algorithm, *FSKD*, Singapore.

[381] H. C. Kraemer (1992), *Evaluating Medical Tests: Objective and Quantitative Guidelines*, Sage Publications.

[382] M. A. Krogel and T. Scheffer (2004), Multi-Relational Learning, Text Mining, and Semi-Supervised Learning from Functional Genomics, *Machine Learning*, Vol. 57, 61–81.

[383] A. Krogh and J. Vedelsby (1995), Neural Network Ensembles, Cross Validation and Active Learning, in D.S. Touretzky (Ed.), *Advances in Neural Information Processing Systems (NIPS)*, 7, Morgan Kaufmann, 231–238.

[384] V. Krueger and S. Zhou (2002), Exemplar Based Face Recognition from Video, *7th European Conf. on Computer Vision (ECCV)*, Copenhagen, Denmark.

[385] J. B. Kruskal (1964), Non-Metric Multidimensional Scaling: A Numerical Method, *Psychometrika*, 29, 115–129.

[386] S. Kshirsagar, T. Molet, and N. M. Thalmann, (2001), Principal Components of Expressive Speech Animation, *Proc. Computer Graphics Int.*, 38–44.

[387] M. Kudo and J. Sklansky (2000), Comparison of Algorithms that Select Features for Pattern Classifiers, *Pattern Recognition*, 33, 25 - 41.

[388] M. Kukar and I. Kononenko (2002), Reliable Classifications with Machine Learning, *13th European Conf. on Machine Learning (ECML)*, Helsinki, Finland.

[389] B. B. K. V. Kumar (1986), Minimum Variance Synthetic Discriminant Functions, *J. Opt. Soc. Am. A* 3, 1579–1584.

[390] B. B. K. V. Kumar, M. Savvides, C. Xie, K. Venkataramani, J. Thornton, and A. Mahalanobis (2004), Biometric Verification with Correlation Filters, *Applied Optics* 43, 391–402.

[391] M. Lades, J. C. Vorbruggen, J. Buhmann, C. Malsburg, R. P. Wurtz, and W. Konen (1993), Distortion Invariant Object Recognition in the Dynamic Link Architecture, *IEEE Trans. on Computers*, Vol. 42, 300–311.

[392] H. Lai and H. Wechsler (2006), Recognition-by-Parts of Occluded and Disguised Faces Using Adaptive and Robust Correlation Filters (in preparation).

[393] J. H. Lai, P. C. Yuen, and G. C. Feng (2001), Face Recognition Using Holistic Fourier Invariant Features, *Pattern Recognition*, 34, 95–109.

[394] K. M. Lam and H. Yan (1996), Locating and Extracting the Eye in Human Face Images, *Pattern Recognition*, Vol. 29, No. 5, 771–779.

[395] K. Lander, F. Christie, and V. Bruce (1999), The role of Movement in the Recognition of Famous Faces, *Memory and Cognition*, Vol. 27, No. 6, 974–985.

[396] A. Lanitis, C. J. Taylor, and T. F. Cootes (1995), Automatic Face Identification System Using Flexible Appearance Models, *Image and Vision Computing* 13, 393–401.

[397] A. Lanitis, C. J. Taylor, and T. F. Cootes (1997), Automatic Interpretation and Coding of Face Images Using Flexible Models, *IEEE Trans. on Pattern Analysis and Machine Intelligence*, Vol. 19, No. 7, 743–756.

[398] A. Lanitis, C. Draganova, and C. Christodoulou (2004), Comparing Different Classifiers for Automatic Age Estimation, *IEEE Trans. on Systems, Man, and Cybernetics, Part B: Cybernetics*, Vol. 34, No. 1, 621–628.

[399] G. D. Lassiter (2002), Illusory Causation in the Courtroom, *Current Directions in Psychological Science* 11, 204–208.

[400] P. C. Lauterbur (1973), Image Formation by Induced Local Interaction: Examples Employing Nuclear Magnetic Resonance, *Nature*, 242, 190–191.

[401] N. Leavitt (2004), Are Web Services Finally Ready to Deliver?, *Computer*, Vol. 37, No. 11, 14–18.

[402] D. D. Lee and H.S. Seung (1999), Learning the Parts of Objects by Non-Negative Matrix Factorization, *Nature*, Vol. 421, 788–791.

[403] J. C. Lee and E. Milios (1990), Matching Range Images of Human Faces, *3rd Int. Conf. on Computer Vision (ICCV)*, Osaka, Japan, 722–726.

[404] K. C. Lee, J. Ho, M. H. Yang and D. J. Kriegman (2003), Video-Based Face Recognition Using Probabilistic Appearance Manifolds, *Computer Vision and Pattern Recognition (CVPR)*, Madison, WI, 313–320.

[405] S. Lefevre, J. Holler, and N. Vincent (2003), A Review of Real-Time Segmentation of Uncompressed Video Sequences for Content Based Search and Retrieval, *Real-Time Imaging*, Vol. 9, 73–98.

[406] D. A. Leopold, A. J. O'Toole, T. Vetter, and V. Blanz (2001), Prototype-Referenced Shape Encoding Revealed by High-Level Aftereffects, *Nature Neuroscience*, Vol. 4, No. 1, 89–94.

[407] M. S. Lew (1996), Information Theoretic View-Based and Modular Face Detection, *2nd Int. Conf. on Automatic Face and Gesture Recognition (FGR)*, Killington, VT, 198–203.

[408] P. Lewicki (1986), Processing Information About Covariations that Can Not Be Articulated, *J. of Experimental Psychology: Learning, Memory and Cognition*, 12, 135–146.

[409] M. B. Lewis and R. A. Johnston (1999), A Unified Account of the Effects of Caricaturing Faces, *Visual Cognition*, 6, 1–41.

[410] B. Li and R. Chellappa (2002), A Generic Approach to Simultaneous Tracking and Verification in Video, *IEEE Trans. on Image Processing*, Vol. 11, 530–544.

[411] F. Li (2005), *Object Recognition Using Strangeness and Transduction*, PhD Thesis, George Mason University.

[412] F. Li and H. Wechsler (2003), Open World Face Recognition with Credibility and Confidence Measures, *4th Int. Conf. on Audio and Video-Based Biometric Person Authentication (AVBPA)*, Surrey, UK.

[413] F. Li and H. Wechsler (2004), Watch List Face Surveillance Using Transductive Inference, *1st Int. Conf. on Biometric Authentication (ICBA)*, Hong Kong.

[414] F. Li and H. Wechsler (2005), Open Set Face Recognition Using Transduction, *IEEE Trans. on Pattern Analysis and Machine Intelligence*, Vol. 27, No. 11, 1686–1697.

[415] F. Li, J. Kosecka, and H. Wechsler (2006a), Strangeness Based Feature Selection for Part Based Recognition, *Computer Vision and Pattern Recognition (CVPR) Workshop on Beyond Patches*, New York, NY.

[416] F. Li, H. Wechsler, and J. Kosecka (2006b), Face Recognition-by-Parts Using Strangeness and Boosting (in preparation).

[417] M. Li and P. Vitanyi (1997), *An Introduction to Kolmogorov Complexity and Its Applications*, (2nd. Ed.) Springer-Verlag.

[418] S. Z. Li and J. Lu (1999), Face Recognition Using the Nearest Feature Line Method, *IEEE Trans. on Neural Networks*, Vol. 10, No. 2, 439–443.

[419] S. Z. Li , X. W. Hou, and H. J. Zhang (2001), Learning Spatially Localized Parts-Based Representation, *Computer Vision and Pattern Recognition (CVPR)*, Vol. 1, 207–212.

[420] S. Z. Li, Q. D. Fu, L. Gu, B. Scholkopf, Y. M. Cheng, and H. J. Zhang (2001), Kernel Machine Based Learning for Multi-View Face Detection and Pose Estimation, *8th Int. Conf. on Computer Vision (ICCV)*, Vancouver, Canada.

[421] S. Z. Li and Z. Q. Zhang (2004), FloatBoost Learning and Statistical Face Detection. *IEEE Trans. on Pattern Analysis and Machine Intelligence*, Vol. 26, No. 9, 1112–1123.

[422] S. Z. Li and A. K. Jain (Eds.) (2005), *Handbook of Face Recognition*, Springer.

[423] Y. Li, S. Gong and H. Liddell (2001), Modelling Faces Dynamically Across Views and Over Time, *8th Int. Conf. on Computer Vision (ICCV)*, Vancouver, Canada, 258–263.

[424] Y. Li, S. Gong and H. Liddell (2003a), Constructing Facial Identity Surfaces for Recognition. *Int. Journal of Computer Vision*, Vol. 53, No. 1, 71–92.

[425] Y. Li, S. Gong and H. Liddell (2003b), Recognising Trajectories of Facial Identities Using Kernel Discriminant Analysis, *Image and Vision Computing*, Vol. 21, 1077–1086.

[426] Y. Li (2004), On Incremental and robust subspace Learning, *Pattern Recognition*, Vol. 37, No. 7, 1509–1518.

[427] Z. Li and X. Tang (2004), LDA-Based Face Recognition Using Different Training Data, *CISST*, 179–182.

[428] C. Y. Lin, M. Wu, J. A. Bloom, M. L. Miller, I. J. Cox, and Y. M. Lui (2001), Rotation, Scale, and Translation Resilient Watermarking for Images, *IEEE Trans. on Image Processing*, Vol. 10, No. 5, 767–782.

[429] N. Littlestone (1988), Learning Quickly When Irrelevant Attributes Abound: A New Linear-Threshold Algorithm, *Machine Learning*, Vol. 2, 285–318.

[430] C. Liu and H. Wechsler (2000), Evolutionary Pursuit and Its Application to Face Recognition, *IEEE Transactions on Pattern Analysis and Machine Intelligence*, Vol. 22, No. 6, 570–582.

[431] C. Liu and H. Wechsler (2001), A Shape- and Texture-Based Enhanced Fisher Classifier for Face Recognition, *IEEE Trans. on Image Processing*, Vol. 10, No. 4, 598–608.

[432] C. Liu and H. Wechsler (2002), Gabor Feature Based Classification Using the Enhanced Fisher Linear Discriminant Model (EFM) for Face Recognition, *IEEE Trans. on Image Processing*, Vol. 11, No. 4, 467–476.

[433] C. Liu and H. Wechsler (2003), Independent Component Analysis of Gabor Features for Face Recognition, *IEEE Transactions on Neural Networks*, Vol. 14, No. 4, 919–928.

[434] C. H. Liu, C. A. Collin, S. J. M. Rainville, and A. Chaudhuri (2000), The Effects of Spatial Frequency Overlap on Face Recognition, *J. of Experimental Psychology: Human Perception and Performance*, Vol. 29, 729–743.

[435] F. Liu, X. Lin, S. Z. Li, and Y. Shi (2003), Multi-Modal Face Tracking Using Bayesian Network, *Workshop on Analysis and Modeling of Face and Gesture (AFMG)*, Nice, France, 135–142.

[436] J. Liu, A. Harris, and N. Kanwisher (2001), Stages of Processing in Face Processing: an MEG Study, *Nature Neuroscience*, Vol. 5, No. 9, 910–916.

[437] Q. Liu, J. Cheng, H. Lu, and S. Ma (2004), Modeling Face Appearance with Nonlinear Independent Component Analysis, *6th Int. Conf. on Automatic Face and Gesture Recognition (FGR)*, Seoul, Korea.

[438] X. Liu and T. Chen (2003), Video-Based Face Recognition Using Adaptive Hidden Markov Models, *Computer Vision and Pattern Recognition (CVPR)*, Madison, WI, Vol. 1, 340–345.

[439] X. Liu, T. Chen, and S. M. Thornton (2003), Eigenspace Updating for Nonstationary Process and its Application to Face Recognition, *Pattern Recognition*, Vol. 39, No. 9, 1945–1959.

[440] Y. Liu, K. L. Schmidt, J. F. Cohn, and R. L. Weaver (2002), Facial Asymmetry Quantification for Expression Invariant Human Identification, *16th Int. Conf. on Pattern Recognition (ICPR)*, Quebec-City, Canada.

[441] Y. Liu, K. L. Schmidt, J. F. Cohn, and S. Mitra (2003), Facial Asymmetry Quantification for Expression Invariant Human Identification, *Computer Vision and Image Understanding*, Vol. 91, 138–159.

[442] M. López, D. Lloret, J. Serrat, and J.J. Villanueva (2000), Multilocal Creaseness Based on the Level Set Extrinsic Curvature, *Computer Vision and Image Understanding*, Vol. 77, 111–144.

[443] D. G. Lowe (2004), Distinctive Image Features from Scale-Invariant Key Points, *Int. Journal of Computer Vision*, Vol. 60, No. 2, 91–110.

[444] K. Ma and X. Tang (2001), Discrete Wavelet Face Graph Matching, *Int. Conf. on Image Processing (ICIP)*, Thessaloniki, Greece, 217–220.

[445] A. Mack (2000), Editorial, *Social Research*, Vol. 67, No. 1.

[446] N. C. Macmillan and C.D. Creelman (1991), *Detection Theory: A User Guide*, Cambridge Univ. Press.

[447] A. S. Mackassy, F. J. Provost, and M. L. Littman (2003), Confidence Bounds for ROC Curves, IS-03-4, Stern School of Business, Net York University.

[448] A. Mahalanobis, B. V. K. Vijaya Kumar, and D. Casasent (1987), Minimum Average Correlation Energy Filters, *Applied Optics*, Vol. 26, 3633–3630.

[449] M. W. Mak, W. D. Zhang, and M. X. He (2001), A New Two-Stage Scoring Normalization Approach to Speaker Verification, *Int. Symp. on Intelligent Multimedia, Video and Speech Processing*, Hong Kong, 107–110.

[450] S. Mallat (1989) A Theory for Multiresolution Signal Decomposition: the Wavelet Representation. *IEEE Trans. on Pattern Analysis and Machine Intelligence*, Vol. 11, No. 7, 674–693.

[451] D. Maltoni, D. Maio, A. K. Jain, and S. Prabhakar (Eds.) (2003), *Handbook of Fingerprints Recognition*, Springer.

[452] B. Mandelbrot (1982), *The Fractal Geometry of Nature*, W. H. Freeman.

[453] M. C. Mangini and I. Biederman (2004), Making the Ineffable Explicit: Estimating the Information Employed for Face Classification, *Cognitive Sciences*, 28, 209–226.

[454] T. Mansfield, G. Kelly, D. Chandler, and J. Kane (2001), *Biometric Product Testing Final Report*, Centre for Mathematics and Scientific Computing, National Physical Laboratory, UK.

[455] T. Mansfield and J. L. Wayman (2002), *Best Practices in Testing and Reporting Performance of Biometric Devices*, Centre for Mathematics and Scientific Computing, National Physical Laboratory, UK.

[456] S. Marcel (2004), Improving Face Authentication Using Symmetric Transformations, *6th Int. Conf. On Automatic Face and Gesture Recognition (FGR)*, Seoul, Korea.

[457] A. Martin et al. (1997), The DET Curve in Assessment of Detection Task Performance, *EuroSpeech*, 1895–1898.

[458] A. M. Martinez (2002) Recognizing Imprecisely Localized, Partially Occluded and Expression Variant Faces from a Single Sample per Class, *IEEE Trans. on Pattern Analysis and Machine Intelligence*, Vol. 24, No. 6, 748–763.

[459] A. M. Martinez and R. Benavente (1998), The AR Face Database, CVC Technical Report #24, Purdue University.

[460] A. M. Martinez and A. C. Kak (2001), PCA versus LDA, *IEEE Trans. on Pattern Analysis and Machine Intelligence*, Vol. 23, No. 2, 228–233.

[461] B. C. Martinson, M. S. Anderson, and R. de Vries (2005), Scientists Behaving Badly, *Nature* 435, 737–738.

[462] M. Matsuda (1996), *The Memory of the Modern*, Oxford University Press.

[463] A. Matsui, S. Clippingdale, F. Uzawa, and T. Matsumoto (2004), Bayesian Face Recognition Using a Markov Chain Monte Carlo Method, *17th Int. Conf. on Pattern Recognition (ICPR)*, Cambridge, UK, Vol. 3, 918–921.

[464] R. Mauro and M. Kubovy (1992), Caricature and Face Recognition, *Memory and Cognition*, Vol. 20, No. 4, 433–440.

[465] S. A. McIlraith, T. C. Son, H. Zheng (2001), Semantic Web Services, *IEEE Intell. Syst.*, Vol. 16 No. 2, 46–53.

[466] S. J. McKenna, S. Gong, and Y. Raja (1997), Face Recognition in Dynamic Scenes, *British Machine Vision Conference (BMVC)*, Vol. 1, 140–151.

[467] S. J. McKenna and S. Gong (1998), Recognising Moving Faces, in H. Wechsler et al. (Eds.), *Face Recognition: From Theory to Applications*, NATO ASI Series F., Springer, Vol. 163.

[468] S. J. McKenna, S. Gong, and Y. Raja (1998), Modelling Facial Colour and Identity with Gaussian Mixtures, *Pattern Recognition*, Vol. 31, No. 12, 1883–1892.

[469] S. J. McKenna, S. Jabri, Z. Duric, H. Wechsler, and A. Rosenfeld (2000), Tracking Groups of People, *Computer Vision and Image Understanding*, Vol. 80, No. 1, 42–56.

[470] M. McKeown (2000), Detection of Consistently Task - Related Activations in fMRI Data with Hybrid Independent Components, *NeuroImage*, Vol. 11, 24–35.

[471] E. McKone, P. Martini, and K. Nakayama (2001), Categorical Perception of Face Identity in Noise Isolates Configural Processing, *Journal of Experimental Psychology: Human Perception and Performance*, Vol. 27, No. 3, 573–599.

[472] D. McNeill (1998), *The Face - A Natural History*, Little, Brown and Company.

[473] G. Medioni and Q. Chen (2001), Building 3-D Human Face Models from Two Photographs, *The Journal of of VLSI Signal Processing*, 127–140.

[474] G. Medioni and B. Pesenti (2002), Generation of a 3D Face Model from One Camera, *16th Int. Conf. on pattern Recognition (ICPR)*, Quebec City, Canada, 667–671.

[475] G. Medioni and R. Waupotitsch (2003), Face Recognition and Modeling in 3D, *Int. Workshop on Analysis and Modeling of Faces and Gestures*, 232–233.

[476] T. Melluish, C. Suanders, I. Nouretdinov, and V. Vovk (2001), The Typicalness Framework: A Comparison with the Bayesian Approach. TR, Dept. of Computer Science, Royal Holloway College, University of London, http://www.clrc.rhul.ac.uk/tech-report/.

[477] R. J. Micheals and T. Boult (2001), Efficient Evaluation of Classification and Recognition Systems, *Computer Vision and Pattern Recognition (CVPR)*, Kuai, HI, 50–57.

[478] S. Mika, A.J. Smola, and B. Schölkopf (2001), An Improved Training Algorithm for Kernel Fisher Discriminants, in T. Jaakkola and T. Richardson (Eds.), *AISTATS*, Morgan Kaufmann, 98–104.

[479] K. Mikolajczyk and C. Schmid (2001), Indexing Based on Scale Invariant Interest Points, *8th Int. Conf. on Computer Vision (ICCV)*, Vancouver, Canada, 525–531.

[480] K. Mikolajczyk and C. Schmid (2003), A Performance Evaluation of Local Descriptors, *Computer Vision and Pattern Recognition (CVPR)*, 257–263.

[481] K. Mikolajczyk, C. Schmid, and A. Zisserman (2004), Human Detection Based on a Probabilistic Assembly of Robust Part Detectors, *8th European Conf. on Computer Vision (ECCV)*, Prague, the Czech Republic, 69–82.

[482] M. Minsky (1986), *The Society of Mind*, Simon and Shuster.

[483] T. M. Moeslund and E. Granum (2001), A Survey of Computer Vision-Based Human Motion Capture, *Computer Vision and Image Understanding*, Vol. 81, 231–268.

[484] B. Moghaddam and A. Pentland (1997), Probabilistic Visual Learning for Object Representation, *IEEE Trans. on Pattern Analysis and Machine Intelligence*, Vol. 19, No. 7, 696–710.

[485] B. Moghaddam, T. Jebara, and A. Pentland (2000), Bayesian Face Recognition, *Pattern Recognition*, Vol. 33, No. 11, 1771–1782.

[486] B. Moghaddam and M. H. Yang (2002), Learning Gender with Support Faces, *IEEE Trans. on Pattern Analysis and Machine Intelligence*, Vol. 24, No. 5, 707–711.

[487] A. Mohan, C. Papageorgiou, and T. Poggio (2001), Example-Based Object Detection in Images by Components, *IEEE Trans. on Pattern Analysis and Machine Intelligence*, Vol. 23, No. 4, 349–361.

[488] P. Moulin and J. A. O'Sullivan (2003), Information-Theoretic Analysis of Information Hiding, *IEEE Trans. on Information Theory*, Vol. 49, No. 3, 563–593.

[489] P. Moulin and R. Koetter (2003), *Data Hiding - Theory and Algorithms*, Tutorial at Nat'l Univ. of Singapore.

[490] P. Moulin and R. Koetter (2005), Data Hiding Codes, *Proc. IEEE*, Vol. 93, No. 12, 2083–2127.

[491] M. Moscovitch, G. Winocur, and M. Behrmann (1997), What is Special About Face Recognition? *Journal of Cognitive Neuroscience* 9, 555–604.

[492] D. Mumford (1992), On the Computational Architecture of the Neo Cortex: II. The Role of the Cortico-Cortical Loops, *Biological Cybernetics*, 66, 241–251.

[493] S. O. Murray, P. Schrater, and D. Kersten (2004), Perceptual grouping and the Interactions Between Visual Cortical Areas, *Neural Networks* 17, 695–705.

[494] K. Nakahara and Y. Miyashita (2005), Understanding Intentions: Through the Looking Glass, *Science* 308, 644–645.

[495] S. Narayanan and S. McIlrath (2002), Simulation, Verification and Automated Composition of Web Services, *World Wide Web Conference*, Honolulu, HI.

[496] C. Nastar (1998), Face Recognition Using Deformable Matching, in H. Wechsler et al. (Eds.), *Face Recognition: From Theory to Applications*, Springer, 206–229.

[497] S. Nayar and T. Poggio (Eds.) (1996), *Early Visual Learning*, Oxford University Press.

[498] A. V. Nefian (2002), Embedded Bayesian Networks for Face Recognition, *Int. Conf. on Multimedia*, Vol. 2, 26–29.

[499] E. Newton, L. Sweeney, and B. Malin (2003), Preserving Privacy by De-identifying Facial Images, TR, CMU-CS-03-119, Carnegie-Mellon University.

[500] A. Y. Ng and M. I. Jordan (2001), On Discriminative vs. Generative Classifiers: A Comparison of Logistic Regression and Naïve Bayes, *NIPS*, 14, 841–848.

[501] K. Nigam, A. K. McCallum, S. Thrun, and T. M. Mitchell (2000), Text Classification from Labeled and Unlabeled Documents Using EM, *Machine Learning*, Vol. 39, Nos. 2/3, 103–134.

[502] A. Nikolaidis and I. Pitas (2000), Robuts Watermarking of Facial Images Based on Salient Geometric Pattern Matching, *IEEE Trans. on Multimedia*, Vol. 2, No. 3, 172–184.

[503] L. O'Gorman (2003), Comparing Passwords, Tokens, and Biometrics for User Authentication, *Proc. IEEE*, Vol. 91, No. 12, 2021–2040.

[504] Y. Ohta (1985), *Knowledge-Based Interpretation of Outdoor Natural Scenes*, Pitman, London, UK.

[505] E. Oja (1982), A Simplified Neuron Model as a Principal Component Analyzer, *J. Math. Biol.* 13, 267–273.

[506] K. Okada and C. von der Malsburg (1999), Automatic Video Indexing with Incremental Gallery Creation: Integration of Recognition and Knowledge Acquisition, *3rd Int. Conf. on Knowledge-based Intelligent Information Engineering Systems*, Adelaide, Australia, 431–434.

[507] B. A. Olshausen and D.J. Field (1996), Emergence of Simple-Cell Receptive Field Properties by Learning a Sparse Code for Natural Images, *Nature*, Vol. 381, 607–609.

[508] A. Opelt, M. Fussenegger, A. Pinz, and P. Auer (2004), Weak Hypotheses and Boosting for Generic Object Detection and Recognition, *8th European Conf. on Computer Vision (ECCV)*, Prague, the Czech Republic, 71–84.

[509] N. M. Orlans, T. Piszcz, and R. J. Chavez (2003), Parametrically Controlled Synthetic Imagery Experiment for Face Recognition Experiment, *ACM SIGMM Workshop on Biometrics Methods and Applications*, Berkeley, CA, 58–64.

[510] A. Ortony and T. J. Taylor (1990), What's Basic About Emotions, *Psychological Review* 97, 315–331.

[511] A. J. O'Toole, K. A. Deffenbacher, D. Valentin, and H. Abdi (1994), Structural Aspects of Face Recognition and the Other Race Effect. *Memory and Cognition*, Vol. 22, 208–224.

[512] A. J. O'Toole, T. Vetter, H. Volz, and E. M. Salter (1997), Three-Dimensional Caricatures of Human Heads, *Perception*, 26, 719–732.

[513] A. J. O'Toole (1998), The Perception of Face Gender: The Role of Stimulus Structure in Recognition and Classification, *Memory and Cognition*, 146–160.

[514] A. J. O'Toole, T. Vetter, and V. Blanz (1999), Three-Dimensional Shape and Two-Dimensional Surface Reflectance Contribution to Face Recognition: An Application to Three-Dimensional Morphing, *Vision Research*, 39, 3145–3155.

[515] Z. Pan, G. Healey, M. Prasad, and B. Tromberg (2003), Face Recognition in Hyperspectral Images, *IEEE Trans. on Pattern Analysis and Machine Intelligence*, Vol. 25, No. 12, 1552–1560.

[516] I. S. Pandzic and R. Forchheimer (Eds.), *MPEG-4 Facial Animation: The Standard, Implementation, and Applications*, Wiley.

[517] S. Pankanti, S. Prabhakar, and A. Jain (2002), On the Individuality of Finger-prints, *IEEE Trans. on Pattern Analysis and Machine Intelligence*, Vol. 24, No. 8, 1010–1025.

[518] J. Panksepp (1982), Toward a General Psychobiological Theory of Emotions, *Behavioral and Brain Sciences*, 5, 405–467.

[519] F. I. Parke and K. Waters (1996), *Computer Facial Animation*, A.K. Peters.

[520] V. V. G. Patnaik, K. S. Rajan, and B. Sanju (2003), Anatomy of 'A Beautiful Face & Smile', *J. Anat. Soc. India*, Vol. 52, No. 1, 74–80.

[521] I. Pavlidis, N. L. Eberhardt, and J. Levine (2002), Human Behavior: Seeing through the Face of Deception, *Nature*, Vol. 415, No. 6867.

[522] J. Pearl (1988), *Probabilistic Reasoning in Intelligent Systems: Networks of Plausible Inference*, Morgan Kaufmann.

[523] J. Pearl (2000), *Causality*, Cambridge University Press.

[524] P. Penev and J. Atick (1996), Local Feature Analysis: A General statistical Theory for Object Representation, *Network: Computation in Neural Systems*, Vol. 7, 477–500.

[525] P. S. Penev and L. Sirovich (2000), The Global Dimensionality of Face Space, *4th Int. Conf. on Face and Gesture Recognition (FGR)*, Grenoble, France.

[526] A. Pentland (2000), Perceptual Intelligence, *Comm. of ACM*, Vol. 43, No. 3, 35–44.

[527] A. Pentland (2005), Socially Aware Computation and Communication, *Computer*, Vol. 38, No. 3, 33–40.

[528] A. Pentland, B. Moghaddam, and T. Starner (1994). View-based and Modular Eigenspaces for Recognition, *Conf. of Computer Vision and Pattern Recognition (CVPR)*, Seattle, WA.

[529] A. Pentland, T. Choudhury, N. Eagle, and P. Singh (2005), Human Dynamics: Computation from Organizations, *Pattern Recognition Letters*, Vol. 26, 503–511.

[530] I. S. Penton-Voak and D. I. Perrett (2000), Consistency and Individual Difference in Facial Attractiveness Judgments: An Evolutionary Perspective, *Social Research*, Vol. 67, No. 1, 219–244.

[531] V. Perlibakas (2006), Face Recognition Using Principal Component Analysis and Log-Gabor Filters.

[532] D. I. Perrett, K. A. May, and S.Yoshikawa (1994), Facial Shape and Judgement of Female Attractiveness, *Nature*, 368, 239–242.

[533] F. Perronnin and J.L. Dugelay (2003), Discriminative Face Recognition, *4th Automatic Video-Based Person Authentication (AVBPA)*, Guilford, UK, 446–453.

[534] F. Perronnin, J. L. Dugelay, and K. Rose (2005), A Probabilistic Model of Face Mapping with Local Transformations and Its Application to Face Recognition, *IEEE Trans. on Pattern Analysis and Machine Intelligence*, Vol. 27, No. 7, 1157–1171.

[535] F. A. P. Petitcolas (2000), Watermarking Scheme Evaluation, *Signal Processing*, Vol. 17, No. 5, 58–64.

[536] F. A. P. Petitcolas, R. J. Anderson, and M. G. Kuhn (1999), Information Hiding-A Survey, *Proc. IEEE*, Vol. 87, No. 7, 1062–1078.

[537] A. Pfitzmann and M. Köhntopp (2000), Anonymity, Unobservability and Pseudonymity - A Proposal for Terminology, *Int. Workshop on the Design Issues in Anonymity and Observability*, Berkeley, CA, 1–9.

[538] T. V. Pham, M. Worring, and A. W. M. Smeulders (2002), Face Detection by Aggregated Bayesian Network Classifiers, *Pattern Recognition Letters*, Vol. 23, 451–461.

[539] P. J. Phillips, H. Wechsler, J. Huang, and P. J. Rauss (1998), The FERET Database and Evaluation Procedure for Face-Recognition Algorithms, *Image and Vision Computing*, 16, 295–306.

[540] P. J. Phillips, A. J. O'Toole, Y. Cheng, B. Ross, and H. A. Wild (1999), Assessing Algorithms as Computational Models for Human Face Recognition, NISTIR 6348, NIST.

[541] P. J. Phillips, H. Moon, S. A. Rizvi, and P. J. Rauss (2000), The FERET Evaluation Methodology for Face Recognition Algorithms, *IEEE Trans. on Pattern Analysis and Machine Intelligence*, Vol. 22, No. 10, 1090–1104.

[542] J. P. Phillips and E. M. Newton (2002), Meta-Analysis of Face Recognition Algorithms, *5th Int. Conf. on Face and Gesture Recognition (FGR)*, College Park, MD.

[543] P. J. Phillips, P. Grother, R.J. Michaels, D. M. Blackburn, E. Tabassi, and M. Bone (2003), Face Recognition Vendor Test 2002, NIST.

[544] P. J. Phillips, P. J. Flynn, T. Scruggs, K. W. Bowyer, J. Chang, K. Hoffman, J. Marques, J. Min, and W. Worek (2005), Overview of the Face Recognition Grand Challenge, *Computer Vision and Pattern Recognition (CVPR)*, New York, NY.

[545] R. Picard (1998), *Affective Computing*, MIT Press.

[546] J. B. Pierrot et al. (1998), A Comparison of a Priori Threshold Setting Procedures for Speaker Verification in the CAVE Project, *ICASSP*, 125–128.

[547] S. Pigeon and L. Vandendorpe (1997), Profile Authentication Using a Chamfer Matching Algorithm, *1st Automatic Video-Based Person Authentication (AVBPA)*, Crans-Montana, Switzerland, 185–192.

[548] S. Pigeon and L. Vandendorpe (1998), Multiple Experts for Robust Face Authentication, *SPIE II*, Vol. 3314, 166–177.

[549] G. Pike, R. Kemp, N. Towell, and K. Phillips (1997), Recognising Motion Faces: The Relative Contribution of Motion and Perspective View Information, *Visual Cognition*, Vol. 4, No. 4, 409–438.

[550] S. Pinker (2002), *The Blank Slate*, Penguin Books.

[551] R. Pless (2003), Image Spaces and Video Trajectories Using Isomap to Explore Video Sequences, *9th Int. Conf. on Computer Vision (ICCV)*, Nice, France.

[552] R. Pockaj and F. Lavagetto (2001), An Efficient Use of MPEG-4 FAP Interpolation for Facial Animation at 70 bit/Frame, *IEEE Trans. Circuits, Systems and Video Technology*, Vol. 11, No. 10, 1085–1097.

[553] T. Poggio and D. Beymer (1995), Learning Networks for Face Analysis and Synthesis, *Int. Workshop on Automatic Face and Gesture Recognition (FGR)*, Zurich, Switzerland, 160-165.

[554] T. Poggio and S. Smale (2003), The Mathematics of Learning: Dealing with Data, *Notices of ASM*, 537–544.

[555] T. Poggio, R. Rifkin, S. Mukherjee, and P. Niyogi (2004), General Conditions for Predictivity in Learning Theory, *Nature*, Vol. 428, 419–422.

[556] N. Poh and S. Bengio (2006), Database, Protocols and Tools for Evaluating Score-Level Fusion Algorithms in Biometric Authentication, *Pattern Recognition Letters*, Vol. 39, 223–233.

[557] D. Pollen and S. Ronner (1981), Phase Relationships Between Adjacent Simple Cells in the Visual Cortex, *Science*, Vol. 212, 1409–1411.

[558] K. Popper (2002), *The Logic of Scientific Discovery*, Routledge.

[559] K. Preston, Jr. (1965), Computing at the Speed of Light, *Electronics* 38, 72–83.

[560] K. Proedrou, I. Nouretdinov, V. Vovk, and A. Gammerman (2001), Transductive Confidence Machines for Pattern Recognition, TR CLRC-TR-01-02, Royal Holloway, University of London.

[561] M. Proesmans, L. Van Gook, and F. Defoort (1997), One-Shot 3D Shape and Texture Acquisition of Facial Data, *1st Int. Conf. on Audio- and Video- Based Person Authentication (AVBPA)*, Crans-Montana, Switzerland, 411–418.

[562] A. Pujol, J. J. Vilalnueva, and H. Wechsler (2001), Learning and Caricaturing the Face Space Using Self-Organization and Hebbian Learning for Face Processing, *ICIAP*, 273–278.

[563] A. Pujol and H. Wechsler (2002), Tracking and Recognition Using Caricatures (unpublished manuscript).

[564] J. R. Quinlan (1993), *C4.5: Programs for Machine Learning*, Morgan Kaufmann.

[565] L. Rabiner (1989), A Tutorial on Hidden Markov Models and Selected Applications in Speech Recognition, *Proc. of IEEE*, Vol. 77, No. 2, 257–286.

[566] V. S. Ramachandran (1998), *Phantoms in the Brain*, William Morrow and Co.

[567] R. P. Rao and D. H. Ballard (1999), Predictive Coding in the Visual Cortex: A Functional Interpretation of Some Extra-Classical Receptive Field Effects, *Nature Neuroscience*, Vol. 2, No. 1, 79–87.

[568] R. Raskar, A. Ilie, and J. Yu (2004), Image Fusion for Context Enhancement and Video Surrealism, *Int. Symp. on Non-Photorealistic Animation and Rendering (NPAR)*, 85–152.

[569] C. E. Rasmussen and J. Quinonero-Candela (2005), Healing the Relevance Vector Machine through Augmentation, *22nd Int. Conf. on Machine Learning*, Bonn, Germany, 689–696.

[570] N. K. Ratha, J. H. Connell, and R. M. Bolle (2001), Enhanced Security and Privacy in Biometrics-Based Authentication Systems, *IBM Systems Journal*, Vol. 40, No. 3, 614–634.

[571] T. R. Raviv and A. Shashua (2001), The Quotient Image: Class Based Re-Rendering and Recognition with Varying Illumination, *IEEE Trans. on Pattern Analysis and Machine Intelligence*, Vol. 23, No. 2, 129–139.

[572] B. Raytchev and H. Murase (2002), VQ - Faces Unsupervised Face Recognition from Image Sequences, *16th Int. Conf. on Image Processing (ICPR)*, Quebec-City, Canada, 809–812.

[573] B. Raytchev and H. Murase (2003), Unsupervised Recognition of Multiview face Sequences Based on Pairwise Clustering with Attraction and Repulsion, *Computer Vision and Image Understanding*, Vol. 91, No. 12, 22–52.

[574] P. Refregier (1991), Optimal Trade-off Filters for Noise Robustness, Sharpness of the Correlation Peak, and Horner Efficiency, *Opt. Lett.*, Vol. 16, 829–831.

[575] D. A. Reynolds, T. F. Quatieri, and R. B. Dunn (2000), Speaker Verification Using Adapted Gaussian Mixture Models, *Digital Signal Processing*, Vol. 10, 19–41.

[576] G. Rhodes (1996), *Superportraits: Caricatures and Recognition*, Hove: The Psychology Press.

[577] G. Rhodes , S. Carey, G. Byatt, and F. Proffitt (1998), Coding Spatial Variations in Faces and Simple Shapes: A Test of Two Models, *Vision Research*, Vol. 38, 2307–232.

[578] M. D. Richard and R. P. Lippman (1991), Neural Network Classifiers Estimate a Posteriori Probabilities, *Neural Computation*, 3, 461–483.

[579] C. K. Richardson, D. Bowers, R. M. Bauer, K. M. Heilman, and C. M. Leonard (2000), Digitizing the Moving face During Dynamic Displays of Emotion, *Neuropsychology*, 1028–1039.

[580] T. Riopka and T. Boult (2003), The Eyes Have It, *Computational Neuroscience*, 9–16.

[581] D. Roark, A. O'Toole, and H. Abdi (2003), Human Recognition of Familiar and Unfamiliar People in Naturalistic Video, *Int. Workshop on Analysis and Modeling of Faces and Gestures*, 36–41.

[582] J. Rohlf and L. F. Marcus (1993), A Revolution in Morphometrics, *Trends in Ecology and Evolution*, Vol. 8, 129–132.

[583] S. Romdhani, V. Blanz, and T. Vetter (2002), Face Identification by Fitting a 3D Morpahable Model Using Linear Shape and Texture Error Functions, *7th European Conf. on Computer Vision (ECCV)*, Copenhagen, Denmark, 3–19.

[584] A. Rosenfeld and H. Wechsler (2000), Pattern Recognition - Historical Perspective and Future Directions, *Int. Journal of Imaging Systems and Technology*, Vol. 11, No. 2, 101–116.

[585] A. Ross and A. K. Jain (2004), Multimodal Biometrics: An Overview, *12th European Signal Processing Conference (EUSIPCO)*, Vienna, Austria, 1221–1224.

[586] S. T. Roweis and L. K. Saul (2000), Nonlinear Dimensionality Reduction by Locally Linear Embedding, *Science*, Vol. 290, 2323–2326.

[587] J. J. K. O. Ruanaidh and T. Pun (1998), Rotation, Scale, and Translation Invariant Spread Spectrum Digital Image Watermarking, *Signal Processing* 66, 303–317.

[588] Y. D. Rubinstein and T. Hastie (1997), Discriminative vs. Informative Learning, *Knowledge and Data Discovery (KDD)*, 49–53.

[589] D. L. Ruderman (1994), The Statistics of Natural Images, *Network: Computation in Neural Systems*, Vol. 5, 517–548.

[590] C. Rudin, I. Daubechies, and R. S. Schapire (2004), Dynamics of AdaBoost: Cyclic Behavior and Convergence of Margins, *J. of Machine Learning Research* 5, 1557–1595.

[591] Y. Rui and Z. Liu (2004), ARTiFACIAL: Automated Reverse Turing Test Using FACIAL Features, *11th ACM Int. Conf. on Multimedia*, Berkeley, CA, 295–298.

[592] R. V. Rullen, J. Gautrais, A. Delorme, and S. Thorpe (1998), Face Processing Using One Spike per Neuron, *BioSystems*, Vol. 48, 229–239.

[593] R. V. Rullen and S. Thorpe (1999), Spatial Attention in Asynchronous Neural Networks, *Neurocomputing*, Vol. 26–27, 911–918.

[594] D. E. Rumelhart, G. E. Hinton, and R. J. Williams (1986), Learning Internal Representations by Error Propagation, in D. E. Rumelhart, J. L. McClelland, and the PDP Research Group (Eds.), *Parallel Distributed Processing: Explorations in the Microstructure of Cognition, Vol. 1: Foundation*, 318–362, MIT Press.

[595] R. Russell (2003), Sex, Beauty, and the Relative Luminance of Facial Features, *Perception*, Vol. 32, 1093–1107.

[596] R. Russell and P. Sinha (2001), Perceptually-based Comparison of Image Similarity Metrics, AI Memo 2001 - 14 / CBL Memo 201, MIT AI Lab.

[597] R. Russell, P. Sinha, M. Nederhouser, and I. Biederman (2004), The Importance of Pigmentation for Face Recognition, *J. of Vision*, Vol. 4, No. 8, 418a.

[598] J. Sadr, B. Fatke, C. Massay, and P. Sinha (2002), Aesthetic judgments of faces in Degraded Images. *J. of Vision*, 2, 743.

[599] J. Sadr, I. Jarudi, and P. Sinha (2003), The Role of Eyebrows in Face Recognition, *Perception*, 32, 285–293.

[600] J. Sadr, B. C. Duchaine, and K. Nakayama (2004), The Perception of Facial attractiveness in Prosopagnosia, *Vision*, 4 (8), 914a.

[601] T. Sakai, M. Nagao, and S. Fujibayashi (1969), Line Extraction and Pattern Recognition in a Photograph, *Pattern Recognition*, 1, 233–248.

[602] A. Samal and P. K. Iyengar (1992), Automatic Recognition and Analysis of Human Faces and Facial Expressions: A Survey, *Pattern Recognition*, Vol. 25, No. 1, 65–77.

[603] F. Samaria and S. Young (1994), HMM-based Architecture for Face Identification, *Image and Vision Computing*, Vol. 12, No. 8, 537–543.

[604] T. D. Sanger (1989), Optimal Unsupervised Learning in a Single-Layer Linear Feedforward Neural Network, *Neural Networks*, Vol. 2, 459–473.

[605] D. Santa-Cruz and T. Ebrahimi (2000), A Study of JPEG 2000 Still Image Coding Versus Other Standards, *10th European Signal Processing Conf.*, Tampere, Finland.

[606] S. Santini and R. Jain (1999), Similarity Measures, *IEEE Trans. on Pattern Analysis and Machine Intelligence*, Vol. 21, No. 9, 871–883.

[607] L. K. Saul and S. T. Roweis (2003), Think Globally, Fit Locally: Unsupervised Learning of Low Dimensional Manifolds, *J. of Machine Learning Research*, Vol. 4, 119–155.

[608] C. Saunders, A. Gammerman, and V. Vovk (1999), Transduction with Confidence and Credibility, *16th Int. Joint Conf. on Artificial Intelligence (IJCAI)*, Stockholm, Sweden.

[609] D. Schilling and P. C. Cosman (2002), Image Quality Evaluation Based on Recognition Times for Fast Image Browsing Applications, *IEEE Trans. on Multimedia*, Vol. 4, No. 3, 320–331.

[610] D. Schmorrow and D. McBride (20040, Augmented Cognition (special issue), *Int. Journal of Human-Computer Interaction*, Vol. 17, No. 4.

[611] H. Schneiderman and T. Kanade (2000), A Statistical Method for 3D Object Detection Applied to Faces and Cars, *Computer Vision and Pattern Recognition (CVPR)*, 746–751.

[612] H. Schneiderman (2004), Learning a Restricted Bayesian Network for Object Detection, *Computer Vision and Pattern Recognition (CVPR)*, Washington, D.C., 639–646.

[613] B. Schneier (1999), The Uses and Abuses of Biometrics, *Comm. of ACM*, Vol. 42, No. 8, 136.

[614] B. Schölkopf and A. Smola (2002), *Learning with Kernels: Support Vector Machines, Regularization, Optimization and Beyond*, MIT Press.

[615] E. L. Schwartz (1981), Cortical Anatomy, Size Invariance, and Spatial Frequency Analysis, *Perception*, Vol. 10, 455–468.

[616] J. Searle (1969), *Speech Acts*, Cambridge University Press.

[617] A. W. Senior (1999), Recognizing Faces in Broadcast Video, *Workshop on Recognition, Analysis and Tracking of Faces and Gestures in Real Time Systems*, Kerkyra, Greece.

[618] A. Serjantov and G. Danezis (2002), Towards an Information Theoretic Metric for Anonymity, *2nd Int. Workshop on Privacy Enhancing Technologies*, San Francisco, CA, 41–53.

[619] G. Shafer (1976), *A Mathematical Theory of Evidence*, Princeton University Press.

[620] G. Shakhnarovich, J. W. Fisher, and T. Darrell (2002), Face Recognition from Long Term Observations, *7th European Conference on Computer Vision*, Copenhagen, Denmark.

[621] G. Shakhnarovich, P. Viola, and T. Darell (2003), Fast Pose Estimation with Parameter-Sensitive Hashing, *9th Int. Conf. on Computer Vision (ICCV)*, Nice, France

[622] Y. Shan, Z. Liu, and Z. Zhang (2001), Model-Based Bundle Adjustment with Application to Face Modeling, *8th Int. Conf. on Computer Vision (ICCV)*, Vancouver, Canada, 644–651.

[623] R. E. Shapire (2002), The Boosting Approach to Machine Learning - An Overview, *MSRI Workshop on Nonlinear Estimation and Classification.*

[624] R. E. Shapire, Y. Freund, P. Bartlett, and W. S. Lee (1998), Boosting the Margin: A New Explanation for the Effectiveness of Voting Methods, *Ann. Stat.*, Vol. 26, No. 5, 1651–1686.

[625] J. Shawe-Taylor and N. Cristianini (2004), *Kernel Methods for Pattern Analysis*, Cambridge University Press.

[626] L. Shen, L. Bai, and P. Picton (2004), Facial Recognition/Verification Using Gabor Wavelets and Kernel Methods, *Int. Conf. on Image Processing (ICIP)*, Singapore, 1433–1436.

[627] Y. Sheng and C. Lejeune (1991), Invariant Pattern Recognition Using Fourier-Mellin Transforms and Neural Networks. *J. Optics (Paris)*, Vol. 22, No. 5, 223–228.

[628] J. Sherrah (2004), False Alarm Rate: A Critical Performance Measure for Face Recognition, *6th Int. Conf. on Automatic Face and Gesture Recognition (FGR)*, Seoul, Korea.

[629] P. Shih and C. Liu (2005), Comparative Assessment of Content-Based Face Image Retrieval in Different Color Spaces, *Automatic Video-Based Person Authentication (AVBPA)*, New York, NY.

[630] B. Shneiderman and P. Maes (1997), Direct Manipulation vs. Interface Agents. *Interactions*, 4, 643–661.

[631] L. Sigal and S. Sclaroff (2000), Estimation and Prediction of Evolving Color Distributions for Skin Segmentation Under Varying Illumination, *Computer Vision and Pattern Recognition (CVPR)*.

[632] P. Simard, B. Victorri, Y. LeCun, and J. Denker (1992), Tangent Prop - A formalism for Specifying Selected Invariances in Adaptive Networks, in J. E. Moody, S. J. Hanson, and R. P. Lippmann (Eds.), *Advances in Neural Information Processing Systems (NIPS)*, 3, Morgan Kaufmann, 895–903.

[633] H. Simon (1982), *The Science of the Artificial*, MIT Press.

[634] R. Simon, J. Nolan, and A. Sood (2001), A Light-Weight Agent Architecture for Collaborative Multimedia Systems, *Information Sciences*, Vol. 140, No. 1-2, pp. 53–84.

[635] R. Simon, W. Chang, and J. M. Pullen (2003), An Agent Architecture for Network Support of Distributed Simulation Systems, *7th Int. Symp. on Distributed Simulation and Real Time Applications (DSRT)*, Delft, The Netherlands, 68–75.

[636] R. Simon, W. S. Chang, and J. M. Pullen (2004), Using Distributed Agents to Improve the Efficiency of End-Host Multicast, *Simulation Interoperability Workshop*, Arlington, VA.

[637] P. Sinha (2002), Recognizing Complex Patterns, *Nature Neuroscience Supplement*, 5, 1093–1097.

[638] P. Sinha and T. Poggio (1996), I Think I know That Face, *Nature*, Vol. 384, 404.

[639] P. Sinha and S. Gilad (2004), Face Recognition with 'Contrast Chimeras', *Vision*, 4 (8), 216a.

[640] F. Smeraldi (2003), A Nonparametric Approach to Face Detection Using Ranklets, *4th Int. Conf. on Audio- and Video-Based Biometric Person Authentication (AVBPA)*, Guilford, UK, 351–359.

[641] F. Smeraldi and J. Bigun (2002), Retinal Vision Applied to Facial Features Detection and Face Authentication, *Pattern Recognition Letters* 23, 463–475.

[642] D. J. Smith, J. S. Redford, L. C. Gent, and D. A. Washburn (2005a), Visual Search and Collapse of Categorization, *J. of Experimental Psychology: General*, Vol. 134, No. 4, 443–460.

[643] D. J. Smith, J. S. Redford, L. C. Gent, and D. A. Washburn (2005b),Specific-Token Effects in Screening Tasks: Possible Implications for Aviation Security, *J. of Experimental Psychology: Learning, Memory and Cognition*, Vol. 31, No. 6, 1171–1185.

[644] A. Smola and B. Schölkopf (1998), A Tutorial on Support Vector Regression, NeuroCOLT NC-TR-98-030, Royal Holloway College, University of London, UK.

[645] R. Snelick, U. Uludag, A. Mink, M. Indovina, and A. Jain (2005), *IEEE Trans. on Pattern Analysis and Machine Intelligence*, Vol. 27, No. 3, 450–455.

[646] J. Sochman and J. Matas (2004), AdaBoost with Totally Corrective Updates for Fast Face Detection, *6th Int. Conf. on Automatic Face and Gesture Recognition (FGR)*, Seoul, Korea.

[647] D. A. Socolinsky, A. Selinger, and J. D. Neuheisel (2003), Face Recognition with Visible and Thermal Infrared Imagery, *Computer Vision and Image Understanding*, Vol. 91, 72–114.

[648] X. Song, C. Y. Lin, and M. T. Sun (2004), Cross-Modality Automatic Face Model Training from Large Video Databases, *Workshop on Face Processing in Video*, Washington, D. C.

[649] C. Soutar, R. Gilroy, and A. Stoianov, Biometric System Performance and Security, *IEEE Auto. Identification Advanced Technology.*

[650] R. M. Sreenath and M. P. Singh (2004), Agent-Based Service Selection, *J. Web Sem.*, Vol. 1, No. 3, 261–279.

[651] M. V. Srinivasan and M. Davey (1995), Strategies for Active Camouflage of Motion, *Proc. R. Soc. Lond. B* 259, 19–25.

[652] M. Stoerring, H. J. Andersen, and E. Granum (1999), Skin Colour Detection Under Changing Lighting Conditions, *7th Int. Symposium on Intelligent Robots Systems*, 187–195.

[653] T. J. Stonham (1986), Practical Face Recognition and Verification with WIZARD, in M. Jeeves, F. Newcombe and A. Young (Eds.), *Aspects of Face Processing*, Nijhoff Publishers, Dordrecht.

[654] J. Stone (2001), Face Recognition: When a Nod is Better than a Wink, *Curr Biol*, 11: R663–R664.

[655] C. J. Stone (1977), Consistent Nonparametric Regression, *Ann. Statist.* 5 595–645.

[656] M. Stone (1977), Asymptotics for and Against Cross-Validation, *Biometrika*, Vol. 64, No. 1, 29–35.

[657] J. V. Stone, J. Porrill, N. R. Porter, and I. D. Wilkinson (2002), Spatiotemporal Independent Component Analysis of Event-Related fMRI Data Using Skewed Probability Density Functions, *NeuroImage*, Vol. 15, No. 2, 407–421.

[658] R. Sukthankar and R.Stockton (2001), Argus: the Digital Doorman, *IEEE Intelligent Systems*, Vol. 16, No. 2, 14–19.

[659] R. S. Sutton and A. G. Barto (1998), *Reinforcement Learning*, MIT Press.

[660] K. Suzuki, T. Kyryu, and T. Nakada (2002), Fast and Precise Independent Component Analysis for High Field Time Series Tailored Using Prior Information on Spatiotemporal Structure, *Human Brain Mapping*, Vol. 15, No. 1, 54–66.

[661] M. J. Swain and D. H. Ballard (1991), Color Indexing, *Int. J. of Computer Vision*, Vol. 7, No.1, 11–32.

[662] P. N. Tan, M. Steinbach, and V. Kumar (2006), *Introduction to Data Mining*, Pearson-Addison Wesley.

[663] X. Tang and X. Wang (2004), Face Sketch Recognition (2004), Face Sketch Recognition, *IEEE Trans. on Circuits, Systems and Video Technology*, Vol. 14, No. 1, 50–57.

[664] B. Takacs (1998), Comparing Face Images Using the Modified Hausdorff Distance, *Pattern Recognition*, Vol. 31, 1873–1881.

[665] B. Takacs and H. Wechsler (1998a), A Dynamic and Multiresolution Model of Visual attention and its Application to Facial Landmark Detection, *Computer Vision and Image Understanding*, Vol. 70, No. 1, 63–73.

[666] B. Takacs and H. Wechsler (1998b), Face Recognition Using Binary Image Metrics, *3rd Int. Conf. on Automatic Face and Gesture Recognition (FGR)*, Kyoto, Japan, 294–299.

[667] X. Tan, S. Chen, Z. H. Zhou, and F. Zhang (2004), Robust Face Recognition from a Single Training Image per Person with Kernel-based SOM-Face, *ISNN* (1), 858–863.

[668] X. Tan, S. Chen, Z.-H. Zhou, and F. Zhang (2005), Recognizing Partially Occluded, Expression Variant Faces from Single Training Image per Person with SOM and Soft kNN Ensemble, *IEEE Trans. on Neural Networks*, Vol. 16, No. 4, 875–886.

[669] A. Tankus and Y. Yeshurun (2000), A Model for Visual Camouflage Breaking, *Biologically Motivated Computer Vision*, 139–149.

[670] J. B. Tenenbaum, V. de Silva, and V. Langford (2000), A Global Geometric Framework for Nonlinear Dimensionality Reduction, *Science* 290 2319–2322.

[671] A. Teoh, S. A. Samad, and A. Hussain (2004), Nearest Neighbourhood Classifiers in a Bimodal Biometric Verification System Fusion Decision Scheme, *J. of Research and Practice in Information Technology*, Vol. 36, No. 1, 47–62.

[672] A. Teoh and D. C. L. Ngo (2005), Cancelable Biometric Features with Tokenized Random Number, *Pattern Recognition Letters* 26, 1454–1460.

[673] J. C. Terrillon, M. David, and S. Akamatsu (2000), Detection of Human Faces in Complex Scene Images by Use of a Skin Color Model and of Invariant Fourier-Mellin Moments, *15th Int. Conf. on Pattern Recognition (ICPR)*, Barcelona, Spain.

[674] D. Terzopoulos and K. Waters (1993), Analysis and Synthesis of Facial Image Sequences Using Physical and Anatomical Models, *IEEE Trans. on Pattern Analysis and Machine Intelligence*, Vol. 15, No. 6, 569–579.

[675] N. P. H. Thian, S. Marcel, and S. Bengio (2003), Improving Face Authentication Using Virtual Samples, *ICASSP*, Hong Kong, 233–236.

[676] D'Arcy Thompson (1917), *On Growth and Form*, Cambridge University Press.

[677] K. Thoresz and P. Sinha (2001), Qualitative Representations for Recognition, *J. of Vision*, Vol. 1, No.3, 298a.

[678] R. Thornhill and S. W. Gangestad (1999), Facial Attractiveness, *Trans. Cognitive Sciences*, 452–460.

[679] S. Thorpe, D. Fize, and C. Marlot (1996), Speed of Processing in the Human Visual System, *Nature*, Vol. 381, 520–522.

[680] K. Tieu and P. Viola (2004), Boosting Image Retrieval, *Int. J. of Computer Vision*, Vol. 56, No. 1-2, 17–36.

[681] C. F. Tippet et al. (1968), The Evidential Value of the Comparison of Paint Flakes from Sources other than Vehicles, *Journal of the Forensic Science Society*, Vol. 8, 61–65.

[682] S. Tong and D. Koller (2001), Support Vector Machines Active Learning with Applications to Text Classification, *Journal of Machine Learning Research*, Vol. 2, 45–66.

[683] F. de la Torre, R. Gross, S. Baker, and B. V. J. V. Kumar (2005), Representational Oriented Component Analysis (ROCA) for Face Recognition with One sample Image per Training Class, *Computer Vision and Pattern Recognition (CVPR)*, San Diego, CA.

[684] A. Trachtenberg (2000), Lincoln's Smile: Ambiguities of the Face in Photography, *Social Research*, Vol. 67, No. 1, 1–23.

[685] E. Trucco and A. Verri (1998), *Introductory Techniques for 3-D Computer Vision*, Prentice Hall.

[686] F. Tsalakanidou, D. Tzocaras, and M. Strintzis (2003), Use of Depth and Color Eigenfaces for Face Recognition, *Pattern Recognition Letters*, Vol. 24, 1427–1435.

[687] T. Tsao and V. Chen (1993), Gabor-Wavelet Pyramid for the Extraction of Image Flow, *Proc. of SPIE Mathematical Imaging: Wavelet Applications in Signal and Image Processing*.

[688] T. Tsuda, K. Yamamoto, and K. Kato (2004), A proposal for a Person/Photograph Distinction Method with Applications to Security Systems, *6th Int. Conf. on Automatic Face and Gesture Recognition (FGR)*, Seoul, Korea.

[689] Z. Tu, X. Chen, A. L. Yuille, and S. C. Zhu (2003), Image Parsing: Unifying Segmentation, Detection, and Recognition, *9th Int. Conf. on Computer Vision (ICCV)*, Nice, France..

[690] M. Turk and A. Pentland (1992), Eigenfaces for Recognition, *J. Cognitive Neuroscience*, Vol. 13, No. 1, 71–86.

[691] P. Tuyls and J. Goseling (2004), Capacity and Examples of Template-Protecting Biometric Authentication Systems, *ECCV Workshop BioAW*, Prague, Czech Republic, 158–170.

[692] U. Udulag, S. Pankanti, S. Prabhakar, and A. K. Jain (2004), Biometric Cryptosystems: Issues and Challenges, *Proc. IEEE*, Vol. 92, No. 6, 948–960.

[693] S. Ullman and R. Basri (1991), Recognition by Linear Combinations of Models, *IEEE Trans. on Pattern Analysis and Machine Intelligence*, Vol. 13, No. 10, 992–1006.

[694] D. Valentin, H. Abdi, A. J. O'Toole, and G. W. Cottrell (1994), Connectionist Models of Face Processing: A Survey, *Pattern Recognition*, Vol. 27, 1209–1230.

[695] T. Valentine (2001), Face-Space Models of Face Recognition, in M. J. Wenger and J. T. Townsend (Eds.), *Computational, Geometric, and Process Perspectives on Facial Recognition: Contexts and Challenges*, Lawrence Erlbaum Associates, Mahwah, New Jersey, 83–113.

[696] T. Valentine (2004), Better the Devil You Know? Non-Conscious Processing of Identity and Affect of Famous Persons, *Psychonomic Bulletin & Review*, 11, 469–474.

[697] L. H. Van Trees (1968), *Detection, Estimation, and Modulation Theory*, Vol. 1, Wiley.

[698] V. N. Vapnik (1998), *Statistical Learning Theory*, Wiley.

[699] V. N. Vapnik (2000), *The Nature of Statistical Learning Theory* (2nd ed.), Springer.

[700] N. Vasconcelos and A Lippman (2005), A Multiresolution Manifold Distance for Invariant Image Similarity, *IEEE Trans. on Multimedia*, Vol. 7, No. 1, 127–142.

[701] T. Vetter and T. Poggio (1997), Linear Object Classes and Image Synthesis from a Single Example Image, *IEEE Trans. on Pattern Analysis and Machine Intelligence*, Vol. 19, No. 7, 733–742.

[702] P. Viola and M. J. Jones (2004), Robust Real-Time Face Detection, *Int. Journal of Computer Vision*, Vol. 57, No. 2, 137–154.

[703] J. Vokey and J. D. Read (1992), Familiarity, Memorability, and the Effect of Typicality on the Recognition of Faces, *Memory and Cognition*, 20, 291–302.

[704] V. Vovk, A. Gammerman, and C. Saunders (1999), Machine-Learning Application of Algorithmic Randomness, *Int. Conf. on Machine Learning (ICML)*, Bled, Slovenia..

[705] V. Vovk, I. Nouretdinov and A. Gammerman (2003), Testing Exchangeability On-Line, *20th Int. Conf. on Machine Learning (ICML)*, Washington, DC., 768–775.

[706] V. Vovk, A. Gammermann, and G. Shafer (2005), *Algorithmic Learning in a Random World*, Springer.

[707] L. Vygotsky (1976), *Mind in Society*, Harvard University Press.

[708] G. Wahba (1990), *Splines Models for Observational Data, Series in Applied Mathematics*, Vol. 59, SIAM, Philadelphia, PA.

[709] C. Wallraven, B. Caputo, and A. Graf (2003), Recognition with Local Features: the Kernel Recipe, *9th Int. Conf. on Computer Vision (ICCV)*, Nice, France, 257–264.

[710] D. Walther, U. Rutishauser, C. Koch, and P. Perona (2005), Selective Visual Attention Enables Learning and Recognition of Multiple Objects in Cluttered Scenes, *Computer Vision and Image Understanding*, Vol. 100, 41–63.

[711] L. Wang and J. M. Mendel (1992), Fuzzy Basis Functions, Universal Approximation, and Orthogonal Least-Squares Learning, *IEEE Trans. on Neural Networks*, Vol. 5, 807–814.

[712] X. Wang and X. Tang (2004), Hallucinating Face by Eigen Transformation with Distortion Reduction, *1st Int. Conf. on Biometric Authentication*, Hong Kong, 88–94.

[713] Y. Wang, C. Chua, and Y. Ho (2002), Facial Feature Detection and Face Recognition from 2D and 3D images, *Pattern Recognition Letters* 23, 1191–1202.

[714] Y. H. Wang, T. N. Tan, and A. K. Jain (2003), Combining Face and Iris Biometrics for Identity Verification, *4th Int. Conf. on Audio and Video-Based Biometric Person Authentication (AVBPA)*, Guilford, UK.

[715] S. Watanabe (1960), Information-Theoretical Aspects of Inductive and Deductive Inference, *IBM J. Res. Dev.* 4, 208–231.

[716] L. J. Wayman (1999), Error-Rate Equations for the General Biometric System, *IEEE Robotics & Automation Magazine*, March, 35–48.

[717] H. Wechsler and L. Zisserman (1988), 2D Invariant Object Recognition Using Distributed Associative Memories, *IEEE Trans. on Pattern Analysis and Machine Intelligence*, Vol. 10, No. 6, 811–821.

[718] H. Wechsler (1990), *Computational Vision*, Academic Press.

[719] H. Wechsler, V. Kaddad, J. Huang, S. Gutta, and V. Chen (1997), Automatic Video-Based Person Authentication Using the RBF Network, *1st International Conference on Audio and Video-Based Biometric Person Authentication (AVBPA)*, Crans-Montana, Switzerland, 85–92.

[720] H. Wechsler, P. J. Phillips, V. Bruce, F. F. Soulié, and T. S. Huang (Eds.) (1998), *Face Recognition - From Theory to Applications*, Springer.

[721] H. Wechsler, Z. Duric, F. Li, and V. Cherkassky (2004), Motion Estimation Using Statistical Learning Theory, *IEEE Trans. on Pattern Analysis and Machine Intelligence*, Vol. 26, No.4, 466–478.

[722] H. Wechsler, J. Yven, and M. Mannucci (2005), W5+ Architectures for Smart Interfaces, *11th Int. Conf. on HCI*, Las Vegas, Nevada.

[723] M. S. Weiss and C. A. Kulikowski, *Computer Systems That Learn*, Morgan Kaufmann.

[724] C. Westbury (1999), *Review for A. Young, Face and Mind*, University of Oxford.

[725] J. Weston, F. Perez-Cruz, O. Bousquet, O. Chapelle, A. Elisseeff, and B. Schölkopf (2003), Feature Selection and Transduction for Prediction of Molecular Bioactivity for Drug Design, *Bioinformatics*, Vol. 19, No. 6, 764-771.

[726] B. Weyrauch, J. Huang, B. Heisele, and V. Blanz (2004), Component-based Face Recognition with 3D Morphable Models, *1st IEEE Workshop on Face Processing in Video*, Washington, D.C.

[727] M. Williams and J. Mattingley (2006), Do Angry Men Get Noticed?, *Current Biology* 16, R402-404, June 6.

[728] O. Williams, A. Blake, and R. Cipolla (2005), Sparse Bayesian Learning for Efficient Visual Tracking, *IEEE Trans. on Pattern Analysis and Machine Intelligence*, Vol. 27, No. 8, 1292-1304.

[729] R. Wilson (1995), Wavelets: Why so many varieties?, *Symp. on Applications of Time-Frequency and Time-Scale Methods*, University of Warwick, Coventry, UK.

[730] L. Wiscott, J. M. Fellous, N. Kruger, and C. von der Malsburg (1997), Face Recognition by Elastic Bunch Graph Matching, *IEEE Trans. on Pattern Analysis and Machine Intelligence*, Vol. 19, No. 7, 775-779.

[731] L. Wolf and A. Shashua (2003), Kernel Principal Angles for Classification Machines with Applications to Image sequence Interpretation, *Computer Vision and Pattern Recognition (CVPR)*, Madison, WI.

[732] J. D. Woodward (1997), Biometrics: Privacy's Foe or Privacy's Friend? *Proc. IEEE*, Vol. 85, No. 9, 1480-1492.

[733] C. Wu, H-Y. Shum, Y-Q. Xu, and Z. Zhang (2004), Automatic Eyeglasses Removal from FACE Images, *IEEE Trans. on Pattern Analysis and Machine Intelligence*, Vol. 26, No. 3, 322-336.

[734] E. P. Xing, A. Y. Ng, M. I. Jordan, and S. Russell (2003), Distance Metric Learning with Application to Clustering with Side-Information, S. Becker, S. Thrun and K. Obermayer (Eds.), *NIPS 15.*

[735] O. Yamaguchi, K. Fukui, and K. Maeda (1998), Face Recognition Using Temporal Image Sequence, *3rd Int. Conference on Face and Gesture Recognition (FGR)*, Kyoto, Japan.

[736] P. Yan and K. W. Bowyer (2005a), Empirical Evaluation of Advanced Ear Biometrics, *Workshop on Empirical Evaluation Methods in Computer Vision*, San Diego, CA.

[737] P. Yan and K. W. Bowyer (2005b), Ear Biometrics Using 2D and 3D Images, *5th Int. Conf. on Audio and Video-Based Biometric Person Authentication (AVBPA)*, New York.

[738] Z. Yan and C. Yuan (2004), Ant Colony Optimization for Feature Selection in Face Recognition, *1st Int. Conf. on Biometrics Authentication (ICBA)*, Hong Kong, 221-226.

[739] J. Yang, D. Zhang, A. F. Frangi, and J. Y. Yang (2004), Two-Dimensional PCA: A New Approach to Appearance-Base Face Representation and Recognition, *IEEE Trans. on Pattern Analysis and Machine Intelligence*, Vol. 26, No. 1, 131-137.

[740] M. H. Yang (2002a), Extended Isomap for Pattern Classification, *18th AAAI*, Edmonton, Alberta, Canada.

[741] M. H. Yang (2002b), Face Recognition Using Kernel Methods, *5th Int. Conf. on Face and Gesture Recognition (FGR)*, Washington, DC, USA, 215-220.

[742] M. H. Yang, D. Kriegman, and N. Ahuja (2002), Detecting Faces in Images: A Survey, *IEEE Trans. on Pattern Analysis and Machine Intelligence*, Vol. 24, No. 1, 34-58.

[743] P. Yang, S. Shan, W. Gao, S. Li, and D. Zhang (2004), Face Recognition Using Ada-Boosted Gabor Features, *6th Int. Conf. on Face and Gesture Recognition (FGR)*, Seoul, Korea, 356-361.

[744] Y. Yeshurun, D. Reisfeld, and H. Wolfson (1991), Symmetry: A Context Free Cue for Foveated Vision, in H. Wechsler (Ed.), *Neural Networks for Pattern Recognition* (Vol. 1.), Academic Press.

[745] A. Yip and P. Sinha (2002), Role of Color in Face Recognition, *Perception*, Vol. 31, 995-1003.

[746] G. Yovel and N. Kanwisher (2004a), Face Perception: Domain Specific, Not Process Specific, *Neuron*, Vol. 44, 889–898.

[747] G. Yovel and N. Kanwisher (2004b), Face Perception Engages a Domain-Specific System for Processing both Configural and Part-Based Information about Faces, *Vision*, 4 (8), 133a.

[748] A. L. Yuille (1991), Deformable Templates for Face Recognition, *J. Cognitive Neuroscience*, Vol. 3, No. 1, 59–70.

[749] Y. Zhai and M. Shah (2005), A General Framework for Temporal Video Scene Segmentation, *10th Int. Conf. on Computer Vision (ICCV)*, Beijing, China.

[750] L. Zhang, S. Z. Li, Z. Y. Qu, X. Huang (2004), Boosting Local Feature Based Classifiers for Face Recognition, *1st IEEE Workshop on Face Processing in Video*, Washington, D.C., USA.

[751] Q. Zhang and A. Benveniste (1992), Wavelet Networks, *IEEE Trans. on Neural Networks*, Vol. 3, No. 6, 889–898.

[752] T. Zhang and B. Yu (2005), Boosting with Early Stopping: Convergence and Consistency, *Ann. Statist.* 33, No. 4, 1538–1579.

[753] W. D. Zhang, K. K. Yiu, M. W. Mak, C. K. Li, and M. X. He (1999), A Priori Threshold Determination for Phrase-Prompted Speaker Verification, *Eurospeech*, Vol. 2, 1023–1026.

[754] Y. Zhang and Q. Ji (2005), Active and Dynamic Information Fusion for Facial Expression Understanding from Image Sequences, *IEEE Trans. on Pattern Analyisis and Machine Intelligence*, Vo. 27, No. 5, 699–714.

[755] Z. Zhang and R. S. Blum (1999), A Categorization of Multiscale-Decomposition-Based Image Fusion Schemes with a Performance Study for a Digital camera Applications, *Proc. IEEE*, Vol. 87, No. 8, 1315–1326.

[756] W. Zhao, R. Chellappa, P. J. Phillips, and A. Rosenfeld (2003), Face Recognition: A Literature Survey, *ACM Computing Surveys*, Vol. 3, No. 4, 399–458.

[757] S. K. Zhou and R. Chellappa (2002), A Robust Algorithm for Probabilistic Human recognition from Video, *16th Int. Conf. on Pattern Recognition (ICPR)*, Quebec-City, Canada.

[758] S. K. Zhou, V. Krueger, and R. Chellappa (2003), Probabilistic Recognition of Human Faces from Video, *Computer Vision and Image Understanding*, Vol. 91, 214–245.

[759] S. K. Zhou and R. Chellappa (2004), Probabilistic Identity Characterization for Face Recognition, *Computer Vision and Pattern Recognition (CVPR)*, Washington, D. C.

[760] S. K. Zhou, R. Chellappa, and B. Moghaddam (2004), Visual Tracking and Recognition Using Appearnce-Adaptive Models in Particle Filters, *IEEE Trans. on Image Processing*, Vol. 13, No. 11, 1491–1506.

[761] S. K. Zhou and R. Chellappa (2005), Beyond One Still Image: Face Recognition from Multiple Still Images or video Sequence, in W. Zhao and R. Chellappa (Eds.), *Face Processing: Advanced Modeling and Methods*, Academic Press.

[762] H. Zouaki (2003), Representation and Geometric Computation Using the Extended Gaussian Image, *Pattern Recognition Letters*, Vol. 24, No. 9–10, 1489–1501.

Index

Printed in the United States of America.